Core Jini

W. KEITH EDWARDS

Prentice Hall PTR, Upper Saddle River, NJ 07458
http://www.phptr.com

Library of Congress Cataloging-in-Publication Date
Edwards, W. Keith.
Core Jini / W. Keith Edwards.
p. cm. -- (The Sun Microsystems Press series)
ISBN 0-13-0114469-X
1. Electronic data processing--Distributed processing. 2. Jini. 3. Title. II. Series
QA76.9.D5E38 1999
004'.36--dc21 99-35672
CIP

Editorial/Production Supervision: Joanne Anzalone
Acquisitions Editor: Tim Moore
Editorial Assistant: Bart Blanken
Development Editor: Ralph Moore
Marketing Manager: Bryan Gambrel
Manufacturing Manager: Alexis Heydt
Cover Design: Anthony Gemmallaro
Cover Design Direction: Jerry Votta
Art Director: Gail Cocker-Bogusz
Technical Reviewers: Peter van der Linden and Marty Hall

Reprinted with corrections Sept, 1999.

Prentice-Hall, Inc.
Upper Saddle River, NJ 07458

Prentice Hall books are widely used by corporations and government agencies for training, marketing, and resale.
The publisher offers discounts on this book when ordered in bulk quantities. For more information, contact Corporate Sales Department, Phone: 800-382-3419; FAX: 201- 236-7141;
E-mail: corpsales@prenhall.com
Or write: Prentice Hall PTR, Corporate Sales Dept., One Lake Street, Upper Saddle River, NJ 07458.

Printed in the United States of America

10 9 8 7 6 5 4 3 2 1

ISBN 0-13-014469-X

Prentice-Hall International (UK) Limited, London
Prentice-Hall of Australia Pty. Limited, Sydney
Prentice-Hall Canada Inc., Toronto
Prentice-Hall Hispanoamericana, S.A., Mexico
Prentice-Hall of India Private Limited, New Delhi
Prentice-Hall of Japan, Inc., Tokyo
Prenticd-Hall (Singapore) Pte. Ltd., Singapore
Editora Prentice-Hall do Brasil, Ltda., Rio de Janeiro

This book is gratefully dedicated to Mark Weiser, who started me down this path in the first place.

Contents

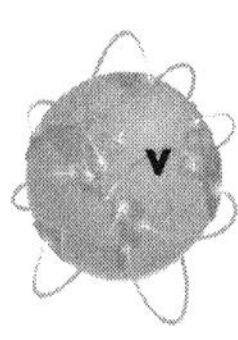

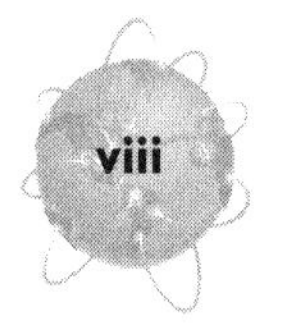

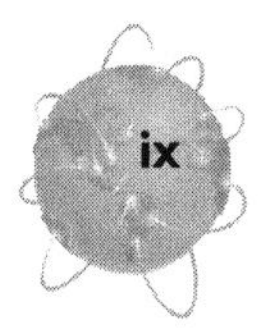

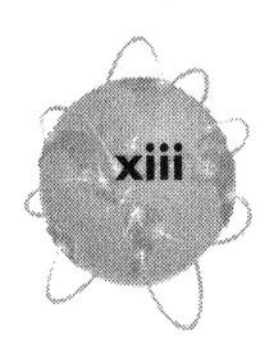

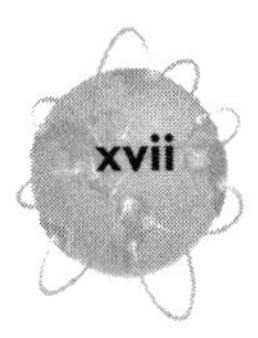

Foreword

Twenty years ago I was a student at U.C. Berkeley, working on what would become a popular version of the UNIX operating system. At the time computers were mostly used by professionals, and had software that was relevant to this use. In the last twenty years we have seen the emergence of the personal computer, with much wider use, but the complexity of the systems today has exceeded the professional systems of twenty years ago, creating untold frustration. A better way of constructing new systems is needed, to reduce this frustration and better match the computing devices to human uses.

Almost a decade ago I came across a book by Jacques Attali called *Lignes d'Horizon*. A colleague, John Gage, and I were traveling a lot together, and John was translating this book from French to English for his personal use. In this book we found great speculations about the computing world of the future, the idea of "nomadic computing," and we saw a linkage between these concepts and our desire for simpler, more reliable, and more human-centered computing. This set us off toward the design of a new computing substrate for the imagined future world of nomadic devices and pervasive embedded computing.

Hence Jini. Jini leverages the Java programming language to provide a simple substrate for distributed computing. Distributed computing is different, mostly because partial failures occur. If we don't handle failure, distributed systems paradoxically become less reliable as they get larger, rather than

more reliable as the existence of redundant parts would suggest. Jini provides the tools for dealing with this and for dealing with the limited bandwidth and latency inherent in distributed computation.

The computing world of the future is a connected world, where "The Network is the Computer®." Java brings reliable object-oriented programming to the network. Its rapid rise reflects the power of objects to structure software, and the additional reliability and productivity that results from its modern design. Jini extends Java's benefits to distributed applications, which are structured as a set of communicating Java applications without requiring complicated underlying operating systems to be understood to understand the meaning of a distributed program.

Because Jini is simple we can teach it, and the principles of distributed programming, to Java programmers in just a few days. By learning about the Jini philosophy, the uses of remote objects, leasing, distributed events and transactions you will be learning about both the essential elements of Jini and some basic principles of distributed programming. Core Jini will aid both the student, the professional programmer writing a production application, and those curious about this new approach and new basic platform for distributed computing.

Bill Joy
Aspen, Colorado
June 1999

Foreword

Much of the early history of the Jini technology has been documented and, at least anecdotally, is well known. Most people who have followed the evolution of this technology over the past six to twelve months know that Bill Joy provided the inspiration and initial direction, and that Jim Waldo—as lead architect—is the creator; without whom this truly revolutionary technology would not exist.

Most people also know that the work on which the Jini technology is based began within Sun Microsystems Laboratories at Sun's east coast facility just outside Boston. While with "the labs" Jim Waldo ran the Large Scale Distribution research project and, along with Ann Wollrath, Peter Jones and Ken Arnold, investigated and developed some of the key Jini concepts. The concepts developed in those early days, concepts such as leasing, distributed events and lightweight transactions, addressed issues in the field of distributed computing in a way that was contrary to the standard approach of attempting to hide distinctions between local and remote systems (sadly for some, this is still the standard approach).

The team of Waldo, Wollrath, Jones and Arnold made up the kernel of the Jini engineering team. The team eventually moved from the labs into the JavaSoft product group where they began to investigate how a language-centric approach could be applied to the distributed computing concepts developed in the labs. As a result of this collaboration, Ann Wollrath created Java RMI which has become one of the most interesting and useful components in the Java language; and Ken Arnold created the JavaSpaces technology as well as having begun work on what would become the Jini lightweight transaction model.

What people probably don't know about the early history of the Jini technology is that when Bill Joy asked the team to expand their prior work to design a new platform for distributed computing, the team was moved out of JavaSoft in order to provide insulation from the kind of large company politics that can kill a new and radical idea. As a matter of fact, the Jini project actually began life in Sun Microsystems' Human Resources division! It was at about this time that Bob Scheifler (of X Consortium fame), Bryan O'Sullivan and Mark Hodapp joined the Jini team as architects and manager respectively. These individuals provided the missing pieces necessary for the project to continue to grow and thrive. The team eventually grew to include about fifteen development engineers. To this day, the development team here on the east coast remains small, focused and highly productive. The Jini team is made up of some of the finest people and brightest minds I have ever had the pleasure of knowing.

Until the summer of 1998, very few people—both internal and external to Sun—were aware of the existence of the Jini project. Just as with the Java language, there were moments where the future of the project was tentative at best. The project owes a debt of gratitude to Bill Joy and Mike Clary, both of whom put their professional reputations on the line to fight for the project's survival. Ultimately, the project survived because of these individuals, and because of the dedication of the team and the vision of Sun's CEO, Scott McNealy.

The Jini project once again demonstrates Sun's ability to think and act in revolutionary ways. Where other companies could never allow themselves to move beyond the safety of the status quo, Sun continues to shatter it. Just as the now legendary story tells how the Java language (known as Oak at the time) was one demo away from cancellation, the Jini project similarly rose from the ashes of pending cancellation. The project was only able to do so because the culture established within Sun allows—even encourages—such things.

You should note that the Jini technology is radical not only in its technical design, but also in its business model. The concept of the Sun Community Source License (SCSL—pronounced "scuzzle") originated within the Jini project. Although some might say this move was not bold enough, placing a key technology under community source requires great vision and courage, especially when such an action represents a move away from the safety of traditional models. The SCSL represents a "call to arms" within the developer community. Through the SCSL, *anyone* can participate in the growth and evolution of the Jini technology.

I joined the Jini project in 1997. At the time, I was designing and implementing middleware for a fairly large telco-based distributed system at another company. The project was exciting and the work environment was one of the best I had ever experienced. When I was contacted about the possibility of joining the Jini development team, the Jini project was in its infancy and its future was still in doubt. Although the project's status might have made some people question the prudence of joining a project with such an uncertain future, five minutes into the description of the Jini vision, I knew this is where I wanted to be. I remember thinking to myself (with apologies to Jon Landau and Bruce Springsteen), "I've seen the future of software, and its name is Jini." The concepts being described to me, even at that early stage (and even though they were being presented by a manager!), were so elegant and so compelling that I knew this was an opportunity to be a part of something that could change the world.

When I was approached about reviewing this book, my first reaction was reluctance. A book review is certainly a lot of work. But more importantly, when a new technology gains notoriety, it is not uncommon for many poor quality texts attempting to "cash in" on the popularity of the latest "hot" technology to begin to appear. I thought this text might possibly be in that category. When I learned that not only was this book to be part of Prentice Hall's respected "Core" series, but also that the author was Keith Edwards of Xerox's Palo Alto Research Center (PARC), I began to understand that this book had the potential to be something special. To my delight, I was not disappointed!

Keith Edwards clearly understands the concepts behind the Jini technology. He has thoroughly analyzed the Jini specifications and presents the designs reflected in those specifications in a way that will be accessible to the beginner as well as the hardened veteran. Keith also presents an accurate description of the Jini philosophy on distributed computing, emphasizing the differences between local and remote systems; a description that remains true to the intent of the Jini architects. Keith's explanations of key concepts such as discovery, lookup, leasing, distributed events and transactions are excellent, and even the experienced reader will benefit from them.

The text covers everything you need to know to build clients and services that run in a Jini environment and which must behave as good "Jini citizens." The explanations are thorough and easy to follow, and are supplemented with example code that accurately demonstrates all the important concepts. Although much of the publicity surrounding the Jini technology emphasizes the role of devices in a Jini environment, Keith stresses through his well-written explanations and examples that the power of this technology can be applied to the enterprise as well as to devices.

Thus, whether you are a beginner or an experienced Java programmer, whether your world involves devices or software services for the enterprise, this book will help you gain a thorough understanding of this new and exciting technology called the Jini technology. Jump in and have fun as Keith introduces you to a radically new way to build distributed systems.

Brian Murphy
Sun Microsystems
Burlington, Massachusetts
June 1999

Introduction

To Alpha 1.1 Release Printing

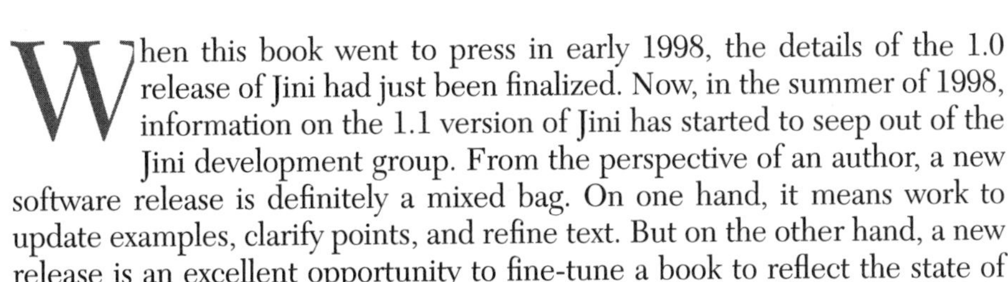

When this book went to press in early 1998, the details of the 1.0 release of Jini had just been finalized. Now, in the summer of 1998, information on the 1.1 version of Jini has started to seep out of the Jini development group. From the perspective of an author, a new software release is definitely a mixed bag. On one hand, it means work to update examples, clarify points, and refine text. But on the other hand, a new release is an excellent opportunity to fine-tune a book to reflect the state of the world since its first release.

While I can't give you firm details about what will or will not be in 1.1—because these details haven't been finalized yet—I have had the opportunity to update the book to present information about 1.1, as best I know it, to you. The updates reflect information in the alpha release of the new 1.1 specs.

Hence this new preface to Core Jini, which provides a high-level overview of the proposed new features in 1.1. In addition, I've made changes in the body of the text to alert you to possible 1.1-related issues, where appropriate. These changes are located in the *1.1 Updates*, found at the ends of chapters.

Most of the new APIs in 1.1 are in the form of some utility classes to make writing Jini services and clients easier, and in the form of some new "standard" services that will ship with the Jini release. These additions do not alter the basic Jini programming model, and if you're used to programming with Jini 1.0, you won't have to "unlearn" any of your current ways of doing things. The 1.1 release builds on what came before, rather than radically changing it.

I haven't updated the examples in the book to reflect new 1.1 APIs, since in almost all cases the versions of the programs shown here should continue to work. Also, I didn't feel it prudent to set new examples in stone when information about 1.1 is still in a very early state (and, particularly, since there is no publicly accessible implementation of the new 1.1 features!) Instead, I have tried to point out possible areas where 1.1 features may be useful to you. If 1.1 is out by the time you read this, you should hopefully be able to make a smooth transition to the new release.

In the rest of this preface, I'll briefly highlight details about the helper classes that may appear in the 1.1 release, and then give information about the new standard services that Sun is working on. Be sure to note that all of the details below are tentative, based on the alpha version of 1.1, and are subject to change.

New Utility Classes in 1.1

The 1.1 release proposes some minor changes to several existing classes and interfaces, as well as one brand-new class designed to make clients easier to write.

Updates to the Discovery Interfaces

In 1.0, the classes used for discovery largely consist of the `LookupDiscovery` class, which performs multicast discovery based on group names, `LookupLocatorDiscovery`, which performs unicast discovery based on `LookupLocator` URLs, and the `DiscoveryListener` interface, which should be implemented by objects that need to respond to discovery events.

In 1.1, the APIs necessary for performing discovery have been better factored. In 1.1, there are new interfaces for each aspect of discovery. These interfaces represent different portions of the "total" discovery API set, and can be used in broader situations. The idea is that classes may implementation one or more of these interfaces, perhaps in different ways. But the rest of the Jini APIs are defined in terms of these interfaces, so that different implementations can be plugged in as needed.

The `DiscoveryManagement` interface has the methods needed to add and remove `DiscoveryListeners`, get the currently discovered set of lookup services, discard lookup services that are not responding, and terminate the discovery process. Essentially, `DiscoveryManagement` is the interface for providing basic control over the discovery process and notifications about discovery.

The `DiscoveryGroupManagement` interface has methods for controlling multicast discovery. These methods allow you to add and remove groups from the set of groups being searched for, set the groups, and fetch the groups.

DiscoveryLocatorManagement is the unicast analog of the DiscoveryGroupManagement interface. DiscoveryLocatorManagement has methods for controlling aspects of unicast discovery; it allows you to add and remove locators from the set of locators being searched for, and get the current set of locators.

With these new interfaces in place, the Jini discovery utilities from 1.0 have been slightly changed to reflect the new interfaces. For example, the LookupLocatorDiscovery class, present in 1.0, is updated to now implement both DiscoveryManagement and DiscoveryLocatorManagement. While the actual APIs supported by this class have not changed, the class now is declared to implement the particular discovery interfaces.

The 1.1 version also adds a particularly nice class for managing all of the discovery-related tasks of a Jini application. In 1.0, clients and services need to use both the LookupDiscovery class (for multicast discovery) and the LookupLocator class (for unicast discovery). (Of course, services use these indirectly, through a JoinManager.) New in 1.1 is the LookupDiscoveryManager, which unifies both unicast and multicast discovery in an easy-to-use way. This class implements all three new discovery-related interfaces—DiscoveryManagement, DiscoveryGroupManagement, and DiscoveryLocatorManagement—to participate in all forms of the discovery protocols. It will call out to any DiscoveryListeners that have been registered with it.

From 1.1 onward, most Jini applications will use this class for their discovery needs, rather than using the separate LookupDiscovery and LookupLocatorDiscovery classes.

Taken together, these changes to the discovery APIs both segregate disparate functionality nicely into component interfaces, and unify the programming model through easy-to-use implementations of these interfaces. Of course, the "old" classes—LookupDiscovery and LookupLocatorDiscovery—are still around and will continue to work, so you should face few migration issues when moving to 1.1.

Changes to JoinManager

The JoinManager class, which provides a convenient way for services to manage their participation in the Jini join protocol, is updated to use the new DiscoveryManagement classes discussed above. These changes are quite minimal.

In the 1.0 implementation of the JoinManager, the code would use LookupDiscovery and LookupLocatorDiscovery instances internally to find lookup services. In 1.1, users can pass an instance of DiscoveryManagement to the JoinManager, and the JoinManager will use this object when searching for lookup services. If you pass null in place of this object, then the Join-

Manager will create a default LookupDiscoveryManager set to join the public group, which is basically the same semantically as the behavior in the 1.0 release.

Why this extra parameter? What does it buy you to be able to specify how the discovery process will take place? In a nutshell, by passing in your own class that implements DiscoveryManagement, you can plug in new discovery implementations for your service while reusing the rest of the JoinManager code. One key reason you might want to do this is if you have implemented new versions of the discovery protocol on top of, say, a non-TCP/IP network (such as an infrared communications link), or have other particular requirements of the discovery protocol.

Once you've set the DiscoveryManagement instance that will be used to manage the discovery process, you can retrieve this instance via a call to getDiscoveryManagement().

Since you can now pass in (and later retrieve) a DiscoveryManagement object to handle discovery, the discovery-related methods on JoinManager have gone away. So instead of calling addGroups(), addLocators(), and friends, you would just access the DiscoveryManagement object being used by the JoinManager and change the discovery parameters on it.

This cleaner separation of functionality between the JoinManager and DiscoveryManagement classes has few implications for portability between 1.0 and 1.1, but can result in cleaner designs and greater functionality.

Client Lookup Utilities

One handy addition to the toolkits of client writers is the new ClientLookupManager class being proposed for 1.1. This class takes over many of the responsibilities of discovery and lookup interactions for clients, in the same way that the JoinManager takes over discovery and lookup duties for services.

While many simple clients may still use the "raw" ServiceRegistrar interfaces for lookup as described in this book, the ClientLookupManager does offer some helpful tools.

Using the ClientLookupManager, clients never interact directly with lookup services or discovery. Instead, they specify what services they are looking for via a ServiceTemplate which will be used to search for desired services at any discovered lookup service, and a ServiceFilter which can cull the list of returned matches, looking for particular services. The ClientLookupManager builds a list of found services, allowing clients to quickly scan over all of the services available in a community. Clients can also receive (local) events telling them about changes in the state of services available to them.

The APIs supported by this proposed class are convenient enough that I expect the `ClientLookupManager` to quickly become the de facto means by which client writers interact with discovery and lookup.

New Standard Services in 1.1

When I was originally writing *Core Jini*, I felt that there were two services that would be particularly appropriate in a book of this sort: a leasing service and an event mailbox service. These services make for fine examples because they not only illustrate basic concepts about building Jini services but, at the end, they give the reader two working and useful services that can be used as infrastructure in a Jini community.

Sun apparently felt the same way, because early information indicates that 1.1 will come with both of these services as "standard" components in the Jini release!

From a writer's perspective, this is both good and bad. It's bad because there's now a bit of redundancy between the code the book presents and what you can (or will be able to) get from Sun. But I feel that it's also good, since the examples here present a solid overview of these two services—technologies that Sun felt were so important that they should be in the toolkits of all Jini developers.

I plan to leave in my versions of both of these services, as they will no doubt be significantly smaller and simpler than whatever comes out of Sun. The issues that these services bring up will be important for writers of many other types of services, and illustrate essential ideas. So you should be aware that by the time you read this, there may be "industrial strength" implementations of these two services widely available. But the descriptions of how to build services like these will still hold true.

In addition to these two services, the 1.1 release may contain a third new service that performs discovery and lookup on behalf of other services. In the sections below, I'll talk about these three services that may be finding their way into the Jini distribution shortly.

The LookupDiscoveryService

One interesting new service proposed for Jini 1.1 is the `LookupDiscoveryService`. This is a service that can perform discovery duties—searching for lookup services—on behalf of its clients (which themselves may be Jini services).

You may be wondering about the utility of such a service—after all, to find a `LookupDiscoveryService`, a client must be able to perform discovery anyway. But the LookupDiscoveryService is actually of great value, particularly in the case where services make use of the RMI activation framework to deactivate themselves when they are not being used.

Imagine a community of services in which many of the services are dormant for periods of time. If a new lookup service is added to the community, these inactive services will not notice the new registrar. Remember that the activation framework only reactivates objects in response to an RMI method call, but the discovery protocols use simple "raw" multicast sockets.

In such a situation, the inactive services could delegate their discovery duties to the LookupDiscoveryService. This service would notice the presence of new lookup services and could inform inactive services (via an RMI method call) about their presence. These services could then become active to register themselves, search for other needed services, and so on.

The programming model of the LookupDiscoveryService is quite simple: Clients of the service register themselves with it, using leased registrations. They specify the groups and lookup locators that they are interested in and provide a RemoteEventListener to be notified when new lookup services are discovered, or when non-responding lookup services are discarded. When any discovery-related event occurs, the clients will receive a RemoteDiscoveryEvent from the LookupDiscoveryService, containing details about what happened, and a list of the ServiceRegistrar proxies for the affected lookup services.

The LeaseRenewalService

Proposed for Jini 1.1 is a new LeaseRenewalService, which performs essentially the same functions as the leasing service described in Chapter 10 of this book—taking over lease management from services that may be inactive for periods of time, or are otherwise unable to perform their own lease management.

The 1.1 LeaseRenewalService supports a rather different API than the service presented in this book. The code in 1.1 uses the notion of LeaseRenewalSets, which are groups of leases that a LeaseRenewalService will manage on behalf of a client. Clients can create new sets of leases via the createLeaseRenewalSet() method on the service, and then add leases to it to be managed.

The LeaseRenewalService supports a number of event notification mechanisms whereby a client can be informed when a lease could not be renewed or when a set of leases is about to expire. One interesting detail of the programming model of the LeaseRenewalService is that clients of the service lease entire sets of leases from the service—essentially, when a client requests the LeaseRenewalService to renew a set of leases, this request comes with a requested lease time. The LeaseRenewalService will generate an event to the client when its lease on this set is about to expire.

Presumably, the LeaseRenewalService would grant leases to its services for durations far greater than those likely to be granted by other particular lease grantors. And, because the LeaseRenewalService will notify clients before the lease on a set is about to expire, activatable clients can easily be awakened to handle their "long-term" leasing.

The EventMailbox Service

Chapter 14 of this book presents the EventMailboxService, a service designed to provide stable queueing for remote events. The Jini 1.1 release proposes a new standard service, called EventMailbox, which performs essentially the same role as the service in this book.

The EventMailbox allows clients to lease storage for their events from an upstream event generator, and then retrieve their stored events at a later time. While the proposed EventMailbox works much the same as the service presented in this book, there is one difference. The Sun EventMailbox allows clients to ask it for a listener, which can be installed as the event listener for any "upstream" generators. The EventMailbox will then denote *any* events received by that listener as being destined for the client. This is unlike the mailbox code presented in this book, which segregates events based on type IDs.

Much like the LeaseRenewalService, I believe the presentation of the EventMailboxService in Chapter 14 has pedagogical value, even if a similar service is available from Sun—although I do expect (and recommend) most developers to use the Sunversion when it becomes available, as it will certainly become a standard tool in the Jini toolbox.

Summary

This preface presents proposed elements of the upcoming Jini 1.1 release. By the time you read this, the 1.1 release may already be available, perhaps in a form similar to that described here, and perhaps very different. Be sure to keep tabs on the Jini Web resources mentioned throughout the book for details on release information.

Introduction

This book provides a comprehensive guide to Jini, the new distributed systems technology from Sun Microsystems. Jini has the potential to revolutionize the way we build networked software. In a sense, Jini signals a change from a world in which devices are *networked* (meaning that computers simply have the ability to talk to one another) into one in which devices join together to form a true *distributed system*—a collection of networked components working together.

The distinction between networked devices and true distributed systems is an important one. Simple networked systems have simple communication patterns (usually peer-to-peer or client/server), and tend to be static, long-lived entities. Distributed systems, on the other hand, are composed of numerous constituent pieces. Any of these pieces can come or go without bringing down the whole system, and the system can respond to changes in its environment and its constituency in reliable and predictable ways. In a nutshell, Jini moves us from a world in which the "system" is the individual networked device, to one in which the "system" is the collection of all these devices working together.

This book serves two purposes. First, it provides a broad introduction to the core technologies of Jini. This introduction will be useful to Java developers who need to understand Jini, and to other technically-savvy readers who need to understand how Jini fits into the world, and why it is significant. Second, the book provides a deep understanding of how to build working software that leverages Jini. This second focus is intended for a range of developers, including those who are building Jini-enabled software for small devices such as PDAs, to those building LAN-based networked systems such

as for the small-office/home-office (SOHO) or remote-office/home-office (ROHO), all the way up to enterprisewide network services and possibly the Internet itself.

These two goals of the book are largely represented by the book's two parts. Part I introduces Jini history, looks at Jini's place in the world—in particular, how Jini is different from what came before it—and provides some details on getting started with the technology and deploying it in actual use. Part II provides an in-depth look at the core Jini concepts, such as leasing, lookup, discovery, and transactions, as well as some extensive examples that illustrate particular aspects of Jini. Finally, the remainder of the book provides appendices and reference materials.

The philosophy taken by this book is that developers learn by reading code. You will no doubt notice if you page through this book, especially the chapters in Part II, that there are a great many code examples here. Some of these are "stand-alone" Jini programs—they typically introduce some concept in the smallest number of lines possible, in the interest of clarity. Others are utility programs that cover "holes" in the Jini APIs. These programs will find their way into the toolchests of programmers working with Jini.

Throughout this book, though, I have provided a number of longer examples that share a common theme: Taken together, these examples can be used as applications in "live" Jini networks, and can interoperate with each other. This approach is very much in keeping with the Jini design philosophy itself—large numbers of cooperating applications working together to provide some service—and happens to be a good way to illustrate the ideas in Jini by using discrete chunks of code rather than monolithic, multithousand line applications. Each of these examples illustrates one or more key points of the Jini architecture. They can be extended by you, and applied to any number of domains, from small, intelligent devices all the way up to enterprise software systems.

One thing this book does not provide is an introduction to Java itself. Jini is a layer atop Java—much like the Java Foundation Classes (JFC) or Java Database Connectivity (JDBC). Like these other layers, Jini introduces some new concepts and extends the Java programming model, but at its core, Jini remains pure Java. This book assumes that you are familiar with Java programming and, with one exception, does not cover the facilities available in the core Java class libraries or the language.

The one exception is the Java Remote Method Invocation system (RMI). RMI is used extensively in Jini. In fact, Jini leverages new features in RMI that only appeared in Java 2 (also popularly known as JDK1.2), such as the RMI activation framework. Thus, there is an RMI primer in Appendix A of this book that serves as an introduction to this technology for those who may be unfamiliar with it.

A Roadmap

Part I of this book, "Foundations," provides some necessary background reading on Jini. This information will be useful for savvy readers who just need to understand Jini, what it does, and how it works. But it's also "required reading" for developers who want to build actual, running Jini programs—the chapters in this part highlight the philosophical differences between Jini and "classical" networked and distributed systems technologies. If you have a good understanding of this material, you're ready to build software that's consistent with the Jini aesthetic.

Chapter 1, "A New Computing Paradigm," looks at the history and motivation of Jini. You'll see how Jini is really the fulfillment of the original Java promise: of collections of software and hardware, working together simply and without administration. This chapter also covers the process of getting and installing the Jini software.

Chapter 2, "Distributed Systems," provides a glimpse at the basics of distributed systems, and how Jini differs from traditional distributed systems software. Even if you're a handy network programmer, you may want to take a look at this chapter. Jini is fairly unique in the distributed systems world, and it's interesting to see the roots of Jini and understand what problems it's good at solving.

Chapter 3, "The Jini Model," introduces the basic concepts in Jini. Fortunately there are very few of these—only five. Understanding these concepts and how they connect to each other will make later reading much easier.

Chapter 4, "Deployment Scenarios," covers some scenarios for deploying Jini services. These are development targets, if you will—ways that you as a developer can deploy Jini code that you write. Jini is perhaps unique in all the Java libraries provided by Sun, in that it is specifically designed to support devices which may *not* have Java Virtual Machines (JVMs) embedded in them. Jini can be used to connect devices with only limited computational ability, just as it can be used to connect large servers and other machines running full-fledged JVMs. This chapter will help you understand the options available to you if you're designing for Jini.

These first four chapters comprise Part I of this book—they provide a broad introduction to the Jini technology and how it fits into the world. Part II, "Building with Jini," is a very in-depth look at particular aspects of Jini. It is designed for the professional Java developer who is writing new Jini services or building Jini-enabled devices. Some of the chapters in this part are *In Depth* chapters that dive deeply into a particular aspect of the Jini technology. Others are structured around large examples that show Jini being applied to real problems.

Chapter 5, "Getting Started with Jini," begins with a series of programs designed to introduce you to the core Jini concepts. This series is a set of "Hello, World" style programs that are evolved to illustrate ideas such as lookup, discovery, leasing, and remote events. This chapter is your first introduction to building Jini software from scratch, and covers almost all the basic Jini ideas, as well as an example of using the RMI activation framework.

Chapter 6, "In Depth: Discovery," is an in-depth chapter looking at Jini's discovery protocols. These are the means by which Jini services notify the world of their existence, and Jini client applications learn about the clusters or "communities" of services that are available to them. We'll look under the hood at these protocols—understanding what's really going on there is key to using them effectively. By the end of this chapter you should understand these protocols well enough to be able to implement them "by hand" if you need to.

Chapter 7, "Using Attributes to Describe Services," talks about the Jini notion of *attributes*. Attributes are objects that can be associated with services to provide descriptive information about them, or even provide additional functionality (such as user interfaces) to extend the behavior of services. This chapter talks about how to use attributes, and how the Jini attribute model meshes nicely with JavaBeans.

Chapter 8, "In Depth: Using Lookup Services," moves on to the next major phase in a Jini application's life cycle, the use of the Jini lookup service. Lookup is how applications learn about particular services within a particular community. In this in-depth chapter, you'll see how both clients and services use lookup, and learn how to use some high-level "convenience" APIs to simplify the responsibilities of services with regard to lookup. We'll pay special attention to the issues around federating and connecting Jini communities into larger structures.

At this point you should understand the basics of what you need to know to build a very functional and useful Jini client application that can participate in the discovery and lookup process, and allow you to find and browse any Jini service on the network. Chapter 9, "A Jini Lookup Service Browser," introduces a long application that exercises the ideas in the previous chapters. This application is a browser that can find lookup servers and the services registered there, and allow you to view and control the attributes of those services. The code in this chapter builds up a toolkit of useful components for displaying and using service information, which you can reuse in your own applications.

Chapter 10, "In Depth: Leasing," gives in-depth coverage of the notion of leasing, which is how Jini manages resources held by remote systems. Leasing is also the key to Jini's ability to "self-heal" a large distributed system. In this chapter, we'll talk about the benefits of leasing, and cover some common idioms that arise again and again when programming with leases.

While Chapter 10's focus is on the ideas behind leasing, and in particular how clients can use leasing, Chapter 11, "Exporting Leased Resources," talks about how Jini services can implement leasing. This is the other half of the leasing equation that is started in Chapter 10. With these two chapters, you can "close the loop," exporting a leased resource to a client, which then uses the lease consumer APIs to control it.

While the chapters on discovery, lookup, and leasing provide the *basics* of what you have to do to write a functional Jini service, Chapter 12, "The Well-Behaved Service," provides a summary of the extra steps you can take to provide a *useful* and *useable* service. This chapter talks about service administration, the join protocol—which governs how services interact with their communities—and how to provide user interfaces for services.

After this coverage of what it takes to be a "good" service, we're ready to build a complete, sophisticated Jini application. Chapter 13, "A Complete Example: The Print Service," presents a long example of a service that allows clients to connect to it to print documents. This program supports administration, persistence, and self-description through attributes, and can serve as the basis for many of the services you will write. And, of course, you'll be able to use this service in conjunction with the other examples in this book.

Next, Chapter 14, "In Depth: Remote Events," provides a look at how Jini supports asynchronous notifications between programs. Jini extends the local Java event model with events that can be sent between objects in different JVMs. This remote event model has different semantics than the usual JavaBeans event model—this chapter looks at why this is, and explores some common idioms for using remote events. The remote event model lends itself to the creation of event "adaptors" that can plug into the event pipeline to provide such services as forwarding or storage of events. One of the examples here looks at an "event mailbox" adaptor that can be a useful service in many Jini communities.

While the preceding chapters cover topics that are considered core and fundamental to Jini, the next two chapters are a bit different. The next chapters cover topics that are actually implemented as services *atop* the core Jini infrastructure.

Chapter 15, "JavaSpaces," provides an introduction to Sun's JavaSpaces service. This service provides an extremely useful object storage engine. Many applications that use Jini will need a way to store persistent data, and share it for use by other applications. JavaSpaces provides an easy object-based way for them to do this. And JavaSpaces can even serve as the basis for new styles of distributed computation. This chapter looks at the JavaSpaces programming model and philosophy.

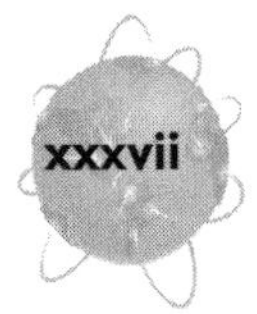

Chapter 16, "Distributed Transactions," covers transactions, which are one of the most technical concepts in Jini. Transactions are a way for cooperating processes to ensure the integrity of their data. Essentially, transactions are a way to make sure that either an entire set of operations happen completely, or that none of them happen at all. Those of you familiar with database programming are no doubt familiar with transactions, and their power in preventing partial failures. The Jini model, while based on the familiar two-phase commit protocol used in database systems, is actually somewhat different. This chapter explores those differences, and shows how to build programs that can use transactions to safely group their operations.

Finally, the two appendices in this book provide some useful reference and background material. Appendix A is a primer on the RMI technology, in particular, the features that have been added as of the Java 2 release. The RMI activation framework, which provides a way for objects to be automatically reconstituted from persistent storage when needed, will be used heavily by many Jini applications, and is important to understand. In general, a good grounding in the ideas of RMI is necessary for getting the most from Jini.

Appendix B provides a reference to the various system properties that can be useful when developing with Jini. You can use these properties to control and tune the behavior of Jini, as well as some basic Java features, in your applications.

Conventions Used in This Book

This book follows a number of conventions to help you get the most out of it. Throughout the text, you'll see a number of callouts that designate particular items of interest. These callouts, called Core Note, Core Alert, and Core Tip, provide useful information that is important enough that it should not be lost in the text. Core Alerts are used for potential pitfalls in developing Jini applications. Examples might include portions of the Jini API that are unimplemented or perhaps behave differently than the specs indicate. Core Tips are pointers to common and useful ways to accomplish particular results. Examples might include common idioms or patterns that can make your life as a developer easier. Core Notes are extra information that might help you make sense of some aspect of Jini, or just provide fodder for Silicon Valley cocktail party conversations.

Getting Sample Code from the Internet

All the code samples in this book have been collected together, and are available electronically from the Prentice Hall ftp site. To download the code, point your web browser at `ftp://ftp.prenhall.com/pub/ptr/sunsoft_books.w-053/corejini`. Save the file to your computer's hard disk, and extract the contents. If you're on Windows, use your favorite unzipping utility, such as WinZip. On Solaris and other UNIX platforms, use a command like `unzip corejini.zip`.

The unzip process will create a directory called `corejini` under whatever directory you ran the unzipper. For consistency with the rest of this book, I'd recommend unzipping the contents into `C:\files\corejini` (on Windows) and `/files/corejini` (on Solaris).

Under the `corejini` directory you'll find separate subdirectories for each of the chapters in this book that contain code samples.

Feedback

No book is perfect, especially one that covers a topic as new and as rich as Jini. Even though this book has been thoroughly reviewed a number of times, I have no doubt that errors do remain, or that improvements can be made. If you find a "bug," either in the text or in one of the example programs, or if you think of anything that might make this book more useful to you or other readers, please drop me a note:

`kedwards@parc.xerox.com`

Further Information

Many of the chapters in this book have a "Further Reading" section at the end of them, with pointers to books, papers, and resources on the Internet that may extend your Jini knowledge.

However, for resources to extend this book itself, you should check out the Prentice Hall Web page for *Core Jini*, to get news on updates, revisions, and so forth:

`http://www.phptr.com`

Acknowledgments

Ipn the fall of 1998, I received an e-mail from Mark Weiser, the Chief Technologist of Xerox PARC, asking me whether I'd be willing to evaluate a new technology called Jini. Mark had been involved for years in a vision of the future called "ubiquitous computing," in which our workspaces are filled with a variety of devices that are not only aware of us, but can work together with us to support us in our jobs. Much of the ubiquitous computing vision is predicated on the belief that technology should be a calming influence in our lives, rather than the often headache-inducing nightmare that it currently is.

When Mark asked me to see if Jini might be a viable substrate on top of which to base some of the grander ideas of ubiquitous computing (not to mention possible Xerox products), I had no idea that his simple e-mail would lead me down the path I've taken for the last few months.

Jini is an important technology. It's important not only because products will ship that are based on it, or because it will help drive up Sun's stock price, or because any number of garages inhabited by two developers, two computers, and a coffee machine may become the birthplaces of huge companies. Jini is important because it has the potential to fundamentally change not only the way we build software, but the way we interact with the technology that is increasingly a part of our lives.

As I learned more about Jini, I became convinced that—even though it is a young technology—it could bring about a shift in what we expect from the

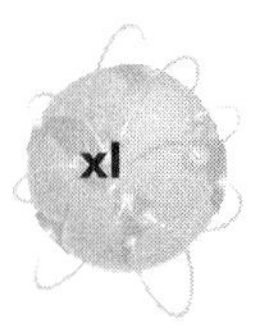

technology in our lives. The ideas in Jini are simple. Perhaps deceptively so, because even simple ideas can be difficult to adopt, when they're so radically different than what's gone before. My goal in writing this book was to help, perhaps just a little bit, to change what we come to expect from our computers. My method has been to focus on these simple ideas in Jini, and dig below the surface to see what the implications of these ideas really are.

Any book—even one with only one author's name on the cover—is always a collaborative effort to some degree. I believe this book has been more collaborative than most.

First, a sincere thanks to Mark Weiser for pointing me toward Jini in the first place, for encouraging me, and for setting *my* expectations about what a technology should be. Mark is, in many ways, the reason I came to Xerox PARC; I'm even more indebted to him after this project. Sadly, Mark passed away before this book could be published; the fact that this book is dedicated to him is appropriate, but doesn't begin to reflect his contributions to PARC and the world.

PARC's management team has been wonderfully supportive of this project, not only in terms of personal encouragement, but also by giving me the time to work on it. Richard Bruce, who is the manager of the Computer Science Lab, deserves thanks for allowing me to get so wrapped up in the writing. And a special thanks to Karin Petersen, my direct manager, for her constant support not only in terms of motivation, but also by giving me the freedom and flexibility to work on the book.

In hindsight, a word of thanks is due to Beth Mynatt, who through her encouragement managed to give me a solid shove off the face of this cliff, while somehow remaining safely on the edge herself. The edge of a precipice is a prime spot for spectators, and Beth has certainly gotten to observe my plummet for the last few months. Her turn will come...

My editors at Prentice Hall, Tim Moore and Ralph Moore (no relation, as Tim always tells me...I'm never sure if Ralph should be offended or relieved!), made this a smooth and *almost* enjoyable process!

I've had the extreme and unwarranted good fortune to have a truly stellar group of technical reviewers on this project. Peter van der Linden, whom many of you will know from his books such as *Deep C Secrets*, and *Just Java*, provided excellent comments, especially on the book's examples. Marty Hall, author of *Core Web Programming*, provided great feedback throughout the early chapters, and also provided kind words in his first reviews that kept me from giving up hope. And a very special thanks to Brian Murphy. Brian is a member of the Jini team, and provided substantial comments on every single chapter in the book. Without his insight and feedback, this book would be far

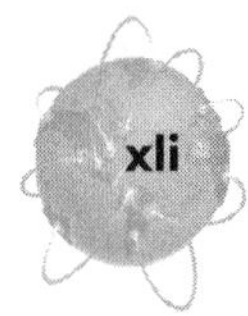

less useful, less accurate, and less clear than it is. Any readers who wish to thank Brian personally should certainly do so; take my word for it—he's saved you hours of aggravation.

A number of "unofficial" technical reviewers have also contributed to the book, especially in its early stages. Anind Dey provided great comments on the first few chapters. Beki Grinter, a dyed-in-the-wool Bell-head, provided excellent and insightful feedback on the telephone example in the first chapter. Beki, if I'd had the room, I would have expanded it into a full chapter, I promise.

My family, and especially my mother, will no doubt be single-handedly responsible for at least half of the sales of this book. I fully expect them to be handed out to old schoolmates, acquaintances from church, and casual passers-by on the streets. Go mom!

Finally, a special word of thanks and appreciation to Beki, who has certainly been the light at the end of this long tunnel. Thanks for supporting me, encouraging me, and not killing me during my mental and physical absences during the past few months.

And now, if you'll excuse me, I'm going to dig out from under the papers, books, and code littering my house, and resume my life where I left off.

Part 1

FOUNDATIONS

A NEW COMPUTING PARADIGM

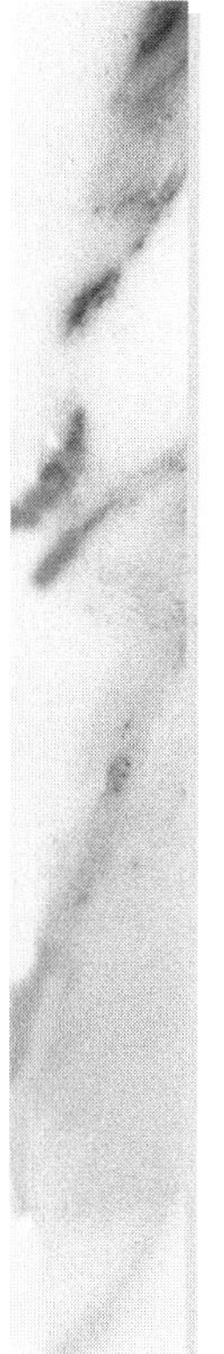

Topics in This Chapter

- The history of Jini
- Sun's licensing model for Jini
- Getting and installing the software
- Running Jini services from the command line

Chapter 1

The computer on your desk is a remarkable device. It provides computational power, storage, and speed that would have been unthinkable only a few years ago. The fact that this statement is now such a cliché is only a testament to the incredible changes that have occurred in our industry.

Yet despite such advances, the basic structure of our computers remains much the same as it was in the 1950s: We have central processing units, memory, and disks. And, despite the fact that we now use computers with power that would have been unimaginable 40 years ago, to play games and balance our checkbooks, we fundamentally interact with these machines in the same ways that our predecessors did: We install software on them, run applications, and manage the (always scarce) disk resources of our systems. A mainframe systems administrator from 1950 would understand these tasks immediately. In fact, in some sense, we've *all* become systems administrators—now each of us has to manage our own machines, doing tasks that would be familiar to systems administrators of an earlier era. The increase in speed and decrease in size has not brought about a qualitative change in how we manage, install, and use these machines.

The situation in desktop computers stands in stark contrast to the situation in telephony. The telephone network has grown exponentially since its humble beginnings, both in terms of raw capacity, and the number of phones connected to the network. One can pick up a standard telephone virtually anywhere in the world and, nearly instantly, create a pipeline suitable for voice or data transfer to anyplace else in the world. And while this system's complexity has grown exponentially, it is largely hidden from its users. My perception of the phone system doesn't grow more complex as users in China come on line. The interface for connecting to any other place in the world stays largely the same, even as more of the world becomes accessible. And installation and maintenance of the small part of the global phone network that's housed in my residence couldn't be simpler—I simply plug in new devices and they become reachable from anywhere in the world. My own minute chunk of the phone network is owned by me and, if such a term even makes sense here, *administered* by me as well. And yet everything still "just works."

If we expect our computers to be useful—or even useable—as the number of interconnected devices on the network explodes, we have to reach this level of reliability, ease of deployment, and ease of administration. The most administration we have to do with the telephone system is the occasional replacement of a handset; why then should we take as a given that our current computers and computer networks require so much hand holding to work properly?

Jini History

In some ways, the history of Jini is the history of Java—Jini is really the fulfillment of the original Java vision of groups of consumer-oriented electronic devices interchanging data and bits of code. Java started out as a language called Oak, designed as a portable way to write programs for embedded processors, at Sun Microsystems Labs in 1990. As the project matured, the language found its way into new types of devices. One of the first experiments resulted in Oak running on a handheld computer called the Star-7. In this guise, the language was used to build interfaces for digital TV and entertainment applications. In fact, the creator of Oak, James Gosling, decided to write the new language only after the team had tried to work with C++ and found it too complicated and "programmer unfriendly."

In its second incarnation, Oak found its way onto the Web. In 1994, two engineers at Sun, Patrick Naughton and Jonathan Payne, wrote a Web browser completely in Oak. This browser, called WebRunner, later became the basis for the HotJava browser, and became famous for its ability to download executable programs, called applets, from Web servers and execute them securely within the browser. The language—rechristened Java for its launch in April 1995—was released with the browser and made Internet history.

Many of the goals of the original consumer electronics vision of Java—the ability to move code from device to device regardless of CPU type, security, compactness, and so on—made the language a natural for its new home on the Web.

The Jini Vision

Although Java got its start in consumer electronics, it is most commonly thought of as a tool for building applets. The original vision never died within Sun, however. A group of engineers realized that the original idea was still compelling. And although Java makes this idea *possible*—what with its ability to send portable code from machine to machine and execute it securely—there are other problems that must be solved to make the vision of constellations of easily administered devices work in *practice*.

This vision requires mechanisms that we don't typically associate with desktop computers.

- The software infrastructure for these devices must be incredibly robust. Toasters and TV sets simply cannot fail with a message asking "Abort, Retry, Ignore?" The software must not only allow, but *encourage*, the development of reliable systems.
- The devices have to support true, effortless "plug and play." They should be the Internet equivalents of the telephone: You plug them in and they just work. There are a couple of requirements that this desire for plug-and-play imposes. First, devices must be easy to use. Much like a telephone, typical consumer devices may have only limited interfaces. Certainly not every device at home will have a mouse and high-resolution display. In fact, we probably don't *want* such interfaces for these devices—if they require a mouse, chances are they're too hard to use. Second, these devices must be easy to administer. We'd like to just plug them in and use them, without having to configure IP addresses for them, set up gateways and routers, install (and possibly remove) drivers, and so on. Upgrades of software are an important issue here—if an administrator has to be called in to upgrade the software for all the TVs in a large hotel, chances are the TVs simply won't get upgraded.
- Software systems for the Internet age must be evolvable. While creating software for stand-alone devices, such as the CPU in a microwave, is challenging enough, the potential problems are multiplied by the fact that networked devices must be able to communicate with any number of peer devices on the Internet.

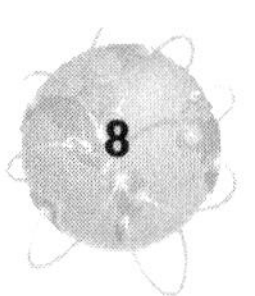

And, perhaps more problematic, the creator of the original device may not even know about the existence of new devices that will appear later. We'd like our software services and devices to be able to use each other without massive reconfiguration of the network.

- Devices like these will form spontaneous communities: Imagine a digital camera that's brought into proximity to a color printer. We'd like to be able to simply print the snapshots on the printer, without having to explicitly tell either device about the other. In many cases, the effort that would be required to tell the devices about one another would overwhelm the potential benefit to be gained from using them together—which is one reason we don't typically reconfigure our current networks at the drop of a hat. In this world, networking would become much more dynamic, and less the fixed, static organization that we have today.

The vision of legions of devices and software services working together, simply and reliably, had been espoused by a number of researchers and computer industry leaders before. Mark Weiser of the Xerox Palo Alto Research Center called this vision "ubiquitous computing," a term meant to connote the ready availability and useability of devices connected to the network. Bill Joy, one of the founders of Sun and the original creator of Berkeley UNIX, believed that the future would continue to hold traditional desktop computers, but also smart "appliances" in homes and vehicles.

With these visions in mind, a group at Sun set out to provide the infrastructure that would bring Java full circle—they intended to build the software layer that would sit atop Java to provide the benefits of reliability, maintainability, evolvability, and spontaneity that such a world would require. These developers set out to define a model that would be easy for programmers to understand, and yet would lend itself to this new way of building software—a way of building software that is probably foreign to many, even those used to writing network-aware code.

This project became known as Jini,[1] and many of the people who created and championed it are the same people who originally created and championed certain aspects of Java: Bill Joy would become one of the inspirations and chief supporters of the project, much as he was for the original Java work. Jim

1. The creators of the system explain that Jini was chosen because it is an energetic and easy-to-remember word that begins with "J" and has the same number of letters as "Java." Although some of them will joke that Jini stands for "Jini Is Not Initials." The word is pronounced just like "genie."

Waldo inspired much of the early work on Jini and would become the chief architect and designer of the system. Ann Wollrath invented Java's Remote Method Invocation (RMI) facility, and continues her work in the context of Jini, where she has been one of the key designers of the system. And Ken Arnold would define Jini's transaction and storage models. One of the key Jini players who came from outside Sun is Bob Scheifler, who once led the X Consortium and has defined the Jini lookup and discovery protocols.

There are any number of exotic programming models that have attempted to solve the problems of distributed computing. The Jini designers could have selected one of these models—such as temporal logic, weakly-consistent databases, or agents—as the basis of a system to address the challenges that Jini addresses. But these systems typically require you to "start from scratch" when learning them, because their programming models are so radical. Fortunately, the designers built their system on a set of core concepts that, at least individually, will be commonplace to Java developers: mobile code, strongly typed interfaces, and separation of interface and implementation. To this mix of old Java standbys they add some new concepts that are unique to Jini. These include a distributed storage model that can be used as a general-purpose facility for storing and retrieving objects. This storage model is based on the Linda system from David Gelernter at Yale. Jini also exposes a concept that has been used "under the covers" in RMI for years—the notion of "leasing" as a means to regulate access to resources on a network. Finally, Jini makes heavy use of periodic multicast to notify cooperating Jini applications and services of one another.

Again, the basic notions in Jini are familiar to any Java programmer. Jini adds a number of incremental changes to Java to extend it to this new world of lightweight distributed computing, but doesn't require developers to invest in learning entirely new programming paradigms from the ground up.

Not Just for Consumer Electronics

Interestingly, many of the attributes that are desirable in consumer devices turn out to be desirable in desktop and enterprise software as well. If you are a network or system administrator, you're probably well aware of the problems of maintaining even stand-alone computers, much less a whole network of machines! PC networks have many of the same needs as consumer devices. We'd like them to be truly "plug and play" (not the weak sort of plug-and-play found on today's PCs, but real, reliable networking by just plugging into the wall). We'd like them to be evolvable in a consistent and reliable way—if I install an OS upgrade on one machine on the network, I'd like it (and the rest of the machines on the network) to keep working. These abilities are as important in home networks as they are in workgroup networks.

Enterprise systems have even more stringent requirements. Servers are meant to stay running for months or even years, so they need to be reliable. We'd like to be able to upgrade the software services on them without requiring a reboot or otherwise breaking the world. And we'd like to have much more flexibility in how we configure the services on the network—if my database server is underpowered, I'd like to be able to just move it to a new machine without having to touch every client to tell it where the database now lives.

This need for "administration free" networking goes beyond simple convenience—it can actually allow us to do things that were so difficult as to be impractical before. For example, Jini enables a world in which you can visit a remote site—say, a customer's place of business—and be able to use all of the software services and devices on that remote network. Printers, fileservers, and scanners, as well as any number of purely software services become accessible without any configuration, administration, or driver installation. Jini's administration-free properties lend themselves to the creation of spontaneous, ad hoc networks of computers, formed whenever and wherever needed.

Jini Becomes Public

The Jini project went on at Sun, hidden from public eyes, until *New York Times* technology reporter John Markoff broke the story in a front page article in 1998. Shortly thereafter, Jini—although still officially unannounced—appeared on the cover of *Wired* magazine. The technology was finally introduced to the public on January 25, 1999, with a host of licensees already on board.

These partners are building Jini-enabled services and devices, including disk drives, digital cameras, printers, and scanners. For its part, Sun is rapidly aligning behind Jini, in much the same way it aligned around Java back in 1995.

Licensees

At the time of this writing, Jini has already been licensed by nearly 40 companies that span a huge gamut from device vendors to enterprise software companies. These include disk drive manufacturers such as Quantum and Seagate, cellular phone manufacturers Nokia and Ericsson, printer vendors including Xerox, Canon, Epson, and Hewlett-Packard, camera manufacturer

Kodak, networking vendors Cisco and 3Com, software producers BEA Systems, Novell, and Inprise, and a huge number of consumer electronics companies including Sony, Sharp, Philips, and Toshiba. Jini has also been licensed for use by companies as diverse as AOL and Kinko's.

Community Source Licensing

Sun provides access to Jini source code under what they call the Sun Community Source License (SCSL). This license is designed to provide virtually free and easy access to all the Jini source code by developers, while allowing Sun to ensure that Jini products remain compatible with one another, and that the Jini source doesn't "splinter" into incompatible versions.

The community licensing model has many similarities to the "Open Source" movement. The Open Source movement espouses freely-available source code, available to anyone who needs it. This approach to software development has many benefits—look at the rapid development of large software systems such as Linux, for example. But it does have drawbacks. Most importantly, most Open Source arrangements either have minimal controls over the definition of the software (meaning that anyone can introduce an incompatible change), or they require anyone using the software to submit modifications they make back to an organizing body. The first drawback means that the original developer of the technology may be unable to prevent it from splintering into a morass of incompatible versions. The second drawback means that many companies who might otherwise be eager to develop for the technology may be reluctant to be required to turn over their intellectual property to a third party.

The community license model allows very open access to source code, while promoting compatibility among the developer community. And yet it does not require companies or developers to hand their developments back to Sun. How does it work? The SCSL defines three levels of usage of the source code, with increasing responsibilities for each.

At the first level, you can obtain the source code for *Research* use. This allows you complete access to the source for personal, research, and educational uses, or to evaluate the source for possible deployment. The license itself is just a "click through" page on the Sun download site; in fact, the core Jini downloads that we'll look at later in this chapter include source code. At this level, there are virtually no requirements for you. You are free to learn about the technology, modify the source, create new implementations of the Jini components, and try it out in your applications. You can even create "clones" of the code, as long as you include the proper notices in the source.

At the next level is the *Internal Use* license. If you've been using the Jini software under the research arrangement, you can move to this level of access and responsibility without any extra legal overhead—there is nothing to sign, and you do not need to notify Sun of your new use of the technology. The only requirement is that if you use the Jini source code to deploy an internal application that you've created, you must follow the Jini naming conventions and be compatible with the Jini Technology Compatibility Kit, which is freely available from Sun. You can "clone" the technology as long as it passes the compatibility tests. These requirements are designed to ensure that you will have complete interoperability and compatibility between your services and Jini implementations and third-party Jini code that your organization may buy or download from the Internet.

Finally, if you're planning to sell new products based on the Jini source code, you must graduate to the *Commercial Use* arrangement. Unlike the two previous usage models, which you are free to use and move between with virtually no overhead or participation with Sun, selling a product based on Jini source code requires you to sign the commercial use community source license with Sun. This license still imposes only minimal requirements on you, though: You must pass the freely available Jini Technology Compatibility Kit, and you must sign a separate Jini Compatibility logo license (which incurs a minimal fee).

These guidelines allow you to have unfettered access to the source code for learning, experimenting, and teaching. As your code becomes more and more public, though—first to others in your organization, and then to others in the world—the community source license requires that your responsibilities to maintain compatibility increase as well. There are no requirements for you to hand over any of your code to other developers or to Sun. If you wish, however, you can choose to donate any code you write back to the community, in which case Sun or other developers can redistribute it.

What does this mean for you? If you're developing a service for Jini that only depends on the Jini run-time framework and the Jini binaries as posted on the Sun Web site, you can distribute your program without having any source license at all, although you cannot redistribute the Jini binaries themselves (Sun does require a commercial license to redistribute their binaries). The SCSL model deals with access, modifications, and redistribution of the Jini *source* code, not the binaries. Only if you plan to use the source in your applications or make modifications to it will you need to follow the guidelines in the SCSL.

Sun intends the community licensing approach to afford the best of both worlds—easy and relatively unfettered access to source code, while still ensuring some degree of compatibility and co-evolution of the code. The

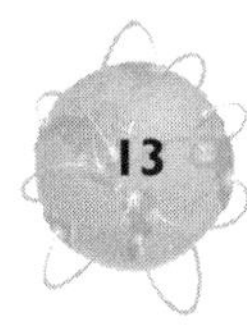

SCSL process is still evolving, and Sun is actively soliciting feedback on their licensing strategies.

Full details of Jini's community licensing model are available from Sun's Web site. If you have any questions about the SCSL, you should definitely consult this page. Since the SCSL is still evolving, there's a good chance that the dictates of the license have changed since the writing of this book.

```
http://java.sun.com/products/jini/licensing/
```

Getting and Installing Jini

Obviously before you can start programming with Jini, you need to get the software set up! Chances are, if you're a Java developer, you've already got Java 2 installed on your system. If you don't have this version (or a later Java 2 point release), you're going to need it, because Jini requires some features that are only in Java 2.

Here's the checklist for getting Jini up and running.

1. Install Java 2, if you don't have it already.
   - Download the Java 2 software from Sun
   - Unpack the distribution
   - Examine the distribution
2. Install the Jini release.
   - Download Jini from Sun
   - Unpack the distribution
   - Examine the distribution
3. Set up your environment.
   - Make sure the Java binaries are in your PATH
   - Edit your CLASSPATH for Jini
4. Start the Jini run-time services, using either the GUI or the command line.
   - Configure and start the HTTP server
   - Configure and start the RMI activation daemon
   - Configure and start the Jini Lookup Service
5. Run the sample programs to make sure you've got everything correctly configured.

The remainder of this chapter details the steps required to download and install the Java 2 JDK and Jini. The instructions for setting up Java 2 are particular to the Windows and Solaris implementations of the JDK that are available from Sun; if you run on a different platform—or simply use a different JDK implementation on one of these two platforms—then you should check with your operating systems vendor for instructions on how to download and install Java 2.

Since the sample implementation of Jini that comes from Sun is itself implemented *completely* in Java, there is one version of the code for all platforms. The installation instructions given here for Jini should be useful for all machines and operating systems.

Core Note: Jini sample implementations and specifications

Jini, much like Java, is defined as a set of core specifications that detail how the software must work. And just as any operating system vendor or group of developers can create an alternate implementation of Java that conforms to these specifications, there can be multiple implementations of Jini as well.

But just as Sun provides "sample" implementations of the Java technology for Windows and Solaris, it also provides a sample implementation of the Jini specifications. Sun's implementation is pure Java, and so should run on any platform with a fully conformant Java 2 implementation. This Jini sample implementation has been tested on the reference implementations of Java for Windows and Solaris; the Jini development team actively encourages developers to test Jini on other JDK implementations.

The installation and set-up instructions here detail the procedures for the sample implementations of both Java and Jini.

Installing Java 2

First, let's look at downloading and installing Java 2.

Downloading the JDK from Sun

The most current Java 2 JDK releases are always available from:

```
http://java.sun.com/products/jdk/1.2/
```

Click on the appropriate link for your OS (currently either Windows or Solaris) and save the resulting file to your hard disk. A note for Solaris users: even though Sun provides both a reference and a "production" implementation of Java for the Solaris operating system, at the time of this writing the Jini team recommends using only the reference implementation of the JDK with Jini.

There is also a documentation bundle separately available from the download site. You may wish to copy this bundle—which is available either as a ZIP file or as a compressed "tar" file—to your local system, if you don't otherwise have access to the Java 2 documentation.

Unpacking the Distribution

Next you need to unpack and actually install the JDK.

For Windows: If you're on the Windows platform, you've just downloaded a self-installing EXE file. You can just double-click on the file to install it. The installation script will copy two separate sets of files to your hard disk: the first is the Java Development Kit proper, which contains the compiler, debugger, and associated tools. The second is the Java Runtime Environment, which contains the Java Virtual Machine and the class libraries for the language. In almost every case, simply installing these files to the default location suggested by the installer is fine.

For Solaris: Solaris users wind up with a self-installing shell script. You can run this script by invoking `sh` (the UNIX command shell interpreter) on the file you downloaded. For example, if you named the file `Solaris-install.bin`, you would type:

```
sh Solaris-install.bin
```

You'll be asked to accept the license agreement and provide a directory to unpack into.

Examining the Distribution

Once you've downloaded and installed the JDK, you should probably familiarize yourself with where all the important pieces live. Table 1–1 presents a list of the most important components of the JDK; we'll assume that you unpacked the contents into a directory called `jdk1.2`. It's important to understand where the essential components live, so that you can make sure your environment is properly configured for running Java.

Table 1–1 Layout for the JDK 1.2 Release

`jdk1.2`	This is the root of the JDK installation.
`jdk1.2/bin`	Contains the Java executables, including `java`, which is the Java Virtual Machine; `javac`, the Java compiler; `rmic`, the RMI compiler; `rmid`, the RMI "activation daemon;" and `rmiregistry`, the RMI name server.
`jdk1.2/demo`	Various demonstration applets and programs.
`jdk1.2/doc`	Documentation for the Java platform, in HTML format. Note that this directory will *only* be available if you downloaded and unpacked the separate documentation bundle.
`jdk1.2/jre`	This directory contains the "Java Runtime Environment." This is the minimal set of tools and libraries required to run—but not develop—Java programs.
`jdk1.2/jre/ext`	This directory is for extensions to the Java platform. You can place JAR files here, as well as supporting native code, and the Java Virtual Machine will make it available to all Java applications in the VM.
`jdk1.2/lib`	This directory contains the JAR files for the Java class libraries, as well as supporting libraries that are not part of the Java API and are not directly callable by Java programs.

Installing Jini

Next, let's look at installing the Jini sample implementation on your system.

Downloading Jini from Sun

As of the writing of this book, the Jini code is available from the Java Developer's Connection Web site. This site requires a free registration before you can access the code there. (In general, if you're a Java developer, you should probably register at this site—it's the source of early access Java releases from Sun, bug listings, and many helpful articles on Java development.)

The version of Jini that this book is written against is called the "Jini System Software 1.0" release, or just "Jini 1.0." Before downloading from the Java Developer's Connection site, you should check at Sun's home page for Jini software to see if newer releases have become available since the writing of this book. The Jini home page is at:

```
http://www.javasoft.com/products/jini/
```

To download the software from the Developer's Connection, register with the site (if you haven't already), and then go to:

```
http://developer.javasoft.com/developer/products/jini/
index.html
```

This page has information on the latest versions of Jini, as well as information on how to submit bugs or requests for improvements. The "Product Offerings" link is where the actual downloadable Jini code comes from. There are a number of separate Jini-related downloads available.

- Jini Starter Kit. This download has the fundamental pieces of the Jini infrastructure, including the interfaces and library code that allow Java programs to interact with the key Jini services, as well as the Jini specifications for those services. This package includes not only public interfaces to the Jini software, but also implementations of several key Jini services. The Starter Kit also includes source code for the basic Jini classes.
- Jini Technology Compatibility Kit. This download contains code that can be used to test the compatibility of Jini services and applications. If you create custom services, or reimplement any of the core Jini interfaces, you should download the compatibility kit to test that your code will work properly when deployed against the Jini reference implementation.
- JavaSpaces Technology Kit. JavaSpaces is a "storage service" built atop Jini, which we will discuss in Chapter 15. This download includes implementations and interfaces for the JavaSpaces services, as well as documentation.

At this point, you only need to download the Jini Starter Kit. In Chapter 15, when we look at building JavaSpaces applications, we'll download the JavaSpaces Technology Kit. In general, the compatibility kit is most useful for developers writing commercial Jini services or creating custom reimplementations of the core Jini functionality.

1.1 Update

At the time of this third printing of Core Jini, the 1.1 release of Jini is being actively developed by Sun. Some preliminary specifications are already starting to become available, and it's possible that by the time you read this, the 1.1 release will be out. Be sure to check the URLs above for details, if this is the case. While the specifics of the 1.1 release are not finalized at the time of writing, I'll try to highlight relevant information about 1.1 as I understand it, where

appropriate. And as always, check the Prentice-Hall web pages for this book, mentioned in the Introduction, for details about updates.

Unpacking the Distribution

Once you've downloaded the Jini Starter Kit ZIP file, which is called `jini10.zip`, you're set to unpack and install it. If you have decided to download the compatibility kit or the JavaSpaces kit at this time, you should first install the basic Jini Starter Kit, and then install the other packages "on top" of it. Again, however, you only need the Starter Kit until later chapters of this book, so here we'll only talk about installation of this package.

For Windows: You can use your favorite ZIP extraction utility, such as WinZip. If you want the Jini code to live under the `c:\` directory on your PC, you can extract to `c:` and the unzip utility will create a directory called `jini1_0` to hold the extracted software. Open the Starter Kit ZIP file and extract the contents to your desired directory.

For example:

```
cd c:\
unzip -d jini10.zip
```

For Solaris: Copy the ZIP files for the Starter Kit to the directory you want to contain the software, for example, `/files`, then unzip the file:

```
mkdir /files
cd /files
unzip jini10.zip
```

(Note that the `-d` option is not needed on Solaris.)

This process will create a directory called `jini1_0` under the directory in which you ran `unzip`.

Examining the Distribution

We'll use the code here pretty extensively during the course of this book, so you should make sure you understand what you've just unpacked and where everything lives. Table 1–2 shows the most important contents of the `jini1_0` directory.

Table 1–2 Layout of the Jini 1.0 Release

`jini1_0`	This is the root of the Jini installation.
`jini1_0/index.html`	The `index.html` file is the root of all the documentation that ships with the Jini release.

`jini1_0/doc`	This directory contains documentation for the Jini release, including JavaDocs for the APIs, specifications, a glossary, and hints on running the Jini examples.
`jini1_0/doc/api`	This directory contains the API documentation for the system.
`jini1_0/doc/specs`	All the Jini specifications, which describe the Jini distributed computing model and all the core Jini services, live here.
`jini1_0/example`	The 1.0 DC release of Jini ships with a number of example programs. These include a ray tracing example and a distributed book bidding application. While the actual code for these examples lives in the `lib` directory, along with the rest of the Jini implementation, this directory contains security "policy" files that support these applications.
`jini1_0/lib`	This directory contains the JAR files that constitute the Jini implementation and interfaces. The `jini-core.jar`, `jini-ext.jar`, and `sun-util.jar` files contain the basic Jini interfaces that application writers will use. Other JAR files include the examples, the implementations of the core services, and some utility classes.
`jini1_0/source`	This directory contains the source code for the Jini distribution, under Sun's community source license.

Once you've downloaded and unpacked the files, you should read the `index.html` file to make sure that the installation and configuration instructions have not changed—the information below describes how to install and configure Jini for the release that was current at the time this book was written.

Set Up Your Environment

Jini can at times appear to be fairly complex; one of those times is when you're configuring your environment to use the software. The main reason for this apparent complexity is that Jini can be used in a number of different development situations—you may be writing new Jini services, applications that make use of Jini services, or you may even be providing your own, custom implementations of the core pieces of the Jini infrastructure.

This section describes how to set up your environment for the most common type of Jini development: creating new services and applications that need to be clients of the core Jini facilities.

Setting Your PATH

The first thing you need to do is make sure that the `bin` directory from the Java 2 release is in your PATH. Setting your PATH correctly will ensure that all of the java binaries—including the compiler and RMI stubs generator—are accessible; these binaries will "automatically" augment your CLASSPATH to find the basic Java libraries when they are run.

For Windows: Type the following:

```
set PATH=c:\jdk1.2\bin;%PATH%
```

In this and later examples, you can change your Windows environment permanently by updating the Environment control pane under the System control panel.

For Solaris: The particular syntax varies depending on the shell that you use. If you use the common C-Shell, use the following command line and then type `rehash` to cause your change to the PATH variable to be reevaluated:

```
setenv PATH=/usr/java1.2/bin:${PATH}
```

You can make this change permanent by editing your `.cshrc` file.

Setting Your CLASSPATH

First off, if you're just going to be running the demonstration programs that come with Jini, you don't need to do *anything* to your CLASSPATH—the JAR files that come with Jini use the "executable JAR" facility, introduced in Java 2. This mechanism allows a JAR file to include a "default" application class, which will be invoked automatically when the JAR file is invoked. You can then simply pass the appropriate JAR files to the `java` executable to invoke the services and examples that you wish to run. This is a great convenience for getting the run-time Jini services up and running on your network.

Because you bought *Core Jini*, though, chances are you're going to want to be writing some actual code rather than just running demos. So you'll need to modify your CLASSPATH to point to the JAR files that you'll need for custom development.

There are three primary JAR files you'll need for development. The first is `jini-core.jar`, which contains the "core" interfaces that are part of the Jini specifications. The second is `jini-ext.jar`, which contains some "nonstandardized" interfaces that are useful for building Jini applications. Finally, `sun-util.jar` contains some Sun-provided utility classes that will come in handy in the code examples. All of these JAR files are located in the `jini1_0/lib` directory.

In Chapter 5, we'll look at some specific guidelines for how to configure your environment to effectively develop Jini clients and services. One of these guidelines will entail passing the JAR files required for development on the command line to the Java compiler, rather than using a CLASSPATH. I recommend that you follow the instructions there, but you can set a CLASSPATH if you want to get up and running quickly. Treat the instructions below as a stop-gap until Chapter 5.

For Windows: Type the following:

```
set CLASSPATH=c:\jini1_0\lib\jini-core.jar;
      c:\jini1_0\lib\jini-ext.jar;
      c:\jini1_0\lib\sun-util.jar;%CLASSPATH%
```

For Solaris: Again, depending on your shell, the syntax will vary somewhat. On the C-Shell, type the following:

```
setenv CLASSPATH
      $HOME/files/jini1_0/lib/jini-core.jar:
      $HOME/files/jini1_0/lib/jini-ext.jar:
      $HOME/files/jini1_0/lib/sun-util.jar:
      ${CLASSPATH}
```

You should remember that this CLASSPATH should be used for developing new Jini applications; you should need no special CLASSPATH to run the standard Jini services—and indeed, to prevent confusion, you should probably make sure that you have no CLASSPATH set when you run these services.

Core Note: Other JAR files in the distribution

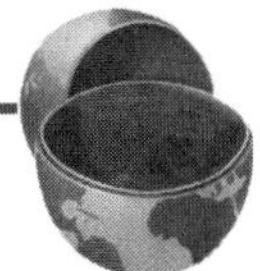

You'll no doubt notice that there are a number of other JAR files in the lib directory of the distribution; many of these end in "`-dl`*". These JAR files contain code that is meant to be downloaded to clients as they run. So, for example, you'll see* `reggie.jar` *(which contains Sun's implementation of the Jini lookup service) as well as* `reggie-dl.jar` *(which contains only the code that clients need to use the lookup service). When you begin to create your own Jini applications, you may wish to make a similar separation, with the implementation of your application in one JAR file and the parts that will need to be downloaded to clients in another.*

Start the Jini Run-time Services

You've probably skimmed through the preceding sections with no problems whatsoever. Now, though, you're going to need to slow down a bit and take the time to start up the services that Jini needs at run time. The bad news is that figuring out the parameters and configurations needed to run these services can be a bit of work. The good news is that you rarely—if ever—have to restart them once they're going.

Jini depends on quite a bit of network infrastructure at run time. In a deployment setting, you would probably run most of these services on a compute server, or perhaps several compute servers for redundancy. To use Jini effectively, you will need one instance of most of these services running somewhere on your LAN; other services are more effectively deployed on every (or at least several) hosts. If you're doing your own development and experimentation with Jini, you can just run these services on your desktop computer, if you like.

The Jini distribution comes with the basic services needed to support Jini, as well as a few other "optional" services. The list below enumerates the various services that are *required* to run Jini applications on your network. In addition to these, there are two other services—the Jini "transaction manager" and the JavaSpaces "storage service"—which come with the distribution, that you should be aware of, but aren't required for most Jini work. So I won't talk about these last two until later in this book. But for development, you should go ahead and start all of the required services as described below. You can leave them running indefinitely, and pretty much forget that they're there.

The services that Jini requires are

- A simple Web server. Jini requires this facility because when downloaded code is needed through RMI, the actual transmission of the code happens via the HTTP protocol. Jini comes with a very simple HTTP server that's sufficient to supply code to applications that need it. A common configuration is to run an HTTP server on each host that needs to provide downloadable code to other applications.
- The RMI *activation daemon*. Despite its frightening name, the activation daemon is a very simple to use and very useful piece of Java infrastructure. This process allows objects that may be invoked only rarely to essentially "go to sleep," and be automatically awakened when they are needed. This situation

commonly arises in remote systems programming, where you may have a long-lived server object that is only rarely used. The RMI activation daemon manages the transition between active and inactive states for these objects, and is used extensively by the other core Jini run-time services. At a minimum, you will need to run the activation daemon on each host that runs a lookup service, described below.

- A lookup service. As you shall see, the lookup service is really the core of Jini. A lookup service keeps track of the currently active Jini services that are available on a LAN. Sun provides its own implementation of a lookup service that's custom-built for Jini. When you read the Jini documentation, you may notice that the RMI registry server that comes with the JDK can be used as a lookup service. While this option *can* be used, it is not recommended—the lookup service that comes with Jini is much more full featured. We won't examine how to use the RMI registry as a lookup service in this book, because there is no good reason to use it. The lookup service relies on activation to recover its state after crashes or restarts. So you must run the activation daemon on each machine that runs a lookup service.

This may seem like a lot of work. But these processes can be spread across the machines in your network, and are largely self-maintaining: Once you start them, they need virtually no caretaking. In the course of my Jini development, I leave these processes running for weeks or even months. Many times I'm surprised to see one still running on a server that I'd completely forgotten about.

There are two ways to start these services. If you want to get up-and-running quickly, you can use a graphical user interface that comes with the Jini distribution. This interface is only capable of starting Jini services on the *local* machine, which is definitely not appropriate for debugging Jini applications that will be run in multimachine environments! Still, the GUI can help you get started more quickly than you could otherwise. I'll discuss this method first.

Most serious developers, though, will want to get "under the hood" to understand how to run the individual services "by hand" and pass any necessary arguments to them. So we'll also look at how to do this.

The next section discusses running the required Jini services via the graphical user interface; the following section gives more in-depth guidelines for running these services from a command line on either Windows or Solaris.

Starting Required Services via the GUI

Jini ships with an easy-to-use GUI for starting the required Jini services. When you use this interface, you start these services on the local machine—typically the same machine on which you will be doing development. The GUI doesn't hide all the details of these services—it just makes the most common configurations easy.

If you wonder about the various options for these services, read the next section on how to start these services from the command line. In general, having an understanding of the options for these services will be useful as you get more skilled in using Jini—so understanding how to start these services from the command line is important.

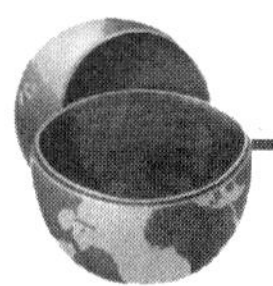

Core Alert: Bug in StartService GUI

There's a bug that prevents certain services from being started on a PC using the StartService GUI application. This bug may be fixed by the time you read this, but you should be aware of it just in case.
The bug arises from the way URLs are generated by the GUI application. URLs are specified to have forward slashes ("/"), the same as paths on UNIX. The StartSpace application mistakenly creates a URL by using the Java File separator character, which is set to a backward slash ("\") on PCs, resulting in a misformatted URL.
This problem prevents the GUI from successfully starting a Jini lookup service, although the other basic services can be started fine. If you have problems starting a lookup service using the GUI application, you will have to use the "by hand" instructions later in this chapter to start the lookup service.

Running the GUI

Once you've got your PATH set up, you can easily launch the configuration application. To do this, just run the following.

On Windows:

```
java -cp C:\jini1_0\lib\jini-examples.jar
      com.sun.jini.example.service.StartService
```

On Solaris:

```
java -cp /files/jini1_0/lib/jini-examples.jar
      com.sun.jini.example.service.StartService
```

Be sure, of course, to replace the "files" directory with the directory that you've installed Jini into. The `-cp` option sets the CLASSPATH for the JVM to include the `jini-examples` JAR file; the last argument is the fully qualified name of the service starting GUI.

Once this program launches, a window opens with a number of tabbed panes containing controls for launching the various services, as shown in Figure 1–1. The initial pane, *Jini Jar Files*, is the most important for us now. This pane contains the names of the various JAR files needed by the runtime services. The first entry here, *Path to Jar Files*, should be edited to point to the directory containing the JAR files from the Jini distribution. For example, if you installed Jini in `C:\jini1_0`, you should set this field to `C:\jini1_0\lib`. Unless you're doing strange things by renaming the files from the distribution, you can leave everything else on this pane set at its default value.

Next, click on the *Web Server* tab to bring up the panel shown in Figure 1–2. There is only one entry here that you are likely to change: The *Top Level Web Document area* field should be set to point to the directory containing the Jini code that is available for download. Because you've (hopefully) installed all of the Jini code in the same place, you should set this to the `lib` directory in your Jini installation—which is the same directory you used for the *Path to Jar Files* field previously. The *Port* field here can be used to change the port on which the Web server will run; if you change this, make

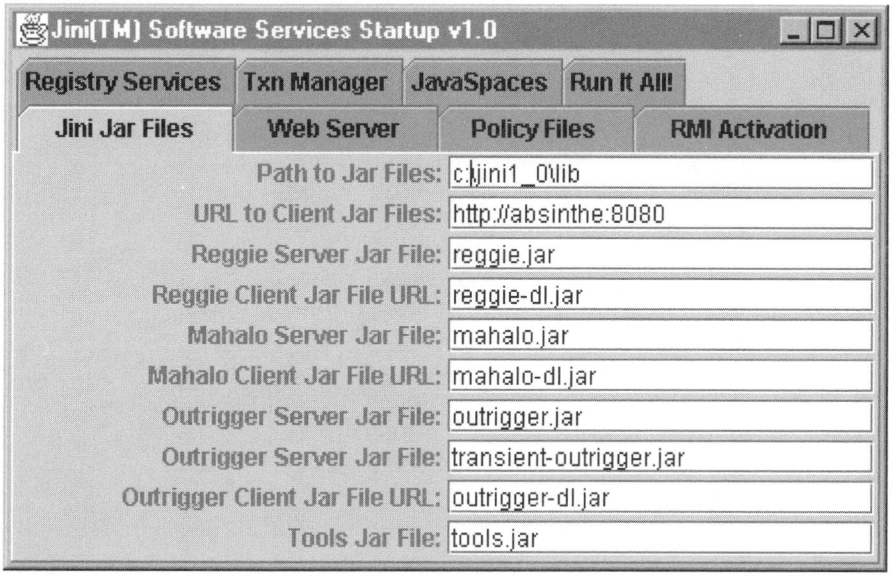

Figure 1–1 Setting thepPath to the JAR files

sure you change the *URL to Client Jar Files* field on the previous pane. The two checkboxes on this pane cause JAR files in the top-level directory to be searched whenever a single class is asked for (rather than returning an error), and turn on logging of code downloads, respectively.

Next, click on the *Policy Files* pane, as shown in Figure 1–3. Several of the run-time services require that the JVM that runs them be started with a special security policy file. The notion of security policies was introduced in Java 2 as a way to provide fine-grained control over the rights of Java code running in a JVM. If you're interested in the details of why these are needed for particular services, see the longer descriptions in the section on starting services from the command line. For now, however, all you have to do is edit the paths here to point to the locations of the policy files that ship with Jini, for example, the ones in the `C:\jini1.0\example` subdirectories, as shown.

The next panel, *RMI Activation*, controls the start up of the RMI activation daemon. Fortunately, this service is simple enough that you don't need to configure anything to make it work. So skip it and go to the *Registry Services* panel, shown in Figure 1–4. As mentioned, Jini allows you to start either the RMI registry or the Jini lookup service for naming. The radio buttons here allow you to select which, if either, of these to start. Select *Lookup Services* to use the Jini lookup service, and set the *Log Directory* field to be the absolute path of a directory in which to store the service's logging information. On Windows, `C:\tmp\reggie_log` is a good choice—you may need to

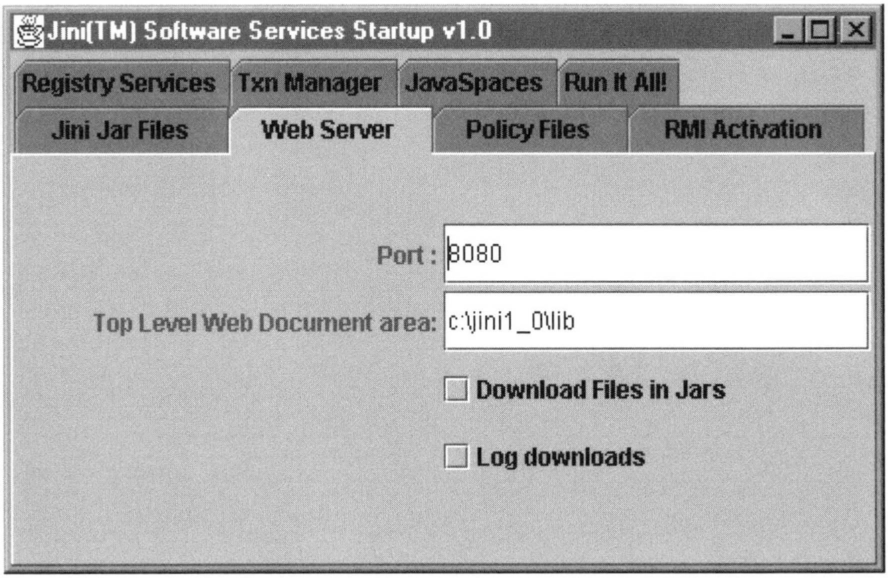

Figure 1–2 Setting the path to downloadable code

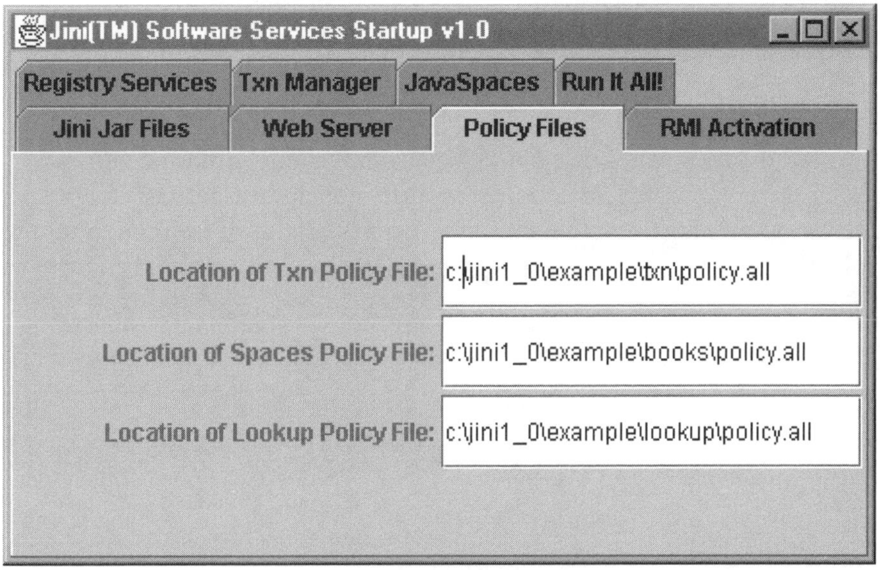

Figure 1–3 Setting the location of the security policy files

create a \tmp directory, though; on Solaris, you can use /tmp/reggie_log. You should make sure that all the directories leading up to the log directory exist; in particular C:\tmp may not exist by default on Windows. The Jini services will, when run, create the actual log directory (reggie_log in this case), but not any leading directories.

Be sure to watch out for the bug mentioned in the **Core Alert** a bit earlier—there may be problems starting the lookup service on a PC using this application, in which case you will have to start that service manually.

We'll skip the next two panels—*Transaction Manager* and *JavaSpaces* configuration—since we won't be using these for a while.

Finally—finally!—we've configured all of the parameters we need to start our run-time services. Go to the final panel (Figure 1–5) called *Run It All!* to start these services. Go in order down the list, starting the services you need: First start the HTTP daemon, then RMID (the RMI activation daemon), and finally the lookup service. Don't start the Transaction Manager or JavaSpaces yet. This panel also allows you to stop a service, if you've found that you've misconfigured it and need to change some of its settings.

At this point, you're set to start running some Jini examples. As mentioned earlier, getting the various services set up can be a pain, largely because of all the options that are needed, and uncommon JVM parameters (such as secu-

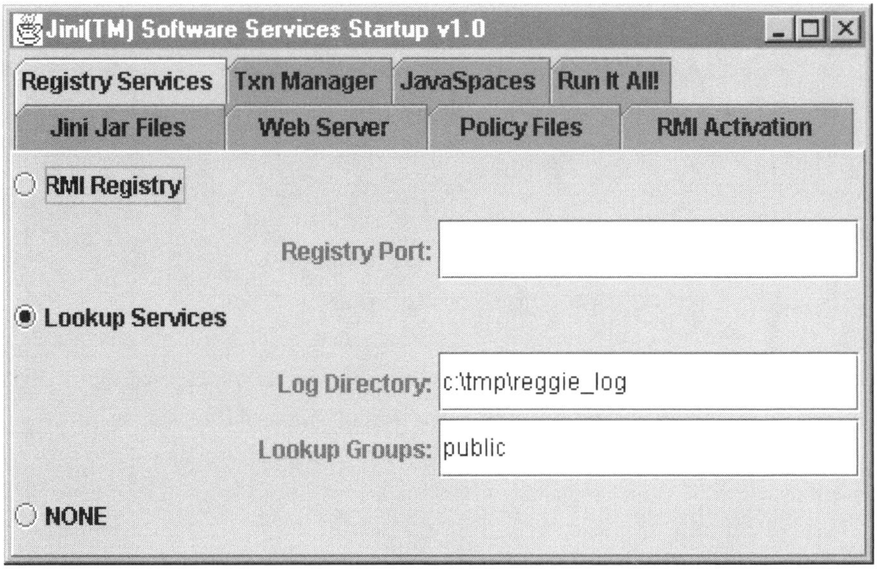

Figure 1–4 Setting the lookup service parameters

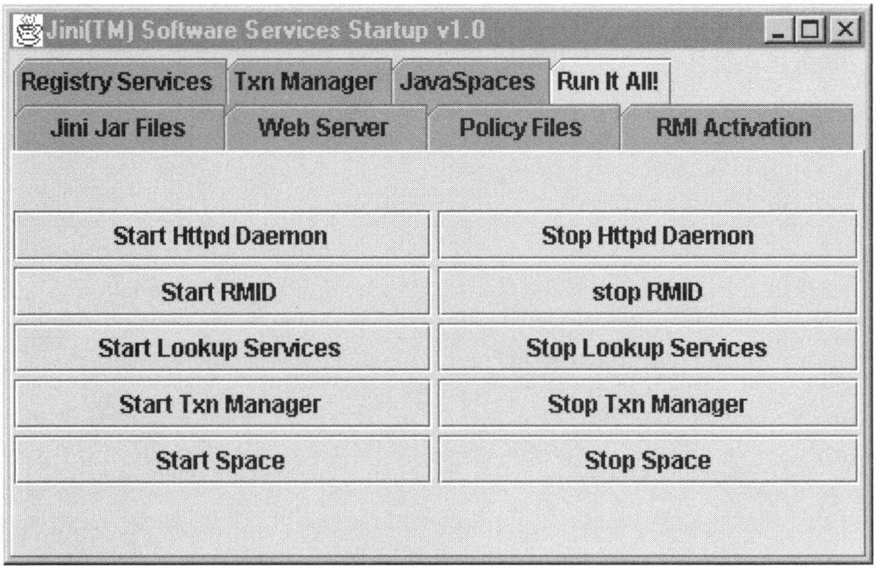

Figure 1–5 Starting the Jini runtime services

rity policies) that have to be used. But once you've set up these services, you can likely leave them running for long stretches of time.

For those with a serious interest in how the Jini services work, I'll now present the details of starting these services from the command line, along with some helpful scripts for getting things going. If you're going to be starting these services automatically when servers boot, you need to understand how to launch them manually. The next section also looks behind the curtains at some of the options that we glossed over in the GUI walk-through.

Starting Required Services via the Command Line

If you have already started the required services from the GUI, you can skip over this section if you like. The purpose of spelling out how to run these by hand is to give you a bit more information about what the options for the various services are, and what common configurations of the Jini services are useful. And knowing how to start these services by hand is essential if you need to configure your machine to start Jini services at boot time.

This is the nitty-gritty on how to run these components. Let's walk through the steps required to start these services. In general, you should start them in the order listed. For each of these services, I'll provide short scripts for both Windows and Solaris that will save you time.

Start the Web Server

As mentioned, to support the downloading of code, you need to have an HTTP server running somewhere on your network that can provide the code needed by applications. The requirements of this server are minimal—it only really needs to support the "get" operation, so any old Web server that you're already running is probably sufficient.

Jini comes with a utilitarian Web server in its `tools.jar` package, though, so I'll show you how to get it running.

In the most basic case, all you have to do is type the following to run the HTTP server:

On Windows:

```
java -jar C:\jini1_0\lib\tools.jar
        -port 8080 -dir C:\jini1_0\lib
        -verbose
```

On Solaris:

```
java -jar /files/jini1_0/lib/tools.jar
        -port 8080 -dir /files/jini1_0/lib
        -verbose
```

Obviously, substitute whatever directory in which you have installed the Jini release. Here we see an example of an executable JAR file that has a default program that will be run when it is launched by the Java Virtual Machine.

There are a number of options you can pass to this server to customize its behavior. By default, the HTTP server runs on the port of 8080. If you already have a Web server running there, you may wish to launch the Jini HTTP server on a different port by passing the `-port <portnum>` option, as shown here. You can also set the root directory that will be served by passing `-dir <directory>` to the server; here I've shown the HTTP root directory to be set to the Jini lib directory, so that all of the core Jini code can be exported. Finally, the `-verbose` option is useful for debugging—it will cause the HTTP server to display each request made to it as well as where the request came from. You may wish to check the documentation that comes with the Jini release for more options, or in case you have specific configuration needs.

In general, any code that may need to be downloaded across the network has to be accessible from an HTTP server. This server doesn't have to be a full-blown, general-purpose Web server; it can be as simple as the HTTP service that comes with Jini. You can collect up all the downloadable code together and have one Web server serve it, or you can have a number of small servers running on your network. For development purposes, since Jini applications are generally deployed into multimachine environments, you will probably want to start multiple HTTP servers, one for each service.

How do you know whether or not code will need to be downloadable? This question will become clear as we delve into the Jini architecture. For now, you can assume that any core Jini component—such as the lookup service, the transaction manager, or JavaSpaces—may need to download code into other processes, and therefore their code should be accessible to at least one HTTP server running somewhere on your network.

Start the RMI Activation Daemon

Starting the RMI activation daemon couldn't be easier. The executable for this process lives in `jdk1.2/bin/rmid`. If you've added this directory to your path, simply type `rmid` to run it. An instance of the activation daemon must run on each host where activatable objects reside. This includes the Jini lookup service, the transaction manager, and JavaSpaces. And, of course, if you create any activatable objects yourself, you will need to run an instance of the activation daemon on the machines that host those objects.

Start the Lookup Service

The Sun implementation of the lookup service is called "reggie," and it lives in the `reggie.jar` file that comes with the distribution. Starting this service is a little more complicated than starting the others. For one thing, there are more arguments that you need to pass to the program to tell it how to behave. Also, you need to pass some options to the Java Virtual Machine that will be running reggie so that it can properly configure its security parameters.

The basic form of running the lookup service is as follows:

```
java -Djava.security.policy=<security_policy>
      -jar <reggie jar file>
      <lookup client codebase>
      <lookup policy file>
      <log directory>
      <lookup groups>
```

This is quite an eyeful, so let's look at these options in a bit more detail. The `-Djava.security.policy` option is letting us provide a pointer to a *security policy file* that the JVM will use when it runs this program. Security policy files are a new introduction in Java 2, and govern what resources a program will be able to use when it runs.

Chances are, you've never run a Java program that has required you to set a security policy before it would work. Providing a security policy is required in this case, because the lookup service needs to have permission to access certain system properties, write to its log directory, and create and listen on socket connections to clients. Jini ships with a security policy that's appropriate for the lookup service in `jini1_0/example/lookup/policy`.

The next part of the command line is the actual JAR file that contains the code we wish to run. The `-jar` option specifies that the `main()` routine for the program is contained in the specified JAR file; here, you should pass in the JAR file for the reggie service, `reggie.jar`, which lives in the `lib` directory of the Jini distribution.

Next we get to the arguments that are passed to the reggie program itself, rather than to the JVM that runs reggie. The next part of the command line is the *codebase* that specifies where code that will be downloaded to clients lives. The argument that you pass here should be a URL that points to the `reggie-dl.jar` file, which contains code used to access reggie that needs to be downloaded to callers. If you know *for certain* that all of your Jini services and applications will always run on the same machine, you can simply use a `file:` URL that points to the directory containing this JAR. As is more likely, though, you'll be running code all over your network. In this case, you should pass a URL for the machine running your Web server that will be used to serve up code, for example, `http://hostname/reggie-dl.jar` (replace "hostname" with the name of the machine that the Web server is running on, of course). You should make sure that the Web server can access the `reggie-dl.jar` file under its root directory.

Core Note: A word about codebase

There's a certain art to figuring out how to set the codebase property which, unfortunately, eludes many newcomers to RMI and Jini. The codebase property is used as a way for the server—a program which supplies callable code to a client—to inform the client of where the code can be retrieved from.

When you set the codebase property on a program, you're explicitly telling the server that, when it serializes an object for transmission to a client, it should "annotate" the serialized object with the codebase URL that says where to fetch the code for that object.

Serialization only transmits the member data within an object, not the code itself. Using codebase is a way for a server to tell a client how to download the code as well.

In general, an HTTP server will be running on each server machine that will export code. This HTTP server may be a separate process, such as you see here, or may be an extremely lightweight entity that lives within the server application itself.

There are two common mistakes to watch out for when using codebase. The first is that you should take great care when using file: URLs. File: URLs specify that the code for a service is accessible through the filesystem. This will work great as long as both the client and the server share the same filesystem. But if one of these components is moved to a different host, your once-working code will now break, since the common filesystem is no longer accessible.

A second precaution is to never use "localhost" in a codebase URL. The hostname "localhost" is a shortcut for referring to the host that is evaluating the hostname. If you specify `localhost` *in a codebase, this means that clients will attempt to load code from their own machines, rather than the server's machine. This is certainly not what you want, and the source of potentially hard-to-track bugs!*

You should always use the name or the IP address of the host on which the HTTP service will run—which is usually the same host that the Jini service itself will run on. We'll discuss codebase a bit more in the appendix on RMI.

Next we see another security policy file. Reggie, like many Jini services, registers itself with the RMI activation daemon. The activation daemon ensures that, should reggie crash, it will be restarted the next time it is needed. The activation daemon takes care of this restart for us. Unlike the first policy file, which is used to grant permissions to the JVM executing the reggie process, the security argument here is passed as an argument to the RMI activation subsystem so that, whenever it reactivates a reggie process, it will begin running with the correct security permissions. You'll see multiple security policies used in a number of these Jini run-time services; typically, they are used in the same way they are used here, to set security for the JVM and to set security for future activations of the service via the activation daemon.

The next option is a directory into which reggie will write its logs. You can pass any directory that is accessible on the filesystem where reggie is running; make sure you use an absolute path name here. You should create any leading directories up to the actual log directory itself—although reggie will create its own log directory, it won't create any missing directories earlier in the path. You'll see many of the Jini services using log directories. These are used so that the services can checkpoint their state periodically, and recover after a crash. If you're planning on leaving the services up for long periods, you'll want to use a log directory that's on a stable, persistent filesystem.

Finally, we pass a list of *groups* for which our lookup server will provide service. Groups are further discussed a bit later, but essentially they are names that can be used to group clusters of Jini services together. Reggie understands two "special" group names that have particular meanings. Passing "public" here indicates to use an unnamed public group in which, by convention, services should register by default; passing "none" means to use no group at all (which is not of much value to us). For now, just use "public" as the group.

Here's a complete command line for starting reggie.

On Windows:

```
java
        -Djava.security.policy=
               c:\jini1_0\example\lookup\policy
        -jar c:jini1_0\lib\reggie.jar
        http://hostname/reggie-dl.jar
        c:\jini1_0\example\lookup\policy
        c:\temp\reggie_log public
```

On Solaris:

```
java
       -Djava.security.policy=
              /files/jini1_0/example/lookup/policy
       -jar /files/jini1_0/lib/reggie.jar
       http://hostname/reggie-dl.jar
       /files/jini1_0/example/lookup/policy
       /tmp/reggie_log public
```

Listings 1–1 and 1–2 offer scripts for Windows and Solaris (which will probably work on most variants of UNIX) that you can use to start the lookup service; these scripts are available from the Prentice-Hall FTP site as mentioned in the introduction.

Listing 1–1 `lookup.bat` Script for Windows

```
REM Set this to wherever Jini is installed
set JINI_HOME=C:\jini1_0
REM Set this to the host where the web server runs
set HOSTNAME=hostname

REM Everything below should work with few changes
set POLICYFILE=%JINI_HOME%\example\lookup\policy.all
set JARFILE=%JINI_HOME%\lib\reggie.jar
set CODEBASE=http://%HOSTNAME%:8080/reggie-dl.jar
set LOOKUP_POLICYFILE=%POLICYFILE%
set LOG_DIR=C:\temp\reggie_log
set GROUP=public

java -Djava.security.policy=%POLICYFILE% -jar %JARFILE%
    %CODEBASE% %LOOKUP_POLICYFILE% %LOG_DIR% %GROUP%
```

Listing 1–2 `lookup.sh` Script for Solaris

```
#!/bin/sh

# Set this to wherever Jini is installed
JINI_HOME=/files/jini1_0

# Set this to wherever the web server is running
HOSTNAME=hostname

# everything below should work with few changes
POLICYFILE=$JINI_HOME/example/lookup/policy.all
JARFILE=$JINI_HOME/lib/reggie.jar
CODEBASE=http://$HOSTNAME:8080/reggie-dl.jar
LOOKUP_POLICYFILE=$POLICYFILE
LOG_DIR=/tmp/reggie_log
GROUP=public

java -Djava.security.policy=$POLICYFILE -jar $JARFILE \
    $CODEBASE $LOOKUP_POLICYFILE $LOG_DIR $GROUP
```

Running the Sample Program

At this point, you should have all of the required Jini services running on your machine, and you're ready to make sure everything works. We'll fire off a simple example—a browser application—that comes with the Jini distribution. To try out the browser, use the following command line:

On Windows:

```
java -cp c:\jini1_0\lib\jini-examples.jar
      -Djava.security.policy=
            c:\jini1_0\example\browser\policy
      -Djava.rmi.server.codebase=
            http://hostname:8080/jini-examples-dl.jar
      com.sun.jini.example.browser.Browser
```

On Solaris:

```
java -cp /files/jini1_0/lib/jini-examples.jar
      -Djava.security.policy=
            /files/jini1_0/example/browser/policy
      -Djava.rmi.server.codebase=
            http://hostname:8080/jini-examples-dl.jar
      com.sun.jini.example.browser.Browser
```

Be sure, of course, to substitute the paths you used to install the Jini JAR files, and to use the correct URL for your Web server, if you changed any of the default configurations.

You'll note that the browser requires its own codebase property—this is because it actually downloads code into the various Jini run-time services as it runs. So if you're running this application on a separate machine, you will want to start a new HTTP server on the machine on which the browser will run, so that it can export its code to other Jini services.

At this point, you should see the browser application shown in Figure 1-6 running on your screen. This application lets you look at the Jini services running on your network, control them, and change the attributes associated with each of them. You can leave this application running to monitor the status of any Jini lookup services running. For now, most of the controls in this application may not make much sense to you—we'll soon learn about Jini services and attributes, though. For now, you should see at least one Jini lookup service running—the one you just started.

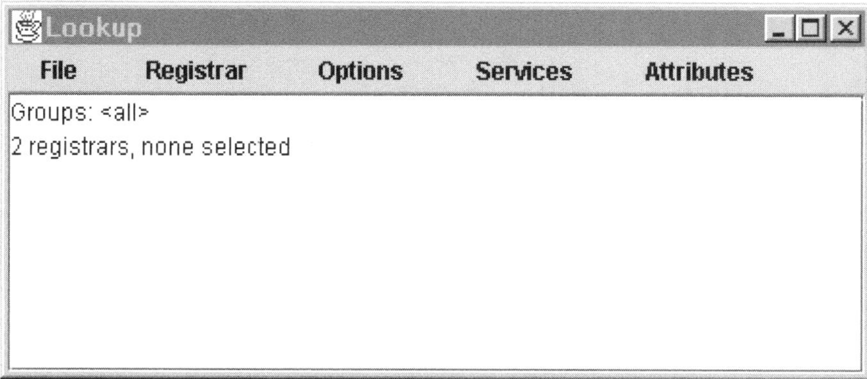

Figure 1–6 Example Jini browser

Further Reading and Resources

If you want to read more about the early history of the Java project (as well as see a photo of the Star-7 device), you can check out James Gosling's home page, which has an excellent introduction to the history of the project

```
http://java.sun.com/people/jag/green/index.html
```

If you're curious about the integration of nondesktop computers into our daily lives, and how computers can be made to "disappear" into the fabric of our surroundings, you may want to check out Mark Weiser's vision of ubiquitous computing.

`http://ubiq.com/hypertext/weiser/UbiHome.html`

The *New York Times* article that broke the scoop on Jini still makes for some interesting reading.

`http://www.nytimes.com/library/tech/98/07/biztech/articles/15sun.html`

Finally, the *Wired* interview with Bill Joy talks about Jini and the future visions of computing that inspired the Jini project.

`http://www.wired.com/news/technology/story/13744.html`

An excellent resource for Jini developers is the JINI-USERS mailing list. To subscribe, send mail to `listserv@java.sun.com`; the body of your message should contain the line `subscribe jini-users`. To unsubscribe, send a message to the same address, with the body containing `signoff jini-users`.

The RMI-USERS mailing list is also a great resource for getting help with RMI-related questions. To sign up, send a note to `listserv@java.sun.com` containing `subscribe rmi-users`. To sign off, send a note to the same address containing `signoff rmi-users`.

Finally, Sun has a website for the use of the larger Jini commnity. This website is a good place to check for code donated by community members, news, and upcoming Jini events. Registration is required, but grants you access to code from other community members, and gives you a space in which to upload you own code:

`http:/www.jini.org`

DISTRIBUTED SYSTEMS

Topics in This Chapter

- The problems with distributed systems
- Why "classical" approaches aren't sufficient
- The Java model of distributed computing
- What dynamically downloadable code means for system designers

Chapter 2

We've all seen the error messages: *NFS server not responding; unable to locate the server; please check the server name and try again; no route to host; host unreachable.* As fallible as our desktop computers seem to be, somehow adding a network to the mix seems to make things break even faster than before.

There are a number of pretty apparent reasons for this fragility. Obviously, new ways for things to break exist in a networked system. The failure of a key router is a type of problem that can bring down a networked application, but simply has no effect on a truly *local* system—meaning an isolated, standalone application running on a single machine and in a single address space.

But there are deeper reasons for why distributed and networked systems are harder to build than stand-alone systems. In fact, these reasons point out *why* you cannot simply paper over the network, making remote resources look exactly like local ones, with exactly the same programming models, and expect your code to work.

This chapter looks at networked and distributed systems, and draws a distinction between the two. Most software these days, particularly with the advent of the Web, is networked. Jini, however, represents a more complex beast: a true dynamic distributed system. We'll look at the differences between these two types of software, and look at why there are some tough issues that an infrastructure for distributed systems programming needs to solve. Jini builds on Java to provide some particularly nice solutions to the problems of distribution; we'll look at what makes this Java-based approach different from what has come before.

What's So Hard about the Network?

To understand why building robust software for the network is difficult, it's useful to look at what approaches have been taken to solve the problems of network programming, and where those approaches break down.

Classical Networked Systems

A lot of the history of networked systems programming is about making the network appear to go away. If we look at the "classical" work in infrastructure for networked systems, we see a couple of common themes. First, they provide a way to move the data to the computation. Second, they provide a way to specify what we want to have done to that data, out of a constrained set of possible options.

Finding a way to move the data to the computation is necessary because we cannot assume that the code needed for a particular operation will be available everywhere on the network. The fact that code has to be *compiled* and *installed* for a particular machine makes it difficult to have the code running everywhere. Thus, it's far easier to move the data to the code. But moving the data is no easy trick itself, because the machines on the network have different notions of byte order, floating-point format, word length, and so on. Data description tools such as XDR (External Data Representation, a Sun protocol from the mid-1980s used to package data for portability) make the network "disappear" by hiding the differences in machine-data formats so that any type of CPU can make sense of data it receives. These tools work by standardizing on a particular, portable wire format, which is independent of any machine-specific byte ordering, word length, etc. These tools let data flow around the network, so that it can make its way to wherever it may be needed.

The task of specifying what is to be done to this data once it has been shipped has typically been done via a Remote Procedure Call (RPC) or remote object system. Remote procedure call systems attempt to make the call of a function on a different machine look (to the programmer) like the call of a local function in the same address space. Remote object systems such as CORBA and DCOM raise the level of programming from function calls to method invocations on objects, but essentially still try to mimic the semantics of local invocation. They are not *qualitatively* different than the remote procedure call technology of the past 20 years.

There's one particularly good reason for these attempts to hide the network: Programmers are brought up to understand basic, local programming techniques practically from the time they are weaned. They *know* how to build reliable stand-alone programs. Adding specialized programming models to the mix just increases the time needed to learn the new models, and brings with it headaches, slipped deadlines, and hair loss.

All of these systems, therefore, try to make the network *transparent;* that is, they make the network simply "go away" from the perspective of the programmer.

The Network Is Not Transparent

Unfortunately, this simplification often turns out to be an oversimplification. These systems bring with them the implicit assumption that introducing a network wire between two software components will not affect the correctness of the program, only its performance. In fact, in traditional distributed object systems, hiding the location of a particular object is often seen as desirable—much as hiding the implementation of a function behind its interface is a desirable aspect of object-oriented programming. The behavior of a component in the face of network failures or poor performance is seen as another aspect of its implementation, not of its interface, or its contract with the rest of the system.

As it turns out, the hardest parts of building reliable distributed systems are not the parts that these systems address: packing data into portable forms, causing the invocation of a remote procedure somewhere on the net, and so forth. Instead, the hardest parts of building reliable distributed systems have to do with precisely those things about the network that *cannot* be ignored by the programmer—the fact that the time required to access a remote resource may be orders of magnitude larger than accessing the same resource locally; the fact that networks fail in ways that stand-alone systems do not; and the fact that networked systems are susceptible to partial failures of computations that can leave the system in an inconsistent state.

Computer scientist Peter Deutsch recognized these problems years ago, and called them "The Seven Fallacies of Distributed Computing." I won't go into all seven here, but see the sidebar for details. Even with the support of all of these classical systems, building reliable, scalable, robust distributed systems is still difficult—which is why we're all so familiar with the error messages at the start of this chapter. The problems come because the classical systems fool the unwary into believing that they can ignore the unhideable issues that lurk in distributed systems programming. I'll talk about some of these next.

Sidebar: The Seven Fallacies of Distributed Computing

Computer scientist Peter Deutsch has written about what he calls "The Seven Fallacies of Distributed Computing." Here are the fallacies, along with an introduction by him.

"Essentially everyone, when they first build a distributed application, makes the following seven assumptions. All prove to be false in the long run, and all can cause *big* trouble and *painful* learning experiences."

- The network is reliable
- Latency is zero
- Bandwidth is infinite
- The network is secure
- Topology doesn't change
- There is one administrator
- Transport cost is zero

Much of the work in Jini is designed to explicitly acknowledge these fallacies, rather than pretend they don't exist.

Performance and Latency

Clearly, accessing some resource—a file or an object—over a network is slower than accessing it locally. We all know this, and we know that the differences in access times, often several orders of magnitude, are enough to make the difference a *qualitative* one, rather than just a quantitative one.

But you may be saying to yourself, "What's the big deal? Accessing cache memory is orders of magnitude faster than accessing main memory, and accessing main memory is orders of magnitude faster than accessing the disk. Isn't this just yet another tier of performance?" The reason this is an issue in networked systems is that the differences in performance often make it impossible to distinguish a *failed* component from a *slow* component. Even though main memory is faster than a disk, both have performance characteristics that tend to stay within fairly fixed bounds. But as anyone who has used a Web browser can tell you, network performance can vary wildly, even within a short span of time. Access times in local systems simply cannot affect the program in quite the same way as do remote access times.

And yet, systems such as RPC and CORBA do not even address these performance issues. By this, I don't mean that they should somehow work some magic to make the network hundreds of times faster so that the differences in latency go away. Obviously they cannot do this. But RPC and CORBA don't even consider performance and latency as part of their programming models—they simply ignore the issue entirely, treating it as a "hidden" implementation detail that the programmer must implicitly be aware of and deal with.

The fact that it is *possible* to ignore these differences when developing (because remote accesses are made to resemble, as closely as possible, local ones) means that designs can arise that not only have extremely poor performance, but may be unable to handle the variations in performance that can happen in distributed systems. If the interfaces between objects in a system are designed before the "implementation detail" of location or "remoteness" is considered, very likely the system will have communication patterns that make it unacceptably slow, or not very robust.

Rather than ignoring the "remoteness" of components until late in a design, we must consider these architectural details at the same time that the interfaces for communicating between objects are designed.

New Failure Modes

Networked systems can fail in ways in which stand-alone systems cannot: Routers can fail, users can—intentionally or unintentionally—yank an ethernet cable out of the wall, key machines with name servers and database servers can crash. A piece of code written to work in a stand-alone environment will be unprepared to deal with the new failure modes that can result if that same code is run in a networked environment.

Consider a simple example: a function to read a file from disk. This code fragment may be used over and over again in a large application, say a spreadsheet, and may be perfectly written for its original intended setting. It may catch and intelligently handle all sorts of errors, from the filesystem filling up to permission violations.

Now imagine this same application running in a situation where the file is on a disk attached to a network file server somewhere. This same code, which could handle all types of local failures in an intelligent way, must now deal with network failures as well. The fileserver machine may crash, or it may become unreachable. The application may, if it is lucky, fail in a "normal" way that mimics what would happen if one of the local error situations were to arise—it may treat a "server down" condition as a permissions violation, for example. But it may also crash in unexpected ways. Certainly, the code won't be able to respond intelligently to network errors, by retrying if the server is unreachable, or asking the user for a secondary fileserver if the primary one crashes.

You may be saying to yourself, again, "So what? We can just check to see whether a failure occurred after performing any operation that involves the network. The situation is the same in local programming—after writing to the disk you check to make sure that the data was actually written." The reason this doesn't work is the fact that, very often in distributed settings, it may be difficult or impossible to even determine *if* an error occurred. In a local system, we can attempt to write some data to the disk and then check to see that the data has actually been written. But in a distributed setting there is often *no* centralized entity—like an operating system—which can be used to determine success or failure. Even "reliable" protocols like TCP/IP don't solve this problem—no matter how reliable TCP/IP is, it cannot distinguish between an application that has crashed and an application that is simply slow to respond; and there is no centralized entity that can detect the difference.

If our systems don't expose the types of failures that can occur in networked situations as part of the contract of dealing with resources—that is, in their interfaces—then these "hide the network" programming paradigms permit programmers to ignore them. By declaring the potential for remoteness in the interfaces to these objects, we can require programmers—via the compiler—to address these issues.

Concurrency and Consistency

Both of these differences between local and remote computing—performance and latency differences, and differences in failure modes—are significant, but they aren't nearly as devastating as the problems of concurrency and consistency that arise in distributed computing. When software components fail in a local setting—an application crashes, say—the failure is typically an all-or-nothing affair. If an entire machine goes down, all work on that machine is going to stop, regardless of what else is happening around the network. And if one of a set of components involved in some cooperative operation fails—say one of two applications involved in a cut-and-paste operation—a central component such as the operating system can detect this and signal the other involved parties.

Such a situation is not the case in distributed computing, however. In distributed computing, individual components can fail in ways that leave other components running and—as is often the case—unaware of their failure. This situation, called *partial failure*, is particularly insidious, and is the source of most of the evils that turn up in distributed computing. *Total failures*, which tend to crop up in local-only applications, are actually *easier* to deal with because at least the system winds up in a known state.

For example, think about a shared whiteboard application that allows a set of participants around the net to mark up and share a common drawing space. When one user makes a mark, the update must be sent to the other participants in the session. This update can be sent via repeated unicast—sending the same message repeatedly to each participant—or via multicast—sending once to a special network address that multiple parties can listen on. In either case, it is possible that one recipient's computer may crash or may become unreachable during the update process.

What happens now? If the sender cannot detect the failure (perhaps because the write routine was originally borrowed from some stand-alone application, or because the operating system simply cannot determine if a message has been delivered or not), it will have no way of knowing that one participant is out of sync with the rest. If the network is restored a moment later, the missed recipient will continue running, none the wiser that it has missed an update.

You may be thinking, well, obviously the thing to do is ensure that the sender is made aware when a message is not received by the recipient. Even if the operating system does not provide such notifications, application programmers can code them in by stamping messages with serial numbers and having recipients explicitly acknowledge receipt of updates. (The actual protocol that would be used is more complicated than this, because the sender of a receipt may not know that its receipt has been delivered correctly.) Even in this case, though, what's the original sender to do if it detects that an update has not been delivered to a recipient? One heavy-handed solution would be to assume that the recipient has crashed and will never come back up, and drop that participant from the session. A kinder, gentler solution would be to have the sender save the update, in the hopes that the recipient comes back on line at some point in the future and the message can be resent. But how long should the sender hold on to that update, and all future updates that happen before the recipient returns? We probably don't want the sender to queue *all* messages in the hopes that some recipient will eventually return, as this causes the sender to consume excess resources because of problems that aren't local to it.

This relatively trivial case—a shared whiteboard application—shows the problems that arise when the intricacies of distributed development are hidden below a veneer of library code. As detrimental as the problems of performance and failure modes are, the problems of partial failure, and maintaining consistency among participants, is the real show-stopper for distributed computing. The classical solutions that try to paper over the differences between local and remote computing simply have nothing to say about these issues. And, in fact, one could argue that they *cannot* say anything about them: How to handle partial failures and consistency violations is an issue that each application writer must decide for themselves—it cannot be pushed into the operating system or tool kit and solved in a general way for all applications. Applications have different requirements, and will implement code to handle partial failures in different ways. An application that positively must have complete consistency may simply shut down if it detects some partial failure from which it cannot guarantee recovery. Another application may be willing to tolerate inconsistencies among participants, perhaps for some short period of time. The point of all of this is that our systems must rely on application code to deal with the handling of partial failures—programmers must acknowledge and deal with the possibility of these sorts of failures in their systems.

In all these cases, the developers of the distributed system have to consciously acknowledge the differences between networked and local programming, and decide what solution or set of trade-offs makes best sense for their applications. This is why building reliable distributed software remains so hard, even after 30 years of research into distributed computing—all of the work into making data portable and being able to move it to where computation occurs is necessary. It just isn't the hard part of the problem.

New Paradigms in Distributed Computing

Although not a panacea, Java makes some strong progress on the issues that make distributed systems programming hard. First off, Java provides a solution to many of the problems classical systems have focused on. Other problems that classical systems have addressed are simply not present in the Java world. The reason for this is that Java has the advantage of being a language-oriented system: The entire platform—from the run-time JVM, to the class libraries, to the bytecode verifier, to the security architecture—assume the existence of objects expressed using Java bytecodes. This assumption can greatly simplify many of the aspects of building distributed systems. In contrast to systems like CORBA and DCOM, where distribution is a bolted-on accessory to one or more languages, Java's approach to distributed computing assumes the existence of a *particular* language everywhere, with a favored data format and a favored code format.

For example, moving data around is no longer hard. The size and format of primitive types such as integers, floating-point numbers, strings, arrays, and even objects are defined by the Java specifications. No complex machinations are needed to handle conversions between the native data formats on one machine and the native formats on another. This is in stark contrast to C, where the language itself says little about the size or format of primitive types, and we have to rely on external, outside-the-language tools for describing portable data.

Even better, in addition to defining the primitive types, Java defines the format of complete *objects*, including such details as subclassing, method protection attributes, and type signatures. Assuming this lingua franca of data obviates the need for schemes such as XDR to homogenize data into portable forms.

Also, one of the key assumptions of pre-Java distributed computing—that data needs to move to the code, because the inverse is impractical—is done away with. Using Java, it's as easy for code to move from machine to machine, even machines with different operating systems or CPUs, as it is to move data. The Java bytecode format is the universal interchange format for executable code. Further, Java's security mechanisms ensure that code, once moved into your system, can execute with a degree of safety not found in other approaches. Although your operating system may support dynamic linking of, say, C code through shared object files or dynamic link libraries, Java's facilities for safe dynamic loading go far beyond what is possible in other environments.

For example, Java allows fine-grained access control to machine resources based on security policies. Code can be digitally signed, giving cryptographically secure guarantees about the authorship of classes. And, perhaps more importantly, Java's strong type safety, combined with the ability of the bytecode verifier to assure that malformed code will never be run, means that remotely loaded code can execute with a reduced chance of bringing down the entire process. For example, in C it is possible—even easy—for a dynamically loaded piece of code to follow a null pointer, provide an out-of-bounds array index, or corrupt the heap, bringing down an otherwise long-running server. In Java, it is impossible to obtain a reference to unused data, and it is impossible to forge a new reference to an object you have not been explicitly given access to. Furthermore, in C a function may return arbitrary (and possibly unexpected) values from a function to indicate errors. In Java, exceptional conditions must be declared as part of the signature of a method, *forcing* those who call the code to deal with them. These safety attributes of Java limit the ability of dynamically loaded code to corrupt the system.

The ability to move code from machine to machine is a dramatic change. Now, servers can be dynamically updated and maintained from authorized clients. Agent code can traverse the net, gaining performance by moving close to needed data. Systems built around rigidly defined, static interfaces can be dynamically evolved by supplying them with new implementations of those interfaces as needed.

So Java provides some novel solutions to many of the problems that classical systems have focused on, and makes some of the problems that those systems have addressed simply vanish. But what about the truly hard problems of distributed computing that we opened this chapter with? What does Java do to promote the distinction and fundamental differences between local and remote objects?

To understand how Java begins to address some of these harder problems, we first have to look at Java's model for strongly typed distributed computing. As we'll see, while Java doesn't provide magical solutions to the problems discussed earlier, its model of distributed computing explicitly acknowledges the differences in local and remote computation, and provides a toolset that allows programmers to deal with them.

The Need for Strong Typing

The previous section talked a lot about Java's ability to send code to running processes on demand. But is this really what we want? Is a world where executable code is flying around really maintainable and understandable? As a language-based approach, Java is able to take the benefits that strong typing, true object orientation, and polymorphism bring to local computing and extend these benefits out to the Internet.

In Remote Method Invocation (RMI), the Java language's type definition facility is used to describe the interfaces for remote communication. This may seem like a subtle point, but it's actually very important—local types that you create when you declare a Java class or interface, as well as the types that are found in the Java libraries, are defined using the exact same mechanisms as the types used for remote communication. This means that a protocol for communicating with some remote server *is* a Java interface, which can be implemented by a class. Here's an example of an interface definition that would be found in a program using Java RMI.

```
public interface RemoteServer extends Remote {
      public int getLength(String s) throws RemoteException;
}
```

Now this example is actually defining a remote "protocol" between two remote processes—it defines the terms of interaction between two processes, including what is sent, what you can do, and what you might get back. This protocol will, of course, be implemented atop some lower-level protocol such as TCP/IP at run time—RMI will handle all the "convenience" tasks of setting up and tearing down sockets, and so forth—but the definition here provides the specification for how two processes will communicate at the *application* level. In a nutshell, the example says that a client can send a single message that transmits a string to a remote server, and the server returns an integer as a reply to this message. But—and this is perhaps the key idea with RMI—this example also defines a first-class interface in the Java language, that can be implemented by classes, composed with other interfaces via multiple interface inheritance, passed as parameters, returned from methods, and introspected at run time.

You may be asking, "What's the big deal?" Other systems, such as CORBA's Interface Definition Language (IDL), for example, expose the remote protocol used for communication with services as a type in the native language. The difference is that in RMI it is this type that completely defines the protocol. It represents "the truth" about the definition of the protocol, and can be manipulated freely in the Java language to extend and change the protocol. Systems like IDL, on the other hand, use some external expression of the protocol (typically a protocol definition written in a language-neutral format) to describe "the truth" about that protocol. The manifestation of the protocol as a Java type is done after the fact, and the Java (or other language) type is only a reflection of the protocol definition; it is not the protocol definition itself. Manipulating the Java type that results from an IDL specification, through subclassing, composition, or reflection, will do nothing to change the protocol used for communication, and it's likely to break your code.

Again, this may sound like a subtle, somewhat academic, distinction. But its importance is hard to overstate. By making protocol definitions first-class objects in a modern object-oriented language, we bring all of the power of object orientation that works so nicely in a single address space out to the world of distributed computation.

Polymorphism works in this world. For example, I can now define remote interfaces that are subinterfaces of other remote interfaces. The usual rules apply here—I can pass the more general interface around, cast it to the more specific interface if I need to, and reflect or use `instanceof` at run time to see what type of entity I am talking to. Just as interfaces allow multiple implementations, I can have any number of Java classes that implement a particular remote interface, and the compiler ensures that I live up to my obligations by implementing the methods I need to, with the correct signature. I can even write classes that implement multiple remote interfaces, just as I can write classes that implement multiple local interfaces.

Practical Remote Polymorphism

Even more radically than supporting polymorphism in remote interfaces, RMI supports full-fledged polymorphism in the types of objects passed as parameters or returned as results to or from remote methods. Consider this code example.

```
public interface MatrixSolver extends Remote {
      public Matrix crossProduct(Matrix m1, Matrix m2)
                                    throws RemoteException;
}
```

This code defines a remote interface for doing matrix math (presumably the remote object that implements this interface is running on some high-end processor that can do matrix math so quickly that the time required to send the parameters and receive the results is low relative to the time savings). This interface takes two instances of type `Matrix`, computes the cross product of them, and returns the result, also as a `Matrix`.

Clearly the designer of this remote interface expects callers to send and receive `Matrix` objects, and to understand the semantics of this class. Suppose, however, that I am a signal processing engineer, and I have developed my own special class for dealing with matrices that contain very few data elements. My implementation, called `SparseMatrix`, is far more space efficient than the standard `Matrix` class that I subclass, so I use it everywhere in my program. I'd like to be able to take advantage of the matrix math remote object written by another group and running on a fast compute server, but the remote object that implements the math functions only understands the basic `Matrix` class, and has never heard of my `SparseMatrix`.

Clearly, in the local-only case, the polymorphism of the Java type system would give me what I want: I pass in `SparseMatrices` to code that expects plain `Matrices`, but the `crossProduct()` function works fine because it is written to use only the `Matrix` "part" of my class. A cleverly written `crossProduct()` function will even call `clone()` on one of its input parameters to create a new object of the same type as the input to stuff its result into, so that the return will be of the same type as one of the inputs.

But what happens in the remote case? If you're using RMI, the same thing as the local case! Even if the remote matrix math server object has never heard of `SparseMatrix`, even if the code for that class doesn't even exist on its machine, RMI can package up instances of `SparseMatrix`, and ship the data in these instances along. More importantly, RMI will even transmit the *code* for this class, if it is needed. It will ensure that `SparseMatrix` is an actual subclass of `Matrix`, and implements all of its required methods so that it can be used safely and reliably wherever a `Matrix` is used.

Here we've seen a very pragmatic example. Dynamic, mobile code need not only be used for avant garde applications like active agents. It can play a very useful role in extending the benefits of object-oriented programming to the networked world.

Remoteness Is Part of the Interface, Not the Implementation

You'll also note from the short code examples in the preceding section one of the other benefits RMI brings to the table. The "remoteness" of an object—its ability to be used from another address space—is a part of the object's interface. This is another subtle change with big ramifications. It forces the developer to "design in" remoteness from the beginning, rather than adding it on as an afterthought. This choice by the RMI designers means that programmers must think upfront about the communication patterns they will support in their applications. The remoteness of a method is something that must be declared; it is not hidden as part of the implementation of the object. And, just like everything else in the Java type system, the remoteness of an object can be strongly typed at compile time and introspected at run time.

RMI requires that all interfaces that define a remote communications protocol extend the interface `java.rmi.Remote`. This interface is common to all "remotable" objects, so it is easy to test at run time or compile time whether something is remote or not. These objects have different semantics than simple local objects—their notions of equality are different, for example. Equality is based on whether two objects that implement `Remote` *refer* to the same remote object that lives on some server somewhere, not whether they *are* the same object. That is, if you have a reference to a remote object, what you actually refer to is a local proxy for the remote object, called a "stub." When you compare two such references, you do not want to know if they refer to the same local stub—you care about whether those stubs reference the same remote object on a different machine some place. So the notion of equality of references is extended to work in the remote case.

Perhaps more importantly, every remotely callable method on a remote object is declared to raise the exception `java.rmi.RemoteException`. This exception, along with its subclasses, defines the failure modes that can happen in a networked setting. By explicitly declaring these failures in the method signatures, RMI forces those who would use remote objects to provide exception-handling code to deal with these extra failure cases. And because Java declares exceptions as part of the signature of a method, any code that calls remote code will have to either handle the error conditions that remote exceptions represent, or propagate them up to code that can handle them—The compiler will not allow the programmer to ignore these conditions.

While the Remote Method Invocation facility is certainly not a panacea, and it won't make problems with distributed systems go away, or make distributed systems as easy to build as local ones, it is a step in the right direction. RMI uses the Java type system, but makes a clear semantic distinction between local and remote objects. It forces developers to handle the failure modes that can occur in a distributed setting, and requires them to decide about distribution "up front" rather than hiding it as an implementation detail. By leveraging the power of the Java language, RMI takes advantage of strong typing, extending it to the network domain. RMI makes the problems of data portability simply go away. And, by supporting secure and safe code motion, RMI allows the benefits of object-oriented programming to now work across the network boundary, supporting flexible and evolvable remote code. It provides a powerful bag of tools for addressing the problems that developers face in building distributed applications.

Of course, Java is famous for mobile code, and not just in the context of RMI. The sidebar below contrasts the use of mobile code in RMI with other uses in Java.

Sidebar: Mobile Code in Other Contexts

We've seen several examples of the usefulness of mobile code in the preceding sections. How do these examples compare with mobile code in other settings... say, in applets? Let's summarize some of the contexts in which mobile code is used, and see what mobile code buys us in each circumstance.

(continued)

- Applets. In Java's best-known role, applets provide a way for small applications to be installed automatically wherever they are needed, and removed when their users are through with them. In this context, mobile code is used as a way to remove the hassles of installing traditional applications on a system. With applets, installation of an application is as easy as browsing a Web page.
- Agents. In the agent paradigm, small, autonomous bits of code travel the Internet, searching out desired data. For example, a "travel agent" might scour the Net looking for the best deals on a flight to Atlanta. In this context, mobile code is used for two things: performance and autonomy. Agents may provide a performance gain because code moves "nearer" the data (in the network sense). Autonomy is essential for agents because the user who started the agent may log off or shut down his or her machine. Once the agent has left the originator's computer, it can continue to run even if the originator disconnects.
- RMI. Java Remote Method Invocation is really an infrastructure for building many types of distributed systems, rather than a single distributed system itself. Thus, RMI can be used for automatic application installation (much as applets are), or to build agent-based systems. In its most basic uses, however, mobile code in RMI is primarily useful for extending the benefits of object-orientation to networked systems, and for supporting evolvability by allowing new implementations of remote objects, and new implementations of parameter and return types.
- Jini. Although we haven't yet talked about Jini proper, Jini leverages RMI and uses mobile code as a way to achieve maintenance, evolvability, and ease of administration for networked devices and services. But, because it is layered atop RMI and takes full advantage of the Java language, all of the other benefits of code motion are available to programs using Jini.

Java is the first widely available and commercially viable system to support such a rich range of uses for mobile code.

All of the features of mobile code, mobile data, and strong typing (necessary for robustness) signal the possibility for a shift toward true dynamic distributed systems in which the "system" is composed of a number of components, all working together to achieve some result. This is in contrast to standard networked systems, where the "systems" are the individual components, which happen to connect to each other in fairly static patterns.

Let's look a bit more closely at some of the attributes of dynamic distributed systems.

- Dynamic distributed systems can potentially be called on to scale to very large numbers of machines.
- To scale, their code must be present on large numbers of machines. To be present on large numbers of machines, the code must be ubiquitously available. To be ubiquitously available, the code must be easy to install.
- Once deployed, dynamic distributed systems may need to stay running for long periods of time, even months or years. Thus, they must be robust and reliable, and be able to "self-heal" when errors occur.
- Any system that is in place for long periods of time will doubtless have to evolve to account for new network topologies, the presence of new devices, and the refinement of both interfaces and implementations. Thus, dynamic distributed systems must be easily adaptable and evolvable.

All of these attributes point to a class of software in which the system is composed of multiple discrete units that, when in the presence of others, offer a sort of emergent behavior—all of the components work together to create a symbiotic, self-healing system that is greater than the sum of its individual components.

In the next chapter, we will take our first look at Jini, a software system explicitly designed to support the creation of true dynamic distributed systems.

Further Reading

Much of the inspiration for this chapter comes from two sources. The first is a lecture that Peter Deutsch gave to me after a presentation I made at Sun Labs, where I claimed "network transparency" as a benefit of a system I was working on. Peter—in his inimitable way—quickly convinced me that what I had claimed as a feature was really a devastating bug.

The second inspiration for this chapter comes from an excellent report written by Jim Waldo, Geoff Wyant, Ann Wollrath, and Sam Kendall, also at Sun Labs. If some of these names sound familiar, it's because these folks have been some of the brains behind the development of RMI and Jini. This report predates Jini by a few years, but it's just as true today as it was when it was written; reading it will give you some sense of where the Jini designers considered the big problems of distributed computing to be.

`http://www.sunlabs.com/technical-reports/1994/abstract-29.html`

THE JINI MODEL

Topics in This Chapter

- The goals of Jini
- What Jini is; what Jini isn't
- Basic concepts: Discovery, Lookup, Leasing, Remote Events, Transactions
- Downloadable proxies as the key to service delivery

Chapter 3

Now that we've looked at the benefits Java can bring to distributed computing, it's time to see what Jini brings to Java. The Jini vision is simply this: You can walk up with any Jini-enabled device—be it a digital camera, a new printer, a PDA, or a cell phone—plug it into a TCP/IP network, and be able to automatically see and use the variety of other Jini-enabled devices in your vicinity. Any resource available on the network is available to your Jini-enabled device, as if it were directly attached to it, or the device had been explicitly programmed to use it. And adding a new device to this "network community" is as simple as plugging it in.

In this chapter, we'll look at what Jini is: both in terms of the "center of gravity" of its design—what aspects the Jini developers considered crucial to focus on—and in terms of the five key concepts Jini introduces.

Jini Design Center

In this section, we'll look at Jini's "design center." This is the set of areas that the Jini designers felt were the most important to focus on.

Simplicity

Bill Joy, one of the inspirations and champions of Jini, once stated, "Large successful systems start out as small successful systems." This philosophy is very much a part of the Jini motivation. Essentially, if you already know Java, you almost know Jini. Jini is built using the fundamental Java concepts—especially as they relate to the distributed computing issues discussed in the last chapter—and adds only a thin veneer to allow devices and services on the network to work with each other more easily.

This is important: Jini is, at its heart, about how services connect to one another—not about what those services are or what they do or how they work. In fact, Jini services can even be written in a language other than Java; the only requirement is that there exists, somewhere on the network, a bit of code that *is* written in Java that can participate in the mechanisms Jini uses to find other Jini devices and services.

I've been using the terms "devices" and "services" pretty interchangeably so far. But from the Jini perspective, everything—even a device such as a scanner or printer or telephone—is really a service. To use an object-oriented metaphor, everything in the world, even hardware devices, can be understood in terms of the interfaces they present to the world. These interfaces are the services they offer, so Jini uses the term "service" explicitly to refer to some entity on the network that can be used by other Jini participants. The services these entities offer may be implemented (here's the O-O terminology again) by some hardware device or combination of devices, or some pure software component or combination of components.

Reliability

I've said that Jini provides the infrastructure that allows these services to find and use one another on a network. But what does this really mean? Is Jini simply a name server like the Internet's Domain Name Service (DNS) or the Lightweight Directory Access Protocol (LDAP) within an organization? As it turns out, Jini does have similarities to a name server; it even provides a service for finding other services in a community (though this service is actually much richer than a traditional name service, as we will see). But there are two essential differences between what Jini does and what simple name servers do.

- Jini supports serendipitous interactions among services and users of those services. That is, services can appear and disappear to other Jini participants in a very lightweight way. Interested parties can be automatically notified when the set of cooperating services changes. Jini allows the set of known services to change fluidly, without requiring any static configuration or administration. In this way, Jini supports what might be called "spontaneous networking"—services close to one another form a community automatically, with no need for explicit user involvement. This means that you don't have to edit configuration files, shut down or restart name servers, configure gateways, or anything else to use a Jini service—You literally just plug it in and Jini does the rest. Furthermore, every device or service that connects to a Jini community carries with it all the code necessary for that device to be used by any other participant in the community.

- Communities of Jini services are largely self-healing. This is a key property built into Jini from the ground up: Jini doesn't make the assumption that networks are perfect, or that software never fails. Given time, the system will repair damage to itself. Jini also supports redundant infrastructure in a very natural way, to reduce the possibility that services will be unavailable if key machines crash.

Taken together, these properties make Jini virtually unique among commercial-grade distributed systems infrastructures. These properties ensure that a Jini community will be virtually administration free. The spontaneous networking abilities of Jini mean that the configuration of the network can be changed without involving system administrators, and the ability to take advantage of devices previously unknown in a Jini community means that there is no need for driver or software installation to use a particular service (other than the installation of the core Jini software itself, of course). Furthermore, the self-healing nature of the system also reduces administrative load, and user headaches. A cooperating group of Jini services will be resilient to changes in network topology, service loss, and network partitions in a clean way. Jini services are able to cope with network failures. Perhaps they will not be able to fully do their jobs (even the telephone network may report errors to the user at times), but at least they will work predictably in the face of failures, and will recover by themselves over time.

Scalability

I've said that groups of Jini services join together in cooperating sets. In Jini, these groups of services are called *communities*; all services in a community are aware of each other and able to use each other.[1]

So Jini services band together to form communities. But how large are these communities? What did the Jini designers envision as the "target" size for a community? This is an important question. If Jini's design favors very large groups—say, a group composed of every Jini-enabled device in the continental United States—it will have very different performance and interaction characteristics than a design that favors very small groups. The key issue here is *scalability*—how Jini is designed to accommodate varying numbers of services, from the very large to the very small.

Jini addresses scalability through *federation.* Federation is the ability for Jini communities to be linked together, or federated, into larger groups. Ideally, the size for a single Jini community is about the size of a workgroup. That is, the number of printers, PDAs, cell phones, scanners, and other devices and network services, needed by a group of 10 to 100 people. The reason for this workgroup focus is that, most often, people tend to collaborate with those they work closely with. Jini makes it easy to bring together this group of people into a community, and makes their resources shareable.

Even if you're part of a small community used by your workgroup, you may occasionally need access to resources "further" away (in the network sense)—for example, that fast, new color laser printer up in marketing. Jini supports access to services in other communities via federating them together into larger units. Specifically, the Jini lookup service—the entity responsible for keeping track of all the services in a community—is *itself* a Jini service. Thus, the lookup service for a given community can register itself in other communities, essentially offering itself up as a resource for users and services there. (As we'll see later, Jini actually bootstraps itself: Many of the core Jini features are themselves Jini services that can be shared and used by other services using the normal Jini mechanisms.)

The topology of these communities is very lightweight. When you install the Jini software, the system will, by itself, create communities that form

1. If you peruse some older Jini technical documentation, you may see the word *djinn* used to refer to a community of Java services. Rather than using an obscure word (the original Arabic word from which "genie" is derived) I'll stick to the more meaningful "community." Often you may see the word "federation" used to describe a Jini community, and some wags, particularly those with a bent toward Star Trek, may refer to a Jini community as a "collective," reminiscent of the Borg.

along network boundaries. So, for example, if your engineering and marketing departments are on different networks, each will form a unique Jini community. If you want to federate these communities, it's trivial to do a tiny bit of administration to ensure that the lookup services for each community are known to the other.

Core Note: Jini and administration

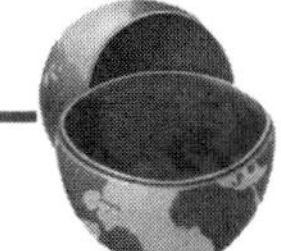

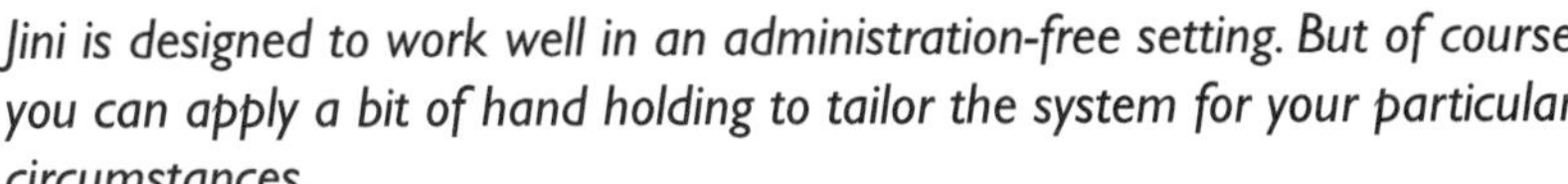

Jini is designed to work well in an administration-free setting. But of course you can apply a bit of hand holding to tailor the system for your particular circumstances.

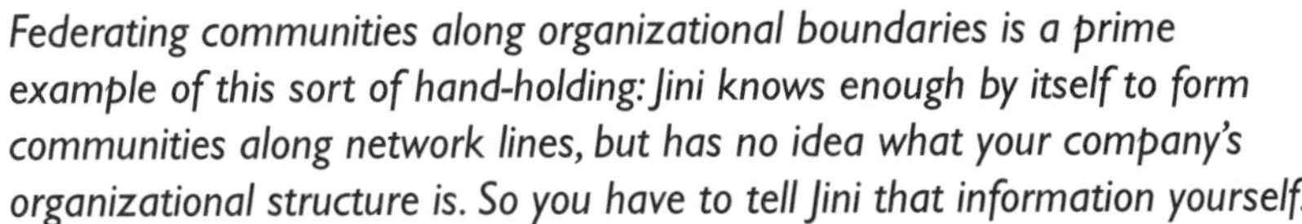

Federating communities along organizational boundaries is a prime example of this sort of hand-holding: Jini knows enough by itself to form communities along network lines, but has no idea what your company's organizational structure is. So you have to tell Jini that information yourself.

Device Agnosticism

This was alluded to in the previous section, but is important enough that it deserves restating: Jini is agnostic with regard to devices. What does this mean? Essentially it means that Jini is designed to support a wide variety of entities that can participate in a Jini community. These "entities" may be devices or software or some combination of both; in fact, it's generally impossible for the user of one of these things to know which it is. This is one of the key contributions of Jini. To use something you don't have to know—and indeed, don't even care—whether that something is hardware or software. You only have to understand the interface it presents.

If an actual hardware device is connected to the network, Jini is flexible about how much computational power it needs to have. Jini can work with full-blown desktop or server computers, capable of running multiple JVMs and connecting with each other at gigabit speeds. It can also work with such devices as PDAs and cell phones that may have only limited Java capabilities—say, an Embedded or Personal Java implementation with a limited set of class libraries.

In fact, Jini is actually designed to accommodate devices that are so simple they may have no computation on them at all. As we shall see in the next chapter, Jini can accommodate devices with the computational intelligence of—literally—a light switch. The only requirement is that some other, perhaps shared, computational resource exist that can participate in the Jini community-building protocols on behalf of that device.

Furthermore, and this may be somewhat surprising, Jini doesn't even require that the device or service be written in or understand Java! Again, all that is required is that some Java-speaking device be willing to act as a proxy on behalf of the Java-challenged device or service.

What Jini Is Not

Now that I've talked a bit about what Jini is, I should say a few words about what Jini is not.

Jini Is Not a Name Server

As mentioned previously, Jini is not just a name server. Some of what Jini does—like keeping track of the services known within a community—looks like a name server, and even uses the Jini lookup facilities, which provide functionality similar to (but not quite the same as) a name server. But Jini is much more. It is a paradigm for building distributed systems that support spontaneous appearance and disappearance in a community, and the ability to self-heal when things go wrong.

Jini Is Not JavaBeans

JavaBeans provides a way for software components—called beans—to find each other, use services provided by other beans, introspect each other, and so forth. But JavaBeans has a very different design center from Jini. Beans is largely intended for use within a single address space: The mechanisms used for communication between beans are based on direct method invocation, not remote protocols. The beans model, flexible as it is, is also far less dynamic than Jini. When a new bean appears on your system, the current beans in your application don't suddenly know about it and start using it. You—the designer of the system—have to explicitly link the bean into your application and "wire it up" to the other beans. JavaBeans is intended largely for design time, and to a lesser degree for run time use in a single address space. Jini is all about run-time use across address spaces. (This isn't to say that Jini and JavaBeans are incompatible systems, however. Jini can leverage

JavaBeans in some nice ways. Later, we'll look at how to use the JavaBeans event model from Jini, and how to attach beans to Jini services.)

Jini Is Not Enterprise JavaBeans

Likewise, Jini is not Enterprise JavaBeans (EJB). EJB has, on the surface, some characteristics of Jini. It provides the notion of services on the network. Enterprise beans can, and usually do, live in different address spaces. But again, the design center of EJB is quite different than that of Jini. EJB is designed to hook together legacy enterprise systems, covered by Java wrappers, to form the back-end business logic of enterprise applications. It is designed to support easy construction of this logic, and leverages the transaction, messaging, and database services already on the enterprise network. As such, EJB is largely used to configure relatively static pathways between enterprise software components. As long as the logic of the system doesn't change, there's probably little need to reorganize the connections between the beans. Again, defining how these connections will take place happens mostly at design time. In contrast, Jini is about dynamic, run-time discovery of services and run-time connectivity between them.

Jini Is Not RMI

Jini is not the same thing as Java RMI. While Jini *uses* RMI extensively, particularly its facilities for mobile code, Jini is a set of services and conventions built atop RMI. As such, services that speak Jini can enjoy the full benefits of Jini's spontaneous networking and self-healing abilities. While it would be possible (although a lot of work) to build these abilities into a generic RMI application, they are not a part of RMI itself and generic RMI applications do not see these advantages.

Jini Is Not a Distributed Operating System

Finally, Jini is not a distributed operating system. In some ways, it is much larger than a distributed operating system—because pieces of it must run atop some platform that provides a JVM at a minimum, but in other ways it is much smaller—the facilities offered and the concepts used by Jini are very limited. Jini only has the notion of services, and the facilities for finding those services. True distributed operating systems provide all the services of traditional operating systems (file access, CPU scheduling, user logins), but do this over a connected group of machines. Jini allows much simpler devices to participate in Jini communities than would devices that rely on running a copy of a full-blown distributed operating system.

The Five Key Concepts of Jini

I've said that conceptual simplicity is one of the explicit goals of Jini, and now we get to see what that means in practice. All of Jini's ability to support spontaneously created, self-healing communities of services is based around five key concepts. Understanding these concepts is all you need to know to use Jini.

The concepts are

- Discovery
- Lookup
- Leasing
- Remote Events
- Transactions

These concepts are implemented as a set of software libraries and conventions that are used by code that participates in Jini communities.

Discovery is the process used to find communities on the network and join with them. Discovery is the part of Jini that is responsible for the spontaneous community-building properties of the system.

Lookup governs how the code that is needed to use a particular service finds its way into participants that want to use that service. Lookup fulfills the role of a directory service within each Jini community, and provides facilities for searching and finding services that are known within a community. What lookup does is actually more complex than a simple name server—whereas a name server simply maps string names onto objects, Jini's lookup facilities understand Java's type hierarchy. So a lookup operation can search based on the type of an object, and even consider inheritance relationships during a search. The functionality provided here is quite a bit more complex (and useful in Jini's context) than a simple string-based name service.

Leasing is one of the most important concepts in Jini, simply because it is used so extensively. Leasing is the technique that provides Jini's self-healing nature. It ensures that a community will, after a while, recover from the loss of any key services that were a member of that community. Leasing also ensures that long-lived services (such as lookup) don't "accrete" information about their communities; without leasing, such long-lived services might eventually grow in size without bound.

Remote events are the paradigm Jini uses to allow services to notify each other of changes in their state. Because lookup is itself a service, it can use remote events to notify interested parties when the set of services available to a community has changed. The Jini remote event model is similar to, but not the same as, the JavaBeans event model. We'll explore the reasons for this in Chapter 14, "In Depth: Remote Events." But essentially remote events must incorporate all of the semantics of "remoteness" discussed in the previous chapter, as well as supporting a key requirement of Jini, namely that any entity can be made to receive any type of event.

Finally, *transactions* are Jini's mechanism for allowing computations that may involve multiple services to reach a "safe" state. By this, I mean that the caller can be assured that the computations have either all completed, or that none of them have completed. In either case, the system is returned to a known state. Jini's transaction model helps guard against the evils of partial failures in a distributed system, helps address the concurrency problems posed by distributed systems as discussed in Chapter 2, and can provide services with a great deal of robustness and resilience to network failures. While Jini's model of transactions resembles the "classical" transaction model often used in database programming, it is significantly different under the covers.

The rest of this chapter presents an overview of these key concepts, and looks at how they work together in practice. By the end of this chapter, you'll understand all the basic mechanisms upon which Jini is built. In later chapters, we'll harden this conceptual knowledge into actual programming skills that you'll use to build working Jini services and applications.

Discovery

Before a Jini-aware entity—either a service or application—can take advantage of other Jini services, it must first find one or more Jini communities. The way an entity does this is by finding the lookup services that keep track of the shared resources of that community—this process of finding the available lookup services is called *discovery.* The Jini discovery protocol is the means by which Jini-aware code finds Jini communities. Once a community has been found, the Jini-aware service can step through a series of conventions called the *join protocol* to allow itself to be used by other applications and services in that community.

There is not necessarily a one-to-one mapping of communities to lookup services. Each lookup service on a network may provide service for one or more communities; each community may have one or more lookup servers that support it. Lookup services are started explicitly by administrators—in fact, this is the *only* Jini service which is required to be running for Jini communities to form.

The Discovery Protocols

There is not just a single discovery protocol—Jini supports several, useful in different situations.

- The Multicast Request Protocol is used when an application or service first becomes active, and needs to find the "nearby" lookup services that may be active.
- The Multicast Announcement Protocol is used by lookup services to announce their presence. When a new lookup service that is part of an existing community starts up, any interested parties will be informed via the Multicast Announcement Protocol.
- The Unicast Discovery Protocol is used when an application or service already knows the particular lookup service it wishes to talk to. The Unicast Discovery Protocol is used to talk directly to a lookup service, which may not be a part of the local network, when the name of the lookup service is known. Lookup services are named using a URL syntax with `jini` as the protocol specifier (`jini://turbodog.parc.xerox.com` specifies the lookup server running on the host `turbodog.parc.xerox.com` on the default port, for example). Unicast lookup is used when there is a need to create static connections between services and lookup services, such as when explicitly federating lookup services together.

The end result of the discovery process is that the entity—the object doing the discovery—is handed one or more references to the lookup services for the requested community. Using these references, services can advertise the facilities they offer, and both clients and services can determine what services are available in a community. A number of other operations, such as soliciting events, can be performed on lookup services (see the section entitled "Lookup," later in this chapter, for the details on what you can do with a lookup service).

While applications such as browsers may obtain references to lookup services in order to display a list of available services, in many cases the entity doing discovery is a Jini service that intends to make itself available to the other members of the community. The process of publishing a service to make it available to the others in a community is called *joining* that community. A service that wishes to join a community performs discovery to find the lookup services for that community, and then joins them using operations on the lookup service references returned from the discovery process (again, see the following section entitled "Lookup.") To ensure that services are well-behaved, Jini dictates the *join protocol* that services should follow to join a community. This "protocol" isn't really a protocol in the network sense, but rather a set of conventions that services should follow.

Supporting Multiple Communities

In Jini, communities can have names. In the Jini APIs, these names are called "groups," and during the discovery process, a service or application can specify the groups it wishes to find. The discovery protocols will return all of the lookup services it can find that are members of those groups. Lookup services can be members of multiple groups, just as any service can be a member of multiple groups.

You can, in most cases, think of "groups" and "communities" as being the same things—groups are simply the notion that Jini uses in its APIs to specify and represent communities. The most important difference to note between communities and groups is that because of network separation, different communities may have the same group name—the "public" group at Xerox PARC does not refer to the same "public" group at JavaSoft, for example. Even though the names are the same, these names can refer to different actual communities depending on the context of their use. Put a different way, group names are not globally unique, nor are they necessarily globally accessible. But, for most purposes, you can think of groups and communities as being interchangeable.

How does a service know which community to join? In most cases, services will simply look for the "default" group, which is named by the empty string and—by convention—is treated as a "public" community, and then use the multicast protocols to connect to any and all lookup services they can find. The multicast protocols are designed to ensure that the discovery process will only reach lookup services running on the local network, to keep from blasting the entire Internet with discovery protocol packets.

In some cases, a service may need to join a nondefault community. For example, a product development lab may test out new Jini services in an "experimental" community that happens to exist on the same subnet as the "production" community, which might be the default. These two communities can share resources (if services join both communities), and even share lookup services (if the lookup services are members of both communities). To join the nondefault experimental community, services would use the group name "experimental" to find the lookup services that are members of the community named "experimental."

In other cases, a service may need to explicitly connect to only some specific set of lookup services—say, a special "administrators only" lookup service with special authorizations and restrictions. In this case, a privileged backup service might use unicast discovery to connect only to that one special lookup service, even if the lookup service and the backup service are running on different networks. The ability to use the unicast discovery protocol allows Jini to be flexible in creating its community structure.

While Chapter 6 goes into quite a bit of detail on the various discovery protocols, using them in practice is thankfully easy. Most applications and services need only implement the `DiscoveryListener` interface and do some simple bookkeeping to participate in discovery and find out about the Jini communities nearby.

Lookup

While discovery is the process of finding lookup services, *lookup* refers to the things you can do to those lookup services. Think of the lookup service as a name server—it's essentially a process, usually long-running, that keeps track of all of the services that have joined a Jini community. But unlike a traditional name server, which provides a mapping from string names to stored objects, the Jini lookup service supports a richer set of semantics. You can search the Jini lookup service for particular types of objects and, since the lookup service understands Java type semantics, you can even search by looking for superclasses and superinterfaces of stored objects. After discovery has successfully found a lookup service for you, it returns a reference to an object that implements the lookup interfaces (this interface is actually called `ServiceRegistrar`. Calling it `Lookup` might have been a better idea).

How the internals of the lookup service are actually implemented is hidden from you. It may be built using a simple hashtable that gets saved to disk periodically, or it may be a high-powered directory service with lightning-fast lookups and logged writes to persistent storage. All you as the user of a lookup service knows is that the object returned from discovery implements `ServiceRegistrar` and knows how to talk to whatever actual lookup service is running on some machine on the network. You do not know the details of this communication—it may be using Java RMI, vanilla sockets, or smoke signals for all you know. This permits multiple, wildly varying implementations of the lookup service, with all of the details hidden behind the object you get that implements the lookup interfaces.

Publishing a Service

So now that you've done discovery, and you've got one or more of these lookup objects, what can you do with them? Abstractly, you can think of the lookup service as maintaining a list of "service items." Each service item contains an object that other participants in the community can download to use that service, and a list of attributes that are used to describe the service. In Figure 3–1, we see a lookup service that's holding three service items. Each service item contains a "proxy" object as well as attributes that describe the service. As we shall see shortly, this proxy object can be downloaded by clients that need to use the service. Even though a given client may know nothing about the implementation of a particular service, it can use the service's proxy as a "front end" for interacting with the service.

If you are a service (say, a printer) and wish to publish yourself to your community (that is, make your printing service available to anyone who wants to use it), you *join* all the lookup services returned from the discovery process. The `ServiceRegistrar` interface has a method called `register()` that lets you join a lookup service.

Core Tip: Join every lookup service for your community

Note that any given community (that is, each unique group name on a given network) may have any number of lookup services supporting it. For fault-tolerance purposes, many redundant lookup services may be active.

Typically, a service that needs to join a community will join all the lookup services that support that community, so that if one lookup service fails, others can stand in for it. Unless you have some special need, or need to explicitly limit the scope of visibility of your service, you should usually join all of the lookup services that you discover.

You invoke the `register()` method by passing in a service item object as an argument. You fill in the attributes with objects that may describe your service. There are some standardized attributes provided by Jini for this purpose—service name, service location, comments, and so on. If your company

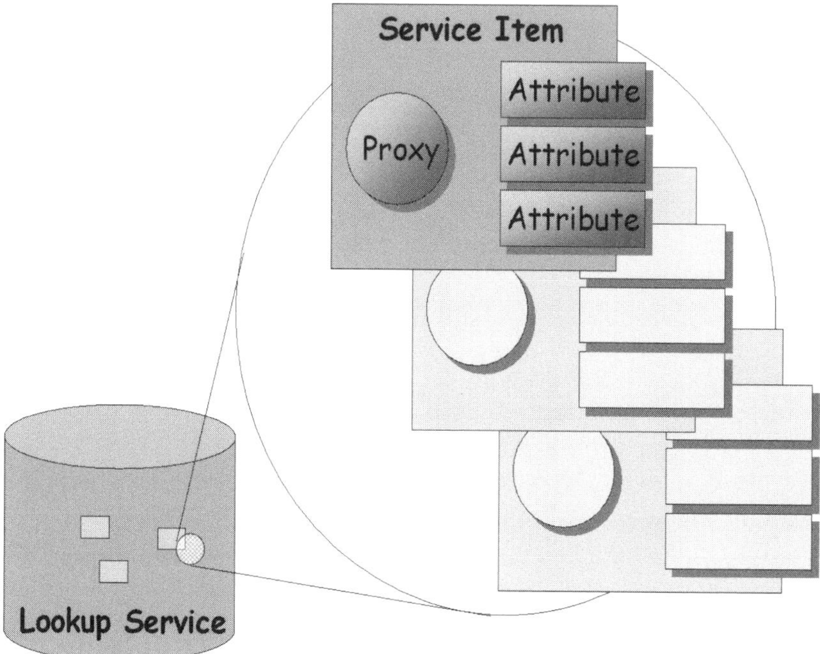

Figure 3–1 Lookup servers maintain lists of service items

sells a number of Jini services, you may even have your own standardized set of attributes that reveal extra information about the services.

Downloadable Proxies

The most important thing in the service item is unique to your service, however. You supply an arbitrary serializable Java object in the service item, called the *service proxy*. Whenever any other entity—whether it's another Jini service, or simply an application that wishes to take advantage of your service—finds your service item, this proxy object will be copied to their Java Virtual Machine, and they will make calls on it to use your service.

This idea of downloadable service proxies is the key idea that gives Jini its ability to use services and devices without doing any explicit driver or software installation. Services publish the code that can be used to access them. A printer, for instance, publishes a proxy that understands how to control that particular printer. A scanner publishes a proxy that knows how to talk to that particular scanner. An application that uses the service downloads the proxy and uses it without needing any understanding of how the proxy is implemented or how (or even whether) it talks to any back-end device or process.

In some ways, Jini proxies are analogous to Java applets: applets provide a zero-administration way to acquire and use an application. Jini proxies provide a zero-administration way to acquire and use the "glue logic" for communicating with any arbitrary back-end service or device. But whereas applets are typically designed for "human consumption"—meaning that they usually appear in a web page when a user asks for them, and come with a graphical interface—Jini proxies are designed to be found, downloaded, and used programmatically. Jini proxies can be thought of as secure network-aware device drivers that are downloaded on demand to the clients that need them, when they need them.

The particulars of how the proxy object interacts with your service are completely up to you. There are a number of common scenarios, though.

- The downloaded proxy object performs the service. In this case, the object that is sent to consumers of the service does everything that the service claims to do, by itself (and therefore, calling it a "proxy" is really unfair). This strategy would be used when the service is implemented purely in software, and there are no external resources that need to be used. An example might be a language translation service that is completely implemented as a chunk of Java code that can be downloaded to a consumer and executed. In this case, there is no need for the downloaded code to talk to any external processes to do its job.
- The downloaded object is an RMI stub for talking to some remote service. This case is commonly used where there is some centralized RMI-based process somewhere on the network that implements the service. This situation represents a minimal approach for turning an RMI-based program into a Jini service--simply use the automatically-generated stub object for the RMI service as the proxy. Here, the stub is very minimal, and only has the "intelligence" necessary to speak RMI.
- The downloaded object is a "smart" proxy that can speak any private communication protocol for talking to the service. This strategy is most commonly used in two cases. The first is where there is some legacy software system involved. Jini is ideal for making non-Java systems accessible through Java. All a developer has to do is write the "glue"--the small downloadable

> Java object that implements the desired interface to the legacy service. This proxy object would then communicate using the legacy system's expected protocols--sockets, proprietary database languages, whatever--and yet provide a pure Java interface that is easily accessible and usable. For example, you could provide Jini access to an IMAP (Internet Mail Access Protocol) server by writing a Java object that speaks the IMAP protocol but exposes an easy-to-use Java interface. The second use for this strategy is when the service is actually provided by some hardware device. In this case, the proxy acts essentially like a downloadable device driver. If the hardware device is a printer, the proxy object exposes some "printerlike" interface to its consumers, and is implemented to speak whatever proprietary back-end protocols are needed to communicate with the printer. In either of these cases, the details of this implementation are hidden from the consumer.

The proxy object is the key to Jini's ability to have services and devices carry with them the code needed to use them. The proxy, particular to the implementation of a service, and typically written by the developer of that service, will be downloaded to consumers of that service whenever they need it. The code of this downloaded object will be executed securely by the consumer. Even better, the consumer has no idea how the particular proxy that connects his or her code to the actual service is implemented. All the user of a printer service has to know is that the proxy implements the `Printer` interface—not the particulars of how it will talk to any specific printer. Figure 3–2 shows an overview of the joining process. Here we see a newly created service publishing its service proxy on the two lookup services it finds.

Figure 3–2 A service joins a Jini community

Finding a Service

We've seen how services join communities to publish their services. Now we can look at how consumers of services find and use the services that are members of a community.

Once it has a reference to a lookup service, a consumer (which may itself be a service that has joined a community) can search all the service items to find services of interest. Jini provides a number of ways to search—you can search based on the type of the downloadable proxy object contained in each service item, you can search by the unique identifier of the service (if you know it), or you can search the attributes contained in each service item. This process of finding the services that are of interest to you is the core of lookup. (And, not surprisingly, the `ServiceRegistrar` interface has a method called `lookup()` that does exactly this.) However you do it, once you've specified the search parameters and called `lookup()`, the value that is returned to you is the proxy object from the service item. In Figure 3–3, we see a client application (a consumer of a Jini service) downloading the proxy for a particular service from a lookup service. Once the proxy has been downloaded, the client uses that proxy as a "front end" to communicate directly with the service's "back end," which is typically a long-lived process or a hardware device connected to the network. The proxy can be as complex or as simple as required. For example, some "smart proxies" may implement private communication protocols with the back end. Others may be simply the RMI-generated stubs that are used to communicate with a remote object in the back end.

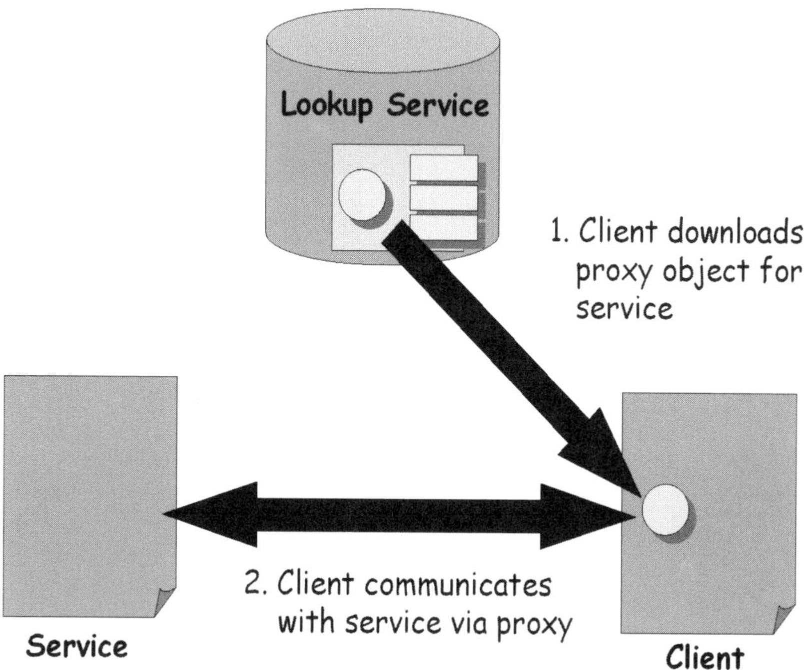

Figure 3–3 Using a Jini service

Say you are writing the software for a digital camera. The camera exposes itself as a service (perhaps implementing a `DigitalCamera` interface, with methods to `snapShutter()` and `copyOutPicture()`), and you want to make printing of the images directly from the camera possible whenever you detect that a printer is nearby. The first part, making your services available to anyone who is interested, is handled by the join process that we've already talked about. For the second part, however, being able to print on any available printers, the camera will be a consumer of another service—a print service.

In this case, the most likely scenario is that the camera does a search of all the lookup services in its community, looking for service items that contain proxies implementing the `Printer` interface. The lookup services may return one or more proxies that implement this interface, and the camera may choose to present them, possibly annotated with name, location, or comment information from their attributes, to the user on the LCD display of the camera. When the user prints a picture to a particular printer, the `Printer` methods on the front-end proxy object are invoked, and output is sent to the printer.

Common Interfaces, Divergent Implementations

You may be asking yourself, "How did the camera know to look for service items for the `Printer` interface?" Clearly, services and applications need to have at least *some* understanding of the semantics of the interfaces they are calling. You, as the writer of the digital camera software, may not know *how* the `Printer` interface works, but you have at least a basic idea of *what* it does—it causes things to be sent to the printer. If you were to encounter an interface with some unintelligible name, say the `Fleezle` interface, you would have no idea what it did, or what to pass as arguments to its methods, or what to do with its return values. In such a case, it's impossible to really use this unknown interface programmatically, without some end-user involvement to tell you what to do. For this reason, most Jini services will be written to implement well-known interfaces, and to expect the other services in a community to implement well-known interfaces. This is the only way they can know *how* to programmatically interact with those services once they see them.

Sun, along with its partners and the wider Jini community of users, is working to define a set of common interfaces for printers, scanners, cellular telephones, storage services, and other common network devices and services. Development of these is ongoing at the time of this writing. If at all possible, writers of new services should use standardized interfaces wherever appropriate to ensure that Jini services can take advantage of each other.

It is, of course, possible to use unknown interfaces if the user can tell you what to do with them. For this reason, Jini supports storing arbitrary serialized Java objects—including full-blown user interfaces—as attributes in service items. Consumers of services can search based on attributes, as well as on the type of the service proxy, as we saw previously. For example, a digital camera may search for all services in its community that have an attribute that's a `java.awt.Component`. These attributes will be user interfaces that can be displayed to a user, and may allow users to interact "manually" with the service, even if the camera's code does not know how to interact with unknown services programmatically. Thus, a user might recognize the `Fleezle` service from its user interface, and control it directly from the camera, even if the camera's software could not.

I've talked a good deal about downloaded code through the service proxy. It's worth mentioning that the Jini lookup infrastructure itself actually uses this mechanism to allow Jini services to talk to different lookup implementations. When discovery is performed, all the answering lookup services actually respond with a service proxy for talking to their particular implementations of the lookup service. The same facilities that allow arbitrary Jini services to be used, regardless of their implementations or what communication mechanisms they use, is leveraged by lookup.

Leasing

So far I've talked about discovery and lookup, the aspects of Jini that allow communities of services to spontaneously form, and to exchange code to allow services to interact with each other. But I haven't talked yet about how to ensure that these communities are stable, self-healing, and resilient in the face of (inevitable) network failures, machine crashes, and software errors. The issue of reliability is especially important when software systems are intended—as Jini communities are—to be long-lived entities that can stay running and responsive over a period of months or even years, with little or no operator intervention.

Consider an example: Suppose our digital camera service joins a community by registering itself with a lookup service for that community (presumably this happens whenever the camera is placed in its network-connected docking cradle, or attached to a computer that is itself on the network). The camera publishes the fact that it is available for use, and all is well. That is, all is well until the user unceremoniously yanks the camera out of its cradle without turning it off first. What happens here? To the other members of the community, this may look like a classic partial failure situation—they may not be able to tell if the remote host to which the camera is connected has gone down, if it's simply slow to answer, if it's not answering network traffic because of a change in its configuration, if the camera's software has crashed, or even if the camera has been smashed with a hammer. But, regardless of how it was disconnected, it has not had a chance to unregister itself before it disconnects because of the abrupt termination of the camera's communication to the network.

The result of the user disconnecting the camera without shutting down properly—a completely understandable and common occurrence—is that, without some special facilities, a "stale" registration will linger in the lookup service for the community. Services that wish to use the camera will see it registered but will not be able to use it. But even more severe are the problems that the lookup service itself will encounter—if the registrations for services it has seen are never properly cleaned up, it will accrete registrations and slowly bog down under the weight of stale data.

This accumulation of state is a serious problem in long-lived distributed systems. We simply cannot ensure that services will never crash or become disconnected before they've had a chance to deregister themselves.

In the case we've described, the camera holds a *resource* in the lookup service—it is asking the lookup service to use some of its (possibly scant or expensive) storage and computation to maintain the camera's registration. If the Jini infrastructure used a traditional approach to *resource reservation*, the registration would simply stay active until it was canceled, or until some human system administrator went through the logs and cleaned out stale services.

Obviously, this solution violates everything that we want from Jini. First, it doesn't ensure that the system self-heals: Partial failures aren't recognized and cleaned up, and services that hold resources on behalf of others may grow without bound. Second, and perhaps even worse, it requires explicit human intervention to administer the system.

Time-Based Resource Reservation

To get around these problems, Jini uses a technique called *leasing*. Leasing is based on the idea that, rather than granting access to a resource for an unlimited amount of time, the resource is "loaned" to some consumer for a fixed period of time. Jini leases require demonstrable proof-of-interest on the part of the resource consumer to continue to hold on to the resource.

Jini leases work much like leases in "real life." Jini leases may be denied by the grantor of the lease. They can be renewed by the holder. Leases will expire at a predetermined date unless they are renewed. They can be canceled early (and, unlike in real life, Jini imposes no penalty on early lease cancellation). Finally, leases can be negotiated, but, as in real life, the grantor has the final word on the terms of the lease that is offered.

Leases provide a consistent means to free unused or unneeded resources throughout Jini: If a service goes away, either intentionally or unintentionally, without cleaning up after itself, its leases will eventually expire and the service will be forgotten. Leases are used extensively in the lookup service and, as we shall see, in other aspects of the system. Therefore, it's important to understand how to effectively use leases when you're building or using Jini services.

One of the great aspects of leases is that they make it very hard to screw up the entire system: The system acts conservatively, so if you forget to do lease management, or a programming bug causes you to never renew your leases, your unreliable code simply drops out of the community without causing widespread damage to others. Jini unifies the handling of certain programming bugs (lease renewal failures) with network errors and machine crashes. All the provider of a resource sees is that the service's lease has expired, and that it is no longer available.

The second great aspect of leasing is that it makes the persistent storage used by the members of a Jini community virtually maintenance free. A system administrator will never have to crawl through logs, trying to determine which services are active, which are inactive, and which have left stale data scattered throughout the system. Given a bit of time, the community will identify unused resources and free them, like antibodies attacking a virus. Certainly it would be a great day if we could erase all traces of unwanted applications, unused drivers, and obsolete OS upgrades from our PCs so easily.

Third-Party Leasing

There is one important difference between Jini leases and most leases in the real world: Jini leases are designed to allow a *third party* to take out a lease on behalf of someone else. This third party goes through the mechanics of acquiring the lease, but the lease is actually in the "name" of the lessor. This would be as if your mother-in-law rented a nice beach house in your name, for you to live in.

Core Note: Leasing analogies

Actually, a much closer analogy is that of power of attorney. When you delegate power of attorney to an individual, you give that person "signing authority" on your behalf to enter into contracts. Although the attorney is doing the signing, you are still the one bound to the contract.

There are few, if any, situations in Jini where an unscrupulous third party would take out a lease on your behalf and gain any benefit from it. So third-party leasing is almost entirely used as a convenience by the lessor.

Why would one want such an arrangement? There are several reasons. The most important is convenience for the lessor. If I just want to worry about writing my service and forget about all of the leasing APIs, lease renewals, lease expirations, and so forth, I can delegate the process of lease renewal to a third party. I ask the third party to continue renewing my lease on my behalf for some fixed period of time, or until I tell it to stop. The third party then worries about contacting the lease grantor, negotiating the lease duration, and renewing the lease before the time expires. Presumably, the third party will tell me if the grantor ever decides to not renew my lease for some reason. This situation is closest to the previous "power of attorney" analogy —it is done for the convenience of the lessor.

The third-party arrangement is also convenient when, for whatever reason, the service holding a lease intends to be extremely long-lived, and yet rarely active. For example, a service that does monthly backups of a disk drive only needs to run once a month. Such a service will probably just "go to sleep" for the rest of the time, probably using the Java RMI *activation framework*, a means for Java objects to be automatically written to persistent storage, and then reconstituted at a later date. While this service would be alive, yet asleep, for an extremely long period of time (maybe even years), the duration of its leases with the lookup service might be orders of magnitude shorter, perhaps even on the order of minutes. If the monthly backup service had to wake up every 10 minutes to renew its lease, a huge amount of computational resources would be spent reviving and saving the service throughout the day—in fact, the work required to do this would probably dominate the actual, once-a-month chore the service is intended to do.

In this situation, third-party leasing is the solution. The monthly backup service delegates its lease renewal to a third party. This third party may itself be a service, and may have published the fact that it is willing to do long-term lease renewals on behalf of other services. (And, therefore, this lease renewal service is likely to be shared among a number of long-lived services.) This third party works just like the third party in the previous example: It manages lists of leases, renews them before they expire, and notifies lessors when it cannot obtain new leases for them.

Third-Party Leasing and Delegation

Those of you familiar with the AWT event model (from JDK1.1 onward) or with JavaBeans programming will notice a parallel between third-party leasing and the "delegation" event model. Delegation allows third parties to handle events on behalf of other objects. This model is in contrast to the original AWT event model, where an event had to be handled by the actual object to which the event was sent. Delegation is far more flexible, and supports programming patterns such as centralized event managers, event chaining, and so forth. Third-party leasing offers many of the same benefits. This sidebar shows how this works in Jini.

Sidebar: Lease Delegation

We'll look at lease delegation extensively in Chapter 11. But now is a good time to start to look at just a bit of code, to give you a feel for how lease delegation looks to a programmer, and to show you how easy it is in practice.

In this example, the code below is registering a new service with a Jini lookup service. The `ServiceRegistration` object that is returned from the registration includes in it a lease.

This lease can be handed to a third-party leasing delegate that will take care of the renewals for it. In this case, the leasing delegate is a class called `LeaseRenewalManager`, which ships with Jini in the `sun-util.jar` file as unsupported code.

```
// myService is the service item for the service I'll
// be publishing. It contains the proxy object for the service
// as well as any attributes I want to be associated with it.
// We won't look at all the details of ServiceItem here.
ServiceItem myService = new ServiceItem(/* ... */);

// lookup is a ServiceRegistrar--a lookup service that I've
// found via discovery. Here I'm registering my service item
// and requesting an initial lease duration of 5 minutes
// (expressed in milliseconds).
ServiceRegistration reg =
        lookup.register(myService, 1000 * 60 * 5);

// I don't want to manage my leases myself, so I'll use
// a LeaseRenewalManager. I can just create one and ask
// it to renew my lease for me. The Lease.ANY parameter says
// to keep renewing the lease until I tell the manager
// otherwise. The null is an optional "listener" object
// that I can pass in that will be notified of lease
// renewal problems.
LeaseRenewalManager mgr = new LeaseRenewalManager();
mgr.renewUntil(reg.lease, Lease.ANY, null);
```

(continued)

In this case, we're delegating the handling of our lease to a "library" class called `LeaseRenewalManager`. The instance of this class that manages our leases is internal to the JVM that the lease owner is in. But we could also delegate lease management to a completely external process—or even a Jini service—that lives in a separate JVM.

We'll look at all the details of this in Chapter 11, but this code snippet should give you a sense of the flavor of lease delegation.

Using Leases in Practice

So far, I've described what leasing is, but not talked about how it works. In Jini, any operation that causes some resource to be held typically takes as a parameter a requested duration, and returns a lease object. For example, the lookup service grants leases to service registrations, rather than granting them in perpetuity. The `register()` method on the `ServiceRegistrar` takes as an argument a long integer representing the number of milliseconds for which the service wants its lease to last. The lookup service responds with a result of type `ServiceRegistration`, which contains information about the just-registered service. One of the members of the `ServiceRegistration` is a `Lease` object. This object represents the lease that the lookup service has granted, and can be used to manipulate the lease—renewing or canceling it, for example.

There are a couple of points to make from this example. First, the "negotiation" process is minimal—there is only one "round" of negotiation. The party attempting to acquire a lease requests a duration, and the party granting the lease can either deny the lease entirely, grant the lease for the requested duration, or grant the lease for a shorter duration. This quick negotiation is sufficient for almost all applications, and does away with multiple time-consuming round-trip messages between the lease requestor and the lease grantor.

The second point to make is that leases are always done in terms of time *duration*. That is, lease times are described relative to the current time, rather than as some fixed absolute time in the future. Why is this? To see why Jini uses relative time, let's imagine how a leasing system based on absolute time would work. Suppose you were able to ask for a lease that expires at an absolute time, say 10:00 AM on Sunday. You're making this request to a process running on a different machine, somewhere across the network. This machine's clock may not be synchronized to yours—in fact, that machine may already think that the requested lease expiration time has passed. Keeping clocks on machines across a network in sync is a tricky problem.

The alternative used by Jini—specifying leases in terms of duration—is much more workable, because it guards against situations where two machines on a network have wildly varying notions of what the time of day is. Even if the lease grantor's clock is off by days, asking for a lease of one hour will yield pretty much one hour of lease time.

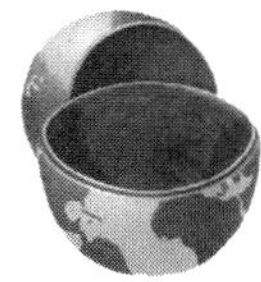

Core Note: How accurate is relative time?

Of course, sending the message to ask for the lease will take some time. And, presumably, if the grantor's clock is wrong it is because the machine's clock is running fast or slow, so your notion of one hour may not exactly equal the grantor's notion of one hour.

Still, the amount of clock error that will accumulate during a typical lease period is far, far less than the total accumulated error that may exist between the two clocks.

While not perfect (nothing involving time in a distributed system can be perfect), the Jini approach presents a simple and workable solution to the problem of expiration times in a distributed system.

The `Lease` object returned from calls that reserve resources is associated with whatever bookkeeping information the grantor is using to track the leases it has granted. Thus, if you suspect you will ever need to perform any operations on this lease such as canceling it or renewing it (and chances are that you will), then you should hold on to this object so that you can use it in the future.

The management of leases, especially when keeping track of multiple leases and the resources with which they are associated, with potentially different expiration times, can be a headache. In fact, dealing with lease management is one of the most substantial issues when writing Jini services. Fortunately, the lease interfaces themselves are very simple (you only really ever need to use two methods, `renew()` and `cancel()`), and the handling of leases can be done pretty automatically by library code. This book provides some handy utility classes for automating much of lease management.

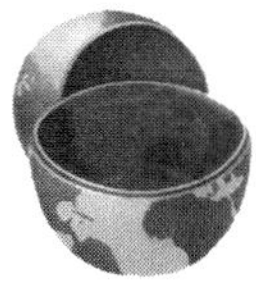

Core Tip: How long should your leases be?

While we've talked about leases, we haven't answered one important question—how long should leases be? The answer to this question really depends on the application. If your service is very short lived, or connects and disconnects from the network very frequently, a lease period of a few minutes is probably what you want.

On the other hand, if your service is constantly up, awake, and connected to the network, you might ask for a much longer lease (hours or even days) to reduce the network traffic of lease renewal. Of course, there is no guarantee that any grantor will actually issue you a lease for this long. Just remember that the longer your lease, the longer it will take your community to heal itself if your service crashes or the network goes down. For this reason, leases of a few minutes are probably appropriate. In fact, the current Jini lookup service will by default only grant five minute leases on service registrations, even if callers ask for more time.

Leasing versus Garbage Collection

Those of you with experience with Garbage Collection (GC) may be thinking that leasing is essentially a duplication of what Java currently does with its garbage collector. In a sense, this is accurate: Both garbage collection and leasing have to do with clearing out unused resources from a system. And Java's RMI facility even comes with a distributed garbage collector that can free up a resource across a network when no *remote* reference to it exists.

So what's the difference? The key difference is that garbage collection is used to free resources when there is no active reference in a program that could be used to reach the resource. In leasing, there are typically *never* any references to the resource to begin with. For example, our digital camera service may sit happily on its lookup service, never to be used by any other Jini participant. Just because this service hasn't yet been used doesn't mean that it should be unregistered and deleted—someone may come along later and want to use it. Leasing is the appropriate solution for resources that are stored for later use by some party; unlike GC, leasing works even if the party that originally stored the resource no longer has any use for it, or any outstanding references to it.

Just as an aside, RMI's distributed garbage collector has used leases internally since the beginning. In RMI, leases are used as a tool to implement the distributed GC algorithms robustly, and solve many of the same problems in RMI that they do in Jini. For example, one of the key differences between local and remote garbage collection is that in the local case, all references to objects are known when the garbage collector begins to run. In the remote case, a program may have shipped off a reference to some internally held object to another machine. The distributed garbage collector must try to determine whether that other machine still holds a reference to the object in order to make a decision about whether it is collectible. Leasing is used as part of the distributed garbage collection process to allow the collector to free resources referenced by clients that may have crashed. RMI hides leases by using them only internally; Jini exposes leases and makes them available as one of the core elements of its programming model.

Remote Events

Jini services, like many software components in a system, whether distributed or local, occasionally need to be notified when some interesting change happens in the world. For example, in the local programming model, a software component may need to be notified when the user clicks a mouse, or when the user closes a window.

These are examples of *asynchronous notifications*. They are messages sent directly to a software component, and they are handled outside the normal flow of control of the component. That is, rather than continually polling to see whether some interesting change has occurred, a method on the component will be "automatically" called when the change occurs. The asynchronous nature of these notifications can often simplify the programming of components—the writer of a component does not have to insert code to periodically check the state of some external entity.

Jini, like most of Java, uses the notion of *events* to do asynchronous notifications. An event is an object that contains information about some external state change that a software component may be interested in. For example, in AWT, a `MouseEvent` is sent whenever the mouse changes state—whenever it moves, or a mouse button is pressed or released. Events are injected into the system by some *event generator* that is watching for state changes. In AWT, there is a thread called the `AWTEventGenerator` that performs this service. In Java, once an event is introduced into the system, it is "sent" to the interested parties that want to hear about it. In this regard, Jini's event model works exactly the same as the standard event model used by JavaBeans and the Java Foundation Classes—all of these models support events and asynchronously call methods on listeners when events arrive.

Remote versus Local Events

But the Jini event model has some differences with the "normal" Java event model. Why this distinction? Aren't the Java event models good enough? As it turns out, the Java models are fine for what they were designed for: delivering asynchronous notifications within a single Java Virtual Machine. The distributed computing world is a very different place, though, and calls for a slightly different event model to fully accommodate the kinds of programs that will run there.

There are a number of very important differences between events that are intended to be delivered locally and events that are intended for distributed delivery.

- In the local case, it's much easier to cause events to be delivered in the order they were generated. This is because local event delivery schemes typically use a centralized queue that acts as a "choke point," forcing the events into a serial order. Distributed systems, because they lack this centralized event manager, and because of the issues of transporting the events over the network, cannot make this guarantee without serious performance penalties. (Java's AWT event dispatch mechanisms actually do *not* provide this guarantee of deterministic ordering for local events—but in general, local event delivery schemes can implement such an ordering relatively easily.)
- In the local case, an event that is sent will always be delivered, barring catastrophic failure (such as a crash of the entire application). Stand-alone systems are not susceptible to the kinds of partial failures that distributed systems are. Partial failures in a distributed system, whether a machine crash or a network partition, can cause events to go undelivered.
- The cost of sending a local event is typically small compared to the work that may be done to handle the event. Typically, "sending" an event is simply a method call to tell the interested party that the event has arrived. The computation that the recipient does as a result of the event delivery will likely dwarf the time required to send the event. In the remote case, the situation is reversed. Delivery of the event may require orders of magnitude more time than the local case, and dominate the time spent in handling the event. The performance differences mean that distributed systems are likely to be architected to generate as few events as possible.
- Finally, in the local case, if a component has asked to be a recipient of events, the sender knows that it can safely deliver the event to the consumer. The remote case is far more complicated. The remote recipient of an event may be temporarily disconnected from the network, in which case the

sender should probably keep trying to send. The recipient may have crashed, in which case the sender may wish to discard the event. Or, the recipient may be "inactive" for a period of time and not able to process the event. This last case can happen quite commonly when the recipient is using the RMI activation framework. An inactive object may wish to have the sender store events destined for it, and wake up periodically and check the events that are waiting.

As you can see, there are many more *policy* decisions to be made in the remote case—many more "knobs" that are available for turning. Does the order of delivery of events matter? Should events be delivered at all costs? If the recipient cannot be contacted, should the event be dropped? Stored until asked for? Resent?

There are no single answers to these questions. Each application must make its own decisions about what makes sense for it. An on-line banking application will almost certainly require very conservative answers to these questions—events should arrive, in order, and at all costs. If a recipient is down, the events should be logged until they can be resent. Other applications may have far less stringent requirements. An on-line game may be able to tolerate a few missed or badly sequenced events and still be fine.

How Jini Uses Events

Now that we see what the Jini event model has to accomplish, we can begin to talk about what it does and why one would want to use it.

There are many cases when a Jini service, or an application that is a consumer of Jini services, may need to receive some asynchronous notification of a change in state of the world. Way back in the section on lookup, I gave the example of a digital camera that wants to be able to use any printers available in its Jini community. I said that this camera would contact all of the lookup services it could find, and then search for services that implement the `Printer` interface. This example makes a grievous assumption that I completely glossed over: It assumes that the printers will be connected to the network and available for use *before* the camera. What if the inverse is true? In this case, there are no printers available when the camera first connects, although printers may come on line later. Certainly, we'd still like to be able to print, regardless of the order in which we plug in our devices.

The answer is that the camera needs the ability to be notified when any services that it might be able to use appear in a community. It's easy to imagine the user interface to such a camera. The "print" button on the LCD is grayed out. You plug a printer into the network, and suddenly the print button comes alive! The camera has just received a notification that a printer is now active on the network.

This is only one example of how events are used in Jini. Obviously, the lookup service will generate events to interested parties when services appear, disappear, or change. But other Jini entities may generate or consume events as well. The `Printer` service may let other services listen for events that denote special printer conditions, such as `OutOfPaper` or `PrinterJammed`. Thus, events don't just have to go between the existing Jini infrastructure and services; they can fly among services themselves.

Event-Programming Model

Let's look at the programming model Jini provides for remote events. These APIs will look very familiar to those of you with experience with JavaBeans or Java Foundation Classes (JFC) programming—and this is good, because the programming models *are* quite similar. But there are some subtle differences that are required by the demands placed on Jini by its distributed setting.

The most noticeable, and least surprising, difference is that the key interface used by objects that wish to receive events, `RemoteEventListener`, is an RMI `Remote` interface. This means that its single method, `notify()`, can be invoked via RMI by objects in other address spaces and may potentially raise `RemoteException`. In practice, this will mean nothing to classes you write that implement `RemoteEventListener`, except that you may have to deal with some new exception types.

The second most noticeable difference between the Jini and "normal" event models is how *narrow* the Jini model is. By narrowness I mean that there are surprisingly few classes and methods. All objects that want to receive remote events implement a single interface, `RemoteEventListener`, with its single method `notify()`. And, in Jini, there is only one class for remote events called, logically enough, `RemoteEvent`. This is in stark contrast to JFC, where there are a plethora of specific event classes for describing state changes in everything from the mouse to the keyboard to the windows on the screen. And, in JFC, each of these event types has its own supporting cast of listener interfaces and adapter classes.

Jini provides a much sleeker set of classes, with its one type of event and one type of listener. Jini provides no generic way of signaling interest in events. (That is, there is no Jini-supplied interface that provides an `addRemoteEventListener()` method.) Rather, each component that may be a source of events decides the circumstances under which it will fire off events, and provides its own way for recipients to express interest.

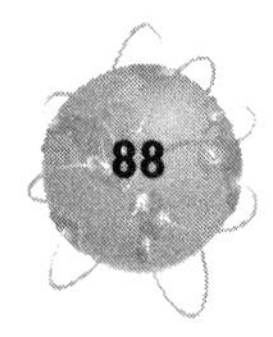

Generic Delegates

Why this simplicity? Does Jini sacrifice expressive power—the ability to capture very specific state changes and represent them in very specific event classes—by forcing everything into `RemoteEvent`? As it turns out, while there is some loss of expressiveness, the narrowness of the interfaces is necessary for one crucial feature of the Jini remote event model: the ability to create delegates that can work with any event source, regardless of what that event is or where it comes from.

I've talked about delegation to third parties quite a bit already in the section on leasing, and as we've seen, delegation is also used extensively in the JavaBeans/JFC local event model. Jini remote events also use delegation, but the form of delegation they support is different than Beans and JFC: Jini has the ability to create *generic third-party event listeners* that can respond to any event type.

Let's look at what this means. Suppose I want to write a class that can receive all of the various JFC events, log them to a file, and then forward them along to their original destinations. If I had such a class, I could simply plug it in as a listener for all of the various event generators in my JFC application (making it implement `MouseListener`, `ActionListener`, `WindowListener`, and so on). Then, the bits of my application code that actually handle these events—responding to mouse clicks and so on—would add themselves as listeners to the third-party object. Essentially, the third party would be inserted into a chain of event deliveries so that it could notice all events and then "call through" to the original listeners.

While I could create such an arrangement using the local Java event model, it would be a lot of work. My event logging class would have to implement *all* of the dozen or so JFC event listener interfaces, with all of the specialized methods in all of those interfaces, and would have to "understand" all of the various JFC event types in order to log them appropriately. If a new event type came along (say, because a new control that generates a specialized event is added to the JFC tool kit), my logger would not work because it had never seen this new event type before.

Jini, on the other hand, is able to support generic third parties. By "generic" I mean that the third-party objects can use, forward, and store Jini remote events without having to have specialized knowledge of what those events "mean." This is because all Jini events are already of a class that the third parties understand—everything is simply a `RemoteEvent`. The third parties don't need any special smarts to understand more specific types, and they only need to implement the one `notify()` method to be able to receive all Jini events, now and forever.[2]

The great thing about Jini third-party event listeners is that, once I've written one that adds some new behavior to my event processing, I can use it everywhere that generates or consumes Jini events. And all I have to do to write one of these generic third parties is implement the single method in the `RemoteEventListener` interface, and use the new object anywhere I would use a "normal" Jini event listener.

Adding Application Behaviors to the Event Pipeline

With all of our talk earlier in this section about out-of-order delivery, guarantees of delivery, and so on, you may be surprised that the Jini remote interfaces have nothing to say about such quality of service policies. This is because Jini takes the approach that the underlying event infrastructure cannot possibly be so general as to capture all of the possible event delivery policies that applications may want. It's easy to imagine what such an API might look like—dozens of methods, each with many parameters specifying the "knobs" that control event delivery. Such an approach would be unwieldy at best and would likely still be insufficient to allow every application to specify what it needs from the event delivery subsystem.

Developers need to decide, *on an application-by-application basis*, what guarantees they need from event delivery. So, instead of providing an API with hundreds of parameters and controls, Jini makes use of the generic delegate mechanism we've just discussed. This mechanism is used to allow new constraints and behaviors to be added to the process of sending, storing, and delivering events.

If a particular service needs to have its events stored, so that if it goes down it can retrieve them later, it can simply plug in an "event storage" delegate that has this behavior. The delegate would listen for all remote events, write them to persistent storage, and deliver them when asked. To the generator of events, the storage delegate would look like any other event consumer. The original event consumer would see the storage delegate as a producer of events.

If a particular service needs to guarantee that each event is reliably delivered, it can plug in a "guaranteed delivery" delegate that catches all

2. Several Jini interfaces and classes use methods called notify(); these are distinct from, and have nothing to do with, the Object.notify() method defined by Java.

events, saves them to persistent storage, and repeatedly tries to deliver the event to the destination until it gets an acknowledgment that it has succeeded. Again, this delegate looks like a consumer to the original generator, and like a generator to the original consumer. Either the original consumer or the original generator can use this delegate to extend its basic event processing behavior.

The fact that the listener interface is so simple also means that delegates can be composed together—you can "stack" a logging delegate with a guaranteed delivery delegate, for example. By combining multiple delegates together you can create a "pipeline" of event processing in which the results of one stage are forwarded on to the next. The clean interfaces mean that the delegates just "snap" together seamlessly. These interfaces also make it easy for *any* of the involved parties—the event generator, the event receiver, or some other interested Jini participant—to add delegates into the event pipeline. Figure 3–4 shows how these delegates connect together. The "notches" on the blocks show how the simple event interfaces plug together to form chains of delegates. See the sidebar for more details.

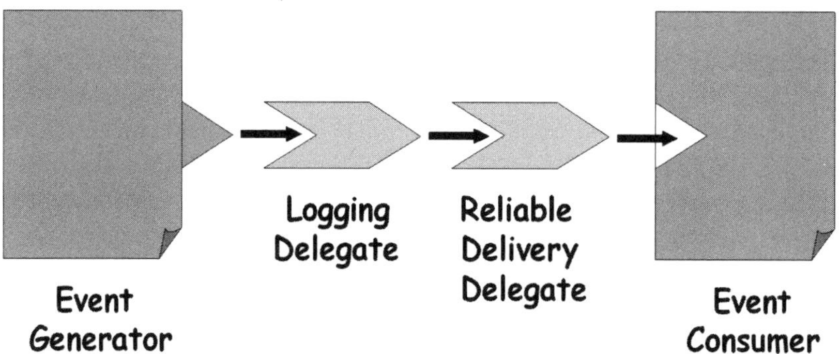

Figure 3–4 Composing multiple event delegates

Sidebar: Stacking Event Delegates

Let's look at a bit of code that illustrates how to snap together a series of delegates to add behavior to an event pipeline. This is a hypothetical example—as of the time of this writing, Jini doesn't come with any event delegates. We'll see in Chapter 14 how to write delegates, but the code below is meant to give you a flavor of how to stack delegates together.

Suppose we've written a Jini service that needs to get reliable delivery of events from a lookup service. Furthermore, imagine that this service will be inactive most of the time—so having the service continually activated just to receive an event is an inefficient use of resources. So what we'd like to do is connect together a few delegates that can (1) make sure that we don't lose any events, and (2) collect events together and send them periodically—maybe once a day or once a week.

The key to this behavior is that our new service is implements `RemoteEventListener`, so it can receive events. The `LoggingDelegate` and `ReliableDeliveryDelegate` also are `RemoteEventListeners`. So when our new service asks the Jini lookup service for events, it says to send the events to the `LoggingDelegate` rather than to it. And likewise it asks the `LoggingDelegate` to send its events on to the `Reliable-DeliveryDelegate`. Since each of these delegates implements the required interface, it can be used in any API that expects a `RemoteEventListener`.

Let's look a bit at how this might work:

```
// First, create a reliable delivery delegate. The
// constructor of this class might take a RemoteEventListener
// to forward any events it receives on to. Since we want
// it to send events to our service, we pass 'this' (the
// object that is calling this code must implement
// RemoteEventListener).
ReliableDeliveryDelegate rdd =
            new ReliableDeliveryDelegate(this);
// Next, we want to interpose a logging delegate further
// up the pipeline (closer to the event generator). So
// we create a logging delegate and have it send its output
// to the reliable delivery delegate that we created earlier.
LoggingDelegate ld = new LoggingDelegate(rdd);
```

(continued)

```
// Now the situation is that any events received by the
// logging delegate will be sent to the reliable delivery
// delegate which will send them to us. The only thing
// missing is to plug the original up-stream event generator
// into the pipeline. Here, lookup is a Jini lookup service.
// The register() method is how we ask for events. We'll
// skip some of the details of how register() works for
// now--including what particular types of events you can
// ask for--and instead focus on how to build the pipeline.
// Here, the 'rdd' parameter to register() should be of type
// RemoteEventListener, and specifies where the lookup
// service should send its events to.
EventRegistration reg1 = lookup.register(/* ... */, rdd);
```

For this code to be useful, the delegate classes—`LoggingDelegate` and `ReliableDeliveryDelegate`—must actually create or reuse some external entity. Clearly, if the delegates live "purely" inside the service that created them, then we haven't gained anything—if our process has to be contacted every time an event is sent to do the logging, then we might as well ditch the logging delegate and just handle the events ourselves. So these delegates will be implemented by creating—or reusing—some external process that is separate from the code that created them. Most likely, this external process will itself be a Jini service that is found via lookup.

The result of all of this is that we've constructed the pipline shown in Figure 3–4. We haven't looked at other issues here—such as how to handle leasing in these delegates—but we'll investigate such issues in Chapter 14.

Again, the actual delegates shown here are hypothetical—no such delegates currently ship with Jini. But Jini was explicitly designed to support exactly this type of composition of functionality.

Different applications have different needs from an event delivery policy, which, as I've stated, is the main reason for Jini's generic third-party event delegate mechanism. Still, there are a number of common cases. In Chapter 14, in which we look at events in greater detail, you'll find some handy utility classes that implement some convenient event delegates. These can provide store-and-forward delivery of events, filter out events based on some service-supplied parameters, and act as a "mailbox" for events, saving events until the service explicitly asks for them, perhaps when it becomes active or reconnects to the network.

Events and Leasing

Now that we've talked about both leasing and events, we can ask an obvious question: What happens if I register myself as being interested in events, and then I crash or disconnect from the network? Does the event generator keep me in its list of event recipients in perpetuity? The obvious answer is that your interest in receiving events is itself leased from the event generator.

Just as in the lookup service, leasing ensures that the system cleans up after itself. If you claim you want to receive event notifications, you have to periodically offer proof of interest to continue to receive events. If you don't offer this proof, either because you crash, or have bugs, or there are problems with the network, then your registration of interest expires and you will receive no more events from that source. Programmatically, the process works much the same as registering a new service on the lookup server. Most event generators will support a `register`-like function, and will return an object that implements the `EventRegistration` interface. This interface allows access to the `Lease` object that represents the duration of interest in the event.

Even though Sun's implementation of the Jini lookup service provides separate mechanisms for service registration leases and event registration leases, there is no requirement that other services work this way. If you write a custom service you may choose to provide only one leasing mechanism, perhaps expiring all of a client's leases together.

In general, though, a service should not attempt to send events to a client whose service registration has expired—such behavior is considered "bad Jini citizenship."

Sequence Numbers and Transactions

Although I won't discuss them in detail here, I should mention a couple of other aspects of events that are important for services that need to make guarantees about event delivery. Every `RemoteEvent` carries with it a *sequence number* that can be used to order it relative to other events generated by the same event source. Listeners (including third-party listeners) that care about ordered event delivery can examine these sequence numbers to reorder events, or determine if they have missed events.

Sequence numbers also interact with Jini transactions (discussed in the next section). But this is an advanced topic, so I'll defer more discussion of sequence numbers and the interactions of events and transactions until Chapter 14 on events.

Transactions

It's now time to deal with the last of the five key Jini concepts: *transactions*. Unfortunately, this concept is probably the most difficult one to master in Jini, but luckily many applications will never have to use transactions.

We've talked a lot about the need for reliability and robustness in distributed systems, and the evils that partial failures can cause. Recall that partial failures are when one stage of a computation fails, or when one component that's needed in a computation fails. If *every* stage that participated in the computation failed, then recovery would be easy—you would know that none of them had successfully completed, and you could simply retry the entire computation later. And, obviously, if every stage succeeded, then you would have no need to recover at all.

But the worst scenario, from the programmer's perspective, is when only a subset of the work that has to be done completes. Let's look at a classic example from database programming that exists in the local case. Bank databases need to be reliable, because millions or billions of dollars are moved through the databases each day. Many of the monetary exchanges are in the form of transfers between two accounts: The money is extracted from one account and added to another. Think about how you would program this transfer. Likely, you would write a bit of code to decrement the total in account A, and then write a bit of code to increment the total in account B by the same amount.

This is all simple and obvious, until you think about ways the transfer can fail. What if you crash just after you've decremented the total in account A? Account A may be out millions of dollars, but the money hasn't gone to B! It's simply lost in the ether, the victim of an accounting error caused by a program that wasn't resilient to partial failures.

Distributed systems compound the problems of partial failures. If you're on a network, each stage of your computation may involve contacting components that live somewhere on the network. These components may crash, or the network may become unstable, at some point midway through the computation. What do you do now? You need to either keep trying to contact the unreachable components (and you'd better succeed before you, yourself, crash), or you need to contact the successful components and tell them to undo whatever changes they've made. And, of course, there's always the chance that only a subset of the undo orders would succeed.

Ensuring Data Integrity

This is where transactions come to the rescue. Transactions are a way to group a series of related operations so that there can be only two possible outcomes: Either all of the operations succeed, or all of the operations fail. In either case, the system moves to a known state in which it is relatively easy to do the right thing—either move on if the transaction succeeds, or try again later if the transaction failed.

Transactions provide what are often called the "ACID" properties to data manipulations, so called because of the initials of the four individual properties.

- Atomicity. Either all of the operations grouped under a transaction succeed, or they all fail: They execute as if they were a single atomic operation.
- Consistency. After the transaction completes, the system should be in a consistent, understandable state. The notion of "consistency" is something that may only be discernible by the human users of the system—therefore, transactions are merely a way to help ensure consistency, not guarantees of consistency itself.
- Isolation. Transactions don't affect one another until they complete. That is, the effects of a transaction that is in the middle of executing will appear "invisible" to other computations outside of that transaction. This property ensures that computations won't be based on bogus data that may change if a transaction fails.
- Durability. Once a transaction completes successfully—meaning that all of its changes have been made permanent—then these changes must not be lost due to any subsequent failure or crash. The results of the transaction must be at least as persistent as the entities that use them.

Transactions work by coordinating all of the cooperating parties through a centralized entity. Essentially, this pushes the burden of getting all the parties to agree or all disagree, and tracking their states, into a piece of software called a *transaction manager*. Because the transaction manager is centralized with respect to the participants, it can have a "privileged" viewpoint, from which it watches all of the participants.

In the local cases, such as the bank database of our example, this centralized transaction manager is typically the database itself. Commercial databases have extensive facilities to ensure that sets of operations in a transaction either all complete or fail together. The database keeps logging information so that it can know whether a transaction has completed or failed if it crashes in the middle of executing a transaction.

Distributed databases—or any system that involves components running on multiple machines—are a little more complicated, though. In the local case, the crash of the database means that all of the operations in the transaction that were in progress also stopped at that point. The database can keep logs that are accurate, because all of the operations in a transaction happen locally to the database (they happen "within" the database itself).

In distributed databases, operations may be executed on remote machines that the database has no direct control over; the database may not be able to determine if an operation running on a remote machine has successfully completed or failed. In this case, we need to follow a slightly more complicated formula to ensure the ACID properties of our data.

Two-Phase Commit

The "protocol" commonly used by such systems is called *two-phase commit.*[3] The name comes from the fact that the protocol has two phases, or stages, that all participants must go through before the transaction as a whole either succeeds or fails.

Let's look at how two-phase commit works conceptually in traditional transaction managers such as databases. Of course, real databases may make all kinds of optimizations here, but this is an easy way to think about two-phase commit.

At a high-level, two-phase commit works like this. First, all the results of a set of operations are calculated and saved in temporary storage. Next, the stored results are moved from temporary storage to permanent storage. This strategy ensures that all of the operations can be done without having to touch any permanent data until they've all completed—if the system crashes half way through, nothing will have been written out and the system can attempt to restart the operations when it comes back up.

While this simple definition is accurate, it glosses over some of the details of the protocol. And, unfortunately, two-phase commit uses a bit of terminology that shows up when we look at it a little more closely. Since this terminology—as well as a more precise definition of what two-phase commit actually does—will be important later, let's expand our simple definition of the proto-

3. You'll sometimes see two-phase commit abbreviated as "2PC."

col and introduce some terms that we'll see again when we talk about Jini transactions.

First, the transaction manager collects all of the constituent operations that comprise the transaction together. These are called the *participants* in a transaction. Next, the manager signals each of these to go into a *precommit* phase. This means that the participants all compute whatever results they would normally compute but, rather than making these changes permanent (actually writing them into the database or to the disk or whatever), they simply keep them handy in a temporary area. Each of these operations returns an indicator to the manager that tells whether it has successfully moved into this precommit phase.

The precommit phase is really a request by the transaction manager to each of the individual participants that they should be prepared to go either way—towards abort or towards commit—at the next signal. Figure 3-5 shows what happens in this first phase. Here we see that the transaction manager asks each of the three operations participating in the transaction if they are ready to commit. In this case, each replies that it is ready.

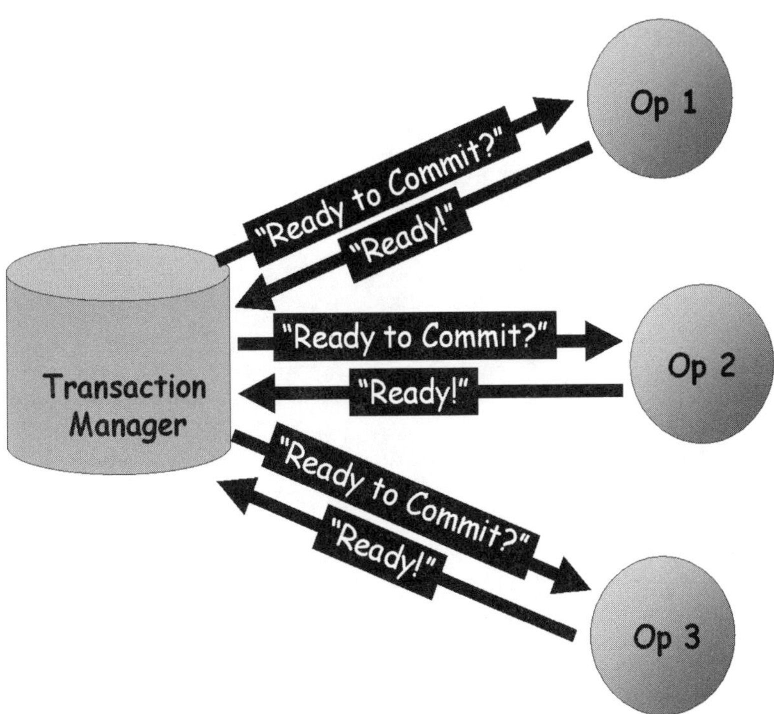

Figure 3–5 A database executes the precommit phase

Next, the transaction manager collects all of the results of the individual participants that it has asked to precommit. If any one of these failed, the manager tells every participant to *abort*. What this means is that the participants can forget their temporary results, and write nothing to stable storage. But, if all of the participants are ready to go, the manager tells each of them to *commit*, which causes them to make their changes permanent. Either all the participants abort or all commit. Figure 3-6 shows this second state of the protocol, where the database tells each participant operation that it should commit its changes.

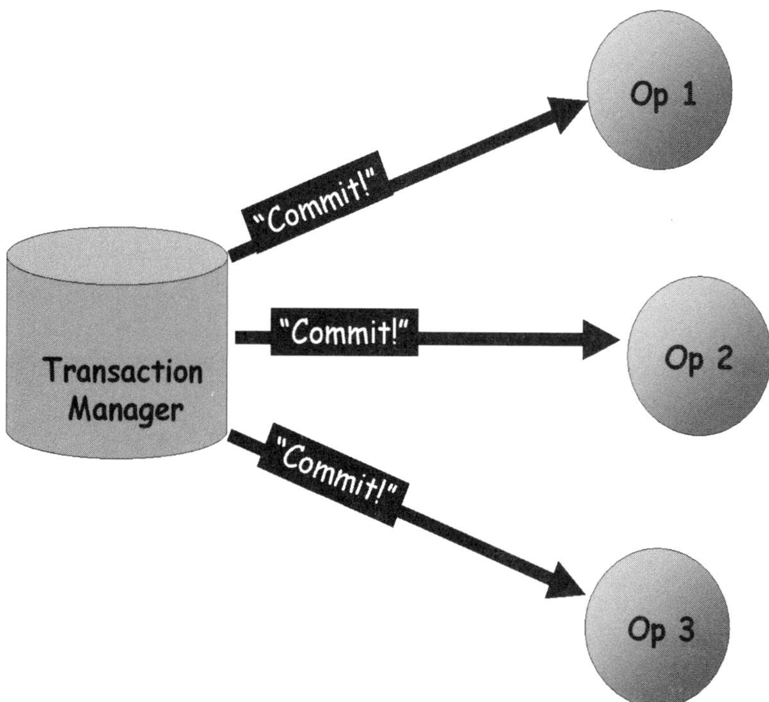

Figure 3–6 A database executes the commit phase

The transaction manager is responsible for lining up all of the participants, and hand holding them all through each of the stages of the process—precommit, and then abort or commit.

So what happens if any component of the system fails during the two-phase commit process? Every individual participant that's involved in the two-phase commit process, including all operations and the transaction manager itself, keep logging information that records the states they have successfully attained. When a participant receives the precommit message, it writes a log entry to stable storage that says that it is ready to either commit or abort, and contains the unchanged value of its data that would be permanent if the operation aborted, as well as the updated value of its data that would be put in place if the operation committed. It is important that the operation "remember" what state it is in so that if it crashes after returning from telling the transaction manager that it is ready to commit, it can recover that state again.

The transaction manager writes to its log whenever it receives all of the replies from its request to precommit. If all of the replies indicate that the participants are willing to go forward with the operation, the manager writes an "ok" record and then issues the commit message. Otherwise, if any one of the operations reports that it cannot continue, the manager writes this information in its log and tells all operations to abort.

The writing of this message in the transaction manager's log is what signals the actual change from Phase 1 to Phase 2 of the protocol. If the manager crashes before this log update is made, it can assume that the precommit phase was never completed and restart it. If it finds a positive entry in the log, it can restart the commit phase of the protocol.

You don't really need to understand all of the details of how this works. The description here is how databases use two-phase commit, which is slightly different than how Jini does it. But having a grounding in the basics of the protocol is important to help you understand how transactions work.

Two-Phase Commit in Jini

Now that we've seen how databases do it, we can look at how Jini implements two-phase commit. The surprising fact is that Jini *doesn't* really implement two-phase commit. The Jini transaction model takes a very lightweight (and very object-oriented) approach: Jini says that two-phase commit is simply a protocol, an interface if you will (see sidebar TransactionParticipant Interface). And the actual particulars of what happens when that protocol is run—when the interface methods are called—is up to the implementation.

This approach means that all the participants in a Jini transaction implement the `TransactionParticipant` interface. The methods in this interface have names that suggest the standard two-phase commit protocol: `prepare()`, `commit()`, and `abort()`. But this is only an interface—Jini says nothing about what the participants in a transaction actually *do* when these methods are called. The implementation of the transaction semantics are up to the implementation of the class that is participating. See the sidebar for details.

Sidebar: TransactionParticipant Interface

To see just how closely the TransactionParticipant interface mirrors the terminology and semantics of two-phase commit, let's look at the interface itself.

```
public interface TransactionParticipant {
    public int prepare(TransactionManager mgr, long id);
    public void commit(TransactionManager mgr, long id);
    public void abort(TransactionManager mgr, long id);
    public int prepareAndCommit(TransactionManager mgr,
                                long id);
}
```

If you're exporting some operation in your service that can be run in the context of a transaction, you can implement the `TransactionParticipant` interface. The transaction manager will then call out to your code through these methods as it walks through the two-phase commit process. You can implement these however you see fit, but the semantics of your implementation should mirror what clients "expect" to see in two-phase commit.

The `prepare()` method indicates that the manager wishes the participant—your code—to move to the precommit phase. The arguments here inticate the `TransactionManager` that is running the protocol, as well as an ID that identifies the transaction. Your code here would return a value indicating whether you had successfully moved into the precommit phase, or needed to abort.

The `commit()` method will be called by the transaction manager once all participants have reported that they have successfully moved into the precommit phase; `abort()` will be invoked if any participant wasn't able to precommit. Your code should make the tentative operation permanent when `commit()` is called, or back the change out if `abort()` is called.

Finally, `prepareAndCommit()` is used as an optimization by the transaction manager. If your code is the last participant in a transaction, and all previous participants have signalled that they are ready to commit, the manager can call this method to indicate that you should prepare and commit immediately, if possible. You can return a failure value here to indicate that you were not ready to commit, in which case all previous precommitted participants will be aborted.

We'll discuss transactions more fully in Chapter 16, but this should give you some sense for how the APIs work in practice.

Unlike a database transaction manager, which takes rigorous steps to ensure that no operation performed within a transaction can overstep its bounds and escape from its constraints, the Jini transaction manager simply runs the two-phase commit protocol on behalf of its participants. It walks through the protocol, invoking the `TransactionParticipant` methods on all the participants, rolling them forward or back depending on group results, and finally calls either the `commit()` or the `abort()` method on all the participants. What these participants do when these methods are called is completely up to them.

As you can see, Jini provides a much less restrictive, and potentially much less safe, notion about what a transaction is. Jini *allows* objects to participate in transactions, rather than *requiring* them to.

In practice this has an upside, however: Jini services know what their data integrity constraints are, and can be written to use as little or as much of the transaction infrastructure as needed. That is, if you're writing a banking application in Jini, you can provide secure transaction semantics that essentially mirror what you would get running under two-phase commit on a commercial database. If you're writing an on-line "chatroom," however, you may decide to take a much lighter-weight approach, perhaps not ensuring full data integrity even in the face of nuclear explosions or collapsing suns.

Using Jini Transactions

Fortunately, using transactions in practice is pretty easy, for three reasons. First, chances are you won't have to do a lot with transactions. Of the current Jini services, only the JavaSpaces storage service actively makes much use of transactions. So, if you never have to see a transaction, dealing with them is quite easy!

Second, even when you do have to deal with transactions, you really don't have to understand any of the mechanics of how two-phase commit works to use them effectively as a *client*. (If you are *providing* an operation that can work in a transaction, then you have to do more work, though.) The end-programmer transaction APIs are quite simple: You just create a transaction, pass it to all the operations you want to be grouped, and then tell it to start the two-phase commit protocol, which will either succeed or fail.

Finally, even though Jini doesn't specify how services should implement the various phases of the two-phase commit protocol, you really don't have to worry about data consistency if you're simply a client of transactions. Jini defines what it calls the *default semantics* of transactions—this is the standard "meaning" of what a transaction does. And, fortunately, it's what most applications will use because Jini provides support for doing it.

The default semantics are implemented by a collection of classes that provide "normal" transaction semantics that have the ACID properties discussed earlier. When you use these transaction classes, you can expect that transactions will behave with all the properties of atomicity and persistence that you'd like to have.

If you're using transactions to cause a set of operations on different services to be grouped, you simply use the Jini `TransactionFactory` to create a `Transaction` object with the default semantics. Every service that knows how to participate in transactions will accept a `Transaction` parameter to its operations. You can just pass in the default object returned by the `TransactionFactory` to cause these operations to be grouped together and to have the default transaction semantics. Once you've invoked the various operations on these services with a `Transaction` argument, you can then call either `commit()` or `abort()` on the `Transaction` object to cause the operations to either try to run or give up. Calling `commit()` starts the two-phase commit process among all of the participants. If the operations all complete successfully, then `commit()` returns. If the transaction cannot be guaranteed, then all operations are undone and `commit()` raises a `CannotCommitException`.

Jini also comes with some classes that can ease the burden of services that wish to be `TransactionParticipants` and can allow their operations to be grouped into transactions.

Because transactions are likely to be one of the aspects of Jini that you use the least, we'll save our in-depth discussion of them until near the end of this book.

What's Next?

I've introduced the five basic ideas in Jini: discovery, lookup, leasing, remote events, and transactions. We've talked about how these notions work conceptually, but haven't seen many details yet on how to actually program with these ideas in Jini.

If you're writing Jini clients—consumers of Jini services—then you need to have some understanding of discovery and lookup, and depending on what you want to do, perhaps events, leasing, and to a lesser degree transactions.

If you're building new Jini services, you need to have a greater understanding of how to be a good citizen in your Jini communities. You need to fully understand how to participate in discovery and lookup, and may need to be an event generator if you wish to asynchronously notify clients of changes in your state. You'll have to have well-behaved leasing, and you may even take the step of allowing your operations to participate in transactions. Fortunately, even though services have a great deal of responsibilities they must take on in the area of bookkeeping, Jini provides some handy classes to make the jobs involved in being a service easier.

In the chapters in Part II of this book, we'll look at these five key concepts in greater detail. We'll also highlight—through the use of extensive examples—how to build both Jini clients and services that are well-behaved and can take advantage of the facilities that Jini offers. These chapters will dive into the programming details of Jini.

But first, before we move on to actual building, we should look at one more broad issue in Jini: How to actually deploy Jini in a network. Now that we understand the basic blocks in the Jini picture, we can look at ways to implement Jini in small devices, software services, and combinations of hardware and software. On to Chapter 4!

DEPLOYMENT SCENARIOS

Topics in This Chapter

- What are Jini services?
- Using Jini on desktop and general-purpose computers
- Jini on devices with on-board Java
- Using Jini to interconnect legacy services and devices

Chapter 4

This chapter completes our broad look at the Jini technologies by examining the common ways that Jini can be deployed and used by devices and services. The Jini model is designed to accommodate a range of situations—from full-blown general-purpose computers running Java Virtual Machines, down to devices such as light switches that may have only a single bit of I/O and no computational power whatsoever.

What Does It Mean to Be a Jini Service?

Now that we know what Jini is, we can talk about what it means to "speak" Jini—what are the minimum requirements for a device or piece of software that wishes to interact with the Jini infrastructure?

The minimum requirements are quite small. Let's look at what a device or service that wants to make itself available through Jini needs to do. If you are a service or device, you, or another piece of software on your behalf, must do the following:

- Be able to connect to a TCP/IP network. This means that your device or service—or a piece of software on your behalf—

should have an IP address and a complete TCP stack with the ability to send and receive multicast messages.

- Participate in the discovery process to find at least one lookup service. Nearly all services will use multicast discovery, and well-behaved services will allow themselves to be configured with a static set of lookup services to connect to through the unicast discovery protocol.
- Register with the lookup service by providing it with a proxy object that clients can download to use the service. This proxy object may call back to a back-end process or device, or may implement the service entirely by itself.
- Ensure that its leases for its lookup registrations are renewed for as long as the service is available.

That's it! At a minimum, all you have to do is ensure that a proxy object gets published in a lookup service so that others can use the service you provide. And the tasks listed above can be done by the entity that implements your service, or by another piece of software on your behalf.

The requirements above represent the *minimum* that is required to participate in Jini. Of course, services can do a bit more work to be better behaved. For example, they can manage the set of lookup services that are discovered and discarded over the lifetime of the service, and they can manage their event registrations and leases. But the proxy publishing mechanism is the star of Jini; everything else is just supporting cast.

You've no doubt noticed that I repeatedly said that another piece of software could enroll a device or service in a Jini community on its behalf. This use of third parties is the key to using Jini to control such devices as light switches and thermostats that may not have embedded JVMs in them as well as legacy software services.

Let's look at what the consumer of a Jini service needs to be able to do.

- The consumer of a service (which need not be a service itself, although it might be) needs to be able to use the discovery process to find one or more lookup services. Nearly all consumers will use the multicast discovery process. In some cases, a consumer may have a URL for a *specific* lookup service and go directly to it using the unicast discovery protocol.
- The consumer must then retrieve the proxy object for the service it wishes to use, where this proxy can be a "pure" RMI stub, a "smart" proxy, or a simple nonremote serialized object. It can do this by searching through the attributes of the services

registered at the lookup service, or it can search by the interface it is looking for, or—if it knows this information—it can search specifically for the service's ID.

- Optionally, but highly recommended, if the desired service isn't found, the consumer may wish to solicit notifications from the lookup services it knows about, so the consumer will be informed if the desired service becomes registered.

Again, this is pretty easy stuff. After the service proxy is found, it is downloaded automatically to the client, which then uses it just as it would a class that was found at compile time.

Minimal Jini services and consumers of services don't have to understand remote events, or transactions, and only need some minimal (and easily automatable) support from leasing. But they do have to be able to use the discovery protocols and interact with lookup services.

How to Use Jini for Your Devices and Services

We'll now look at some common scenarios for making your devices and networked services participate in Jini. As I've mentioned, Jini is designed to support a wide variety of hardware platforms, and can bring together hardware ranging from the very cheap (under a dollar) to the very expensive (million-dollar servers).

Understanding the options available to you when you decide to Jini-enable your product is crucial, because each of the options has different benefits and costs associated with it. In general, there are three common options for deployment. In many cases, the particular option will be dictated for you by the type of device or service you are producing. The options are

- Use Jini on a general-purpose computer. By "general purpose" I mean that the machine has its own network connection, enough computational power to run a full-fledged Java Virtual Machine, and tends to stay up and connected to the network for long periods of time.
- Use Jini on a device with its own embedded JVM. These devices differ from general-purpose computers in that they have much less computational power (and, typically, a much

lower cost), are only sporadically connected to the network, and tend to have much lower bandwidth to the network. Also, these devices may only be able to run a subset of Java, typically either Embedded Java (eJava) or Personal Java (pJava).[1] (See sidebar "Java Variants.")

- Use Jini to control a device with no JVM. In this situation, a shared Jini-enabled computer is used to control a set of devices that have very limited—and sometimes no—computing power, but do have a small amount of I/O capability. This scenario is ideal in the case of things like switches around the home. Each switch may have a single bit I/O "port" (actually, a wire coming out of it) connected to a centralized Jini-enabled computer that handles communication with the switches, and exposes them as Jini services. Note that the centralized computer here need not be very powerful. It may be as simple and as small as a wall-mounted thermostat, or it can be a normal desktop PC.

We'll look at each of these scenarios, and examine their relative strengths and weaknesses.

Jini on General-Purpose Computers

While much of the media focus surrounding Jini hypes its ability to link together small devices, Jini is perfectly at home running on a general-purpose computer as well. There are any number of services that can run on such machines, and Jini makes sense for exposing all of these to other members of a Jini community. For example, every desktop PC has a disk drive in it. There's no reason that this storage space couldn't be exposed to such devices as digital cameras (for picture storage), cellular telephones (for keeping backups of the on-board phone book), the answering machine (for providing long-term message storage), or even the VCR (to allow video to be digitized directly to the hard disk). This storage service would run directly on the PC, and would make the PC's hard drive accessible to any and all services that participate in Jini.

1. A third Java variant, JavaCard, lacks the networking functionality required to participate fully in Jini on its own. But again, a third party can participate in Jini on the behalf of JavaCard devices to bring such devices into a Jini community.

A little further up the scale, Jini can be run on large servers to provide a way to conveniently and robustly manage corporate data services. Jini in the enterprise can make corporate networks extremely reliable and resilient to network failures. It can also cut down on administration time. Consider a Jini service that collects statistics from the machines on a corporate network. Because it may be available redundantly on any number of lookup services, it is extremely reliable—a desirable attribute in systems administration, because you typically want your network diagnostic tools to be the last thing to crash. This service could provide a user interface for viewing these statistics on any Jini-enabled device with a display. It could also easily plug into other services—perhaps generating e-mail or pager messages through a communications service when a disk fills up or a machine crashes.

General-purpose machines such as these make the ideal hosts for Jini services that need to stay connected to the network for long periods of time (these include the "native" Jini services, such as lookup). There is a cost efficiency here, because multiple services can be run on a single computer. And they also provide convenient development platforms, because the services can be developed on the same machines on which they will be deployed.

Furthermore, the advantage of having a full-blown JVM cannot be overstated. Services that run on this platform would be able to take advantage of RMI to communicate with their service proxies once they have been downloaded into clients. Additionally, RMI could be used to *upload* new code to the server, enabling on-the-fly maintenance and upgrades of the services running there. Such services can also connect to corporate databases using Java Database Connectivity (JDBC) software. And, by providing a complete JVM, with the entire Java class libraries, we also ensure that virtually all downloadable code will run—which may not be the case when using a Java subset such as eJava or pJava.

Figure 4–1 shows an example of a Jini service running on a general-purpose computer, and using RMI to communicate with its service proxy embedded in a client. And note that even though RMI, Jini, and JDBC are shown as peer class libraries atop the JVM in this diagram, these services may use each other.

The downside of this strategy, obviously, is that it requires a general-purpose computer. But in many situations, general-purpose machines will be on hand anyway, and using Jini on them does not significantly increase their load. In the context where general-purpose desktop or server machines are already available, running Jini services on these machines makes perfect sense.

Sidebar: Java Variants

There are two primary subsets of Java that have been endorsed by the industry: these are called Personal Java (shortened as pJava) and Embedded Java (eJava). Both of these are small-footprint versions of full-blown Java. And while they run the same bytecodes and have exactly the same language semantics as full-blown Java, they have significantly reduced sets of class libraries available to them.

Personal Java is largely intended for programmable devices that have interfaces on them—devices such as cell phones and PDAs, for example. These devices are usually able to download applet code, and have at least AWT and sometimes the Java Foundation Classes available for user interfaces. The main things missing from pJava are the "enterprise"-oriented APIs: database connectivity, CORBA communication, and (sometimes) RMI. As of the time of this writing, pJava is based against the JDK1.1 specification, not Java 2. So some of the features required by Jini from Java 2's implementation of RMI are not present. Sun promises an update to pJava to support Java 2 sometime in 1999.

Assuming an update to pJava to support Java 2, pJava is the Java subset you are most likely to encounter in the Jini context. Fortunately, the pJava platform is very close to its full-blown Java cousin. And pJava devices that are intended to work with Jini will almost certainly support RMI.

For Embedded Java devices, the situation is somewhat more restricted. Fortunately, eJava devices are less likely to be found in the Jini context. Embedded Java is a more limited subset of Java and Personal Java—it makes most of the user interface classes optional, along with most of the networking classes (obviously, however, these would have to be present on an eJava device that is participating in Jini). These devices may run Java bytecodes directly out of ROM, and many do not support downloaded code (although, again, an eJava device in a Jini setting would have to support downloaded code). For most purposes, an eJava device with networking support and the ability to download and run new code would be capable of using most Jini service proxies, except those that have user interface components.

Of course, even an eJava device can participate in Jini if another piece of software is working on its behalf to make it visible through Jini.

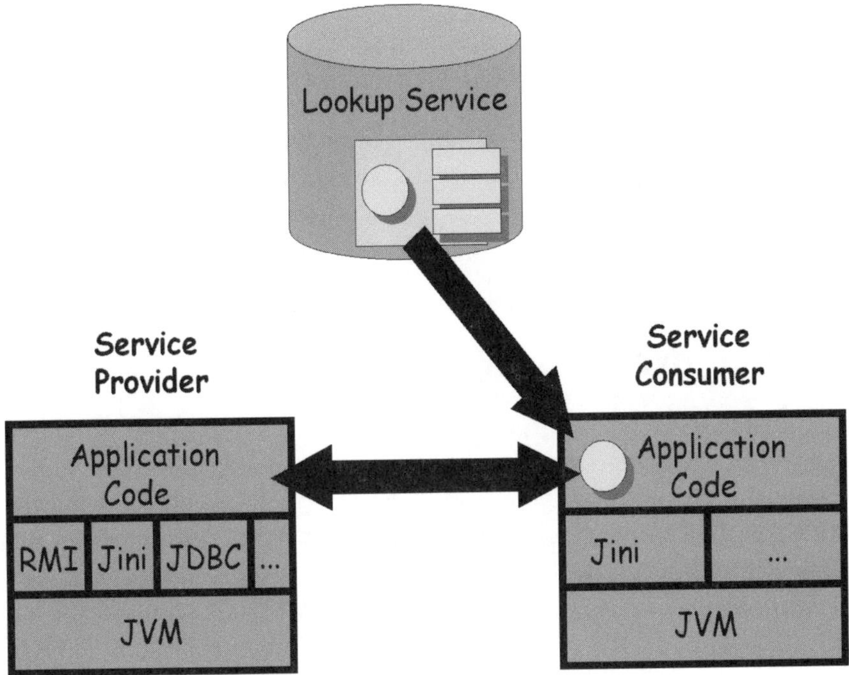

Figure 4–1 Using Jini on a general-purpose computer

Jini on Java-Enabled Devices

As more and more devices in the world become Java-enabled, the option of deploying Jini on small devices with their own embedded JVMs becomes more common. More and more, devices such as cell phones, PDAs, printers, scanners, and cameras are coming with their own JVMs. In many ways, there is not much to distinguish this scenario from the previous one—in both cases, the devices are network connectable, and capable of executing the Java programs already contained on them, and, usually, downloading and running Java bytecodes from the network.

There are a few significant differences between running Jini on small devices and on general-purpose computers, however.

- Small devices may only run a subset of the entire Java platform.

- Small devices may only be intermittently connected to the network.
- Small devices typically have much less computational power and network bandwidth than their general-purpose cousins.

Of these, only the first is a real issue. Although you wouldn't want to run the Jini lookup service itself on a device that is off the network more than it is on, or that has extremely limited computing power, you're not likely to want to have the sole lookup service on your network running on a toaster or microwave oven anyway.

Jini and Java Subsets

The issue of coping with different versions of Java is a significant problem for small devices. Such devices, because they are generally inexpensive, may have only a small subset of the full Java platform available to them, and may have very limited ability to display graphical interfaces. In some cases, they may have *no* ability to display an interface.

Think about how Jini works and you'll see why this is a problem. At the heart of Jini is the ability for a service to essentially embed part of itself, its service proxy, in a client. When the service proxy is written, the developer makes an implicit assumption about what class libraries will be available on the client platform—if the service proxy uses JFC, for example, he or she assumes that JFC will be available wherever the proxy is run. This may not be the case if the more limited Java environments are being used as consumers of Jini services.

The two primary subsets of Java mentioned earlier—Personal Java (pJava) and Embedded Java (eJava)—have more restricted sets of class libraries available to them than full-blown Java. So certain service proxies may have problems executing in those contexts.

Even More Limited Java Environments

Note that the problems from the preceding section all deal with using limited-capability Java devices as *consumers* of Jini services. You may think that a limited-Java device that only publishes a service is in better shape. But recall that even service providers are themselves consumers of the lookup service—the lookup service downloads its own service proxy into the service providers. So at a minimum, an eJava or pJava device would have to be able to download and run the lookup service's service proxy.

There is another option, however. A device could run a *custom* subset of the JVM that works with Jini even without the option of downloading code.

Such a device would "hard code" the discovery protocols, and would carry with it the code for talking to particular implementations of the Jini lookup service. Such a device would be very restricted—It would not work outside its expected setting. If the implementation of the lookup service changed (perhaps because a vendor begins selling a newer, faster service that uses a different protocol for talking to lookup users), the device would not work.

One clear implementation strategy for such devices is that they could carry on them their own *custom* implementation of the lookup service that only holds the proxy for the device itself. This would limit the required interaction of the device with the rest of the Jini community—it would only have to be able to serve up a proxy for its custom lookup service that clients can use to retrieve the device's proxy.

The benefit here is that the footprint of the JVM and class libraries required for such a device is *greatly* reduced. Because no code could be downloaded, there would be no need for the bytecode verifier or security manager. And the class libraries installed on the device could be pared down to the bare minimum required to participate in discovery and lookup.

Such a device would only be able to publish Jini services; it would not be able to consume Jini services, because using a service requires the ability to download its proxy. While these trade-offs are severe, they may be worthwhile in some circumstances.

Versioning

The eJava and pJava problems are instances of a more general problem, one of ensuring that the version of the host platform is compatible with the version of Java expected by a service proxy. The solution is to agree on a set of conventions—allowing service proxies to be stored with attributes that indicate the minimum level of Java functionality they require. Such an attribute would have information about needed class libraries, JVM versions, and so forth. Before attempting to use a service proxy, a consumer could check its attributes to make sure it was runnable.

At the time of this writing, the Jini community has not standardized on a set of such attributes. There are some steps you can take to create services that can run on as wide a set of host platforms as possible though. Most importantly, you can limit the dependencies your proxy object has on the host platform. Usually this means excising dependencies on libraries that may not be present everywhere. If your service can be partitioned into chunks of functionality—some of which only depend on core libraries, and others that depend on less prevalent libraries—then the extra functionality can often be attached to the service as attributes. By keeping questionable code out of the proxy, you ensure that clients can always download and use the proxy objects. Other code—such as user interfaces—can be bundled and sent along separately, allowing clients to optionally use them.

Jini Using Device Proxies

This third approach is the one that will likely be taken by a large class of devices, including printers, scanners, and other devices that are attached to a host computer, as well as extremely lightweight and cheap devices such as switches around the house.

In this approach, a machine capable of running a JVM is physically attached to one, and usually more, devices. This machine acts as a Jini *proxy* on behalf of these devices—it participates in the lookup and discovery protocols, handles their service proxies, and manages their leases for them. In this case, the connection between the machine running the JVM and the device is typically not a network cable—more likely it's an RS-232, USB, Firewire, or perhaps even an X10 "home automation" connection.[2]

The machine running the JVM may either run full-blown Java (as in the general-purpose computer case mentioned previously), or may run a Java subset such as eJava or pJava. Such a machine may actually *be* a general-purpose computer, say a spare PC in someone's basement, or it could be specialized for use as a Jini control box. Imagine a Jini controller that plugs into your stereo equipment, making your CD and DVD players, tuner, VCR, and television all accessible to your home Jini community. An even smaller device could resemble a wall-mounted thermostat, and would provide Jini services on behalf of your home alarm system, light switches, door locks, and so on. Whatever the shape of the controller, once the devices have been connected to it, they are fully available in the home Jini community.

A likely short-term scenario is a proxy application that runs on PCs. This application starts when the machine boots, and examines the Windows plug-

2. Current and older desktop computers are likely to connect with a standard, serial RS-232 connection. Newer machines may use the faster Universal Serial Bus (USB) serial port. Firewire is a high-speed serial connection used in many high-end consumer electronics devices. And X10 is a set of technologies designed for building home automation and control systems. Sun's alliance with the HAVi group means that Firewire may serve a common role in connecting Jini stereos, VCRs, and DVD players—see the note at the end of this chapter.

and-play database to see if new hardware is added. If a recognized device, such as a printer or scanner, is added, the proxy application publishes services for these new devices, making them available on the network. Figure 4–2 shows an example of devices sharing a JVM that serves as a Jini proxy for them.

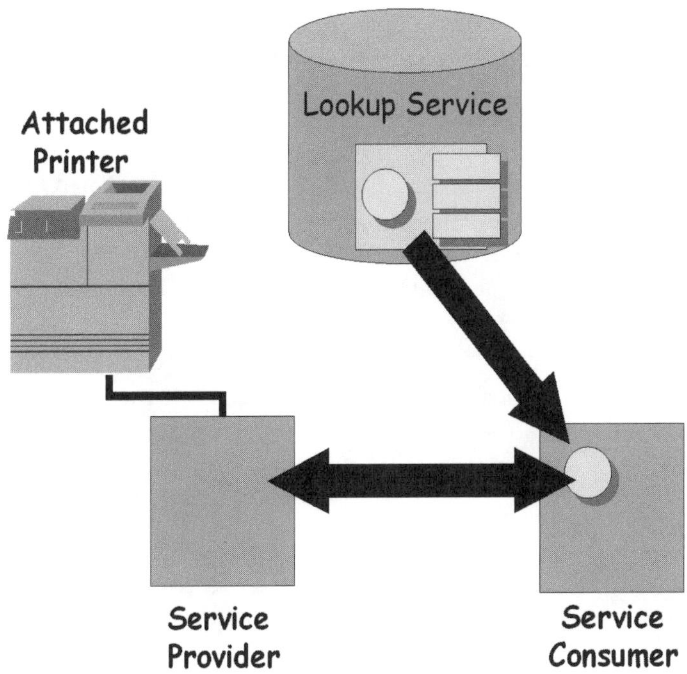

Figure 4–2 Devices share a Jini proxy

There are obvious benefits to this approach. First, it enables "legacy" hardware to participate in Jini. There are huge numbers of printers, scanners, and other devices in the world that do not (yet) run Java; by installing a bit of software on a host computer, these devices are brought into the Jini world. One could even imagine a Jini "converter box" that plugs in between a host computer and a printer that makes the printer Jini accessible.

Second, the proxy approach allows very cheap devices to be brought into a Jini community. If we all had to use light switches with embedded JVMs and eight megabytes of memory, chances are that not many of us would be buying them. If, on the other hand, large numbers of cheap devices can share a single Jini host, and be indistinguishable from devices that run full JVMs, then we may begin to see more and more inexpensive Jini devices in the home.

Requirements for Jini Infrastructure Services

The preceding sections talked about what platform requirements exist for running Jini services and consumers of Jini services. But what about the core pieces of the Jini infrastructure themselves? Recall that many of the key parts of the Jini infrastructure are themselves Jini services, with requirements about where they can be run.

Jini defines interfaces to its services, not implementations. So a particular implementation of a Jini service may have more or less stringent requirements than an alternative implementation. For example, one lookup service may be built atop a full-blown commercial database, requiring JDBC support, while another may use an in-memory hashtable. But, while we cannot make generalizations about what particular implementations these key services may require, we can talk about the absolute *minimum* functionality needed—this is the level of functionality required by the interfaces to these components.

While Jini defines two services as particularly key—the lookup service and the transaction manager—the lookup service is the really important one. Barring any strange requirements imposed by the implementation of a particular transaction manager, you can run this service anywhere, given the same guidelines for "generic" services that we've talked about previously.

Sun's current reference implementation of the lookup service is really at home on a general-purpose computer, running real, live Java. But a more minimal lookup service can actually be run on a far less-capable platform. You usually do, however, want your lookup services running on a server machine to minimize downtime.

The most basic requirement for the host platform for a minimal lookup service is that it support IP multicast network traffic over sockets. The discovery protocols make use of this protocol to find lookup servers, and lookup servers are expected to be able to respond. The response that a lookup server gives is a serialized Java object representing the service proxy that clients will use to connect back to the lookup service. This serialized object, when reconstituted on a lookup client, can call back to the lookup service using any custom protocol, over any desired transport.

As the "bootstrapping" service for Jini, lookup can run on platforms that are little more than a box with a network cable coming in.

When Is Jini Appropriate?

Now that we've looked at some common scenarios for enabling your device or service to participate in Jini, we can look at situations where using Jini may be appropriate from a technological or market perspective. These really boil down to a few common cases.

- If there exists, or you expect there to exist, Jini services that your device or software service could use to become more valuable, then Jini may be an appropriate solution for you. If you sell scanners, for example, and you see small Jini software services appearing that can provide image-to-e-mail or image-to-fax gateways, your scanner can easily use these to add value to itself. By making your scanner a consumer of Jini services, you enable it to appear as if it can directly scan to an e-mail message or a fax. You take instant advantage of all the developers in the world building these services. Essentially, you make these developers *your* developers.
- If your device can add value to other Jini services that exist, or you expect to exist, then Jini may be appropriate. For example, if you are in the market of selling printers, and you see Jini-enabled digital cameras coming to market, you have an opportunity to pitch your wares as an easy printing solution for digital photography.
- If your device already has an embedded JVM, or is usually deployed attached to a general-purpose computer, then adding Jini is likely a no brainer. Once you've got Java on or near your machine, the work required to support Jini is minimal, and the potential gain is huge.
- If your software service is running on a general-purpose computer that can run a Java Virtual Machine—and practically all can, these days—then you can easily create a Jini wrapper for your service that makes it available in the Jini world. This is one of the great benefits of Jini—that it's easy to write a small bit of glue logic that makes an entire software service, even one not written in Java, accessible to any other Jini device or service.
- If you have a software service that can be easily decomposed into constituent pieces, then it may make sense to represent each of those pieces as a Jini service. For example, an

enterprise-scale document management system may have components that act as document storage repositories, document service engines, query engines, and so forth. By creating separate Jini services for each, you gain a number of benefits. First, you can easily move components to different machines as needed, without any need for reconfiguration or administration. Second, you gain built-in redundancy. Need a spare backup instance of one of these services? Just run another copy! Finally, by opening your architecture, you enable easy extensibility down the road.

- If you are creating a device that will typically be connected to other devices, then Jini may be a useful enabling technology for controlling these connections. For example, the components in a rack of stereo equipment are usually interconnected in a jumble of wires. Wouldn't it be nice if my preamp knew what devices were on the rack with it, what their levels and inputs were, and configured its controls accordingly?
- Finally, if your device can benefit from programmability, Jini may be a nice solution. Because Jini enables code downloading, your programmable devices can be upgraded on-the-fly. Even better, they can automatically control other devices in their Jini communities—imagine a central MIDI control panel that adds a new user interface for controlling a drum machine as soon as the drum machine is plugged in.

As Java appears on more and more devices and computers, and as more and more of our devices and software systems connect to each other, Jini becomes a logical solution for managing this interconnectivity. And—perhaps the point that will most encourage its adoption—if you've already got Java on your device or on your general-purpose computer system, adding Jini is trivial.

When Is Jini Not Appropriate?

Because Jini was explicitly designed to cover such a wide range of possible deployment scenarios—all the way from servers down to light switches—there are few hardware situations where Jini is not appropriate. There are a few factors that might argue against the cost of adding Jini to a device, however.

- First, if your device is *truly* isolated—meaning there isn't even a wire going to it—or is so fundamentally uninteresting that no one would want to use it over the network, then Jini is probably not for you. But fewer and fewer devices these days are truly isolated. And what would you be doing trying to sell a boring device?
- If your device is unlikely to be near any devices with a JVM, and needs to be so cheap that it cannot have a JVM embedded on it, then Jini is not a viable solution. Java has to exist *somewhere* in the loop for devices to participate in Jini.

Further Reading

If you're a fan of high-end audio and video equipment for the home, you might want to check out the *Home Audio/Video Interoperability* (HAVi) Web site. This group is a consortium of big A/V vendors who are promoting a set of very interesting standards. HAVi devices connect to one another via Firewire—an extremely high-speed serial connection, also known as IEEE1394 by those with a fondness for standards committees, and as i.LINK by Sony—and can transmit not only control information but also digital audio and video content from device to device.

Sun and the HAVi vendors have recently (at the time of this book's writing) agreed to integrate Jini with the HAVi technology. So we may soon be seeing "plug-and-play" stereo gear that both uses and provides Jini services.

`http://www.havi.org`

What's Next?

This chapter completes our broad look at the Jini technologies. In the next Part, we'll start to build real Jini services, and look at the core Jini technology in depth.

Part 2

BUILDING WITH JINI

GETTING STARTED WITH JINI

Topics in This Chapter

- Guidelines for building, testing, and deploying Jini services
- Exploring Lookup and Discovery with HelloWorldService
- Using Remote Events to detect changes in a community
- Implementing Leasing to enhance reliability and self-healing
- Using RMI and the activation framework

Chapter 5

In this chapter, you'll start building some actual Jini services, and the client applications to use them. The first pair of programs we'll look at are a "Hello, World" service and client. These are the minimal Jini programs—they use discovery and find a lookup service; the service publishes a service proxy, and the client fetches and uses it. The proxy for this service is pretty trivial—it returns the string "Hello, World" when asked. In this case, the proxy *is* the service, as it is capable of performing this task completely on its own. But it demonstrates how to begin working with Jini.

After this initial program, we'll begin iterating to show more and more Jini features. First, we'll expand the client to use events, so that it can be notified when services register with lookup services after it does.

The next iteration adds more sensible leasing. In the first version, the service never renews the leases it holds on its registrations with lookup services. So we'll extend it to continually renew the leases it holds, so that the service's proxy will not "disappear" from the Jini community. Similarly, the client application needs to renew the leases it holds on its event registrations; in this iteration we'll extend it to manage its event registration leases so that it can be informed of changes in the state of its community.

Finally, we'll build a more complicated version of the "Hello, World" service that uses a service proxy that communicates back to a server process. In this case, the proxy uses RMI to communicate back to the server to get the message to display. While the example is simple, it shows the way most Jini

services will be architected—with a "thin" proxy communicating back to a "fat" server, which bears the burden of implementing the service. This example also illustrates how to use the RMI activation mechanisms to create a back-end service that is only active when it is needed.

This chapter starts to turn some of the abstract notions we learned about Jini in Chapter 3 into actual code. We'll do this progressively, improving our examples with each iteration, so that we can focus in on each feature as we present it.

Running the Jini Services

Before you can start writing your program, you need to make sure that the required Jini services are up and running. Check Chapter 1 for details on getting your environment set up to run Jini. For the examples in this chapter, you will not need to run a JavaSpaces storage service, or a transaction manager. All of the iterations of "Hello, World" require only that a lookup service, an RMI activation daemon, and an HTTP daemon be running somewhere on the network. The RMI activation daemon (`rmid`) will need to run on the same host as the lookup service, since Sun's implementation of the lookup service uses activation. Also, in the last example in this chapter, we'll create our own custom activatable service. For this example, you'll also need to have `rmid` running on the same machine as the service. (If you're running the example on the *same* machine as the lookup service, you do not need to run a separate instance of `rmid`—you only need one per machine, no matter how many activatable services you run there.)

Here's the checklist for getting set up.

- Configure your PATH, as per the instructions in Chapter 1.
- Run the RMI activation daemon. You should run this on the same machine that you'll be running the lookup service on, and the activation daemon should be started *before* the lookup service. For the last example, you'll also need to run the activation daemon on the same host as the example program.
- Run the Jini lookup service. You should run this service on a machine on the same network subnet that you intend to run the sample programs—this is because Jini's multicast discovery protocols are, by default, only configured to find lookup services running "nearby" the object doing discovery.[1]

- Run a Jini HTTP server. This particular instance of the HTTP server will supply downloadable code for the Jini lookup service; this server can be run on the same machine as the lookup service. You can set its "root" directory to point to the "lib" directory from the Jini distribution—this will ensure that your code will be able to download the classes in the `reggie-dl.jar` file, which contains the code needed by your programs to use the lookup service. Also, all of the example programs we'll write need to be able to supply code to Jini services and to each other. So you'll also need to run an HTTP service to supply the code from these examples. I'll talk more about how to do this once we get into the example code itself.

That's it! This configuration of services should allow you to run all of the programs that follow. There are, however, some steps you can take to make your life easier when you get around to testing and deploying Jini services; we'll look at these steps in the next section.

We'll also look at the specific instructions for each example as we come to it. Note that the examples in this chapter consist of both a Jini service—the entity that publishes a service proxy; as well as a Jini client—essentially just an application that uses discovery and lookup to find a service proxy that it is interested in using. In many cases, services will use other services, so a Jini program is often both a service and a client. In the interest of simplicity, though, the client programs here are simple "stand-alone" applications.

While you can run all of these programs, lookup services, HTTP servers, activation daemons, clients, and servers on the same machine, I strongly advise you to read the next section. If you develop Jini applications in the same way that you probably develop "stand-alone" Java applications—by doing everything on one machine with the same CLASSPATH—you're likely to run into trouble when you deploy these programs on multiple machines. The next section offers some strategies for tuning your environment that can minimize these problems.

---

1. In Chapter 6, when we look in depth at the discovery process, we'll find out exactly what Jini means by "nearness" in the network sense. But for now, you can be assured that any two machines on the same subnet are near enough to one another to share the same community.

Developing with Deployment in Mind

Clearly, in the "real world," virtually all Jini services and clients will be run in multimachine environments. This means that services may be scattered across any number of machines on a network. The downloadable code for these services may be served by any number of HTTP servers, and clients may be connecting to these services from any machine.

But often—whether through convenience or necessity—you need to develop and test your code on only one machine. It's quite easy to run into problems in such cases, simply because by running everything on one machine you're not exercising parts of your code that may cause things to break when the components of your distributed system run on different hosts.

Let's look a bit more closely at what this means. For most Jini development, you will have three Jini-aware applications running: a lookup service, the service you're testing, and a client that uses that service (these applications are in addition to whatever other programs are needed, such as HTTP servers and RMI activation daemons). If all of these programs run on the same machine, and share the same resources (the same CLASSPATH, the same HTTP server, and so on), then potential problems with dynamic class loading or with security may be masked. Developing and testing in such an environment can allow problems to lurk unnoticed in your code.

This is the great danger to only testing "locally." The apparent early convenience of taking the easy way out can result in greater headaches down the road. So even though a multimachine environment may require more "up-front" work, such as starting more HTTP servers, setting security policies, and so on, you'll be rewarded for this effort by easier debugging and deployment later. For this reason, it's a good idea to get in the habit of thinking about multimachine environments, and even "simulating" such environments when you develop and test.

Fortunately this "simulation" is fairly easy to do. There are some simple tips you can follow when you run and test your code to ensure that it will work in such a multi-machine environment, even if you're developing on only one computer. These tips address most of the common problems in a multi-machine setting.

Here are the tips you should follow when developing.

- Run a separate HTTP server for each program that provides downloadable code to other programs.
- Watch out for codebase problems.
- Always set a SecurityManager.
- Pay attention to security policies.
- Take care with CLASSPATH.
- Consider bundling downloadable code into a JAR file.

Let's look at each of these in turn.

Run Multiple HTTP Servers

It's a good idea to run a separate HTTP server for each and every program that needs to provide downloadable code to other programs. This strategy allows you to clearly separate the downloadable code for each program from that of every other program. An alternative, like running one HTTP server with a root directory that points to the top of your Java development tree, will almost certainly be more convenient—because all of the classes you write will be accessible anywhere—but will keep you from identifying dependencies in your downloadable code that might keep your applications and services from working if they need to be moved to different machines.

If you can clearly separate all the downloadable code for a given program on one HTTP server, and then run that program with a codebase property that instructs clients of the program to fetch code only from that HTTP server, then you can tell when you don't have all the necessary code together in one place—the clients will complain that they cannot load certain needed classes.

Watch Out for Codebase Problems

Recall that the codebase property is set on a *server* (a program that exports downloadable code) to tell its *clients* (consumers of that code) where to load the required classes from. Appendix A has more details on codebase.

There are a few good general tips you should follow when setting the codebase property, though. First, never use `file:` URLs. If a server passes a `file:` URL to a client, the client will try to download any needed code from its own local filesystem. If you're developing and testing both your client and your server on the same machine, your code may work—since the class files will live in the same place for both client and server. But if you ever run the client and server on separate machines that do not share a filesystem, your code will suddenly break.

Likewise, never use "localhost" in a codebase as a hostname. "Localhost" is used to refer to the current host, so if a server sets the codebase to a URL containing `localhost`, the client will evaluate this codebase and attempt to load the code from *its* system, rather than the server's. Again, this situation *may* deceptively work if you're testing the client and the server on the same machine, as you're likely to do. But if you use actual hostnames in codebase URLs, and run separate HTTP servers for each, as noted above, then you can identify potential problems in code loading early.

Always Set a Security Manager

Any Java program that will *use* downloadable code should set a security manager by calling `System.setSecurityManager()`. The security manager ensures that any classes that are loaded remotely—through a codebase that is provided via RMI—do not perform any operations they are not allowed to perform.

If you do not set a security manager, then no classes will be loaded other than those found in the application's CLASSPATH. So, if you only test locally, and do not set a security manager, your code may still work because the classes that would otherwise have to be downloaded may be found in your CLASSPATH. But your application will definitely fail in a multimachine setting.

Pay Attention to Security Policies

When you run a program with a security manager, the Java 2 security machinery will—by default—use a standard security policy. This standard policy is, unfortunately, often too restrictive to allow Jini applications to run. So in almost all cases you will need to specify a new policy file that allows your program to run.

In these examples, I've used a very promiscuous security policy—it allows our example applications free and unfettered access to any resources. While this policy is fine for testing "known" code—meaning code that you have written—it's definitely not suitable for a production environment.

Take Care with CLASSPATH

As you've probably noticed, most of these development tips have to do with preventing unwanted sharing of resources—primarily, the sharing of code through unanticipated and nonrobust means, such as `file:` URLs or shared HTTP servers. One other way that code can be shared between two applications—and this is the way that most of us are familiar with—is by running the applications on the same machine and with the same CLASSPATH. If both a client and a server are sharing class files off the disk, then it's virtually impossible to tell what specific classes these programs will need to access remotely. So to prevent unanticipated sharing of class files, you may consider running *without* any CLASSPATH at all. Instead, try passing the `-cp` option to the `java` bytecode interpreter. This option lets you specify a series of directories and JAR files to load class files from. Even if you're developing your client and server on the same machine, you can keep the class files for each in separate directories, unset your CLASSPATH, and use a different `-cp` argument to the `java` interpreter for each to ensure that no unwanted cross talk exists between your applications.

Furthermore, it's a good habit to get into to provide *only* those classes the application needs to do its job, rather than all class files "just to be sure." You can start off with the three Jini JAR files in the `-cp` argument (`jini-core.jar`, `jini-ext.jar`, and `sun-util.jar`), and then copy in your own specific application class files as needed. The compiler is a great help in identifying which class files you need to install, as it will complain if it cannot find needed classes.

Under no circumstances should you put the `-dl` JAR files (`reggie-dl.jar` and so on) from the Jini distribution into your directory of classes—these are meant to be dynamically downloaded from the core Jini services. If you put these in with your application classes, you'll simply be ensuring that you're using the versions of these files that you got with Jini, and not the version that the lookup service *expects* and *tells* you to use.

Consider Bundling Downloadable Code into a JAR File

Perhaps the best way to make sure that you've isolated any unwanted dependencies from your code, and that you're providing exactly and only the code that other programs will need to download, is to create a JAR file that contains the classes that clients will have to download to use your program. This is the strategy taken by the core Jini services—the lookup service, for example, has the classes it needs for its implementation in `reggie.jar`, and the classes that will be downloaded to clients in `reggie-dl.jar`. The HTTP server that exports the lookup service's downloadable code has its root directory set to a directory containing `reggie-dl.jar`. The codebase property for the lookup service provides a URL naming the HTTP server that specifies where clients should download the classes in `reggie-dl.jar`.

You should consider breaking your classes into chunks for the implementation and the downloadable components. Creating separate JAR files for each is also handy when you need to move your service, or change where clients download your service's code.

Summary

These tips are designed to simulate the isolation that would exist between two Jini programs run on different machines—they share no common filesystem and no CLASSPATH. Security must be considered, since programs must go off-machine to access resources. And, in a real deployment setting, you cannot guarantee the existence of one global HTTP server for the network that contains all downloadable class files; instead, you must plan on separating class files for each service, and accessing them through individual HTTP servers.

Setting up your development environment in this way is a bit of trouble; but it can pay off in a big way as you begin to develop more complex services and applications.

Now that we've looked at strategies for developing Jini software, let's get into writing some actual code!

A First Jini Program: Hello, World

Let's look at the minimal Jini programs. We'll build a simple service, and a client application to use that service, and step through how each of them works. The first thing we should have is an interface, such as in Listing 5–1, that defines what our service will do. The service proxy object will implement this interface, and the client will use it whenever it searches the lookup services. In all of these examples, I'll include a package name that reflects where the code

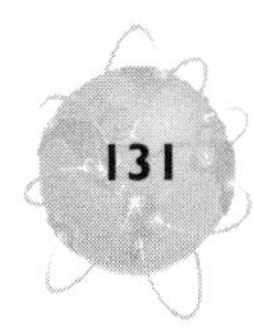

lives in the FTP'able bundle you can get from the Prentice-Hall FTP server. This will help to keep the code from different chapters partitioned.

Listing 5–1 `HelloWorldServiceInterface.java`

```
// This is the interface that the service's proxy
// implements

package corejini.chapter5;

public interface HelloWorldServiceInterface {
    public String getMessage();
}
```

This interface defines one simple method: When a caller asks for a message, a string is returned. The proxy object for the service will implement this interface.

Now let's look at our service. In this simple case, the "service" is really just the proxy object—which is perfectly capable of returning a string on its own without talking to any device or back-end process.

We will, however, need a process that finds a lookup service, publishes the proxy, and, in later examples, handles the leasing for our proxy to make sure that the lookup services holding it don't throw it away. This is called the "wrapper" process—it has a `main()` that takes care of the interactions with Jini needed to publish the proxy.

There are a few things to note about this example, as well as a few conventions that I'll be following in the code examples in the rest of this book. First, most of the Jini code lives in the `net.jini` package. This naming scheme follows the convention of using inverted domain names as package names—Bill Joy's Aspen SmallWorks, one of Sun's research labs, registered the domain "jini.net" in early 1997.

Second, Jini partitions its package namespace to reflect what is a core part of the system and what is built on top of the core. So the `net.jini.core.*` packages contains core, standard interfaces that constitute the heart of the system. These packages live in the `jini-core.jar` file. The `net.jini.*` packages contain libraries built using the core packages; this code lives in `jini-ext.jar`. Finally, Sun provides a set of "helper" classes in the `com.sun.jini.*` packages. These are considered "nonstandard" and subject to change. These classes reside in the `sun-util.jar` file.

In the code listings, I'll follow the convention of explicitly importing all of the Jini classes, so that you can tell which classes live in which packages.

The code in Listing 5–2 shows, in less than 100 lines of code, how to participate in a Jini community.

Listing 5–2 `HelloWorldService.java`

```
// This is the first iteration of a Hello, World
// service--it publishes a proxy that returns
// a string when asked by clients.

package corejini.chapter5;

import net.jini.discovery.DiscoveryListener;
import net.jini.discovery.DiscoveryEvent;
import net.jini.discovery.LookupDiscovery;
import net.jini.core.lookup.ServiceItem;
import net.jini.core.lookup.ServiceRegistrar;
import net.jini.core.lookup.ServiceRegistration;
import java.util.Hashtable;
import java.io.IOException;
import java.io.Serializable;
import java.rmi.RemoteException;
import java.rmi.RMISecurityManager;

// This is the proxy object that will be downloaded
// by clients. It's serializable and implements
// our well-known HelloWorldServiceInterface.
class HelloWorldServiceProxy implements Serializable,
    HelloWorldServiceInterface {
    public HelloWorldServiceProxy() {
    }
    public String getMessage() {
        return "Hello, world!";
    }
}
// HelloWorldService is the "wrapper" class that
// handles publishing the service item.
public class HelloWorldService implements Runnable {
    // 10 minute leases
    protected final int LEASE_TIME = 10 * 60 * 1000;
    protected Hashtable registrations = new Hashtable();
    protected ServiceItem item;
    protected LookupDiscovery disco;
```

Listing 5–2 `HelloWorldService.java` **(continued)**

```
    // Inner class to listen for discovery events
    class Listener implements DiscoveryListener {
        // Called when we find a new lookup service.
        public void discovered(DiscoveryEvent ev) {
            System.out.println("discovered a lookup " +
                               "service!");
           ServiceRegistrar[] newregs = ev.getRegistrars();
            for (int i=0 ; i<newregs.length ; i++) {
               if (!registrations.containsKey(newregs[i])) {
                   registerWithLookup(newregs[i]);
               }
            }
        }

        // Called ONLY when we explicitly discard a
        // lookup service, not "automatically" when a
        // lookup service goes down.  Once discovered,
        // there is NO ongoing communication with a
        // lookup service.
        public void discarded(DiscoveryEvent ev) {
           ServiceRegistrar[] deadregs = ev.getRegistrars();
            for (int i=0 ; i<deadregs.length ; i++) {
                registrations.remove(deadregs[i]);
            }
        }
    }

    public HelloWorldService() throws IOException {
        item = new ServiceItem(null, createProxy(), null);

        // Set a security manager
        if (System.getSecurityManager() == null) {
            System.setSecurityManager(
                          new RMISecurityManager());
        }

        // Search for the "public" group, which by
        // convention is named by the empty string
        disco = new LookupDiscovery(new String[] { "" });

        // Install a listener.
        disco.addDiscoveryListener(new Listener());
    }
```

Listing 5–2 `HelloWorldService.java` **(continued)**

```
    protected HelloWorldServiceInterface createProxy() {
        return new HelloWorldServiceProxy();
    }

    // This work involves remote calls, and may take a
    // while to complete.  Thus, since it's called from
    // discovered(), it will prevent us from responding
    // in a timely fashion to new discovery events.  An
    // improvement would be to spin off a separate short-
    // lived thread to do the work.
    protected synchronized void
        registerWithLookup(ServiceRegistrar registrar) {
        ServiceRegistration registration = null;

        try {
            registration = registrar.register(item,
                                              LEASE_TIME);
        } catch (RemoteException ex) {
            System.out.println("Couldn't register: " +
                               ex.getMessage());
            return;
        }

        // If this is our first registration, use the
        // service ID returned to us.  Ideally, we should
        // save this ID so that it can be used after
        // restarts of the service
        if (item.serviceID == null) {
            item.serviceID = registration.getServiceID();
            System.out.println("Set serviceID to " +
                               item.serviceID);
        }

        registrations.put(registrar, registration);
    }

    // This thread does nothing but sleep, but it
    // makes sure the VM doesn't exit.
    public void run() {
        while (true) {
            try {
                Thread.sleep(1000000);
            } catch (InterruptedException ex) {
            }
        }
    }
```

Listing 5–2 `HelloWorldService.java` **(continued)**

```
    // Create a new HelloWorldService and start
    // its thread.
    public static void main(String args[]) {
        try {
           HelloWorldService hws = new HelloWorldService();
           new Thread(hws).start();
        } catch (IOException ex) {
           System.out.println("Couldn't create service: " +
                              ex.getMessage());
        }
    }
}
```

Let's walk through the example. The first thing we have to do is import the required Jini classes to use discovery and lookup. There are a number of classes here that we'll use, primarily from the `net.jini.core.lookup` and `net.jini.discovery` packages.

Writing the Service Proxy

Following the imports, you'll see the class definition for our service proxy, which here is called `HelloWorldServiceProxy`. There are a handful of points to make about this class.

- You'll notice it implements the `java.io.Serializable` interface. This is a *requirement* for a service proxy, because an instance of the class will have to be "pickled" and sent to each lookup service we contact, and then on to each client from there. Being serializable means that the proxy can be saved to a byte stream, sent down a socket to a remote system, and reconstituted at the other end.
- The service proxy also implements an interface, `HelloWorldServiceInterface`, that is known to the client. This is because, in the example, the client program will search the lookup services for service proxies that implement this interface. In general, you should try to use well-known interfaces wherever possible to make it easy for clients to know what your service does. In other words, the client must know what to ask for.

- The service proxy has a public, no-argument constructor. This is a requirement for all classes that will be serialized and deserialized.
- In this example, the proxy is declared as a "top-level" but nonpublic class in the same file as the "wrapper" application that publishes it. The arrangement used here is fine—remember that the client will not need compile-time access to the proxy, so having it hidden here is not a problem.[2] The client gains access to this proxy at run time via serialization and code downloading. You can even declare a proxy as a nested inner class with one caveat—inner classes have a "hidden" reference to the instance of the class that created them. When an object is serialized, all of the nontransient, nonstatic references within it are serialized as well, which would cause the *wrapper* class to be bundled up with the proxy. This is almost certainly never what you want. If you declare your proxy as an inner class, be sure to declare it as a *static* inner class to avoid this problem. The keyword *static* on an inner class means that the class is nested simply for structural convenience—not for any run-time association between the nested and outer classes.[3] Static inner classes don't have the "hidden" reference to their enclosing classes, so your wrapper classes won't be serialized.

Core Alert: Forgetting serialization

If, as will sometimes happen, you either do not make your service proxy `Serializable`*, or leave off the no-argument constructor, the compiler cannot detect this error. Instead, you will get a run-time error when you attempt to register this proxy with a lookup service. The exact exception that will be raised is* `java.io.NotSerializableException`.

The `ServiceItem` *class, which is the class containing the service proxy that is passed to the registration process, is defined to hold an instance of type Object as the service's proxy. So you can pass any type of object here—although you should be aware that you will not get any compile-time warning if the object is not serializable.*

---

2. Although the client *will* need compile-time access to the *interface* that the proxy implements. Otherwise it would not know how to use the proxy programmatically.
3. Strictly speaking, "static" makes the class a "nested top-level class," not an inner class. But most people call it an inner class anyway.

The "Wrapper" Application

Now let's look at the application that will find lookup services and publish the proxy. This program isn't involved in helping the proxy perform its service; it only helps it manage its Jini responsibilities. In the example, the class that does this is called `HelloWorldService`. This class contains the `main()` function that begins the discovery process.

There is another inner class here that is used to interact with the Jini discovery system. The class, called `Listener`, implements the `DiscoveryListener` interface. By breaking the discovery-oriented code out into a separate inner class (as opposed to making the `HelloWorldService` wrapper class itself do discovery), we can clean up the design a bit and keep a nice separation between the work required to participate in discovery and the work required by our particular service. We'll come back to the `Listener` class and describe how it works in just a bit.

After the declaration of the inner class for discovery, we get into the meat of this program. The constructor for `HelloWorldService` does four things. First, it creates an instance of `ServiceItem`. Instances of this class are what get passed to the lookup services during the registration process.

You'll notice three arguments to this constructor. The first is the *service ID* for the service. The service ID is a globally unique identifier for your service—even if you register the service on different lookup services, at different times, the service ID should be the same each time. This requirement that services remember their service IDs entails some bookkeeping on their part. This service isn't particularly well-behaved, as it requests a new service ID each time it is run.

To make the job of constructing an initial service ID easier, Jini uses a convention where, if you pass `null` as a service ID the first time you register it, the lookup service will assign a globally-unique service ID to us. Subsequent registrations should use this ID. We'll soon see how to do this for our simple service. Chapter 8, which discusses lookup in depth, has more details on service IDs, their lifetimes, and how they are generated; we'll also see some convenient ways to manage this bookkeeping.

The second argument is an instance of the service proxy. This object will be serialized and, whenever a lookup service is discovered, sent to that lookup service to await a client who wants it. Here I've placed the construction of the proxy object in its own method, `createProxy()`, for clarity and for the ability of future subclasses to override this method.

The final argument, also `null` here, can contain a list of attributes we wish to associate with the service proxy. Interested clients can search these attributes. So, for example, if you are registering a printer, you might attach attributes that indicate the location and model of the printer. Clients could then retrieve this information for display to a user, or use it programmatically to find a particular printer. This argument is typed as an array of objects implementing the `Entry` interface. We'll see some examples of using attributes in future examples, but for now, we'll not attach any attributes to our service proxy.

Once we've created the `ServiceItem` that we'll register in the lookup services we discover, we set a security manager, if one is not yet set. Recall that any Java program that will download code—meaning load it from some location other than from a local directory specified by the CLASSPATH—must have a security manager to prevent that code from performing unauthorized operations. Since the service will need to download the proxy object for any lookup services we find, we *must* set the security manager here.

After setting the security manager, we create an instance of `LookupDiscovery`. This class provides the mechanisms for using the Jini discovery protocol. Using it is amazingly simple. We want to be told whenever a lookup service that is a member of the public group is found, so we pass in an array of group names including only the empty string. (Recall that a "group" is simply a name that can be given to a Jini community. By convention, the group named by the empty string is taken to be a "public" community that services will join by default. Most of the time, using the approach taken here of passing the empty string is the appropriate one. If, on the other hand, you are running an experimental service, you might pass the string "experimental" here to look for that community. You would also have to run a lookup service somewhere on your network that is configured to support that group name.)

The `LookupDiscovery` object can call out to a `DiscoveryListener` whenever a new lookup service is found. The nested listener class implements this interface, so the constructor for `HelloWorldService` adds a new instance of `Listener` as the listener for discovery. After this, the discovery subsystem will call out to the `Listener` instance on the `DiscoveryListener` methods whenever a lookup service is found.

Core Note: The Discovery API has an asynchronous look-and-feel

Clearly, if I want to write a Jini service that can be asynchronously notified whenever a new lookup service appears, I have to implement some listener interface so that the Jini libraries can call me back whenever a lookup service is started.

But why use an "asynchronous" interface—one in which notification is done outside the main flow of control—if I only want to connect to lookup services that are already running? Can I not get a "synchronous" API that blocks until it can return the lookup services to me?

The Jini APIs use this asynchronous style exclusively for discovery. The reason is that, in almost every case, a Jini service needs to be able to handle lookup services that start after it does. So using an asynchronous API everywhere has a number of advantages. First, it encourages "proper" behavior because services will have to be written to understand notifications of lookup services anyway. Second, it means that there is only a single way to get information about lookup services, so service code is simplified (as opposed to having both a blocking and a nonblocking API). Finally, even if you know for a fact that lookup services are already running somewhere on your subnet, you don't know how long it will take them to respond to you. So, because you wouldn't know how long to block waiting for a response from a lookup service anyway, the asynchronous API is appropriate here to.

In general, the issues of designing good APIs that encourage the building of correct applications, and that make things that should be easy actually easy, are important to the Jini design. I'll highlight API design issues as they come up in later chapters.

Using Discovery and Lookup

Let's now look at how to build the code to support discovery. Recall that the code shown here uses an inner class called `Listener` to perform discovery. This class implements the `DiscoveryListener` interface, which has two methods: `discovered()` and `discarded()`. The former will be called whenever a lookup service is found that matches the group we're looking for. The latter is called to indicate that a previously discovered lookup service should no longer be considered valid. Usually this happens because a lookup service has ceased to respond, and so you call the `discard()` method on `LookupDiscovery` to tell it that you are dropping the lookup service from the set you have found. The `discarded()` method may also be called if you change the groups you are searching for. This change would cause any lookup services you found previously that do not service your new groups to be discarded. Each of these methods will be passed a `DiscoveryEvent` object that describes the lookup services that have been discovered or discarded.

Core Tip: Understand when to discard lookup services

The `discarded()` method on `DiscoveryListener` will be called in two circumstances. First, when the set of groups you're looking for changes, and `LookupDiscovery` needs to inform you of which lookup services you hold references to are no longer valid for that set of groups. And second, when you explicitly discard a lookup service from the set of groups you are managing. The latter case is by far the more common.

Why would you ever explicitly discard a lookup service? If you are performing an operation on a lookup service and get a `RemoteException`, chances are the lookup service has gone down or is otherwise not accessible. When this happens you should call the `discard()` method on `LookupDiscovery` to tell that class to drop the lookup service from the set of services it has found. Once this happens, `LookupDiscovery` will call out to your implementation of `discarded()` so that you can clean up your state.

By discarding a failed lookup service, you're in a position to rediscover it once it returns to the network.

Misunderstanding how the `discarded()` method is called is a common problem for beginning Jini programers—they mistakenly believe that when a lookup service crashes, some special post-mortem communication happens that causes the `discarded()` method to be called. This is not the case—once a lookup service has been found, there is no ongoing communication with it other than whatever methods you may call on it. So you're responsible for dropping lookup services that begin to report errors.

Look at the example's implementation of `discovered()`. We keep a hashtable that records all of the lookup services we have found. Whenever the discovery protocol tells us that new lookup services have been found, we fetch them out of the `DiscoveryEvent` that we've been handed, and iterate through them to make sure we don't already have them in our hashtable. If the lookup service is indeed a new one, we store it in the hashtable and register with the lookup service by calling `registerWithLookup()`.

Core Note: Redundant lookup services

In our example, we do a bit of work to track the lookup services that we've already seen, and ensure that we don't register with them twice. This isn't strictly necessary. A second registration at the same lookup service would simply overwrite the first one.

But tracking the registrations will turn out to be useful for managing leases anyway (something we'll get to later in this chapter), so keeping the hashtable is something we'd have to do anyway if we care about our service's leasing behavior—which almost certainly we do. Plus, making sure that we don't somehow do redundant registrations cuts down a bit on network traffic.

The process of registration with a lookup service is easy: We simply get the `ServiceRegistrar` instance that corresponds to the lookup service we've discovered, and call the `register()` method on it. As you see, this call takes two arguments. The first is our service item, created earlier, and the second is the requested duration of the lease. This is the amount of time we ask the lookup service to hold on to our proxy without hearing from us again. In this case, we ask for a 10-minute lease. Recall that the lookup service, as the grantor of the lease, may deny our request, or may grant a shorter lease. The status of the lease is returned in the `ServiceRegistration` object that results from this call. This result value allows a number of useful operations to be performed on it: We can get the ID of our newly registered service—this is how we can get the service ID assigned to us the first time we run. The returned `ServiceRegistration` also allows us to get the `Lease` object associated with the registration, and change the attribute set associated with the service item.

Core Tip: Do registration in a separate thread

In the example shown here, the work done by `registerWithLookup()` *happens in the same thread that does discovery—that is, registration happens in response to a* `DiscoveryEvent`, *and occupies that thread until registration completes.*

In most cases, this work should be done in a separate thread of control, because the registration process involves a remote call which may take a relatively long amount of time to return: for example, the lookup service may crash, which means that a time out would occur before the call would return.

No other lookup services can be discovered while this registration process is in progress. So that lookup services can be discovered in a timely fashion, a better approach is to use a separate, short-lived thread to handle the registration tasks. The approach shown here should only be used when you really do want to block discovery until registration completes, but the code here is appropriate for illustrating the basics of how to do discovery and registration.

After we register our service proxy, we check to see if this is the first time we've been registered. If this is the first time, we write the service ID that's been returned to us into our service item, so that future registrations will use this same ID. We also stash the registration result into a hashtable so that we can retrieve it in the future, if we need to.

The code here follows that maxim that services should register themselves with any and all lookup services that they encounter for their specified groups. This way, if multiple lookup services are running on a network, we get built-in redundancy.

Note that this example shows the bare minimum necessary to register a service. There are a number of obvious and fairly important improvements we could, and will, make in the next iterations of this program. Most crucial is leasing. As currently written, this program will register a service that will go away after 10 minutes, or whatever time the lookup service grants us as a registration duration. Secondly, there is very little error checking going on here. For example, what if the `register()` method fails? Remember that registration is defined so that if I re-register a service, it simply overwrites all previous registrations. Therefore, it's safe to simply retry a registration if it fails. This code gives up after the first attempt. We'll solve many of these problems in later iterations, but for now, it's important to get the basic concepts.

Last Details

The rest of the code is pretty much boilerplate. Our service's class implements `Runnable`. We do this to ensure that our little application won't simply stop when `main()` finishes. Without at least one active (non-daemon) thread in the application, it would simply terminate when `main()` "ran off the end" of available statements, likely before any lookup services would be able to report their existence to us. So our service implements `Runnable` and causes a simple thread to be started that sleeps forever. If you happen to be doing any AWT or Swing work in your application, you won't need to start your own thread, as the Java windowing system starts its own threads as soon as you create any windows. But because we're not doing graphics here, we'll have to start our own thread. Note that the back-end program will run forever, or until you kill it, as we've made no provision for breaking out of this thread.

The `main()` routine simply creates a `HelloWorldService` instance and starts the background thread to keep the application alive.

Now let's look at a simple client application (Listing 5–3) that can use our service.

Listing 5–3 `HelloWorldClient.java`

```
// A simple Client to exercise the HelloWorldService

package corejini.chapter5;

import net.jini.discovery.DiscoveryListener;
import net.jini.discovery.DiscoveryEvent;
import net.jini.discovery.LookupDiscovery;
import net.jini.core.lookup.ServiceRegistrar;
import net.jini.core.lookup.ServiceTemplate;
import java.util.Vector;
import java.io.IOException;
import java.rmi.RemoteException;
import java.rmi.RMISecurityManager;

public class HelloWorldClient implements Runnable {
    protected ServiceTemplate template;
    protected LookupDiscovery disco;

    // An inner class to implement DiscoveryListener
    class Listener implements DiscoveryListener {
        public void discovered(DiscoveryEvent ev) {
           ServiceRegistrar[] newregs = ev.getRegistrars();
            for (int i=0 ; i<newregs.length ; i++) {
                lookForService(newregs[i]);
            }
        }
        public void discarded(DiscoveryEvent ev) {
        }
    }

    public HelloWorldClient() throws IOException {
        Class[] types = { HelloWorldServiceInterface.class
};

        template = new ServiceTemplate(null, types, null);

        // Set a security manager
        if (System.getSecurityManager() == null) {
            System.setSecurityManager(
                                 new RMISecurityManager());
        }
```

Listing 5–3 `HelloWorldClient.java` **(continued)**

```
        // Only search the public group
        disco = new LookupDiscovery(new String[] { "" });

        // Install a listener
        disco.addDiscoveryListener(new Listener());
    }

    // Once we've found a new lookup service, search
    // for proxies that implement
    // HelloWorldServiceInterface
   protected Object lookForService(ServiceRegistrar lusvc)
{
        Object o = null;

        try {
            o = lusvc.lookup(template);
        } catch (RemoteException ex) {
            System.err.println("Error doing lookup: " +
                                 ex.getMessage());
            return null;
        }

        if (o == null) {
            System.err.println("No matching service.");
            return null;
        }

        System.out.println("Got a matching service.");
        System.out.println("Its message is: " +
                          ((HelloWorldServiceInterface)
                                    o).getMessage());
        return o;
    }

    // This thread does nothing--it simply keeps the
    // VM from exiting while we do discovery.
    public void run() {
        while (true) {
            try {
                Thread.sleep(1000000);
            } catch (InterruptedException ex) {
            }
        }
    }
```

Listing 5–3 `HelloWorldClient.java` **(continued)**

```
    // Create a HelloWorldClient and start its thread
    public static void main(String args[]) {
        try {
            HelloWorldClient hwc = new HelloWorldClient();
            new Thread(hwc).start();
        } catch (IOException ex) {
            System.out.println("Couldn't create client: " +
                               ex.getMessage());
        }
    }
}
```

This client program has some similarities with the server. It has an inner class that implements `DiscoveryListener`, as it has to participate in the discovery protocols. It spawns off a background thread so that its main program won't simply exit before any lookup services are found. And it installs a security manager since it will need to download and use the service proxy from the `HelloWorldService`.

But, instead of registering a service, this client program will *search* for a service proxy that implements `HelloWorldServiceInterface`. Whenever `discovered()` is called, we know that we've found one or more lookup services through the discovery protocol. For each of these, we'll look for our desired service. We do this by using a `ServiceTemplate` object, which is a way to describe the services we're looking for.

Using Service Templates to Search for a Service

Each `ServiceTemplate` has three fields in it that control how we search. Here's part of the definition of a `ServiceTemplate`.

```
public class ServiceTemplate {
      public ServiceID serviceID;
      public Class[] serviceType;
      public Entry[] attributeSetTemplates;
      // ... other details elided ...
}
```

The `ServiceTemplate` code acts like a query specification. When you pass a `ServiceTemplate` to a lookup server, the server searches all of its registered services for a match. A template matches a service if

- The service ID in the template matches the ID of a registered service, or if the template's service ID field is null; *and*
- The registered service is an instance or a subtype of *every* type in the template's `serviceType` field, or the template's type field is null; *and*
- The service's list of attributes contains at least one attribute that matches every entry in the template, or the template's attribute field is null. (Exactly what it means to "match" an attribute will be discussed in Chapter 7 on attributes.)

By using a `ServiceTemplate`, you can search for services that match a known class or interface, or that have a desired set of attributes, or that have a specific service ID (if you happen to know it). Since Java type relationships are considered by the matching process, you can search for services that are subtypes of known types. For example, if class B extends class A, and if A is in the template, then a search will return all objects of type A or type B registered in the lookup service. Leaving one of the fields in a template set to null essentially makes it a wild-card value. A template with all fields set to null will match all services.

Core Tip: Finding the proxy for the lookup service

The proxy object for a lookup service is itself stored along with the set of registered services. So when you match all services, the call to `lookup()` *will return a reference to the lookup service itself, in addition to whatever other services are registered with the lookup service. Many users expect* `lookup()` *to return all services except the lookup service.*

Of course, you can always do a search for proxies that implement `ServiceRegistrar` *to return only proxies for lookup services.*

In our example, we create a template that searches based on the type of the service. In our case, we create a template that's initialized by an array of `Classes` containing only the class of our desired interface, `HelloWorldServiceInterface`. Leaving the service ID and attributes fields blank means that our search will match any service that implements `HelloWorldServiceInterface`, no matter what its service ID is, or what attributes may be associated with it.

Looking Up a Service

We do the actual search by calling `lookup()` on the `ServiceRegistrar` object that represents a lookup service. This method contacts the lookup service and performs the search. If a match is found, the lookup service transmits the matching service's proxy object back to the client. This method returns either the proxy for the service, deserialized and ready to use, or `null` if there was no match.

Note that it's completely possible that a given Jini community may contain any number of services that implement our desired interface or, more generally, match any given query we use to search. The form of the `lookup()` call we use here only returns a single match—typically the first service found that matches the query. There is another form of the `lookup()` method that takes an extra parameter specifying the maximum number of matches to be returned.

In general, though, returning the first match from a specified query is good enough for most applications. If I create a query that only specifies the interface I'm searching for, I'm implicitly telling the lookup service that the interface is the only thing that matters to me. In such a case, one `HelloWorldServiceInterface` is as good as any other. Likewise, if I issue a query that essentially specifies "any unjammed color printer on the third floor," then any single match satisfying that query is probably good enough.

If you need a very specific service, particularly if you need to find one that cannot be easily specified by using the matching facilities available in `ServiceTemplates`, then you can write a more general query to fetch a set of matching services, and then refine these (perhaps by presenting them to a user) to isolate a single service that you'll use. And clients like browsers will typically want to fetch all of the services they can find.

For our application, getting a single match is fine. Once we get a match, we can just cast it to its known type and use it! And while this particular service proxy is trivially simple, the fact that its implementation details are completely hidden means that a client can interact with arbitrarily complex services while knowing only their interfaces.

Compiling and Running the Examples

Once you've got the code typed in or downloaded, you can compile and then run the programs. For the examples in this chapter, I'll be following the somewhat tedious set of tips that I discussed earlier that are designed to "simulate" clients and services running on different hosts. I'd strongly recommend that you follow these steps, although if you want to jump in quickly, you can leave all the classes in your development directory and share a

CLASSPATH. But if you do this, please come back to this example and walk through the procedure before you go on! The sidebar below presents a summary of the conventions that I'll be using in the rest of the book.

Sidebar: Conventions I'll Be Using

All the code examples in this book follow the set of guidelines presented earlier that are meant to mirror the effects of running clients and services on separate machines. Some of these guidelines may seem like a lot of extra work to you—after all, you want to jump in and get to coding!

But most of the problems that starting Jini programmers face have to do with problems with security and code loading: problems that are often hidden if you do not follow these guidelines.

In all the instructions for building and testing the code samples in this book, I've followed a set of conventions for where to put the code and how to run the services.

Most examples consist of a Jini service as well as a client that exercises that service. To ensure that the service and the client aren't inadvertently sharing class files, I will place the class files for each in a separate directory.

Likewise, in many of the examples, both the service and the client may need to export some downloadable code to another entity in the Jini community—services, for example, need to be able to export their proxy objects to Jini lookup services and to the clients that will use them. Clients often need to export downloadable code for their remote event listeners. In all these examples, I will also create and use a separate directory for the downloadable code that each entity exports; so the portions of the client that are meant to be downloadable are in a directory separate from the rest of the client's code, as are the portions of the service that are meant to be downloaded.

To simulate the effects of each of these bundles of downloadable code being on separate machines, I also will run separate HTTP servers to export the code in the service's export directory and the client's export directory; each will have its "root" directory set to point to one of the directories containing downloadable code. These HTTP servers can be run on the same physical machine, as long as they use different port numbers. In this book, I'll run the HTTP servers for services and clients on different ports: Port 8085 for the services and Port 8086 for the clients. The codebase properties for the client and the server will refer to the particular instance of the HTTP server that is exporting their code.

(continued)

Table 5–1 summarizes the conventions that I'll be using for directories, on both Windows and Solaris.

Table 5–1 Class file directory conventions

Directory Contents	*Windows Location*	*Solaris Location*
Class files needed for the implementation of the service	`C:\service`	`/files/service`
Class files that the service makes available for download to other entities	`C:\service-dl`	`/files/service-dl`
Class files needed for the implementation of the client	`C:\client`	`/files/client`
Class files that the client makes available for download to other entities	`C:\client-dl`	`/files/client-dl`

When compiling a client, I'll set the class path for the compiler to point to not only the three Jini JAR files, but also the client implementation directory, as specified above. This is necessary so that the compiler can find and use class files already generated for use by the client. Likewise, when compiling services, I'll set the class path to the three Jini JAR files and the service's implementation code directory.

One advantage of this arrangement—in addition to maintaining separation between class files used by the client and the service—is that it's easy to create JAR files from these separate directories. Once your code has been partitioned like this, you can take the class files in each directory and create implementation and download JAR files for both the client and the service, much as the Jini reference implementation does (such as `reggie.jar` and `reggie-dl.jar`).

Refer back to the section, "Developing with Deployment in Mind," earlier in this chapter, for the rationale of these conventions.

Let's get ready to build and run the examples. First, unset your CLASSPATH to ensure that no extraneous class files leak across this boundary into either the client or the service; we'll be specifying the paths to find classes on the command line. Second, make sure that the source code for these examples is together in a well-known place. I suggest `C:\files\corejini` on Windows and `/files/corejini` on Solaris or other UNIX operating systems.

Compiling

Next, let's compile the programs. We want to keep the class files for the client and the service separated since, in general, clients and services share no code at compile time and will have no special knowledge of one another, other than some shared interfaces that the service's proxy may implement. We also need to separate code used in the implementation of a program from code meant to be downloaded *to* another program. In this case, the only application-specific downloadable code we have is the proxy object. Both our client and our service will, of course, need to be able to download the lookup service's proxy, but you should have already configured an HTTP server somewhere on your network that exports the `reggie-dl.jar` file, when you started the lookup service.

To keep the code separate, we'll tell the `javac` compiler to output class files into separate directories. In fact, we'll create a directory called `client` for the client-side implementation, `service` for the service-side implementation, and `service-dl` for the downloadable code that the server exports (this is the downloadable code that the client will use; note the conventions being used for directory names here). You can create these directories under `C:\` on Windows and under `/files` on Solaris, and then pass the `-d` flag to the compiler to tell it where to output the class files it creates.

On Windows: First, create the directories you will need, and go to the directory that contains the sources you will compile.

```
mkdir c:\client
mkdir c:\service
mkdir c:\service-dl
cd c:\files\corejini\chapter5
```

Next, compile the source files needed for the service. The service relies on both `HelloWorldService.java` and `HelloWorldServiceInterface.java`. The `-d` option says to drop the resulting class files into `C:\service`.

```
javac -classpath C:\jini1_0\lib\jini-core.jar;
                         C:\jini1_0\lib\jini-ext.jar;
                         C:\jini1_0\lib\sun-util.jar;
                         C:\service
  -d C:\service
  C:\files\corejini\chapter5\HelloWorldServiceInterface.java
  C:\files\corejini\chapter5\HelloWorldService.java
```

Now, compile the source files needed for the client. The client also relies on `HelloWorldServiceInterface.java`, as well as `HelloWorldClient.java`. We'll put these files in `C:\client`.

```
java -classpath C:\jini1_0\lib\jini-core.jar;
                         C:\jini1_0\lib\jini-ext.jar;
                         C:\jini1_0\lib\sun-util.jar;
                         C:\client
  -d C:\client
  C:\files\corejini\chapter5\HelloWorldServiceInterface.java
  C:\files\corejini\chapter5\HelloWorldClient.java
```

Note that even though we already compiled the interface source file when we built the service, we need to make sure that the resulting class file is present in both the client and the server directories, since it's required by both. So here we compile it into the client's directory as well.

Finally, in this example, the only code we've written that will be downloaded is the proxy's class file. This file should have been created when we compiled the service, since the proxy is a nested class within the service. You can just copy this file from the `C:\service` directory to the `C:\service-dl` directory:

```
cd C:\service\corejini\chapter5
copy HelloWorldServiceProxy.class C:\service-dl
```

On Solaris: First, create the directories you will need, and go to the directory that contains the sources you will compile.

```
mkdir /files/client
mkdir /files/service
mkdir /files/service-dl
cd /files/corejini/chapter5
```

Next, compile the source files needed for the service. The service relies on both `HelloWorldService.java` and `HelloWorldServiceInterface.java`. The `-d` option says to drop the resulting class files into `/files/service`.

```
javac -classpath /files/jini1_0/lib/jini-core.jar:
                            /files/jini1_0/lib/jini-ext.jar:
                            /files/jini1_0/lib/sun-util.jar:
                            /files/service
  -d /files/service
  /files/corejini/chapter5/HelloWorldServiceInterface.java
  /files/corejini/chapter5/HelloWorldService.java
```

Now, compile the source files needed for the client. The client also relies on `HelloWorldServiceInterface.java`, as well as `HelloWorldClient.java`. We'll put these files in `/files/client`.

```
javac -classpath /files/jini1_0/lib/jini-core.jar:
                            /files/jini1_0/lib/jini-ext.jar:
                            /files/jini1_0/lib/sun-util.jar:
  -d /files/client
  /files/corejini/chapter5/HelloWorldServiceInterface.java
  /files/corejini/chapter5/HelloWorldClient.java
```

Note that even though we already compiled the interface source file when we built the service, we need to make sure that the resulting class file is present in both the client and the server directories, since it's required by both. So here we compile it into the client's directory as well.

Finally, in this example, the only code we've written that will be downloaded is the proxy's class file. This file should have been created when we compiled the service, since the proxy is a nested class within the service. You can just copy this file from the `/files/service` directory to the `/files/service-dl` directory:

```
cd /files/service/corejini/chapter5
cp HelloWorldServiceProxy.class /files/service-dl
```

Start an HTTP Server for the Service

Now that we've segregated our class files, we can start an HTTP server that will export the downloadable class files that clients will need to use the service. In this example, the service is the only entity that needs to export downloadable code (in addition to the lookup service, that is, which should have its own HTTP server already running), so we can run an HTTP server with a root directory set to the location of the service's downloadable class files.

If you're developing everything on one machine, you're probably running the HTTP server that provides the class files for the core Jini services on your machine already. If this is the case, then you should pick a port number for the new HTTP server that's different than the one already running (which defaults to port 8080). Here, I'm starting the server on port 8085. In the rest of this book, I'll always run the HTTP server that exports code for services on this port.

On Windows: Launch the HTTP server that comes with Jini:

```
java -jar C:\jini1_0\lib\tools.jar
            -dir C:\service-dl -verbose -port 8085
```

On Solaris: Launch the HTTP server that comes with Jini:

```
java -jar /files/jini1_0/lib/tools.jar
            -dir /files/service-dl -verbose -port 8085
```

Set Up a Security Policy File

Since our example programs have a security manager set, they need to have a security policy provided for them at run time that tells the Java Virtual Machine what these programs are allowed to do. The policy file shown here in Listing 5–4 is very "promiscuous," in that it allows the programs to essentially do anything. This is fine in our testing environment, since we've written the code and know what it does. But you should not use this policy file in a production environment. Read the JavaSoft security tutorial, or *Just Java 1.2* by Peter van der Linden for more information on policy files.

Listing 5–4 A promiscuous policy file

```
grant {
    // Allow everyone access to everything
    permission java.security.AllPermission;
};
```

Drop this file into `C:\policy` on Windows, or `/files/policy` on Solaris. You'll need to pass the path to it on the command line when you run the programs.

Running

Now (finally!) you're ready to run the programs. One caveat with the version of the example programs shown in this section: You have to start the `HelloWorldService` program *first*. This is because the client application only searches for services that are already in existence when it runs—there is no way for the client to be notified if the desired service comes along after the client has started. This is a problem that will be remedied in the next iteration of the example.

First, run the service. Make sure that you replace "myhost" in the codebase URL with the hostname on which the service's HTTP server is running.

On Windows:

```
java -cp C:\jini1_0\lib\jini-core.jar;
                  C:\jini1_0\lib\jini-ext.jar;
                  C:\jini1_0\lib\sun-util.jar;
                  C:\service
            -Djava.rmi.server.codebase=http://myhost:8085/
            -Djava.security.policy=C:\policy
      corejini.chapter5.HelloWorldService
```

On Solaris:

```
java -cp /files/jini1_0/lib/jini-core.jar:
                  /files/jini1_0/lib/jini-ext.jar:
                  /files/jini1_0/lib/sun-util.jar:
                  /files/service
            -Djava.rmi.server.codebase=http://myhost:8085/
            -Djava.security.policy=/files/policy
      corejini.chapter5.HelloWorldService
```

After you see the service report that it has "discovered a lookup service," run the client. Note that the client doesn't need to have a codebase property specified, as it is providing no downloadable code to other programs.

On Windows:

```
java -cp C:\jini1_0\lib\jini-core.jar;
                  C:\jini1_0\lib\jini-ext.jar;
                  C:\jini1_0\lib\sun-util.jar;
                  C:\client
            -Djava.security.policy=C:\policy
      corejini.chapter5.HelloWorldClient
```

On Solaris:

```
java -cp /files/jini1_0/lib/jini-core.jar:
                 /files/jini1_0/lib/jini-ext.jar:
                 /files/jini1_0/lib/sun-util.jar:
                 /files/client
          -Djava.security.policy=/files/policy
      corejini.chapter5.HelloWorldClient
```

The client will contact the lookup services, download the service proxy from the lookup service, as well as the code for the proxy from HTTP server associated with the service, and execute it. You should see output like the following:

From the service:

```
discovered a lookup service!
Set serviceID to e91bb61d-b18e-447e-8935-adfd8bd741f5
```

From the client:

```
Got matching service.
Its message is: Hello, world!
```

Success! Our client has contacted a Jini community, searched for a service that implements a particular Java interface, and downloaded code that implements that interface. All the setup here may seem at first like a lot of work with little payoff—certainly the Hello, World service isn't very compelling on its own. But we'll be able to extend this basic paradigm to richer and richer functionality. And—painful though it may be—following the tips to simulate a multimachine environment in which clients and services share no CLASSPATH will keep problems from cropping up later.

Now we're ready to move on and extend our client code by enabling event handling.

Extending Hello World with Events

The previous example highlighted the basics of interacting with the discovery and lookup programming models. And, while unencumbered by some of the other Jini concepts, we would have to do a bit more to make these programs reliable and better behaved in a Jini community.

In this section, we extend the client class with the ability to respond to remote events. By using remote events, we'll gain the ability to run the "Hello, World" service *after* the client has started. This is flexibility that's essential for a real-world application, and is missing from the prior iteration of the example.

As we revise the example to make it more complex, and add needed functionality, we'll subclass our previous work. This makes it easy to see what has changed between iterations, and cuts down on the amount of redundant code that you as the reader have to parse.

For this example, we can keep most of the code the same—`HelloWorldService` and `HelloWorldServiceInterface` will stay exactly the same. We only need to extend the functionality of the `HelloWorldClient` code, as shown in Listing 5–5, to make it handle events properly.

Listing 5–5 `HelloWorldClientWithEvents.java`

```
// Extend the client so that it can receive events
// when new services appear.

package corejini.chapter5;

import net.jini.core.lookup.ServiceEvent;
import net.jini.core.lookup.ServiceItem;
import net.jini.core.lookup.ServiceRegistrar;
import net.jini.core.event.RemoteEvent;
import net.jini.core.event.RemoteEventListener;
import net.jini.core.event.UnknownEventException;
import java.util.Vector;
import java.io.IOException;
import java.rmi.RemoteException;
import java.rmi.server.UnicastRemoteObject;

public class HelloWorldClientWithEvents
            extends HelloWorldClient {
    // 10 minute leases
    protected final int LEASE_TIME = 10 * 60 * 1000;

    // An inner class to listen for events.
    class MyEventListener
        extends UnicastRemoteObject
        implements RemoteEventListener {
        public MyEventListener() throws RemoteException {
        }
```

Listing 5–5 `HelloWorldClientWithEvents.java` **(continued)**

```
        // Called when an event is received.
        public void notify(RemoteEvent ev)
            throws RemoteException, UnknownEventException {
            System.out.println("Got an event from: " +
                               ev.getSource());
            if (ev instanceof ServiceEvent) {
              ServiceEvent sev = (ServiceEvent) ev;
              ServiceItem item = sev.getServiceItem();
              HelloWorldServiceInterface hws =
                (HelloWorldServiceInterface) item.service;

              System.out.println("Got a matching service.");
              System.out.println("Its message is: " +
                                 hws.getMessage());
            } else {
               System.out.println("Not a service event, " +
                                  "ignoring");
            }
        }
    }

    protected MyEventListener eventCatcher;

    // Same as superclass, only create an event
    // listener
    public HelloWorldClientWithEvents()
                throws RemoteException, IOException {
        eventCatcher = new MyEventListener();
    }

    protected Object lookForService(ServiceRegistrar lu) {
        Object o = super.lookForService(lu);

        if (o != null) {
            return o;
        } else {
            try {
                registerForEvents(lu);
            } catch (RemoteException ex) {
               System.err.println("Can't solicit events: "
                                  + ex.getMessage());
                // Discard it, so we can find it again
                disco.discard(lu);
            } finally {
                return null;
            }
        }
    }
```

Listing 5–5 `HelloWorldClientWithEvents.java` **(continued)**

```
    // Ask for events from the lookup service
    protected void registerForEvents(ServiceRegistrar lu)
        throws RemoteException {
        lu.notify(template,
                ServiceRegistrar.TRANSITION_NOMATCH_MATCH,
                 eventCatcher, null, LEASE_TIME);
    }

    // Start the client.
    public static void main(String args[]) {
        try {
            HelloWorldClientWithEvents hwc =
                    new HelloWorldClientWithEvents();
            new Thread(hwc).start();
        } catch (IOException ex) {
            System.out.println("Couldn't create client: " +
                                    ex.getMessage());
        }
    }
}
```

This version of `HelloWorldClient` is a subclass of the original, and inherits all its functionality. The new code adds the ability to receive events from lookup services when a desired service is registered after the client has already done a `lookup()` operation. The changes needed to support this are quite small, and will be easily repeatable boilerplate for most applications.

Writing a Remote Event Listener

The most obvious feature of this revision of the client program is the inclusion of a nested class that will catch any events for us. The Jini remote event model is based on RMI—that is, remote events are sent from a remote process to our program by calling the `notify()` method, which is exposed as a method on a remote object. Here, I have created a new, nested class, called `MyEventListener`, whose sole purpose is to receive these events. In general, there's no reason that the class that registers the service cannot be the same class that receives the events. But, creating a separate class for listeners—whether local or remote—often results in a much cleaner design. In this case, the listener must extend the RMI class `UnicastRemoteObject`, so I have no choice but to create a separate nested class. Using separate nested classes for listeners is good practice in most cases.

If you are unfamiliar with RMI, now may be a good time to check out the RMI primer in Appendix A of this book. Basically, by making the listener class inherit from `UnicastRemoteObject`, we've said that its methods may be called from an object in a different JVM, either on the same host or on different hosts. In this case, the `notify()` method will be called by the lookup service to deliver an event whenever the desired service appears.

This event listener class needs to do several things.

- It must inherit from `UnicastRemoteObject` so that its methods can be called by objects in another Java Virtual Machine to deliver events.
- It must implement `RemoteEventListener`, which includes the `notify()` method. This method will be invoked whenever an event comes in.
- To work correctly with RMI, the class must declare that its constructor and any remotely callable methods may raise `RemoteException`. You'll notice that this is done in the example.

Now that we've defined a class to receive events for us, we can start up the client. The constructor for our extended client program, and also creates an instance of `MyEventListener` that will be used to receive events. Note that, as of now, we've only declared and created one of these listeners—we haven't actually "plugged it in" yet, because we haven't yet found any lookup services from which we can receive events.

Soliciting Events via Notify()

The next change is in the `lookupService()` method. This implementation again calls its superclass—the behavior shown in the first `HelloWorldClient` is fine for the case when the service already exists when the client starts. But, if the superclass version of `lookupService()` doesn't find a service, we then solicit events from that lookup service.

This is done by calling the `notify()` method on the lookup service. The `notify()` method is used to ask for event notifications from the lookup service. Thus, `notify()` is really a registration process, and its semantics involve a use of templates that is similar to the use of the `lookup()` method discussed earlier. We specify a template on which to search, and get informed of any matches. The difference is that `lookup()` finds matches that *already* exist in the lookup service; `notify()` finds matches *in the future*. Once you call `notify()`, you're asking the lookup service to hold on to your query, and inform you via an event whenever the service items in the lookup service change in way that makes the query match.

There are a number of parameters to `notify()`.

- The first is the `ServiceTemplate`. This argument works just like it does in the `lookup()` method—you can specify explicit service IDs, service types, or attributes to match on. In our example, we use the same `ServiceTemplate` that we use for doing the original `lookup()`, because we're searching for the same thing in both cases—a proxy that implements `HelloWorldService`.
- The second is the "transition" parameter. This value indicates when an event should be sent to you—when the lookup service changes so that a previously matching value no longer matches (indicated by the constant `TRANSITION_MATCH_NOMATCH`), when a matching value appears (indicated by `TRANSITION_NOMATCH_MATCH`), or simply when a matching value changes in some way (indicated by `TRANSITION_MATCH_MATCH`). By using this parameter, you can get notifications when services appear, disappear, or are modified. These values can be bitwise OR'ed together to solicit multiple types of matches. In our example, we care about when services start up that didn't exist previously, so we use `TRANSITION_NOMATCH_MATCH`.
- The third parameter indicates the object that should receive the events. This object must implement the `RemoteEventListener` interface. Here, we use the instance of our event listener that we created in the constructor.
- The fourth parameter, which is `null` here, is a `MarshalledObject` that will be returned to the caller when the event occurs. Any value that you pass here will be saved by the lookup service and returned to you in the `RemoteEvent` that you receive. By using this parameter, you can associate arbitrary extra data that may be meaningful to your application with events, and use this data to distinguish different contexts in which events were solicited. The `MarshalledObject` class is new in Java 2; see the sidebar if you are unfamiliar with it.

- The final parameter is the requested duration of the lease. Recall that event registrations, just like lookup service registrations, are leased to requestors. In our example, we have requested a 10-minute lease. Again, this example does not have adequate leasing behavior—it never renews its leases, so if you run the service after the client's event registration leases have expired, the client will receive no notifications. We'll remedy this in the next iteration.

Sidebar: MarshalledObjects

The MarshalledObject class is a new addition to Java 2. It represents the serialized form of an object—essentially the raw bits that can be reconstituted into a "live" object upon demand.

When you write out a Serializable object to an output stream, the Java serialization machinery is called to create a representation of the object that can be recreated as needed. A MarshalledObject is simply an object that represents the actual bytes that result from the serialization process. The MarshalledObject class itself can be thought of as the container for the bytes that result from serialization; the class only supports a few methods—basically just the ability to reconstitute the object, and the ability to compare two MarshalledObjects without having to reconstitute them into "live" objects again.

While the Jini APIs could have used a Serializable parameter here, using a MarshalledObject can be more efficient—the object has already been serialized at this point, and can be shipped around, and compared without the overhead of reconstituting it into a "live" object each time it is needed. And if the client code wishes to use the same data in each event registration, it can "preserialize" the data into a MarshalledObject and use it over and over again.

Once we've called `notify()`, the lookup service will send us an event whenever there is a match for the combination of template plus transition that we have specified. In this example, since we have specified `TRANSITION_NOMATCH_MATCH`, we'll get an event whenever a service that matches the template is added to the lookup service. Whenever such a match occurs, the `notify()` method we've implemented on the `MyEventListener` class will be invoked. Our class implements this method by simply casting the found service to `HelloWorldServiceInterface` and printing out the message returned from the proxy.

The actual event that gets delivered when a match occurs is a subclass of `RemoteEvent` called `ServiceEvent`. So our implementation of `notify()` casts the event to a `ServiceEvent`, which contains detailed and specific information about the match. The event is set so that its source is the lookup service that matched the query. The `ServiceEvent` also has a `getServiceItem()` method which returns the service item that caused the event (or null if the event was sent because of a service item disappearing), a `getServiceID()` method that returns the ID of the service that caused the event, and a `getTransition()` method that returns the type of transition that caused the event to be sent. Here, we get the service item from the event so that we can fetch and use the proxy.

With the addition of this bit of code, we've made our little distributed system much more robust. Now, the client and service can be started in any order.

Compiling and Running the Code

Because our new class uses RMI to provide remote objects, there's one extra step in the compilation process: We need to run the RMI stub generator, called `rmic`, on the class files for our remote code to create "stub" classes for it. These stub classes are used internally by RMI to manage the over-the-wire communication with remote objects, and are downloaded to callers who need to invoke remote methods. Essentially, the stubs provide a bit of code that lives in the caller that takes care of the mechanics of performing the remote method invocation on the remote object. Also, we've added another entity to our system that must export downloadable code—since the client needs to pass the stubs for its listener class to the lookup service, it must deposit the necessary code in a directory so that the lookup service can access it.

Compiling

First, however, let's compile the classes. Again, we'll follow the rather intricate steps from before to ensure that we prevent unnecessary code sharing.

On Windows: Compile the client source file, and put the resulting code into `C:\client`.

```
javac -classpath C:\jini1_0\lib\jini-core.jar;
                 C:\jini1_0\lib\jini-ext.jar;
```

```
                              C:\jini1_0\lib\sun-util.jar;
                              C:\client
  -d C:\client
  C:\files\corejini\chapter5\HelloWorldClientWithEvents.java
```

On Solaris: Compile the client source file, and put the resulting code into `/files/client`.

```
javac -classpath /files/jini1_0/lib/jini-core.jar:
                              /files/jini1_0/lib/jini-ext.jar:
                              /files/jini1_0/lib/sun-util.jar:
                              /files/client
  -d /files/client
  /files/corejini/chapter5/HelloWorldClientWithEvents.java
```

Generating the RMI Stubs

Generating the RMI stubs is an easy task—one call to the `rmic` stubs compiler will do the trick, producing the code that will allow the lookup service to call the `notify()` method in the client remotely. We do, however, want to create a new directory for the downloadable code that the *client* provides. Although we created a directory for downloadable code from the *service* in the last example, here we need to export code from the client so that the lookup service can call the client. The stubs code necessary to call the `notify()` method remotely needs to be downloadable to callers, so it'll have to go in this download directory.

Core Alert: Bug in RMIC

As of JDK1.2, there is a bug in `RMIC` *where specifying the* `-classpath` *option completely overrides the system classpath. This means that you cannot specify just the locations of your application class files in the* `-classpath` *argument, or* `RMIC` *will complain that it cannot find various core Java classes (such as* `java.lang.Object`*).*

In the following examples, I've explicitly included the `rt.jar` *file, which contains Java's core classes, in the* `-classpath` *argument. You may want to try leaving the* `rt.jar` *file off the first time you try these examples, in case the bug has been fixed by the time you read this.*

On Windows: First, create the directory for downloadable code

```
mkdir C:\client-dl
```

Then generate the RMI stubs. Make sure you use the correct path to `rt.jar`:

```
rmic -classpath C:\jdk1.2\jre\lib\rt.jar;
                         C:\jini1_0\lib\jini-core.jar;
                         C:\jini1_0\lib\jini-ext.jar;
                         C:\jini1_0\lib\sun-util.jar;
                         C:\client
       -d C:\client-dl
corejini.chapter5.HelloWorldClientWithEvents.MyEventListener
```

On Solaris: First, create the directory for downloadable code

```
mkdir /files/client-dl
```

Then generate the RMI stubs. Make sure you use the correct path to `rt.jar`:

```
rmic -classpath /usr/java1.2/jre/lib/rt.jar:
                         /files/jini1_0/lib/jini-core.jar:
                         /files/jini1_0/lib/jini-ext.jar:
                         /files/jini1_0/lib/sun-util.jar:
                         /files/client
      -d /files/client-dl
corejini.chapter5.HelloWorldClientWithEvents.MyEventListener
```

Once you've run `rmic`, you can look in the `client-dl` directory and you'll now see the generated stub file:

```
HelloWorldClientWithEvents$MyEventListener_Stub.class
```

Start an HTTP Server to Export the Client's Downloadable Code

You'll now need to start an HTTP server that can serve up the RMI stub files that the client needs to export. When you run the client, you'll set a codebase property that tells any interested parties where to find this code relative to the HTTP server. Since the client will be sending stubs to the Jini lookup service so that the lookup service can call the client's methods remotely, we'll actually be downloading a bit of custom behavior into a core Jini service. Nifty!

Once again, you may need to use a different port number, if you've got multiple HTTP services running on one machine. In this book, I'll use port 8086 for the HTTP server that exports clients' code.

On Windows: Launch the HTTP server that comes with Jini:

```
java -jar C:\jini1_0\lib\tools.jar
            -dir C:\client-dl -verbose -port 8086
```

On Solaris: Launch the HTTP server that comes with Jini:

```
java -jar /files/jini1_0/lib/tools.jar
            -dir /files/client-dl -verbose -port 8086
```

Running

Now we can run the example programs. Running the examples works just like before, with the exception that you can now run the client and the service in either order. You can use the exact same service we created earlier with this new client.

But since we want to see the event behavior in action, run the client first. Make sure that you replace "myhost" in the codebase URL with the hostname on which the client's HTTP server is running; this is the HTTP server we just started. Also note that, unlike the previous version of the client, here we have to set a codebase, since we need to tell the lookup service where to download code from. And, since the client needs access to not only its implementation classes but also its stub at runtime, the `client-dl` directory should also be its classpath.

On Windows:

```
java -cp C:\jini1_0\lib\jini-core.jar;
                  C:\jini1_0\lib\jini-ext.jar;
                  C:\jini1_0\lib\sun-util.jar;
                  C:\client;
                  C:\client-dl
            -Djava.rmi.server.codebase=http://myhost:8086/
            -Djava.security.policy=C:\policy
      corejini.chapter5.HelloWorldClientWithEvents
```

On Solaris:

```
java -cp /files/jini1_0/lib/jini-core.jar:
                  /files/jini1_0/lib/jini-ext.jar:
                  /files/jini1_0/lib/sun-util.jar:
                  /files/client:
                  /files/client-dl
            -Djava.rmi.server.codebase=http://myhost:8086/
            -Djava.security.policy=/files/policy
      corejini.chapter5.HelloWorldClientWithEvents
```

Finally, you can run the service, just as you did before.

On Windows:

```
java -cp C:\jini1_0\lib\jini-core.jar;
                  C:\jini1_0\lib\jini-ext.jar;
                  C:\jini1_0\lib\sun-util.jar;
                  C:\service
            -Djava.rmi.server.codebase=http://myhost:8085/
            -Djava.security.policy=C:\policy
      corejini.chapter5.HelloWorldService
```

On Solaris:

```
java -cp /files/jini1_0/lib/jini-core.jar:
                  /files/jini1_0/lib/jini-ext.jar:
                  /files/jini1_0/lib/sun-util.jar:
                  /files/service
            -Djava.rmi.server.codebase=http://myhost:8085/
            -Djava.security.policy=/files/policy
      corejini.chapter5.HelloWorldService
```

If there are instances of the service running when the client starts, it will act exactly as it did before. Otherwise, it will simply wait for a `HelloWorldService` to appear, and display nothing.

From the client:

```
No matching service.
```

From the service:

```
discovered a lookup service!
Set serviceID to e91bb61d-b18e-447e-8935-adfd8bd741f5
```

From the client:

```
Got an event from: com.sun.jini.reggie.Registrar-
Proxy@9b559fd1
Got a matching service.
Its message is: Hello, world!
```

You should see the client detect the start of the new service and display the output from the proxy.

In this example, the client and the service can be started in any order. There's only one more extension to this code that we need to make: We must ensure that our leases, on both lookup and event registrations, are properly renewed. We'll solve this in the next iteration.

Hello World with Leasing

The final major flaw in our example program is that it never renews—or even checks—the leases returned to it for lookup service registrations or event solicitations. To address this problem, our service should be extended so that it tracks the leases that are returned from each lookup service it registers itself with, and renews these before they expire, for as long as it wishes to make the service available. On the client side, the client should similarly renew its event solicitations from the lookup services for as long as it wishes to be informed about new services appearing. Finally, both applications should be "well-behaved" by canceling any leases they hold when they shut down. While this isn't a strict requirement—because the whole idea of leases is that they provide a way for the system to clean up after applications that don't or cannot clean up after themselves—it does allow the lease grantors to free up resources as soon as possible. We don't do this in our examples—because they never shut down—but canceling your leases just before you terminate is an easy task in most applications.

Lease management in Jini is, unfortunately, one of the more cumbersome aspects of developing services and applications. However, for most applications, lease management turns out to be a pretty mechanical affair—they simply need to keep renewing all of their leases until they shut down.

A Simple Approach

We will discuss strategies for effective leasing, including the use of external "leasing services," in Chapter 10. For now, though, we will add leasing directly to our "Hello, World" service and client applications. Once again, we'll subclass the code we've already written to add the new functionality we need.

Leasing is similar in both the client and service cases: We need to keep track of the leases that have been returned to us—for event registrations in the client, and for lookup service registrations in the service—and then renew them before they expire. In the earlier applications, we saw that we started a thread that essentially did nothing. This thread was only used to keep the process alive so that our application could receive discovery or event notifications, even after `main()` had "run off the end" and completed.

In the next examples, we'll actually put this thread to good use. To use leasing properly, this thread will sit in the background, waking up when needed to renew leases. As we shall see, the structure of both the lease-augmented client and service are similar. First, let's look at a version of the "Hello, World" service, extended to do better leasing, as shown in Listing 5–6.

Listing 5–6 `HelloWorldServiceWithLeases.java`

```
// Extend HelloWorldService to renew its service
// registration leases.

package corejini.chapter5;

import net.jini.core.lookup.ServiceRegistrar;
import net.jini.core.lookup.ServiceRegistration;
import net.jini.core.lease.Lease;
import net.jini.core.lease.UnknownLeaseException;
import java.util.Vector;
import java.util.Enumeration;
import java.io.IOException;
import java.rmi.RemoteException;

public class HelloWorldServiceWithLeases extends Hel-
loWorldService {
    protected Thread leaseThread = null;
```

Listing 5–6 `HelloWorldServiceWithLeases.java` **(continued)**

```
public HelloWorldServiceWithLeases() throws IOException {
}

// Not only register, but also cause the lease
// thread to wake up.
protected void registerWithLookup(ServiceRegistrar lu) {
    super.registerWithLookup(lu);
    leaseThread.interrupt();
}

// run now maintains our leases
public void run() {
    while (true) {
        try {
            long sleepTime = computeSleepTime();
            Thread.sleep(sleepTime);
            renewLeases();
        } catch (InterruptedException ex) {
        }
    }
}

// Figure out how long to sleep.
protected synchronized long computeSleepTime() {
    long soonestExpiration = Long.MAX_VALUE;
    Enumeration enum = registrations.elements();
    while (enum.hasMoreElements()) {
        Lease l = ((ServiceRegistration)
                 enum.nextElement()).getLease();
        if (l.getExpiration() - (20 * 1000) <
                 soonestExpiration) {
            soonestExpiration = l.getExpiration() -
                 (20 * 1000);
        }
    }

    long now = System.currentTimeMillis();

    if (now >= soonestExpiration) {
        return 0;
    } else {
        return soonestExpiration - now;
    }
}
```

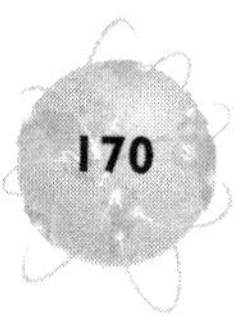

Listing 5–6 `HelloWorldServiceWithLeases.java` **(continued)**

```
    // Do the work of lease renewal.
    protected synchronized void renewLeases() {
        long now = System.currentTimeMillis();
        Vector deadLeases = new Vector();

        Enumeration keys = registrations.keys();
        while (keys.hasMoreElements()) {
            ServiceRegistrar lu = (ServiceRegistrar)
                     keys.nextElement();
            ServiceRegistration r = (ServiceRegistration)
                     registrations.get(lu);
            Lease l = r.getLease();
            if (now <= l.getExpiration() &&
                now >= l.getExpiration() - (20 * 1000)) {
                try {
                    System.out.println("Renewing lease.");
                    l.renew(LEASE_TIME);
                } catch (Exception ex) {
                    System.err.println("Couldn't renew: " +
                                       ex.getMessage());
                    deadLeases.addElement(lu);
                }
            }
        }

        // clean up after any leases that died
        for (int i=0, size=deadLeases.size() ; i<size ; i++) {
            registrations.remove(deadLeases.elementAt(i));
        }
    }

    // Create the service and start the leasing
    // thread.
    public static void main(String args[]) {
        try {
            HelloWorldServiceWithLeases hws =
                     new HelloWorldServiceWithLeases();
            hws.leaseThread = new Thread(hws);
            hws.leaseThread.start();
        } catch (IOException ex) {
           System.out.println("Couldn't create service: " +
                              ex.getMessage());
        }
    }
}
```

While the code for the leasing-enabled version of our service has grown a bit, most of the changes are fairly easy to understand. Let's start by looking at the heart of the changes, in the `run()` method.

Prior to this example, we made our service process create a new thread that essentially did nothing but sleep. While it accomplished no useful work, this thread was actually required to keep the JVM from exiting, because without a live, non-daemon thread, the Java Virtual Machine will exit as soon as `main()` returns. In all of our examples, `main()` simply creates an object representing our service, starts a new thread of control, and then returns (by simply "running off the end" of the available statements).

Here, however, we actually have a need for a thread to do some work for us. In our new service, `run()` handles our lease management. The new implementation of `run()`, which overrides the one from the original `HelloWorldService`, basically loops forever. For each iteration, it determines how long it should sleep until it needs to do some leasing work, sleeps for that amount of time, and then wakes up to renew any leases that are coming due.

Let's look at how this works in more detail. Ignoring the code that handles `InterruptedException` for the moment, we see that for each iteration in `run()`, we first compute the time we should sleep, via `computeSleepTime()`. This method iterates through all of the leases for service registrations that we've received from lookup services and finds the one that expires the soonest. Once we've determined which lease is coming due first, we compute how long we have to sleep in order to wake up just before the lease expires. To do this, we store in the variable `now` the current time (in milliseconds) and compare it to our needed wake-up time. If we've already missed our next wake-up time, we return 0, indicating that we should not sleep at all, but rather should go ahead and try to renew the expiring lease if we can (chances are we may be too late if this happens, though). Otherwise, we return the number of milliseconds we should sleep.

You'll note that this code, rather than using the "raw" expiration time for leases, "fudges" the amount a bit. Here, we adjust the expiration time by 20 seconds. This is meant to give us time to do any processing needed to send the renewal message, allow transit time over the network to the lease grantor, and a bit more time just to be safe.

After we've figured the amount of time the thread should sleep, `run()` sleeps for that amount, and then calls `renewLeases()` to do the actual lease renewal for us.

The `renewLeases()` method again iterates through all the leases. Whenever it finds a lease that expires at any point between now and now plus the

20-second fudge factor, it tries to renew the lease for the 10-minute lease time used in all our examples. If the lease renewal fails for any reason (such as the lease grantor is unwilling to renew it, or the network is down), `renewLeases()` adds it to a list of "dead leases" until it finishes all the renewal attempts. Once it's done with renewals, it then walks through the dead leases and removes them from the list of registrations.

Core Note: Handling "Dead" Leases

This example takes the simple and expedient approach of simply disposing of troublesome leases. An actual service, however, would probably be coded to be a little more persistent than this.

For example, a service may continue to retry the renewal for some period of time. If the registration is with a lookup service that is especially important—perhaps because a human user has told the service to register itself there, for instance—then it may periodically try to re-register itself there.

This example shows lease management in its most basic form—simply waking up periodically to renew leases before they expire. We've seen how `run()` works by computing a sleep time, sleeping, and then renewing all the leases that are about to expire.

But what happens to this code when a new lease is added after the thread starts? Remember that discovery is an asynchronous process. New lookup registrations may happen at any arbitrary point in the future, not just when we start to run the lease thread. If a new lease is added while the thread is blocked in `sleep()`, it may need to wake up sooner than it otherwise would. Perhaps the new lease will expire before the thread is due to wake. To deal with this case robustly, we need to wake the sleeping thread and recompute the sleep interval whenever a new lease is added.

The key to handling this case is already in the code you see here. As you may have guessed, the `try-catch` block to handle the `InterruptedException` in `run()` has something to do with it.

Whenever a new registration is done in the `registerWithLookup()` method, we not only call the superclass version of this method to cause the registration to happen and be recorded, we also interrupt the thread that's doing lease management. The `run()` method, because it catches and handles `InterruptedException`, will simply restart another iteration of its internal loop when it is interrupted. This causes the sleep time to be recomputed, which will correctly account for any change in the set of managed leases.

Notice how the `main()` routine stores the `Thread` object for the lease management thread in the `HelloWorldServiceWithLeases` instance so that this interrupt process can happen.

Let's move on to the client example. Whereas the service used leases to handle its registrations with lookup services, the client uses leases to handle its registrations for events. As we shall see in Listing 5–7, while the basic implementation details are just a bit different, the "big picture" of leasing is exactly the same in the client as it is in the service.

Listing 5–7 `HelloWorldClientWithLeases.java`

```
// Extend the client to renew its event registration
// leases.

package corejini.chapter5;

import net.jini.core.lookup.ServiceRegistrar;
import net.jini.core.event.RemoteEvent;
import net.jini.core.event.RemoteEventListener;
import net.jini.core.event.EventRegistration;
import net.jini.core.lease.Lease;
import net.jini.core.lease.UnknownLeaseException;
import java.util.Vector;
import java.io.IOException;
import java.rmi.RemoteException;

public class HelloWorldClientWithLeases
    extends HelloWorldClientWithEvents {
    protected Vector eventRegs = new Vector();
    protected Thread leaseThread = null;

    public HelloWorldClientWithLeases()
        throws RemoteException, IOException {
    }

    // When we register for events, add the event's
    // registration to the set of managed
    // registrations.
    protected void registerForEvents(ServiceRegistrar lu)
        throws RemoteException {
        EventRegistration evreg;

        evreg = lu.notify(template,
             ServiceRegistrar.TRANSITION_NOMATCH_MATCH,
             eventCatcher, null, LEASE_TIME);
```

Listing 5–7 `HelloWorldClientWithLeases.java` **(continued)**

```
        eventRegs.addElement(evreg);
        leaseThread.interrupt();
    }

    // run maintains our leases
    public void run() {
        while (true) {
            try {
                long sleepTime = computeSleepTime();
                Thread.sleep(sleepTime);
                renewLeases();
            } catch (InterruptedException ex) {
            }
        }
    }

    // Figure out how long to sleep.
    protected synchronized long computeSleepTime() {
        long soonestExpiration = Long.MAX_VALUE;
        for (int i=0, size=eventRegs.size() ; i<size ; i++)
{
            Lease l = ((EventRegistration)
                      eventRegs.elementAt(i)).getLease();
            if (l.getExpiration() - (20 * 1000) <
                      soonestExpiration) {
                soonestExpiration = l.getExpiration() -
                      (20 * 1000);
            }
        }

        long now = System.currentTimeMillis();

        if (now >= soonestExpiration) {
            return 0;
        } else {
            return soonestExpiration - now;
        }
    }

    // Do the lease renewal work.
    protected synchronized void renewLeases() {
        long now = System.currentTimeMillis();
        Vector deadLeases = new Vector();
```

Listing 5–7 `HelloWorldClientWithLeases.java` **(continued)**

```
        for (int i=0 , size=eventRegs.size() ; i<size ; i++) {
             Lease l = ((EventRegistration)
                       eventRegs.elementAt(i)).getLease();
             if (now <= l.getExpiration() &&
                 now >= l.getExpiration() - (20 * 1000)) {
                 try {
                     System.out.println("Renewing lease.");
                     l.renew(LEASE_TIME);
                 } catch (Exception ex) {
                    System.err.println("Couldn't renew: " +
                                       ex.getMessage());

                      deadLeases.addElement(
                                   eventRegs.elementAt(i));
                 }
             }
         }

         // clean up after any leases that died
        for (int i=0, size=deadLeases.size() ; i<size ; i++)
{
            eventRegs.removeElement(deadLeases.elementAt(i));
        }
    }

    // Start the service.
    public static void main(String args[]) {
        try {
            HelloWorldClientWithLeases hwc =
                         new HelloWorldClientWithLeases();
            hwc.leaseThread = new Thread(hwc);
            hwc.leaseThread.start();
        } catch (IOException ex) {
            System.out.println("Couldn't create client: " +
                               ex.getMessage());
        }
    }
}
```

The extensions to the client code to do leasing are much the same as the extensions required in the service code. Here again we see an extended `run()` method, which allows a thread to do lease management duties. We

also see the use of interrupts to cause the leasing thread to recompute the required sleep time after a change in the set of managed leases.

In fact, the only real difference here is that the client and the service use different data structures in which to store their registrations, because we're storing different types of registrations—`ServiceRegistrations` in one case and `EventRegistrations` in the other. So the code to iterate over them is a bit different. The fact that two applications serving two very different roles—client and service—in a Jini community have nearly identical lease management code is a big hint that lease management can be largely automated with some helper classes. We'll look at how to do this in Chapter 10.

For now, though, we've seen the basics of how to manage leases in both clients and services, and we've extended our simple "Hello World" examples through several iterations to the point that they can become full-fledged participants in a Jini community.

Compiling and Running the Code

We've already set ourselves up with HTTP servers for the downloadable code from our services (their proxies), the downloadable code from our clients (the stubs for their event listeners), and our core services (the lookup service). To run the leasing examples, all we have to do is compile the client and the service into their appropriate directories. This extension of the Hello, World examples adds no *new* downloadable code, so we don't have to copy any class files into the download directories that are served by our HTTP servers.

Compiling

Compile the client and the service just as in the previous examples. Here, again, I'm sending the class files that result from the compilation into separate directories, to ensure that the class paths of the two programs are isolated, just as they would be when the programs are running on two different machines on the network.

On Windows: compile the client source file, and put the resulting code into `C:\client`.

```
javac -classpath C:\jini1_0\lib\jini-core.jar;
                               C:\jini1_0\lib\jini-ext.jar;
                               C:\jini1_0\lib\sun-util.jar;
                               C:\client
  -d C:\client
  C:\files\corejini\chapter5\HelloWorldClientWithLeases.java
```

And then compile the service source file, putting the resulting class files into `C:\server`.

```
javac -classpath C:\jini1_0\lib\jini-core.jar;
                        C:\jini1_0\lib\jini-ext.jar;
                        C:\jini1_0\lib\sun-util.jar;
                        C:\service
  -d C:\service
  C:\files\corejini\chapter5\HelloWorldServiceWithLeases.java
```

On Solaris: compile the client source file, and put the resulting code into `/files/client`.

```
javac -classpath /files/jini1_0/lib/jini-core.jar:
                        /files/jini1_0/lib/jini-ext.jar:
                        /files/jini1_0/lib/sun-util.jar:
                        /files/client
  -d /files/client
  /files/corejini/chapter5/HelloWorldClientWithLeases.java
```

And then compile the service source file, putting the resulting class files into `/files/server`.

```
javac -classpath /files/jini1_0/lib/jini-core.jar:
                        /files/jini1_0/lib/jini-ext.jar:
                        /files/jini1_0/lib/sun-util.jar:
                        /files/service
  -d /files/service
  /files/corejini/chapter5/HelloWorldServiceWithLeases.java
```

Running

Now we're set to run the extended example programs. Since the client in this case extends the earlier version that uses events, you can run these programs in either order. And, unlike previous versions, these programs will continually renew their leases so you don't have to run them within a few minutes of one another!

On Windows: Run the service and the client in either order. Here I'm starting the service first.

```
java -cp C:\jini\lib\jini-core.jar;
                  C:\jini1_0\lib\jini-ext.jar;
                  C:\jini1_0\lib\sun-util.jar;
```

```
            -Djava.rmi.server.codebase=http://myhost:8085/
            -Djava.security.policy=C:\policy
       corejini.chapter5.HelloWorldServiceWithLeases

java -cp C:\jini1_0\lib\jini-core.jar;
                  C:\jini1_0\lib\jini-ext.jar;
                  C:\jini1_0\lib\sun-util.jar;
                  C:\client;
                  C:\client-dl
            -Djava.rmi.server.codebase=http://myhost:8086/
            -Djava.security.policy=C:\policy
       corejini.chapter5.HelloWorldClientWithLeases
```

On Solaris: Run the service and the client in either order. Here I'm starting the service first.

```
java -cp /files/jini1_0/lib/jini-core.jar:
                  /files/jini1_0/lib/jini-ext.jar:
                  /files/jini1_0/lib/sun-util.jar:
                  /files/service
            -Djava.rmi.server.codebase=http://myhost:8085/
            -Djava.security.policy=/files/policy
       corejini.chapter5.HelloWorldServiceWithLeases

java -cp /files/jini1_0/lib/jini-core.jar:
                  /files/jini1_0/lib/jini-ext.jar:
                  /files/jini1_0/lib/sun-util.jar:
                  /files/client:
                  /files/client-dl
            -Djava.rmi.server.codebase=http://myhost:8086/
            -Djava.security.policy=/files/policy
       corejini.chapter5.HelloWorldClientWithLeases
```

The output of running this client and service pair is much the same as in the first example: the client will contact the lookup service, download the service proxy (including getting the code for the proxy from the HTTP server associated with the service), and run it. But in this case, both the client and the service will periodically renew their leases. You should see output like the following:

From the service:

```
discovered a lookup service!
Set serviceID to e91bb61d-b18e-447e-8935-adfd8bd741f5
Renewing lease.
Renewing lease.
Renewing lease.
```

From the client:

```
Got matching service.
Its message is: Hello, world!
Renewing lease.
Renewing lease.
Renewing lease.
```

These programs will continue to renew their leases indefinitely, until you kill them.

In the last example of the chapter, we'll extend the Hello, World service once again. This time we'll see two new concepts: how to use RMI to allow a service proxy to communicate with a "back-end" process, and how to make a service's back end activatable.

Using an Activatable Back-End Process

In this last example of the chapter, we'll focus on two technologies that, while not specifically part of Jini, are likely to be used extensively in many Jini programs. These technologies are RMI and activation. As we saw in the event examples, RMI is a convenient way to implement remote communication between two Java objects.

Here, we extend our previous implementation of the service to use RMI to communicate with a "back-end" process. In all of the previous examples, the proxy object for the various versions of the `HelloWorldService` performed the service entirely on their own. Most services, though, will be implemented by both a proxy and a back-end device or process with which the proxy communicates. There is no requirement that these two components—the proxy and the back end—communicate via RMI. They can use raw sockets, IIOP, or any other protocol they desire. But here we'll use RMI both because it's simple and because a good working understanding of RMI is useful for using other aspects in Jini.

So what would a back-end process for our simple little service do? Here, I've architected it as an object that returns different strings from a list of strings each time it is called. The proxy object communicates to the back end to get the next string to display. Now there's nothing extraordinary about returning strings that innately requires the complexity of a back-end process. But the behavior here that the end user sees is different than in the cases where the proxy does all the work itself—the back end acts as a centralized keeper of not only the strings to display, but the knowledge of which string is to be displayed next. So if several clients have fetched the proxy for this service, each call to get another message will return the centralized back-end's notion of what the next string is—not any particular proxy's notion of what the next string is. This illustrates an important concept—back-end processes can serve as centralized coordinators for all their proxies. While the proxies for such a service may be living in any number of clients, doing any number of things, all these proxies have to coordinate with the back end to get their work done. This back-end process acts as a "choke point" for coordinating all the proxies.

Now, clearly having a process sitting around waiting on proxies to ask it for strings is resource intensive. We've got a process that's always active and waiting for connections, even if no proxies for it have been downloaded. While having one or two such processes sitting around may not be so bad, a whole network full of Jini services that are consuming resources while basically doing nothing could be a big performance hit.

The answer is to use the RMI activation framework, which I've alluded to a few times already and the sidebar further explains. The activation framework provides a way for a remote object to consume no memory or CPU resources until it is needed. When a caller tries to invoke a method on it, the object is *activated*, which means that it is brought "back to life" in the state it was in before it was previously *deactivated*. At this point the object is ready to receive calls on it.

Activation provides a nice way to have very long-lived remote objects that don't have to be active when they're not being used. It also provides another benefit—references to these objects can also be long-lived. That is, if I have a reference to an activatable object, that reference is good for as long as the activation framework knows about the object. I can save it, reuse it, and rely on the fact that the object to which it refers will be started if needed.

Sidebar: The Activation Framework

The RMI activation framework was introduced with Java 2. Since it is used extensively by the core Jini run-time services—including Sun's reference implementation of the lookup service, the transaction manager, and the JavaSpaces storage service—and because it can be handy when creating new services, it's good to understand some of the concepts behind activation.

(continued)

Appendix A goes into a bit of detail on activation, and RMI in general, but the basic ideas behind activation can be stated simply. Prior to activation, remote objects that were to be called from external JVMs had to be "live"—that is, running and exported—all the time. Activation brings a way for such objects to be "activated"—that is, recreated—as needed, on demand.

Activation can be a huge win in systems in which there are large numbers of remote objects. Clearly, having so many objects "live" at one time could potentially be a huge drain on resources. Activation provides a means for temporarily unused objects to be made inactive, and reactivated as needed.

The RMI activation daemon (`rmid`) is the entity that handles activating objects on demand. It does this by spawning new JVMs as needed to run the objects it is activating. External JVMs are spawned as child processes of `rmid`, and multiple objects can share these JVMs—a group of objects that can share a single JVM, with its associated security policies and resources, is called an "activation group." In the example that we'll see, we create a new activation group to run the Hello, World service object.

While activation can be a big win for performance in situations where there are large numbers of remote objects, or where remote objects may be rarely used, you should take care when deciding on a policy for activation and deactivation. The overhead required to reactivate an inactive object is rather large: it can entail creating a new JVM, loading and verifying all necessary classes for the object being activated, and deserializing any persistent state. Thus, once an object has been activated, it should employ some strategy for staying up for a "safe" amount of time. Without such a strategy, the object may "thrash" between active and inactive states, consuming lots of cycles and memory. A deactivation strategy could be based on the amount of time since the last call, the number of accumulated calls, or some other metric.

An "activation descriptor" for an activatable remote object describes how the object will be reactivated. One of the nifty things about the activation descriptor is that you can pass to the class's constructor a "restart" flag that indicates whether the object should be automatically restarted whenever `rmid` restarts. The activation daemon remembers the remote objects that have registered with it, and can recreate them, even after restarts of the activation daemon itself. This can be handy for restarting a whole set of services whenever a machine reboots.

(continued)

> The Sun sample implementations of the Jini services use this flag. So, for example, the lookup service will be automatically restarted whenever `rmid` restarts, and it will also be restarted on demand with the first method invocation on it. This feature can be used to make your services quite robust in the face of machine or software failures.

Let's look now at the final example (Listing 5–8), an extension of the `HelloWorldService` that uses RMI to talk to an activatable back-end process.

Listing 5–8 `HelloWorldServiceBackend.java`

```
// Create an extension of the service that uses
// RMI to communicate with an activatable back-end process.

package corejini.chapter5;

import java.util.Vector;
import java.util.Enumeration;
import java.io.IOException;
import java.io.Serializable;
import java.rmi.RemoteException;
import java.rmi.Remote;
import java.rmi.MarshalledObject;
import java.rmi.RMISecurityManager;
import java.rmi.server.UnicastRemoteObject;
import java.rmi.activation.Activatable;
import java.rmi.activation.ActivationID;
import java.rmi.activation.ActivationDesc;
import java.rmi.activation.ActivationGroup;
import java.rmi.activation.ActivationGroupID;
import java.rmi.activation.ActivationGroupDesc;
import java.rmi.activation.ActivationException;
import java.util.Properties;

public class HelloWorldServiceBackend
    extends HelloWorldServiceWithLeases {

    // An interface to define the remote
    // communications protocol between the
    // proxy and the back-end.
    interface BackendProtocol extends Remote {
        public String fetchString() throws RemoteException;
    }
```

Listing 5–8 `HelloWorldServiceBackend.java` (continued)

```
    // This is a nested class that implements the
    // back-end protocol.  It's activatable, so it
    // is already a UnicastRemoteObject.
    public static class Backend extends Activatable
                                implements BackendProtocol {
        int nextMessage = 0;
        String[] messages = { "Hello, World",
                              "Goodbye, Cruel World",
                              "What's Up, Doc?" };

      public Backend(ActivationID id, MarshalledObject data)
            throws RemoteException {
            super(id, 0);
        }

        public synchronized String fetchString()
                    throws RemoteException {
            String str =  messages[nextMessage];
           nextMessage = (nextMessage + 1) % messages.length;
            return str;
        }

        // should put itself back to sleep after a while.
    }

    // We need a new proxy that uses the back-end
    // protocol.  Since this proxy implements the
    // same HelloWorldServiceInterface as the old
    // one, clients can use it transparently.
    static class HelloWorldServiceProxy2
       implements Serializable, HelloWorldServiceInterface
{
        BackendProtocol backend;

        public HelloWorldServiceProxy2() {
        }
        public HelloWorldServiceProxy2(BackendProtocol
                                                backend) {
            this.backend = backend;
        }
        public String getMessage() {
```

Listing 5–8 `HelloWorldServiceBackend.java` **(continued)**

```
            try {
                return backend.fetchString();
            } catch (RemoteException ex) {
                return "Couldn't contact back end: " +
                         ex.getMessage();
            }
        }
    }

    public HelloWorldServiceBackend() throws IOException {
    }

    protected HelloWorldServiceInterface createProxy() {
        try {
             // Create a descriptor for a new activation
             // group to run our back-end object in.
            Properties props = new Properties();
            props.put("java.security.policy", "C:\policy");
            ActivationGroupDesc group =
                     new ActivationGroupDesc(props, null);
            // Register the group and get the ID.
            ActivationGroupID gid =
                ActivationGroup.getSystem().registerGroup(
                                                 group);
            // Now create the group
            ActivationGroup.createGroup(gid, group, 0);

            // Create an activation descriptor
            // for our object
            String location = "http://myhost:8085/";
            MarshalledObject data = null;
            ActivationDesc desc =
                new ActivationDesc("corejini.chapter5." +
                       "HelloWorldServiceBackend$Backend",
                       location, data);

            // Create the 'back-end' object that will
            // implement the protocol.
            BackendProtocol backend =
              (BackendProtocol) Activatable.register(desc);
            return new HelloWorldServiceProxy2(backend);
        } catch (RemoteException ex) {
            System.err.println("Error creating backend: " +
                                 ex.getMessage());
```

Listing 5–8 `HelloWorldServiceBackend.java` **(continued)**

```
            System.exit(1);
            return null;
        } catch (ActivationException ex) {
           System.err.println("Problem with activation: " +
                                     ex.getMessage());
            ex.printStackTrace();
            System.exit(1);
            return null;
        }
    }

    // Create the service and start its lease
    // thread.
    public static void main(String args[]) {
        try {
            HelloWorldServiceBackend hws =
                     new HelloWorldServiceBackend();
            hws.leaseThread = new Thread(hws);
            hws.leaseThread.start();
        } catch (IOException ex) {
           System.out.println("Couldn't create service: " +
                                  ex.getMessage());
        }
    }
}
```

Let's walk through this code. The first thing you'll notice is that there are a few more `imports` here: These are for the RMI and activation classes that are used to build the back-end service. The overall structure of this code is similar to the previous version—the new class, `HelloWorldServiceBackend`, extends the earlier version of the service with leases.

But after this, things start to change. The new wrapper class defines three nested classes and interfaces. The first of these, `BackendProtocol`, is an interface that defines the protocol that the proxy object will use to communicate with the back-end remote object. Recall that in RMI, remote protocols are defined using Java interfaces; here you see one of those interfaces. `BackendProtocol` extends the `Remote` interface (this is what indicates that `BackendProtocol` defines a remote interface for communicating between objects in different JVMs, rather than just local communication between objects in the same JVM). It has a single method, `fetchString()`, which returns a string and may raise `RemoteException` if there is a problem with the communication.

Here I've declared this interface inside the wrapper class. This is fine, because the interface is only used for communication between the proxy and the back-end remote object—effectively, it's an implementation detail of the service that will be hidden from clients, so no one needs to see the details of the protocol.

The next thing to do is define the back-end remote object, called `Backend`. This little class is quite simple. It keeps an array of strings and an index indicating what the next string to return is. Whenever it's asked for a string, it returns the next string in the array and increments the counter. Far more important than the actual work done in this object is the boilerplate that makes it play with RMI and the activation system.

The first thing to notice is that the `Backend` object subclasses `Activatable`. Most of the "smarts" in making an object activatable live in this class. `Activatable` itself is a subclass of `java.rmi.UnicastRemoteObject`, so any object that's activatable will automatically inherit all of the code necessary to make its methods callable from remote JVMs. You'll also see that this class implements `BackendProtocol`. By implementing this interface, you're claiming that the implementation of `Backend` can be used in any remote communication that expects to speak the `BackendProtocol` protocol, which is how the proxy will communicate with the back end.

The only other important detail to note in the `Backend` class is its constructor—here you see a constructor that takes two parameters, an `ActivationID` and a `MarshalledObject`. The RMI activation system requires that activatable objects support a constructor with exactly these arguments. Whenever an object is activated, the activation system will use this constructor to re-instantiate the object. The `ActivationID` parameter uniquely identifies this particular activatable object, and should be passed through to the superclass constructor. (The other "0" argument in the call to the superclass constructor is the port number on which the newly activated object will be bound. Specifying zero here means to use any port number.) The `MarshalledObject` parameter is a way to pass "extra" data into the constructor; when you first register your activatable object with the activation system, you can provide a `MarshalledObject` that will be passed back to you whenever you're activated.

The third and final nested class defined here is a new service proxy. The old service proxy, which served us well in all of the previous examples, simply returned the "Hello, World" string on its own. Here, we're going to "swap in" a more high-powered proxy that knows how to communicate with our back-end object. Even though this proxy has a completely new implementation, it

still implements the familiar `HelloWorldServiceInterface`, so clients cannot distinguish it from the earlier proxy based on its interface.

Our new proxy is called—unimaginatively—`HelloWorldServiceProxy2`. This new proxy keeps a reference to the back-end part of its service. Whenever the proxy is registered with the lookup service, and whenever it's sent back to the client and reconstituted, this reference will be serialized and will arrive intact along with the proxy. The proxy will use this reference to communicate with the back end.

The major difference between this class and the previous proxy is in the implementation of `getMessage()`. In the old case, the method simply returned a string. In this case, the code calls `fetchString()` on the back-end object to get the string to return.

Because the proxy is now communicating with a remote object, network failures can occur. Therefore, the `getMessage()` method has to catch any `RemoteExceptions` that may be raised during the course of getting the string. If an exception occurs, there is no way of returning the "correct" string to the caller, so the code returns the text of the exception.

Core Tip: Plan on remoteness early

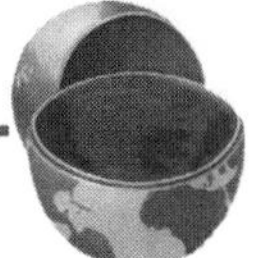

There's an interesting and subtle design error that this code raises. The old version of the proxy didn't declare any exceptions as being raised from its **`getMessage()`** *method—and, in fact, the interface that it implements says that it cannot raise any exceptions in this method.*

So in the example here we're forced into a bad situation—the only way to report the error to the client is to return it through the "normal" channels used for data: as the return value of the function. In a "real-life" service, we would not want to expect our clients to be able to distinguish strings that represent real data from strings that represent exceptional conditions.

Likewise, we could raise a nondeclared run-time exception here. But this would almost certainly cause any clients to exit immediately, as few run-time exceptions are caught by programmers.

The situation we find ourselves in here points to an important design goal for defining the interfaces for your services: Decide early whether any potential implementation of your service may involve remoteness. Even though your particular implementation may not require remote communication now, some future implementation may need it. And, because Java requires the possibility of `RemoteExceptions` *to be declared in the interface, it is extremely hard to evolve a system toward remoteness if the design didn't account for it upfront.*

Both the constructor and the main for the wrapper class are pretty much identical to the earlier versions. But the implementation of `createProxy()` is different. Recall from the very first version of `HelloWorldService` that the `ServiceItem`—the object that gets registered with lookup services—is initialized to contain the proxy object returned by `createProxy()`. In the early version, `createProxy()` simply returned the basic `HelloWorldServiceProxy`. In this new example, things get a bit more complex. Here we need to create the back-end object, make sure it's known to the activation system, and then create the proxy with a reference to this back-end object so that the proxy can call back to it. All of this is done in `createProxy()`.

The first thing this method must do is create the back-end object and register it with the activation system. Let's look at the steps this requires.

- Create a security policy that the *activation group* that runs the back-end service will use. An activation group is simply a representation for the collection of activatable objects that can share a single JVM when they are activated. The activation system may need to launch a new JVM when a new activation group is created, and so we need to tell the activation framework what security policies this JVM should have. These policies define what code executed in the JVM will be allowed to do. Here I've used the same simple policy file, seen earlier, that yields all permissions. You should not use this policy file in real applications, but it'll serve our purposes here. You'll need to change the code to point to the location of the policy file in your environment.
- Create a new activation group to run the back-end service. This entails creating a *group descriptor* for the group that contains information about the environment of any JVM that the group may create. Here, you can pass in any properties that you wish a launched JVM to have.
- Create an *activation descriptor* that describes how the back-end service should be activated, when it is needed. The activation descriptor here contains the fully qualified name of the class that will be activatable, and a URL that points to the class's code (here I've given a URL that points to the HTTP server managing the service's export directory. Make sure this URL is correctly formatted to have a trailing slash). The descriptor can also be created with a `MarshalledObject` that contains

arbitrary data that will be passed to the activatable object's constructor whenever it is activated.

- Finally, register the back-end object with the activation system. This registration doesn't actually create a back-end object. Instead, it tells the activation system *how* to create a back-end object whenever it is needed. Actual creation and activation of the object is done "lazily"—meaning that it is only done when needed.

Once we have the reference to the back-end object, we can create the proxy, initializing it with the reference to this object so that the proxy can communicate with it.

The particular steps required to make an object activatable are described in more detail in Appendix A. If you're unfamiliar with activation, you may want to take a glance there to find out more about what these particular steps do. If you're familiar with activation—or don't care about it just yet—you can treat the lines here as boilerplate that you can drop into your code.

There's one obvious extension to this code that's not shown here in the interest of brevity and clarity. The back-end object could spin off a thread that wakes up periodically to see if the back end has been used recently. If not, the thread could "pickle" the object—move it to an inactive state—so that it will not consume CPU or memory resources until it is needed again. See Appendix A on RMI and activation for details on how to deactivate a remote object.

This example shows a slightly different use of policy files than we've seen before. When we get around to running the example, we'll see that, like before, we need to pass a security policy file to the JVM. This is necessary because the code—through its superclass—sets a security manager, and so we need to use a policy that grants us more permissions than the default policy. For example, the application must be able to connect to the activation daemon via a socket, access the local filesystem, and so on. All of this is the same as we've seen in our other examples.

But here we also specify a policy file directly in the *code* of the application. Unlike the first policy file, which is passed to the JVM running the wrapper application, this policy file will be passed to any JVM created by the activation daemon to run a newly activated back-end object. The "activation group descriptor" for an activatable object specifies the security which the JVM that runs it should have.

This scenario is an example of common usage when doing activation. There is typically one security policy for the wrapper that does discovery and registry, and one for the service itself. And, although I've used the same policy file for both here, generally these two objects will have very different security requirements, and hence different policy files.

If you look back to the instructions in Chapter 1 on how to start Sun's reference implementation of the lookup service, reggie, you'll see an example of this. Reggie is started with a policy file passed via a property to the JVM, and a separate policy file passed as an argument to reggie itself, used to set security in JVMs launched from the activation daemon.

The use of security files may be unfamiliar to you. Unlike JDK1.1 and earlier, in which only applets ran in any type of secure context, in Java 2 any application can also run in a secure setting. Java 2 introduced this notion of security policies that define what privileges a piece of code has—that is, what it is allowed to do and what it is not allowed to do. By default, most applications run with full privileges in Java 2: They can access any file and connect to any host on the network. But applications that run with a security manager have a more restricted set of operations available to them. Policy files provide a flexible way to selectively allow code to perform particular operations.

Core Tip: Security in Java 2 is incredibly flexible

Covering all the ins and outs of security in Java 2 is beyond the scope of this book. In fact, it could easily be material for an entire book on its own.

Our examples in this book will only scratch the surface of what you can do with Java 2 security—the new security model allows you to grant fine-grained privileges to code depending not only on where it was loaded from, but also who signed it.

If you're interested in learning more about Java 2 security, you should definitely consider Just Java 1.2, *by Peter van der Linden. This book has an entire chapter devoted to Java 2 security, and specifically covers such topics as policy files and digitally signing code.*

For a more terse introduction to the subject, you can also look at the JavaSoft Web site for the security tutorial:

```
http://java.sun.com/docs/books/tutorial/security1.2/
index.html
```

Note that the wrapper application here has even more work to do than it did before. Not only does it have to find lookup services, register proxies, and maintain leases, it also has to handle telling the activation system about our new back-end object.

Compiling and Running the Example

Compiling this example is no different than compiling any of the previous examples. Before you compile, make sure that you've edited the code to point to the location of a policy file and the code for the activatable class—in the example here, I've used the Windows pathname for the policy file that I've been using in all of these examples (`C:\policy`). If you're on Solaris or another system, you should change this. Likewise, the URL that specifies where the code for the service can be downloaded from uses `myhost`, which should be changed to whatever the hostname is on which the service's HTTP server is running.

Compiling

Next, compile the Java source file, putting the resulting code into the service's implementation code directory. All the class files resulting from the compilation will be used by the service, and should go in the service's implementation directory. Additionally, the new proxy defined by this service needs to reside in the service's directory of exportable, downloadable code so that it can be fetched by lookup services and clients. So, after compilation, copy the class file for the proxy out to the export directory.

On Windows:

```
javac -classpath C:\jini1_0\lib\jini-core.jar;
                         C:\jini1_0\lib\jini-ext.jar;
                         C:\jini1_0\lib\sun-util.jar;
                         C:\service
  -d C:\service
  C:\files\corejini\chapter5\HelloWorldServiceBackend.java

cd C:\service\corejini\chapter5
copy
     HelloWorldServiceBackend$HelloWorldServiceProxy2.class
     C:\service-dl
```

On Solaris:

```
javac -classpath /files/jini1_0/lib/jini-core.jar:
                         /files/jini1_0/lib/jini-ext.jar:
                         /files/jini1_0/lib/sun-util.jar:
                         /files/service
  -d /files/service
  /files/corejini/chapter5/HelloWorldServiceBackend.java
```

```
cd /files/service/corejini/chapter5
cp HelloWorldServiceBackend$HelloWorldServiceProxy2.class
      /files/service-dl
```

Generating the RMI Stubs

The activatable service uses a nested class, `Backend`, that implements the remote protocol that the proxy will talk to. Since the methods on this nested class will be callable remotely, you need to invoke the RMI stubs compiler (`rmic`) on it to generate the class file for the stubs that callers will use to talk to the back-end object. Since the stubs file will be downloaded to clients as needed, you'll have to tell `rmic` to put its output in the service's downloadable code directory.

Remember the **Core Alert** from the event example previously: as of JDK1.2 there is a bug in `rmic` that requires you to pass the core Java libraries in `rt.jar` via the `-classpath` argument.

On Windows: Make sure you use the correct path to `rt.jar`:

```
rmic -classpath C:\jdk1.2\jre\lib\rt.jar;
                           C:\jini1_0\lib\jini-core.jar;
                           C:\jini1_0\lib\jini-ext.jar;
                           C:\jini1_0\lib\sun-util.jar;
                           C:\service
       -d C:\service-dl
corejini.chapter5.HelloWorldServiceBackend.Backend
```

On Solaris: Make sure you use the correct path to `rt.jar`:

```
rmic -classpath /usr/java1.2/jre/lib/rt.jar:
                           /files/jini1_0/lib/jini-core.jar:
                           /files/jini1_0/lib/jini-ext.jar:
                           /files/jini1_0/lib/sun-util.jar:
                           /files/service
       -d /files/service-dl
corejini.chapter5.HelloWorldServiceBackend.Backend
```

After running `rmic`, if you look in the service's export directory you should see the file:

```
HelloWorldServiceBackend$Backend_Stub.class
```

Now that the service's code is in the implementation directory, and the necessary class files are in the export directory, we're ready to run!

Running

First, since the service is activatable, make sure you're running the activation daemon, rmid, on the system on which the service's back end will run. If you're developing on the same machine that you're running a Jini lookup service on, then there's no need to start a separate rmid—your service and the lookup service can "share" a single instance of rmid.

Next, you can start the service just as before. For the client, you can "reuse" any of the clients we've used before—since the new service simply provides a reimplementation of *exactly* the same interface as before, the clients are none the wiser. This is the power of Jini: you can swap particular implementations of a service in-and-out at run time, and clients will simply use whichever one they find that meets their requirements.

Let's look at how to run the service and the client. Here I'm reusing the leasing client from the previous example. Note that since this version of the service has its own rmi stub in the service-dl directory, you'll have to include this directory in the services classpath so that it can find and use its stub at runtime.

On Windows:

```
java -cp C:\jini\lib\jini-core.jar;
                   C:\jini1_0\lib\jini-ext.jar;
                   C:\jini1_0\lib\sun-util.jar;
                   C:\service;
                   C:\service-dl
             -Djava.rmi.server.codebase=http://myhost:8085/
             -Djava.security.policy=C:\policy
       corejini.chapter5.HelloWorldServiceBackend

java -cp C:\jini1_0\lib\jini-core.jar;
                   C:\jini1_0\lib\jini-ext.jar;
                   C:\jini1_0\lib\sun-util.jar;
                   C:\client;
                   C:\client-dl
             -Djava.rmi.server.codebase=http://myhost:8086/
             -Djava.security.policy=C:\policy
       corejini.chapter5.HelloWorldClientWithLeases
```

On Solaris:

```
java -cp /files/jini1_0/lib/jini-core.jar:
                   /files/jini1_0/lib/jini-ext.jar:
                   /files/jini1_0/lib/sun-util.jar:
```

```
                  /files/service:
                  /files/service-dl
            -Djava.rmi.server.codebase=http://myhost:8085/
            -Djava.security.policy=/files/policy
      corejini.chapter5.HelloWorldServiceBackend

java -cp /files/jini1_0/lib/jini-core.jar:
                  /files/jini1_0/lib/jini-ext.jar:
                  /files/jini1_0/lib/sun-util.jar:
                  /files/client:
                  /files/service-dl
            -Djava.rmi.server.codebase=http://myhost:8086/
            -Djava.security.policy=/files/policy
      corejini.chapter5.HelloWorldClientWithLeases
```

Since the service's proxy is communicating with a back-end process, you'll actually get different results each time you run the client! Even if you start multiple clients at the same time, each will download a separate proxy for the service. Each of these proxy objects will come with the RMI code needed to communicate with the back-end process, which actually determines which string to return.

Here's a sample run:

From the service: This output is the same as before.

```
discovered a lookup service!
Set serviceID to e91bb61d-b18e-447e-8935-adfd8bd741f5
```

From the client: Let's run the service four times in a row and see what happens:

```
Got matching service.
Its message is: Hello, world!

Got a matching service.
Its message is: Goodbye, Cruel World

Got a matching service.
Its message is: What's Up, Doc?

Got matching service.
Its message is: Hello, world!
```

The first time the proxy is invoked, the activation system will activate the `Backend` implementation. And each time the proxy's `getMessage()` method is called, it goes over the wire to the back-end object to fetch the next string.

Here you can see the back-end portion of the service cycling through the strings it provides. Even if the proxies are running in clients on different machines, they will all communicate with the single back-end process to get the string to display. This is a classic—albeit simple—example of using a back-end process as a "choke point" to synchronize multiple clients.

What's Next?

We've seen how to create simple Jini clients and services that do all of the basics—lookup and discovery, leasing and event registration, and even activation. The goal of this chapter was to get your hands dirty by working with the various Jini facilities at a very low level. But while you've seen all of the basics here, this isn't the end-all and be-all of building with Jini. Our services don't do a very good job of remembering their service IDs, and they have no way for users or administrators to interact with them. For example, I cannot tell the `HelloWorldService` that I'd like it to register itself with a lookup service that's not on the local network.

In future chapters, we'll look at convenience APIs that make many of the chores we did "by hand" in this chapter easier. These same APIs make services better behaved by taking over many of the odd details that we ignored here. By now, though, you should have a good grounding in what's going on "behind the scenes" whenever a Jini service or client runs.

In Chapter 6, we'll look in depth at one of the most important topics in Jini: the discovery process.

IN DEPTH: DISCOVERY

Topics in This Chapter

- Multicast and unicast discovery protocols
- How IP multicast works
- Using the LookupDiscovery and LookupLocator classes
- Discovery packet formats

Chapter 6

In this chapter, we'll look in depth at the protocols and APIs used to locate lookup services. The discovery protocols are at the core of Jini, and are the mechanism by which Jini services and applications bootstrap themselves into Jini communities when they start up. Discovery also provides a means for services that may have been separated from the network to reestablish their participation when they are once again in communication with the rest of their communities.

This chapter covers discovery in brutal detail. If you're only interested in building applications and services, then you probably only care about the "higher level" details of discovery—how discovery works and what APIs are available to control it. This chapter covers these aspects of discovery upfront. The first two sections provide an overview of the goals and methods of discovery, while the third section discusses how to use discovery in applications via the various class libraries that Jini provides.

Some of you will want to get under the hood and get your hands dirty, though. This may be because you are interested in how discovery works, or even because you want to build your own lookup service that implements discovery. So later in this chapter we'll look at what the convenient APIs provided by Jini are actually *doing* when you're finding lookup services, and how the various discovery protocols are structured. We'll even look at the raw, on-the-wire formats of the discovery protocols, which you'll need if you're implementing discovery from scratch.

Much of the material in this chapter is equally applicable whether you're building clients or services: The discovery protocols are used by both. There are a number of places, however, where services interact with discovery in particular ways unique to them. I'll highlight those points throughout the text via **Core Notes**.

What's Discovery?

You saw a quick overview of discovery in Chapter 3. Basically, discovery is the process by which Jini applications find the lookup services that serve their communities. A Jini community is a group of services that are available—both to each other and to consuming applications—on the network. All of the members of a community are available and visible to all other members of that community, and to any application that "looks" at that community.

The end result of the discovery process is that an interested party knows about a set of lookup services, and acquires service proxies for those services so that it can interact with them using whatever protocols they speak. Recall that lookup services are accessed through their proxies, just like any other Jini service. But whereas "normal" proxies are retrieved by talking to a lookup service, retrieving the proxies for a lookup service is done via discovery—it's how Jini bootstraps itself. And, of course, like any other service proxy, the actual protocol that the proxy uses to speak to the lookup service is hidden from the proxy's user.

The discovery process is designed so that, by default and without any special knowledge of what communities may exist, a service that starts up will find and register itself with the "nearby" lookup services. The discovery protocol's notion of "nearness" is based on network topology—services that are on the same or a closely connected network will, by default, share the same lookup services. What nearness means for a particular network will largely depend on how that network was configured by its administrator. I'll talk more about network nearness a bit later in this chapter.

The use of network nearness doesn't, however, preclude other forms of nearness, possibly with their own future discovery protocols to support them. For example, a device with an infrared transceiver may join communities based on their physical proximity. Such a device could use a special discovery protocol to find and join communities within IR range. These IR-located communities may or may not be the same, or overlap with, the network-based communities.

Groups Partition the Community Namespace

Typically, one or more lookup services will exist on a subnet. Each of these lookup services will serve a set of "groups," which are essentially names for their communities. Groups might be created for organizational entities within a company ("engineering" or "marketing"), or for physical distinctions that might not be reflected in the network topology ("first floor" or "commons area"), or for deployment distinctions ("production" versus "experimental"). Figure 6–1 shows how a group of lookup services may support a number of groups, and how those groups may be "overlapped" across lookup services. Here we see three groups, called "Engineering," "Marketing," and "Accounting." The engineering and marketing groups share a lookup service that is a member of both of these groups. Marketing and accounting also have their own individual lookup services that are members of only those groups. You can see here that a given group may be supported by multiple lookup services (as in the case of marketing), and that a lookup service can support multiple groups (as in the one supporting both engineering and marketing here).

When a service starts, it may be configured to search out and join certain groups that it finds on its subnet—such a service would either have some persistent state that recorded the groups it should join, or might have a user interface by which an actual human tells it which groups it should become a part of.

In most cases, however, services and applications will always join the *default* group. This is an unnamed, public group that will contain most of the services in a Jini community.

Types of Discovery

Broadly, there are two basic forms of discovery. One form is used to support "serendipitous" interaction between services and lookup services. Serendipitous interaction means that the lookup services and Jini services find each other without any previous configuration or advance knowledge of one another; they discover one another without being explicitly told to search for one another.

This form of discovery is used both when a service starts and needs to find all the lookup services that may (or may not) be running in its vicinity. It's also used when a lookup service starts and needs to announce its presence to any Jini services that may (or may not) be running, in case they wish to register themselves with all lookup services. These two sorts of discovery—discovery that originates from the joining service, versus discovery that originates from

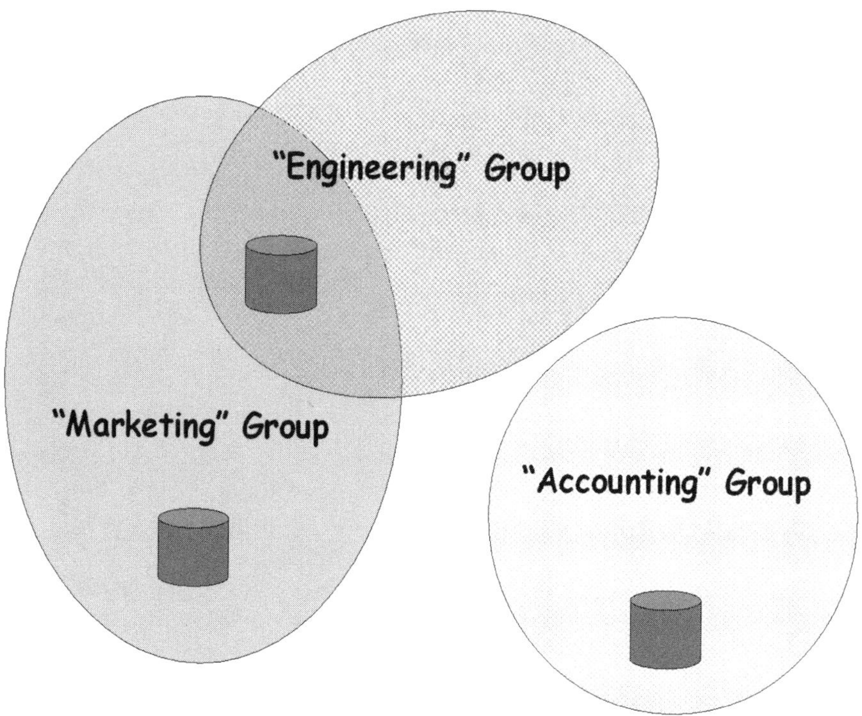

Figure 6–1 Multiple lookup services supporting multiple groups

the lookup service—actually use different but similar protocols. We'll look at these protocols in this chapter.

The second form of discovery is used to "hard wire" a Jini service to a lookup service. Unlike the serendipitous forms of discovery, where services find any and all lookup services in their vicinity, this "direct" form of discovery allows services to contact particular lookup services that they may know about ahead of time. This form of discovery uses its own protocol that is distinct from the serendipitous forms of discovery, and has a URL-based naming scheme for specifying lookup services.

Together, these three protocols—two serendipitous and one direct—form the core of discovery.

Requirements for Discovery

The Jini discovery mechanism has a number of important requirements that are embodied in the individual protocols.

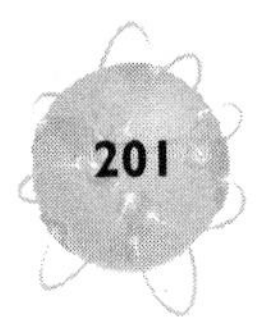

- Discovery should be flexible enough to support a range of community topologies.
- Discovery should promote easy recovery from network partitions and machine failures.
- Discovery should be lightweight enough that it can easily be run on systems with very limited computational ability.

Flexibility comes from the variety of protocols used in discovery, and the ways in which they are applied. The discovery protocols allow three different types of interaction.

- Service-initiated requests for lookup services.
- Lookup service-initiated announcements to other services.
- Direct pairings between lookup services and other Jini services.

The first two support communities that naturally divide themselves on network boundaries. The last supports arbitrary connectivity, where Jini services may register themselves with lookup services across the hallway or across the world.

Recovery is largely handled by the two serendipitous protocols. If a Jini service disconnects from the network and then reconnects, it can send out a request for all of the nearby lookup services to rebuild its sense of the community it is a part of. When a lookup service starts, or reattaches to the network after an absence, it can announce its presence, allowing services to take advantage of its facilities.

The protocols themselves, as we shall see, are very lightweight. They can be run on very limited systems with only a minimal network stack and constrained computing horsepower.

An Overview of Discovery

Let's look at how discovery works in practice. Each of the three discovery protocols is designed to be used in different scenarios, so we'll look at each in turn. But first, we should talk about an important technology that is the basis for two of the discovery protocols: IP multicast. The next section provides a background introduction to this technology.

An IP Multicast Primer

Both of the serendipitous discovery protocols use the IP (Internet Protocol) multicast facility. Multicast is a way to send one message that may be received by any number of parties. It is not broadcast, because it does not go to every party on the network; it only goes to those who are explicitly listening for it. And it is not unicast, which would entail sending a separate message to each intended recipient, and would require that the sender know the IP addresses of each recipient ahead of time. Multicast makes efficient use of network resources, because a message sent to multiple receivers is transmitted as a single message wherever possible. (Of course, if the parties are on two completely different networks, at some point the multicast routers will have to copy the message to reach the recipients on the second network.)

The form of multicast used by Jini is based on the UDP/IP protocol. UDP provides a connectionless, unreliable transport. This means that UDP provides no guarantees that a packet sent will actually arrive, and it provides no guarantees about the order in which a series of packets will arrive. These properties are the same as in normal, unicast UDP. (It should be noted, though, that UDP is pretty reliable in practice.)

In UDP multicast, a range of special IP addresses are used as *multicast groups*. Interested parties can effectively "join" a group by listening for messages sent to that IP address. Any message sent to the address will be received by all parties listening to it.

Each message sent via multicast has a *scope* associated with it, which is used to limit the "distance" the message will travel. The benefit of scoping is that an IP address used as a multicast group for one set of hosts may be invisible to another set of hosts using the same IP address, if the hosts are far enough away and their messages are scoped so that they do not reach each other. In this way, scoping effectively limits the visibility of multicast groups, and allows the addresses used for multicast to be reused many times across the Internet. Parties don't have to agree on which multicast addresses will be "owned" by which organizations. (This situation is in contrast to the domain naming system used to associate host names with IP addresses. Because these addresses are visible globally across the network, they must be registered and owned by a centralized facility.)

Scoping also allows efficiency in routing. If a sender sends a message to a multicast address, it may not know ahead of time if anyone has joined that group (that is, is listening on that address). If the routers had to send the message into every nook and cranny of the Internet, looking for interested recipients, the Internet would be swamped in short order. Instead, a sender can set the scope of its messages, which would cause the routing infrastructure of the Internet to only let the message go so far in its search for recipients.

In UDP multicast, the scope of a message is set by specifying the value of the IP "Time-to-Live" (TTL) parameter. The TTL of a message specifies how many "hops" it will take. When the message is routed through the network, every router that it crosses increments its hop count. Once the hop count exceeds the TTL parameter, the message is dropped. Setting the TTL limits the range of multicast messages. A TTL of 1 will cause the message to only reach machines on the same network segment; longer TTLs can cause a message to span the entire Internet. TTLs effectively let you set a "radius" within which any interested parties will hear your message.

Network administrators can also control message scope. Routers are configured with settings that cause them to drop packets beyond a certain configured radius, to prevent packet storms that can be caused by abusive senders. So the *particular* notion of what constitutes the "nearness" of some host on the network depends largely on the configuration of the network.

Service-Initiated Discovery

When a new service starts and wishes to join the community in its vicinity, it uses the *multicast request protocol*. This protocol is used to find all of the nearby lookup services that may be running. As its name implies, this protocol uses IP multicast to find lookup services. The service sends a multicast message to a well-known multicast address; this address is agreed upon ahead of time by all the Jini lookup services and all other services, and the message is scoped so that it will only travel a set distance. This is how a Jini service finds the lookup services nearby—the scoping limits the discovery request so that it only reaches lookup services that might be listening on a multicast address and are running on the same subnet as the service.

Once a lookup service receives a multicast discovery request, it replies by connecting directly to the requesting service and sending a unicast (point-to-point) message. This message contains the proxy object that the service can use to contact the lookup service. Depending on network latencies and the speeds of the machines running the lookup services, these answer messages may "trickle in" over a short period of time.

Lookup Service-Initiated Discovery

Lookup services periodically announce their existence using the *multicast announcement protocol*. This protocol works much the same as the multicast request protocol, only it is initiated by the lookup services themselves.

In multicast announcement, interested parties on the network listen on a well-known multicast address for announcements about the existence of lookup services. Periodically, all lookup services send a multicast message to this address; the message is scoped so that it only reaches interested parties on the local area network.

Once an interested party has received an announcement of the existence of a lookup service, it can then ask the lookup service for its service proxy. It contacts the lookup service using a direct unicast connection, and the lookup service replies with the proxy object that the client can use to communicate with it.

You may be wondering why the lookup service doesn't just multicast out its proxy object when it announces its presence. This would allow any interested recipients to immediately get the proxy, without requiring them to do a separate round-trip message to fetch it. There are two reasons Jini does not take this approach. The first is that multicast announcements are extremely small—they fit inside a single network packet. Because most announcements are likely to go unused except when a lookup service is just starting or reconnecting to the network, keeping the message size as small as possible can greatly cut down on network traffic. But a second, even more severe, reason is that multicast messages *must* be kept to a reasonable size. The multicast protocol itself dictates a maximum packet size, which is fairly small. Because serialized proxy objects can be arbitrarily large, there is no way to guarantee that they'll fit within the bounds of a multicast message. We'll see later in this chapter why multicast imposes this size restriction.

"Direct" Discovery

In addition to listening on a multicast address for multicast discovery requests from services, each lookup service also listens on a normal, unicast address. This protocol is called the *unicast discovery protocol*. Any service can connect directly to this address to access the lookup service. In this sense, the protocol isn't so much a "discovery" protocol, as a way to contact an already known lookup service in order to download its service proxy. The client sends a message to the lookup service, which replies with its service proxy.

Unicast discovery is based on a URL naming scheme, where lookup services are named using URLs of the form `jini://turbodog.parc.xerox.com:4160/foobar`. The protocol name, `jini`, specifies that the URL represents a Jini lookup service. The next component is the hostname, in this case `turbodog.parc.xerox.com`. The next part, containing the colon and the number is optional—if present, it represents the port number on which the lookup service is listening. Port number 4160 is the default port for Jini lookup.[1] The last part, `/foobar` in this case, while a legal component of a URL, is generally not used in Jini and should not be a part of a Jini URL specification. Jini lookup services are typically not searchable by name, so the part of the URL trailing the host and port specification is superfluous.

Core Note: The service "join" protocol adds more requirements

This chapter just addresses the core mechanisms of discovery; most of these mechanisms are equally valid whether your code is providing a service or simply consuming services that it finds on the network.

There are, however, a few guidelines and conventions that service builders must follow. These guidelines dictate what "well-behaved" services will do, and result in a bit of extra work for services. While much of the extra work that services must do happens after discovery—registering with the lookup service, maintaining leases, and so on—some of the task of being a service also affects how the service interacts with discovery.

Collectively these guidelines are called the service "join" protocol, because they control how services join communities.

These guidelines dictate how services should try to reconnect to lookup services that have disappeared from the network, what services should do if they are specifically configured with unicast URLs to connect to, and so on.

All the details of being a "well-behaved" service are grouped together in Chapter 12. I'll wait until there to cover the join protocol, because join involves details of lookup services and persistence that we haven't covered yet. There, we'll see the particular conventions that govern how services use discovery; in this chapter, we'll look only at the mechanisms that control what discovery does.

---

1. The number 4160 is represented in hexadecimal as 0xCAFEBABE, which also happens to be the "magic number" that identifies Java class files.

Using Discovery in Applications

As you saw in Chapter 5, the basic discovery APIs are quite simple. The discovery API is based on the listener paradigm, common throughout Java. This asynchronous API provides a common model for both of the serendipitous forms of discovery—multicast request and multicast announce. There is a separate API for the direct, unicast form of discovery, though, which we haven't seen yet.

Let's look first at the most common discovery interfaces, those that help out with the multicast protocols.

DiscoveryListeners Are Informed of Discoveries

The basic interface for Jini-aware applications that need to work with discovery is called `DiscoveryListener`. This is a very simple Java interface with only two methods.

```
package net.jini.discovery;

import java.util.EventListener;

public interface DiscoveryListener extends EventListener {
      public void discovered(DiscoveryEvent ev);
      public void discarded(DiscoveryEvent ev);
}
```

Any object that needs to find lookup services through the serendipitous protocols must implement this interface. The first method, `discovered()`, will be called whenever a new lookup service is found via the discovery protocols. The Jini class libraries that implement the discovery protocols will invoke the method "automatically" when necessary.

The second, `discarded()`, is a bit more interesting. This method will be called when a previously found lookup service is no longer relevant. This may happen, for example, when the set of groups you are interested in changes. Any previously found lookup services that do not support one of the new groups will be discarded.

But most often, this method is called whenever problems develop when communicating with a lookup service. If you've implemented a program that communicates with a lookup service, and you begin getting `RemoteExceptions` whenever you try to talk with that lookup service, then chances are that it's crashed or is unreachable. In such a case you can actually tell the discovery machinery to "undiscover" an already discovered lookup service (this is done through a method called `discard()` on the `LookupDiscovery` class that we'll see in a bit). When this happens, the Jini class libraries in your program will call out to the `discarded()` method so that the `DiscoveryListener` can clean up any state to reflect the fact that a lookup service has been discarded.

Many beginning Jini programmers believe that the `discarded()` method is somehow called automatically whenever a lookup service crashes. This isn't the case. Once a lookup service has been found, there is no ongoing communication with it—especially no post mortem communication. Your code is responsible for discarding lookup services that you detect are misbehaving; the `discarded()` method here will be called by the Jini discovery machinery in response to that.

DiscoveryEvents Encapsulate Discovery Information

You'll notice that both `discovered()` and `discarded()` take an instance of `DiscoveryEvent`. Let's look at the relevant parts of that class now.

```
package net.jini.discovery;

import java.util.EventObject;

public class DiscoveryEvent extends EventObject {
      // ... some methods elided ...
      public ServiceRegistrar[] getRegistrars();
}
```

Some of the methods in this class, like the constructor, are not shown here because they will not be used by Jini applications directly (only the lookup service and the internals of the Jini libraries will create new `Discovery-Events`, for example). For receivers of these events, there is only one method of interest—`getRegistrars()`. This method returns an array of `Service-Registrar` instances. Each of these is a service proxy that can be used to talk to a particular lookup service, somewhere on the network. The underlying Jini libraries may batch together multiple `ServiceRegistrars` into one event, which is why an array of `ServiceRegistrars` is returned here.

The `DiscoveryEvent` class extends the `EventObject` class, and therefore inherits a number of methods from it. The only one of importance is `get-Source()`, which returns the instance of `LookupDiscovery` that resulted in

this event being delivered. LookupDiscovery is the basic interface for initiating and controlling the discovery process, and we'll look at it next.

Using LookupDiscovery to Control Multicast Discovery

So far, we've only seen the interfaces used for notifying interested parties about the existence of lookup services—not the mechanics of how to start discovery. Let's look at the LookupDiscovery class to see how to do that.

```
package net.jini.discovery;

public class LookupDiscovery {
      public static final String[] ALL_GROUPS = null;
      public static final String[] NO_GROUPS =
                                new String[0];

      public LookupDiscovery(String[] grps)
                                throws IOException;
      public void addDiscoveryListener(DiscoveryListener l);
      public void removeDiscoveryListener(DiscoveryListener
                                                      l);
      public void discard(ServiceRegistrar reg);
      public String[] getGroups();
      public void setGroups(String[] grps)
                                throws IOException;
      public void addGroups(String[] grps)
                                throws IOException;
      public void removeGroups(String[] grps);
      public void terminate();
}
```

The LookupDiscovery class has methods to start and control the discovery process for an application or service. Most programs that need to do discovery will create one instance of this class by passing an array of the group names they are interested in to the constructor. Passing null to the constructor signifies that *all* groups are considered relevant and should be found. Passing an empty (zero-length) array to the constructor indicates that no groups should be discovered (this can be changed later by adding groups to the set of groups that this LookupDiscovery instance is searching for). The class provides the constants ALL_GROUPS and NO_GROUPS to indicate these special-case values.

Most users of `LookupDiscovery` will pass an array containing a single item, the empty string, to the constructor. This value indicates a default "public" group that is likely to exist on every network.

When a `LookupDiscovery` instance is created, the discovery process begins (unless the `NO_GROUPS` flag is used). The instance begins by performing multicast request to ask for all the lookup services already running in the local area. After a while, the code automatically goes into a mode where it waits for announcement messages.

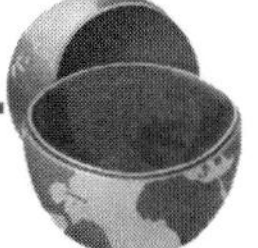

Core Note: Automatic switching between discovery modes

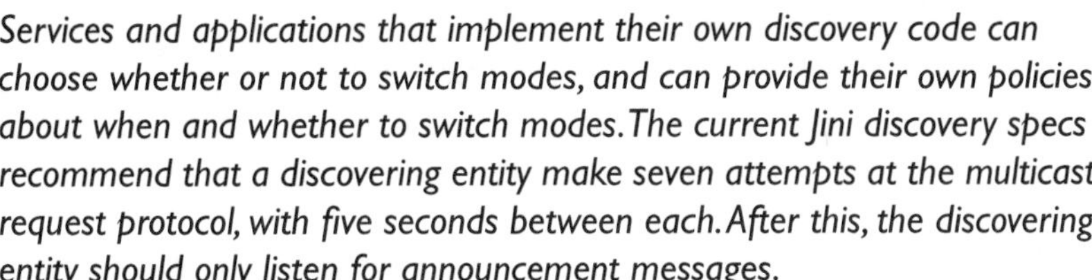

Services and applications that implement their own discovery code can choose whether or not to switch modes, and can provide their own policies about when and whether to switch modes. The current Jini discovery specs recommend that a discovering entity make seven attempts at the multicast request protocol, with five seconds between each. After this, the discovering entity should only listen for announcement messages.

If the set of groups that the discoverer is interested in changes, it may begin multicast request again.

The `LookupDiscovery` *class handles all of this for you, so you don't have to worry about it if you're using the Jini class libraries for discovery.*

If the `LookupDiscovery` instance encounters problems starting the discovery protocols during its construction, it will raise an `IOException`.

Whenever a new lookup service is found either through an answer to a multicast request or through a multicast announcement, the `LookupDiscovery` calls out to all its registered listeners. To add or remove listeners to or from this set, you can call `addDiscoveryListener()` or `removeDiscoveryListener()`, respectively. The `LookupDiscovery` class remembers all the lookup services it has found to date and, when a new listener is added, will report all the previously found lookup services to it. By batching up previous discoveries and sending them to listeners who may be added later on, the `LookupDiscovery` class avoids any potential race condition where discovery is started and a lookup service is found before any listeners have been registered.

Calling the `discard()` method causes the `LookupDiscovery` instance to "forget" about a previously seen lookup service, which allows it to be discovered again. When a lookup service is discarded, all of the registered listeners will have their `discarded()` methods called and, if the service is subsequently re-discovered, their `discovered()` methods will be invoked. Discarding is primarily a way for users of the `LookupDiscovery` class to remove lookup services that are known to be dead, from the set of active services.

Be sure to note the difference between the `discard()` method on `LookupDiscovery` and the `discarded()` method on `DiscoveryListener`. Your service is responsible for calling `discard()` and, because of that call, `LookupDiscover` calls the `discarded()` method on the listener. You don't call `discarded()` to drop a lookup service; that method is invoked "automatically" for you when a lookup service is dropped via `discard()`.

The set of groups that the `LookupDiscovery` instance attempts to discover is managed by a handful of methods. The `setGroups()` method explicitly sets the groups for discovery, overwriting any existing groups. The special constants `ALL_GROUPS` and `NO_GROUPS` work here in the same way they do in the constructor—so passing in a null causes all groups to be searched for, and passing in an empty array causes no groups to be searched for. If the set of groups grows, then the `LookupDiscovery` instance will initiate a new round of multicast requests to find lookup services supporting the new groups.

Addition and deletion of individual groups can be done via `addGroups()` and `removeGroups()`. If groups are dropped from the active search set, either through `setGroups()` or `removeGroups()`, then this may cause already found lookup services to become "uninteresting"—if a lookup service is no longer a member of any of the groups being searched for, then it will be discarded from the set of active lookup services. When this happens, all listeners will have their `discarded()` methods invoked.

Because both `setGroups()` and `addGroups()` may cause the multicast request protocol to begin again, these methods may raise `IOException` if they encounter problems starting the protocol.

The `getGroups()` method returns the current set of groups being searched for, and may return `ALL_GROUPS` or `NO_GROUPS`; in the case of `NO_GROUPS`, the value returned by `getGroups()` is actually the *same* `NO_GROUPS` member in the class, so the return value can be tested against `LookupDiscovery.NO_GROUPS` by using the `==` operator.

Calling `terminate()` ends the discovery process. When this method is called, no more `DiscoveryEvents` will be sent to any already registered listeners, although new listeners added after the call to `terminate()` will be notified of all of the lookup services found prior to the call to `terminate()`. Calling `terminate()` stops the process of discovery irreversibly for the particular instance of `LookupDiscovery` that you call it on—you can never restart discovery again without creating a new `LookupDiscovery`. Trying to change the state of the instance via `setGroups()`, `addGroups()`, or `removeGroups()` after termination will cause an `IllegalStateException` to be raised.

Core Note: Dealing with catastrophic failure

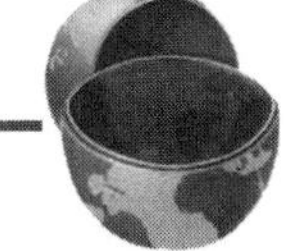

The volume of network traffic required for one service to participate in discovery is relatively small. But imagine a situation where a whole network of machines is coming back up after a power failure or other catastrophic failure that causes an entire network of machines to crash. Hundreds, perhaps thousands, of services would begin at about the same time and begin pummeling their lookup services with multicast requests. In addition to swamping the network with multicast traffic, they will also swamp the lookup services and the machines hosting them.

This situation is called a packet storm, and it is a very real consequence of having network services that need to interact with each other upon start up. A packet storm can easily bring an entire network to its knees and even cause machines running some less-than-robust operating systems to simply crash. Clearly, this is a situation we want to avoid.

Therefore, a well-behaved Jini service should wait for some random period of time before initiating a multicast request. This delay will help to reduce the odds that enough services will start at once to create packet storms and flood the network. This safeguard can help a Jini network restart itself safely after a catastrophic failure. While a service can wait for a random time within any range it desires, a range of 0 to 15 seconds is probably fine.

An Example

Let's look at a short example of how to use multicast discovery in applications, via the `LookupDiscovery` class. This program starts up and participates in both of the multicast discovery protocols—request and announcement—until you hit the return key to stop it. It will print out details about each lookup service that it can find on your local network.

Obviously, to get the most out of this application, you need to be running a lookup service somewhere on your network! If you haven't followed the instructions in Chapter 1 for installing and running the core Jini services, now would be a good time to do that. Without a lookup service on your network, the program in Listing 6–1 will simply sit around doing nothing.

Listing 6–1 `DiscoveryExample.java`

```
package corejini.chapter6;

import net.jini.discovery.DiscoveryListener;
import net.jini.discovery.DiscoveryEvent;
import net.jini.discovery.LookupDiscovery;
import net.jini.core.lookup.ServiceRegistrar;
import java.rmi.RemoteException;
import java.rmi.RMISecurityManager;
import java.io.IOException;

public class DiscoveryExample {
    protected LookupDiscovery disco = null;
    protected Listener listener = null;
    protected String[] groups;

    class Listener implements DiscoveryListener {
        public void discovered(DiscoveryEvent ev) {
            ServiceRegistrar[] regs = ev.getRegistrars();

            for (int i=0 ; i<regs.length ; i++) {
                try {
                    System.out.println("Discovered: ");
                    System.out.println("\tURL:     " +
                                 getURL(regs[i]));
                    System.out.println("\tID:      " +
                                 regs[i].getServiceID());
                    System.out.println("\tGroups: " +
                                 getGroups(regs[i]));
                } catch (RemoteException ex) {
                     System.err.println("Error: " +
                                      ex.getMessage());
                     disco.discard(regs[i]);
                }
            }
        }

        public void discarded(DiscoveryEvent ev) {
            ServiceRegistrar[] regs = ev.getRegistrars();
            for (int i=0 ; i<regs.length ; i++) {
                try {
                    System.out.println("Discarded: ");
                    System.out.println("\tURL:     " +
                                      getURL(regs[i]));
```

Listing 6–1 `DiscoveryExample.java` **(continued)**

```
                } catch (RemoteException ex) {
                    System.err.println("Error: " +
                                    ex.getMessage());
                }
            }
        }
    }

    public DiscoveryExample(String[] groups) {
        this.groups = groups;
    }

    public static String getURL(ServiceRegistrar reg)
         throws RemoteException {
        return reg.getLocator().toString();
    }

    public static String getGroups(ServiceRegistrar reg)
         throws RemoteException {
        String[] groups = reg.getGroups();

        if (groups.length == 0) {
            return "<none>";
        }

        StringBuffer buf = new StringBuffer();
        for (int i=0 ; i<groups.length ; i++) {
            if (groups[i] == null) {
                buf.append("NULL ");
            } else if (groups[i].equals("")) {
                buf.append("PUBLIC ");
            } else {
                buf.append(groups[i]);
            }
        }
        return buf.toString();
    }

    synchronized void startDiscovery() throws IOException {
        if (disco == null) {
        listener = new Listener();
            disco = new LookupDiscovery(groups);
            disco.addDiscoveryListener(listener);
        }
    }
```

Listing 6–1 `DiscoveryExample.java` (continued)

```
    synchronized void stopDiscovery() throws IOException {
        if (disco != null) {
            disco.removeDiscoveryListener(listener);
            disco.setGroups(LookupDiscovery.NO_GROUPS);
            disco = null;
        }
    }

    public static void main(String[] args) {
        String[] groups;
        int index = 0;

        if (System.getSecurityManager() == null) {
            System.setSecurityManager(
                    new RMISecurityManager());
        }

        if (args.length == 0) {
            groups = LookupDiscovery.ALL_GROUPS;
        } else {
            groups = new String[args.length];
        }

        for (int i=0 ; i<args.length ; i++) {
            if (args[i].equals("all")) {
                groups = LookupDiscovery.ALL_GROUPS;
                break;
            } else if (args[i].equals("none")) {
                groups = LookupDiscovery.NO_GROUPS;
                break;
            } else if (args[i].equals("public")) {
                groups[index++] = "";
            } else {
                groups[index++] = args[i];
            }
        }

        try {
            DiscoveryExample ex =
                 new DiscoveryExample(groups);
            ex.startDiscovery();

            System.out.println("Hit return to terminate " +
                               "discovery.");
```

Listing 6–1 `DiscoveryExample.java` **(continued)**

```
            while (((char) System.in.read()) != '\n')
                /* loop */ ;

            System.out.println("Terminating discovery.");
            ex.stopDiscovery();
        } catch (IOException ex) {
          System.err.println("Problems with discovery: " +
                             ex.getMessage());
        }
    }
}
```

When you run this program, you can specify on the command line what groups you're interested in discovering. The `main()` for this program does some argument processing—you can specify the special values "all," "none," or "public" to tell the program that you're interested in finding all groups, no groups, or the unnamed public group, respectively (we have to use a keyword for the unnamed group because it is, after all, unnamed).

The `main()` then passes the array of desired groups into the `DiscoveryExample` class, starts the discovery process by calling `startDiscovery()`, and waits until a return is typed at the keyboard. The discovery process will run in the background continuously until you hit a key, at which point `main()` calls `stopDiscovery()`. Even though we never restart discovery in this example after it is stopped, one certainly might want to do this. So `stopDiscovery()` shuts down the discovery process temporarily by setting the groups to be searched for to `NO_GROUPS` and removes the discovery listener. This arrangement is not irreversible, as calling `terminate()` on the `LookupDiscovery` instance would be.

An inner class called `Listener` implements `DiscoveryListener`, so the program creates and installs one of these as the listener for a `LookupDiscovery` instance that it creates when `startDiscovery()` is called. Using a separate inner class for tasks like discovery is a good idea, since it can lead to a cleaner design than you might get otherwise. Take a look at the `DiscoveryListener` methods on the `Listener` class—`discovered()` and `discarded()`. These methods will print details about each lookup service that is found or subsequently tossed away: the URL that can be used to name the lookup service, its service ID, and the groups it supports. To print out these details, the example calls out to two methods that I've defined: `getURL()` and `getGroups()`. These methods handle the exception processing and return appropriate strings to describe the service. I've made these methods both public and static, because we'll be using these handy printing functions from other classes in later examples.

The `getURL()` class shows something we haven't seen before: How to get the URL for a lookup service. The code here calls `getLocator()` on a `ServiceRegistrar`, which returns a `LookupLocator`. The `LookupLocator` class is used to manage the unicast discovery process, much like `LookupDiscovery` is used to manage multicast discovery. We'll see the ins and outs of this new class a bit later in this chapter.

Be sure to note how the `discard()` method is used in this program. If there is ever an error when communicating with a lookup service—that is, when a `RemoteException` is raised by any of the methods on it—then the code here calls `discard()` on the `LookupDiscovery` class. This causes the errant lookup service to be dropped, and the `discarded()` method on `Listener` to be invoked. If the failed lookup service comes back in the future, it will be rediscovered.

Security and LookupDiscovery

Jini provides a way, using the Java 2 security mechanisms, for you to limit what groups a service or application can join. This can be very useful, for example, if you download new Jini services from the Internet. If you don't trust the source of the service, and cannot guarantee that it won't try to do something malicious, you can restrict it to only connecting to certain groups. An "unsafe" group might exist just for experimenting with untrusted services, for example.

When a service or other application creates a `LookupDiscovery` object, or tries to change the set of groups for which the `LookupDiscovery` object is searching, the code checks to see whether the creator has permission to try to discover each of the set of desired groups. `LookupDiscovery` will raise a `java.lang.SecurityException` if the proper privileges aren't in place.

But permissions need to be set even for *trusted* programs because, by default, applications are allowed to discover *no* groups. So you *must* pass in *some* form of policy file, to allow even lookup services themselves to be able to perform discovery. These same mechanisms can be used to selectively restrict the groups that applications can join.

So to allow a service access to certain groups, you can create a policy file and pass the file to the JVM via the `java.security.policy` property. The policy file would be used to restrict and allow accesses made by the *discovering* application, whether it's a service or a client or a lookup service itself (since lookup services use the normal discovery process to find other lookup services).

Jini introduces its own permissions class just for granting access to groups. This class is called `net.jini.discovery.DiscoveryPermission`, and can be used in a policy file just like any other permission. The permission takes an argument that indicates the group to which access should be allowed, and supports the use of "*" as a wildcard character. Here are some examples. This permission entry in a policy file allows discovery of all groups on the network.

```
permission net.jini.discovery.DiscoveryPermission "*"
```

This entry grants access to one specific group, the "unsafe" group.

```
permission net.jini.discovery.DiscoveryPermission
            "unsafe"
```

And finally, this entry grants access to the default, unnamed group.

```
permission net.jini.discovery.DiscoveryPermission ""
```

You should note that when you set a security policy for a JVM, that policy restricts *all* the code that runs in the JVM by default, not just downloaded code. You can, however, use the features of Java 2 security to create policy files that selectively grant code certain permissions based on where it came from. So, for instance, you could create policy files that grant more permissions to locally loaded classes than downloaded ones, or to classes "digitally signed" by a known person.

Compiling and Running the Program

Let's build the program and try it out. Compilation is pretty easy—the class exports no downloadable code (it isn't a Jini service), and has no remote methods. So you won't have to worry about using the RMI stubs compiler or copying downloadable code to a web server's root directory. But I will follow our standard guidelines here of specifying the classpath on the command line, both when compiling and running.

On Windows:

```
javac -classpath C:\jini1_0\lib\jini-core.jar;
                                C:\jini1_0\lib\jini-ext.jar;
                                C:\jini1_0\lib\sun-util.jar;
                                C:\client
  -d C:\client
  C:\files\corejini\chapter6\DiscoveryExample.java
```

On Solaris:

```
javac -classpath /files/jini1_0/lib/jini-core.jar:
                         /files/jini1_0/lib/jini-ext.jar:
                         /files/jini1_0/lib/sun-util.jar:
                         /files/client
  -d /files/client
  /files/corejini/chapter6/DiscoveryExample.java
```

Now you're set to run the program. Since this program will *use* downloaded code, and since it must perform discovery to find lookup services, you must pass it a policy file. The "promiscuous" policy file that we used in Chapter 5 will work just fine.

On Windows:

```
java -cp C:\jini1_0\lib\jini-core.jar;
                   C:\jini1_0\lib\jini-ext.jar;
                   C:\jini1_0\lib\sun-util.jar;
                   C:\client
       -Djava.security.policy=C:\policy
       corejini.chapter6.DiscoveryExample
```

On Solaris:

```
java -cp /files/jini1_0/lib/jini-core.jar:
                   /files/jini1_0/lib/jini-ext.jar:
                   /files/jini1_0/lib/sun-util.jar:
                   /files/client
       -Djava.security.policy=/files/policy
       corejini.chapter6.DiscoveryExample
```

When the program starts, it will wait for discovery events until you hit the return key. Every time a new lookup service is discovered, some information about it will be printed to standard out.

> *Hit return to terminate discovery.*
>
> *Discovered:*
>
> > *URL: jini://grouper.parc.xerox.com/*
> >
> > *ID: 90afbd9d-3103-48f9-b3de-b7db0b37095b*
> >
> > *Groups: PUBLIC*
>
> *Discovered:*

URL: jini://turbodog.parc.xerox.com/

ID: c498f93c-9c3c-4c71-94b4-92bc63d863e3

Groups: PUBLIC

Discovered:

URL: jini://foundation.parc.xerox.com/

ID: e5020ccd-d079-457a-a696-b8278a8031d4

Groups: <none>

Discovered:

URL: jini://rubberducky.parc.xerox.com:40437/

ID: 8311f536-7f1c-4c69-bfef-f009542f9f8c

Groups: PUBLIC

Terminating discovery.

This program shows the basics of using `LookupDiscovery` to interact with the discovery protocols and find the lookup services that are members of a Jini community.

Using LookupLocator to Control UnicastDiscovery

We've looked at how to use the `LookupDiscovery` class to control the serendipitous, multicast forms of Jini discovery. But there's another set of APIs for interacting with unicast discovery. These interfaces are as easy to use as the multicast interfaces, but use a different programming style.

The multicast interfaces, you will recall, are designed to "trickle in" lookup services as they are found. The design of the protocols, and the role that the protocols are asked to play in Jini, both lend themselves well to the asynchronous, nonblocking design used by the `LookupDiscovery` class. But unicast discovery is a different process. In unicast discovery, you already *know* the name of the lookup service you want to interact with; all you need to do is get the service proxy for it. In this case, either the process succeeds or it fails; there is no trickle in of answers as in the multicast protocol. Because of this reason, the interfaces for interacting with unicast discovery have a traditional, blocking feel.

The class `LookupLocator` provides an interface to unicast discovery.

```
package net.jini.discovery;

public class LookupLocator implements Serializable {
      public LookupLocator(String host, int port);
      public LookupLocator(String url)
                  throws MalformedURLException;
      public String getHost();
      public int getPort();
      public ServiceRegistrar getRegistrar()
            throws IOException, ClassNotFoundException;
      public ServiceRegistrar getRegistrar(int timeout)
            throws IOException, ClassNotFoundException;
}
```

Each `LookupLocator` instance represents the location of a single lookup service somewhere on the net. The lookup service need not be nearby on the local network as in the cast of multicast discovery, since the unicast protocol underlying this class can go directly to any lookup service anywhere on the network, regardless of distance.

You construct a new `LookupLocator` by providing it with the location of the lookup service you want to talk to. The *location* of a lookup service comprises two parts: the address of the host on which the service is running, and the IP port number on which the service is listening for incoming requests. The address of the host may take the form of a fully qualified domain name or an IP address (e.g., 13.2.116.134).

In the first version of the constructor you pass these two parameters in separately. In the second, you pass a specially formatted Jini URL that contains the name of the lookup service. This URL has the form `jini://hostname:port/data` or `jini://hostname/data`. The `port` is optional, and defaults to the standard Jini lookup service port number (4160). The `data` part, while valid in the URL syntax, is meaningless to Jini and should be omitted (in the current implementation, this part of the URL is simply ignored). The constructor that takes a string representation of the URL may raise a `MalformedURLException` if the string isn't a properly formatted Jini URL.

The methods `getHost()` and `getPort()` simply return the values for the host and port extracted from the parameters to the constructor. They do not contact the remote lookup service, and do no validation on the values that were passed to the constructor.

Invoking either of the `getRegistrar()` methods actually initiates the unicast discovery protocol. Each of these methods returns the service proxy for the lookup service specified in the constructor, or raises an exception if it fails. There are two ways that the method may fail. If it runs into trouble with the discovery protocol itself, it raises an `IOException`. If the service proxy that it receives from the lookup service cannot be reconstituted, it raises a `ClassNotFoundException`.

The first version of the `getRegistrar()` method blocks for a predetermined amount of time, currently one minute in the default implementation.[2] The second version takes a parameter that specifies a timeout, expressed in milliseconds. If either form of the method waits for the duration of its timeout period without hearing from the lookup service, it raises `java.io.InterruptedIOException` (which is a subclass of the basic `java.io.IOException`).

An Example

Let's look at an example (Listing 6–2) of how to use the `LookupLocator` class. This program is similar to the one we saw in the section on `LookupDiscovery`—it contacts a lookup service and then prints out details about it. The difference here is that rather than specifying a set of groups that you're interested in on the command line, you provide a URL that names the desired lookup service. The program uses unicast discovery to go directly to the lookup service and fetch its service proxy and other information about it.

Listing 6–2 `LocatorExample.java`

```
package corejini.chapter6;

import net.jini.core.discovery.LookupLocator;
import net.jini.core.lookup.ServiceRegistrar;
import java.io.IOException;
import java.net.MalformedURLException;
import java.rmi.RemoteException;
import java.rmi.rmiSecurityManager;

public class LocatorExample {
    public LocatorExample() {
    }
public ServiceRegistrar getRegistrar(String url)
```

2. The timeout value can be set via the `net.jini.discovery.timeout` property. See Appendix B for a complete list of the Jini and RMI properties that are relevant.

Listing 6–2 `LocatorExample.java` **(continued)**

```
        throws MalformedURLException, IOException,
                ClassNotFoundException {
        LookupLocator loc = new LookupLocator(url);
        System.out.println("Host: " + loc.getHost());
        System.out.println("Port: " + loc.getPort());
        return loc.getRegistrar();
    }
    public static void main(String[] args) {
        if (args.length != 1) {
            System.out.println("Usage:  LocatorExample " +
                                "<URL>");
            System.exit(1);
        }
        if (System.getSecurityManager() == null) {
        System.setSecurityManager(new RMISecurityManager());
        }

        LocatorExample loc = new LocatorExample();
        ServiceRegistrar reg;

        try {
            reg = loc.getRegistrar(args[0]);
            System.out.println("Got registrar: ");
            System.out.println("\tURL:     " +
                    DiscoveryExample.getURL(reg));
            System.out.println("\tID:      " +
                    reg.getServiceID());
            System.out.println("\tGroups: " +
                    DiscoveryExample.getGroups(reg));
        } catch (MalformedURLException ex) {
            System.err.println("Malformed URL. " +
                               "Use a valid jini URL.");
            System.exit(1);
        } catch (Exception ex) {
          System.err.println("Error getting service proxy: "
                                    + ex.getMessage());
            System.exit(1);
        }
    }
}
```

This example is quite straightforward, because there's not all that much you can *do* with a `LookupLocator`. Here we see that `main()` extracts a string from the command line and passes it to our `LocatorExample` instance by calling `getRegistrar()` to attempt to fetch the actual service proxy. The `getRegistrar()` method creates a `LookupLocator`, dumps out some details about it (which it can do without going over the wire—the host and port are simply extracted from the URL), and then tries to get and return its service proxy. The code shown here reuses the methods from our earlier example, `DiscoveryExample`, to display the group and URL information about the lookup service.

If you find yourself needing to use `LookupLocator` classes often, you should read up on `com.sun.jini.discovery.LookupLocatorDiscovery`. This is a useful "helper" class that works much the same way as `LookupDiscovery`. But rather than specifying a list of groups to search for, you specify a list of `LookupLocators`. As each locator is found in turn, `LookupLocatorDiscovery` will call out to a `DiscoveryListener` with a `DiscoveryEvent` that contains the newly found service registrar. Many applications will only need to search by group (and usually only the public group), so `LookupDiscovery` is the more commonly used class. But if you are using locators, `LookupLocatorDiscovery` can be a big help, especially since it lets you reuse your `DiscoveryListener` implementation to respond to both serendipitous and direct discoveries. (The class is in the `com.sun.jini` package because it is not considered to be a "core" part of the Jini APIs. The Jini team debated whether to "promote" this class to `net.jini` but decided to leave it where it was for the first Jini release. Many of the classes in `com.sun.jini` are extremely useful, and you shouldn't be shy about using them just because they're not in `net.jini`.)

Compiling and Running the Program

Let's run this program and see what it does. The compilation instructions are basically the same as for the last example.

On Windows:

```
javac -classpath C:\jini1_0\lib\jini-core.jar;
                             C:\jini1_0\lib\jini-ext.jar;
                             C:\jini1_0\lib\sun-util.jar;
                             C:\client
        -d C:\client
  C:\files\corejini\chapter6\LocatorExample.java
```

On Solaris:

```
javac -classpath   /files/jini1_0/lib/jini-core.jar:
                   /files/jini1_0/lib/jini-ext.jar:
                   /files/jini1_0/lib/sun-util.jar:
                   /files/client
  -d /files/client
  /files/corejini/chapter6/LocatorExample.java
```

Now you're set to run the program. You'll have to pass a valid Jini URL on the command line. You can use one of the URLs that was returned from the `DiscoveryExample` program earlier.

On Windows:

```
java -cp C:\jini1_0\lib\jini-core.jar;
                 C:\jini1_0\lib\jini-ext.jar;
                 C:\jini1_0\lib\sun-util.jar;
                 C:\client
       -Djava.security.policy=C:\policy
       corejini.chapter6.LocatorExample
       jini://turbodog.parc.xerox.com
```

On Solaris:

```
java -cp /files/jini1_0/lib/jini-core.jar:
                 /files/jini1_0/lib/jini-ext.jar:
                 /files/jini1_0/lib/sun-util.jar:
                 /files/client
       -Djava.security.policy=/files/policy
       corejini.chapter6.LocatorExample
       jini://turbodog.parc.xerox.com
```

The program will perform unicast discovery on the URL you provide to it. Once the service registrar proxy has been downloaded, the program will use it to print out some information about the just-discovered lookup service.

Host: turbodog.parc.xerox.com

Port: 4160

Got registrar:

URL: jini://turbodog.parc.xerox.com/

ID: c498f93c-9c3c-4c71-94b4-92bc63d863e3

Groups: PUBLIC

This program illustrates how to use the `LookupLocator` class to discover a lookup service given it's URL-formatted name, and retrieve its service proxy.

Under the Hood: The Discovery Protocols

If you're just writing Jini services and need to have a grasp of the basics of how discovery works, the previous sections should be enough for you. With the overview of discovery and the details about how to actually program against the Jini APIs, you should be all set to tackle most discovery tasks.

But some of you may need more details, either to solve discovery problems, or perhaps because you are building your own custom lookup services that need to correctly interact with services using the discovery protocols. In this section, we'll take an in-depth look at the nitty-gritty details of the three discovery protocols and how they're implemented.

The Multicast Request Protocol

The multicast request protocol is a service-initiated protocol that is used when a service needs to discover all the lookup services that may already exist on a local network. The protocol is implemented using a low-level multicast facility, so it does not require full-fledged Java RMI or CORBA or any other more heavyweight protocol. If, as is usually the case, the multicast request protocol is being run in a standard TCP/IP setting, then multicast UDP datagrams are used as the basis for the protocol. This section describes the implementation of the protocol on top of multicast UDP.

Communication Flow

The initiating service—called the discoverer here, for clarity—sets itself up to both send multicast request messages and receive unicast replies. This is done by creating a couple of sockets, one for outgoing multicast UDP messages and one for incoming TCP messages. Likewise a lookup service that participates in the multicast request protocol will set up a socket for receiving multicast UDP messages (it *joins* the multicast group represented by the address, in multicast parlance) as well as a socket for sending outgoing TCP messages. These sockets are the twins of those on the service side, as Figure 6–2 shows.

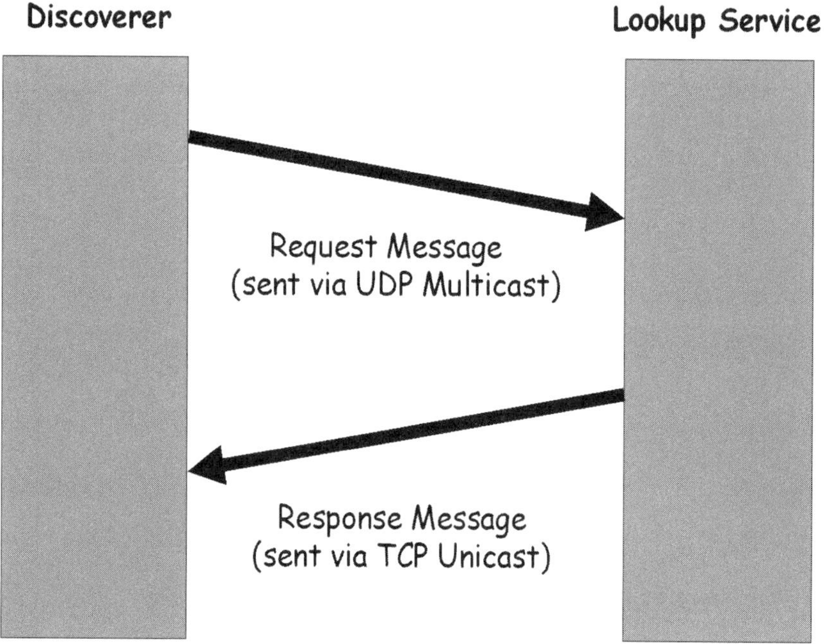

Figure 6–2 The multicast request protocol

The discoverer then sends the multicast request message, which contains the set of groups in which the discoverer is interested. This message must fit in a single packet, so that it can be contained in a single UDP multicast datagram message. This requirement is because UDP provides no guarantees that a message spanning multiple packets will arrive in order or without packet loss; by making the messages simple Jini guards against partial message loss.

Further, the message contains only simple data types—no objects—because the discovery protocols are designed to be easy to implement by very lightweight entities. Since these entities may not even have a Java Virtual Machine available to them, the discovery request cannot take advantage of Java serialization or other features.

Packet Format

Figure 6–3 shows the format of the packet.

Header

Proto Version <int>	Port <int>

Groups

Group Len <int>	Group 1 <string>	Group 2 <string>	...

Heard From

Heard Len <int>	Heard 1 <svc id>	Heard 2 <svc id>	...

Figure 6–3 The multicast request packet

Wherever a data type such as `int` or `string` is used in the protocol, you can assume that the message was written using the same semantics that you would get if you called `DataOutputStream.writeInt()` or `writeUTF()`. That is, integers are written as four-byte (32-bit) values, with the most-significant byte first (that is, in standard network byte order). Strings are written in UTF-8 character encoding; the first two bytes of a string representation will be the length, most significant byte first, and the remaining bytes will contain a representation of the characters in the string. UTF-8 uses one, two, or three bytes to encode each character, depending on its value. Check out the documentation for the `DataOutputStream` class for details on how specific types are written.

The header portion contains the following items:

- The `Protocol Version` is an integer that denotes the version of the discovery protocol being used; explicitly providing the version number allows implementors of future discovery protocols to know when they are speaking with a party that implements an earlier version of the protocol. In the current version of Jini, the version should be set to 1.
- The `Port` field is an integer that should contain the TCP port number that the discoverer is listening on for unicast replies from the lookup service. The lookup service will reply to the port number contained here when it sends its unicast response.

After this short, fixed-length header, come two variable-length chunks of data. The first, called `Groups`, contains the set of groups the discoverer is interested in. All lookup services that are members of one of the specified groups should answer the request.

- The `Group Length` field is an integer containing the number of groups that follow. If the length is zero, then the discoverer is indicating that all groups are being searched for.
- Each `Group` denotes the name of a group that is being searched for. Each item here is a string encoded in UTF-8 format. The number of groups should, of course, match the number indicated in the length field.

Finally, the packet contains a list of lookup services from which the discoverer has already heard, called `Heard From`. If a lookup service receives the multicast request, but is in the "heard from already" set, it should not reply. This allows some optimization of the protocol.

- The `Heard Length` field is an integer containing the number of heard-from lookup service identifiers that follow. The length may be zero if no lookup services have yet been heard from.
- Each `Heard` item is a representation of a Jini service ID. Each ID is a 128-bit value that will uniquely identify a lookup service (see Chapter 8 for more details on service IDs). Each item is written as a 16-byte chunk, with the most significant byte first.

Jini requires that any message sent via multicast be, at most 512 bytes long (see the section Other Internal Discovery Issues, later in this chapter, for details on why this is so). Since there are two components of the request that are variable length, either or both may cause the size of the packet to exceed the size limit of 512 bytes. The Jini discovery specifications dictate that if the `Groups` component causes the packet to exceed 512 bytes, then a discoverer should perform multiple requests. Each request should have a subset of the total group list such that there is no overlap between the groups specified in each request.

If the `Heard From` component causes the packet to exceed 512 bytes, then the set of lookup service IDs from which the discoverer has already heard must be left incomplete. Remember that this is only an optimization, so excluding lookup services from the list, while unfortunate, will not "break" anything. How a discoverer chooses to exclude lookup service IDs from this list is up to it—however, simply truncating the request to 512 bytes is not an option. No matter what solution you take, the packet must be correctly formatted, with a `Heard Length` that correctly denotes the number of service IDs, and no partially sent service IDs.

Once a lookup service receives the multicast message it can reply to the discoverer. To do this, it must figure out where to send the reply. It builds the internet address to send its response to by using the port number from the request, and getting the host address by determining the source of the incoming request, using the `getAddress()` call on `java.net.DatagramPacket`.

The message it sends is essentially the same as the response used in the unicast discovery protocol, which we discuss later. This response transmits a serialized service proxy for the lookup service back to the discoverer, at which point it can reconstitute the object and use the lookup service.

Using the Multicast Request Protocol

Once the discoverer has set itself up for sending requests and receiving responses, it periodically sends multicast request messages. These messages are sent to a well-known address that Jini lookup services listen on (the IP address is 224.0.1.85 and the port number is 4160). While the interval between requests is up to the service, five seconds is a good number to use. As responses come in, the discoverer adds the service IDs of the discovered lookup services to the set of lookup services it has heard from. After some period of time, the discoverer ceases using multicast request, presuming that it has found all active lookup services already running. While the length of time that a service will use multicast request is up to it, seven rounds of messages is recommended by the Jini specifications. After this point it can stop sending messages and shut down the socket it has been using for receiving requests. Most discoverers at this point will switch over to listening for multicast announcement messages to detect lookup services that start in the future or that reconnect to the network.

As mentioned in the description of the join protocol, services should wait for some random period of time before initiating multicast request. This random wait helps to reduce "packet storms" that may flood a network after a power outage or other large failure.

Remember that the details here of using the multicast request protocol are primarily for developers who need to implement the protocol "by hand" for some reason. The Jini class libraries providing the nice set of APIs discussed in this chapter make the job of discovery easier.

The Multicast Announcement Protocol

The multicast announcement protocol is used by lookup services to announce their presence to any interested parties that may be listening and "in range" of the multicast scope of the lookup service. Unlike multicast request, which typically only is used during the start up phase of a service or when the set of groups it wishes to be a member of changes, multicast announcement is used for the duration of the life of a lookup service. It will periodically announce its existence to any parties that may care to listen.

Communication Flow

The announcement protocol is a bit simpler than the request protocol. The lookup service creates a multicast UDP socket on which to send messages, and a unicast TCP socket on which it will receive messages from interested parties. Services and other applications that wish to receive announcements of new lookup services, again called discoverers here, create a socket to listen for the multicast UDP announcements.

When discoverers receive an announcement from a lookup service they have not heard from, they can contact it by creating a TCP socket and sending a message to the TCP socket the lookup service is listening on for requests. This second half of the protocol is essentially the same as the unicast discovery protocol, which will be discussed shortly. The first half is literally only used to announce the presence of lookup services, so that discoverers can then use the unicast discovery protocol to find out more information about them. The communications flow is shown in Figure 6–4.

Packet Format

Figure 6–5 shows the format of the outgoing announcement message that lookup services will send. This packet has essentially the same requirements as the multicast request that discoverers send in the multicast request proto-

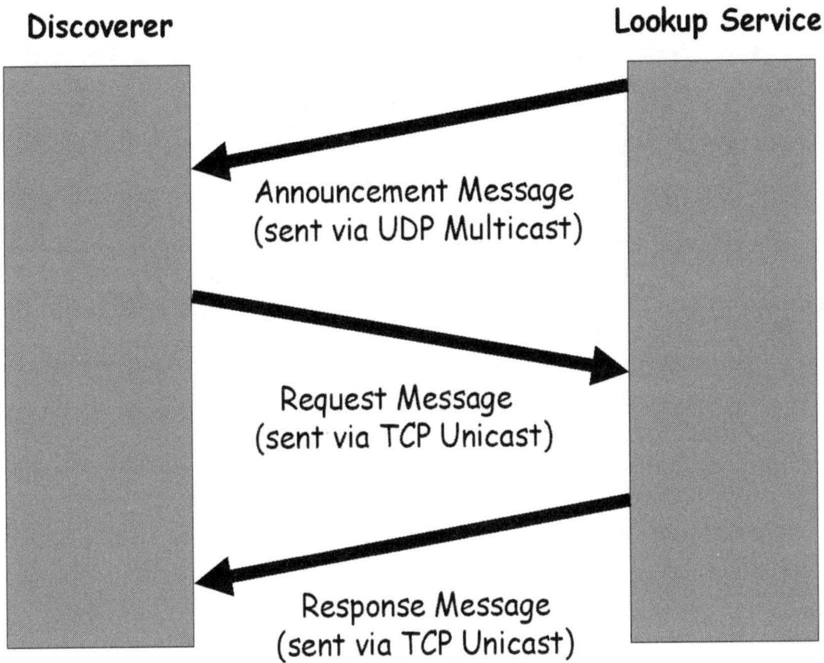

Figure 6–4 The multicast announcement protocol

col: it must be no longer than 512 bytes, and should be as simple as possible to encode and decode (thus, it cannot require Java serialization, since the lookup service may not be implemented using Java).

Just as in the request protocol, all data elements are written as if encoded via a `java.io.DataOutputStream`. So integers are written in standard network byte order (most significant byte first), and strings are encoded as UTF-8, with the character data preceded by two bytes containing the length. The header of the message contains the following items.

- The `Protocol Version` is an integer, indicating the version of the protocol to accommodate possible future revisions. In the current Jini implementations, this value should always be set to 1.
- The `Host` field is a string containing the name of the host on which the lookup service is running. A discoverer can use this hostname to connect to the lookup service using the unicast discovery protocol.

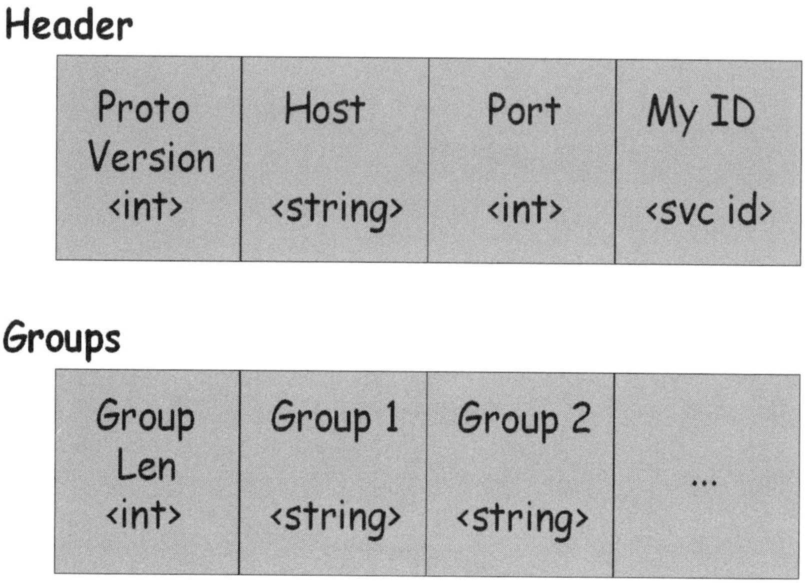

Header

Proto Version <int>	Host <string>	Port <int>	My ID <svc id>

Groups

Group Len <int>	Group 1 <string>	Group 2 <string>	...

Figure 6–5 The multicast announcement format

- The `Port` field contains the port number on which the lookup service is listening for incoming unicast discovery requests. This value is also needed for the discoverer to initiate the second half of the discovery protocol.
- The `Service ID` field represents the globally unique identifier for the lookup service generating the announcement. It represents a `net.jini.lookup.ServiceID` object, a 128-bit value that discoverers can use to determine whether they have heard from this lookup service already. It is encoded as a 16-byte chunk, written with the most significant byte first.

After this fixed-length header, a variable length component called `Groups` indicates the names of the groups of which the lookup service is a member.

- The `Group Length` field is an integer that indicates the number of group names to follow.
- Each `Group` item is a string, encoded as UTF-8, that represents one of the groups of which the lookup service is a member. The number of groups should, of course, match the length specified.

Since the variable length portion of the message may cause the packet to exceed 512 bytes, the lookup service must generate multiple announcements if it supports too many groups to fit into a single message. These messages will each contain a subset of the groups that the service supports, organized in such a way that there is no overlap between messages.

Using the Multicast Announcement Protocol

When a lookup service starts, it creates a UDP multicast socket on which to send its announcement messages. This socket is bound to the well-known address on which discoverers will listen for announcements (the IP address is 224.0.1.84 and the port number is 4160). It also creates a TCP socket to listen for incoming unicast messages from discoverers that have heard the announcements and wish to fetch the lookup service's proxy object using unicast discovery. The lookup service then periodically sends announcement messages. The time between sends is up to the lookup service, but the Jini specifications recommend 120 seconds between announcements.

A discoverer that wishes to receive announcements creates a multicast UDP socket and "joins" this socket to the well-known multicast address on which lookup services will announce themselves. When the discoverer receives an announcement on this socket, it looks at the service ID and list of groups contained in the message. If the service ID is one that the service has already seen, or if the group list doesn't contain any groups the discoverer is interested in, it can ignore the message. Otherwise, it adds the service ID to the list of IDs it has heard from and may initiate unicast discovery to fetch the lookup service's proxy object.

Core Note: Knowing when groups change

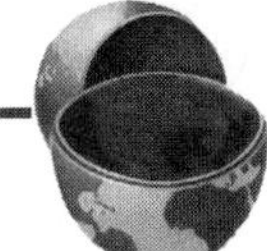

The actual implementation of the protocol may be a bit trickier than this, because the set of groups of which a lookup service is a member may change. There is no indication in the multicast announcement protocol when a lookup service suddenly joins, and therefore begins to support, new groups. Therefore, interested parties should also track the set of groups joined by each of the lookup services it has seen. Then, if a lookup service was ignored because it previously belonged to no interesting groups, the discoverer can see whether an interesting group has been added and continue on to unicast discovery.

The `LookupDiscovery` *class does this for you, which is yet another reason to use these convenience APIs if at all possible.*

Like in multicast discovery, the standard Jini APIs provide an easy way to use multicast announcement—in fact, the fact that there is a distinction between multicast request and multicast announcement is hidden from the programmer behind a listener-style interface. The preceding information is primarily for developers who need to get under the hood with discovery, perhaps to implement their own lookup service.

The Unicast Discovery Protocol

Both of the multicast protocols are used in situations where lookup services and other Jini services that are located on a local area network need to find each other. These protocols, since they both involve some element of periodicity—that is, the discovery process continues at intervals for a period of time—also help Jini communities repair themselves after network, machine, and software crashes.

But sometimes services need to search or join groups associated with lookup services that may not be nearby in the network sense. In these cases, a service needs to be able to retrieve a proxy for a lookup service that may be running on the other end of the building or the other side of the planet. The unicast discovery protocol is used in these situations. And, as we've seen, unicast discovery is also used during the course of the two multicast protocols: when multicast request runs, the service proxy is delivered using the lookup service-to-discoverer half of the unicast discovery protocol. And in multicast announcement, once a discoverer has been made aware of a lookup service, it requests its service proxy using unicast discovery.

In both of these contexts, the multicast protocols are essentially used as a way to "jump start" the unicast discovery process. Unlike multicast, where lookup services and discoverers find each other merely via the fact that multicast will reach all hosts within range, unicast requires *explicit* information about the location of the lookup service. This information includes the name of the host that the lookup service is running on, and the port that the lookup service is listening on for incoming requests. Essentially, in the two serendipitous protocols, multicast is used as a convenient way to provide this information about the location of the lookup service so that unicast can proceed from there.

In this section we'll look at the basic unicast discovery protocol, which may be used as part of multicast request, multicast announcement, or as a "stand-alone" protocol for connecting to lookup services whose location is already known.

Communication Flow

The unicast discovery protocol is very simple. It involves a simple request to the lookup service and a response back to the discoverer. The response always contains the service proxy for the lookup service.

The initial request can come from a number of sources. If unicast discovery is being used as a "stand-alone" protocol, then a discoverer will, through some means, have obtained the location (hostname and port number) of the lookup service, possibly through direct user configuration. It will then make a connection to the lookup service, which will respond with the proxy. Figure 6–6 shows the communication flow for stand-alone discovery.

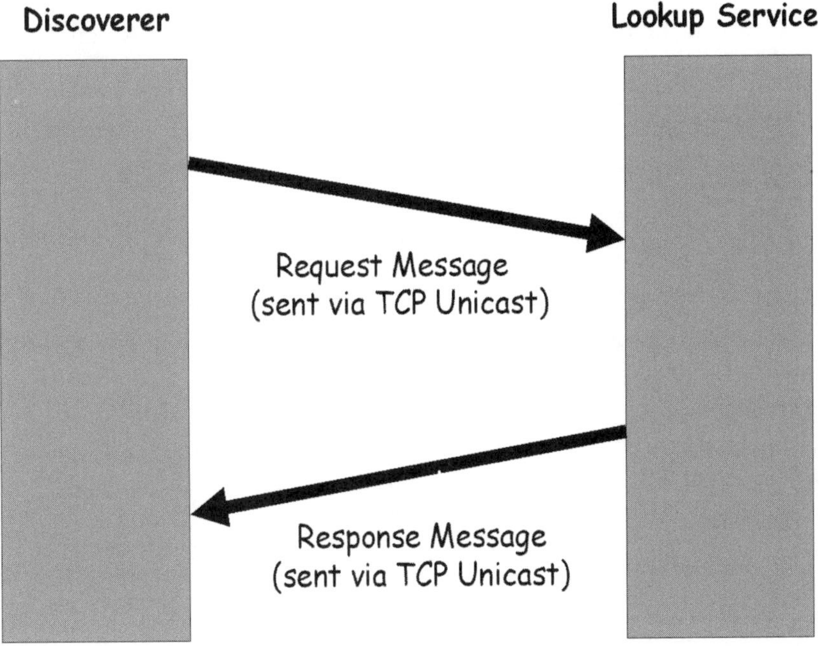

Figure 6–6 The unicast discovery protocol

If unicast discovery is being used as a part of the multicast request protocol, the multicast request message serves as the initial request for unicast discovery. It contains all the information needed for the lookup service to respond with its service proxy. In Figure 6–2, which shows the complete multicast request protocol, the final message in the protocol is a unicast discovery response.

If unicast discovery is being used as a part of multicast announcement, then the protocol works just like in the stand-alone case. Announcement distributes the location of the lookup service, and discoverers are then free to use full unicast discovery to get the service proxy. In Figure 6–4, which shows the complete multicast announcement protocol, the second half of the exchange is unicast discovery.

In all these cases, the lookup service can determine the host of the discoverer (which it needs in order to send back its service proxy) by getting the source of the incoming request. The lookup service still needs to know the port number at which the discoverer is listening for its response, though. When unicast discovery is being used as a "stand-alone" protocol, or as part of multicast announcement, the lookup service always connects to the default port (4160) on the discoverer's host. When unicast discovery is being used as part of multicast request, the port number is included as part of the original multicast request message.

Packet Format

Let's look at the request that a discoverer uses to initiate unicast discovery. This message is used in stand-alone unicast discovery, or in the second half of the multicast announcement protocol. As mentioned, in multicast request, there is no need for a discoverer to send a separate unicast discovery request, as the multicast request message serves this purpose without requiring that the discoverer already know the location of the lookup service.

The unicast discovery request message is very simple—it contains only one field. Figure 6–7 shows the format of the packet. The one field of the packet is

- The `Protocol Version` field, an integer, indicating which version of the protocol is being used. This field allows for possible future expansion of the protocol. In all current Jini implementations, this field should be set to 1.

Like all Jini discovery messages, the field here is encoded using network normal byte order.

The response is only slightly more complicated. This is the response message that is the end result of *all* the discovery protocols—it delivers a lookup service's service proxy, as well as a list of the groups that it supports. Figure 6–8 shows the format of the packet. Here are the fields of the response.

Figure 6–7 The unicast discovery request format

- The message begins with the `Service Proxy` for the lookup service. This is a representation of a `java.rmi.MarshalledObject` for the proxy, written out using Java object serialization.
- The `Group Length` field is an integer containing the number of group names that follow.

Each `Group` item that follows is a UTF-8 encoded string representing the name of a group of which the lookup service is a member. Obviously, the number of group names here should match the length sent.

Using Unicast Discovery

As we discussed, unicast discovery is used as a part of the other discovery protocols. A discoverer can initiate unicast discovery using a number of means: multicast request, multicast announcement, or "directly." Initiating direct discovery means that the discoverer has, somehow, learned the location of a lookup service and has sent a unicast discovery request to it. Such a location could be provided by a user or as part of the discoverer's persistent configuration.

The lookup service replies with the response format just given. Once the discoverer receives this response, it can deserialize the `MarshalledObject` included in it, and then call the `get()` method that `MarshalledObject` supports to get the actual service proxy. This proxy implements the `net.jini.lookup.ServiceRegistrar` interface and can be used to communicate with the lookup service.

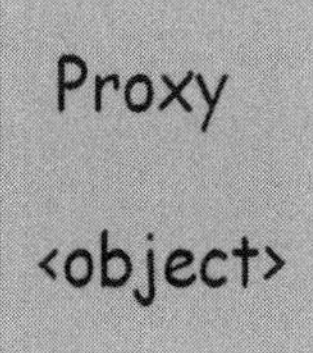

Figure 6–8 The unicast discovery response format

An Example

Let's look at one last example program in this chapter. This is the "lowest level" example here, because it shows how to build the "consumer" side of one of the discovery protocols by hand. The code here implements the requestor half of unicast discovery. As you'll note, it includes *none* of the Jini discovery packages, as it completely implements the protocol itself.

While the example here (Listing 6–3) is of the unicast protocol, which is the simplest of all the discovery protocols, the basic layout of the code here will be the same for any of the protocols.

Listing 6–3 `Unicast.java`

```
package corejini.chapter6;

import net.jini.lookup.ServiceRegistrar;
import java.net.Socket;
import java.rmi.MarshalledObject;
import java.io.*;
```

Listing 6–3 `Unicast.java` **(continued)**

```
public class Unicast {
    public static final int protoVersion = 1;

    public Unicast() {
    }

    public ServiceRegistrar getRegistrar(String host,
                                         int port)
    throws IOException, ClassNotFoundException {
        Socket sock = new Socket(host, port);

        // send the request
        DataOutputStream out =
             new DataOutputStream(sock.getOutputStream());
        out.writeInt(protoVersion);
        out.flush();

        // receive the reply
        ObjectInputStream in =
             new ObjectInputStream(sock.getInputStream());
        MarshalledObject mobj =
             (MarshalledObject) in.readObject();

        System.out.println("Received serialized proxy.");

        int groupLen = in.readInt();
        String[] groups = new String[groupLen];

        System.out.println("Registrar supports " +
                           groupLen + " groups.");
        for (int i=0 ; i<groupLen ; i++) {
            groups[i] = in.readUTF();
            System.out.println("Group " + i + ": " +
                               groups[i]);
        }

        // Convert the marshalled object into a "live" reg
        ServiceRegistrar reg = (ServiceRegistrar) mobj.get();

        return reg;
    }
```

Listing 6–3 `Unicast.java` **(continued)**

```
    public static void main(String[] args) {
        String host = null;
        int port = 4160;

        if (args.length >= 1) {
            host = args[0];
        }
        if (args.length == 2) {
            try {
                port = Integer.parseInt(args[1]);
            } catch (NumberFormatException ex) {
               System.err.println("Expected a number: " +
                                   ex.getMessage());
               System.exit(1);
            }
        }
        if (args.length == 0 || args.length > 2) {
            System.err.println("Usage: Unicast <host>" +
                                 " [<port>]");
            System.exit(1);
        }
         if (System.getSecurityManager() == null) {
         System.setSecurityManager(new RMISecurityManager());
         }

        Unicast unicast = new Unicast();
        ServiceRegistrar reg;

        try {
            reg = unicast.getRegistrar(host, port);

            System.out.println("Got registrar: ");
            System.out.println("\tURL:     " +
                         DiscoveryExample.getURL(reg));
            System.out.println("\tID:      " +
                         reg.getServiceID());
            System.out.println("\tGroups: " +
                         DiscoveryExample.getGroups(reg));
        } catch (Exception ex) {
            System.err.println("Error getting proxy: " +
                               ex.getMessage());
        }
    }
}
```

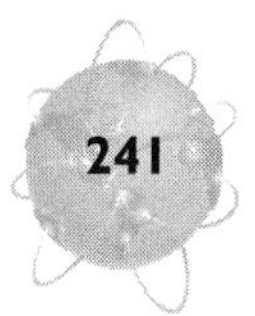

From the user's standpoint, this program works almost the same as the one we did in the `LocatorExample` code. Both do essentially the same thing—download the service proxy for a lookup service—only they do it in different ways. Here we handle the protocol ourselves, directly, rather than relying on `LookupLocator` to do it for us. From the user's perspective, the only difference is that a hostname and port number for a lookup service get passed on the command line, rather than a URL (this is just to save the tedium of dissecting the URL in this short example). If no port number is provided, the code will default to 4160, the standard Jini discovery port.

The `Unicast` class does the work. When `getRegistrar()` is called with a host and port number, it creates a socket bound to the address of the lookup service. It then wraps the socket's `OutputStream` in a `DataOutputStream` and writes the protocol version number to the lookup service. The version number is the only outgoing component of the unicast request.

Next, `getRegistrar()` needs to assemble the reply from the lookup service. It gets the socket's input stream and wraps it in an `ObjectInput-Stream`, because it'll be reading a serialized object from this stream—the actual raw service proxy of the lookup service just found. The code here fetches the proxy, which is stored as a `MarshalledObject` on the stream, and then gets the number of supported groups, and the groups themselves. Once it's got all of the contents of the reply, the code reconstitutes the `Marshalle-dObject` back into a "live" `ServiceRegistrar` and returns it.

Compiling and Running the Program

Let's compile this last example of the chapter and give it a run. The compilation instructions are basically the same as for the last example.

On Windows:

```
javac -classpath C:\jini1_0\lib\jini-core.jar;
                              C:\jini1_0\lib\jini-ext.jar;
                              C:\jini1_0\lib\sun-util.jar;
                              C:\client
  -d C:\client
  C:\files\corejini\chapter6\Unicast.java
```

On Solaris:

```
javac -classpath    /files/jini1_0/lib/jini-core.jar:
                    /files/jini1_0/lib/jini-ext.jar:
                    /files/jini1_0/lib/sun-util.jar:
                    /files/client
```

```
  -d /files/client
  /files/corejini/chapter6/Unicast.java
```

Now you're set to run the program. Remember that instead of a URL, this program takes a hostname and, optionally, a port number on the command line instead of a URL.

On Windows:

```
java -cp C:\jini1_0\lib\jini-core.jar;
                   C:\jini1_0\lib\jini-ext.jar;
                   C:\jini1_0\lib\sun-util.jar;
                   C:\client
       -Djava.security.policy=C:\policy
       corejini.chapter6.Unicast
       turbodog.parc.xerox.com
```

On Solaris:

```
java -cp /files/jini1_0/lib/jini-core.jar:
                   /files/jini1_0/lib/jini-ext.jar:
                   /files/jini1_0/lib/sun-util.jar:
                   /files/client
       -Djava.security.policy=/files/policy
       corejini.chapter6.Unicast
       turbodog.parc.xerox.com
```

The program will perform unicast discovery on the URL you provide to it. Once the service registrar proxy has been downloaded, the program will use it to print out some information about the just-discovered lookup service.

Registrar supports 1 groups.

Group 0:

Got registrar:

URL: jini://turbodog.parc.xerox.com/

ID: c498f93c-9c3c-4c71-94b4-92bc63d863e3

Groups: PUBLIC

This program essentially does the same thing as the `LookupExample` earlier—it uses unicast discovery to find a lookup service and download its service proxy. But in this case, we've implemented the entire client side of the unicast protocol "by hand."

Other Internal Discovery Issues

In this section we'll discuss some other issues that may concern implementors of new lookup services that will use discovery, and network administrators who plan to deploy Jini lookup services. We'll also look at the rationale for one of the restrictions imposed on the multicast discovery protocols—namely, that protocol messages must fit in one packet.

Multicast Restrictions and Guidelines

As mentioned, the multicast discovery protocols require that all multicast data fit in packets with maximum length of 512 bytes. The reason for this is that multicast is based on UDP, which makes no guarantees that a series of packets will arrive in the correct order, or even arrive at all. Rather than layering a more heavyweight control protocol atop UDP multicast to ensure that multipacket chunks of data arrive intact, Jini simply requires that each message fit in a single packet, and that each packet be understandable by a receiver without any other context.

The 512 byte requirement comes from the fact that this is the smallest size that IP mandates to be supported by all implementations. So, no matter what the actual transport IT is running over, IP guarantees that packets of this size or less will arrive intact if they arrive at all.

When multicast protocols are in use, senders should take care to ensure that they limit the scope of their transmissions to keep from flooding a large portion of the network. While the scope of messages is not mandated by the Jini specifications, a TTL (Time-to-Live) value of 15 is recommended for the UDP multicast environment.

While the "under the hood" details in this chapter cover the implementation of the discovery protocols atop TCP and UDP multicast, it is possible to implement a protocol for communication between a discoverer and a lookup service over other protocols, even reliable ones. Jini takes the approach that the protocol used for communication *may* run over an unreliable, connectionless transport that makes no guarantee about the order of delivery of packets. By imposing such "lowest common denominator" demands on the network, the Jini concepts should map well to other transports.

Multicast Routing Infrastructure

While most modern IP routers support multicast, there are still some older machines on the net that do not. If a router connecting two network segments does not support multicast, then multicast traffic originating on one segment will not be forwarded on to the second segment (although it would still appear on the first and be available to hosts there).

If your network is in such a situation, there are a number of options available to you. The first is simply to run a Jini lookup service on each network segment. This means that only services on the same segment will be able to find each other, unless you explicitly federate your lookup services by providing each lookup service with the name of its peer and having them use unicast discovery to join each other.

A second alternative is to "bridge" between the two segments in such a way that multicast traffic passes between them, even though the routers do not support it. In IP multicast, this technique is called *multicast tunneling*, and is fairly easy to set up. You could even write a simple tunnel yourself: you just create a program that joins a multicast group and forwards all messages it receives on to an IP address for a host on another network segment. The program also reads from a standard socket and relays messages received there on to the multicast socket. By running two of these on machines on different segments, you can relay multicast traffic on distinct segments using unicast IP.

Security

Be forewarned—in the current Jini implementation and specifications, there is no authentication performed on either the discovery requests or responses. This means that it is impossible to know whether the entity contacting you is a "legitimate" lookup service or other service, or what actual human user "owns" those processes.

Sun promises to extend Jini with better distributed security based on the RMI security model being proposed for a future version of Java.

Host and Network Requirements

Let's look at the minimal software support required to run each side of discovery—the requirements for lookup services and the requirements for parties finding lookup services.

In order to run the portions of the discovery protocols required by a lookup service, your machine must have a network stack that can support both multicast TCP and unicast UDP protocols. Implicit in this requirement is that the machine has an IP address. Other than these two requirements, the Jini discovery protocols impose no other burdens on the machine that will host a lookup service. There is not even a requirement for a JVM on this machine—the portion of the discovery protocols that run in the lookup service could easily be implemented in C or any other language. Of course, a particular implementation of a lookup service that uses these protocols may impose its own requirements on the host platform, over and above these.

Parties that are searching for a lookup service have slightly expanded requirements of their host platforms. First, like lookup services, they must have a properly configured network stack capable of UDP multicast and TCP unicast messages. They must also, however, have a Java Virtual Machine available to them. The JVM is needed by these parties because any lookup services that are found will transmit to them a serialized Java object that will be used to communicate with the lookup service. These applications will need a JVM in order to reconstitute and run the proxy objects returned from discovery.

Interfaces for Discovery Implementors

This chapter has gone into some fairly nitty-gritty details about the discovery protocols and how messages are encoded. Most developers who need this information will be building their own lookup services, possibly with different performance and administration characteristics, or that use different network transports. Others may use this information to create alternative APIs to the discovery process, perhaps because the default APIs discussed in this chapter are not flexible enough.

If you find that you need to implement the discovery protocols yourself, you should know that Jini provides a set of APIs that encapsulate the encoding for the messages in the discovery protocols. Writing code that does the actual encoding and decoding of the data in the messages is one of the most potentially error-prone tasks that a discovery implementor could face. To ensure that the on-the-wire format of the discovery messages is the same, the `net.jini.discovery` package provides classes to do this for you.

While the description of these classes is outside the scope of this book—because they will be used by very few people—you should know that the classes exist, and where to find them. Table 6–1 gives a list of these classes.

Table 6–1 Classes for Discovery Implementors

Class Name	*Description*
`OutgoingMulticastRequest`	Marshals a multicast discovery request into an array of instances of class `java.net.DatagramPacket`
`IncomingMulticastRequest`	Unmarshals a single `Datagram-Packet` into a class with methods to access the relevant message fields
`OutgoingMulticastAnnouncement`	Marshals a multicast announcement message into an array of `Datagram-Packets`
`IncomingMulticastAnnouncement`	Unmarshals a single `Datagram-Packet` into a class with methods to access the relevant message fields
`OutgoingUnicastRequest`	Marshals a unicast discovery request onto an `OutputStream`
`IncomingUnicastRequest`	Unmarshals a unicast request from an `OutputStream`
`OutgoingUnicastResponse`	Marshals a unicast discovery response onto an `OutputStream`
`IncomingUnicastResponse`	Unmarshals a unicast discovery request from an `OutputStream` into a class with methods to obtain the service proxy and supported groups.
`Constants`	Provides a number of useful static constants and methods for accessing common discovery constants, such as addresses and port numbers.

Summary

This chapter has shown how the Jini discovery protocols allow services to come together to form communities. The discovery protocols can support "serendipitous" connectivity—so that spontaneous communities can form based simply on the "nearness" of services to one another—and can also support "direct" connectivity, in which explicit associations are created between services and communities.

A thorough understanding of the protocols underlying discovery is essential if you ever need to debug problems with discovery, or are just curious about how Jini's much-lauded spontaneous networking actually works. But for most developers, the handy `LookupDiscovery` class will be just about all they ever need to use discovery.

1.1 Update

One of the changes being proposed for the 1.1 release of Jini is a set of minor modifications to the current discovery classes, as well as a new class that unifies both the multicast discovery services provided by LookupDiscovery and the unicast services provided by LookupLocatorDiscovery. This new class is called the LookupDiscoveryManager, and should become the default interface for developers building Java applications in the 1.1 world.

A new set of interfaces partition the basic discovery APIs; the existing discovery classes, as well as the new LookupDiscoveryManager, are defined to be implementations of these APIs in 1.1. These particular changes don't actually introduce any new APIs to the existing discovery classes though; they just provide a way to better support multiple discovery implementations with the same interfaces. See the Preface to the Third Printing, earlier in this book, for more details.

What's Next?

Now that you know how to find the lookup services in a Jini community, it's time to move on. The next chapter talks about how to *describe* the services that you find using Jini's notion of *attributes*. The techniques we'll see there will allow you to attach arbitrary Java objects to services, and retrieve and use them later.

USING ATTRIBUTES TO DESCRIBE SERVICES

Topics in This Chapter

- What are attributes?
- Search using attributes
- The Jini standard attributes
- Writing new attributes
- Attributes and JavaBeans

Chapter 7

As you saw in the example programs in Chapter 5, services create and publish records called `ServiceItems` that contain information about themselves. These `ServiceItems` contain the proxy object for the service, the service's unique ID, and also any *attributes* that may describe the service. You've already seen the basics of how `ServiceItems` get published, and when we discuss the Jini lookup facilities in depth in Chapter 8, we'll look more closely at this topic, and also see how client applications can search for services.

Before delving into how services and clients use lookup, though, we need to spend some time talking about attributes, the subject of this chapter. Jini attributes provide a rich and very flexible way for services to annotate their proxy objects with information describing the service. Clients can, when searching for services, look at these attributes to find particular services that they're looking for.

Jini provides a set of "standard" attributes—essentially well-formatted information that both clients and servers understand and can use to communicate with one another. But service developers can also write their own custom attributes. We'll look at how to do this, and also explore the integration of attributes with the JavaBeans framework.

Having a good grounding in how to use attributes is important for creating well-behaved services, and will be essential for our exploration of how to effectively use lookup in the next chapter.

Attributes Basics

In the examples in Chapter 5, you saw how to register services using the `ServiceRegistrar` object returned from the discovery process, and how clients can search for services using this same object. When the "Hello, World" services published their proxy objects, they created a `ServiceItem` containing a service ID, the proxy object, and a set of attributes. Likewise, when the clients from that chapter connected to a lookup service, they could search by providing template objects that could contain an ID, the class of a proxy, and some attributes.

In all the examples so far, though, we haven't actually *used* any attributes. All of the examples in Chapter 5 simply passed in a null array of `Entry` objects for the attributes.

It's time now to look at what attributes are, how to use them, and what you can do with them. This chapter lays the groundwork for a more in-depth look at how services and clients use lookup in the next chapter. Many of the tasks that Jini programs need to do involve using the lookup service and managing attributes. Understanding attributes gives you not only a great tool for describing your services to clients (and end users), but also gives you powerful ways to search for particular services that you need to use.

What Are Attributes?

Attributes are Java objects that are attached to service proxies. Services attach these attributes when they publish their service proxies, and clients can search lookup services by looking for certain attribute patterns, and can download the attributes of a service to examine them closely.

Attributes are used to associate extra descriptive information with a service than might otherwise be available. So, for example, a printer service might have a location attribute that specifies where the printer is, as well as a status attribute that indicates whether the printer is out of paper. These two attributes—location and status—would be Java objects that you created and attached to your service proxy.

Every Java object that you wish to use as an attribute must implement the `net.jini.core.entry.Entry` interface. This interface is a subinterface of `java.io.Serializable`, but adds no new methods itself. Much like `Serializable`, it's merely a "marker" or "tag" interface that you use to indicate that you're allowing a certain class to be used in a certain way.

The Special Semantics of Attributes

While you can think of attributes as simply arbitrary serializable Java objects—because that's what they are—Jini doesn't use all the "objectness" of these objects in performing its searches. To Jini, a searchable attribute is simply a collection of its data fields. All of the methods of the object are ignored for purposes of search, as are various "special" data fields: static, transient, nonpublic, or final fields. Likewise, all fields that are primitive types (such as ints and booleans) are ignored; only references to other objects within an attribute are considered for searching.

In fact, the best way to think of `Entries` is not as single Java objects—they should be thought of as *collections* of Java objects, because what really matters from the search standpoint are the individual fields in an `Entry`. Each member in an `Entry` is a separate item in the collection, independent from all others for purposes of search. Figure 7–1 illustrates this notion.

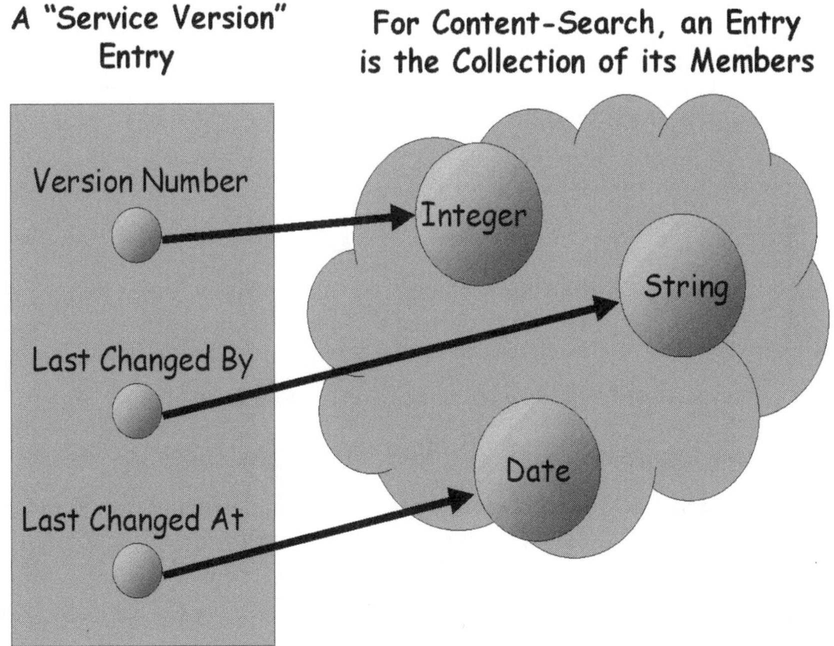

Figure 7–1 Entries are collections of objects

Paring down the searchable parts of objects to this bare minimum means that Jini can implement attribute searching very simply, and without requiring the writers of attributes to implement any special code. One could imagine an alternative where every attribute had to have a `searchMe()` method that participated in the search process; Jini uses nothing so complicated, and thus allows more types of objects to be useable as attributes.

`Entry` objects are `Serializable`, so they can be transmitted to lookup services when a service registers itself, and they can be downloaded to clients when service proxies are retrieved. Like all `Serializable` objects, `Entry`'s must have a no-argument constructor.

But `Entry` objects have a few more special semantics than regular objects, even regular `Serializable` objects. First, all the fields of a given entry are serialized separately and independently from one another. This means that if a given entry has two fields that refer to the same object, two copies of that object will be serialized. This is different than the standard serialization behavior, where normally any object written to a serialization stream twice will result in only one copy of the object being stored. When such an `Entry` is reconstituted, each of its fields will point to a separate copy of the object.

Why is this so? Why do Jini attributes diverge from the normal semantics of serialization? Remember that Jini considers `Entries` to be collections of the objects that are referenced by the fields of the attribute, not the attribute itself. So, by serializing each field separately, Jini allows each field to be accessed independently from every other field. In addition to this "philosophical" reason of serializing fields separately to reinforce the notion of `Entry` objects as collections rather than single objects, there's also an important pragmatic reason why Jini does this. If all references in an entry were "chunked" together into one serialized stream, searching for particular references would involve either deserializing the entire `Entry` (an expensive operation), or "understanding" the serialized format well enough to crawl through it, looking for particular references. Because the ability to search on individual fields in an object is essential, serializing members separately means that search code can provide this behavior while executing quickly, with no understanding of the particular serialized format of an attribute.

Figure 7–2 shows how this works. On the left is an `Entry` object before it has been serialized. Note that two of its member references point to the same object. On the right, we see this same object after it has gone through the process of serialization and reconstitution. Note that the references that originally pointed at the same object now point to two separate objects. Each of these is a copy of the original, created because the original was serialized separately for each of the two references to it.

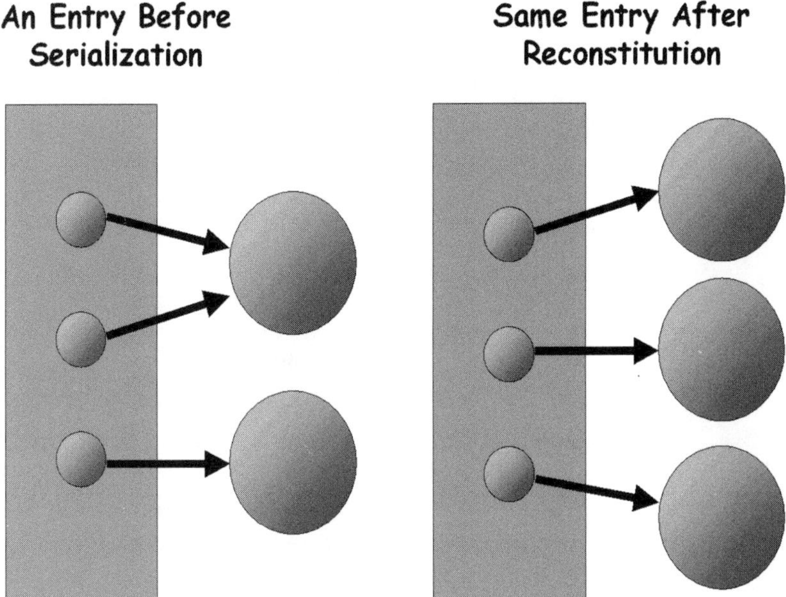

Figure 7–2 An entry before and after serialization

The peculiar semantics of `Entry`'s have implications for you as a writer of services and service consumers. Even though only the public, nonstatic, nonfinal, nontransient object references "matter" from the standpoint of search, you can still use whatever code, data, and methods in your attributes that you want. These attributes can be transmitted to clients who can use them just as they would any other object returned through RMI or dynamically loaded via a class loader. You simply have to realize that all of the data members in your object will be reconstituted separately when the attribute is reconstituted at the client. This is the real reason that Jini has the `Entry` "tagging" interface that adds no methods—it is to ensure that you have considered the implications of using your code as an attribute when you write it.

If, for some reason, your attribute cannot be properly deserialized (probably because it contains a reference to a nonserializable object), any client that tries to retrieve your attribute will get a `net.jini.core.entry.UnuseableEntryException` when they try to fetch it. We'll look at this exception, and at how clients search for and fetch attributes, a bit later in this chapter. For now, however, let's continue our look at how attributes are used.

Search Using Attributes

Jini's attribute mechanisms are designed to make searching for particular attributes simple, quick, and effective. Think about what it might mean to "search" for an arbitrary Java object, however. What would you specify as the search criterion? You could imagine searching based on the class of the object, which would certainly be useful. By using this form of searching you could find every attribute that is of a certain type. If you were writing a client application that presented a list of all the printers in a building, you might search for all service proxies of type `Printer` that have an attribute of type `Location` on them.

But this form of searching alone is somewhat limited. Suppose you want to find only those printers on the third floor. If you can search only on the type of the attribute, you'd have to find all printers that have a `Location`, and then manually check each of these to see if the printer is on the third floor. So a more powerful form of searching that would help us here would let us match attributes based on the *contents* of attributes, not just on their *types*.

Content-based searching allows you to ask the lookup service to only send back those service proxies whose attributes contain data that match some pattern you supply. And, importantly, you don't have to provide the *exact* value of the attribute object to match it. If the attribute contains a number of fields, you can specify which you are interested in matching and which you don't care about.

Think about a `Location` attribute. In an office setting, such an attribute might include several fields, including building, floor, and office number. Jini's attribute searching mechanisms allow you to formulate a query that will match any printer in a specified building, any printer on the third floor of *any* building, or any combination of matches on these fields.

The facilities in Jini support both of these styles of search: type-based and content-based.

Let's look at how attribute searching works. This type of search is typically done when a new client starts up and needs to find a select group of services. As you'll see a bit later in this chapter, clients can control search in a number of ways—they can search for specific services by looking for their IDs, they can find services that implement particular interfaces, or, as described here, they can look for services that have certain attributes attached to them.

Attribute search uses the notion of *attribute templates* that are checked for *matches* against the set of attributes attached to a service. It works like this: When you perform a search, you give it a template. A template is itself just an attribute—no more and no less. The template is compared to all of the stored attributes to see if any match. For the template to match an attribute, the attribute must be of the same class, or a subclass, of the template. Further, the data fields in the template that are non-null must match *exactly* the corresponding data fields in the attribute. If a template has a null data field, it is considered to be a "wildcard" that matches any value in the attribute.

When I say that a data field must "match exactly" the value in the template, I mean that two data fields, when serialized, produce the same bytes. In the lookup service, the fields of templates and attributes are stored in their already serialized forms as `MarshalledObjects`. Comparison of two fields calls the `equals()` method on `MarshalledObject`, which reports true if the fields serialize to the same sequence of bytes, except for the codebase that may be attached to the serialization by RMI. Note that the `equals()` method on the `Object` class, as well as any `equals()` method that may exist on the attribute class, is never called. So you cannot override this method to change matching behavior.

The template matching scheme is convenient because it allows a program to search based on any part of an attribute that it considers salient—a program need not match the *entire* attribute completely to have a match; it can use wildcards for fields that it doesn't care about, and specify those that it does care about.

Because templates can potentially match attributes that are of the same class or a subclass of the attribute, templates can be used to find extensions of types known to the searching program.

The template matching mechanisms used by Jini are simple, intuitive, and easy for the system to implement. They allow wildcard searches without necessitating any changes to the objects that you're searching for, or complicated edifices of pattern matching code. But you should be aware of one minor limitation of the way Jini templates work—because a null field is "reserved" to indicate a wildcard value, there is no way for you to explicitly search for attributes whose fields are set to null. To find an attribute that has a null field, you must use a template with a wildcard that will match *any* value in that field. You will then need to retrieve all matching attributes, and skim out only the ones that have the null fields you are looking for.

Who Changes Attributes?

I've talked about the fact that attributes are used to describe services. Occasionally, the description of a service may need to change—if a printer is moved, the location attribute on it must be updated; if it runs out of paper, its status attribute should reflect this fact.

Who is actually responsible for changing these attributes that describe services? Clearly, the service itself can take charge of some of these. If a printer can tell that it's out of paper, there's no reason it shouldn't advertise this fact via an attribute; requiring a human to notice that the printer is out of paper and attach a status attribute to it is just extra work that we don't need to do. So some attributes represent information that the service and the service alone should have control over.

Other attributes reflect information that a particular service may have no inkling of, however. If you pack up and move a printer to a new office, the printer will have no idea where it is. Some human, likely the printer's owner, will have to explicitly set the location attribute of the printer, if he or she wants to advertise its location to the rest of the world. In cases like this, there is no way the service can know the correct value of an attribute ahead of time, and an actual human *must* set the value, if it is to be set.

There are actually a wealth of human-attachable attributes that one might want to add: attributes to comment on a particular service, to leave helpful hints about its use, or to leave the e-mail address of the resident expert on using the service. So in general, Jini services should provide a way for users to create and add new attributes; some of these may be from the "standard" set of attributes, and others may be "home grown" attributes that have meaning only to a particular individual or organization.

Jini provides a convention that attribute writers can use to describe which type of attribute they are creating. If an attribute is meant to be changed *only* by a service, it should implement the `net.jini.lookup.entry.ServiceControlled` interface. This interface, much like `Entry`, is merely a "tagging" interface that says that the attribute should not be changed by anyone or anything other than the service that added it. This interface has no methods; it's merely a way for Jini to tell what kind of access control to grant to a particular attribute that implements it.

An attribute that does not implement `ServiceControlled` is effectively saying that it is freely writable, and can be used by humans, other services, or applications to squirrel away information that may be useful in the future.

Services that wish to change the set of attributes associated with themselves can use the various interfaces available to services, described in the next chapter. But how do users and client programs change the attributes on a service? The answer is that services should *allow* them to add attributes to their proxies. Most services in Jini should provide an "administration" interface, that allows client programs—as well as users, through those client programs—to change the set of attributes on a service. These same administration interfaces can often be used to start or stop a service, change the set of groups it joins, and change the set of explicit lookup services it registers itself with.

Chapter 12 has all the details on service administration. For the discussion of attributes here, all you need to know is that certain attributes are controllable by either users or the services that published them, while others "belong" solely to the service. This latter type of attribute should implement the `ServiceControlled` interface.

The Standard Attributes

The Jini class libraries provide a number of "standard" attribute types that should be used to provide information about services. By agreeing on a set of these types, services can publish information about themselves in a well-understood format, and clients can have an idea of what they should be searching for.

The Jini standard attributes are defined in the `net.jini.lookup.entry` package. Hopefully, as the industry gains more experience with Jini, more and more types of attributes will become standardized, and applications can be written to expect these types. Sun believes that the Jini community process will lead to the creation and adoption of new attribute types.

Table 7–1 provides a list of the basic standard attribute types.

Table 7–1 Standard Jini Attributes

Attribute	*Purpose*
`Address`	Provides information on the geographical location of a service, such as country, city, and street address. This attribute type is distinct from `Location`, which describes a location within an organization. This attribute is not `ServiceControlled`.
`Comment`	Used to provide a free-form string comment on a service. This attribute is not `ServiceControlled`.
`Location`	Provides information on the location of a service within an organization—building, floor, and room number. This attribute is not `ServiceControlled`.
`Name`	Used to designate a human-readable name for the service that will be seen by its users. The name of a service should be something that users will naturally understand, like "Fred's VCR." This attribute is not `ServiceControlled`.

Table 7–1 Standard Jini Attributes (continued)

Attribute	*Purpose*
`ServiceInfo`	Used to provide generic information about a service's manufacturer, model name, serial number, and so on. This attribute has a name field, which should provide the "generic" name of the product, rather than the specific name of an instance of the product (so, "Fleebtix VideoStar 1500" rather than "Fred's VCR," for example). This attribute is `ServiceControlled`.
`ServiceType`	Used to associate human-readable information that can describe a service. The `ServiceType` attribute includes a localized name for the service, a short description for it, and an icon to use for it. This attribute is `ServiceControlled`.
`Status`	Used to provide information on the current operating state of a service. The `Status` class is meant to be used as a superclass for service-specific types of status. The class, along with its supporting `StatusType` class, supports the designation of multiple error levels, from `NORMAL` up through `ERROR`. Users can search for particular error levels without having to understand the specifics of the `Status` subclasses used by individual services.

Writing New Attributes

The Jini standard attributes provide tools to associate information with services in ways that will be understood by nearly every Jini-aware application that will be written. Because these attributes are standardized and included with Jini itself, information such as comments and locations and manufacturer details will be encoded using these types, and applications will be written to look for and use them.

But sometimes you may need to create your own attributes. Sometimes the standard types are insufficient for the information you'd like to reveal about your service, and sometimes your organization may have decided on its own set of conventions for the kinds of information to associate with services. In these situations, you should create your own attribute types to store information about your service. Creating new attribute classes is easy—nearly as easy as just writing a Java object—and gives you complete freedom in how to represent the information that you will attach to your service.

You should, however, try to use the standard attributes wherever possible. Jini services can have any number of attributes attached to them, and can even have multiple attributes of the same type attached to them (a computer may have multiple `Name` attributes, for example). Because so many applications will expect the standard attributes, you should use them in addition to whatever extra information you provide.

We've already covered most of the details of writing new attribute classes: For the most part, you simply have to create a class that implements the `Entry` interface. Because this interface requires no methods, "implementing" it is trivial. `Entry` is a subinterface of `Serializable`, so you do have to take the normal steps that you would take to write a `Serializable` class—have a default, no-argument constructor, ensure that anything you *don't* want to be serialized is flagged with the `transient` keyword, or is static, and make sure that all the data that you reference is itself `Serializable`. This last requirement—making sure that all objects you reference are `Serializable`—is easily forgotten and can lead to great pain and misery when debugging.

Also, remember to take into consideration the special semantics of `Entry` objects with regard to searching and serialization. Searches involve only the public, nontransient, nonstatic, nonfinal object reference fields in an attribute. So, if you want clients to be able to search your attributes based on some data they contain, make sure that the data is stored as an object, and that the reference to it is public, nonstatic, nonfinal, and nontransient.

With regard to serialization, recall that all object reference fields in an attribute are serialized independently from one another, and will be reconstituted independently from one another when a client downloads your attribute. You must take special care to ensure that your object has no cross-field dependencies that will cause strange or broken behavior after reconstitution.

If you are writing a simple attribute that doesn't need to inherit from some preexisting class, you can use the Jini `AbstractEntry` as your attribute's superclass. This class, which lives in `net.jini.entry`, provides some handy methods that override some of the methods in the `Object` class: `AbstractEntry` provides new implementations of `equals()`, `hashCode()`, and `toString()` that are useful in the context of `Entrys`. For example, `toString()` returns a string containing each field's name and value. And `equals()` performs the `Entry` comparison test—it sees if the relevant (nonstatic, public, etc.) fields in two `Entries` match.

You don't have to use the `AbstractEntry` class, but if you're not already subclassing an existing class, you may find it useful. All of the Jini standard attributes use `AbstractEntry` as their superclass.

Finally, you should plan on human readability of your new attribute type. At a minimum, you should provide a sensible implementation of the `toString()` method, so that users who view your attribute will be able to read it. If you are implementing complex attribute types, you should also consider providing ways to integrate your attribute with the JavaBeans framework, as described in the next section.

An Example: A Capacity Attribute

Let's look at an example of a new attribute. Many services and devices have some innate capacity associated with them. For example, a storage service may have a maximum number of bytes that it can store; a digital camera can only store so many pictures before it exceeds its limits.

We can define a *capacity* attribute that captures this sort of information. A "generic" capacity attribute could be reused by many services, because it is not dependent on the "units" of storage (megabytes, or photos, or documents).

Let's look at how such an attribute might be implemented in Listing 7–1.

Listing 7–1 `Capacity.java`

```
package corejini.chapter7;

import net.jini.entry.AbstractEntry;
import net.jini.lookup.entry.ServiceControlled;

public class Capacity extends AbstractEntry implements Ser-
viceControlled {
    public Integer maxCapacity;
    public Integer inUse;
    public Integer freeSpace;

    public Capacity() {
        maxCapacity = new Integer(0);
        inUse = new Integer(0);
        freeSpace = new Integer(0);
    }

    public Capacity(int max, int used) {
        maxCapacity = new Integer(max);
        inUse = new Integer(used);
        freeSpace = new Integer(max - used);
    }
}
```

This new `Capacity` attribute starts off by extending the `AbstractEntry` class. By extending this class, it inherits useful implementations of `toString()` and other methods. The new class also implements `ServiceControlled` because the amount of free space in a service is intrinsic to that service and should not be altered directly by a user or a client (of course, the free space available in a service can and will change through administration of the service. But the attribute itself should never be changed or overwritten by anyone other than the service itself).

Although this class is straight forward, there is one interesting design point to make. Here, the three aspects of capacity—the maximum amount of storage, the amount of storage currently in use, and the amount of storage currently available—are stored as separate `Integers`. At first glance this may appear wasteful. Certainly, given any two of these you could compute the other one.

The reason for "breaking out" these details as separate objects is to facilitate search over them. Some searches may be interested in all storage services that have a maximum total capacity of a certain size. Other searches may be looking for storage services with a given amount of free capacity. Yet others may be looking for heavily used storage services that are holding some given number of items. By using individual members for each of these, they can be searched individually. You could imagine other computed values that might be of interest and could be stored as separate members in this attribute. A "percent full" member might be of interest to some applications, for instance.

Unfortunately, there is no way for a query to perform comparisons of data members in an attribute. So there is no way for an application to directly ask for all services with a maximum capacity *over* a given amount. A client that needed to do this sort of query would retrieve everything with a capacity and then look for those with particular values. We'll build on this simple `Capacity` attribute as we explore the relationship of attributes and JavaBeans.

Attributes and Beans

As said many times in this chapter, attributes are simply Java objects, albeit with some special serialization behavior to make searching more effective. As full-blown Java objects, you can set member fields in attributes and call methods on those attributes, if they have them.

But, just as "normal" Java objects can sometimes be difficult to work with—because they may not follow certain design patterns that indicate how to use them—attributes can also be somewhat opaque. In the Java world, special objects that follow certain design patterns are called *beans*. A bean is simply a Java object, just like any other, but it follows a set of conventions about how it will work and what its methods will be named.

For example, all beans have a no-argument constructor. Most beans are `Serializable`. If a bean has data in it that is accessible from outside the bean, it must have "get" and "set" methods that allow access to the data; these methods must follow JavaBeans-prescribed naming conventions.

All of these requirements are so that programs—particularly development tools—can *introspect* these objects and, if not understand *what* they do, at least get a sense of *how* they might do it. That is, they can figure out what methods are available to change the bean's state, and get some idea of how those methods work together. The JavaBeans `Introspector` class has the intelligence to look at a class that follows the bean conventions, and report on how to interact with the bean.

Beans also follow conventions that allow them to provide extra information describing their use. Any bean class will typically also come with a corresponding `BeanInfo` class that provides details on the fields and methods of the bean, as well as extra useful information such as icons that can be used to represent the bean on a palette of tools.

If an attribute followed the bean conventions or, alternatively, there were a way to associate a bean with an attribute at run time, then we could leverage all the power of the JavaBeans framework when working with attributes.

Using Entry Beans to Map Entries to Beans

Fortunately, Jini provides just such a facility. Jini uses the notion of *entry beans*, which are beans that correspond to particular `Entry` classes. An entry bean for a given entry will provide "get" and "set" methods for every data member that the `Entry` contains. Entry beans "wrap" normal `Entries`, and allow them to participate in the JavaBeans framework. In Jini, all beans that represent entries implement the `EntryBean` interface.

Let's look at how you create and use entry beans. If you have an entry—whether as a service or as a client—and you want to create an associated bean for it so that you can use the bean programmatically or introspect on it, you go through the `net.jini.lookup.entry.EntryBeans` class. This class provides some static utility methods for finding and instantiating entry beans for a given `Entry`. Let's look at the methods it provides.

```
package net.jini.lookup.entry;

public class EntryBeans {
        public static EntryBean createBean(Entry ent)
                    throws ClassNotFoundException,
                                 IOException;
        public static Class getBeanClass(Class c)
                    throws ClassNotFoundException;
}
```

The `createBean()` method instantiates an `EntryBean` given a particular `Entry` instance. The method will search for an `EntryBean` class that corresponds to the specified `Entry`, instantiate it, connect it to the `Entry` instance you passed in, and return it.

The `getBeanClass()` method simply tries to load the class of the `EntryBean` that corresponds to the `Entry` class you pass in (if you pass the class of something that's not an `Entry`, you'll get a `ClassCastException` run-time error). Once you've got the class, you can instantiate it yourself.

How Are Entry Beans Found?

The scheme that the `EntryBeans` utility class uses to find beans is simple, and is very similar to the method used by the "regular" JavaBeans bean-loading facilities. For an `Entry` with a given class name, say `Foo`, the `EntryBeans` class tries to find a class called `FooBean`. It tries to find this class by calling first the class loader that originally loaded the `Entry`, and then by calling its own default class loader.

The fact that the `EntryBeans` class first tries the class loader that was responsible for loading the `Entry` means that you can engineer some quite elegant code with beans. For example, if the original `Entry` was loaded remotely, say via RMI, then the code that implements the entry's bean can be stored on the same HTTP server and will be transmitted to the caller when it is needed. Once a bean is loaded, you can use the same class loader to fetch any extra information, such as `BeanInfo` classes, that may exist to describe how to use the bean.

If you create your own attribute classes, you should definitely consider creating corresponding `EntryBeans` and storing the code for them on the same server that manages the code for your `Entry` classes.

The Entry Bean Class

The Jini `net.jini.lookup.entry` package contains an interface that should be implemented by all entry beans. This interface is called, logically enough, `EntryBean`. If you create a new attribute type and want to make a new bean to go along with it, there are a few standard steps that you must take.

1. Create your bean class by implementing `EntryBean`.
2. Name your bean class by taking the name of your `Entry`'s class and appending "Bean" to it. So, for example, if your `Entry` is of class `Fleezle`, your bean should be of class `FleezleBean`. The bean should be in the same package as your `Entry` class.
3. Make sure your bean has a public, no-argument constructor and implements `Serializable` (so that it can be transmitted to clients as needed).
4. For every significant data member in the `Entry`, provide "get" and "set" methods in your bean. So, for example, if your `Entry` has a reference to an object called `foo`, you should provide methods called `getFoo()` and `setFoo()`, following the standard Java capitalization conventions.

The `EntryBean` interface is quite simple: it requires that you implement only two methods. Let's look at that interface.

```
package net.jini.lookup.entry;

public interface EntryBean {
        public void makeLink(Entry e);
        public Entry followLink();
}
```

The first method, `makeLink()`, is used to "wire up" the bean to an existing `Entry`. By calling this method, you create the association between a particular bean and a particular attribute. Your implementation of this method will typically be quite simple: you stash the reference to the `Entry` in your bean, and then all of your "get" and "set" methods simply access the data members in that `Entry`. If, for some reason, a caller passes in an `Entry` which is of the wrong type for your bean, you should raise a `ClassCastException`.

The next method, `followLink()`, simply provides a way to access the original `Entry`, given the bean.

While the requirements of implementing the `EntryBean` interface are practically trivial, you should make sure that you do, in fact, implement this interface. The `EntryBeans` utility class will complain loudly (through the use of `ClassCastExceptions`) if your bean doesn't implement this interface, even if it is named correctly.

If the `Entry` class that you're wrapping is particularly complex, you may want to consider making your bean a `java.awt.Component` or `javax.swing.JComponent` or some other "active" entity so that it can be displayed and edited properly. Ensuring that actual human users can understand, use, and edit your attributes is an important requirement, and providing a user interface for your attributes via a bean is an easy way to do this.

The Standard Entry Beans

Just as Jini provides a standard set of attributes, it also provides a standard set of beans that can wrap those attributes. In fact, for each of the standard `Entry` types, the `net.jini.lookup.entry` package contains a corresponding `EntryBean`.

In their current implementation, these bean classes only wrap their corresponding `Entry` classes; they do not provide any extra `BeanInfo` descriptions or icons or anything fancy like that. In future Jini releases, we should see a richer set of `Entry` classes, along with more complex beans to support them.

An Example: A Capacity Bean

Let's look at a minimalist bean for the `Capacity` attribute in Listing 7–2. This bean is simply a wrapper for a `Capacity` instance.

Listing 7–2 `CapacityBean.java`

```
package corejini.chapter7;

import net.jini.core.entry.Entry;
import net.jini.lookup.entry.EntryBean;
import java.io.Serializable;

public class CapacityBean
            implements EntryBean, Serializable {
    protected Capacity assoc = null;

     public CapacityBean() {
     }
```

Listing 7–2 `CapacityBean.java` **(continued)**

```
    public Entry followLink() {
       return assoc;
    }
    public void makeLink(Entry e) {
        if (e != null && !(e instanceof Capacity)) {
            throw new ClassCastException(
                "Expected corejini.chapter7.Capacity");
        }
        assoc = (Capacity) e;
    }
    public Integer getMaxCapacity() {
        return assoc.maxCapacity;
    }
    public void setMaxCapacity(Integer maxCapacity) {
        assoc.maxCapacity = maxCapacity;
    }
    public Integer getInUse() {
        return assoc.inUse;
    }
    public void setInUse(Integer inUse) {
       assoc.inUse = inUse;
    }
    public Integer getFreeSpace() {
       return assoc.freeSpace;
    }
    public void setFreeSpace(Integer freeSpace) {
       assoc.freeSpace = freeSpace;
    }
}
```

Here you see the basics of creating a bean for an attribute. The `CapacityBean` class implements `EntryBean` and is `Serializable` because, obviously, it will be downloaded to clients as needed. The class implements the simple `makeLink()` and `followLink()` methods by using an internal reference to a `Capacity` entry; note that `makeLink()` raises a `ClassCastException` if a caller tries to create a link to an `Entry` that's not a `Capacity`.

By following the bean naming conventions, you can allow the data in a `Capacity` object to be introspected and used programmatically—all of the members of the attribute are mapped into "get" and "set" functions that access the wrapped `Capacity`.

Once you've created a bean class for your attribute, you can go further and create extra information that can describe how to use the bean. For example,

you can create `BeanInfo` and `BeanDescriptor` classes that provide guidelines on how the bean should be used. If you define any exotic types in your attribute, you can provide bean `PropertyEditors` that allow users to display and edit these types, or `Customizers` that allow users to interact with the entire bean as a whole.

Listing 7–3 shows an example of a `BeanInfo` class for the above bean. It's pretty simple: Because `Capacity` defines no unusual types, there is no need for specialized `PropertyEditors` or `Customizers`. The only "extra" information provided here is a `BeanDescriptor` that has an extended description of the `CapacityBean`.

Listing 7–3 `CapacityBeanBeanInfo.java`

```
package corejini.chapter7;

import java.beans.BeanInfo;
import java.awt.Image;
import java.beans.BeanDescriptor;
import java.beans.MethodDescriptor;
import java.beans.EventSetDescriptor;
import java.beans.PropertyDescriptor;

public class CapacityBeanBeanInfo implements BeanInfo {
    protected BeanDescriptor beanDesc = null;

      public CapacityBeanBeanInfo() {
      }

      public BeanInfo[] getAdditionalBeanInfo() {
         return null;
      }
      public BeanDescriptor getBeanDescriptor() {
         if (beanDesc == null) {
             beanDesc = new BeanDescriptor(
                      corejini.chapter7.CapacityBean.class,
                      null);
             beanDesc.setShortDescription(
                  "This Jini attribute shows the capacity " +
                  "of a storage service.");
               }
         return beanDesc;
      }
      public EventSetDescriptor[] getEventSetDescriptors() {
         return null;
      }
```

Listing 7–3 `CapacityBeanBeanInfo.java` **(continued)**

```
    public int getDefaultEventIndex() {
        return -1;
    }

    public PropertyDescriptor[] getPropertyDescriptors() {
        return null;
    }
    public int getDefaultPropertyIndex() {
        return -1;
    }

    public Image getIcon(int param1) {
        return null;
    }
    public MethodDescriptor[] getMethodDescriptors() {
        return null;
    }
}
```

For most of the `BeanInfo` methods, the class returns null, indicating that it is providing no special information over what can be determined by the JavaBeans `Introspector` class. If you wanted, you could return extra information here, describing which parts of the `CapacityBean` are considered to be for "expert" use only, and provide icons for your bean.

Here, I've implemented the `getBeanDescriptor()` method to return a new `BeanDescriptor` with a short description of the `CapacityBean`. This is meant to be a human-readable message that can be presented to users.

The JavaBeans loading facilities dictate how `BeanInfo` objects must be named. A `BeanInfo` class for a given bean is named by taking the name of the original bean and appending "BeanInfo" to it. So here, I've named the class `CapacityBeanBeanInfo` so that it can be found at run time.

A Second Bean Example: Using GUI Beans

The `CapacityBean` is certainly a JavaBean—it follows all of the patterns and naming conventions of the beans framework—but it doesn't provide much other value. The information contained in a `Capacity` object is amenable to a graphical presentation, so you could create a new `CapacityBean` class that is a graphical component.

This new bean would still follow all of the bean conventions, and would implement all of the methods shown above. But it would also be a full-fledged component that clients could drop into GUI applications as needed.

Let's look at such a bean in Listing 7–4.

Listing 7–4 Another Version of `CapacityBean.java`

```
package corejini.chapter7;

import net.jini.core.entry.Entry;
import net.jini.lookup.entry.EntryBean;
import java.io.Serializable;
import javax.swing.JLabel;
import javax.swing.JPanel;
import javax.swing.JProgressBar;
import javax.swing.BoxLayout;

public class CapacityBean extends JPanel
            implements EntryBean, Serializable {
    protected Capacity assoc = null;

    public CapacityBean() {
        super(true);
        setBackground(java.awt.Color.white);
        setLayout(new BoxLayout(this, BoxLayout.Y_AXIS));
        add(new JLabel("Not initialized"));
    }

     public Entry followLink() {
        return assoc;
     }
     public void makeLink(Entry e) {
        if (e != null && !(e instanceof Capacity)) {
            throw new ClassCastException(
                 "Expected corejini.chapter7.Capacity");
        }

        assoc = (Capacity) e;

        init();
    }
```

Listing 7–4 Another Version of `CapacityBean.java` (continued)

```
    protected void init() {
        // clear out anything lingering from a
        // previous init()
        removeAll();

        JLabel label = new JLabel("Max = " +
                                  getMaxCapacity() +
                                 ", used = " + getInUse() +
                                  ", free = " +
                                  getFreeSpace());
        JProgressBar slider = new JProgressBar(0,
                              getMaxCapacity().intValue());
        slider.setValue(getInUse().intValue());

        add(slider);
        add(label);
    }

    public Integer getMaxCapacity() {
        return assoc.maxCapacity;
    }
    public void setMaxCapacity(Integer maxCapacity) {
        assoc.maxCapacity = maxCapacity;
    }
    public Integer getInUse() {
        return assoc.inUse;
    }
    public void setInUse(Integer inUse) {
        assoc.inUse = inUse;
    }
    public Integer getFreeSpace() {
        return assoc.freeSpace;
    }
    public void setFreeSpace(Integer freeSpace) {
        assoc.freeSpace = freeSpace;
    }
}
```

This class is a reimplementation of the first `CapacityBean`. The most notable difference is that the new implementation is a subclass of `JPanel`. This means that it inherits full functionality as a Swing component—it can be nested within other components and used just as you would any other widget in the Swing package.

Let's look at how this code works. First, notice that the class implements all of the "standard" get and set methods that are required if our code is to be a bean for the `Capacity` class. But here, whenever `makeLink()` is called, `CapacityBean` initializes two subcomponents that provide a graphical view of the capacity of a service. The code creates a `JLabel` and a `JProgressBar` that provide a view of current capacity.

To use GUI beans such as this, clients must do the following:

- For a given attribute, fetch its bean.
- Introspect the bean, to see if it is a subclass of `Component`.
- If the bean is a component, it can be displayed on the screen.
- Otherwise, the client should create a default label or other display by calling the `toString()` method on the original attribute.

If you write your clients to test whether beans it retrieves are `Components`, you can greatly enhance the appearance and usefulness of your code.

Core Note: User interfaces for Jini services

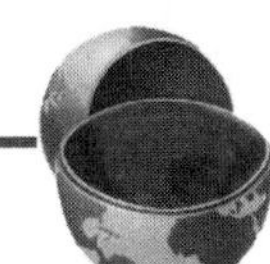

Actually, as you'll see in Chapter 12, there are a number of options available to you when you want to associate a user interface with a Jini service or attribute. Each of these approaches has different trade-offs. Check out Chapter 12 for a discussion of some strategies for building user interfaces for Jini; there is no single strategy that is best for all applications.

Further Reading

If you're new to the world of JavaBeans, a great way to get your feet wet is to check out *How to be a Good Bean*, a short tutorial on what a class needs to do to play well with other JavaBeans. This is a short but informative paper from JavaSoft, written by Eduardo Pelegri-Llopart and Larry Cable

```
http://java.sun.com/beans/docs/goodbean.pdf
```

The on-line tutorial from JavaSoft is a more comprehensive introduction to the world of JavaBeans.

```
http://java.sun.com/docs/books/tutorial/javabeans/
```

IN DEPTH: USING LOOKUP SERVICES

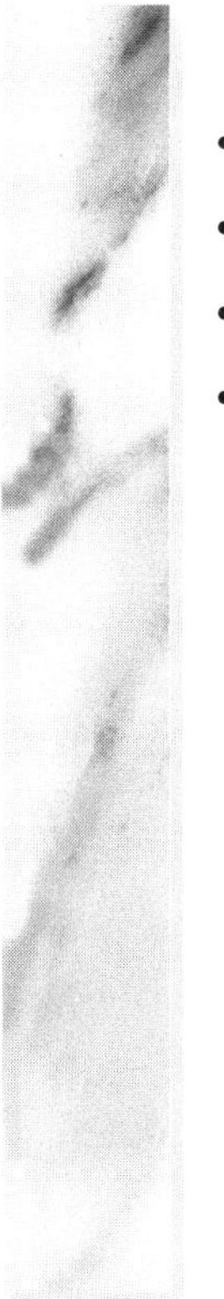

Topics in This Chapter

- Overview of Lookup
- Using the JoinManager class
- Searching for services
- Federating and administering lookup services

Chapter 8

In Chapter 6 we looked at how to find lookup services for Jini communities via the process of discovery. Now we'll look at what to actually *do* with those lookup services once we've found them. The collection of lookup services that support a Jini federation are the heart of that community—they have shared responsibility for keeping an accurate picture of the services available to the community up-to-date.

Jini lookup services provide a rich but simple set of APIs for service producers and consumers, both of which use the lookup facilities. Services use lookup to store their service proxies, and to describe these proxies by attaching attributes to them. Consumers of services use lookup to search for services, and to be notified when new services become available. Consumers can, of course, fetch the attributes associated with a service, and use them programmatically or present them to users. We'll look at how both service producers and consumers use lookup in this chapter.

We'll also take a look at quite a few examples that show off how to use lookup services to search for services and ask for events to be delivered when the set of services available from lookup changes. We'll also see some rather complex examples of how to administer lookup services, and control how services are made visible.

Overview of Lookup

We saw a basic overview of what Jini lookup services do and how to use them in Chapters 3 and 5. Basically you can think of a lookup service as a big networked storage engine. Each lookup service stores a set of `ServiceItems` that describe the particular services that the lookup service knows about. When a new service starts, it tells the lookup services about itself by *registering* `ServiceItems` with them. When a new client starts up and wants to use a service, it contacts any lookup services it finds and *searches* for the desired service.

Both clients and services find lookup services by using the discovery mechanisms outlined in Chapter 6. Clients typically use the discovery APIs directly; as we shall see, services can take advantage of some higher-level APIs that manage discovery for them. The discovery process results in the delivery of an object that implements the `ServiceRegistrar` interface to the discovering program. `ServiceRegistrar` is the interface that *all* Jini lookup services must implement, and so it forms the most basic API for dealing with lookup services. After discovery, programs that need to interact with lookup services can invoke the methods on `ServiceRegistrar`, either directly, or through an intermediate class library.

Lookup Services Are Jini Services

These `ServiceRegistrar` objects are actually service proxies for particular Jini lookup services; users of lookup services download and use these proxies just as users of "normal" services do when they download and use these service's proxies.

In fact, Jini lookup services *are* full-fledged Jini services, and support all the abilities and properties of other Jini services. They have unique service IDs, they manage leases, they publish proxies and attributes that describe those proxies, and they can be administered using the same mechanisms as other services. The only difference between a lookup service's proxy and any other service proxy is that lookup proxies can be found by the discovery process; this is how Jini applications bootstrap themselves into a community.

As we shall see, the fact that lookup services are Jini services means that you can configure groups of lookup services in very powerful ways: Any given lookup service can, in addition to whatever other service proxies it holds, keep a reference to its *own* proxy, as well as proxies for other lookup services.

Why would a lookup service want to hold on to proxies for itself and other lookup services? There are three reasons. First, proxies that are stored in a lookup service can have attributes associated with them. So a lookup service can "annotate" itself by attaching attributes to its service proxy. Clients can, when they connect to a lookup service, search for that lookup service's `ServiceItem`, and view any attributes attached to it.

Second, allowing access to the lookup service's service proxy through the lookup service itself provides a very uniform and elegant way to access resources on a Jini network: A lookup service holds proxies for *all* the services it knows about, including itself. So an application that iterates over all the service proxies held by a lookup service will actually get every service proxy available to it, including the lookup service's.

Finally, by making lookup services themselves Jini services, Jini supports the ability to *federate* lookup services together. You can make one Jini community reachable through another one by having the first community's lookup service register itself with the second community. By connecting communities, you can create arbitrary structures of Jini communities—groups of lookup services can be organized into a hierarchy, for example, or all the communities in your organization can also connect to a larger "clearing house" lookup service that only maintains pointers to other lookup services. We'll look at an example in this chapter of federating lookup services together.

How Services Use Lookup

You've seen some simple examples of how services use lookup in Chapter 5. The basic plotline is simple: A service creates a `ServiceItem` object that will hold its service proxy object and any attributes that the service wants to attach to it. It then uses discovery to find lookup services. While virtually all services will use multicast discovery, well-behaved services should also be configurable to try to connect to any explicitly provided Jini URLs that users may have specified.

Every service has an ID that uniquely identifies it and distinguishes it from its neighbors. Recall that service IDs are very long (128-bit) identifiers that uniquely name a service. The very first time a service is run, it will have no service ID; the first time a given service connects to a lookup service, the lookup service will assign it a service ID. The service must remember this and use it when it registers itself with all lookup services in the future.

The actual details of how services use their IDs, as well as the other particulars of interacting with lookup services, are called the service *join protocol*. This "protocol"—actually it's a series of conventions that dictate how services interact with discovery and lookup, rather than any network protocol—controls a number of aspects of services. The join protocol dictates how services will use discovery, what they will do if they lose a connection to a lookup service, which lookup services they will attempt to join, and so on. The particular requirements of the join protocol are somewhat complex; I'll discuss them more fully in the next few pages. But, fortunately, Jini provides some handy classes that automate the process.

When a service registers itself with a lookup service, the lookup service returns to it a lease that should be renewed for as long as the service is active. If the service ever "goes away" it should cancel its leases to ensure that the lookup service will forget about it as quickly as possible, and can free up any resources it was using to maintain the registration for the service.

How Clients Use Lookup

Client applications—meaning programs that only consume services, and don't provide them—can use lookup in a number of ways. First, they can search for any services that may have registered themselves with a lookup service. There are a few ways clients can search. We'll look at them in great detail in this chapter, but basically you can search for services based on the interfaces that the service proxy implements, the attributes that are attached to it, or explicitly using the service's ID (if you know it).

Depending on the particular search API used, the lookup service will either return to the client a single service proxy object, or a set of `ServiceItems`, each of which contains a proxy as well as any attributes associated with the proxy. Once a client has a proxy in its hands, it can invoke methods on the proxy to interact with the service.

In addition to searching, clients can also ask a lookup service to send it notifications when new services appear, existing services change, or previously registered services go away. The mechanisms for asking for events are very similar to the mechanisms used to search. In fact, the actual calls are almost identical. You can think of lookup services as providing two kinds of search—one for services that were registered in the past, and one for services that will be registered in the future. The tools used for describing what you're interested in are virtually the same in either case.

In the rest of this chapter, we'll look at the particulars of how different classes of applications interact with lookup services. First, we'll look at how a service provider publishes its service proxy. This process involves getting service IDs and knowing how to interact with lookup services using the join protocol. After this, we'll look at how clients use lookup services to search for services, and to solicit events so that they'll be informed of new services that

appear in the future. Finally, we'll look at administration of lookup services, see how to federate them together, and look at some examples of how to do this.

Publishing a Service Proxy: The Join Protocol

From the earlier examples, you've seen that publishing a proxy for a service is a pretty easy task—even when you're managing your interactions with a lookup service "by hand" as in the examples in Chapter 5. The most basic steps that a service needs to do are

- Create a `ServiceItem` that holds both the proxy object for the service and any attributes that describe it.
- Publish the service by calling `register()` on any `ServiceRegistrars` found through the discovery process.
- Maintain the leases on service registrations returned from the lookup services.

These are the most *basic* steps that need to happen when a service makes itself available. But, as alluded to in Chapter 5, there are many other things that well-behaved services should do in order to play nicely with other members of a Jini community.

Some of these were discussed in the chapter on discovery—services should switch from multicast request to waiting for multicast announcement after a period of time; services should wait some random amount of time before attempting discovery; and so forth.

But other requirements concern how services interact with lookup services. These requirements are collectively called the *join protocol*, because they regulate how services join communities. The basics of join are exactly as those just described, and exactly what you saw in Chapter 5: Services simply publish proxies and remember their IDs. But well-behaved services need to do this in a constrained way, in particular

- Services should use unique service IDs, even across restarts of the service and across whatever lookup services they are registered with. The first time—meaning the *very first time ever*—that a service is run, it needs to ask for a service ID from the first lookup service it contacts.

- Services should keep a list of *specific* lookup services that they are expected to join. This list may be configured by a human user or administrator. The list should be "remembered" to persistent storage when the service shuts down so that it can recover it later.
- When a service starts, it should register itself with all of the specific lookup services named in this list. The service uses unicast discovery to turn these lookup service URLs into `ServiceRegistrars` for the lookup services.
- Services renew their leases on registrations. If, at any point, communication with a lookup service fails, what steps the service takes depend on how the lookup service was discovered. If the lookup service was discovered through multicast discovery, the service should explicitly "forget" about it by calling `discard()` on the `LookupDiscovery` object that is managing the discovery process. If the lookup service later recovers, it will announce its presence via multicast announcement and will be rediscovered. If the lookup service was discovered through unicast discovery—that is, it was one of the explicit lookup services to which to connect—then the service should try periodically to reconnect. The join protocol dictates this because explicit lookup services were likely configured by humans, and should be remembered at all costs; also, since these lookup services are likely to be on a different network, they will not be discovered automatically via the serendipitous forms of discovery.
- If a service changes the set of attributes that it keeps—or is *asked* by a user or administrator to change the set of attributes—then it makes this change at *every* lookup service it is registered with. This stipulation is because a user or administrator ideally wants to be able to simply change *one* instance of an attribute and have it propagated to whatever lookup services are necessary.
- If a service changes the set of groups it is a member of—or is *asked* by a user to change the set of groups—then it must drop its registration at any discovered lookup services that are not members of the new groups. If groups are added, the service should begin discovery again to find lookup services that are members of these groups.

As you can see, while services at a *minimum* need only call `register()` to publish their proxies, there is quite a bit more work that needs to happen for services to interact cleanly with their communities. All the requirements of the join protocol are designed to make services easy to administer and maintain.

Clearly, there is a lot of bookkeeping that needs to happen for services to use the join protocol. Services need to *persistently*—meaning even across restarts of the service—remember a number of details, including their service IDs, the set of groups they are members of, the set of explicit lookup services they are to connect to, and any attributes attached to them.

The "Hello, World" service examples in Chapter 5 showed only the bare minimum of how to register with a lookup service in the interest of clarity. Now it's time to see how to "really" do it.

The JoinManager Class

Clearly, if you were a masochist, you could implement all of the requirements of the join protocol yourself, using the simple `ServiceRegistrar` interface described earlier. This interface is, in fact, the "base" level interface that describes all that you can guarantee a lookup service knows how to do. But fortunately, Jini provides some convenient classes to help you manage the process. The most important of these is called `JoinManager`, and lives in the `com.sun.jini.lookup` package.

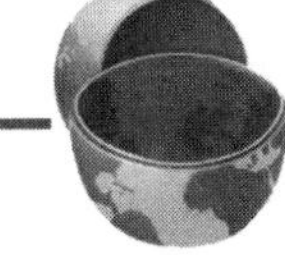

Core Alert: Join Manger is not a "core" package

This is one of the first major pieces of code we've seen that lives under the `com.sun.jini` *package, and not the* `net.jini` *or* `net.jini.core` *packages. This is because the code here is considered to be "library" code, built on top of the basic Jini foundations and interfaces. As we shall see,* `JoinManager` *requires the use of a few other pieces of code that are built atop the Jini foundation interfaces in* `net.jini`*. Be alert: The fact that these classes are in* `com.sun.jini`*, rather than* `net.jini`*, means that they are more likely to change than the underlying packages. Sun makes no guarantees that these classes will continue to exist or even be supported; in fact, Sun actively requests feedback on ways to improve these classes. But it's virtually certain that Sun will continue to provide a class that provides either the same or even greater functionality than* `JoinManager`*, since the task of participating in the join protocol can be pretty onerous otherwise.*

The JoinManager class provides all of the functionality necessary to implement the join protocol, with the exception of persistent storage. The JoinManager will even "take over" the process of discovery from you, so that it can decide when to restart multicast discovery after groups are added, maintain the unicast discovery list, and so on.

Let's look at some of the relevant parts of API for the JoinManager class.

```
package com.sun.jini.lookup.JoinManager;

public class JoinManager {
        public JoinManager(Object proxy, Entry[] attrs,
                           ServiceIDListener listener,
                           LeaseRenewalManager mgr);
        public JoinManager(Object proxy, Entry[] attrs,
                           String[] groups,
                           LookupLocator[] locs,
                           ServiceIDListener listener,
                           LeaseRenewalManager mgr);
        public JoinManager(ServiceID id, Object proxy,
                           Entry[] attrs,
                           String[] groups,
                           LookupLocator[] locs,
                           LeaseRenewalManager mgr);
        public void addAttributes(Entry[] attrs);
        public void addAttributes(Entry[] attrs,
                                  boolean checkSC);
        public void addGroups(String[] groups);
        public void addLocators(LookupLocator[] locs);
        public Entry[] getAttributes();
        public String[] getGroups();
        public ServiceRegistrar[] getJoinSet();
        public LookupLocator[] getLocators();
        public void modifyAttributes(Entry[]
                                     attrTemplates,
                                     Entry[] attrs);
        public void modifyAttributes(Entry[]
                                     attrTemplates,
                                     Entry[] attrs,
                                     boolean checkSC);
        public void removeGroups(String[] groups);
        public void removeLocators(LookupLocator[]
                                         locs);
        public void setAttributes(Entry[] attrs);
        public void setGroups(String[] groups);
        public void setLocators(LookupLocator[] locs);
        public void terminate();
}
```

From just perusing this API you can see that using `JoinManager` will make the job of participating in the join protocol much easier. The `JoinManager` takes care of participating in discovery, propagating attributes, handling group membership changes, and additions and deletions of explicit lookup service names. You can control all of these easily, just by using the methods that control the state of the various parameters.

Let's walk through the API. The first thing you see are the constructors. The `JoinManager` class provides three constructors, which can be used at different times during a service's life cycle. The first constructor is used when a service *first* starts, before it has a service ID, has been configured to join any groups, or has any specific lookup URLs to process. This constructor essentially does exactly what the old "Hello, World" service did: It publishes the proxy object, attaching the desired attributes to it, and registers the service in the unnamed public group.

Here, however, are a couple of extra parameters we haven't seen before. The first is the `ServiceIDListener`. This is an object that will receive notification when the service ID has been set; likely, this object will try to save the service ID to persistent storage so that it can be reused if the service ever shuts down or restarts. The listener doesn't, however, have to do anything special to tell the `JoinManager` about the service ID. The `JoinManager` automatically notices that an ID has been assigned to the service and will use it in any future registrations until it shuts down or the service goes away (recall that the `JoinManager` doesn't handle persistent state itself—so it's up to the user of `JoinManager` to take care of remembering things like service IDs across runs). If you leave off the `ServiceIDListener` by just passing in null, the `JoinManager` will continue to work, but you will not be called when the ID is first set.

The second parameter is a thing called a `LeaseRenewalManager`. This is simply an object that takes care of managing and renewing leases for you, much like the "helper" code we wrote in Chapter 5. The `LeaseRenewalManager` lives in the `com.sun.jini.lease` package, and so is subject to change in future releases. Basically a `LeaseRenewalManager` will automatically try to renew any leases that it manages, and can call out to a listener if a renewal ever fails. We'll see a few examples of how it works in this chapter, and we'll explore it more fully in Chapter 10 (we'll also, in that chapter, see how to go about building custom lease renewal services).

If you don't need any specialized lease renewal behavior, and don't care to be informed whenever leases cannot be renewed, you can just pass in null here. The `JoinManager` will create a "default" `LeaseRenewalManager` to handle leasing for you.

The second constructor is also used when a service first starts. In this case, though, the service has been configured ahead of time to join a specific set of groups and try to connect to a specific set of lookup services. This constructor is much the same as the first—including the use of a `ServiceIDListener` to inform you when a service ID has been assigned—but allows you to pass in an initial set of groups and `LookupLocators`.

Finally, the third constructor is used when a service is being rerun, perhaps after being shut down for maintenance or being moved to a new machine. The difference between this constructor and the previous two is that this constructor takes the ID of the service as an explicit argument. When the `JoinManager` starts its work, it will use this ID at every lookup service it registers with. Also note that it doesn't have a `ServiceIDListener`, since the ID is already set and should never change.

The rest of the methods are pretty self-explanatory: they allow you to change the set of groups a service tries to join, the set of lookup services it explicitly contacts, and the attributes it maintains. All of these methods are a great time saver, because they allow you to perform operations across *all* of a service's registrations with one method call. Calling, for example, `setAttributes()` doesn't just change the set of attributes cached locally in the `JoinManager`. It actually goes out and updates all of the service's current registrations to have the new attributes. Likewise, any future registrations will acquire the new attributes. We'll look at how to use these methods a bit later in our examples.

Managing Service IDs

I've talked both in this chapter and in Chapter 5 about the need to keep service IDs unique, and for services to use the same service ID across runs and on every lookup service they register with. Why is this?

To answer this question, we need to look at how Jini applications use service IDs. If you are a client application that wishes to use, say, a printer service, you start out by contacting all of the lookup services you can find. A well-written printer service will have registered itself with all the lookup services for the groups it wishes to join. If this printer service used a different ID each time it registered, the client would have no way of knowing that the registrations at each lookup service represented the *same* printer. It might display to its users a list of dozens of printers, each of which was actually the same device. By requiring services to use the same ID at each lookup service, we can *know* that two `ServiceItems` with the same IDs actually represent the same device or service.

So this is why services use the same IDs at each lookup service they find. But why is it so important for services to remember their IDs across crashes, and use the same ID after they've been restarted, or even if they're disconnected, moved to a different computer, and reattached?

The answer is that you, as the service writer, cannot ensure that a given client will not hold on to your service ID indefinitely. Say that your service controls a printer. Another service, say a digital camera, might be a *consumer* of your service—When a printer is available, the "print" button on the camera's display highlights to mean that printing is possible. If there are several printers on the network, the user of the camera may have configured the camera to print to *your* printer, and so the camera has recorded the service ID of your print service as the "preferred" printer.

Now suppose the printer is disconnected momentarily from the network—either because the computer it attaches to crashes, or maybe because someone needed to rework its cabling to add a scanner or other device. If the printer were to come back up with a new ID, the camera would have no way to find the printer's proxy using the information it retains—the old ID of the service. In this case, the user's configuration of the camera would be lost, and he or she would have to reset the default printer for the camera. This is the sort of unhappy and frustrating chore that gives computers a bad name, and is exactly the thing that Jini is designed to prevent.

The solution is for the printer to remember its ID and reuse it when it reconnects to the network. Because the writer of the printer service can't guarantee that no client will be holding on to its ID, it should make every effort to reuse the ID that it was originally granted.

The underlying key to all of this is a simple concept: service IDs uniquely represent services. That is, a service ID will globally and for all time refer to *exactly* one printer, or camera, or software service, even if that printer, camera, or software moves to a different machine or disappears off the net for long periods of time. You can think of the service ID as the "serial number" of a service. Even two cameras from the same manufacturer, identical in every other regard, still have different serial numbers to identify them as different cameras. Like serial numbers, each *instance* of a Jini service has a unique identifier—even if I have one class that implements a printer service, each instance of that class would represent a different physical printer and thus would have its own ID. And also like many serial numbers, Jini service IDs are quite large so that they can uniquely distinguish all the potential Jini-enabled devices that may come along—Jini service IDs are 128 bits long, more than enough to last virtually *forever.* (Even if the world's population reaches 100 billion, and each of these people have, say, a million Jini-enabled

VCRs, cameras, and DVD players to their name—a situation that would make Sun quite happy indeed— assigning unique IDs to these devices would only take around 64 bits of the service ID address space.)

But unlike a serial number, which is typically burned into a device or piece of software when it leaves the factory, Jini assigns service IDs to services when they first run. This practice is in keeping with Jini's philosophy of decentralized control—there is no need for any central, global registry to keep track of all service IDs and dole them out to applicants. There is likewise no bureaucratic paperwork to go through to get a unique service ID assigned to your service. All you have to do is use the proper constructors of `JoinManager` to ensure that a service ID that is globally unique and yours for all time is assigned to you the first time you run. The `JoinManager` gets the service ID from the first Jini lookup service that happens to respond to it.

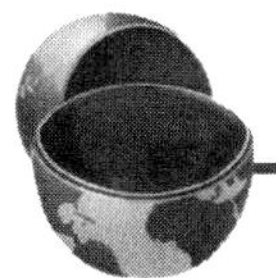

Core Note: How are service IDs generated?

The fact that programs that need an ID that is theirs forever, across all space and time, can simply have one handed to them is great. But how does this actually work? What's the magic that allows any Jini lookup service to create one of these almighty IDs? The truth is that there's no magic. In fact, the size of the bit space makes it rather improbable that any two 128-bit random numbers ever generated would be the same, as long as they start from different seed values. Jini uses a somewhat more sophisticated technique than just cranking out random 128-bit numbers, though. I won't go into the details here; see the Further Reading section at the end of this chapter if you really care. But basically the service ID is created by stuffing together 60 bits of system clock, expressed in 100 nanosecond chunks since the year 1582, a bunch of random "noise" thrown in for good measure, and, on some implementations, a unique host address for the lookup service (usually its ethernet address, if it has one). This scheme guarantees unique numbers until the year 3400 A.D., at which point the clock rolls over. Even then, however, the host identifiers and random number components will likely provide uniqueness, although it can no longer be guaranteed. (And, by that time, the smart money says that any Jini printers bought in the late 20th or early 21st century will be out of warranty so you should probably consider upgrading anyway.)

Using the JoinManager in Applications

It's time to look at how to use the `JoinManager` to implement services. In this example, you'll see the use of a new kind of service wrapper. Recall that a service wrapper is a process that publishes a service proxy and takes care of the chores of renewing leases for it.

In the examples in Chapter 5, the "Hello, World" services all used a process that continually ran to manage their simple service proxies. In all of these cases, the wrapper simply handled lease management (although the last example of Chapter 5 did use a "back-end" object that the proxy communicated with to accomplish its service—this back end was separate from the wrapper, however).

Here you'll see an example of a service wrapper that uses the `JoinManager` APIs. You'll also see how to use persistence to store some of the state that services need to keep between runs—the service ID, attribute sets, groups, and explicit lookup URLs. In the "Hello, World" examples, every time we ran the service, it "forgot" all of its old state—it would try to acquire a brand new service ID for each run, and it did nothing to store the state of any attributes or other data.

The example here (Listing 8–1) will "checkpoint" its state to persistent storage whenever it first receives a service ID from a lookup service. When subsequently run, it will recover this state from persistent storage, and use it to reset all its internal data, including its service ID. In this simple example, there is no way for users to *change* the set of groups, attributes, or lookup URLs that the wrapper uses. You can easily extend this program to provide a way to programmatically change these parameters; the wrapper can then checkpoint these whenever they are updated.

Let's look at the wrapper code.

Listing 8–1 `ServiceWrapper.java`

```
// a basic wrapper that uses JoinManager

package corejini.chapter8;

import java.io.*;
import net.jini.core.lookup.ServiceID;
import net.jini.core.discovery.LookupLocator;
import net.jini.core.entry.Entry;
import com.sun.jini.lookup.JoinManager;
import com.sun.jini.lookup.ServiceIDListener;
import java.rmi.RMISecurityManager;
```

Listing 8–1 `ServiceWrapper.java` (continued)

```
    class MyProxy implements Serializable,
            corejini.chapter5.HelloWorldServiceInterface {
    public MyProxy() { }
    public String getMessage() {
        return "Bonjour, my little turnip...";
    }
}

public class ServiceWrapper implements Runnable {
    protected JoinManager join = null;
    protected File serFile = null;
    protected Object proxy = new MyProxy();

    // note static!
    static class PersistentData implements Serializable {
        ServiceID serviceID;
        Entry[] attrs;
        String[] groups;
        LookupLocator[] locators;

        public PersistentData() {
        }
    }

    class IDListener implements ServiceIDListener {
        public void serviceIDNotify(ServiceID serviceID) {
            System.out.println("Got service ID " +
                                                  serviceID);
            PersistentData state = new PersistentData();
            state.serviceID = serviceID;
            state.attrs = join.getAttributes();
            state.groups = join.getGroups();
            state.locators = join.getLocators();

            try {
                writeState(state);
            } catch (IOException ex) {
                System.err.println("Couldn't write: " +
                                   ex.getMessage());
                ex.printStackTrace();
                join.terminate();
                System.exit(1);
            }
        }
    }
```

Listing 8–1 `ServiceWrapper.java` **(continued)**

```
    public ServiceWrapper(File serFile,
            boolean firsttime)
          throws IOException, ClassNotFoundException {
        this.serFile = serFile;

        if (System.getSecurityManager() == null) {
            System.setSecurityManager(
                new RMISecurityManager());
        }

        if (firsttime)
            register();
        else
            reregister();
    }
    public void run() {
        while (true) {
            try {
                Thread.sleep(Long.MAX_VALUE);
            } catch (InterruptedException ex) {
            }
        }
    }

    protected void register() throws IOException {
        if (join != null) {
            throw new IllegalStateException(
                                 "Wrapper already started.");
        }


        System.out.println("Starting...");
        join = new JoinManager(proxy, null,
                   new IDListener() , null);
    }

    protected void reregister()
        throws IOException, ClassNotFoundException {
        if (join != null) {
            throw new IllegalStateException(
                             "Wrapper already started.");
        }
```

Listing 8–1 `ServiceWrapper.java` **(continued)**

```
        PersistentData state = readState();

        System.out.println("Restarting:  old id is " +
                                         state.serviceID);

        join = new JoinManager(state.serviceID,
                                         proxy, state.attrs,
                                         state.groups,
                                         state.locators, null);
    }


     protected void writeState(PersistentData state)
                                   throws IOException {
        ObjectOutputStream out =
            new ObjectOutputStream(
                         new FileOutputStream(serFile));

        out.writeObject(state);
        out.flush();
        out.close();
    }

    protected PersistentData readState()
        throws IOException, ClassNotFoundException {
        ObjectInputStream in =
            new ObjectInputStream(
                         new FileInputStream(serFile));

        PersistentData state = (PersistentData)
                                   in.readObject();
        in.close();
        return state;
    }

    static void usage() {
        System.err.println("Usage: ServiceWrapper " +
                "[-f] serialization_file");
        System.exit(1);
    }
```

Listing 8–1 `ServiceWrapper.java` **(continued)**

```
    public static void main(String[] args) {
        boolean firsttime = false;
        String serFileName = null;
        File serFile = null;

        if (args.length < 1 || args.length > 2) {
            usage();
        }

        if (args.length == 2) {
            if (args[0].equals("-f")) {
                firsttime = true;
                serFileName = args[1];
            } else {
                usage();
            }
        } else {
            serFileName = args[0];
        }

        serFile = new File(serFileName);

        try {
            ServiceWrapper wrapper =
                 new ServiceWrapper(serFile, firsttime);
            new Thread(wrapper).start();
        } catch (Exception ex) {
            ex.printStackTrace();
        }
    }
}
```

This is a fairly involved example that shows how a service might make its state persistent between runs. Here, because the point is to show how to use `JoinManager` and how to make the data that `JoinManager` needs be persistent, rather than to show off any particularly fancy service, I've reused the "Hello, World" interface from our earlier examples.

The first thing to notice is that the code required to deal with the mechanics of discovery and lookup is actually significantly *shorter* than the prior examples. And, not only is the code shorter, it is actually better behaved as well: This version has proper leasing behavior and fully participates in the join protocol.

Let's look at how the wrapper works. When you run the `main()` provided here, you need to specify a file in which to store the persistent state between runs. Also, if this is the first time that the service is being brought up, you specify `-f` on the command line, to indicate that this is the service's "first time." Here I'm using the special command-line arguments for flags and to specify the storage location so that I can simplify the concepts being illustrated. Your services will most probably automatically detect whether they are being run for the first time by looking to see if a service ID has already been written to persistent storage. And, rather than specifying the location of that storage on the command line, they will support selectively changing the storage location through the service administration interfaces we'll talk about in Chapter 12.

Once the wrapper class is instantiated, `main()` checks the command-line arguments, and calls `register()` if this is the first time it's been run, or `reregister()` otherwise. The `register()` call simply instantiates a `JoinManager` to handle the wrapper's participation in the join protocol. It then passes the proxy object, registers an instance of a nested listener class as the `ServiceIDListener` for the protocol (the code must be informed when it gets a `ServiceID` for the first time, so that it can checkpoint it), and passes in null for the attribute list and a lease manager. Recall that if you use a null lease manager, `JoinManager` will create one to renew your leases until you shut down or tell it to stop.

The first time a `ServiceID` is assigned, `serviceIDNotify()` will be called by virtue of the fact that the wrapper is registered with the `JoinManager` as a `ServiceIDListener`. This is where the service checkpoints its state out to stable storage. In this particular case, the `ServiceID` is the *only* thing that can change. It's easy to imagine an extension of this code that allows users to set attributes, groups, and lookup URLs, however, and the wrapper could just as easily checkpoint these when they change.

When the wrapper checkpoints its state, it saves everything as an instance of `PersistentData`, a class defined here to collect together all the parameters in the `JoinManager` that may change. Note here that `PersistentState` is a *static* nested class. If this class weren't declared static, it would have an implicit reference to the `ServiceWrapper` that created it, causing the entire wrapper to be saved to the disk along with it! This clearly isn't what we want; declaring the class static means that it's nested purely for purposes of scoping, not because of any run-time association between the nesting and the inner class.

Data is written to stable storage by extracting any state we want to save out of the `JoinManager`, putting it in a `PersistentData` object, and then calling `writeState()`. The `writeState()` call simply creates an `ObjectOutputStream` for the file being saved to, and writes the object.

If the service is terminated—or crashes—and is run again later, you can leave off the `-f` flag and the `reregister()` method will be invoked. This method loads in the persistent state by calling `readState()`, which works just the same as `writeState()` but in reverse. It wraps an `ObjectInputStream` around the data file and loads in the `PersistentData` object that was written earlier. A new `JoinManager` is created from this data—note how `reregister()` passes in the service ID and other data that were retrieved from stable storage so that it registers itself in the same state it had the last time it was run.

Compiling and Running the Example

This example program is a service, so it both needs to consume downloadable code and export downloadable code (its service proxy). So, following the conventions we've been using so far in this book, you'll need to compile the service and then copy any class files that are meant to be downloadable out to the `service-dl` directory. This is the directory that's exported by the HTTP server that's handling the downloadable code from services. You'll also need to provide the name of a file for persistent storage, and the `-f` flag the first time you run.

On Windows:

```
javac -classpath C:\jini1_0\lib\jini-core.jar;
                 C:\jini1_0\lib\jini-ext.jar;
                 C:\jini1_0\lib\sun-util.jar;
                 C:\service
            -d  C:\service
        C:\files\corejini\chapter8\ServiceWrapper.java

cd C:\service\corejini\chapter8
copy MyProxy.class
                 C:\service-dl\corejini\chapter8

java -cp C:\jini1_0\lib\jini-core.jar;
                      C:\jini1_0\lib\jini-ext.jar;
                      C:\jini1_0\lib\sun-util.jar;
                      C:\service;
                      C:\service-dl
        -Djava.security.policy=C:\files\policy
        -Djava.rmi.server.codebase=http://myhost:8085/
        corejini.chapter8.ServiceWrapper -f C:\temp\foo
```

On Solaris:

```
javac -classpath /files/jini1_0/lib/jini-core.jar:
                 /files/jini1_0/lib/jini-ext.jar:
                 /files/jini1_0/lib/sun-util.jar:
                 /files/service
             -d  /files/service
        /files/corejini/chapter8/ServiceWrapper.java

cd /files/service/corejini/chapter8
copy MyProxy.class
                 /files/service-dl/corejini/chapter8

java -cp /files/jini1_0/lib/jini-core.jar:
                      /files/jini1_0/lib/jini-ext.jar:
                      /files/jini1_0/lib/sun-util.jar:
                      /files/service:
                      /files/service-dl
        -Djava.security.policy=/files/policy
        -Djava.rmi.server.codebase=http://myhost:8085/
        corejini.chapter8.ServiceWrapper -f /tmp/foo
```

Using Attributes through the JoinManager

Let's look now at how to add and change attributes on your service through the `JoinManager` interface. The `JoinManager` supports a handful of calls to control attributes on a service: `addAttributes()` allows new attributes to be added to the existing set of attributes; `removeAttributes()` discards a set of attributes for the service; `setAttributes()` overwrites the current attributes with new ones; `getAttributes()` fetches the current set of attributes for the service; and `modifyAttributes()` changes sets of attributes according to pattern-matching rules similar to those used for search.

All of these calls share one thing in common—any change they make to the set of attributes is used for all future registrations, and is also propagated to all current registrations. These methods provide an extremely convenient way to change whole batches of attributes across all the lookup services that a particular service is registered with.

Most of these methods are self-explanatory, but a few deserve some extra attention. The first thing to note is the `modifyAttributes()` method. This is a fairly complex—but very useful—method that can be used to change a whole series of attributes in one shot.

The `modifyAttributes()` call takes two parameters, each an array of `Entries`. The call modifies the current set of attributes based on these parameters. The first parameter, called the *attribute templates*, is used to specify which attributes to change. The second parameter, called the *attributes set*, specifies what to do to attributes that match the templates.

Here's how it works. Both of the arrays of `Entries` must be the same length; if they are not, an `IllegalArgumentException` is thrown. Next, the method iterates through the arrays, looking pair-wise at `Entries` from both the attribute template and attribute set arrays (so, for the third iteration, the method will look at `attrTemplate[3]` and `attrSet[3]`).

For each attribute template, the method finds all attributes attached to the service that match the template—this means that the system finds all attributes that have the same class as the template's class, and any non-null fields in the template exactly that match the corresponding field in the attribute being tested for a match.

Once all the matches for the template have been found, the method looks at the corresponding element in the attribute set array (that is, the element that has the same index as the template it just tested). The value of the `Entry` in the attribute set array determines what will happen to the matches. If the attribute set `Entry` is null, then all matched attributes are deleted. Otherwise, every non-null field in the `Entry` is copied into the corresponding field of every matched attribute.

Using `modifyAttributes()` lets you make wholesale changes to entire sets of attributes—removing groups of attributes that match a template, and making prescribed changes to groups of attributes—all in one operation.

Restricting Changes to ServiceControlled Attributes

As you no doubt noticed, the `JoinManager` class provides two versions of each of the `addAttributes()` and `modifyAttributes()` methods. The first version of each of these methods, the ones without the boolean `checkSC` parameter, are meant to be used by the service itself to add and change any of its attributes. These calls simply perform the requested change when they are invoked.

There are second versions of each of these methods, however, that take a boolean called `checkSC`. The `checkSC` parameter says whether to check if the attributes being added or changed implement the `ServiceControlled` interface. If any added or changed attribute *does* implement this interface, and `checkSC` is true, then a `SecurityException` will be raised. This version

of the call is meant to be used when an attribute addition or change may originate with an external client application or end user.

Recall the details of service administration from the last chapter: Services should provide some means for users and programs to change their attributes. Typically, this will be done through an object that implements one or more service administration APIs. Service consumers will typically ask the service proxy for its administration object, and any method calls on this administration object will—in a service-specific way—make their way back to the service's back end for processing.

This is where the `checkSC` versions of these methods come in. A client may interact with a service's proxy object to cause new attributes to be added. The proxy bundles this request up however it sees fit—using RMI or sockets or whatever—and transmits it back to the "back-end" process or device that handles the service proxy's registration. This back-end process will most likely be a wrapper like the one we've already seen; and this wrapper, if it is implemented in Java will almost certainly be built using the `JoinManager` class. So, when these client-originated requests for attribute changes come in, the back-end process can simply pass them through the `checkSC` versions of the `addAttributes()` and `modifyAttributes()` methods of the `JoinManager`. If the client is attempting to add or change an attribute that should be under the sole control of the service, a `SecurityException` will be raised and the back-end process can abort the change.

Figure 8–1 shows the basic idea—a client asks for an administration object by calling `getAdmin()`. Once it has this delegate object which it can use to administer a service, it can call methods defined on it to interact with the service. In this illustration, calling `addAttribute()` on the administration object will cause a message to be sent to the wrapper for the service, which will then invoke the "safe" version of `addAttribute()` defined by the `JoinManager`. If the client attempts to change any `ServiceControlled` attributes, the call will fail with a `SecurityException`. The exact way in which an administration object calls back to the wrapper is dependent on the way in which the service author chose to build administration.

How Clients Use Lookup Services

So far in this chapter we've seen how services use the lookup facilities in Jini to publish their service proxies, and we've taken an in-depth exploration at how attributes work to describe services. Now it's time to look at how client applications interact with lookup services.

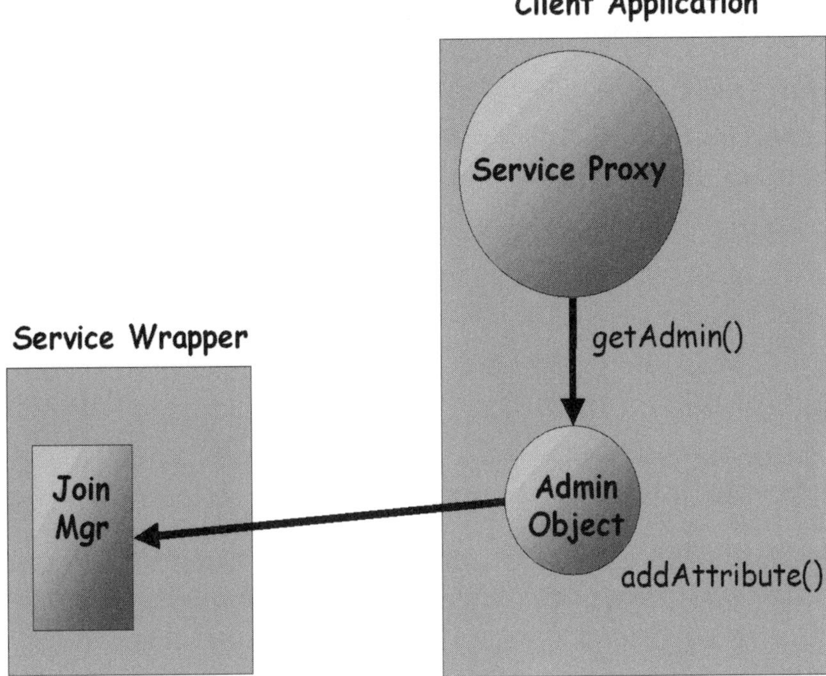

Figure 8–1 Attributes are added through administration delegates

When we wrote our first Jini programs, the "Hello, World" examples way back in Chapter 5, we saw the `ServiceRegistrar` class. In those examples, we used the `ServiceRegistrar` interface to lookup services *directly*; `ServiceRegistrar` is the low-level, core interface that all lookup services support.

In this chapter, we saw that services could use the `JoinManager` class, which is built on top of `ServiceRegistrar`, to make the jobs they need to do when registering service proxies easier.

Clients, however, have no such "utility" classes to help their interactions with lookup services—they use the "raw" `ServiceRegistrar` interfaces directly. The good news is that clients don't really *need* any fancier facilities to help them get the most out of lookup. For the most part, client interactions with lookup services are limited to two operations: searching for services, and soliciting events so that they can be notified when the set of available services changes.

In this section, we'll revisit the `ServiceRegistrar` API, and look at how searching and event solicitation work from the client's perspective. As we shall see, the basic mechanisms for both searching and events work in much the same way.

The Client Life Cycle

Clients begin their search for services in the same way that services begin their lives: they use discovery to find lookup services. Services can use the `DiscoveryListener`, `LookupDiscovery`, `LookupLocatorDiscovery`, and `LookupLocator` APIs that we explored in Chapter 6 or, as we saw earlier in this chapter, they can let the `JoinManager` take care of their discovery tasks for them.

Clients, on the other hand, use the discovery APIs directly and, once they've found one or more lookup services, typically interact directly with the `ServiceRegistrar` interface. *How* exactly they use these APIs depends on the client; there is no equivalent of the "join protocol" for clients. Whereas services need to follow a rigorously prescribed set of steps to ensure that they are manageable, administrable, and reliable, clients can essentially be ad hoc in regard to how they interact with discovery and lookup.

Why is this? The extra requirements on services are dictated by the fact that services are, typically, longer-lived entities than clients. Services are meant to be started and run virtually autonomously for long stretches of time. The rules of the join protocol are intended to make services as maintenance free as possible, by constraining how and when they contact lookup services, how they store their attributes and groups, and which lookup services they connect to.

On the other hand, many clients are short lived. An application like a service browser (which we will see in the next chapter) is started at the request of a user, and runs only until the user has accomplished some task, at which point it is shut down. Clients don't *provide* any services of their own, so no other Jini entities can have dependencies on them to behave correctly in any way. Even long-lived clients—such as a "background" program that runs on your PC to detect new Jini devices and software services and then make them visible to applications by updating the Windows registry—can follow the guidelines implied by their particular application niche for how to save persistent state and interact with discovery and lookup.

Because the requirements for how clients interact with discovery and lookup, and how they record any persistent state they may need, are so minimal, there is no equivalent of the `JoinManager` for clients. Clients use the discovery APIs directly to retrieve `ServiceRegistrar` instances. Once they have these instances, they communicate directly with lookup services to typi-

cally do two things: search for services, and ask the lookup services to send them events when the set of services known to them changes.

Let's look at searching first.

Searching for Services

We took a somewhat shallow look at the APIs for searching in Chapter 7. In that chapter, we saw that searching was based on a simple idea: You submit a *template* that describes the service you are searching for to the lookup service. The lookup service then returns the matches for your template.

The Search APIs

The `ServiceRegistrar` interface supports two variants of a method called `lookup()` for performing searches. One variant is intended for clients that can completely specify the service they need by using the template mechanism. The other is appropriate either if a client cannot fully specify the service it is looking for using a template, or for "browser"-style applications that may need to find all available services. Here are the two versions of the `lookup()` method:

```
Object lookup(ServiceTemplate tmpl)
                              throws RemoteException;
ServiceMatches lookup(ServiceTemplate tmpl, int maxMatches)
                              throws RemoteException;
```

All the classes and interfaces used here are part of the `net.jini.core.lookup` package, since they are the foundation for interaction with lookup services.

In both versions of the `lookup()` method, the client provides a template that describes the services it is searching for. This template is represented as a class, called `ServiceTemplate`. In the first version of `lookup()`, the client provides a template which causes the lookup service to perform a search. If no services match the template, then null will be returned to the client. Be sure to test the reference you get back to see if it is null—assuming that the template will always match and return a non-null value is a common programming error in Jini.

If one or more services match, however, then *one* will be selected by the lookup service as the matching service. The proxy object of this service will be returned to the caller.

This version of the `lookup()` method is quite simple to use, because it trades potential complexity for some inflexibility. Even though multiple services may match the template you specify, only one will be returned; you have no control over *which* matched service will be returned.

In practice, this limitation will not be a problem for the clients that use this version of `lookup()`; there are two situations in which using this version of the method may be acceptable to clients. First, they may be capable of *fully* specifying the service that they want using the template mechanisms, in which case there will be only one service that matches. This situation might be the case for a Jini "universal remote control" that needs to talk to *exactly* one particular DVD player in your house, and knows this device by its service ID or by enough descriptive information that it can uniquely identify it. Either the desired DVD player is there, or it isn't, and no fancier search techniques are needed to determine whether it's there.

Alternatively, for a particular application, as long as the desired service can be specified *well enough* by the template, the client may not *care* which of a number of possible choices it gets back. If a client needs a TIFF to JPEG image format conversion service, it can simply formulate a query that asks for any such converter. If multiple TIFF to JPEG services are running on a network, the client doesn't particularly care which one is returned—any of the alternatives will do, as long as it meets the needs that the client has specified.

You should be aware of a second limitation of this method, however. This version of `lookup()` returns *only* the service proxy object for the matched service. There is no way to get the service ID of the matched service, or any of its attributes. This method is the "quick and dirty" version of search, where clients know exactly what they want, and intend to use the service proxy returned with a minimum of fuss.

The second version of `lookup()` is more flexible, but also not as easy to use as the first. In this version, the client again passes in a `ServiceTemplate` that describes the services it wishes to find. But it also passes in an integer, describing the maximum number of matches it wishes to have returned to it. For its part, the `lookup()` method, rather than simply returning a single service proxy, returns an object called `ServiceMatches` that contains an array of complete `ServiceItems` (containing proxy, service ID, and attributes) that matched the query. If you need to find *all* the services known to a lookup service, you can pass in `Integer.MAX_VALUE` as the number of items to find. This is the largest number that can fit in 32 bits, which should far outstrip the number of individual services registered with any one lookup service.

The `ServiceMatches` class is simply a container for an array of `ServiceItems`. Here are the relevant parts of that class.

```
package net.jini.core.lookup;

public class ServiceMatches
            implements Serializable {
        public ServiceMatches(ServiceItem[] items,
                              int totalMatches);
        public ServiceItem[] items;
        public int totalMatches;
}
```

The `items` array is public, so once you get back a `ServiceMatches` object from the `ServiceRegistrar`, you can just grab this array to see all the return results. The `ServiceItem` class contains public members for the service proxy, the service ID, and any attributes that are associated with the service. You already saw in the earlier examples how services create `ServiceItems` when they join a Jini community; the `ServiceItems` returned from `lookup()` are simply copies of the same `ServiceItems` published by services. Here are the relevant portions of that class.

```
package net.jini.core.lookup;

public class ServiceItem implements Serializable{
        public ServiceItem(ServiceID serviceID,
                           Object service,
                           Entry[] attributeSets);
        public ServiceID serviceID;
        public Object service;
        public Entry[] attributeSets;
}
```

The `service` field here is the proxy object for the service. This is the same object that would be returned from the simpler version of `lookup()` we saw before.

Once a client retrieves this array of `ServiceItems`, it can iterate over them to look for exactly the services it needs or, in the case of browser-style applications, simply display them all to the user.

How Are Templates Matched?

I've talked about how the `lookup()` method takes a template which will be *matched* against the services known to the lookup service, but haven't yet said anything about how this is done. The Jini service template matching system is extremely flexible and yet simple to use. When searching, you can find ser-

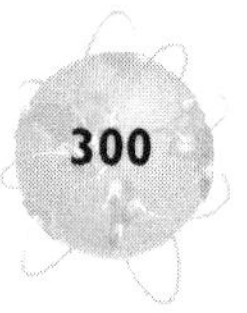

vices based either on the set of attributes associated with them (using the content-based attribute matching rules already described in this chapter); you can search for one *explicit* service by looking it up via its service ID; and you can search for services that implement particular interfaces that your client knows how to use.

The way you describe what you'd like to search for is by using the `ServiceTemplate` class. Each `ServiceTemplate` has fields for specifying service IDs, service types, and desired attributes. Any or all of these can be null to specify a "wild card" value which will match any service. Here are the relevant parts of the `ServiceTemplate` definition.

```
package net.jini.core.lookup;

public class ServiceTemplate
            implements Serializable {
        public ServiceTemplate(ServiceID serviceID,
                               Class[] serviceTypes,
                               Entry[] attrSetTmpls);
        public ServiceID serviceID;
        public Class[] serviceTypes;
        public Entry[] attrSetTemplates;
}
```

When you create a `ServiceTemplate`, you simply "fill in" the fields that you care about with appropriate values. If you know the ID of the service you're searching for, you can fill it in and leave the other fields null. Likewise, if you know the class of the service you're searching for, or any of its attributes, you can fill these in and leave other fields empty.

In Chapter 7, I briefly outlined the rules that govern whether a match occurs; let's review them here. A given service item stored in a lookup service matches a template if

- The service ID in the template matches the ID of a registered service, or if the template's serviceID field is null; *and*
- The registered service is an instance of *every* type in the template's `serviceType` field, or the template's type field is null; *and*
- The service's list of attributes contains *at least* one attribute that matches *every* entry in the template, or the template's attribute field is null.

To boil these rules down, a template matches a service item if every field in the template matches the corresponding field in the service item. Fields that are null in the template always count as matches. And the attributes field is matched using the standard attribute matching rules we've already discussed.

The array fields, `serviceTypes` and `attributeSetTemplates`, allow you to specify multiple "tests" that a service item must pass. If you provide multiple classes in `serviceTests`, for example, you're saying that for any service to match, its proxy must implement every one of the types (classes or interfaces) that you specify.

An Example: Searching for Service Information

Let's look at an example of searching. In Listing 8–2 we see how a client searches using the `ServiceRegistrar` to look for all services that have a specific type of attribute. In this case, we're looking for all services that have a `ServiceInfo` attribute, with any values in that attribute. Such a function might be used by a Jini browser, for example, to show to users all of the services that have human-readable information attached to them.

This example also shows how client code can distinguish among multiple `ServiceItems` that they may receive from a collection of registrars by looking at their `ServiceIDs`. Since any given service uses its unique ID everywhere it registers itself, clients can eliminate duplicates by examining the IDs of newly found services with those of services they've already seen.

Listing 8–2 `ServiceInfoSearcher.java`

```
// Find and print services that have ServiceInfo
// attributes.

package corejini.chapter8;

import net.jini.discovery.LookupDiscovery;
import net.jini.discovery.DiscoveryEvent;
import net.jini.discovery.DiscoveryListener;
import net.jini.core.lookup.ServiceMatches;
import net.jini.core.lookup.ServiceItem;
import net.jini.core.lookup.ServiceTemplate;
import net.jini.core.lookup.ServiceRegistrar;
import net.jini.lookup.entry.ServiceInfo;
import net.jini.core.entry.Entry;
import java.util.Hashtable;
import java.rmi.RemoteException;
import java.rmi.RMISecurityManager;
import java.io.IOException;
```

Listing 8–2 `ServiceInfoSearcher.java` **(continued)**

```
public class ServiceInfoSearcher implements Runnable {
  protected Hashtable registrars = new Hashtable();
  protected Hashtable services = new Hashtable();
  protected ServiceTemplate tmpl;

  class Discoverer implements DiscoveryListener {
      public void discovered(DiscoveryEvent ev) {
         ServiceRegistrar[] newregs = ev.getRegistrars();
          for (int i=0 ; i<newregs.length ; i++) {
              addRegistrar(newregs[i]);
          }
      }
      public void discarded(DiscoveryEvent ev) {
         ServiceRegistrar[] newregs = ev.getRegistrars();
          for (int i=0 ; i<newregs.length ; i++) {
              removeRegistrar(newregs[i]);
          }
      }
  }

  public ServiceInfoSearcher() throws IOException {
      if (System.getSecurityManager() == null) {
          System.setSecurityManager(
              new RMISecurityManager());
      }

      // build our template
      Entry[] attrTemplates = new Entry[1];
      attrTemplates[0] = new ServiceInfo(null, null,
                                        null, null,
                                        null, null);
      tmpl = new ServiceTemplate(null, null,
                                        attrTemplates);

      // set up for discovery
      LookupDiscovery disco =
          new LookupDiscovery(
                           LookupDiscovery.ALL_GROUPS);
      disco.addDiscoveryListener(new Discoverer());
  }
```

Listing 8–2 `ServiceInfoSearcher.java` **(continued)**

```
     protected synchronized void addRegistrar(
                                  ServiceRegistrar reg) {
        if (registrars.contains(reg.getServiceID()))
            return;

        registrars.put(reg.getServiceID(), reg);
        findServices(reg);
    }

    protected synchronized void removeRegistrar(
                                  ServiceRegistrar reg) {
        if (!registrars.contains(reg.getServiceID()))
            return;

        registrars.remove(reg.getServiceID());
    }

    void findServices(ServiceRegistrar reg) {
        try {
            ServiceMatches matches =
                     reg.lookup(tmpl, Integer.MAX_VALUE);

            for (int i=0 ; i<matches.totalMatches ; i++) {
                if (services.contains(
                             matches.items[i].serviceID))
                    continue;


                addService(matches.items[i]);
            }
        } catch (RemoteException ex) {
            System.err.println("Couldn't search: " +
                                  ex.getMessage());
        }
    }

    protected void addService(ServiceItem item) {
        services.put(item.serviceID, item);
        System.out.println("New service found: " +
                                     item.serviceID);
        printServiceInfo(item);
    }
```

Listing 8–2 `ServiceInfoSearcher.java` **(continued)**

```
    protected void printServiceInfo(ServiceItem item) {
       for (int i=0 ; i<item.attributeSets.length ; i++) {
           if (item.attributeSets[i]
                                    instanceof ServiceInfo) {
               ServiceInfo info = (ServiceInfo)
                                    item.attributeSets[i];
               System.out.println("    Name = " +
                                         info.name);
               System.out.println("    Manufacturer = " +
                                         info.manufacturer);
               System.out.println("    Vendor = " +
                                         info.vendor);
               System.out.println("    Version = " +
                                         info.version);
               System.out.println("    Model = " +
                                         info.model);
               System.out.println("    Serial Number = " +
                                         info.serialNumber);
           }
       }
    }

    public void run() {
        while (true) {
            try {
                Thread.sleep(Long.MAX_VALUE);
            } catch (InterruptedException ex) {
            }
        }
    }

    public static void main(String args[]) {
        try {
            ServiceInfoSearcher searcher =
                                new ServiceInfoSearcher();
            new Thread(searcher).start();
        } catch (Exception ex) {
           System.err.println("Error starting searcher: " +
                                  ex.getMessage());
            ex.printStackTrace();
        }
    }
}
```

The search program participates in discovery to find all lookup services on its local network. The program does some bookkeeping as results come in—it records all the registrars it finds by putting them in a hash table keyed by the ID of the service. As it finds lookup services, it executes a query by calling `lookup()` on the `ServiceRegistrars` for each of the discovered lookup services.

The `ServiceTemplate` we submit to do the query is created by initializing the service ID to null (since we're not looking for specific IDs) and by setting the types array to null also (since we're not looking for specific types of services). We *do* however pass in a template for the attribute we're looking for: we create an empty `ServiceInfo` entry, which is one of the standard Jini attribute types, and make sure that all its fields are set to null. This will cause it to match *any* `ServiceInfo` attribute, regardless of contents.

Whenever services are returned from the search, the code scans a list of all services found so far, looking for each returned service's ID. If a newly found service is just a duplicate of one that has already been seen, it is ignored. Otherwise the code adds it to the hash table of all known services on the network, and prints the details it can learn about it from its `ServiceInfo`. This keeps duplicate registrations from showing up as separate services.

Compiling and Running the Example

This example is one of the more simple to compile and run. This code is only a consumer of downloadable code (the proxies for the lookup services it finds) and it exports no downloadable code of its own. I'll compile the program into the `client` directory since it doesn't export a service.

On Windows:

```
javac -classpath C:\jini1_0\lib\jini-core.jar;
                              C:\jini1_0\lib\jini-ext.jar;
                              C:\jini1_0\lib\sun-util.jar;
                              C:\client
                -d C:\client
        C:\files\corejini\chapter8\ServiceInfoSearcher.java

java -cp C:\jini1_0\lib\jini-core.jar;
                      C:\jini1_0\lib\jini-ext.jar;
                      C:\jini1_0\lib\sun-util.jar;
                      C:\client
        -Djava.security.policy=C:\files\policy
        corejini.chapter8.ServiceInfoSearcher
```

On Solaris:

```
javac -classpath /files/jini1_0/lib/jini-core.jar:
                         /files/jini1_0/lib/jini-ext.jar:
                         /files/jini1_0/lib/sun-util.jar:
                         /files/client
                -d /files/client
        /files/corejini/chapter8/ServiceInfoSearcher.java

java -cp /files/jini1_0/lib/jini-core.jar:
                      /files/jini1_0/lib/jini-ext.jar:
                      /files/jini1_0/lib/sun-util.jar:
                      /files/client
        -Djava.security.policy=/files/policy
        corejini.chapter8.ServiceInfoSearcher
```

Soliciting Events from a Lookup Service

Searching is a tool that you can use to see what services are *already* registered at a particular lookup service. But you can also ask lookup services to tell you when *new* services arrive by requesting that it send you events. Jini lookup services are capable of generating events so that clients can be notified of changes in the state of a lookup service without having to contact the lookup service to poll it for its changes. Events are a far more efficient way for clients to become aware of changes in lookup service state, since messages are sent *only* when a change actually occurs.

The process of asking for a lookup service to send you an event is called *soliciting* the event. The Jini facilities for event solicitation are very rich—not only can you become informed when new services appear, you can also be informed when existing services go away, or when the set of attributes on a service changes in an "interesting" way. And you don't simply ask the lookup service to send you an event when anything happens to it—you can specifically describe which changes you wish to be informed of.

Specifying When Events Should Be Sent

The facilities for describing when lookup services should send events are very similar to the facilities for describing search queries. In both cases, you use a `ServiceTemplate` that describes the types of services you consider interesting. In searching, any services matching that template will be returned to you. Event solicitation allows you to have some richer control over how the template is used to determine when to send events.

When you ask for events to be sent to you, you provide a special flag that determines how the template is used. This flag can have any or all of three possible values, indicating that an event should be sent when

- A service suddenly matches the provided template.
- A service which *used* to match the template no longer does.
- A service which matches the template changes in some way, while still matching the template.

The first case is used when you are looking for particular types of services, or services with particular attributes associated with them, and want to be informed when one of these registers itself. For example, if you're an application that needs a storage service, you may ask for events to tell you when any new storage services appear in a community. If you're a printer administration client, you may ask that an event be sent to you when any printer service suddenly has an "out of paper" status attribute attached to it.

The second case is used to detect when services are unregistered with a lookup service (possibly because the service crashes and its leases expire), or when an attribute on a service goes away. For example, a browser application may clean up its display, removing icons for services that are no longer registered with a lookup service. Our printer administration application may remove a printer from it's trouble logs once it determines that an error condition has been corrected.

Finally, the third case is used simply to keep clients' views of the state of the community up-to-date. By using this flag value, you can determine when the set of attributes on a service changes in some way, even if that change does not cause it to no longer match the template. For example, if a user adds a comment to a service, you could detect the change with this flag value, and update any display you were presenting to a user.

Using Notify() to Ask for Events

In this section, we'll only look at the basics of how to use events to retrieve information from lookup services. We won't go into a full-blown design discussion of how events in Jini work, or some of the interesting ways you can alter the Jini event behavior—these topics will have to wait until Chapter 14, in which we take an in-depth look at events.

But we can learn enough here to deal with nearly all the requirements that lookup clients have when using events. Clients ask for events by calling the `notify()` method on a `ServiceRegistrar`. Here is the definition of that method, along with the definition of the "transition" flags that govern when events are sent.

```
int TRANSITION_MATCH_NOMATCH = 1 << 0;
int TRANSITION_NOMATCH_MATCH = 1 << 1;
int TRANSITION_MATCH_MATCH = 1 << 2;

EventRegistration notify(ServiceTemplate tmpl,
                         int transitions,
                         RemoteEventListener l,
                         MarshalledObject data,
                         long leaseDuration)
                             throws RemoteException;
```

The arguments here are mostly self-explanatory. You pass in a ServiceTemplate that describes a pattern to match, and a transitions flag to indicate how the template should be used. The valid values of transitions are specified by the integer flags shown here. TRANSITION_MATCH_NOMATCH indicates that an event should be sent when the template ceases to match a given service; TRANSITION_NOMATCH_MATCH indicates that an event should be sent when the template begins to match a service; and TRANSITION_MATCH_MATCH means that an event should be delivered when a previously matched service changes in some way, yet still matches the template. The flag values shown here can be bitwise OR'ed together so that you can specify that any or all of these transitions should result in events.

Next, you specify a RemoteEventListener. This is an object that the lookup service will call when an event is generated; this should be an object in your client that implements the RemoteEventListener interface and is equipped to deal with messages from the lookup service. RemoteEventListener is an RMI remote interface, so the object that implements this interface must fit into the RMI framework—by extending UnicastRemoteObject, and so on. (We'll see an example of how to do this in this chapter; see Appendix A if you need some background information on how RMI works.)

The third parameter to notify() is a MarshalledObject that specifies an arbitrary, preserialized Java object that you wish to be returned to you when an event is sent. You can use this parameter to store any information that you may need to process the event once it arrives; by having necessary information returned in the event itself, you can often simplify your bookkeeping.

Finally, the last parameter is a requested duration for the lease on your event solicitation. Remember that event solicitations, just like lookup service registrations, are leased in Jini. You have to request that the lookup service send you events in the future, and you must renew the lease that's returned to you if you want to continue receiving events.

The `notify()` method returns an `EventRegistration` to you. This is a simple container class that contains the source of the event (which, in the case of events from lookup services, will be the `ServiceRegistrar` that generated the event), the lease for the event registration, and a few other pieces of data that we'll look at later. When you receive an `EventRegistration`, you should hold on to the lease that comes with it so that you can renew it when you need to.

Receiving Events

When you request that events be delivered to you, you provide an object that implements the `RemoteEventListener` interface to receive the events. The `RemoteEventListener` interface is extremely simple—it only has one method. Here's the interface.

```
package net.jini.core.event;

public interface RemoteEventListener
            implements java.rmi.Remote,
                       java.util.EventListener {
        public void notify(RemoteEvent ev)
            throws java.rmi.RemoteException,
                       UnknownEventException;
}
```

Whenever the lookup service changes state in such a way that an event should be sent to you, it will construct an event, and deliver it by calling the `notify()` method on the `RemoteEventListener` you specified when you originally solicited the event.

The implementation of `notify()` that you create for your listener will be declared to take a `RemoteEvent` parameter. The lookup service actually delivers to you a *subclass* of `RemoteEvent` that provides extra information about the change that took place in the lookup service. This subclass is called `ServiceEvent`.

```
package net.jini.core.lookup;

public class ServiceEvent extends RemoteEvent {
        // ... some details elided ...
        public ServiceID getServiceID();
        public ServiceItem getServiceItem();
        public int getTransition();
}
```

When your listener receives the event, it can cast it to `ServiceEvent` and then access details about the change that occurred in the lookup service. The `getServiceID()` method returns the id of the service that caused the event to be triggered. The `getServiceItem()` method returns the complete service item that caused the event to be sent. This item is the *new* state of the service item, if it changed, or null if the service was deleted. Finally, `getTransition()` returns a flag value indicating what type of transition occurred—a service matched, a previously matched service disappeared, or a matching service changed in some way.

An Example: Using Events to Find Services

Let's look now at an extension of the previous attribute-based search example. This new example (Listing 8–3) subclasses the previous `ServiceInfoSearcher` to display information for when services with `ServiceInfo` attributes start up, go away, or have their attributes changed.

Listing 8–3 `ServiceInfoWatcher.java`

```
// like lookup searcher, only uses events

package corejini.chapter8;

import net.jini.core.lookup.ServiceRegistrar;
import net.jini.core.lookup.ServiceEvent;
import net.jini.core.lookup.ServiceItem;
import net.jini.core.event.RemoteEvent;
import net.jini.core.event.EventRegistration;
import net.jini.core.event.RemoteEventListener;
import net.jini.core.lease.Lease;
import com.sun.jini.lease.LeaseRenewalManager;
import java.rmi.RemoteException;
import java.rmi.server.UnicastRemoteObject;
import java.util.Hashtable;
import java.io.IOException;

public class ServiceInfoWatcher extends ServiceInfoSearcher {
    protected Listener listener;
    protected LeaseRenewalManager mgr;
    protected Hashtable leases = new Hashtable();
    protected int transitions =
            ServiceRegistrar.TRANSITION_MATCH_NOMATCH |
            ServiceRegistrar.TRANSITION_NOMATCH_MATCH |
            ServiceRegistrar.TRANSITION_MATCH_MATCH;
```

Listing 8–3 `ServiceInfoWatcher.java` **(continued)**

```
    class Listener extends UnicastRemoteObject
        implements RemoteEventListener {

        public Listener() throws RemoteException {
        }

        public void notify(RemoteEvent ev)
                                  throws RemoteException {
            if (!(ev instanceof ServiceEvent)) {
                System.err.println("Unexpected event: " +
                                  ev.getClass().getName());
                return;
            }

            ServiceEvent serviceEvent = (ServiceEvent) ev;

            switch (serviceEvent.getTransition()) {
            case ServiceRegistrar.TRANSITION_NOMATCH_MATCH:
                addService(serviceEvent.getServiceItem());
                break;
            case ServiceRegistrar.TRANSITION_MATCH_NOMATCH:
                removeService(
                         serviceEvent.getServiceItem());
                break;
            case ServiceRegistrar.TRANSITION_MATCH_MATCH:
                serviceChanged(
                         serviceEvent.getServiceItem());
                break;
            }
        }
    }

    public ServiceInfoWatcher()
                    throws IOException, RemoteException {
        mgr = new LeaseRenewalManager();
        listener = new Listener();
    }

    protected void removeService(ServiceItem item) {
        services.remove(item.serviceID);
        System.out.println("Service no longer available: "
                                    + item.serviceID);
        printServiceInfo(item);
    }
```

Listing 8–3 `ServiceInfoWatcher.java` **(continued)**

```
    protected void serviceChanged(ServiceItem item) {
        services.put(item.serviceID, item);
        System.out.println("Service updated: " +
                                          item.serviceID);
        printServiceInfo(item);
    }

    // overrride addRegistrar and removeRegistrar to
    // have them ask for/terminate event solicitations
    // whenever we find a lookup service.
    protected void addRegistrar(ServiceRegistrar reg) {
        try {
            super.addRegistrar(reg);

            EventRegistration er = reg.notify(tmpl,
                                              transitions,
                                              listener,
                                              null,
                                              10*60*1000);
            // do something with lease
            leases.put(reg.getServiceID(), er.getLease());
            mgr.renewFor(er.getLease(),
                                    Long.MAX_VALUE,
                                          null);
        } catch (RemoteException ex) {
            System.err.println("Can't solicit event: " +
                               ex.getMessage());
        }
    }

    protected void removeRegistrar(ServiceRegistrar reg) {
        try {
            super.removeRegistrar(reg);

            // terminate leases on this dude.
            Lease lease = (Lease)
                        leases.get(reg.getServiceID());

            if (lease == null)
                return;
```

Listing 8–3 `ServiceInfoWatcher.java` **(continued)**

```
            leases.remove(reg.getServiceID());
             // May raise unknown lease exception or
             // remote exception. Should be ok to ignore
             // here...
            mgr.cancel(lease);
        } catch (Exception ex) {
        }
    }

    public static void main(String[] args) {
        try {
            ServiceInfoWatcher watcher =
                                 new ServiceInfoWatcher();
            new Thread(watcher).start();
        } catch (Exception ex) {
            System.err.println("Error starting watcher: " +
                               ex.getMessage());
        }
    }
}
```

This code is a subclass of `ServiceInfoSearcher`, so it reuses all of the existing behavior for searching over the services registered at lookup services. Unlike the search example, here we have to use RMI to receive remote events; this adds a bit of complexity that wasn't in the search version of the program.

Before we look at how RMI works in this case, look at the `addRegistrar()` and `removeRegistrar()` methods. This overrides the previous implementations from the search example so that it can solicit events whenever it finds a new lookup service. Let's look at `addRegistrar()` first. Here, the code calls the superclass version of `addRegistrar()`, so that it still gets all of the default searching behavior. But it also solicits events from the newly found registrar. Here, I've used the same template we use for searching—basically any service that has a `ServiceInfo` attribute on it. The code specifies that it's interested in any type of transition of those services, passes in a listener object for remote events (more on this in a bit), and requests an initial lease time of 10 minutes.

The call to `notify()` returns an `EventRegistration` which contains the lease for the registration. Here again, the code has to do a bit of extra bookkeeping. We will want to be able to cancel our event leases whenever a lookup service goes away. So the code stores the lease in a hash table, keyed by the lookup service's ID. That way, if we ever learn that a lookup service is being dropped (perhaps because it no longer supports a group we are interested in), we can find its lease and cancel it. Here we also see that the code is asking a `LeaseRenewalManager` to take care of its leases for it. We'll look at lease managers in Chapter 10 when we talk about leasing in depth. For now, you can just rest easy knowing that the lease renewals will be taken care of until the `ServiceInfoWatcher` program shuts down or until you tell the lease manager to cease renewing this lease.

The reimplementation of `removeRegistrar()` also calls out to the superclass version of `removeRegistrar()`, so that it can update its bookkeeping of active lookup services. But here the code also finds the event registration it had on the newly irrelevant lookup service and asks the lease manager to cancel it. The lease is also removed from the bookkeeping hash table.

You should note that the `cancel()` method on the lease manager may raise exceptions if it runs into trouble canceling the lease (it may raise either an `UnknownLeaseException` or a `RemoteException`). Since the reason for calling `cancel()` in the first place is to tell the manager to stop trying to renew leases with a lookup service that seems to be failing, ignoring the exceptions in this *particular* case is ok.

All of this work is to properly solicit events and manage event leases. Let's now look at how the actual delivery of an event works.

`ServiceInfoWatcher` defines a class called `Listener` that will receive remote events from lookup services. Note the format of this class, because the basics will be common to all receivers of remote events: it's a `java.rmi.server.UnicastRemoteObject`, because its `notify()` method needs to be callable from the lookup service running in a separate address space. It implements `RemoteEventListener`, because this is the way Jini knows to deliver remote events.

Whenever an event is delivered to this class—indicating that the state of services registered with a lookup service has changed in some way—the `notify()` method will be invoked, and a `RemoteEvent` will be delivered. The lookup service will actually send a subclass of `RemoteEvent` called `ServiceEvent`, which contains details of the service that has changed.

When the `ServiceEvent` comes in, the implementation of `notify()` looks at the transition in the event that specifies what type of change occurred. If a new service has appeared, it calls the `addService()` method that was defined in the `ServiceInfoSearcher` superclass. If the transition indicates that a service has been removed or changed in some way, `notify()` calls `removeService()` or `serviceChanged()`, respectively. These simply

update the bookkeeping required to track the known services and print out details of the affected service.

Compiling and Running

This program not only uses proxy objects downloaded from the lookup services it finds, but it also needs to export the stubs for its `RemoteEventListener` implementation to lookup services. So in addition to compiling, you'll have to use `rmic` to generate RMI stubs, and be sure to set a codebase so that lookup services can find the implementation of the stubs.

You should consider leaving this program running; it'll allow you to see how services come and go in your Jini community as you run other examples from this book.

On Windows:

```
javac -classpath C:\jini1_0\lib\jini-core.jar;
                              C:\jini1_0\lib\jini-ext.jar;
                              C:\jini1_0\lib\sun-util.jar;
                              C:\client
                -d C:\client
        C:\files\corejini\chapter8\ServiceInfoWatcher.java

rmic -classpath C:\jdk1.2\jre\lib\rt.jar;
                              C:\jini1_0\lib\jini-core.jar;
                              C:\jini1_0\lib\jini-ext.jar;
                              C:\jini1_0\lib\sun-util.jar;
                              C:\client
                -d C:\client-dl
        corejini.chapter8.ServiceInfoWatcher.Listener

java -cp C:\jini1_0\lib\jini-core.jar;
                      C:\jini1_0\lib\jini-ext.jar;
                      C:\jini1_0\lib\sun-util.jar;
                      C:\client;
                      C:\client-dl
        -Djava.security.policy=C:\files\policy
        -Djava.rmi.server.codebase=http://myhost:8086/
        corejini.chapter8.ServiceInfoWatcher
```

On Solaris:

```
javac -classpath /files/jini1_0/lib/jini-core.jar:
                         /files/jini1_0/lib/jini-ext.jar:
                         /files/jini1_0/lib/sun-util.jar:
```

```
                            /files/client
                -d /files/client
        /files/corejini/chapter8/ServiceInfoWatcher.java

rmic -classpath /jdk1.2/jre/lib/rt.jar:
                            /files/jini1_0/lib/jini-core.jar:
                            /files/jini1_0/lib/jini-ext.jar:
                            /files/jini1_0/lib/sun-util.jar:
                            /files/client
                -d /files/client-dl
        corejini.chapter8.ServiceInfoWatcher.Listener

java -cp /files/jini1_0/lib/jini-core.jar:
                        /files/jini1_0/lib/jini-ext.jar:
                        /files/jini1_0/lib/sun-util.jar:
                        /files/client:
                        /files/client-dl
        -Djava.security.policy=/files/policy
        -Djava.rmi.server.codebase=http://myhost:8086/
        corejini.chapter8.ServiceInfoWatcher
```

Other Client Issues

Search and event solicitation are the two most important items in your bag of tricks as the developer of a Jini client. Using these simple APIs you can select the services you need to do your job.

There are, however, a few more details that you might need to be aware of. These aren't new APIs or new programming techniques that you need to master; they're merely bits of information that you may need to know to build more effective clients.

You Cannot Change a Service's Attributes Without Going through the Service

First, you should be aware that there is no API on the `ServiceRegistrar` class to change the attributes associated with a service. This means that clients have no *direct* way to update, modify, or remove any attributes attached to the services they find.

While search and notification may return to you a list of `ServiceItems`, which contain attributes for the services you've found, these are merely *copies* of the attributes that reside in the lookup service. In almost every case, any changes you make to these attributes will have no effect on the attributes stored in a lookup service. (One exception is if the attributes are themselves remote objects. In this case, calling methods on these objects to change them will change some centralized object, and the change you make will be visible everywhere.)

This restriction is by design—clients cannot just rampage over the set of attributes associated with a service without telling that service. If Jini allowed this sort of operation, it would have to provide security primitives that would allow services to dictate exactly what changes could be made to which attributes. Also, if a client could change a service's attributes directly, the service may have no way of detecting this change, and would be unable to propagate the change out to the other lookup services it is registered with—a requirement of the join protocol.

So then how do client applications change service attributes, say to add a comment or to update a location? The answer is that the client *must* go through an API provided by the service to do this. By going through the service, Jini allows the service a chance to veto any proposed change that it does not approve of. And this approach also gives the service a chance to "notice" the change, so that it can write the attribute to persistent storage and propagate it out to any other lookup services it may be registered with.

Jini provides conventions that services can use to allow clients to change their attributes. These conventions are made manifest through the *service administration* APIs—these are a set of interfaces that services may implement which allow clients to change their attributes, set the groups they are members of, and so on. I'll talk more about service administration, and how to make your services administrable, in Chapter 12. For now, however, just remember that you shouldn't make the mistake of trying to change an attribute that you get back from search or from an event, and expect it to affect any attributes stored in a lookup service.

Downloaded Service Proxies Are Not Leased

A second point to make is that once you've downloaded a service proxy to your client, it's yours until you decide you no longer need it. Even if the back-end part of the service goes away, there is no part of the system that will take the proxy out of your hands. So, for example, if you're using an image conversion service through its proxy, and the service crashes, your client needs to be written to realize that if the "convert" methods on the proxy are raising exceptions, then perhaps the service is no longer available.

Unlike a service's registrations with a lookup service, a client's copy of a service proxy is not leased; it will not be automatically cleaned up if the service crashes. Why is this? There is both a philosophical and a pragmatic reason for this decision.

Philosophically, services and clients are very different entities. Services are essentially passive—they sit around, waiting until someone needs them before they do anything. Once started, they're largely autonomous. Leasing provides a way for "the system"—meaning the collection of all of these autonomous services—to ensure that it returns to a safe state, without requiring the participation of any one member. Even if a service goes berserk, leasing ensures that the system as a whole will clean up after it, even if the individual services that make up the greater system are poorly written or ill-behaved.

Client applications, on the other hand, are assumed to be acting at the behest of a user or another program on behalf of a user, and can be written to provide whatever degree of safety the application writer deems necessary. In large part, the behavior of a client in the face of failure should *not* be determined by the rest of the system; it should be the responsibility of the application writer to deal with failures in a way that makes sense for his or her application.

To sum it up, leasing is a tool to protect the *system* as a whole; not to ensure that any one *application* works without fail. And, since leasing provides a "semantically neutral" solution—if a lease expires the resource becomes unavailable, no matter what else happens—this approach may not be best for particular clients.

The pragmatic reason that proxies downloaded to clients are not leased to them is that the basic model of leasing—that the user of a resource continually proves interest to the grantor of that resource—makes no sense here. Who is the "grantor" of the resource? Is the service the grantor, since it provides the use of its services to the client? In this case, the client would be the one who would have to renew the lease, which would provide no way for us to tell when the service crashed! If we consider the client to be the grantor of the resource—perhaps because it provides storage and computational cycles for the service's proxy to be run—then we require that the service continually renew its lease with the client. The client now has to implement all of the machinery to manage and expire leases on behalf of the services that *it* is using! We're making the wrong entity pay the costs of lease management in this case.

Because leasing is inappropriate in the case of proxies downloaded to clients, the writer of a client must make sure that it has some way to detect if a service crashes while the client is using it. Typically, the client will catch any

exceptions raised by methods on the service's proxy, and consider certain errors (such as `RemoteException`) as indications that the service has crashed. Clients can also, once they've downloaded a service's proxy, solicit events from the lookup service that the proxy came from. These events can tell the client if the service has failed to renew its lease, and may have disappeared. Doing this is simple—once you download a proxy, you create a template that has the ID of the service, and tell the lookup service to send you an event if the service ever disappears.

This approach is not an *alternative* to catching and dealing with exceptions raised by the service's proxy—because, depending on the duration of the registration's lease, the service may crash some time before you ever get an event telling you that the service is no longer available. But it can provide you with extra information about what's going on in your Jini community.

Service IDs Are Unique Across Lookup Services

Finally, the fact that service IDs are unique across all space and time is of great importance to client writers. Once you've found a service, you know that any time you encounter that service's ID, it represents the same service. So, if your client application contacts multiple lookup services (as it is almost certain to do), you can "prune" the lists of services you find at each one to eliminate multiple registrations of individual services.

Likewise, since service IDs are the same across time, if you ever find an ID for a service you wish to use, you can safely store that ID away, and know that it will *always* refer to that service. Of course, there is no guarantee that the service will be up and reachable when you want to use it, but know you can always *try* to find and use the service given its ID.

Miscellaneous Lookup APIs

In addition to the basic APIs that clients use for searching for services, and soliciting notifications, lookup services support a handful of methods designed to simplify the creation of browsers.

These methods allow you to contact a lookup service and download all the classes that any registered service proxies implement, or the values of particular fields in the attributes of registered services. These APIs are typically not used by most clients—most commonly, they're used by browsers that may need to quickly determine what services are registered, or get a "slice" of the values of some attributes, without having to download the attributes themselves.

This book doesn't go into detail on these browser convenience APIs, but you should know that they exist. Look at the documentation for the `getEntryClasses()`, `getFieldValues()`, and `getServiceTypes()` methods on `ServiceRegistrar` for more details. The methods are easy to use and quite self-explanatory.

Federating and Administering Lookup Services

I've alluded a few times in this chapter to the ability of services to be controlled through a set of administrative interfaces. We'll talk about how to build administrable services in quite a bit of detail in Chapter 12, and look closely at all of the various administrative interfaces that are available for controlling services.

Lookup services, you will remember, are themselves Jini services. And, as Jini services, they provide a set of administrative interfaces that can be used to control them. Through these interfaces, you—or your programs—can tune various parameters to control a lookup service. For example, you can change the set of groups of which a lookup service is a member, and you can cause it to register itself with specific lookup URLs that represent other lookup services. You can change the attributes that the lookup service attaches to its service proxy. You can also change the logging directory that a lookup service uses for checkpointing its data, and even shut down a lookup service.

In this section I'll focus just on the interfaces that govern how lookup services may be administered. I'll save the more general discussion of service administration until Chapter 12.

A Quick Overview of Service Administration

Services use a "delegation" model of administration. This means that you can ask a service for an object that can be used to administer it. Once you have this administration object, you can test it to see if it implements certain standard interfaces for controlling the service.

Jini services that are administrable will have service proxies that implement the `net.jini.admin.Administrable` interface. This interface has only one method on it:

```
package net.jini.admin;

public interface Administrable {
        public Object getAdmin()
                throws java.rmi.RemoteException;
}
```

If you want to administer a service, you test its proxy to see if it is implements `Administrable` and, if it does, call the `getAdmin()` method on it to fetch an object that can be used to administer the service. The `getAdmin()` method is declared to raise a `RemoteException`. This is because certain services may implement `getAdmin()` by contacting a back-end process to retrieve an administrative object. Declaring this exception in the interface gives service writers freedom in how they choose to fetch and return administration objects to callers.

Once you've gotten an administrative object, you can test whether it implements various well-known interfaces that can be used to control a service. Most services will provide a single administrative object that implements a handful of different administrative interfaces.

Jini defines one core administrative interface that is used to control a service's participation in the join protocol. This interface, called `net.jini.admin.JoinAdmin`, can be used to set the groups that a service tries to join, the lookup URLs it contacts when it starts, and the attributes it attaches to its proxies.

Other, specialized services may implement their own administrative interfaces on top of the core ones. In fact, Jini defines one such interface that the administrative objects of all lookup services should implement.

Lookup Administrative Interfaces

The interface `net.jini.lookup.DiscoveryAdmin` is used to control a lookup service. Through its methods, you can read or change the set of groups of which a lookup service is a member, and read or change the port that the lookup service uses for unicast discovery.

Be sure to note the distinction between `JoinAdmin` and `DiscoveryAdmin`. The former controls which lookup services a Jini service joins, while the second controls which groups a lookup service supports for discovery. While a lookup service may implement `JoinAdmin` to allow it to become a member of multiple groups, it may answer discovery requests for a potentially different set of groups.

```
package net.jini.lookup;

import java.rmi.RemoteException;
import java.io.IOException;

public interface DiscoveryAdmin {
        public void addMemberGroups(String[] groups)
                    throws RemoteException;
        public String[] getMemberGroups()
                    throws RemoteException;
        public int getUnicastPort()
                    throws RemoteException;
        public void removeMemberGroups(String[] groups)
                    throws RemoteException;
        public void setMemberGroups(String[] groups)
                    throws RemoteException;
        public void setUnicastPort(int port)
                    throws RemoteException, IOException;
}
```

The methods on this interface should be mostly self-explanatory. The `addMemberGroups()`, `setMemberGroups()`, and `removeMemberGroups()` methods change the set of groups that the lookup service *supports*. This is not the set of groups that the lookup service registers its own proxy with; instead it is the set of groups for which this lookup service will answer a discovery request.

Calling `setUnicastPort()` changes the port number on which the lookup service listens for unicast discovery requests. If you set the port to zero, the lookup service will try to establish itself on the default port, and then choose an arbitrary port if it cannot acquire the default one.

In addition to the `DiscoveryAdmin` interface, which all administrable lookup services are required to implement, most lookup services will also implement a handful of other administrative interfaces. Many of these are "suggested" administrative interfaces that live in `com.sun.jini.admin`; these interfaces can be used to shut down a service, or to change where the service keeps its persistent storage.

A particular lookup service also may implement any number of interfaces specific to it. So, for example, a lookup service based on an SQL database implementation may provide an administrative interface for tuning the database, setting database permissions, and so forth.

Administering the Reggie Lookup Service Implementation

Sun provides a default lookup service implementation that ships with Jini. This service, called *reggie*, is administrable through all the standard interfaces. Calling `getAdmin()` on its service proxy returns an object that implements not only `net.jini.admin.JoinAdmin` and `net.jini.lookup.DiscoveryAdmin`, but also two "optional" administrative interfaces from `com.sun.jini.admin`: `DestroyAdmin` and `StorageLocationAdmin`, which are used to shut down services and change a service's persistent storage location.

Additionally, reggie's administrative object also implements the `com.sun.jini.reggie.RegistrarAdmin` object. This object allows clients to control reggie-specific parameters, such as how the internal algorithm used by reggie to grant lease times is used, and how the logging file is used.

I won't go into all of the details of how to administer reggie here. For most uses, the standard lookup service administrative interfaces are sufficient for anything a client application or an administrator will need to do. If you're seeing poor lease performance on your network, or need to manage the growth of reggie's log files, then you can use the reggie-specific administrative interfaces to do this. See the documentation on the `com.sun.jini.reggie.RegistrarAdmin` class that comes with Jini for more details.

Federating Lookup Services

By default, the multicast forms of discovery will only find lookup services that are "nearby," in a network sense. As discussed in the chapter on discovery, this is because of the way that multicast works, and Jini's desire to support workgroup-sized communities easily and with no administration. "Nearness" depends on the number of "hops" a packet requires to travel to a destination, which in turn depends on the local network configuration.

But often, you may need to take the ad hoc collection of communities that Jini lookup services will naturally create, and shape it into a form that represents boundaries other than simple network dividing lines. For example, you might wish to create a hierarchy of Jini communities that mirrors an organizational structure in your company. Or, if you're in a large building, you may want to connect a group of Jini communities together in a way that mirrors the physical layout of your work space.

Both of these cases are examples of how you may need to *federate* Jini communities together into new topologies that do not necessarily reflect simple network boundaries. In Jini, complex organizational structures like this are created by explicitly connecting the lookup services for various communities to one another.

Let's look at an example. Suppose I want to create an enterprise-wide collection of Jini communities that will allow me access to any resource, anywhere on my company's network, anywhere in the world.

One solution I could take to this problem is to create *one* Jini community, and have each and every service be configured with a set of URLs that point to the lookup services supporting this community. In this case, my entire enterprise is one huge Jini community.

This approach may not be the best one, however. I'm putting a huge load on each of the lookup services in this case—every one of them needs to be able to hold the entire set of services that are available. If you work for a large company, you'd better be running these lookup services on some pretty high-powered machines! Even worse, having a centralized set of lookup services means that most services will live far away (networkologically-speaking) from the lookup services back at company HQ. If a branch office's connection to HQ is severed, all work stops. Even though my computer may be sitting right next to a printer at the branch office, I cannot use it because I cannot contact the central lookup services back at headquarters. This set up also increases your administrative workload—every service that anyone in the company brings up must be explicitly configured with the "magic" URLs for the HQ lookup services.

A far better approach is to create clusters of interlinked communities that reflect natural working patterns. In this approach, every branch office might have its own Jini community that supports only the services available locally; since these services only talk to local lookup services, they require no extra administration. Another lookup service might represent the sales division of my company. This service would support a "community of communities," linking all of the branch offices together. All of the lookup services for each of the branch offices would register themselves in this "metacommunity," and the lookup services for the larger sales division metacommunity would register themselves in the branch office lookup services. I could continue up the organizational hierarchy, finally creating a "root" community that contains proxies for the lookup services supporting sales, engineering, accounting, and so on.

In this example, I have created a hierarchy of Jini lookup services. At each level, the lookup services register both with those "above" them and those "below" them in the hierarchy. When you browse your local community's lookup service, you not only see all the services in your neighborhood, but you see the lookup services for higher-level organizational units. You can "open" these (by searching them) to find other offices that are peers of yours, and to find further parent communities.

This hierarchical arrangement has great benefits. Not only does it provide a structure that mirrors that of the organization—providing clear administrative boundaries—it also means that the services of a local community will *always* be available, even if a network connection to HQ goes down. Each community can function autonomously, even if it is isolated from the others. And, since you only have to set explicit lookup URLs in the federated lookup services, not every service anywhere on the network, this approach keeps the amount of explicit administration work low.

Other topologies are possible. You might create a "star" arrangement, where each local community connects to a centralized community whose job it is to maintain references to all other communities. Or you might have a completely ad hoc organization, where you have Jini "islands" connected to one another as users need to access resources in other communities. Figure 8–2 shows a few of these.

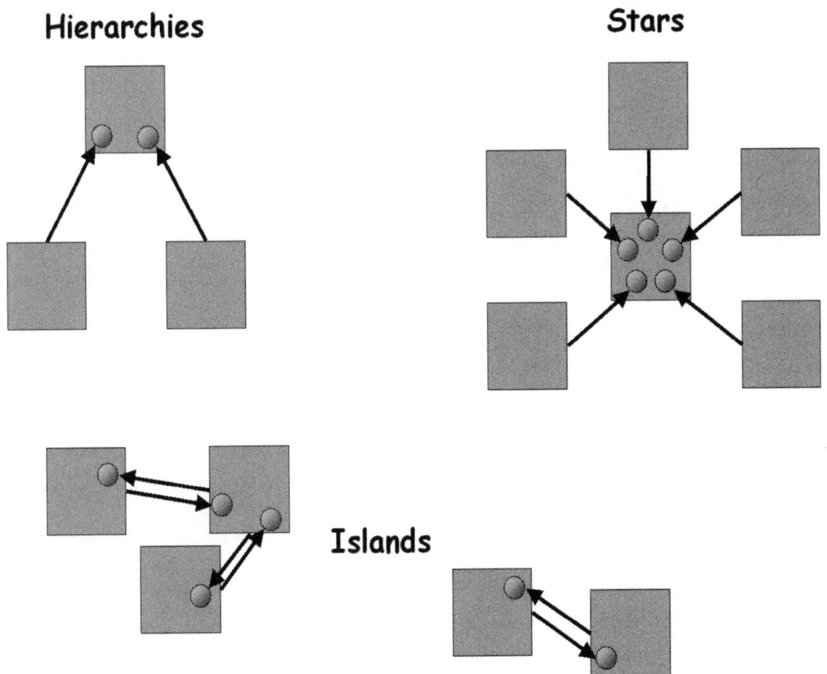

Figure 8–2 Lookup federation topologies

This freedom to federate lookup services together is one of the great strengths of Jini. It allows administrators and users to create connections between clusters of Jini services as needed; every organization or individual is free to create whatever structures it needs across its communities.

Let's look at an example (Listing 8–4) of how to federate two lookup services together. This program would be used by an administrator to create a two-way connection between two lookup services: You provide it with URLs that name two separate lookup services, and the tool creates the link between them. Each lookup service registers itself with the other one.

Listing 8–4 `Federate.java`

```
// Cause two lookup services to register with each
// other.

package corejini.chapter8;

import net.jini.core.discovery.LookupLocator;
import net.jini.core.lookup.ServiceRegistrar;
import net.jini.admin.Administrable;
import net.jini.admin.JoinAdmin;
import java.net.MalformedURLException;
import java.io.IOException;
import java.rmi.RMISecurityManager;

public class Federate {
    public Federate() {
            if (System.getSecurityManager() == null) {
                System.setSecurityManager(
                        new RMISecurityManager());
            }
    }

    public boolean federate(String url1, String url2)
        throws MalformedURLException, IOException,
           ClassNotFoundException {
        // Get service registrars for both servers
        LookupLocator loc1 = new LookupLocator(url1);
        LookupLocator loc2 = new LookupLocator(url2);

        ServiceRegistrar reg1 = loc1.getRegistrar();
        ServiceRegistrar reg2 = loc2.getRegistrar();

        Object admin1 = null, admin2 = null;
```

Listing 8–4 `Federate.java` **(continued)**

```
        if (reg1 instanceof Administrable) {
            admin1 = ((Administrable) reg1).getAdmin();
        } else {
            System.err.println("Registrar " + reg1 +
                               " is not administrable");
            return false;
        }

        if (reg2 instanceof Administrable) {
            admin2 = ((Administrable) reg2).getAdmin();
        } else {
            System.err.println("Registrar " + reg2 +
                               " is not administrable");
            return false;
        }

        if (!(admin1 instanceof JoinAdmin)) {
            System.err.println("Registrar " + reg1 +
                             " doesn't support " +
                               "join administration");
            return false;
        }


           if (!(admin2 instanceof JoinAdmin)) {
            System.err.println("Registrar " + reg2 +
                             " doesn't support " +
                               "join administration");
            return false;
        }

        JoinAdmin jadmin1 = (JoinAdmin) admin1;
        JoinAdmin jadmin2 = (JoinAdmin) admin2;

        // now, actually do the federation
        LookupLocator[] locs = new LookupLocator[1];

        locs[0] = loc1;
        jadmin2.addLookupLocators(locs);

        locs[0] = loc2;
        jadmin2.addLookupLocators(locs);

        return true;
    }
```

Listing 8–4 `Federate.java` **(continued)**

```
    public static void main(String[] args) {
        if (args.length != 2) {
            System.err.println("Usage: Federate " +
                               "<url1> <url2>");
            System.exit(1);
        }

        String url1 = args[0], url2 = args[1];

        Federate fed = new Federate();

        try {
            if (fed.federate(url1, url2)) {
                System.out.println(
                              "Lookup servers federated!");
            } else {
                System.err.println(
                 "Couldn't federate lookup services.");
            }
        } catch (Exception ex) {
            System.err.println(
                    "Error federating lookup services: " +
                                    ex.getMessage());
        }
    }
}
```

This is a rather straightforward program that illustrates a powerful concept. The program takes URLs for two Jini lookup services. The two lookup services represented by these URLs will be registered with each other as services. Any program contacting either one of these lookup services will find the proxy for the other, and can then "jump" to that lookup service simply by downloading and using its proxy. Since we're explicitly providing URLs here, there is no requirement that the federated lookup services exist on the same network; they can exist on opposite sides of the world from each other. (Indeed, the connection of lookup services in different network "regions" is the entire point of federation. Lookup services that are near one another already will likely find each other through multicast discovery.)

This is a minimalist example; you can probably imagine improvements on it. For one thing, rather than connecting individual lookup services, we more likely want to connect entire communities. This would entail finding all the lookup services that support a given group, and connecting them to all the lookup services that support a second group. Once you contact any lookup service in the first group, you should be able to find the other lookup services supporting that group, since they will most likely be registered with the lookup service you just found.

One other point to make about this example is that here we're causing two lookup services to publish their service proxies in one another. Any client that stumbles across the proxy as it scans a lookup service would have to be written to realize that what it has in its hands is, in fact, a federated lookup service that it may want to contact to search for other services. This is behavior that most clients will want to support—since, presumably, the whole point of a user federating two lookup services is to allow clients to make use of services on either one.

But it's easy to imagine—and even easy to build—a more complicated sort of federating tool. We'll look at such a tool as the last example in this chapter.

Compiling and Running

This code exports no remote objects, so you don't have to use `rmic` here. Make sure when you run that you pass in the Jini URLs for two lookup services on the command line.

On Windows:

```
javac -classpath C:\jini1_0\lib\jini-core.jar;
                              C:\jini1_0\lib\jini-ext.jar;
                              C:\jini1_0\lib\sun-util.jar;
                              C:\client
                -d C:\client
        C:\files\corejini\chapter8\Federate.java

java -cp C:\jini1_0\lib\jini-core.jar;
                      C:\jini1_0\lib\jini-ext.jar;
                      C:\jini1_0\lib\sun-util.jar;
                      C:\client
        -Djava.security.policy=C:\files\policy
        corejini.chapter8.Federate
                jini://turbodog.parc.xerox.com
                jini://foundation.parc.xerox.com
```

On Solaris:

```
javac -classpath /files/jini1_0/lib/jini-core.jar:
                         /files/jini1_0/lib/jini-ext.jar:
                         /files/jini1_0/lib/sun-util.jar:
                         /files/client
                -d /files/client
        /files/corejini/chapter8/Federate.java

java -cp /files/jini1_0/lib/jini-core.jar:
                      /files/jini1_0/lib/jini-ext.jar:
                      /files/jini1_0/lib/sun-util.jar:
                      /files/client
        -Djava.security.policy=/files/policy
        corejini.chapter8.Federate
                     jini://turbodog.parc.xerox.com
                     jini://foundation.parc.xerox.com
```

Example: A Lookup Service Tunnel

The last example showed how to federate lookup services by cross-publishing their proxies with each other. I mentioned that clients that come across a lookup service proxy would have to be written to realize that the proxy represents a registrar, and to search it and present the services that exist there.

In this example, you'll see a type of federation that doesn't require *any* special client-side smarts. This example is a *lookup service tunnel*. This program connects two lookup services in a much deeper way than simply asking them to publish their proxies with each other. The tunnel makes the individual services registered with one lookup service *directly* available on another.

The tunnel actively finds all of the services that are known to one lookup service, called the *from* service. It then contacts a second lookup service, called the *to* service. Any services found in the *from* service are registered in the *to* service. The tunnel solicits events from the *from* service so that it

can ensure that its picture of the services available there is up-to-date and reflected in the services it makes available on the *to* lookup service.

Essentially the tunnel is a service that acts as a wrapper for other services. It finds their proxies on a given lookup service (one might say it *absconds* with the proxies for these services), and then republishes them on a different lookup service. It also takes over responsibility for managing the leases on the republished proxies for these services, and ensures that the attributes on them accurately mirror the attributes on the originals.

With a lookup service tunnel, clients don't need *any* special smarts to use services that used to reside on a distant lookup service—because the tunnel makes all of those services locally available.

Let's look at the program as shown in Listing 8–5.

Listing 8–5 `TunnelService.java`

```
// Create a tunnel between two lookup services

package corejini.chapter8;

import java.io.Serializable;
import java.io.IOException;
import java.util.Hashtable;
import java.rmi.server.UnicastRemoteObject;
import java.rmi.RemoteException;
import java.rmi.RMISecurityManager;
import net.jini.lookup.entry.Name;
import net.jini.lookup.entry.ServiceInfo;
import net.jini.core.lookup.ServiceEvent;
import net.jini.core.lookup.ServiceRegistrar;
import net.jini.core.lookup.ServiceTemplate;
import net.jini.core.lookup.ServiceItem;
import net.jini.core.lookup.ServiceMatches;
import net.jini.core.event.RemoteEventListener;
import net.jini.core.event.RemoteEvent;
import net.jini.core.event.EventRegistration;
import com.sun.jini.lookup.JoinManager;
import com.sun.jini.lease.LeaseRenewalManager;
import net.jini.core.discovery.LookupLocator;
import net.jini.discovery.LookupDiscovery;
import net.jini.core.entry.Entry;

class TunnelServiceProxy implements Serializable {
}
```

Listing 8–5 `TunnelService.java` **(continued)**

```
public class TunnelService {
    protected JoinManager join;
    protected ServiceTemplate tmpl =
                new ServiceTemplate(null, null, null);
    protected LeaseRenewalManager mgr =
                new LeaseRenewalManager();
    protected Hashtable leases = new Hashtable();
    protected Hashtable joinManagers = new Hashtable();
    protected LookupLocator toLoc;
    protected ServiceRegistrar fromReg;
    protected int transitions =
            ServiceRegistrar.TRANSITION_MATCH_NOMATCH |
            ServiceRegistrar.TRANSITION_NOMATCH_MATCH |
            ServiceRegistrar.TRANSITION_MATCH_MATCH;
    protected Listener listener;

    class Listener extends UnicastRemoteObject
                     implements RemoteEventListener {
                public Listener() throws RemoteException {
                }
        public void notify(RemoteEvent ev)
                             throws RemoteException {
            if (!(ev instanceof ServiceEvent)) {
                return;
            }

            ServiceEvent sev = (ServiceEvent) ev;
            ServiceItem[] items = new ServiceItem[1];
                items[0] = sev.getServiceItem();

            switch (sev.getTransition()) {
            case ServiceRegistrar.TRANSITION_MATCH_NOMATCH:
                withdrawServices(items);
                break;
            case ServiceRegistrar.TRANSITION_NOMATCH_MATCH:
            case ServiceRegistrar.TRANSITION_MATCH_MATCH:
             // new service has shown up, or an old one
             // has changed--push it to the dest.  if
             // it's a change we'll overwrite
                pushServices(items);
                break;
            }
        }
    }
```

Listing 8–5 `TunnelService.java` (continued)

```
     public TunnelService() throws RemoteException {
             listener = new Listener();

             if (System.getSecurityManager() == null) {
                     System.setSecurityManager(
                             new RMISecurityManager());
             }
    }

    public void createTunnel(String from,
                 String to) throws Exception {
        LookupLocator fromLoc = new LookupLocator(from);
        toLoc = new LookupLocator(to);
        fromReg = fromLoc.getRegistrar();

        publishProxies(fromLoc, toLoc);
        solicitEvents();
        ServiceItem[] fromServices = getServices();
        pushServices(fromServices);
    }

    protected ServiceItem[] getServices()
                     throws RemoteException {
        ServiceMatches matches = fromReg.lookup(tmpl,
                     Integer.MAX_VALUE);
        return matches.items;
    }

    protected void publishProxies(LookupLocator from,
                                    LookupLocator to)
        throws IOException {
        Name name = new Name("Tunnel service");
        ServiceInfo info =
                 new ServiceInfo("Tunnel service",
                              "Prentice-Hall",
                              "Your local bookseller",
                              "v1.0",
                              null, null);
        Entry[] entries = new Entry[2];
        entries[0] = name;
        entries[1] = info;

         LookupLocator[] locators = new LookupLocator[2];
        locators[0] = from;
        locators[1] = to;
```

Listing 8–5 `TunnelService.java` **(continued)**

```
        String[] groups = LookupDiscovery.NO_GROUPS;

        join = new JoinManager(new TunnelServiceProxy(),
                     entries, groups,
                     locators, null, mgr);

        System.out.println("Join manager started...");
    }

    protected void solicitEvents() throws IOException,
            ClassNotFoundException {
        EventRegistration er = fromReg.notify(tmpl,
                                          transitions,
                                          listener,
                                          null,
                                          10*60*1000);

        leases.put(fromReg.getServiceID(), er.getLease());
        mgr.renewUntil(er.getLease(),
                                    Long.MAX_VALUE,
                                    null);
    }

    protected void pushServices(ServiceItem[] items) {
        for (int i=0 ; i<items.length ; i++) {
            try {
                LookupLocator[] toArray =
                        new LookupLocator[] { toLoc };
                System.out.println("Pushing service to " +
                                        toLoc + ": " +
                                items[i].service);
                JoinManager j =
                    new JoinManager(items[i].serviceID,
                            items[i].service,
                            items[i].attributeSets,
                            LookupDiscovery.NO_GROUPS,
                                    toArray, mgr);
                joinManagers.put(items[i].serviceID, j);
            } catch (Exception ex) {
                System.err.println("Couldn't tunnel: " +
                                ex.getMessage());
            }
        }
    }
```

Listing 8–5 `TunnelService.java` **(continued)**

```
    protected void withdrawServices(ServiceItem[] items) {
        for (int i=0 ; i<items.length ; i++) {
            try {
               System.out.println("Withdrawing service " +
                                  items[i].service);
                JoinManager j = (JoinManager)
                    joinManagers.get(items[i].serviceID);
                j.terminate();
                joinManagers.remove(items[i].serviceID);
            } catch (Exception ex) {
                System.err.println("Couldn't withdraw: " +
                                  ex.getMessage());
            }
        }
    }



    public static void main(String[] args) {
        if (args.length != 2) {
            System.err.println("Usage: TunnelService " +
                    "<from_url> <to_url> ");
            System.exit(1);
        }

        String from = args[0], to = args[1];

        try {
            TunnelService tunnel = new TunnelService();
            tunnel.createTunnel(from, to);
        } catch (Exception ex) {
            System.err.println("Error creating tunnel: " +
                    ex.getMessage());
            System.exit(1);
        }
    }
}
```

The tunnel service program is the most complex example we've seen so far. This program is both a service, and a fairly complex client application. The heart of the program is the `createTunnel()` method. This method creates LookupLocator instances from the string URLs it is passed. It then publishes proxies for its service on both the *to* and the *from* lookup services—in the code shown here, this is a "no op" proxy; it is simply published to give a representation of the tunnel service on both of the lookup services. You can easily extend this proxy to implement administrative interfaces that could be used to control the behavior of the tunnel, and save selected parameters to persistent storage.

After registering its proxies, the tunnel solicits events from the *from* lookup service. This step is necessary so that the tunnel will be made aware when the state of the set of services registered there changes—it must update the proxies it will create on the *to* lookup service to reflect changes in the original service.

Once it has solicited events, the tunnel retrieves all of the services currently registered at the *from* lookup service and "pushes" them out to the *to* lookup service.

In this one example you see illustrated many of the concepts we've discussed in this chapter. TunnelService needs to be able to search for services in the *from* registrar, and publish new service proxies on the *to* registrar. It must also be a recipient of remote events—when new services appear, they are pushed to the destination registrar. When services disappear, they are removed. And when they change, their ServiceItems are written to the destination, overwriting whatever attributes were there before.

As new services are pushed, the code in pushServices() is run to create the proxying behavior. Every new service has its own JoinManager that is responsible for its registration. The JoinManager essentially creates a new service, copying the original service's ID, attributes, and proxy. The JoinManager's parameters are set so that it will only connect to the destination lookup service—it will never try to perform multicast discovery, because LookupDiscovery.NO_GROUPS is passed as the set of groups it should connect to.

This code also maintains its own LeaseRenewalManager, which manages the leases for not only the TunnelService's proxy object, but also the leases for event registrations, and all the registration leases for the proxy objects that it tunnels through to the *to* lookup service.

When services disappear from the original lookup service, they are removed from the destination service. This is done by terminating the join protocol—the service's ID is mapped to the JoinManager that was created for it. When the JoinManager is retrieved, the terminate() method is called, and the bookkeeping entry for the service is removed from the hash table that maps from services to their JoinManagers.

Compiling and Running

This is the most complicated example of the chapter to compile and run. First, the program—like any Jini program—needs to be able to use downloaded lookup service proxies, so you must take the usual care to run it with a security policy file. Second, the code exports two downloadable classes: the RMI stub for its event listener, and the proxy for the tunneling service. So you need to run the `rmic` stubs compiler and make sure you copy the proxy class file out to the `service-dl` directory, as well as set a codebase property to tell other program where to find the implementations for these classes.

On Windows:

```
javac -classpath C:\jini1_0\lib\jini-core.jar;
                              C:\jini1_0\lib\jini-ext.jar;
                              C:\jini1_0\lib\sun-util.jar;
                              C:\service
                 -d C:\service
        C:\files\corejini\chapter8\TunnelService.java

cd C:\service\corejini\chapter8
copy TunnelServiceProxy.class
            C:\service-dl\corejini\chapter8

rmic -classpath C:\jdk1.2\jre\lib\rt.jar;
                              C:\jini1_0\lib\jini-core.jar;
                              C:\jini1_0\lib\jini-ext.jar;
                              C:\jini1_0\lib\sun-util.jar;
                              C:\service
                 -d C:\service-dl
        corejini.chapter8.TunnelService.Listener

java -cp C:\jini1_0\lib\jini-core.jar;
                       C:\jini1_0\lib\jini-ext.jar;
                       C:\jini1_0\lib\sun-util.jar;
                       C:\service;
                       C:\service-dl
        -Djava.security.policy=C:\files\policy
        -Djava.rmi.server.codebase=http://myhost:8085/
        corejini.chapter8.TunnelService
                      jini://turbodog.parc.xerox.com
                      jini://foundation.parc.xerox.com
```

On Solaris:

```
javac -classpath /files/jini1_0/lib/jini-core.jar:
                            /files/jini1_0/lib/jini-ext.jar:
                            /files/jini1_0/lib/sun-util.jar:
                            /files/service
                  -d /files/service
         /files/corejini/chapter8/TunnelService.java

cd /files/service/corejini/chapter8
cp TunnelServiceProxy.class
                  /files/service-dl/corejini/chapter8

rmic -classpath /jdk1.2/jre/lib/rt.jar:
                            /files/jini1_0/lib/jini-core.jar:
                            /files/jini1_0/lib/jini-ext.jar:
                            /files/jini1_0/lib/sun-util.jar:
                            /files/service
                  -d /files/service-dl
         corejini.chapter8.TunnelService.Listener

java -cp /files/jini1_0/lib/jini-core.jar:
                        /files/jini1_0/lib/jini-ext.jar:
                        /files/jini1_0/lib/sun-util.jar:
                        /files/service:
                        /files/service-dl
         -Djava.security.policy=/files/policy
         -Djava.rmi.server.codebase=http://myhost:8085/
         corejini.chapter8.TunnelService
                       jini://turbodog.parc.xerox.com
                       jini://foundation.parc.xerox.com
```

Further Reading

If you're interested in the nitty-gritty details about how Jini lookup services generate their globally-unique service IDs, you should check out this draft document from the IETF (Internet Engineering Task Force, the body that decides on all Internet standards) that describes the process. The draft is written by Paul Leach and Rich Salz, and is available at

http://www.ietf.org/internet-drafts/draft-leach-uuids-guids-01.txt

Summary

This chapter has presented an overview of how to use Jini lookup services—how to publish service proxies, how to search for services, and how to solicit events from lookup services. Together with the discovery protocols that allow you to find lookup services in the first place, these operations from the core of Jini. They allow you to create applications that bind together to form communities of services with minimal advance knowledge of each other.

1.1 Update

There are a couple of changes being considered for the Jini 1.1 release that are relevant to the discussions in this chapter. The first is a relatively minor change to the JoinManager constructors. In the current implementation, the JoinManager will internally create and use LookupDiscovery and LookupLocatorDiscovery instances to manage its interactions with the Jini discovery protocols. In 1.1, you can pass in your own implementation of the DiscoveryManagement interface; this allows you to change the implementation of discovery used by the JoinManager. If you pass null for this parameter, the JoinManager will continue to use a default discovery implementation.

A more significant change is the introduction of the ClientLookupManager class. This class is designed to better support the lookup chores of Jini clients. While many Jini clients may continue to use the "raw" ServiceRegistrar interfaces, the ClientLookupManager provides a particularly easy-to-use set of tools for contacting a set of lookup services and keeping a picture of the services available there up-to-date. The ClientLookupManager allows you to specify certain search criteria for services and then be notified whenever a matching service appears in any lookup service. This class handles the details built "by hand" in this chapter, of performing lookup queries and soliciting events.

See the Preface to the Third Printing, earlier in this book, for more details.

What's Next?

In the next chapter, we'll put our newfound knowledge of lookup services to good use: we'll build a complete lookup service browser from the ground up.

A JINI LOOKUP SERVICE BROWSER

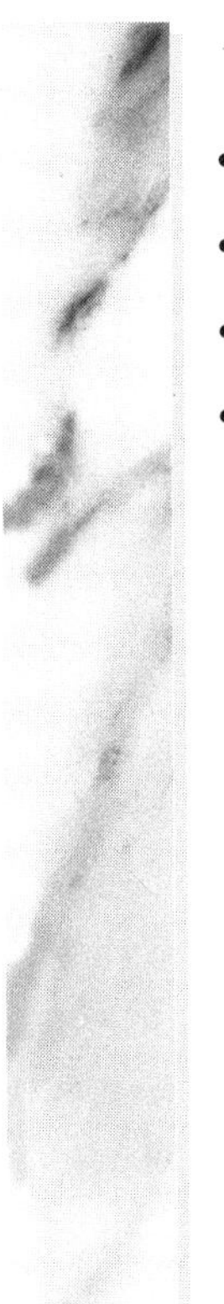

Topics in This Chapter

- Implementing a lookup service browser
- Building interfaces for service administration
- GUI components for Jini services and attributes
- Using JavaBeans attributes in a browser

Chapter 9

This chapter builds on all the tricks of the trade that you've learned in the previous chapters. Here, we focus on one large application: a full-blown Jini service browser. This browser allows you to view the lookup services on your network, find the services available at each, view the attributes associated with services, and administer services.

We'll look at how to apply many of the concepts you learned earlier. For example, you'll see how to retrieve beans from attributes and display them to users, you'll also see how to wrap a service's administrative APIs in easy-to-use GUI components.

While much of the Jini code in this chapter is similar to what you've seen in the individual, smaller examples earlier, here I'll pull all the concepts into one large application. I'll also build a number of Swing GUI components that can be dropped into your custom applications to allow you to view attributes and administer services. In this chapter, I've broken many of the GUI classes out into separable chunks to not only enhance clarity, but also to facilitate reuse of the code in your own applications.

What Does a Browser Do?

There are many possible browsers that one could build for the Jini environment. In general, a browser is a tool that allows users to see a whole set of the services available on a Jini network. How these services are organized and presented is up to the *particular* browser; Jini doesn't dictate how this should be done and, in fact, there are a number of logical choices.

For example, a browser could be "attribute oriented." Such a browser may search for specific attributes, such as GUI components, and only display those services that have rich representations. A "universal remote control" might be this sort of browser—it would display the "control panels" for each of the devices it manages in turn.

Other browsers might be "service oriented." That is, they might show all the services available (removing duplicates of course), and what the attributes of those services are, while hiding details about which lookup services the services came from (and perhaps even hiding the notion of lookup services at all). Such a browser might look like a conventional computer desktop, with icons representing all the available services. Clicking on an icon might open it up to display its user interface or information about the services.

Another type of browser—and this is the type we will see here—is "lookup oriented." This means that, rather than hiding details about what lookup services are out there and which services are registered with particular lookup services, this information is presented to the user. I believe that such a tool is perhaps more useful for debugging a Jini community than as an actual end-user tool. End users most likely do not *care* about where services are registered, and most likely they don't even want to know what a lookup service is. They're just interested in getting work done by interacting with the services made available through each of those lookup services.

But, as a Jini developer, you will certainly have a need to do occasional debugging of your Jini community—to see if your newly created service has registered itself on all the lookup services it can find, and to administer services and lookup services as needed. This example allows you to do that. And, perhaps more importantly, it illustrates a number of idioms for building browsers. At the end of this chapter, you'll have a set of building blocks that you can use in new applications (including new browsers), and can fine-tune as you need.

Using the Browser

Our lookup-oriented browser uses a three-paned display to show lookup services, services registered at a particular lookup service, and the attributes attached to a particular service. This layout is reminiscent of the class browser for the Smalltalk language, which may be familiar to you; Figure 9–1 shows the basic display.

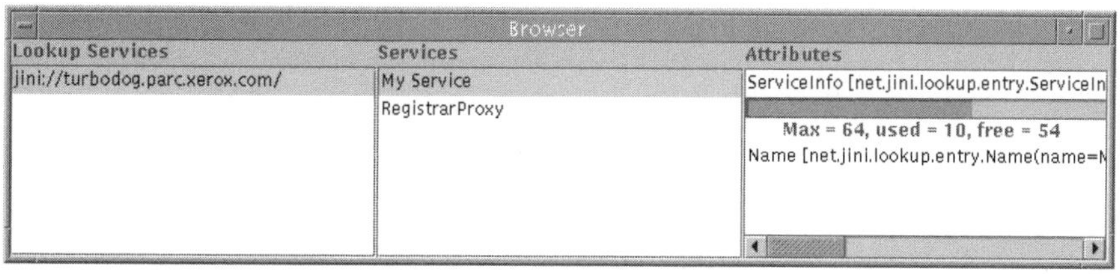

Figure 9–1 A lookup service browser

The left panel displays all the lookup services found through multicast discovery. The center panel shows the services registered at the currently selected lookup service. And the right panel shows all the attributes for the currently selected service.

The browser application we will build also allows graphical administration of any lookup service or service that supports the `Administrable` interface. See Figure 9–4 for an example of what this graphical administration interface looks like. The browser also has a tight integration with the JavaBeans framework. In the screen shot shown here, you see the `CapacityBean` we developed earlier being used as an attribute; the browser will locate beans for attributes and display them in-line if they are graphical components.

Building Administration Components

As mentioned in earlier chapters, most services—and certainly all well-behaved ones—support administration through delegation. What this means is that the proxy for a service may implement the `Administrable` interface, which allows a client to ask the proxy for an object that can be used to control the service.

The returned "administration object" is a delegate that can be used to control the service. How do clients know how to interact with this object? They

test it to see whether it implements one or more well-known administrative interfaces. Services, depending on their type, may implement several different administrative interfaces for controlling the communities a service joins, for adding and removing attributes, for changing the location of its persistent storage, and so on. In addition to a handful of "standard" well-known administrative interfaces, services can implement any number of implementation-specific administrative interfaces that they like. Of course, only clients written to understand these special-purpose APIs will be able to call them programmatically.

Of course, we'd like to be able to make our services afford administration by actual human users—and not merely programmatically by client applications that understand a particular service's administrative interfaces. What we'd like is the ability to take *any* administrative interface, even one we've never seen before, and create a GUI for it to display to a user.

Currently, Jini does not provide any standard conventions for how a service can provide its own GUI for administration. One possibility would be to have the administrative object itself be a full-blown GUI object; clients could test to see whether it subclasses the `Component` class and, if so, display it. This approach has a drawback though: on restricted platforms without the GUI class libraries available, a client would never be able to instantiate this administrative interface because its superclasses would be unavailable. This would prohibit *any* use of it on such platforms, even direct programmatic use through its APIs that never even use the object's "`Component`-ness."

An alternative would be to define a type of attribute, perhaps called `AdministrationGUI`, that contains the GUI for service administration. Once retrieved, a well-known method on the attribute could be called to "activate" it with a service's administration object. Unfortunately, Jini has not yet provided any such conventions for use.

A third option—and the one taken here—is to explicitly create a custom GUI for the administrative object in the client. In the browser example in this chapter, this creation happens by introspecting the administration object to see whether it implements any of a few well-known administrative interfaces. Each of these interfaces has a GUI associated with it that we'll look at shortly. One could get even fancier—perhaps using the JavaBeans introspection facilities to create custom GUIs for a service's administration object *on the fly*. This approach would work much like the way JavaBeans property sheets are created for beans after they are loaded. The on-the-fly approach is beyond the scope of this chapter though, so here we'll just build a set of custom administration GUIs "by hand."

The administrative interfaces this code supports are `DiscoveryAdmin`, `StorageLocationAdmin`, `DestroyAdmin`, and `JoinAdmin`. We will define a component called `AdminPanel` that takes as an argument to its constructor an administration object from a service's proxy. It will then create a tabbed panel with separate GUIs for each of the administrative interfaces that the object implements.

Each of the panes of the tabbed panel is a separate custom GUI that "understands" how to present the features of a particular administrative interface. Let's look at the most simple of these first, and then move up to the more complex examples.

DestroyAdminPanel

The `DestroyAdmin` interface (Listing 9–1) has only one method, which allows a caller to shut down a service. So, as you might expect, the GUI to this interface is equally simple: a single button to invoke the shutdown operation! Like all the separate administrative GUIs we'll see here, the `DestroyAdminPanel` is a subclass of `JPanel`. As such, it inherits all the Swing component functionality, and can be inserted into any other type of container component—so it can be displayed in lists, or inserted into frames, or placed in any other Swing container.

Listing 9–1 `DestroyAdminPanel.java`

```
// A user interface for DestroyAdmin

package corejini.chapter9;

import javax.swing.*;
import java.awt.event.*;
import java.awt.BorderLayout;
import java.rmi.RemoteException;
import com.sun.jini.admin.DestroyAdmin;

// initialize with a ref to the admin object
public class DestroyAdminPanel extends JPanel {
     public DestroyAdminPanel(final DestroyAdmin admin) {
        setLayout(new BorderLayout());
        JLabel label;
        JButton button;
```

Listing 9–1 `DestroyAdminPanel.java` **(continued)**

```
            add(new JLabel("CAUTION:"), BorderLayout.NORTH);
            add(new JLabel("Clicking will terminate " +
                    "the service!"), BorderLayout.CENTER);

            button = new JButton("Terminate");
            button.addActionListener(new ActionListener() {
                public void actionPerformed(ActionEvent ev) {
                    try {
                        admin.destroy();
                    } catch (RemoteException ex) {
                        JOptionPane.showMessageDialog(null,
                              "Couldn't destroy service:\n"+
                              ex.getMessage(), "Alert",
                              JOptionPane.ERROR_MESSAGE);
                    }
                }
            });

            add(button, BorderLayout.SOUTH);
    }
}
```

The constructor for the panel simply creates the button and a couple of labels to warn the user that clicking will shut down the service. The heart of the code is in the `ActionListener` for the button: This code calls the `destroy()` method on the service's administration object. If an error occurs (perhaps because the service has crashed or is disconnected from the network), a `RemoteException` will be raised, which causes a warning dialog box to be displayed.

Figure 9–2 shows the `DestroyAdminPanel` nested in an `AdminPanel` (which we will discuss shortly), along with the other administration interfaces.

StorageLocationAdminPanel

The second simplest standard administrative interface is called `StorageLocationAdmin`. This interface (Listing 9–2) allows a caller to change the location of a service's persistent storage. It supports only two methods—one to get the current storage location, and one to set a new storage location.

Figure 9–2 The DestroyAdminPanel

Let's look at the code:

Listing 9–2 `StorageLocationAdminPanel.java`

```
// A user interface for StorageLocationAdmin

package corejini.chapter9;

import javax.swing.*;
import java.awt.event.*;
import java.awt.*;
import java.rmi.RemoteException;
import com.sun.jini.admin.StorageLocationAdmin;

// Initialize with a ref to the admin object
public class StorageLocationAdminPanel extends JPanel {
    public StorageLocationAdminPanel(final
                                StorageLocationAdmin admin) {
        setLayout(new BorderLayout());
        final JTextField loc = new JTextField();
        JButton button = new JButton("Set");
```

Listing 9–2 `StorageLocationAdminPanel.java` **(continued)**

```
        JPanel panel = new JPanel();
        final JLabel currentLoc = new JLabel();
        panel.setLayout(new GridLayout(2, 2));
        panel.add(new JLabel("Current storage location:"));

        try {
            // get the initial location
            currentLoc.setText(admin.getStorageLocation());
            panel.add(currentLoc);
        } catch (RemoteException ex) {
            JOptionPane.showMessageDialog(null,
                         "Couldn't get location:\n" +
                         ex.getMessage(), "Alert",
                         JOptionPane.ERROR_MESSAGE);
        }
        panel.add(new JLabel("New storage location: "));
        panel.add(loc);
        add(panel, BorderLayout.NORTH);

        button.addActionListener(new ActionListener() {
            public void actionPerformed(ActionEvent ev) {
                try {
                    // try to set the location
                    admin.setStorageLocation(loc.getText());
                    currentLoc.setText(
                         admin.getStorageLocation());
                } catch (Exception ex) {
                    JOptionPane.showMessageDialog(null,
                         "Couldn't set location:\n" +
                         ex.getMessage(),"Alert",
                         JOptionPane.ERROR_MESSAGE);
                }
            }
        });

        add(button, BorderLayout.SOUTH);
    }
}
```

This code is only slightly more complex than the `DestroyAdminPanel` we saw earlier. This example lays out a 2x2 grid. On the top row are two labels which provide the current storage location of the service; the bottom contains a text field and a button to cause any text in the field to be used as the new storage location.

Once again, the heart of this code is in the `ActionListener` attached to the button. This code fetches the text out of the text field and calls `setStorageLocation()` to attempt to change the service's location of its persistent storage. To see if the change took effect, the code then asks the service for its new storage location and displays that in the panel. This allows users to confirm what actually happened when they tried to change the storage location.

An attempt to change a service's storage location can fail for two reasons. First, the network connection to the service may be down, in which case a `RemoteException` will be raised. Second, the user may specify a location that makes no sense for the particular service. Examples of this might include providing a DOS-style path name to a service running on UNIX. Jini makes no assumptions about how services will interpret the storage location passed to them; it's merely a string, which they are free to interpret or reject as they see fit. If a user passes in a bogus storage location, an `IOException` will be raised. Both of these conditions are trapped in this example, and a warning dialog is presented to the user.

Figure 9–3 shows the simple user interface for this administrative API.

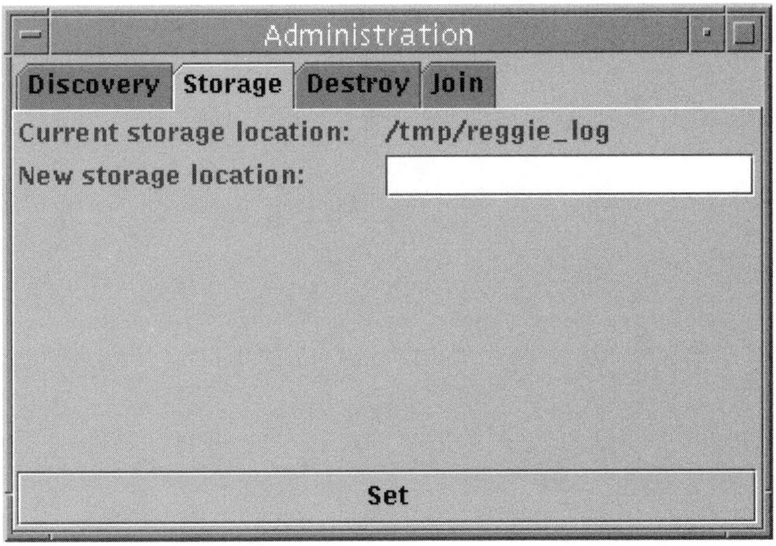

Figure 9–3 The StorageLocationAdminPanel

Both of the next two administrative interfaces are significantly more complex than what we've seen before. And both of them happen to require a particular style of interaction—adding and removing items from a set. Before going on with the next two administrative GUIs, let's take a look at a "helper" class that we'll use to manage sets of items.

A ListBox for Managing Sets

The `JoinAdmin` and `DiscoveryAdmin` APIs have methods for controlling sets of groups a service should join, sets of attributes that should be attached to it, and sets of lookup locator URLs that it should explicitly connect to. To facilitate controlling sets like these, we'll create a `ListBox` class (see Listing 9–3) that allows a user to view the items in a set, and add and remove items from it. The `ListBox` supports "plug in" actions that can be used to map the GUI behavior of the `ListBox` onto what ever particular sort of set it is managing. We'll use this class extensively in our next two administration panel examples.

Listing 9–3 `ListBox.java`

```
// A list component specialized for this application

package corejini.chapter9;

import javax.swing.*;
import javax.swing.event.*;
import java.awt.*;
import java.awt.event.ActionEvent;

public class ListBox extends JPanel {
    protected Action addAction, removeAction, updateAction;
    protected JList list = new JList();
    protected JTextField field = new JTextField();
    protected JButton addButton = new JButton("Add");
    protected JButton removeButton = new JButton("Remove");
    protected Object lastSelected = null;

    public ListBox(String title, int rowCount) {
        this(null, null, null, title, rowCount);
    }
```

Listing 9–3 `ListBox.java` (continued)

```
    // create a ListBox initialized with our actions
    public ListBox(Action addAction, Action removeAction,
                   Action updateAction, String title,
                  int rowCount){
        super();
        this.addAction = addAction;
        this.removeAction = removeAction;
        setLayout(new BorderLayout());
        removeButton.setEnabled(false);
        list.setVisibleRowCount(rowCount);
        list.addListSelectionListener(new
                                  ListSelectionListener() {
           public void valueChanged(ListSelectionEvent ev){
                int idx = ev.getFirstIndex();

                if (idx == -1)
                    lastSelected = null;
                else
                    lastSelected = ((JList)
             ev.getSource()).getModel().getElementAt(idx);

                if (ev.getValueIsAdjusting())
                    return;
                 if (((JList)
                     ev.getSource()).getSelectedIndex()==-1)
                    removeButton.setEnabled(false);
                else
                    removeButton.setEnabled(true);
            }
        });

         setLayout(new BorderLayout());
        JPanel listPanel = new JPanel();
        listPanel.setLayout(new BorderLayout());
        JPanel gridPanel = new JPanel();
        gridPanel.setLayout(new GridLayout(2, 2));

         listPanel.add(new JLabel(title),
                        BorderLayout.NORTH);
        listPanel.add(new JScrollPane(list,
             JScrollPane.VERTICAL_SCROLLBAR_ALWAYS,
             JScrollPane.HORIZONTAL_SCROLLBAR_AS_NEEDED),
                        BorderLayout.CENTER);
```

Listing 9–3 `ListBox.java` (continued)

```
        gridPanel.add(addButton);
        gridPanel.add(field);

        gridPanel.add(removeButton);
        add(listPanel, BorderLayout.CENTER);
        add(gridPanel, BorderLayout.SOUTH);
        if (addAction != null)
            addButton.addActionListener(addAction);

        if (removeAction != null)
            removeButton.addActionListener(removeAction);

        if (updateAction != null) {
            addButton.addActionListener(updateAction);
            removeButton.addActionListener(updateAction);

            updateAction.actionPerformed(new
                                 ActionEvent(this, 0, null));
        }
    }

    // Change the action set
    public void setActions(Action add, Action remove,
                                             Action update) {
        if (addAction != null)
            addButton.removeActionListener(addAction);

        if (removeAction != null)
            removeButton.removeActionListener(
                                             removeAction);

        if (updateAction != null) {
            addButton.removeActionListener(updateAction);
            removeButton.removeActionListener(
                                             updateAction);
        }

        addAction = add;
        removeAction = remove;
        updateAction = update;
```

Listing 9–3 `ListBox.java` **(continued)**

```
        if (addAction != null)
            addButton.addActionListener(addAction);

        if (removeAction != null)
            removeButton.addActionListener(removeAction);

        if (updateAction != null) {
            addButton.addActionListener(updateAction);
            removeButton.addActionListener(updateAction);

            updateAction.actionPerformed(new
                                 ActionEvent(this, 0, null));
        }
    }

    // Some "helper" list methods
    public Object getSelectedValue() {
        return lastSelected;
    }
    public JList getList() {
        return list;
    }
    public JTextField getField() {
        return field;
    }
}
```

This component groups together four controls. There is a list widget within a scrolling pane, a text field, an associated "add" button that attempts to add whatever text is entered in the text field, and a remove button that attempts to remove whatever item in the list is selected.

To be useful for our different administration panels, this component needs to be able to interact with different sorts of lists—lists of attributes, lists of groups, and lists of lookup URLs. And when the add and remove buttons are clicked, the component needs to call out to different code that invokes the appropriate administration methods for whatever type of list is being edited.

The `ListBox` supports editing different types of lists by abstracting out the application behavior that says what to actually *do* when the add or remove buttons are clicked, and by abstracting away the details about how the list gets populated. A caller will pass the `ListBox` three `Action` objects representing the code to invoke whenever the add button is pressed, the remove button is pressed, or when the list needs to be updated.

The `Action` class is an addition to the Java GUI programming model made by the Java Foundation Classes. It provides a way to represent a single callable operation in an object which implements the `ActionListener` interface. `Actions` can be installed in buttons, where they will be automatically invoked whenever the button is pressed, or they can be called "manually" by invoking the `actionPerformed()` method on them.

Our `ListBox` class, in addition to creating its subcomponents, also handles making sure that the remove button is properly enabled or disabled whenever an item is selected or unselected in the list. The `ListBox` also remembers what the last selected item in the list was, by watching for change events in the list.

Whenever the add or remove actions are performed by clicking the appropriate button, the `ListBox` will also manually invoke the update action to cause the contents of the list to be redisplayed. By providing an update action which queries a service for the state of a particular administrable item, clients can cause the `ListBox` to properly reflect the contents of service group, attribute, and locator lists.

The constructor for the `ListBox` also allows callers to pass in two parameters that control aspects of the appearance of the control: the `rowCount` integer specifies the desired minimum number of rows in the list, and the `title` string allows callers to provide a descriptive title over the `ListBox`.

Now that we've built a `ListBox` widget that we can reuse in our examples, let's move on to the next administration panel.

DiscoveryAdminPanel

Jini lookup services will implement the `DiscoveryAdmin` interface. This interface controls the way the service supports Jini communities—it allows callers to change the set of groups in which a lookup service is a member, and also allows them to change the port number on which the lookup service listens for unicast discovery messages.

In this section, we'll build a reuseable GUI component for interacting with `DiscoveryAdmin` objects. This control provides a `ListBox` for viewing, adding, and removing groups from the lookup service's set of supported

groups, and provides a text entry field and a button for changing the lookup service port as shown in Listing 9–4.

Listing 9–4 `DiscoveryAdminPanel.java`

```
// A user interface for DiscoverAdmin

package corejini.chapter9;

import javax.swing.*;
import javax.swing.event.*;
import java.awt.event.*;
import java.awt.*;
import net.jini.lookup.DiscoveryAdmin;

public class DiscoveryAdminPanel extends JPanel {
    protected ListBox listbox;
    protected JTextField portField = new JTextField();
    protected JLabel currentPort = new JLabel();
    protected DiscoveryAdmin admin;

      // An action for adding new groups
    class AddAction extends AbstractAction {
        public void actionPerformed(ActionEvent ev) {
             String[] newGroups = new String[1];

             newGroups[0] = listbox.getField().getText();

             if (newGroups[0].equals("<public>"))
                  newGroups[0] = "";

            try {
                admin.addMemberGroups(newGroups);
            } catch (Exception ex) {
                System.err.println("Couldn't add group: " +
                                           ex.getMessage());
            }
        }
    }
```

Listing 9–4 `DiscoveryAdminPanel.java` **(continued)**

```
    // An action for removing groups
    class RemoveAction extends AbstractAction {
       public void actionPerformed(ActionEvent ev) {
           Object sel = listbox.getSelectedValue();

           if (sel == null) {
               return;
           }

           try {
               String[] items = new String[1];
               sel = (sel.equals("<public>") ? "" : sel);
               items[0] = (String) sel;
               admin.removeMemberGroups(items);
           } catch (Exception ex) {
              System.err.println("Couldn't remove group: "
                                   + ex.getMessage());
           }
       }
   }

   // An action for changing groups
   class UpdateAction extends AbstractAction {
       public void actionPerformed(ActionEvent ev) {
           try {
               String[] members = admin.getMemberGroups();
               for (int i=0 ; i<members.length ; i++) {
                   if (members[i].equals(""))
                       members[i] = "<public>";
               }
               listbox.getList().setListData(members);
           } catch (Exception ex) {
               System.err.println("Couldn't update: " +
                                     ex.getMessage());
               listbox.getList().setListData(new
                                          String[0]);
           }
       }
   }
```

Listing 9–4 `DiscoveryAdminPanel.java` **(continued)**

```
    class SetPortAction extends AbstractAction {
       public void actionPerformed(ActionEvent ev) {
           try {
               admin.setUnicastPort(
                Integer.parseInt(portField.getText()));
               currentPort.setText(
                        Integer.toString(
                            admin.getUnicastPort()));
           } catch (Exception ex) {
               System.err.println("Couldn't change port: "
                                    + ex.getMessage());
           }
       }
    }

    public DiscoveryAdminPanel(DiscoveryAdmin da) {
       admin = da;
       setLayout(new BorderLayout());

       // Create a ListBox and initialize it with our
       // actions
       listbox = new ListBox("Member Groups", 12);
       listbox.setActions(new AddAction(),
                          new RemoveAction(),
                          new UpdateAction());
       JPanel portPanel = new JPanel();
       portPanel.setLayout(new BorderLayout());
       JPanel gridPanel = new JPanel();
       gridPanel.setLayout(new GridLayout(2, 2));
       gridPanel.add(new JLabel("Current port: "));
       try {
           currentPort.setText(
            Integer.toString(admin.getUnicastPort()));
       } catch (Exception ex) {
           System.err.println("Error setting port: " +
                              ex.getMessage());
       }

       add(listbox, BorderLayout.CENTER);
       add(portPanel, BorderLayout.SOUTH);
   }
```

Listing 9–4 `DiscoveryAdminPanel.java` (continued)

```
            gridPanel.add(currentPort);
            gridPanel.add(new JLabel("New port: "));
            gridPanel.add(portField);
            portPanel.add(gridPanel, BorderLayout.CENTER);
            JButton button = new JButton("Set");
            button.addActionListener(new SetPortAction());
            portPanel.add(button, BorderLayout.SOUTH);
        }
}
```

This code is a heavy user of the `ListBox` control shown earlier; it creates three actions that understand how to interact with objects implementing the `DiscoveryAdmin` interface to present lists of lookup groups to a user.

The `AddAction` class retrieves the text out of the `ListBox`'s text field. The text is treated as the name of a group that the lookup service is being asked to support, and so it is passed to the `addMemberGroups()` call to tell the lookup service to begin supporting the named group. The code here allows the user to type "<public>" to indicate the default, unnamed public group; more on this a bit later. Note that this code doesn't have to handle updating the list itself—it only need concern itself with how to add an item to the list. The updating of the list is done by the `ListBox`, which automatically calls out to whatever update action has been installed in it after the add action is invoked.

The `RemoveAction` class fetches the selected item from the `ListBox` that, because of the data our actions install in the list, will be a string. The selected string is then passed to `removeMemberGroups()` to ask the lookup service to remove it from the set of groups it supports. Note here the special handling for the default, unnamed public group. Because the default group is unnamed (or, more precisely, it is named by the empty string), our actions use the convention of showing the string "<public>" in the list instead of an empty list item. So, if the selected item is called "<public>," the `RemoveAction` replaces it with the empty string so that we will properly name the default group. Like `AddAction`, this code doesn't have to update the list after removing an item, because the `ListBox` automatically invokes the update action after removal.

The `UpdateAction` simply asks the `DiscoveryAdmin` object for all the groups in which the lookup service is a member. These are displayed in the list; note that the unnamed group is "translated" into the string "<public>" for display here. If an exceptional condition results from the operation, the list is cleared and an error is reported.

Finally, even though management of the unicast port number isn't done through the `ListBox` class, here I've defined a `SetPortAction` that will be bound to a button to change the port number. This code calls out to `DiscoveryAdmin` to set the port from whatever text is contained in the text entry field, and then sets the displayed port number to whatever the `DiscoveryAdmin` object reports as its true, current port number. Note that, unlike the remove and add actions, this code *must* update the display itself after it is executed—there is no `ListBox` class automatically performing updates for it after invocation.

Figure 9–4 shows this interface.

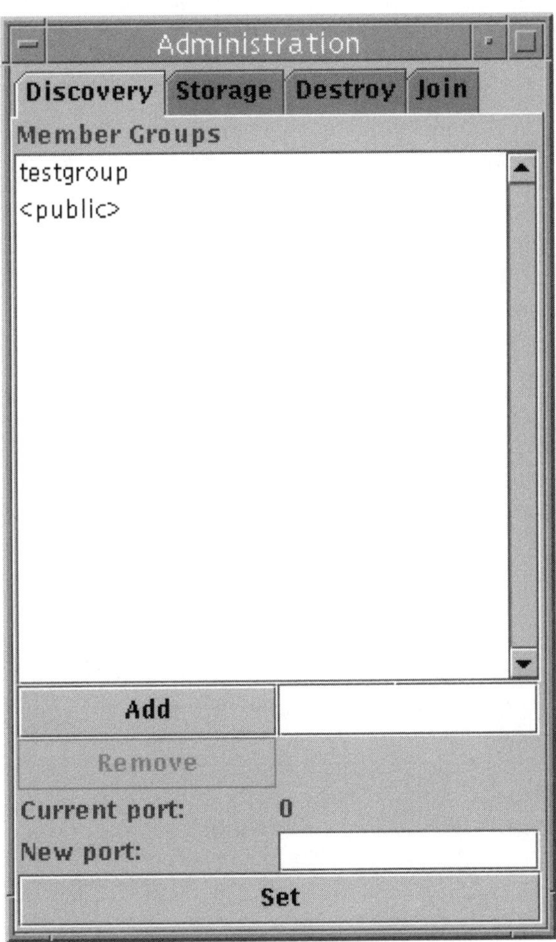

Figure 9–4 The DiscoveryAdminPanel

The rest of the code is in the constructor for `DiscoveryAdminPanel`, and is straightforward. The code creates the layout by constructing a `ListBox` and then the grid of controls for displaying and updating the port number. All the appropriate action classes are instantiated and installed in the `ListBox` so that it will automatically call out to methods to add, remove, and update list elements whenever the `Listbox`'s buttons are pressed.

JoinAdminPanel

Our final administration GUI is the most visually complicated. The `JoinAdminPanel` (Listing 9–5) presents an interface to controlling services that support the `JoinAdmin` interface. This interface should be implemented by every Jini service: it is used to control the groups that a service will try to join, the attributes that should be installed on every one if its registrations, and the set of explicit lookup locator URLs that it should try to connect to. Essentially, this interface controls the aspects of a service's participation in the Jini join protocol.

All three of these controllable parameters—groups, attributes, and locators—are sets from which items can be added and removed. So all three of these can use the `ListBox` class to permit editing. We will, of course, need different action objects to support interacting with the various `JoinAdmin` APIs.

Listing 9–5 `JoinAdminPanel.java`

```
// A user interface for JoinAdmin

package corejini.chapter9;

import javax.swing.*;
import javax.swing.event.*;
import java.awt.event.*;
import java.awt.*;
import java.rmi.RemoteException;
import net.jini.admin.JoinAdmin;
import net.jini.core.discovery.LookupLocator;
import net.jini.core.entry.Entry;
```

Listing 9–5 `JoinAdminPanel.java` **(continued)**

```
public class JoinAdminPanel extends JPanel {
    protected ListBox groupsList, locsList, attrsList;
    protected JoinAdmin admin;

    // An action for adding groups
    class AddAction extends AbstractAction {
        ListBox listbox;

        AddAction(ListBox lb) {
            listbox = lb;
        }

        public void actionPerformed(ActionEvent ev) {
            String newItem = listbox.getField().getText();

            try {
                if (listbox.equals(groupsList)) {
                    String[] items = new String[1];
                    items[0] = newItem;

                if (items[0].equals("<public>"))
                    items[0] = "";

                    admin.addLookupGroups(items);
                } else if (listbox.equals(locsList)) {
                    LookupLocator[] items =
                                 new LookupLocator[1];
                    items[0] = new LookupLocator(newItem);
                    admin.addLookupLocators(items);
                } else if (listbox.equals(attrsList)) {
                    // noop for now...
                }
            } catch (Exception ex) {
                System.err.println("Error adding item: " +
                                      ex.getMessage());
            }
        }
    }
```

Listing 9–5 `JoinAdminPanel.java` **(continued)**

```
    // An action for removing groups

    class RemoveAction extends AbstractAction {
       ListBox listbox;

       RemoveAction(ListBox lb) {
           listbox = lb;
       }

       public void actionPerformed(ActionEvent ev) {
           Object sel = listbox.getSelectedValue();

           if (sel == null)
               return;

           try {
               if (listbox.equals(groupsList)) {
                   String[] items = new String[1];
                   if (sel.equals("<public>")
                       sel = "";
                   items[0] = (String) sel;
                    admin.removeLookupGroups(items);
               } else if (listbox.equals(locsList)) {
                   LookupLocator[] items =
                                 new LookupLocator[1];
                   items[0] = (LookupLocator) sel;
                   admin.removeLookupLocators(items);
               } else if (listbox.equals(attrsList)) {
                   // noop for now...
               }
           } catch (Exception ex) {
               System.err.println("Error removing item: "
                                      + ex.getMessage());
           }
       }
  }
```

Listing 9–5 `JoinAdminPanel.java` **(continued)**

```
// An action for updating groups

 class UpdateAction extends AbstractAction {
    ListBox listbox;

    UpdateAction(ListBox lb) {
        listbox = lb;
    }

    public void actionPerformed(ActionEvent ev) {
        Object[] items = null;
        try {
            if (listbox.equals(groupsList)) {
                items = admin.getLookupGroups();
                for (int i=0 ; i<items.length ; i++) {
                    if (items[i].equals(""))
                        items[i] = "<public>";
                }
            } else if (listbox.equals(locsList)) {
                items = admin.getLookupLocators();
            } else if (listbox.equals(attrsList)) {
                items = admin.getLookupAttributes();
            }
            listbox.getList().setListData(items);
        } catch (Exception ex) {
            System.err.println("Error updating: " +
                                         ex.getMessage());
            listbox.getList().setListData(
                                              new String[0]);
        }
    }
}
 public JoinAdminPanel(JoinAdmin ja) {
     admin = ja;

    groupsList = new ListBox("Lookup Groups", 4);
    groupsList.setActions(new AddAction(groupsList),
                           new RemoveAction(groupsList),
                          new UpdateAction(groupsList));
    attrsList = new ListBox("Lookup Attributes", 4);;
    attrsList.setActions(new AddAction(attrsList),
                          new RemoveAction(attrsList),
                          new UpdateAction(attrsList));
```

Listing 9–5 `JoinAdminPanel.java` **(continued)**

```
        locsList = new ListBox("Lookup Locators", 4);
        locsList.setActions(new AddAction(locsList),
                            new RemoveAction(locsList),
                            new UpdateAction(locsList));

        setLayout(new BorderLayout());
        JPanel panel = new JPanel();
        panel.setLayout(new BoxLayout(panel,
                                      BoxLayout.Y_AXIS));
        panel.add(groupsList);
        panel.add(attrsList);
        panel.add(locsList);

        add(panel, BorderLayout.CENTER);
    }
}
```

The constructor for this class simply creates the three `ListBoxes` and arranges them into a panel. Let's look at the three action classes used by this example, which are where the action is.

The `JoinAdminPanel` uses one add, one remove, and one update action class for all of the three types of lists that it manages (groups, attributes, and locators). The constructors for these actions are parameterized by the particular `ListBox` they are asked to manage. So, in the constructor, you see the creation of three separate instances of `AddAction`, one for each of the three `ListBoxes`. And each of these takes the particular `ListBox` it is associated with as a parameter.

Whenever an action is invoked, it compares the `ListBox` it was passed as a parameter to the three `ListBoxes` it knows are used in this panel. By doing this, it can tell if it is meant to manage groups, attributes, or locators. This "trick" saves us the trouble of creating three separate add action classes, three separate remove action classes, and three separate update action classes, one for each type of list.

Let's look at how `AddAction` works. When it is invoked, it fetches any text from the text entry field of its `ListBox`. It then checks to see whether the `ListBox` it was parameterized by was the groups `ListBox`, the attributes `ListBox`, or the locator `ListBox`. Depending on which list it is managing, it invokes the appropriate method, with the appropriate arguments, on the `JoinAdmin` object. For example, if the `AddAction` is associated with the groups `ListBox`, it calls `addLookupGroups()` and passes the selected string as an argument. If it is associated with the locators `ListBox`, it converts the string to a `LookupLocator` and passes this to `addLookupLocator()`.

Note that this code currently ignores attributes—there is no way to add a new attribute to a service using this GUI as presented. The reason for this is that specifying attributes and filling out all of their member data is a fairly long process—a bit too long to present readily in book format. Properly adding an attribute would require that the GUI allow users to enter the name of an attribute class, load that class, and then introspect on it to determine what member data it supports. The GUI would then allow the users to "fill in" each of these attributes in the appropriate type, probably by using the JavaBeans `PropertyEditor` mechanisms.

One less powerful, but quite easy, alternative would be to simply take the strings that are typed and install them as `Comment` attributes on the current service. As mentioned, though, the code here does not support adding attributes to services.

The `RemoveAction` class is structured much the same as `AddAction`. Depending on the `ListBox` it was parameterized with, it will invoke either `removeLookupGroup()` or `removeLookupLocator()` on the `JoinAdmin` object with the appropriate parameters. Again, this code does not support removing attributes from services. Note here again how this action translates the string "<public>," meant for display in a list, into the empty string for manipulating the default group.

The `UpdateAction` class does this same translation, and invokes the appropriate methods on `JoinAdmin` for fetching groups, locators, and attributes (the code here does allow *viewing* all the attributes on a service in a list).

Figure 9–5 shows the `JoinAdminPanel`.

AdminPanel

Now that we have all of these separate panels, we can group them together so that we have an easy solution for administering all four of these common service behaviors.

The `AdminPanel` class simply provides a panel with a tabbed pane containing separate tabs for each of the four administrative interfaces that a service may implement. You can create one of these by simply passing in the administration object for a service to the `AdminPanel` constructor as shown in Listing 9–6.

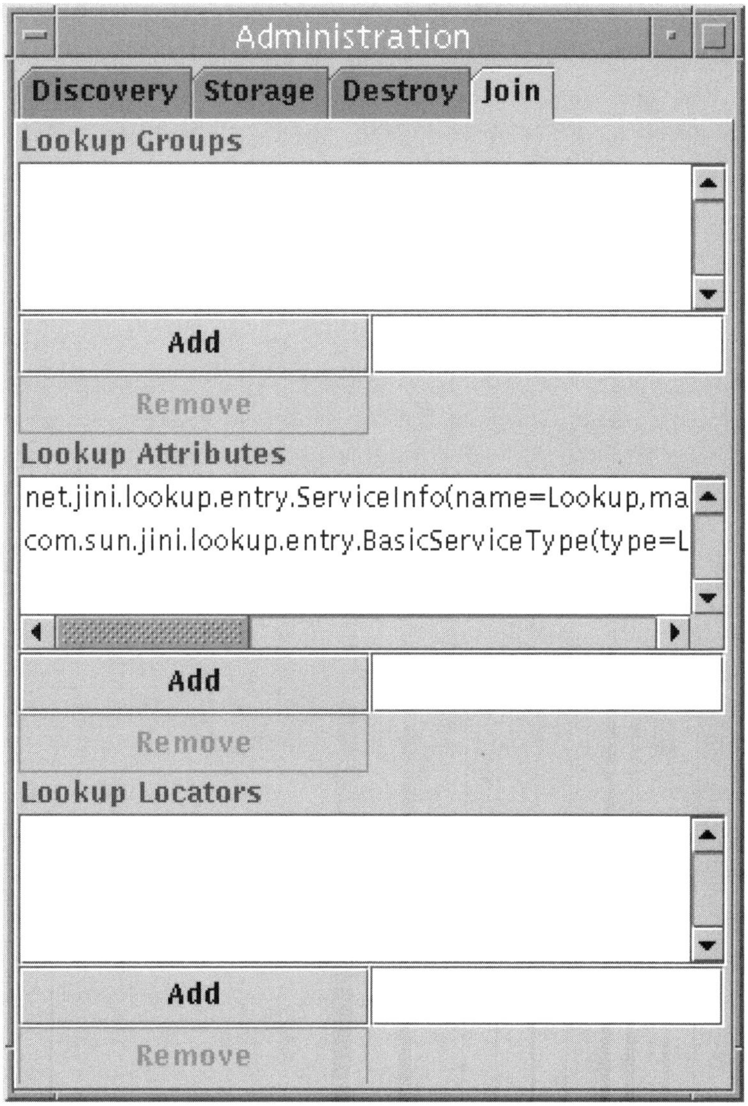

Figure 9–5 The JoinAdminPanel

Listing 9–6 `AdminPanel.java`

```
// This is the overall admininstration GUI. You pass it
// an admin object, it introspects to figure out which
// interfaces it implements, and sets up the tabbed panes.

package corejini.chapter9;

import javax.swing.*;
import java.awt.BorderLayout;
import net.jini.admin.JoinAdmin;
import net.jini.lookup.DiscoveryAdmin;
import com.sun.jini.admin.*;

public class AdminPanel extends JPanel {
    public AdminPanel(Object admin) {
        super();

        setLayout(new BorderLayout());
        JTabbedPane pane = new JTabbedPane();

        if (admin instanceof DiscoveryAdmin) {
            DiscoveryAdminPanel panel =
                new DiscoveryAdminPanel((DiscoveryAdmin)
                                            admin);
            pane.addTab("Discovery", panel);
        }
        if (admin instanceof StorageLocationAdmin) {
            StorageLocationAdminPanel panel =
                new StorageLocationAdminPanel(
                        (StorageLocationAdmin) admin);
            pane.addTab("Storage", panel);
        }
        if (admin instanceof DestroyAdmin) {
            DestroyAdminPanel panel =
               new DestroyAdminPanel((DestroyAdmin) admin);
            pane.addTab("Destroy", panel);
        }
        if (admin instanceof JoinAdmin) {
            JoinAdminPanel panel =
                new JoinAdminPanel((JoinAdmin) admin);
            pane.addTab("Join", panel);
        }

        add(pane, BorderLayout.CENTER);
    }
}
```

This code simply introspects on the administration object passed to it. For each known administrative API that it implements, the constructor creates a new tab in the tabbed pane with the appropriate administration GUI. This class is ready-to-use in your own applications.

JList Cell Renderers for Common Jini Types

We're now ready to move on from our administrative GUI building to other components we'll need for our browser. As you saw in the screen shot of the browser in Figure 9–1, our view of a Jini community is organized as a set of individual lists, displaying lookup services, services contained within those lookup services, and attributes attached to services.

The Swing `JList` class provides some handy facilities for controlling how the items in a list will appear. The `JList` class can contain any type of object as an element in a list. By default, these objects are displayed in the list via `JLabel` instances: in most cases, the text of the label will be set by invoking `toString()` on the object. If the object contained in the list's model is an icon, then the label that displays that object will be set to display that icon instead of any text.

You can, however, override this default behavior by specifying a new `ListCellRenderer` for the `JList`. A `ListCellRenderer` examines each item in a list and returns an appropriate `Component` type to display it. Custom cell renderers can, for example, be used to display a list of `java.awt.Color` objects as color swatches, rather than simply the `toString()` representation of colors stuffed into a label. A cell renderer must simply override one method, called `getListCellRendererComponent()`, to return a custom component for an object stored in a list.

Because the browser organizes lookup services, other services, and attributes into `JLists`, we can take advantage of Swing's custom cell rendering behavior to generate appropriate `Components` for each of these Jini object types. The browser will use these renderers when it creates its display lists. The cell renderers presented here can be reused in your own code when you have a need to display Jini types in a Swing container.

LookupCellRenderer

Let's first look at a `ListCellRenderer` (Listing 9–7) that can help display objects of type `ServiceRegistrar`. These will be the proxy objects for the various lookup services that we discover; by creating a custom cell renderer for these proxies, we can display them in a more sensible form than whatever the implementor happened to provide for the `toString()` return value.

Listing 9–7 `LookupCellRenderer.java`

```
// Draw a ServiceRegistrar as its locator URL

package corejini.chhapter9;

import javax.swing.*;
import java.awt.Component;
import net.jini.core.lookup.*;

public class LookupCellRenderer
                         extends DefaultListCellRenderer {
    public Component getListCellRendererComponent(JList lst,
                                Object value,
                                int index,
                                boolean isSelected,
                                boolean cellHasFocus) {
        Component c =
             super.getListCellRendererComponent(lst, value,
                                    index, isSelected,
                                        cellHasFocus);
        if (c instanceof JLabel) {
            JLabel l = (JLabel) c;
            if (value instanceof ServiceRegistrar) {
                ServiceRegistrar reg =
                                (ServiceRegistrar) value;
                try {
                    l.setText(reg.getLocator().toString());
                } catch (RemoteException ex) {
                    System.err.println("Error getting " +
                                       "locator: " +
                                   ex.getMessage());
                    l.setText(reg.toString());
                }
            }
        }
        return c;
    }
}
```

Here we see a short cell renderer that creates a label containing the ServiceRegistrar's locator URL. Recall that ServiceRegistrar is only an interface—we have no idea what actual class it is, and so cannot predict what APIs it may have available other than those defined in ServiceRegistrar, and cannot know what its toString() method may return. A LookupLocator URL is a common representation of *all* ServiceRegistrars, however, and so I'll use that, rather than an arbitrary toString() result, as the value to display.

Note here how the code interacts with the superclass's implementation of getListCellRenderer(). By subclassing DefaultListCellRenderer, the code has access to all of that class's methods, including the default functionality for creating a new JLabel from an object stored in a list. The behavior in the default cell renderer is actually a bit more complicated than simply creating a label and returning it. It considers whether the object in the list is selected, and whether it has the focus, to properly assign colors and highlighting information to it.

Because we don't want to recreate all of that work in our class, the code reuses the label handed to it from the superclass, and changes the text of it to be the URL for the ServiceRegistrar. This is a fairly simple example of a ListCellRenderer; the next examples will be a bit more complex.

ServiceCellRenderer

The next type of Jini object we'll need to display in lists is a service proxy. Service proxies, as you will recall, are even more free-form than lookup ServiceRegistrars: there are *no* standard interfaces that they typically implement, other than Administrable, which will not help us create an easily recognizable representation of a service.

We'd like to be able to display lists of service proxies in a way that helps users to quickly identify and use them. Again, if we have to rely on whatever toString() implementation the writer of the proxy may—or may not—have provided, we may be in trouble.

Instead, the alternative used here is to search the attributes associated with a service for helpful information on how to display it (see Listing 9–8).

Listing 9–8 `ServiceCellRenderer.java`

```
// Draw a service as its name if it has one, or a
// cleaned-up representation of the proxy's class.

package corejini.chhapter9;

import javax.swing.*;
import java.awt.Component;
import net.jini.core.lookup.*;
import net.jini.lookup.entry.Name;

public class ServiceCellRenderer
                         extends DefaultListCellRenderer {
    public Component getListCellRendererComponent(JList lst,
                                 Object value,
                                 int index,
                                 boolean isSelected,
                                 boolean cellHasFocus) {
        Component c =
             super.getListCellRendererComponent(lst, value,
                                     index, isSelected,
                                     cellHasFocus);

        if (c instanceof JLabel) {
            JLabel l = (JLabel) c;
            if (value instanceof ServiceItem) {
                ServiceItem item = (ServiceItem) value;
                String s = null;
                for (int i=0 ; i<item.attributeSets.length;
                                             i++) {
                    if (item.attributeSets[i] instanceof
                                             Name) {
                        s = ((Name)
                             item.attributeSets[i]).name;
                        break;
                    }
                }
                if (s == null) {
                    s = Browser.declassify(
                     item.service.getClass().getName());
                }
                l.setText(s);
            }
        }
        return c;
    }
}
```

The basic structure of this ListCellRenderer is the same as the previous one—it calls out to its superclass to create a default label, and then changes it based on information it can determine about the object it is displaying.

In this case, I assume that the objects in the lists of services are ServiceItems. When the cell renderer is asked to display a ServiceItem, it scans over the attributes associated with it. If a Name attribute is found (which will contain a human-readable name like "Fred's VCR" or "OCR Service"), it is used as the text of the label. If no Name is associated with the service's proxy, then the class name of the service is used; here I call a method called declassify(), which is defined in the Browser class we'll see shortly, to strip off leading package names from a class. Displaying the name of the proxy's class isn't the best solution—because whatever the proxy's author named the class is really an implementation detail which may not be fit for human consumption—but it's all we have to go on.

You could easily change this example to search for a ServiceInfo attribute and fetch the Icon member out of it to display a graphical representation of the service; most of the services shipped by Sun as a part of Jini do not have such icons, though, so I haven't taken that approach here.

AttrCellRenderer

Now for the fun one: lists of attributes. You'll remember from Chapter 7 that attributes have a nice synergy with beans—the Jini APIs provide a way for developers to associate beans with attribute classes, and clients can take advantage of these beans for display or programmatic purposes.

The cell renderer for attributes (Listing 9–9) follows the same basic paradigm of the others—it asks its superclass for a default Component to be used to display an object. In this case, however, it also uses the beans facilities to see if it can recover a bean for the attribute. If the bean it gets back is itself a Component, then the code can display this instead of the boring old label it gets from the default renderer.

Listing 9–9 `AttrCellRenderer.java`

```
// Draw attributes as components, if they are, or use
// the name of the class along with its toString()
// representation
package corejini.chapter9;

import javax.swing.*;
import java.awt.Component;
import net.jini.core.lookup.*;

public class AttrCellRenderer
                         extends DefaultListCellRenderer {
    public Component getListCellRendererComponent(JList lst,
                                 Object value,
                                 int index,
                                 boolean isSelected,
                                 boolean cellHasFocus) {

        Component c =
        super.getListCellRendererComponent(list, value,
                                         index,
                                         isSelected,
                                         cellHasFocus);
       return getComponentForEntry((Entry) value, c);
     }

     Component getComponentForEntry(Entry e,
                                 Component defaultComp) {
         EntryBean bean = null;

             try {
                    bean = EntryBeans.createBean(e);
             } catch (Exception ex) {
             }
```

Listing 9–9 AttrCellRenderer.java (continued)

```
        // If it's a component return it. If it's null or
        // not a component, return the default.
        if (bean == null || !(bean instanceof Component)) {
            if (defaultComp instanceof JLabel) {
              String cname =
               Browser.declassify(e.getClass().getName());
               ((JLabel) defaultComp.setText(cname + " [" +
                                       e.toString() + "]");
            }
            return defaultComp;
        } else {
            ((Component) bean).setVisible(true);
            return (Component) bean;
        }
    }
}
```

The getListCellRendererComponent() method again calls the superclass to fetch a JLabel which will be the default component to return. But the code also calls getComponentForEntry() to see if a "better" one can be returned. This method takes the Entry for which we're looking for a Component, as well as the default Component which will be returned if we cannot find an alternative.

The getComponentForEntry() method first calls out to the EntryBeans class to try to create a bean for the specified Entry. This will result in an attempt to locate and load a bean that corresponds to whatever Entry class was passed in. The code here ignores any exceptions that may result; if the bean is null then it will just use the default.

After trying to load the bean, the code checks to see if a bean was successfully loaded and, if so, whether the bean is a subclass of Component. If it is, then setVisible() is called on it to make it appear on the screen, and it is returned. If no bean was loaded, or if the loaded bean was not a Component, then the default component (most likely a JLabel) is returned. Here, we try to make sure that the display is somewhat sensible, by setting the label to the de-packaged class name and then appending the toString() representation of the attribute. (And here you see yet another example of why providing intelligent implementations of toString() is so important for classes like this that will be displayed to users.)

With the bag of tricks we've accumulated so far, we can create administrative GUIs for arbitrary services, and create nice-looking and intuitive lists of

services, registrars, and attributes. Now, we're ready to move on to the browser itself.

The Core Browser Framework

Now that we've got a set of building blocks to work from, we can begin looking at the core code of our browser application. The basic functionality of the browser is fairly simple; it needs to do the following things:

- Create the three-paned user interface we saw in Figure 9–1.
- Perform discovery, and be prepared to receive events from the lookup services that we've discovered.
- Monitor for mouse clicks on the list panes; clicks and double clicks will cause other panes to update, and may contact Jini lookup services to find available services, and solicit events from these services.

I've tried to create a "natural" set of bindings between mouse clicks and operations in this interface. Clicking on the various panels will have the actions shown in Table 9–1.

Table 9–1 Operations in the Jini Browser

Lookup Service Clicked	Clicking on a lookup service causes the service list to be updated with the set of services contained in that lookup service. The code will also solicit events from the lookup service so that new services will be found. Event registrations from any previously selected lookup service are canceled.
Lookup Service Double clicked	Double clicking on a lookup service causes the administration panel for that service to appear, if the lookup service is administrable.
Service Clicked	Clicking on a service causes the attribute list to display the set of attributes associated with that service. Any beans that may exist for the attribute classes will be found and, if those beans are `Components`, will be displayed in the list.
Service Double clicked	Double clicking on a service causes the administration panel for that service to appear, if the service is administrable.

Table 9–1 Operations in the Jini Browser (continued)

Attribute Clicked	Clicking on an attribute has no effect in this example. One could extend this example to pop up a panel containing more information about the attribute—such as the short description that can be retrieved from the attribute's bean.
Attribute Double clicked	Double clicking on an attribute has no effect in this example. One could extend this example to pop up a JavaBeans PropertyEditor to edit the attribute, and then set its value through the service's administrative APIs.

Storing Data in Lists

Now that we have some idea of the requirements for the browser, we can begin to flesh out the individual components of the core program. From the screen shot you saw in Figure 9–1, you no doubt noticed that the browser is organized as three lists, each in separate panes. These lists are `JLists`, which are quite flexible in how the data contained in them is represented. If you peruse the documentation for this class, you'll notice that you can create new `JLists` by passing in arrays or `Vectors` of objects, or by passing in something called a `JListModel`. If you pass in a simple type—such as an array or `Vector`—the `JList` class will create a default list model that it will use internally to represent the data stored in it. The *bad* thing about using this default model is that if you ever add, remove, or change anything in the array or `Vector` you passed to the list, the `JList` object will not notice this fact. The default list model expects the input data to be unchanging; if your data will ever change, you need to define a new list model that will "poke" the `JList` whenever it is updated.

Clearly, the data in our lists may change. Services may appear and disappear from the services pane; lookup services may come and go. So the code for the browser creates an extremely simple new list model called the `VectorListModel`. This class implements the various `ListModel` interfaces, and wraps a simple `Vector`. Whenever items are added to or removed from this model, it calls out to any listeners that may be waiting for changes. The visible `JList` components in our application register themselves as listeners for changes in their respective models, so they will be updated as the set of managed list items changes.

Listing 9–10 shows the `VectorListModel` class:

Listing 9–10 `VectorListModel.java`

```
// Contains the data in a list.

package corejini.chapter9;

import java.util.Vector;
import javax.swing.*;

class VectorListModel extends AbstractListModel {
    Vector v = new Vector();

    public Object getElementAt(int index) {
        return v.elementAt(index);
    }
    public int getSize() {
        return v.size();
    }
    boolean contains(Object o) {
        return v.contains(o);
    }
    synchronized void addElement(Object o) {
        v.addElement(o);
        fireIntervalAdded(this, v.size(), v.size());
    }

    synchronized void removeElement(Object o) {
        int index = v.indexOf(o);
        if (index != -1) {
            v.remove(index);
            fireIntervalRemoved(this, index, index);
        }
    }
    synchronized void setData(Vector newVector) {
        int len = v.size();
        v = newVector;
        fireIntervalRemoved(this, 0, len);
        fireIntervalAdded(this, 0,  v.size());
    }
}
```

This simple class extends `AbstractListModel`, so it inherits all the basic `ListModel` functionality. It also contains an enclosed `Vector`, and exposes some handy `Vector`-like methods on it (such as `addElement()`, `contains()`, and so on). Whenever these methods are called to update the contents of the contained `Vector`, any listeners for the model will be messaged.

This list model will serve as the basis for all three of the list panes in our browser example. Next, let's look at some classes we'll use to facilitate the browser's integration with Jini.

Using Discovery

There are two special interfaces that code in the browser will need to implement to be "plugged in" to the Jini run-time system. First, it will have to leverage the `DiscoveryListener` interface to be informed about new lookup services. Second, it will have to use `RemoteEventListener` so that it can be informed of changes in the set of services known to particular lookup services.

There is no reason we couldn't have one big `Browser` class that does all of this by implementing both interfaces. For clarity though, here I've broken out the implementors of these two interfaces into separate classes (see Listings 9–11 and 9–12). These could easily be inner classes, which would allow them to have direct access to the members of the `Browser` class that created them; in the interests of clarity, I've tried to lessen the amount of cross-talk between the classes here and the larger `Browser` class by writing these as separate non-nested classes. Let's look at the one for discovery first.

This class is instantiated by passing it an instance of a `Browser`. Basically all it does is wait around for new `DiscoveryEvents` to be passed to it via its `discovered()` and `discarded()` interfaces. When `discovered()` is called, each registrar is compared to the list of registrars already known to the browser; if the registrar is a new one, it is added to the browser's list of registrars. When a registrar is discarded, it is removed from the browser's list of registrars.

This code requires that the `Browser` implement a method called `getLookups()` that returns a list of lookup services known to it. As we'll see when we look at the `Browser` class, the object that is returned from this call is an instance of the `VectorListModel` we defined earlier. By using this list, the `Discoverer` can simply add and remove registrars, safe in the knowledge that the `Browser`'s lists will be updated appropriately.

Listing 9–11 `Discoverer.java`

```
// A class to manage Discovery for us.

package corejini.chapter9;

import net.jini.core.lookup.*;
import net.jini.discovery.*;

class Discoverer implements DiscoveryListener {
    protected Browser browser;

    Discoverer(Browser browser) {
        this.browser = browser;
    }
    public void discovered(DiscoveryEvent ev) {
        ServiceRegistrar regs[] = ev.getRegistrars();
        for (int i=0  ; i<regs.length ; i++) {
            if (!browser.getLookups().contains(regs[i])) {
                browser.getLookups().addElement(regs[i]);
            }
        }
    }
    public void discarded(DiscoveryEvent ev) {
        ServiceRegistrar regs[] = ev.getRegistrars();
        for (int i=0 ; i<regs.length ; i++) {
            browser.getLookups().removeElement(regs[i]);
        }
    }
}
```

Receiving Service Events

The second interface that we need to implement to play well with Jini is `RemoteEventListener`. Whenever the user selects a new lookup service, the browser needs to search that lookup service to see which services are known to it. It *also* must solicit events from the lookup service so that it will be informed when new services appear, or old services disappear, so that it can update the lists that it presents to users; the `Listener` object will receive these events.

The `RemoteEventListener` interface is implemented by a separate object. Again, this interface could be implemented by the larger `Browser` itself, or by an inner class. But here, I've pulled it out as a separate, non-nested class.

Listing 9–12 `Listener.java`

```
// A class to receive RemoteEvents

package corejini.chapter9;

import java.rmi.server.UnicastRemoteObject;
import java.rmi.RemoteException;
import net.jini.core.lookup.*;
import net.jini.core.event.*;

class Listener extends UnicastRemoteObject
                implements RemoteEventListener{
    Browser browser;

    Listener(Browser browser) throws RemoteException {
        super();
        this.browser = browser;
    }
    public void notify(RemoteEvent ev) {
        if (!(ev instanceof ServiceEvent))
            return;

        // we just update the whole set of services --
        // not efficient, but shorter than mucking our
        // way through the lists.
        browser.updateServices((ServiceRegistrar)
                                      ev.getSource());
    }
}
```

The `Listener` class extends `java.rmi.server.UnicastRemoteObject`, so that its methods can be called by objects in other JVMs. The single essential method in this class is `notify()`, which will be passed a `RemoteEvent` as a parameter. The parameter is tested to see if it is a `ServiceEvent`—meaning that it came from a registrar containing news of service changes—and if it is not, the event is ignored. If it *is* a `ServiceEvent`, however, then the source of the event (which will be the `ServiceRegistrar` object representing the lookup service that generated it) is passed to a method on the browser called `updateServices()`.

Note that the `ServiceEvent` contains details about the changes in the state of services at a particular registrar. So the code here could use this information to update the various lists in the browser directly—by seeing if a changed service was the currently selected and, if so, selectively updating its list of attributes. By passing only the source of the event to `updateServices()`, we're losing much of this information; and in fact, `updateServices()` (as we shall see) simply rebuilds the entire service list when a change is detected. While this is a bit wasteful, the set of services and attributes available to a lookup service will likely not change very often. And, by avoiding a "widening" of the interfaces between `Listener` and `Browser`, we keep the connections between these two classes as simple as possible.

Handling List Events

Finally, before we move on to the large `Browser` class, we can look at one more piece of infrastructure that we will need. As you know if you've done much Java GUI programming, events such as mouse clicks are handled by listener classes that are set up to receive certain events. The most convenient way to create a listener is to make a small inner class—perhaps even an *anonymous* inner class (meaning one that is defined "in line" and has no name)—that implements whatever particular interfaces you need.

From the table of actions that you saw earlier, you know that we'll need some listener class to handle all of the various sorts of clicks and double clicks on our lists. Here is the listener (Listing 9–13) I've defined for the browser. Once again, code like this is most often seen as an inner class, but here it's broken out for better clarity.

Listing 9–13 `ListClickListener.java`

```
package corejini.chapter9;

import java.awt.event.*;
import javax.swing.event.*;
import javax.swing.*;

class ListClickListener extends MouseAdapter {
    Browser browser;

    ListClickListener(Browser browser) {
        this.browser = browser;
    }
    public void mouseClicked(MouseEvent ev) {
        boolean doubleClick = ev.getClickCount() == 2;

        if (ev.getSource() instanceof JList) {
            JList list = (JList) ev.getSource();
             int index = list.locationToIndex(ev.getPoint());

            if (index == -1)
                return;

            if (list.getModel().equals(
                                browser.getLookups())) {
                if (doubleClick) {
                    browser.lookupDoubleClicked(index);
                } else {
                    browser.lookupClicked(index);
                }
            } else if (list.getModel().equals(
                                browser.getServices())) {
                if (doubleClick) {
                    browser.serviceDoubleClicked(index);
                } else {
                    browser.serviceClicked(index);
                }
            }
        }
    }
}
```

You'll note that this code really has nothing to do with Jini, but lots to do with Swing. The listener class extends `MouseAdapter`, which provides default implementations for all the various `MouseListener` methods. The only thing we care about is when the mouse is clicked, so the `ListClickListener` overrides `mouseClicked()`, which will receive a `MouseEvent` whenever a click occurs.

This method determines if the event represents a single or a double click. Then, it checks the source of the event to ensure that it is, in fact a `JList` object (if the source is some other class, then our `ListClickListener` was in all probability installed as a `MouseListener` for some other component on the screen by accident). The method then computes the newly selected index from the *X*, *Y* coordinates of the mouse click. Finally, it asks the source list for its model, and compares it to the `Browser`'s models for the lookup list and the service list. These models stored by the `Browser` are instances of the `VectorListModel` defined earlier, and are accessed by calling `getLookups()` and `getServices()` on the `Browser` instance.

The Browser Class

Now that we've finally looked at all the individual "support" classes we'll be using, we can move on to the `Browser` class itself.

Listing 9–14 shows this rather involved class.

Listing 9–14 `Browser.java`

```
// This is the overall browser, as seen in Figure 9-1
package corejini.chapter9;

import javax.swing.*;
import java.awt.event.*;
import java.awt.*;
import java.util.Vector;
import net.jini.admin.*;
import net.jini.discovery.*;
import net.jini.core.lookup.*;
import net.jini.core.event.*;
import net.jini.lookup.DiscoveryAdmin;
import net.jini.lookup.entry.*;
import net.jini.core.entry.Entry;
import java.rmi.RMISecurityManager;
```

Listing 9–14 `Browser.java` **(continued)**

```
import com.sun.jini.lease.LeaseRenewalManager;
import java.io.IOException;
import java.rmi.RemoteException;
import java.rmi.server.UnicastRemoteObject;
import java.beans.*;

// It's a panel, so it can be embedded in other jcomponents
public class Browser extends JPanel {
    // models for the three panes
    protected VectorListModel lookups, services, attrs;
    protected ServiceRegistrar currentLookup = null;
    // Search for everything
    protected ServiceTemplate template =
        new ServiceTemplate(null, null, null);
    // current event registration
    protected EventRegistration er = null;
    protected Listener eventListener;
    protected LeaseRenewalManager leaseMgr =
                                new LeaseRenewalManager();
    protected LookupDiscovery disco;

    public Browser() throws IOException, RemoteException {
        MouseListener listener =
                        new ListClickListener(this);

        // Make an event listener
        eventListener = new Listener(this);

        // Create the list models
        lookups = new VectorListModel();
        services = new VectorListModel();
        attrs = new VectorListModel();

        GridBagLayout layout = new GridBagLayout();
        GridBagConstraints c = new GridBagConstraints();

        setLayout(layout);

        c.fill = GridBagConstraints.BOTH;
        c.weightx = 1.0;
        c.gridx = GridBagConstraints.RELATIVE;
        c.gridy = 0;
```

Listing 9–14 `Browser.java` **(continued)**

```
// do labels across the top
JLabel label = new JLabel("Lookup Services");
layout.setConstraints(label, c);
add(label);

label = new JLabel("Services");
layout.setConstraints(label, c);
add(label);

label = new JLabel("Attributes");
layout.setConstraints(label, c);
add(label);

// do scrolling lists across the bottom
c.gridy = 1;
c.weighty = 1.0;
JList list = new JList(lookups);
list.addMouseListener(listener);
list.setCellRenderer(new LookupCellRenderer());
JScrollPane scroller = new JScrollPane(list);
layout.setConstraints(scroller, c);
add(scroller);

list = new JList(services);
list.setCellRenderer(new ServiceCellRenderer());
list.addMouseListener(listener);
scroller = new JScrollPane(list);
layout.setConstraints(scroller, c);
add(scroller);

list = new JList(attrs);
list.setCellRenderer(new AttrCellRenderer());
list.addMouseListener(listener);
scroller = new JScrollPane(list);
layout.setConstraints(scroller, c);
add(scroller);
```

Listing 9–14 `Browser.java` **(continued)**

```
        // Set up for discovery
        disco = new
            LookupDiscovery(LookupDiscovery.ALL_GROUPS);
        disco.addDiscoveryListener(new Discoverer(this));
    }

    VectorListModel getLookups() {
        return lookups;
    }
    VectorListModel getServices() {
        return services;
    }
    VectorListModel getAttrs() {
        return attrs;
    }

    // Find all services in "reg"
    void updateServices(ServiceRegistrar reg) {
        ServiceMatches matches;

        try {
            matches = currentLookup.lookup(template,
                                           Integer.MAX_VALUE);
        } catch (RemoteException ex) {
            showDialog("Problem contacting registrar:\n" +
                                        ex.getMessage());
                        disco.discard(reg);
            return;
        }

        Vector newServices =
                         new Vector(matches.totalMatches);
        for (int i=0 ; i<matches.totalMatches ; i++) {
            newServices.addElement(matches.items[i]);
        }

        services.setData(newServices);
    }
```

Listing 9–14 `Browser.java` **(continued)**

```
    // handle single clicks on lookup services--update the
    // list of services
    protected void lookupClicked(int index) {
        unsolicitEvents();
        currentLookup = (ServiceRegistrar)
                            lookups.getElementAt(index);
        updateServices(currentLookup);
        solicitEvents();
    }

    // handle double clicks on lookup services--administer
    // the lookup service
    protected void lookupDoubleClicked(int index) {
        currentLookup = (ServiceRegistrar)
                            lookups.getElementAt(index);

        if (!(currentLookup instanceof Administrable)) {
            System.out.println("Not administrable");
            return;
        }

        Object o;

        try {
            o = ((Administrable) currentLookup).getAdmin();
        } catch (RemoteException ex) {
            showDialog("Problem contacting registrar:\n" +
                                    ex.getMessage());
                    disco.discard(currentLookup);
            return;
        }

        if (o != null) {
            AdminPanel panel = new AdminPanel(o);
            JFrame frame = new JFrame("Administration");
            frame.getContentPane().add(panel);
            frame.pack();
            frame.setVisible(true);
        }
    }
```

Listing 9–14 `Browser.java` **(continued)**

```
    // handle single clicks on services--update the attr
    // list
    protected void serviceClicked(int index) {
        ServiceItem item = (ServiceItem)
                           services.getElementAt(index);
        Vector newEntries =
                 new Vector(item.attributeSets.length);
        for (int i=0 ; i<item.attributeSets.length ; i++) {
            newEntries.addElement(item.attributeSets[i]);
        }

        attrs.setData(newEntries);
    }

    // handle double clicks on services--try to administer
    // them
    protected void serviceDoubleClicked(int index) {
        ServiceItem item = (ServiceItem)
                           services.getElementAt(index);

        if (!(item.service instanceof Administrable)) {
            System.out.println("Not administrable");
            return;
        }

        Object o;

        try {
            o = ((Administrable) item.service).getAdmin();
        } catch (RemoteException ex) {
            showDialog("Problem contacting registrar:\n" +
                                     ex.getMessage());
            return;
        }

        if (o != null) {
            AdminPanel panel = new AdminPanel(o);
            JFrame frame = new JFrame("Administration");
            frame.getContentPane().add(panel);
            frame.pack();
            frame.setVisible(true);
        }
    }
```

Listing 9–14 `Browser.java` **(continued)**

```
    // Ask a lookup service for events
    void solicitEvents() {
        try {
            er = currentLookup.notify(template,
             ServiceRegistrar.TRANSITION_MATCH_NOMATCH |
             ServiceRegistrar.TRANSITION_NOMATCH_MATCH |
             ServiceRegistrar.TRANSITION_MATCH_MATCH,
                    eventListener, null, 10 * 60 * 1000);

            leaseMgr.renewUntil(er.getLease(),
                              Long.MAX_VALUE, null);
        } catch (RemoteException ex) {
            er = null;
            disco.discard(currentLookup);
        }
    }

    // Stop receiving events
    void unsolicitEvents() {
        if (er == null)
            return;

        try {
            leaseMgr.cancel(er.getLease());
        } catch (Exception ex) {
        }
    }

    // clean up a classname (strip off package part)
    static String declassify(String name) {
        if (name == null) return null;

        int idx = name.lastIndexOf('.');

        if (idx == -1)
            return name;
        else
            return name.substring(idx+1);
    }
```

Listing 9–14 `Browser.java` **(continued)**

```
    void showDialog(String message) {
       JOptionPane pane = new JOptionPane(message,
                              JOptionPane.DEFAULT_OPTION,
                              JOptionPane.ERROR_MESSAGE,
                              null, null, null);
       JDialog dialog = new
        JDialog(JOptionPane.getFrameForComponent(this),
                "Alert!");
       dialog.getContentPane().setLayout(new
                                         BorderLayout());
       dialog.getContentPane().add(pane,
                                  BorderLayout.CENTER);
       dialog.pack();
       dialog.show();
    }

    public static void main(String[] args) {
       try {
           if (System.getSecurityManager()==null){
               System.setSecurityManager
                              (new RMISecurityManager());
           }
           JFrame frame = new JFrame("Browser");
           frame.addWindowListener(new WindowAdapter() {
               public void windowClosing(WindowEvent ev) {
                    System.exit(1);
               }
           });
           frame.getContentPane().add(new Browser());
           frame.pack();
           frame.setVisible(true);
       } catch (Exception ex) {
           System.err.println("Couldn't create browser:" +
                                     ex.getMessage());
           ex.printStackTrace();
       }
    }
}
```

The `Browser` class is an extension of `JPanel` so that you can embed it in a `JFrame`, or any other Swing container that needs the ability to browse lookup services and other Jini services. The code here declares three separate `VectorListModels`—these are the models that represent the data stored in the three panes of the interface. It also declares a reference to the currently-selected lookup service, the `EventRegistration` object for event solicitations on that current lookup service, a template for searching for services, the event listener, and a `LeaseRenewalManager` to handle event solicitations.

The constructor for the Browser class sets up the user interface and readies all the objects that we'll need for Jini participation. All the required VectorListModels are created, and JLists are built to view them; each JList has an instance of ListClickListener installed as its MouseListener so that the list data will be updated properly on single and double clicks. Each list is also passed the appropriate list cell renderer for it to draw its contents. And, finally, the constructor initiates discovery by creating a Discoverer and using it as the DiscoveryListener on a LookupDiscovery instance.

The Browser is responsive to several sorts of occurrences: user input on the lists, events from lookup services telling the Browser that the set of services has changed, and discovery events that tell the Browser that the set of lookup services has changed. All of these three types of input are handled by the objects created earlier; but all of these objects call back into the Browser to change its state.

When new discovery events are received, the Discoverer simply updates the list of available lookup services by changing the VectorListModel that represents these services; changes to these models cause the display to automatically update. The other two input handlers have slightly more complex interactions with the Browser though.

When new ServiceEvents are received by the Listener class that handles remote events from lookup services, the updateServices() method on Browser is called. This method simply executes a lookup() search on the changed lookup service, and rebuilds the data stored in the VectorListModel representing the services pane. As discussed when we looked at the implementation of the Listener class, this isn't the most efficient implementation, but it's easy to implement and show here, and the performance hit shouldn't be too bad for most applications. If you have services that continually update their attributes, say several times a minute—which is probably a bad idea anyway—you can change the code to dissect the ServiceEvent and only update those portions of the lists that have been affected.

Note that many of the methods here that contact the lookup service may run into problems if the lookup service is down. These methods (such as solicitEvents()) always catch any RemoteExceptions from the lookup service and call discard() on the LookupDiscovery instance to drop the lookup services from use. The list pane will be updated (since calling discard() causes the discarded() method on Discoverer to be called) and—if the lookup service ever returns—it will be rediscovered.

The ListClickListener calls several methods on Browser that update its state in response to user input. These methods are the "meat" of the code shown here. Let's look at each in turn.

The lookupClicked() method needs to update the services list display to reflect all of the services available on the newly selected lookup service. This method first "unsolicits" events from the currently selected lookup service, if any. This is necessary so that it will not continue to receive events from a lookup service we're not even looking at, and will also reduce the bandwidth requirements the code places on the network. Next, it records the currently selected lookup service, so that it will have it available when it does any event processing. The code then calls the same updateServices() method that is used during ServiceEvent handling. And, finally, it solicits events from the lookup service, so that as services come and go the display of available services will be changed.

Administration of lookup services is done via the lookupDoubleClicked() method. This method simply tests the selected item to see if it implements the Administrable interface and, if it does, creates a new AdminPanel and nests it in a frame to display it.

The serviceClicked() method needs to update the list of attributes to show the attributes for the currently selected service. It fetches the ServiceItem that corresponds to the selected index, and retrieves the attributes out of it, setting the data in the VectorListModel for the attribute list.

The implementation of serviceDoubleClicked() is similar to lookupDoubleClicked()—it fetches the selected item and tests to see whether it is Administrable. If it is, it creates a new frame containing the AdminPanel for the service and displays it.

Most of the rest of the methods on this class are "helpers" that are called from one of the input-handling routines. The solicitEvents() method is used to ask for events from a newly selected lookup service. It uses the stored value of currentLookup to ask for notifications, and saves the returned EventRegistration so that it will be available later when we need to cancel the event leases. It also passes the lease from this registration to our LeaseRenewalManager for automatic renewal.

When the user changes the currently selected lookup service, any previously solicited events must be canceled before new events are requested. The unsolicitEvents() method takes care of this. It finds the current event registration and asks the LeaseRenewalManager to cancel the leases for it.

The other methods in this class are quite simple. The declassify() method is simply a helper to strip any leading package name off a class name, for a cleaner display. It is called from the various ListCellRenderers we saw before. And showDialog() simply displays an error dialog when something goes wrong; it is invoked from several of the methods in Browser.

The `main()` shown here creates a new `JFrame`, and adds a new `Browser` instance to it. Once created, the `Browser` will handle all the Jini interactions and display updates on its own.

Building and Running the Browser

There are three steps to getting this new browser up and running. First, you must compile the source. Follow the guidelines used elsewhere in this book to ensure separation between the browser's class files and the class files of any services that may be on your machine. If you just compile the "main" class, `Browser.java`, then the Java compiler should build the other class files as needed.

Next, you'll have to run `rmic` to generate the stubs for the event listener class. Make sure that these go in the `client-dl` directory, since they'll be downloaded to lookup services.

Finally, you're set the run the browser. Make sure you specify a codebase that refers to the HTTP server that is exporting the RMI stubs class file, and provide a security policy file.

On Windows:

```
javac -classpath C:\jini1_0\lib\jini-core.jar;
                                  C:\jini1_0\lib\jini-ext.jar;
                                  C:\jini1_0\lib\sun-util.jar;
                                  C:\client
                -d C:\client
            C:\corejini\chapter9\Browser.java

rmic -classpath C:\jdk1.2\jre\lib\rt.jar;
                                  C:\jini1_0\lib\jini-core.jar;
                                  C:\jini1_0\lib\jini-ext.jar;
                                  C:\jini1_0\lib\sun-util.jar;
                                  C:\client
                -d C:\client-dl
        corejini.chapter9.Listener

java -cp C:\jini1_0\lib\jini-core.jar;
                        C:\jini1_0\lib\jini-ext.jar;
                        C:\jini1_0\lib\sun-util.jar;
                        C:\client;
                        C:\client-dl
        -Djava.security.policy=C:\files\policy
```

```
        -Djava.rmi.server.codebase=http://myhost:8086/
        corejini.chapter9.Browser
```

On Solaris:

```
javac -classpath /files/jini1_0/lib/jini-core.jar:
                         /files/jini1_0/lib/jini-ext.jar:
                         /files/jini1_0/lib/sun-util.jar:
                         /files/client
                -d /files/client
            /files/corejini/chapter9/Browser.java

rmic -classpath /jdk1.2/jre/lib/rt.jar:
                         /files/jini1_0/lib/jini-core.jar:
                         /files/jini1_0/lib/jini-ext.jar:
                         /files/jini1_0/lib/sun-util.jar:
                         /files/client
                -d /files/client-dl
        corejini.chapter9.Listener

java -cp /files/jini1_0/lib/jini-core.jar:
                      /files/jini1_0/lib/jini-ext.jar:
                      /files/jini1_0/lib/sun-util.jar:
                      /files/client:
                      /files/client-dl
        -Djava.security.policy=/files/policy
        -Djava.rmi.server.codebase=http://myhost:8086/
        corejini.chapter9.Browser
```

What's Next?

This chapter has looked at our first fairly large Jini application. And while most of the Jini-specific interactions shown here should be fairly familiar to you by now, you've seen how to create the "glue" between Jini and Swing applications. Many of the components here can be reused in applications you build in the future.

In the next chapter, we'll continue our in-depth look at Jini by focusing on one of its core concepts: leasing. You'll learn how to use leasing in your applications, and how to create services that export resources through leasing.

IN DEPTH: LEASING

Topics in This Chapter

- Reliability and self-healing
- The leasing paradigm
- Using relative time
- Batching leases for performance
- The low-level leasing interfaces
- Convenience classes for building lease consumers
- A leasing service
- Guidelines for implementing leasing

Chapter 10

In this chapter we'll look in depth at the leasing paradigm used throughout Jini. As we will see, leasing provides a solution to many of the problems inherent in distributed computing—it allows for a distributed system to clean up when parts of it fail, and prevents the accretion of persistent state in long-lived systems.

Leasing is not without its problems, though. In particular, managing leases can be one of the more difficult aspects of building with Jini. Fortunately, most of the lease management chores you will face are mechanical enough that they can be easily automated by class libraries or third-party services.

In our look at leasing, we'll reexamine the rationale for leases as opposed to other solutions for designing reliability into distributed systems. After this introduction, we'll take a close look at the programming interfaces for using, renewing, and canceling leases, and focus on some common idioms that programmers will use to handle leases. We'll turn these common idioms into a set of classes that application writers can use to make the job of managing leases easier.

Being a well-behaved consumer of leases is only half of the story, though. In the chapter after this one, you'll see how you can export resources you hold to other applications via leasing.

Reliability in Distributed Systems

Let's briefly reexamine the problems of designing reliability into a distributed system, and the approach that Jini takes.

Any system, distributed or not, will never be completely reliable: software can crash, machines and networks will fail. Sometimes failures seem as if they must be caused by the phase of the moon or perhaps cosmic rays. But distributed systems—systems comprised of multiple, cooperating components distributed across a network—compound the problems of failure greatly. In a distributed system, the failure of any one component may *potentially* bring down the entire system. And not only do distributed systems suffer because they necessarily have more components that might fail, they also suffer simply because they can fail in ways that stand-alone systems cannot. A dead power supply in a key router is unlikely to bring down a purely stand-alone application; that same failure can cripple a distributed system, however.

The challenge here is not to design distributed systems so that none of their components can fail—this is clearly impossible. Nor is it to design distributed systems that appear to fail in the same ways that stand-alone systems can—work over the years has shown that this is impractical at best, and at worst hides important information that developers need to make informed decisions about how to handle failures.

Instead, the challenge is to design distributed systems using concepts that promote reliability wherever possible, acknowledge the inevitability of failures, and provide a way for the system itself (and not developers) to clean up from failures. The reason that the system itself should be empowered to clean up from failures isn't that programmers are too dim to do it; it's that, often, the software component that would do the cleaning up is itself the one that has failed or become disconnected from the network. So the need for "self-healing" distributed systems is critical.

The Need for Self-Healing

Self-healing also addresses one of Jini's primary concerns—that distributed systems should function for long periods of time without the intervention of a human administrator. If a human has to come in and clean up the mess (reconfigure the software, move machines, reinstall applications, juggle network topologies) every time a component crashes, the system will become simply unworkable as it grows to hundreds, thousands, or even millions of components.

What is inarguably the most successful distributed system in history—the Internet—has many of these self-healing properties. Routing tables are automatically distributed around the world as network configurations change. Domain name service entries are propagated to secondary servers and cached locally as they change. And packets that are unable to reach a destination through one route may be resent along a different one.

The Need for Evolvability

Many distributed systems do, however, share a reliability problem that stand-alone systems also have: they are often designed to run for long periods of time without interruption. While many stand-alone systems, such as web servers and database servers, are designed to stay up for months or even years, distributed systems typically have even greater needs in this area.

There are a couple of reasons for this. The first is that distributed systems potentially reach many, many more people than any application running on a stand-alone machine. Thus, the costs of bringing the entire system down may be astronomically greater. Chances are that it would be impossible to even inform all of the users, distributed across a campus or across the planet, about the impending downtime.

A second reason that distributed systems must be designed to stay up for longer periods of time is simply that distributed systems are hard to control. Because a distributed system is spread across many machines on a network, there may be no centralized point of control for the entire system. Can you imagine what it would even mean to "shut down the Internet" over a weekend for maintenance? These systems, once they've started, rarely stop running.

Both of these facts point to one of the big problems of distributed systems—once started, these systems may be difficult or impossible to upgrade. Think about how tricky it is to introduce new versions of a software program on even a stand-alone computer—file formats change, other applications expect the old version to still exist, and so on. In a distributed system the problem is exponentially compounded because it is impossible to upgrade all the components across the world at the *same time*—you cannot take the system down for maintenance, and even if you could, chances are you wouldn't be able to reach every machine to upgrade everything smoothly without failures. One must be able to evolve or upgrade the system *incrementally*—on a component-by-component basis—rather than upgrading the entire system as a whole. This problem of *software evolution* is a serious one in distributed systems and needs to be specifically addressed by any design for reliability we use in our systems.

Leasing as a Solution

The problems inherent in distributed computing point to the fact that we should design to accommodate these problems explicitly. That is, the concepts and idioms that we use to build our systems should be created based on the understanding that distributed systems can fail, that they should heal themselves wherever possible, and that they may be long-lived beasts once they've been started.

Leasing in Jini is an attempt to address these issues. Jini uses this one central concept—that access to resources is leased to consumers, rather than granted to them in perpetuity—as a way to acknowledge that systems fail. The common idioms of using leases, and the code in the Jini class libraries that supports leasing, are designed to promote self-healing and provide a degree of maintainability in long-running distributed systems.

The Leasing Approach

Let's look at exactly what problems leasing addresses, and how leasing can provide some solutions—not to the problems of keeping components in a distributed system from failing—but to the problem of building software that reacts predictably and safely in the face of those failures.

The primary idea behind leasing is that it requires a continued proof-of-interest on the part of the lease holder if it is to continue holding some resource. If the lease holder fails to demonstrate interest, then the lease expires and the resource is released.

There are a couple of key points to make here.

- The resource that a lease grants access to can be essentially anything—a bit of storage, some computation, a promise for the lease grantor to act in the future on behalf of the requestor. The core Jini services use leases to grant access to event and lookup service registrations; your own services can use leases to grant access to any resources you export.
- The failure of a lease holder to demonstrate proof-of-interest may be because the holder is honestly no longer interested in

using the resource. But it may also be because the lease holder has crashed or become disconnected from the network.

Leasing is a very simple idea conceptually. But the notion that resources are leased, rather than granted indefinitely, provides some real benefits to distributed systems. It also requires a bit of work on the parts of both the lease grantor and holder.

Leasing provides a way to address two central problems in distributed computing. First, failures are guaranteed to be detected. If the system were to grant access to resources indefinitely, then the holder of a resource may crash, perhaps never to return, and the grantor of the resource would be unable to allow its use by other interested parties. By granting a lease, the system guarantees that failures will be detected without requiring any separate component other than the lease grantor to be involved in the process of determining that the failure exists. Leasing also puts a hard deadline on when failures will be detected—if a lease is granted for 10 minutes, then 10 minutes is the longest window during which an unnoticed failure may exist.

Second, leases provide a way for a distributed system to *automatically* clean up after failed components. This is especially important in long-lived software systems. If our system didn't discard irrelevant information, then it would accrete state for all the components that had been a part of the system but hadn't cleaned up after themselves. Clearly, a component that fails won't have the opportunity to free up its resources. Leasing guarantees that irrelevant data will simply be forgotten when leases expire.

The ability of leases to detect failures and to cause unwanted state to be cleaned up happens in a way that is autonomous—the grantor of the resource knows when the lease expires, meaning that possibly a lease holder has crashed and that definitely its resources may be freed. This determination happens completely within the lease grantor. Because there is no need for the holder of the resource or any centralized authority to be involved, you can say the system is self-healing in the face of failures of resource holders.

The fact that a service that does not renew its lease is completely forgotten from the system provides a way to evolve components of a distributed software system in isolation. When a service is cleaned up after its leases expire, you know for a fact that its service proxy is no longer installed in any lookup service, it will never receive any events, and no other service will be able to find it. The entire service and every trace of it has been removed from the Jini community. Once the service is "off line," you are free to run a different version of the same service, perhaps using the same API but with a different implementation, and plug it into all the same communities of which the original service was a member.

Issues in Leasing

Simply saying that "resources are leased rather than granted indefinitely" gives a flavor of Jini leasing, but provides no specifics. The Jini designers had to make a number of other crucial design choices to ensure that leasing works to promote reliability in distributed systems.

Relative versus Absolute Time

The first design choice, which may be unintuitive at first, is that Jini leases are specified using a desired lease *duration*, rather than an explicit lease expiration *time*. While absolute times are useful and natural for many applications, they are unworkable in a distributed system, particularly one where you may not have control over all the computers that are participating in the system.

Suppose leases were specified in terms of absolute time. You might ask a resource provider for a lease that lasts until, say, 10PM Tuesday night. You have no idea what kind of machine the resource provider is running on, how well maintained it is, or even where it is. The clock on the machine may not have been set in years, or it may have missed the last switch to daylight savings time. The two machines involved in this operation—the machine that your service is running on and the machine that the resource provider is running on—may have completely different notions of what absolute time of day it is.

Now look at a lease specified in terms of relative time. In such a system, a resource consumer requests a lease for a duration, say one hour. Even though the systems may have completely different ideas about the time of day, their clocks are probably more-or-less capable of timing the passage of one hour accurately.

But, you may be asking, if the clock of one machine is wildly wrong in the first place, isn't that probably because the machine's clock is keeping inaccurate time? That is true. But the amount of clock skew that can accrue for the typical duration of a lease is far, far less than the total amount of error that the clock may have accumulated since it was last set. So, except in the case of disastrous clock failures of the sort that would likely keep the machine from functioning anyway, specifying leases in terms of duration is more accurate than specifying leases in terms of absolute times.

You may also be wondering about the time required to send the message to renew the lease. If I ask for a lease for one second, how can I guarantee that my message to renew the lease will arrive before the lease expires? The answer is that you should request leases large enough that the time required to send a renewal message will, in all probability, be in the noise. While you cannot guarantee that your renewal request will arrive in *any* fixed time (or even whether it will arrive at the destination at all), you can make some good guesses about the order of magnitude differences between network transmission time and lease duration. So most leases will be on the order of five or ten minutes and will completely dominate the time required to send a renewal message on any network.

Lease Negotiation

A second design choice, perhaps an obvious one, is that leases in Jini are negotiated. Without some form of negotiation, resource consumers could simply ask for an impossibly large lease duration, and we would be back with the problems that happen when access to resources is granted for a virtually infinite period of time.

So Jini works more like "real-life" leases: the grantor and the lease holder (the lessor) must agree on the terms of the lease. And, also like in the real world, the grantor has the final say on the lease that is offered.

Real-life leases may involve many rounds of negotiation. Fortunately Jini uses a much simpler approach that is easy to use by programs. A lease requestor asks for a lease of a given duration, and the grantor replies with the *actual* duration, which may be the requested value, zero (thus denying the lease), or any value in between. At the point that the grantor returns the lease, the receiver effectively holds it; there is no need for it to acknowledge or accept the duration of the lease, and it cannot propose a new duration without going through the normal lease renewal process.

In practice, this approach works well. While it is not as flexible as an involved, multiround lease negotiation, it involves only one round-trip message between the requestor and the grantor, the request process can be done simply via one method invocation, and the process is good enough for nearly all applications.

Leasing Done by Third Parties

A third choice of the Jini designers was that leases could be acquired by third parties on behalf of the resource consumer. This is an interesting design decision—it says that while a resource may be held by the original resource consumer, the task of providing proof-of-interest can be delegated to an external entity.

Clearly, this may make the life of the resource consumer easier: it can delegate all (or at least most) of the mechanics of leasing to someone else, and go about the job of using its resources. And such a strategy may be a requirement in situations where services are running on computationally-impoverished devices that may not have the horsepower, connectivity, or bandwidth to handle all of the chores of lease management. Such devices can hand off the task of leasing to a third party to be done for them.

But third-party leasing can bring with it problems. Most of these problems arise from the separation noted earlier: that the resource still resides in the consumer, but the task of providing proof-of-interest has been removed from the consumer. We'll look at all the implications of third-party leasing, and strategies for services that are using third-party leasing, in this chapter.

The Cost of Leasing

This ability to automatically detect failures and clean up after them is the benefit that leasing brings to a distributed system. But it also brings a bit of a burden to the users—both consumers and grantors—of leasing. In a system where access to resources is granted in perpetuity, the programming model for resource consumers is simple: they simply ask for the resource and, if they get it, continue to use it until they are finished. Well-behaved consumers will hopefully remember to free the resource when they shutdown. Likewise, the job of the resource provider is also easy: it simply grants the resource when asked for it, and forgets about it until the consumer says otherwise.

This simplicity is where the problems come in. Because the provider forgets about the resource until the consumer says otherwise, it may not be able to detect when the consumer has failed. Likewise, for the consumer to notify the provider when it fails, the programmer must remember to put in the code for the notification, and the program must be able to call it—meaning that it has not crashed before it can free the resource.

So leasing presents us with some benefits, but at the cost of a more heavyweight programming model. Leasing requires that a consumer of a resource be actively engaged in showing the provider that it is interested in holding on to that resource. The resource provider must actively keep an eye on the resources it has granted so that it can free them when leases expire.

This chapter looks at leasing from the perspective of a lease consumer. In the next few sections we'll look at the programming interfaces available to resource consumers for managing and using leases. Virtually all of the Jini code you write will be a consumer of resources in some way, so these sections are crucial for writing reliable Jini code. The following chapter looks at how services that grant access to resources can use leasing to manage these resources.

Building Lease Consumers

In this section we'll look at the programming interfaces that are used by lease consumers—that is, services and applications who hold leases on some resource in another service. Here we'll look at the most basic leasing interfaces, which allow you to renew and cancel leases. These are the lowest level leasing APIs, which we've seen in the "Hello, World" examples. There are a number of higher-level APIs built on top of these, which we'll examine a bit later.

The process of *creating* a lease, however, varies depending on how you gain access to the resource that the lease represents. For example, lookup service registrations are leased, so the process of registering a service causes a lease to be returned. Likewise, since event registrations are leased, asking for notifications returns a lease. In these situations, leases aren't ever created directly by the consumer of a lease—instead, they are created by the provider of the lease, and returned as a natural part of asking for access to a particular resource.

Both lookup and event registration mechanisms provide their own APIs that return leases, often bundled together with some other information about the registration. If you write a service that provides some resource to other services and wish to use leasing to control access to that resource, you can choose your own APIs for how the lease is returned to callers.

The Lease Interface

Here, let's assume that—through some means such as service or event registration—a lease has been returned to a consumer. Let's look at the basic `Lease` interface first.

```
package net.jini.lease;

import java.rmi.RemoteException;

public interface Lease {
```

```
        long FOREVER = Long.MAX_VALUE;
        long ANY = -1;

        int DURATION = 1;
        int ABSOLUTE = 2;

        long getExpiration();
        void cancel() throws UnknownLeaseException,
                                        RemoteException;
        void renew(long duration) throws LeaseDeniedException,
                                        UnknownLeaseException,
                                        RemoteException;
        void setSerialFormat(int format);
        int getSerialFormat();
        LeaseMap createLeaseMap(long duration);
        boolean canBatch(Lease lease);
}
```

The first thing to notice here is that `Lease` is an interface, not a class. In Jini, the `Lease` object that is returned to a caller is used to manage the lease. Invoking the remote methods on the `Lease` object causes messages to travel to the lease grantor (the service that controls the underlying resource) to update the grantor's notion of the lease's state. Some of the `Lease` methods are local accessors. The `getExpiration()` method, for instance, returns a value that is stored locally by the `Lease` object. It causes no communication between the lease grantor and the lease holder. The grantor's notion of the state of a lease is, ultimately, the "true" one, since the grantor is the entity that controls the underlying resource that the lease grants access to. The object returned to callers is merely a "proxy" that can be used to effect changes in the state of the grantor's internal lease representations. Figure 10–1 shows an illustration of this—the lease object held by a consumer is a proxy that's used to communicate with a lease grantor; the grantor maintains the actual resource and any information it uses to track the status of leases.

Lease grantors decide how they will communicate with the `Lease` proxy objects that they return to callers. This is why `Lease` is an interface and not a class—different lease grantors may use different mechanisms for communication between the `Lease` proxy objects handed out to callers and themselves. One implementation might use RMI, another might use raw TCP/IP sockets, and a third might use CORBA. But whatever type is actually returned to callers, it must implement the `Lease` interface defined here.

The interface defines a number of constants that can be useful when managing leases. The `FOREVER` token can be used to indicate that the requestor

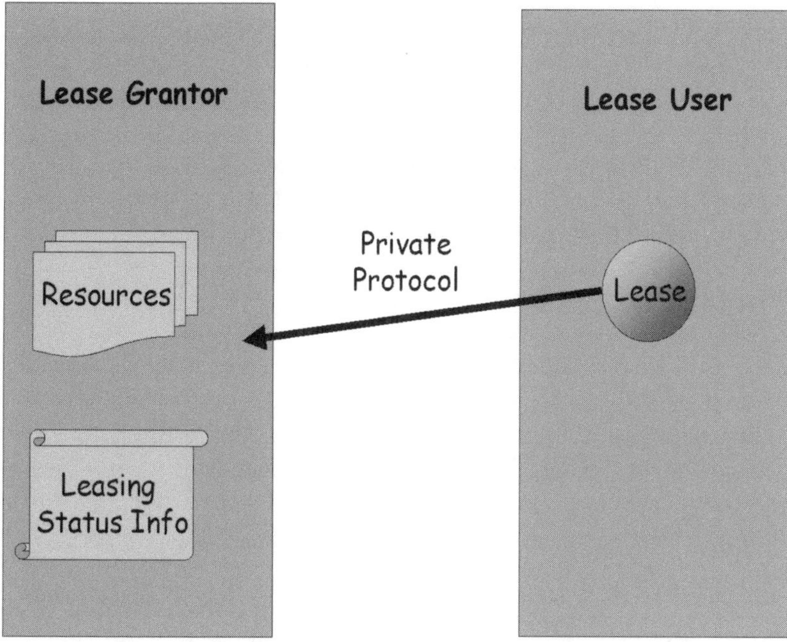

Figure 10–1 Leases are proxies for communication with grantors

wishes a lease granted in perpetuity. Most lease grantors will be unwilling to grant such a lease, as it circumvents the nice "fail and forget" properties that Jini promotes. If a requestor does receive such a lease, however, it should be very conscientious about canceling the lease when it has finished with it.

The `ANY` token indicates that a requestor is asking for a lease of any duration. Usually this will result in the grantor's default lease duration being assigned.

We'll skip the next two constants, `DURATION` and `ABSOLUTE`, for now and come back to them when we talk about serialized formats for leases.

Determining When a Lease Expires

The first method in the interface, `getExpiration()`, returns the expiration time of the lease. The return value is a long, representing the number of milliseconds since the start of "Java time" (January 1, 1970). You'll note that this value is an absolute one. Even though leases are requested in terms of relative time durations, the `getExpiration()` method returns expirations in terms of absolute time as a convenience to the programmer: you can very easily call `System.currentTimeMillis()` to check the current clock against the expiration time of the lease.

The fact that the method expresses time in terms of absolute expirations, rather than durations, doesn't circumvent the desirable properties of using durations in leasing. Durations are still what is transmitted over the wire when requesting leases and doing lease management. But leases will convert durations into absolute times for convenience. This is a local-only operation that is not affected by any differences in machine clocks.

Canceling a Lease

The `cancel()` method does just what its name suggests—it cancels the lease represented by the `Lease` object. A lease that is explicitly canceled has the same effect as a lease that expires through neglect: the resource that the lease grants access to is freed, and possibly made available for others to use. In general, you should not call `cancel()` on a lease that has already expired, as this simply makes extra work for the lease grantor, and increases network traffic.

You'll note that `cancel()` can raise two exceptions. The first, `RemoteException`, is raised if the `Lease` object has trouble communicating with the lease grantor. Remember that the `Lease` object is used for manipulating state in the lease grantor; so methods like `cancel()` must cause some message to be sent to the grantor in order to cancel the lease. The second exception, `UnknownLeaseException`, means that the grantor does not know about the lease represented by the `Lease` object you hold. Most likely this will happen when a lease expires automatically, and yet you still hold the `Lease` object representing it and try to call `cancel()` on it. Lease grantors are free (and encouraged) to clean up all remnants of expired leases. If you hold on to a reference to the `Lease` object representing this lease longer than the grantor does, you can get this exception. Most often it indicates an error in your lease management logic.

Renewing a Lease

The `renew()` method is used to renew an already granted lease. The parameter to this method is the duration, in milliseconds, of the desired lease. If the grantor grants this renewal, the specified duration here will become the *new* lease duration—it is not added to whatever time is left on the old duration.

The `renew()` method returns no value to its caller. Instead, the new duration of the lease is available through the `getExpiration()` method of the `Lease` object as soon as `renew()` returns. If, for some reason, the grantor decides to deny the request entirely, then the `LeaseDeniedException` is raised. If this happens, the original lease duration remains intact and will expire at whatever point in the future it originally would have. Like `cancel()`, `renew()` may raise `RemoteException` if communication with the grantor fails, or `UnknownLeaseException` if the grantor no longer knows about the lease represented by this `Lease` object.

Ensuring That Leases are Serialized Correctly

The next set of methods are used to control how a `Lease` object is serialized. `Leases` are commonly serialized for two reasons. The first is when a `Lease` is transmitted across machines. If a `Lease` is used as a parameter or a return value in an RMI call, it is serialized—written out as a sequence of bytes—sent over the wire, and then reconstituted into a complete `Lease` object at the other end.

The second case is when a service needs to record its persistent state. Services may "checkpoint" themselves from time to time, so that if they crash they can recover the information that they once held. They may also become inactive for a period of time (typically using the Java RMI activation mechanisms), particularly if they only need to do work infrequently. In this case a service may wish to write the `Lease` objects it holds to persistent storage as well as any other important state it needs to maintain.

Whenever a `Lease` is transmitted between two machines via serialization, we need to make sure that the lease expiration time is sent as a duration, rather than an absolute value. This is because we cannot guarantee that the clocks of the two machines are in sync, and is exactly the case that we've talked about earlier in this chapter.

But what happens when we need to save a `Lease` to persistent storage for later retrieval on the *same* machine? If we write those `Leases` to disk in such a way that their expiration times are saved as durations, we are in trouble when we read them back. Suppose that we save our `Leases` to disk, go inactive for a period of time, and then wake up and recover our saved data. The expiration times for our `Leases` are now expressed as a duration relative to the last time we ran. To make sense of these times, we'd also need to store the times at which each `Lease` was granted and do some math to figure out how to normalize the times. This is a lot of extra work, and introduces the potential for errors. The problem would be a lot simpler if, when storing `Leases` for later use on the same machine, we could just tell them to write themselves as absolute times.

This is where the `setSerialForm()` and `getSerialForm()` methods come in. These methods are used to ensure that `Lease` objects have the correct behavior whenever they are serialized, either for transmission to another machine or for persistence on the same machine.

The `Lease` interface provides two constants that can be used as arguments to `setSerialForm()` and are returned as results from `getSerialForm()`. The `DURATION` value is used to indicate that, when serialized, the `Lease` should be written in a form so that times are expressed as durations rather than absolute expirations. This value should be used whenever a `Lease` is to be sent to a different machine on the network, and is the default for all `Leases`. The value of the constant `ABSOLUTE` is used to indicate that whenever a `Lease` object is serialized, its expiration time should be represented as an absolute time, not a duration. This value should be used whenever a `Lease` is serialized for writing to persistent storage for later retrieval on the same machine.

Batching Leases for Performance

In many cases, a resource consumer will have to manage many leases at the same time. For example, a service may have several lookup service registrations, may be registered to receive multiple event notifications, and may have leases on other types of resources owned by other entities.

The `Lease` APIs provide the foundation for *batching* lease operations together to make lease management more efficient, in terms of computation required to do lease management, network bandwidth required for doing lease updates, and programmer effort required to write lease management code.

In lease batching, a number of leases are grouped together using a data structure called a `LeaseMap`, and can all be renewed or canceled at the same time. This permits easier lease management and can drastically cut down on the network traffic required to do renewals or cancellations—if leases are managed individually, each will require a separate round-trip message to the lease grantor to renew or cancel it.

Not all leases held by a lease consumer can be batched together in a `LeaseMap`, however. `LeaseMaps` are designed to group together all the `Lease` objects held by a consumer that can be batched. Typically, this means that a `LeaseMap` can only contain `Leases` that originated from the same lease grantor. `Leases` that come from different grantors each need to talk to their particular grantor in order to do renewals or cancellations, and each of these `Lease` objects may use a different protocol to talk back to the grantor.

Because of these constraints, not all leases can be batched together into a `LeaseMap`. In fact, the decision about whether two `Lease` objects can be batched together depends on the particular implementation of the `Lease`

that is in use; some Leases may support batching in some circumstances, others may not.

The Lease interface has two methods to support lease batching: createLeaseMap() and canBatch(). The canBatch() method is used to determine whether an object from a particular Lease implementation can be batched with another Lease object. The method returns a boolean indicating whether batching is possible; if batching is possible, then these two Lease objects can coexist in the same LeaseMap for efficiency.

Typically, a Lease implementation that supports batching will return true from canBatch() if the argument Lease uses the same implementation and communicates back to the same lease grantor. Smarter implementations could, in theory anyway, batch with Leases of other implementations.

The createLeaseMap() method creates a new LeaseMap object, initialized to contain the Lease instance that the method was called on. The argument to the method associates a duration in milliseconds with the Lease object; whenever the Leases in the LeaseMap are all renewed together, this is the value that will be requested for the duration of that Lease.

The LeaseMap Interface

Let's look now at the API provided by the LeaseMap interface.

```
package net.jini.lease;

import java.rmi.RemoteException;

public interface LeaseMap extends java.util.Map {
      boolean canContainKey(Object key);
      void renewAll() throws LeaseMapException,
                                              RemoteException;
      void cancelAll() throws LeaseMapException,
                                              RemoteException;
}
```

LeaseMap extends the java.util.Map interface, part of the Java 2 collections library. A Map is much like a hash table, and provides a way to associate keys with values; any key can exist only once in the map. Since LeaseMap extends Map, all the usual Map methods for adding and removing key-value pairs from the object are available here. Check out the documentation for the Java 2 Map class for all the basic details of how this form of associative collection works.

The LeaseMap maintains an association between keys which are Lease objects and values which are objects of class Long. These Longs are the desired duration for the Lease. Whenever the leases in the map are renewed, the map will attempt to renew each lease for its associated duration.

The LeaseMap will ensure that any Lease you add to it is compatible with the other Leases already there. That is, it will check that any added Lease can be batched with the Leases already in the map. If you try to add a Lease that cannot be batched with the other Leases in a LeaseMap, an IllegalArgumentException will be raised. So you should be prepared to catch this exception, or—even better—check that the Lease can be added before you try. The method canContainKey() is used to determine whether a candidate Lease would be compatible with the other Leases in a LeaseMap.

The usual Map methods for adding key-value pairs will also raise an IllegalArgumentException if you try to add in a key which is not a Lease or a value which is not a Long.

Once you've added your Leases to your LeaseMap, you can efficiently control all of them at once using the renewAll() and cancelAll() methods. Calling renewAll() will attempt to renew all the Lease objects in the LeaseMap for the duration associated with each. If all the renewals are done successfully, then nothing is returned and control flow continues as normal. If, however, any of the renewals fail, those objects will be dropped from the LeaseMap. This is so that a renewal failure will not cause repeated failures in the future when renewAll() is again called on the LeaseMap. In this case, a LeaseMapException will be raised. This exception contains all the Leases for which renewal failed. The program can then take steps to deal with the failure, most likely by letting the leases expire, or scheduling a retry for sometime in the future—which are the standard strategies to take when a singleton Lease renewal is denied.

The cancelAll() method works in much the same way as renewAll(): the method attempts to cancel all Leases in the LeaseMap. If the operation completes successfully, nothing is returned and the program continues as normal. If any of the cancellations fail, however, they are removed from the LeaseMap and a LeaseMapException is raised which contains the failed cancellations. In this case a program may either let the Lease objects involved in the failed cancellation expire on their own, or may attempt to retry the cancellation at some point in the future.

Let's now look at a portion of the LeaseMapException class and see how to extract bad Leases from it.

```
package net.jini.lease;

import java.util.Map;

public class LeaseMapException extends LeaseException {
      public Map exceptionMap;

      // ... other methods and constructor elided ...
}
```

The `LeaseMapException` class has a public member, called `exceptionMap`, which is a `Map` containing all the `Leases` involved in a failed renewal or cancellation operation. Since this member is publicly accessible, you can just poke around in the contained `Map` to see where the problems are.

The keys in this `Map` are the `Lease` objects involved in failed operations. The values are the `Exceptions` that were raised when the renewal or cancellation was attempted. By using the `Exception` associated with each `Lease`, a program can make a determination about what caused the failure, how to proceed, and how to report the failure to a user.

Higher-Level APIs for Lease Consumers

In Chapter 5 we extended the simple "Hello World" example to use leasing. Clearly, managing the leases used by that simple application was a big part of the programming there. In the case of this trivially simple service, leasing consumed a big fraction of the total number of code lines.

Fortunately, the work that programmers have to do to manage leases is pretty mechanical—a set of leases are acquired and remembered. For most services, these leases will be held for as long as the service lasts. This is because the leases typically represent things like lookup service registrations, which most services want to maintain indefinitely. There's not a lot of fine-grained juggling of leases in most applications.

These characteristics of application behavior lend themselves well to library code that can handle the chore of lease management for us. In the last section we looked at the "foundation" level APIs for leasing, because it's important to understand the groundwork on which higher-level APIs are based. In the next few sections, we'll look at some examples of common leasing idioms, and see how these can be expressed in helpful higher-level lease management tools that developers can use.

The first of these tools is provided by Jini itself, and you've already seen some examples of it in previous chapters. It's called the `LeaseRenewalManager`, and it can offload some of the leasing chores from applications. In this section we'll explore the `LeaseRenewalManager`. A bit later, we'll see how to create and use completely external third-party services to handle leasing.

The `com.sun.jini.lease` package defines a handful of classes that are ready-to-use for lease management. The most important of these is the `LeaseRenewalManager`. The `LeaseRenewalManager` is a class that can manage the renewals for whole sets of leases. The basic programming paradigm is that you create a `LeaseRenewalManager` and give it leases to manage. Whenever you pass it a lease, you also tell it how long the lease should be held. At any point in the future, you can tell the `LeaseRenewalManager` to extend the expiration time on the lease, remove the lease from the set of managed leases, or cancel the lease.

You may be asking yourself, "So what does this buy me? I've still got to figure out how long my leases should be for, and ask the `LeaseRenewalManager` to renew them for me. I'm doing the same work, only I'm talking to this new class, rather than a generic lease object." The big difference between using a `LeaseRenewalManager` and handling "raw" leases by yourself is that you typically ask the `LeaseRenewalManager` for lease expiration times that are *far* longer than a normal lease grantor would provide as a lease duration. The `LeaseRenewalManager` takes care of repeatedly contacting the grantor and renewing the leases, no matter what actual duration the grantor was willing to give for a single duration. So you can ask a `LeaseRenewalManager` for a lease of days, weeks, or even years. It will dutifully continue renewing the lease at whatever duration it can get until the time expires, or you tell the manager to drop the lease.

The fact that you can ask for long leases does not violate the self-healing properties of Jini, because the `LeaseRenewalManager` itself will deal with the shorter leases that services grant. And, if the JVM containing your service terminates, it will bring down the `LeaseRenewalManager` as well. So the failure behavior is the same whether or not you use this class—there's a "window" of error during which an unexpired lease may exist for a client that has gone away.

If a lease cannot be renewed by the `LeaseRenewalManager`, it will call out to a listener that can decide what to do—clean up any state that may be lingering around in the lease consumer, pop up a message to the user, and so on. Users of the `LeaseRenewalManager` can have listeners on a lease-by-lease basis—each lease can have its own listener, so you can use different listeners for, say, leases for event registrations than you use for leases for service registrations. Lease listeners should implement the `LeaseListener` interface, which includes one method, called `notify()`, which receives a `LeaseRenewalEvent` whenever a lease expires.

You've seen the use of the `LeaseRenewalManager` a number of times in the preceding chapters, so here I'll focus on the APIs for the classes you need to use to work with the `LeaseRenewalManager`.

First, let's look at the `LeaseRenewalManager` itself.

```
package com.sun.jini.leases;

import net.jini.core.lease.Lease;
import net.jini.core.lease.UnknownLeaseException;
import java.rmi.RemoteException;

public class LeaseRenewalManager {
      public LeaseRenewalManager();
      public LeaseRenewalManager(Lease lease,
                                 long expiration,
                                 LeaseListener listener);
      public void cancel(Lease lease)
                       throws UnknownLeaseException,
                              RemoteException;
      public void clear();
      public long getExpiration(Lease lease);
      public void remove(Lease lease)
                       throws UnknownLeaseException;
      public void renewFor(Lease lease, long duration,
                                 LeaseListener listener);
      public void renewUntil(Lease lease, long expiration,
                                 LeaseListener listener);
      public void setExpiration(Lease lease,
                                  long expiration)
                       throws UnknownLeaseException;
}
```

A new `LeaseRenewalManager` can be created "empty" (meaning that it manages no leases initially), or can be created with a single initial lease to manage. In the form of the constructor which takes a lease, you see that the call also takes an expiration time (expressed in milliseconds, as you might expect), as well as a `LeaseListener` that will be associated with this lease and will be notified if a request for renewal is ever denied. Using this second form of the constructor is equivalent to creating an empty `LeaseRenewalManager` and then calling `renewUntil()` to add a lease to it.

The `renewFor()` and `renewUntil()` methods are the ways to add new leases to the set of managed leases. These calls work exactly the same, except that `renewFor()` takes a long indicating a duration from the present time, and `renewUntil()` takes a long indicating an absolute expiration time. (Both of these calls still result in relative durations being sent to the lease grantor; the call that takes an absolute expiration time is simply for programmer convenience.)

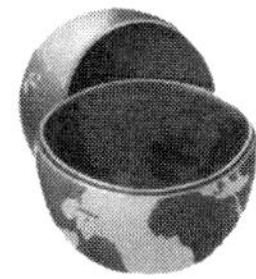

Core Alert: There's a bug in renewFor()

At the time this book goes to press, there is a bug in the implementation of `renewFor()` *in the 1.0 version of the Jini Starter Kit. The* `renewFor()` *method doesn't test for overflow, so if someone inputs the value* `Lease.FOREVER` *(or another large value), overflow will occur because* `renewFor()` *adds the duration input to the current time. This problem doesn't exist in* `renewUntil()`.

The bug has been fixed internally by the Jini team, and will most probably be released by the time you read this. But you should be aware of this bug if you're using the 1.0 version of Jini.

When a lease is added to the managed set, it will be continuously renewed until the requested expiration time passes, or the lease cannot be renewed by its grantor, or it is explicitly canceled or removed from the managed set. If you try to add an already managed lease, the lease will be removed and then added back to the set. This may be useful if you change some parameter of a lease, or renew it "manually" without going through the `LeaseRenewalManager`; adding the lease again gives the manager a chance to refresh its sense of when it should wake up to renew the lease. If you happen to pass in an expiration time that is sooner than the current expiration time, then the current expiration time is not changed.

One very common idiom that is used by most clients and services is to continually renew a lease until the program using the resource goes away. For example, a Jini service browser will typically want to continue to receive events until the user shuts the program down. If you only use the `LeaseRenewalManager` to ask for very long leases, you haven't actually saved yourself much work: you still have to be prepared to wake up and ask the `LeaseRenewalManager` to extend the leases for you.

Fortunately, when you add a lease using `renewUntil()`, you can pass the special token `Lease.ANY`. As you remember from the discussion of the "raw" leasing APIs, the `ANY` flag indicates that the grantor is free to grant a lease for any duration that is most convenient for it. Essentially this is the grantor's "preferred" lease duration. In the context of the `LeaseRenewalManager`, passing this flag as the expiration time for your lease means that the lease will be *continually* renewed in whatever chunks the grantor sees fit to use, until the owner cancels it or the `LeaseRenewalManager` goes away (including when the JVM containing it exits). This is the way most applications will use the `LeaseRenewalManager`—they will use the special `Lease.ANY` flag to renew leases continually until they shut down. Note that you *cannot* pass this flag to `renewFor()`, which renews a lease for a requested duration. Or, more precisely, you *could* add use `Lease.ANY` here, but it will be interpreted purely as a duration, not as a special flag to be used to indicate continuous renewal forever.

Core Note: What happens if you pass Lease.ANY to renewFor()?

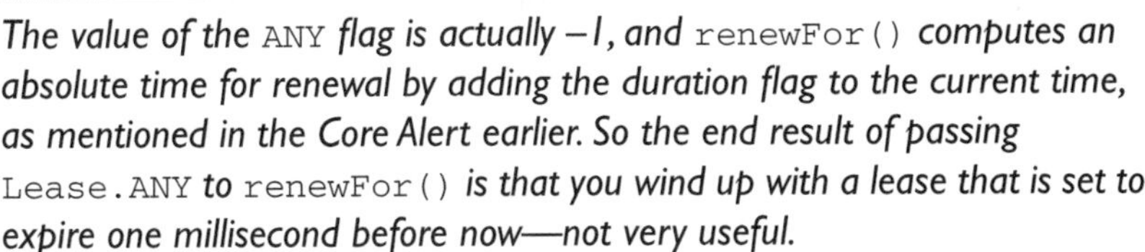

The value of the `ANY` *flag is actually –1, and* `renewFor()` *computes an absolute time for renewal by adding the duration flag to the current time, as mentioned in the Core Alert earlier. So the end result of passing* `Lease.ANY` *to* `renewFor()` *is that you wind up with a lease that is set to expire one millisecond before now—not very useful.*

Confusing the `renewFor()` *and* `renewUntil()` *methods is a common mistake; it would be good if* `renewFor()` *complained if a user passed in* `Lease.ANY` *as a duration, but it doesn't.*

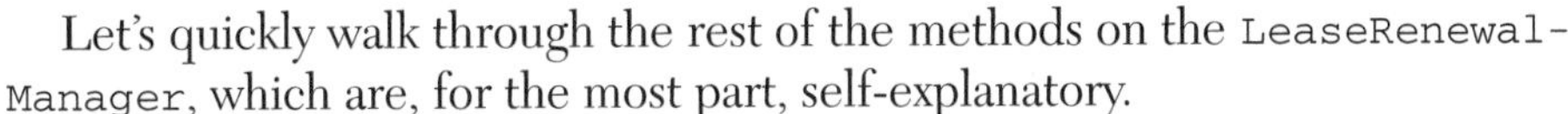

Let's quickly walk through the rest of the methods on the `LeaseRenewalManager`, which are, for the most part, self-explanatory.

Calling `getExpiration()` returns the *desired* expiration time that you passed into the `LeaseRenewalManager`. Note that this isn't what time the lease's currently granted duration runs out—the `LeaseRenewalManager` hides this from you. The return value is the time you've asked the `LeaseRenewalManager` to stop automatically renewing the leases. The `setExpiration()` method allows you to change the desired expiration time for a lease. Calling this method is equivalent to calling `renewUntil()` on a new lease. So you can pass `Lease.ANY` to go into the same renew-forever mode that you get when you pass this flag to `renewUntil()`. Both of the expiration times in these methods are expressed in milliseconds, represented as a long. And both may raise `UnknownLeaseException` if the lease that you're changing isn't known to its grantor for some reason; this may occur if you hold on to a lease outside the lease manager after it's already been canceled or has expired.

The `cancel()` method cancels a lease, if it was in the set of managed leases known to the `LeaseRenewalManager`. The lease is also removed from the set of managed leases. Calling `remove()` simply removes the lease from the set of managed leases, perhaps because a caller wishes to control a particular lease "by hand." And finally, `clear()` removes all leases from the managed set; it does not cancel them, however.

Internally, the `LeaseRenewalManager` creates a new thread that will wake up periodically to renew leases. It also tries to batch leases together into `LeaseMaps` wherever possible.

Let's look a bit now at the way that listeners are notified when leases expire early because they cannot be renewed. Note that listeners are *not* called when a lease expires at the requested time—when it dies a natural death, if you will. Listeners are only called when their requested expirations can not be met. Each lease in a `LeaseRenewalManager` can have its own listener associated with it, which implements the `LeaseListener` interface.

```
package com.sun.jini.lease;

import java.util.EventListener;

public interface LeaseListener extends EventListener {
      public void notify(LeaseRenewalEvent ev);
}
```

A `LeaseListener` need only implement one method, `notify()`. This method will be called with a `LeaseRenewalEvent` as a parameter whenever a lease expires early or cannot be renewed.

```
package com.sun.jini.lease;

import java.util.EventObject;
import net.jini.core.lease.Lease;

public class LeaseRenewalEvent extends EventObject {
      // ... some details elided ...
      public Exception getException();
      public long getExpiration();
      public Lease getLease();
}
```

Since `LeaseRenewalEvent` extends the standard Java `EventObject`, it inherits a `getSource()` method from there that will return the `LeaseRenewalManager` that resulted in this event being sent. The `getExpira-`

tion() method returns the original desired expiration time that was requested of the LeaseRenewalManager for the now-defunct lease; the getLease() method returns the lease itself. Finally, getException() returns an exception that explains why the lease renewal failed. If the lease was denied, this will be a net.jini.core.lease.LeaseDeniedException; if the lease expired, the exception may be any one of net.jini.core.lease.UnknownLease-Exception, java.rmi.RemoteException, or null.

Because the LeaseRenewalManager does such a fine job of handling leases, most lease users will never use the low-level APIs.

A Leasing Service

The LeaseRenewalManager is an example of how a generic class can satisfy leasing on behalf of an application—as the user of leases, you can simply pass your leases to the manager and forget about them.

There are other ways you could imagine delegating lease behavior. Jini's leasing mechanisms are flexible enough that they can support *third-party leasing*, which means that a completely external entity, outside the lease owner's JVM, can take care of leasing for you. Essentially you delegate the chore of lease management to a process running outside your address space.

This section presents an example of just such an entity, which here is implemented as a complete Jini service, called the LeaseService. The LeaseService registers itself in Jini communities and makes its facilities available to all parties on the network; the service can be shared by any number of other services and can perform the leasing operations for all of them. This strategy is useful for services that will be inactive for long periods of time (and therefore will be unable to do their own lease management without waking up continually), but still wish to hold on to leases. It may also be useful for small devices that have very limited computational ability or bandwidth, but tend to be always connected to the network.

While delegating lease renewals to an external process makes good sense in many settings, there are some downsides to the strategy as well. After we walk through the implementation of the lease renewal service, we'll discuss some of the pros and cons of using a facility like this.

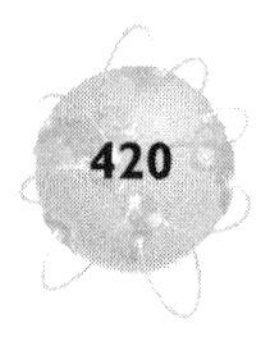

An Overview of a Leasing Service

A leasing service is a complete, stand-alone Jini service that exposes callable methods to other Jini services and applications. In this case, the methods that are exposed help a program to delegate the management of its leases.

The `LeaseRenewalManager` has a solid API that makes the task of delegating the management of leases within a JVM an easy task. So, for the example leasing service that we'll build here, we'll keep the same basic "look and feel" of the interfaces: callers will be able to add new leases to the set of managed leases, using both relative durations and absolute expiration times; callers can cancel and remove leases from the set; and callers can receive notification via a listener mechanism when leases expire prematurely.

There are some niceties of the `LeaseRenewalManager` API that we'll have to work to preserve in this new, remote setting however. In particular, even though the "wire" format of leases is always a duration, the `LeaseRenewalManager` allows lease times to be specified in either relative durations or absolute expiration times. This works great because the owner of the lease and the `LeaseRenewalManager` are running on the same machine—they will both see the system clock, and therefore they can easily convert from absolute to relative times as needed by simply adding or subtracting the current time.

Such is not the case with a remote lease manager, though. If a client asks for an absolute expiration time, this needs to be converted into a relative duration for transmission to the remote manager. Once there, it can be converted into whatever the *manager's* sense of absolute time is. This is because we cannot guarantee that both the client and the lease service have the same sense of absolute time, so working with relative durations is the only way to approach an accurate lease time.

We'll also have to make a few other changes to the basic `LeaseRenewalManager` API. For example, all the methods that callers will use to manage leases will now need to raise `RemoteException` since they involve going "over the wire" to a remote process. For the remote lease service to call back to clients to deliver lease expiration events when their leases expire prematurely, lease listeners will have to be remotely callable objects.

With these considerations in mind, we can begin to flesh out what a remote leasing service might look like. The client-side API should look as close to the `LeaseRenewalManager` as possible; this will be the API that's implemented by the service proxy object that clients use. It will be essentially identical to the methods available on `LeaseRenewalManager` except for the raising of `RemoteExceptions`. The proxy object will communicate with the back-end leasing service using a private protocol that handles the translation to and from relative and absolute times. And clients that wish to receive events when their leases expire early will need to implement a special remote version of the `LeaseListener` interface.

Remote Leasing APIs

Let's start off by looking at the APIs we would like to support. We'll look both at the client-side API (that is, the API supported by the service proxy object as shown in Listing 10–1), as well as the remote interface that's used for communication between the proxy and the back-end part of the service as shown in Listing 10–2.

Listing 10–1 `LeaseRenewalService.java`

```
// interface for the proxy -- clientside api.
package corejini.chapter10;

import net.jini.core.lease.Lease;
import net.jini.core.lease.UnknownLeaseException;
import net.jini.core.event.RemoteEventListener;
import java.rmi.RemoteException;

public interface LeaseRenewalService  {
   public void renewUntil(Lease lease, long expiration,
                          RemoteEventListener listener)
                          throws RemoteException;
   public void renewFor(Lease lease, long duration,
                        RemoteEventListener listener)
                        throws RemoteException;
   public void clear() throws RemoteException;
   public void remove(Lease lease) throws RemoteException,
                                   UnknownLeaseException;
   public void cancel(Lease lease) throws RemoteException,
                                   UnknownLeaseException;
   public long getExpiration(Lease lease)
          throws RemoteException, UnknownLeaseException;
   public void setExpiration(Lease lease, long expiration)
          throws RemoteException, UnknownLeaseException;
}
```

The `LeaseRenewalService` interface is the API which the service proxy will implement, and which clients will use to interact with the leasing service. This API is designed—intentionally—to reflect as closely as possible the interfaces of the LeaseRenewalManager. Since, unlike the LeaseRenewalManager, this interface provides access to remote leasing agents, all the methods are declared to raise RemoteException since they can fail in various network-oriented ways. Other than this, the API is essentially the same as that of the local-only leasing manager.

Let's look now at the interface that the proxy will use for communication with the back-end portion of the service. This interface defines the remote protocol that the back-end part of the service speaks.

Listing 10–2 RemoteLeaseRenewer.java

```
// Defines the remote (RMI) protocol between the proxy and
// the back-end.

package corejini.chapter10;

import net.jini.admin.Administrable;
import net.jini.core.lease.Lease;
import net.jini.core.lease.UnknownLeaseException;
import net.jini.core.event.RemoteEventListener;
import java.rmi.Remote;
import java.rmi.RemoteException;

public interface RemoteLeaseRenewer
            extends Remote, Administrable {
    public void renewAny(Lease lease,
                         RemoteEventListener listener)
                         throws RemoteException;
    public void renewFor(Lease lease, long duration,
                        RemoteEventListener listener)
                        throws RemoteException;
    public void clear() throws RemoteException;
    public void remove(Lease lease)
            throws RemoteException, UnknownLeaseException;
    public void cancel(Lease lease)
            throws RemoteException, UnknownLeaseException;
    public long getRemainingDuration(Lease lease)
            throws RemoteException, UnknownLeaseException;
    public void setRemainingDuration(Lease lease,
                                     long expiration)
         throws RemoteException, UnknownLeaseException;
}
```

You'll note that the APIs defined here are very *similar*, but not exactly the *same*, as the client interfaces. Instead of a `renewUntil()` interface here we see a `renewAny()`. And `getExpiration()` and `setExpiration()` are replaced by `getRemainingDuration()` and `setRemainingDuration()`.

The reason for these differences is that the remote protocol used for communication between the proxy and the service must *only* traffic in relative durations. You can expose the *appearance* of absolute time in the proxy but, whenever you send lease times out across the wire, you must convert them into relative times for the reasons mentioned before.

For most client-side uses of `renewUntil()`, we can simply convert the absolute time passed there into a duration and send that to the service using `renewFor()`. However, recall that one of the uses of `renewUntil()` is to support the perpetually renewing behavior that passing an expiration time of `Lease.ANY` indicates. Since this is a special case behavior that `renewFor()` doesn't support, here I've added a special `renewAny()` that specifically turns on this behavior.

Likewise, `getRemainingDuration()` and `setRemainingDuration()` do simple conversions to and from absolute and relative time.

This interface is defined as a remote interface—by virtue of the fact that it extends `Remote`—which means that the proxy object and the back-end service will communicate using RMI. The interface also extends `Administrable`, so it provides a way for proxies to call back to the service to fetch an administration object for them.

Listing 10–3 shows the implementation of the proxy object that will mediate between these two APIs. You can think of this proxy as essentially a converter box that maps from the client-side interface to the wire protocol used to communicate with the back-end service.

Listing 10–3 `LeaseServiceProxy.java`

```
//
// This intentionally has nearly the same api as
// LeaseRenewalManager, only here we raise
// remote exceptions.
//
// The reason we don't just use the rmi stub for the leasing
// service directly is that the proxy here must translate
// between absolute and relative time.
//
// The backend methods traffic *only* in relative time
//
package corejini.chapter10;
```

Listing 10–3 `LeaseServiceProxy.java`

```
import net.jini.core.lease.Lease;
import net.jini.core.lease.UnknownLeaseException;
import net.jini.core.event.RemoteEventListener;
import net.jini.admin.Administrable;
import java.io.Serializable;
import java.rmi.RemoteException;

public class LeaseServiceProxy
      implements LeaseRenewalService,
                 Serializable, Administrable {
    protected RemoteLeaseRenewer backend;

    public LeaseServiceProxy(RemoteLeaseRenewer backend) {
        this.backend = backend;
    }

    public void renewUntil(Lease lease, long expiration,
                           RemoteEventListener listener)
        throws RemoteException {
        // Translate between time formats.
        if (expiration == Lease.ANY) {
            backend.renewAny(lease, listener);
        } else {
            long duration =
                 expiration - System.currentTimeMillis();
            backend.renewFor(lease, duration, listener);
        }
    }

    public void renewFor(Lease lease, long duration,
                         RemoteEventListener listener)
        throws RemoteException {
        backend.renewFor(lease, duration, listener);
    }

    public void clear() throws RemoteException {
        backend.clear();
    }

    public void remove(Lease lease) throws RemoteException,
        UnknownLeaseException {
        backend.remove(lease);
    }
```

Listing 10–3 `LeaseServiceProxy.java`

```
    public void cancel(Lease lease) throws RemoteException,
            UnknownLeaseException {
        backend.cancel(lease);
    }

    public long getExpiration(Lease lease)
        throws RemoteException, UnknownLeaseException {
        // Translate between time formats
        long dur = backend.getRemainingDuration(lease);
        return System.currentTimeMillis() + dur;
    }
    public void setExpiration(Lease lease, long expiration)
        throws RemoteException, UnknownLeaseException {
        // Translate between time formats
        backend.setRemainingDuration(lease,
                    expiration - System.currentTimeMillis());
    }

    public Object getAdmin() throws RemoteException {
        return backend.getAdmin();
    }
}
```

When the proxy is created, it is passed a reference to an object that implements the back-end protocol; it will use this object to make calls on the service. The rest of the code here is pretty simple; in fact, most of the mappings between the client-side APIs and the server-side APIs are simple "pass throughs," meaning that there is no special conversion to be done.

Only the methods noted earlier have anything special to do. The `renewUntil()` method checks its parameters to see if `Lease.ANY` was passed to it. If it was, then the code maps the method invocation into `renewAny()` on the server; otherwise, it calculates a duration by subtracting the current time from the requested expiration time, and calls `renewFor()` on the server.

Likewise, `getExpiration()` and `setExpiration()` convert to and from the absolute expiration times that are used locally and the durations that must be sent over the wire; these methods call `getRemainingDuration()` and `setRemainingDuration()`, respectively.

Note that the proxy shown here implements `Administrable` by calling back to the remote leasing service. The remote service will return an object that can be used for administration.

Events and Listeners for Remote Leasing

The classes and interfaces used for delivering leasing events from the LeaseRenewalManager will not work in the remote case—LeaseListener is not a remote interface, so listeners cannot be called from JVMs on remote machines, and LeaseRenewalEvent provides a local LeaseRenewalManager as its source, which is not useful in the remote case.

We'll need to develop some new interfaces and classes for dealing with remote leasing services. And here, just like when we defined the interfaces for LeaseRenewalService, we'll try to stay as close to the semantics of the existing classes as possible.

First, let's look at a remote version of LeaseRenewalEvent as shown in Listing 10–4.

Listing 10–4 RemoteLeaseRenewalEvent.java

```
// A subclass of RemoteEvent for lease events
package corejini.chapter10;

import com.sun.jini.lease.LeaseRenewalEvent;
import net.jini.core.lease.Lease;
import net.jini.core.event.RemoteEvent;

public class RemoteLeaseRenewalEvent extends RemoteEvent {
    protected Lease lease;
    protected long expiration;
    protected Exception exception;

    public RemoteLeaseRenewalEvent(long eventID,
                               long seqNum,
                               LeaseRenewalService renewer,
                               Lease lease, long expiration,
                               Exception exception) {
        super(renewer, eventID, seqNum, null);
        this.lease = lease;
        this.expiration = expiration;
        this.exception = exception;
    }
    public Lease getLease() {
        return lease;
    }
    public long getExpiration() {
```

Listing 10–4 `RemoteLeaseRenewalEvent.java` **(continued)**

```
        return expiration;
    }
    public Exception getException() {
        return exception;
    }
}
```

Here I've defined a new event class, which is a subclass of the Jini `RemoteEvent` class, as all good Jini remote events should be. Unfortunately, subclassing `LeaseRenewalEvent` is not really an option here—pragmatically, to initialize a `LeaseRenewalEvent` superclass, we'd have to pass in a `LeaseRenewalManager`, which we don't have in the remote case. Also, making `RemoteLeaseRenewalEvent` a subclass of `LeaseRenewalEvent` really says that the remote event is just a special case of the local event, which isn't exactly true—they're fundamentally different types of events that just happen to report similar occurrences.

All of the methods defined here return exactly the same values that they do in the local case, with one exception. The `getSource()` method, defined by the `EventObject` superclass of `RemoteEvent`, returns the `LeaseRenewalService` that caused the event to be fired, rather than the `LeaseRenewalManager` that's returned in the local case.

There are a few other details here that will be discussed more fully in Chapter 14 when we talk about remote events. For example, the constructor takes an "event ID" and a "sequence number" which are simply passed through to the superclass constructor. These values are used to allow clients to route and order events. For our purposes here, though, you can pretty much ignore them for the time being.

Since the `RemoteLeaseRenewalEvent` is a subclass of `RemoteEvent`, we can just use the regular Jini `RemoteEventListener` interface as the interface that receivers of these events will implement. So we don't need to create any new listener classes here. In other words, the Jini `RemoteEventListener` will become the remote analog of the local `LeaseListener` interface. Note that using `RemoteEventListener` implies that classes that implement it must be RMI server objects, which means that most likely they will be subclasses of `java.rmi.server.UnicastRemoteObject`, so that they can receive the remote method invocation of `notify()`.

Leasing Service Implementation

Now that we've defined the interfaces and protocols used for communication, as well as how events and listeners work, let's focus on building the actual leasing service (see Listing 10–5).

First and foremost, the code shown here *is* a Jini service. So much of the code is involved with creating a `JoinManager` to participate in discovery, and handling persistent state so that the service can recover itself after restarts or crashes.

Since the back-end service shown here needs to communicate via RMI with its proxies in various clients, it extends `UnicastRemoteObject` so that its implementations of the methods in `RemoteLeaseRenewer` can be called remotely.

The code in the service that actually implements lease management is fairly simple. All of the `RemoteLeaseRenewer` calls are implemented by calling out to our old friend, the local `LeaseRenewalManager`! The service essentially wraps up one of these and makes it available to any other services around the network via RMI.

Most of the rest of the code is concerned with two tasks. The first is mapping to and from local `LeaseListeners` (which are what the `LeaseRenewalManager` used by the implementation understands) to `RemoteEventListeners` (which are what clients provide to us). The second is checkpointing lease information out to persistent storage whenever something changes (so that the code can recover the state of its leases after a crash), and recovering that checkpointed state after a restart.

Let's look at the code now.

Listing 10–5 `LeaseService.java`

```
// A service back-end to manage leases.

package corejini.chapter10;

import net.jini.core.lease.Lease;
import net.jini.core.lease.UnknownLeaseException;
import net.jini.core.event.RemoteEvent;
import net.jini.core.event.RemoteEventListener;
import net.jini.core.event.UnknownEventException;
import net.jini.core.discovery.LookupLocator;
import net.jini.core.lookup.ServiceID;
import net.jini.core.entry.Entry;
```

Listing 10–5 `LeaseService.java` (continued)

```
import com.sun.jini.lookup.JoinManager;
import com.sun.jini.lookup.ServiceIDListener;
import com.sun.jini.lease.LeaseRenewalManager;
import com.sun.jini.lease.LeaseRenewalEvent;
import com.sun.jini.lease.LeaseListener;
import java.rmi.RemoteException;
import java.rmi.RMISecurityManager;
import java.rmi.server.UnicastRemoteObject;
import java.util.Hashtable;
import java.util.Enumeration;
import java.io.File;
import java.io.Serializable;
import java.io.IOException;
import java.io.ObjectOutputStream;
import java.io.ObjectInputStream;
import java.io.FileOutputStream;
import java.io.FileInputStream;

public class LeaseService  extends UnicastRemoteObject
    implements RemoteLeaseRenewer, ServiceIDListener {
    protected JoinManager joinManager = null;
    protected LeaseRenewalManager leaseManager =
                 new LeaseRenewalManager();
    protected String storageLoc = null;
    protected LeaseRenewalService proxy;
    protected Hashtable allLeases = new Hashtable();
    protected File file = null;
    protected ServiceID serviceID = null;
    protected long eventID = 0;

    // Maps from local lease listeners to remote event
    // listeners
    class LeaseListenerConduit implements LeaseListener {
        RemoteEventListener remote;
        long eventID;
        long seqNum = 0;

        LeaseListenerConduit(RemoteEventListener remote,
                             long eventID) {
            this.remote = remote;
            this.eventID = eventID;
        }
```

Listing 10–5 `LeaseService.java` **(continued)**

```
    public void notify(LeaseRenewalEvent ev) {
        // Always remove the lease from the set of
        // leases
        allLeases.remove(ev.getLease());
        try {
            checkpoint();
        } catch (IOException ex) {
           System.err.println("Couldn't checkpoint to " +
                              storageLoc +
                              ": " + ex.getMessage());
            System.err.println("Service not removed " +
                                 "from storage.");
        }

        try {
            if (remote != null) {
                remote.notify(remotify(ev, eventID,
                                           seqNum++));
            }
        } catch (RemoteException ex) {
            System.err.println("Couldn't notify " +
                                 "remote listener: " +
                              ex.getMessage());
        } catch (UnknownEventException ex) {
            System.err.println("UnknownEvent: " +
                              ex.getMessage());
            remote = null;
        }
    }

    // Produce a RemoteLeaseRenewalEvent from a
    // local LeaseRenewalEvent.
    RemoteLeaseRenewalEvent remotify(LeaseRenewalEvent ev,
                                     long eventID,
                                     long seqNum) {
        return new RemoteLeaseRenewalEvent(eventID,
                                     seqNum,
                                     proxy,
                                     ev.getLease(),
                                     ev.getExpiration(),
                                     ev.getException());
    }
}
```

Listing 10–5 LeaseService.java (continued)

```
    // This is the state that we need to keep around to
    // manage leases.
    static class LeaseEntry implements Serializable {
        long expiration;
        RemoteEventListener listener;
        long id;    // ID to use when sending events

        LeaseEntry(long expiration,
                   RemoteEventListener listener,
                   long id) {
            this.expiration = expiration;
            this.listener = listener;
            this.id = id;
        }
    }

    // All of this service's persistent data...
    static class LeaseServiceData implements Serializable {
        ServiceID id;
        Entry[] attrs;
        String[] groups;
        LookupLocator[] locs;
        Hashtable leases;

        LeaseServiceData(ServiceID id, Entry[] attrs,
                   String[] groups, LookupLocator[] locs,
                   Hashtable leases) {
            this.id = id;
            this.attrs = attrs;
            this.groups = groups;
            this.locs = locs;
            this.leases = leases;
        }
    }

    public LeaseService(String storageLoc)
        throws RemoteException, IOException,
        ClassNotFoundException {
        if (System.getSecurityManager() == null) {
            System.setSecurityManager(
                        new RMISecurityManager());
        }
```

Listing 10–5 `LeaseService.java` **(continued)**

```
        this.storageLoc = storageLoc;

        proxy = new LeaseServiceProxy(this);

        file = new File(storageLoc);

          // If the file exists, treat this as a re-start.
          // Otherwise it's the first time the service has
          // been run.
        if (file.exists()) {
            restore();
        }

          // We'll use the "initial" form of the join manager
          // constructor if the file didn't exist or
          // restore() didn't work.
        if (joinManager == null) {
            joinManager = new JoinManager(proxy, null,
                                                 this, null);
        }
    }

    protected void checkpoint() throws IOException {
        LeaseServiceData data;

          // Cycle through allLeases and chuck the ones that
          // have expired.
        Enumeration keys = allLeases.keys();
        while (keys.hasMoreElements()) {
            Lease lease = (Lease) keys.nextElement();
            LeaseEntry entry = (LeaseEntry)
                          allLeases.get(lease);
            if (entry.expiration >=
                      System.currentTimeMillis())
                allLeases.remove(lease);
        }

        data = new LeaseServiceData(serviceID,
                              joinManager.getAttributes(),
                              joinManager.getGroups(),
                              joinManager.getLocators(),
                              allLeases);
        ObjectOutputStream out = new
            ObjectOutputStream(new FileOutputStream(file));
```

Listing 10–5 `LeaseService.java` **(continued)**

```
        out.writeObject(data);
        out.flush();
        out.close();
    }

    protected void restore() throws IOException,
                    ClassNotFoundException {
        ObjectInputStream in = new
            ObjectInputStream(new FileInputStream(file));
        LeaseServiceData data =
                (LeaseServiceData) in.readObject();

        if (data == null) {
            System.out.println("No data in data file.");
        } else {
            allLeases = data.leases;
            // fill the lease manager with the leases...
            Enumeration enum = allLeases.keys();
            while (enum.hasMoreElements()) {
                Lease lease = (Lease) enum.nextElement();
                LeaseEntry entry = (LeaseEntry)
                              allLeases.get(lease);

                if (entry.expiration >=
                              System.currentTimeMillis()) {
                    allLeases.remove(lease);
                    continue;
                }

                 LeaseListenerConduit conduit =
                 new LeaseListenerConduit(entry.listener,
                                          entry.id);
                 leaseManager.renewUntil(lease,
                                      entry.expiration,
                                      conduit);
            }
            serviceID = data.id;
            joinManager = new JoinManager(data.id, proxy,
                                          data.attrs,
                                          data.groups,
                                          data.locs,
                                          null);
        }
    }
```

Listing 10–5 `LeaseService.java` **(continued)**

```
    public void serviceIDNotify(ServiceID serviceID) {
        this.serviceID = serviceID;

        try {
            checkpoint();
        } catch (IOException ex) {
            System.err.println("Couldn't checkpoint to " +
                               storageLoc +
                               ": " + ex.getMessage());
            System.err.println("Service ID not saved.");
        }
    }

     // these are the methods of RemoteLeaseListener that our
     // proxy will use to communicate with us.

    public void renewAny(Lease lease,
                         RemoteEventListener listener)
        throws RemoteException {
        long id = eventID++;
        lease.setSerialFormat(Lease.ABSOLUTE);
        allLeases.put(lease,
                 new LeaseEntry(Lease.ANY, listener, id));

        try {
            checkpoint();
        } catch (IOException ex) {
            System.err.println("Couldn't checkpoint to " +
                               storageLoc +
                               ": " + ex.getMessage());
            System.err.println("New lease not saved.");
        }

        LeaseListenerConduit conduit =
            new LeaseListenerConduit(listener, id);

        leaseManager.renewUntil(lease, Lease.ANY, conduit);
    }
```

Listing 10–5 `LeaseService.java` **(continued)**

```
public void renewFor(Lease lease, long duration,
                     RemoteEventListener listener)
    throws RemoteException {
    long id = eventID++;
    lease.setSerialFormat(Lease.ABSOLUTE);
    allLeases.put(lease,
                  new LeaseEntry(duration +
                         System.currentTimeMillis(),
                         listener, id));

    try {
        checkpoint();
    } catch (IOException ex) {
        System.err.println("Couldn't checkpoint to " +
                           storageLoc +
                           ": " + ex.getMessage());
        System.err.println("New lease not saved.");
    }

    LeaseListenerConduit conduit =
        new LeaseListenerConduit(listener, id);

    leaseManager.renewFor(lease, duration, conduit);
}

public void clear() throws RemoteException {
    allLeases.clear();

    try {
        checkpoint();
    } catch (IOException ex) {
        System.err.println("Couldn't checkpoint to " +
                           storageLoc +
                           ": " + ex.getMessage());
       System.err.println("Lease storage not cleared.");
    }

    leaseManager.clear();
}
public void remove(Lease lease) throws RemoteException,
    UnknownLeaseException {
    allLeases.remove(lease);
```

Listing 10–5 `LeaseService.java` **(continued)**

```
        try {
            checkpoint();
        } catch (IOException ex) {
            System.err.println("Couldn't checkpoint to " +
                               storageLoc +
                              ": " + ex.getMessage());
            System.err.println("Lease not removed " +
                                "from storage.");
        }
        leaseManager.remove(lease);
    }
    public void cancel(Lease lease) throws RemoteException,
            UnknownLeaseException {
        allLeases.remove(lease);

        try {
            checkpoint();
        } catch (IOException ex) {
            System.err.println("Couldn't checkpoint to " +
                               storageLoc +
                              ": " + ex.getMessage());
            System.err.println("Lease not removed " +
                                "from storage.");
        }

        leaseManager.cancel(lease);
    }

    // Note the absolute/relative time conversions.
    public long getRemainingDuration(Lease lease)
            throws RemoteException, UnknownLeaseException
{
       long expiration = leaseManager.getExpiration(lease);
       return expiration - System.currentTimeMillis();
    }

    public void setRemainingDuration(Lease lease,
                                       long duration)
       throws RemoteException, UnknownLeaseException {
       LeaseEntry entry = (LeaseEntry) allLeases.get(lease);
        long expiration = System.currentTimeMillis() +
                                 duration;
```

Listing 10–5 `LeaseService.java` **(continued)**

```
        if (entry != null) {
            entry.expiration = expiration;
            allLeases.put(lease, entry);
        }

        try {
            checkpoint();
        } catch (IOException ex) {
            System.err.println("Couldn't checkpoint to " +
                                storageLoc +
                                ": " + ex.getMessage());
            System.err.println("Lease expiration not " +
                                "updated in storage.");
        }

        leaseManager.setExpiration(lease, expiration);
    }

    // For now, don't return an administration object.
    public Object getAdmin() {
        return null;
    }

    public static void main(String[] args) {
        if (args.length != 1) {
            System.err.println("Usage: LeaseService " +
                               "<storage_loc>");
            System.exit(1);
        }

        try {
            LeaseService src = new LeaseService(args[0]);
            while (true) {
                try {
                    Thread.sleep(Long.MAX_VALUE);
                } catch (InterruptedException ex) {
                }
            }
        } catch (Exception ex) {
            System.out.println("trouble: " + ex.getMessage());
            ex.printStackTrace();
        }
    }
}
```

This is a rather involved piece of code, so let's start from the top. The `LeaseService` is an application—meaning it has a `main()` to start it—that extends `UnicastRemoteObject` because some of its methods will be callable remotely, and implements `RemoteLeaseRenewer`, because this is the way that its proxies will communicate with it, and `ServiceIDListener`, because it needs to know its ID so that it can save it to persistent storage.

Let's first look at how the service starts up, how it checkpoints itself to persistent storage, and how it resumes after a restart. The `main()` here takes a single parameter on the command line—the location of the service's persistent storage. If the indicated file does not exist, then the service assumes that this is the first time it is being run, and will use the `JoinManager` to retrieve a fresh `ServiceID` for it. If the file *does* exist, then the service assumes that it is being restarted after a crash or other shutdown. The constructor for `LeaseService` calls `restore()` if the file exists. If the file doesn't exist—or if for some reason `restore()` doesn't create a `JoinManager`, the constructor creates a `JoinManager` using the "initial" form of the constructor and sets its instance up as the `ServiceIDListener` so that the `LeaseService` can be informed when an ID is assigned to it.

The constructor also creates the proxy for the service, which is just an instance of the `LeaseServiceProxy` class you saw earlier. This instance is initialized by passing it a handle to the `LeaseService`, which is the way the proxy will communicate back to the service.

In the case of the leasing service here, there will always be a back-end process, chugging away to do the lease renewals. The approach that you saw in Chapter 5—using the RMI activation framework to have a back-end process sleep until it is needed—doesn't really apply here. The service will spend most of its time working to renew leases; and when no leases need renewing, the `LeaseRenewalManager` used internally just goes to sleep. You could write a version of this code that used the activation framework though. Such a version could deactivate itself if it had no leases to renew and after no clients had contacted it for some period of time. This strategy would allow the back-end service to consume *no* resources until a caller used its proxy. Of course, some other entity would have to be active to renew the `LeaseService`'s registration leases.

The `restore()` method tries to reload all of the saved state of the service. It creates an `ObjectInputStream` from the storage file, and reads in an instance of `LeaseServiceData`, which is a class used here to group all of the persistent state together. This class contains the service's ID, and the set of groups, lookup locators, and attributes it is to use. In addition to all of this state used by the `JoinManager`, `LeaseServiceData` also keeps all the leases that were in use the last time the service was checkpointed, stored as a hash table. This hash table is keyed by the leases themselves, and maintains a `LeaseEntry` for each lease. The `LeaseEntry` class, defined here, is a way to keep track of all of the state that the `LeaseRenewalManager` needs for each lease—its desired expiration time, and the listener that is associated with it. Whenever `restore()` is called, the code fetches all the saved leases and re-inserts them into the `LeaseRenewalManager` so that they will be managed again. As it processes each lease, it eliminates any stored leases that have already passed their expiration times.

Note that this operation doesn't guarantee that leases will be saved across crashes or restarts. If a lease has expired during the time the `LeaseRenewalService` was down, there will be no way for us to renew it. But clearly a leasing service should be as conservative as possible, so the code here dutifully tries to save lease data and restore it when possible. If no leases expired during the time the service was down, it should be able to successfully recover and continue managing all the leases that were in effect before it crashed.

The `checkpoint()` method is the inverse of `restore()`: it writes all necessary data to persistent storage. This method will be called from each and every one of the other methods in `LeaseRenewalService` that cause the state of managed leases to change, or from any code that changes any state that might be needed by the join protocol.

Each time the set of managed leases is checkpointed, any already expired leases are eliminated from the set of `allLeases`. The code does this since there is no "automatic" way to determine when a managed lease has expired—listeners are only called when some "exceptional" condition occurs, such as when a lease expires before the desired period has elapsed. Rather than spinning off a thread to clean up the managed lease set, we simply remove dead leases whenever we checkpoint or resume.

Most of the work described above has little to do with leasing per se. It's more about the things that "good" services have to do to ensure that they can recover properly, rather than specifically about how to build a service that does leasing. In future chapters, I'll expand on the code here to create a generic service framework to handle persistence. But for now, let's look at the code that's specific to leasing.

Let's look now at the `renewFor()` method, since it's typical of the other methods from the `RemoteLeaseRenewer` interface that this service implements. When `renewFor()` is invoked, it is passed a lease, a duration, and a `RemoteEventListener`. The first thing this method does is set the serialization format of the lease so that it will be stored as an absolute time whenever it is checkpointed to disk. Remember that whenever the code saves leases to disk it *must* save them in absolute time format—otherwise, when it wakes up it will have no idea how to convert the stored durations into new absolute times.

Next, the code stores the lease in the `allLeases` hash table, along with a new `LeaseEntry` for it that records the expiration time (computed by adding the duration to the current time—it must always save times as absolutes here), and the listener that was passed to it. Then `checkpoint()` is called to write the change in the state of managed leases out to persistent storage. If the service crashes at this point, it can recover not only the lease itself, but the desired expiration time and the listener that the client wished to be used for it.

Finally, after all the checkpointing, the method actually calls to the local `LeaseRenewalManager` to have it manage the lease. The `renewFor()` implementation passes the lease and the computed duration. But what about the listener? The client has sent us a `RemoteEventListener` class—which they must do since we need to call them back remotely—but `LeaseRenewalManager` only understands the local `LeaseListener` class.

The answer to this conundrum is that we create a custom class that maps between local and remote listeners, called the `LeaseListenerConduit`. This class is an implementation of the `LeaseListener` interface, so it can be used as a listener in the `LeaseRenewalManager`. It takes a `RemoteEventListener` as an argument and saves it, so that whenever its `notify()` method is called it can forward the invocation to the `RemoteEventListener`. Whenever any new lease is passed to the `LeaseService`, it "wraps" the `RemoteEventListener` in a new `LeaseConduit` and passes the conduit to the `LeaseRenewalManager` as the listener for the lease.

Let's look at the `LeaseListenerConduit` a little more closely. The implementation of `notify()` actually has to do a few things. First, it needs to remove the lease from the set of all managed leases. Recall that the listener is called whenever a lease expires prematurely or cannot be renewed. If this happens, the code needs to remove it from the set of managed leases and checkpoint to persistent storage.

The code also invokes the remote listener if it is not null. Clients can easily pass in a null `RemoteEventListener`; the various methods on `LeaseService` still create conduits, though, since they need to make sure that they have a conduit for every lease to remove failed leases from the managed set. So the null check here is necessary so that the code doesn't try to call out to a nonexistent remote listener.

Note here that the invocation of `notify()` passes in an *event ID* and a *sequence number* when it creates the remote version of the event. As we'll see in Chapter 14, Jini remote events should have a unique ID and increasing sequence numbers stored in them. This service doesn't really *use* these numbers in any way, but they should be generated correctly in any case. The strategy taken here is to simply keep a counter for event IDs and assign each new lease registration a new ID. The ID number is stored in the `LeaseEntry` for the lease. Sequence numbers are stored in the conduit and incremented each time an event is generated. Again, if you're curious about how this works and what it does, you can jump ahead to Chapter 14 or—probably better—just ignore it until we get there.

Finally, the code traps any exceptions that may result from calling the remote listener. The `LeaseListener` API doesn't specify any exceptions that may be thrown from `notify()`. So, since the conduit must meet this interface, it cannot raise any exceptions it receives. `RemoteException` may be raised if there is trouble communicating with the receiver. If such an exception is caught, the service simply prints a message but does nothing else. Since it doesn't remove the listener, the service will try to resend events in the future, if any arise. The `UnknownEventException` is an exception type that the Jini `RemoteEventListener` class may raise. We'll look at the full meaning of this exception in Chapter 14, but you can basically treat it as a request to not send future events to this recipient. The service "disables" the recipient by setting the listener to null, ensuring that it will receive no further events.

The implementation of `LeaseService` shown here implements the `getAdmin()` interface required by `RemoteLeaseRenewer`, but it returns null. So in practice, this service is not administrable. We will, however, come back to this service in Chapter 12, when we look at building service administration objects and graphical interfaces. At that time, we'll re-implement this method to do "real" administration.

Compiling and Running the Example

On Windows: first, compile the main program file. The Java compiler should build all of the class files needed by `LeaseService`. You can compile all of the implementation code for the service into the `service` directory.

```
javac -classpath C:\jini1_0\lib\jini-core.jar;
                 C:\jini1_0\lib\jini-ext.jar;
                 C:\jini1_0\lib\sun-util.jar;
                 C:\service
```

```
        -d C:\service
    C:\corejini\chapter10\LeaseService.java
```

Next, you need to ensure that downloadable code is copied to a directory that is being exported by the service's HTTP server. Clients will download the service's proxy, so `LeaseServiceProxy.class` needs to be copied to the `service-dl` directory. Also, the implementation of the proxy depends on `RemoteLeaseRenewer` and `LeaseRenewalService`, so those class files are necessary as well. (If you ever have trouble figuring out what files are needed in the download directory, you can simply try running a client—it will tell you if needed classes cannot be found with a `ClassNotFoundException`.)

```
cd C:\service\corejini\chapter10
copy LeaseServiceProxy.class C:\service-dl
copy RemoteLeaseRenewer.class C:\service-dl
copy LeaseRenewalService.class C:\service-dl
```

The only bit of shared state that both a client of the service and the service itself have is the interface that the service's proxy implements: `LeaseRenewalService`. So here I've also copied that class file out to the `client` directory, where presumably clients would be able to link against it.

```
copy LeaseRenewalService.class C:\client\corejini\chapter10
```

The last step in building things is to run the RMI stubs compiler on `LeaseService`. The stubs also need to be downloadable, so make sure you put them in the `service-dl` directory that's exported by the HTTP server.

```
rmic -classpath C:\jdk1.2\jre\lib\rt.jar;
                         C:\jini1_0\lib\jini-core.jar;
                         C:\jini1_0\lib\jini-ext.jar;
                         C:\jini1_0\lib\sun-util.jar;
                         C:\service
      -d C:\service-dl
corejini.chapter10.LeaseService
```

Finally you're set to run! Make sure you pass in a security policy file, a correct code base, and a file to use for persistent storage for the service.

```
java -cp C:\jini1_0\lib\jini-core.jar;
                   C:\jini1_0\lib\jini-ext.jar;
                   C:\jini1_0\lib\sun-util.jar;
```

```
            C:\service
        -Djava.rmi.server.codebase=http://myhost:8085/
        -Djava.security.policy=C:\policy
    corejini.chapter10.LeaseService C:\temp\leasedata
```

On Solaris: first, compile the main program file. The Java compiler should build all of the class files needed by `LeaseService`. You can compile all the implementation code for the service into the `service` directory.

```
javac -classpath /files/jini1_0/lib/jini-core.jar:
                 /files/jini1_0/lib/jini-ext.jar:
                 /files/jini1_0/lib/sun-util.jar:
                 /files/service
        -d /files/service
    /files/corejini/chapter10/LeaseService.java
```

Next, you need to ensure that downloadable code is copied to a directory that is being exported by the service's HTTP server. Clients will download the service's proxy, so `LeaseServiceProxy.class` needs to be copied to the `service-dl` directory. Also, the implementation of the proxy depends on `RemoteLeaseRenewer` and `LeaseRenewalService`, so those class files are necessary as well. (If you ever have trouble figuring out what files are needed in the download directory, you can simply try running a client—it will tell you if needed classes cannot be found with a `ClassNotFoundException`.)

```
cd /files/service/corejini/chapter10
cp LeaseServiceProxy.class /files/service-dl
cp RemoteLeaseRenewer.class /files/service-dl
cp LeaseRenewalService.class /files/service-dl
```

The only bit of shared state that both a client of the service and the service itself have is the interface that the service's proxy implements: `LeaseRenewalService`. So here I've also copied that class file out to the `client` directory, where presumably clients would be able to link against it.

```
copy LeaseRenewalService.class /files/client/corejini/chapter10
```

The last step in building things is to run the RMI stubs compiler on `LeaseService`. The stubs also need to be downloadable, so make sure you put them in the `service-dl` directory that's exported by the HTTP server.

```
rmic -classpath /jdk1.2/jre/lib/rt.jar:
                           /files/jini1_0/lib/jini-core.jar:
                           /files/jini1_0/lib/jini-ext.jar:
                           /files/jini1_0/lib/sun-util.jar:
                           /files/service
       -d /files/service-dl
corejini.chapter10.LeaseService
```

Finally you're set to run! Make sure you pass in a security policy file, a correct code base, and a file to use for persistent storage for the service.

```
java -cp /files/jini1_0/lib/jini-core.jar:
                     /files/jini1_0/lib/jini-ext.jar:
                     /files/jini1_0/lib/sun-util.jar:
                     /files/service
             -Djava.rmi.server.codebase=http://myhost:8085/
             -Djava.security.policy=/files/policy
      corejini.chapter10.LeaseService /tmp/leasedata
```

Leasing in Practice

In the very first "Hello, World" examples we looked at, you may have wondered about the wisdom of requiring a long-lived server process to sit around on a machine someplace, just to renew the leases for a trivially simple proxy object that never even needs to contact the server. So this raises the question—who *should* do the leasing for a particular service?

As it turns out, there are a number of leasing strategies you might use; which one you actually implement depends almost entirely on how your service is structured. In this section, we'll take a look at some of the strategies and the pros and cons of each.

Who Handles Lease Renewals?

There are three common service architectures used in Jini: services may be implemented using back-end processes, services may be implemented through a combination of hardware and software, or services may be implemented completely in the service proxy object that is sent to clients. In this section we'll look at leasing strategies for each of these architectures.

Many Jini services are implemented as proxies that communicate with back-end software processes. If you build a new network software service, in most cases the service will be implemented as a long-lived process that runs on a machine somewhere on the net; a custom proxy object will be used to communicate with this back end. In nearly all of these cases, it makes sense to have this back end process handle the lease renewals for the proxy. This arrangement is an easy and natural fit for the Jini leasing model, and makes intuitive sense—the service is only "up" for as long as the back end is running; if the back end ever goes away, the leases for its proxy should expire on their own.

There are a couple of mitigating factors that may argue against using this strategy, however, even when a service has a long-lived process associated with it. First, the back end of a service may not be implemented in Java. This will usually be the case when you need to make some legacy software service accessible through Jini. In such situations, it will likely be impossible for a back end written in, say, C to fulfill all of the obligations of Jini lease management (it will not, for example, be able to deserialize and use `Lease` implementations received from lease grantors). With such an arrangement, a *separate* back-end "wrapper" process may be created in Java, solely to handle various Jini chores, and to publish the service proxy that will be used to communicate with the "native" back end. This wrapper can stay active, handling the leasing itself, or it can delegate leasing to an external lease service and exit.

A second mitigating factor is if the back-end process, while long lived, is typically inactive for long periods of time. A service may be idle because it has to do work only infrequently—typically when required by its service proxy or some external scheduling constraints. A monthly disk backup service might fall into this class of application. Services like this can either wake up as needed to manage lease renewals, or they can delegate their lease management to an external lease service, like the one we've already seen in this chapter.

Waking up as needed to perform leasing makes sense if the service can acquire very long leases, or if the service doesn't consume many system resources while it is in its "sleeping" state. Delegating leasing to an external service may be easier though, and allows the back-end process to completely deactivate itself (possibly via the RMI activation mechanisms) when it is not in use. While the external leasing service would have to stay running the entire time, just as the back end would do if it were to manage leases itself, the external service has the advantage that it can be shared among *many* services.

If a service is implemented as a proxy object that communicates with a hardware device, then the approaches are much the same as in the software-only case. If the device has a JVM on it, it can easily do its own lease management during the time it is connected to the network. Much like a software service that consists of a back-end process and a proxy, this architecture is a natural fit for Jini: as long as the device is connected to the network, its proxies will be available since the device itself will manage its participation in a Jini community.

If the device does not have a JVM on it, then the most typical solution is to provide an external Java "wrapper" that does the leasing. This wrapper will typically run on a computer that the device is connected to (the host for a printer, for example). The wrapper may handle leasing itself, which means that it must stay active, or it can delegate lease management to an external service and then exit.

The final common type of service is where the service proxy *is* the service—it contains all the intelligence to implement all of its operations itself, without having to communicate with any external software process or hardware device. The first versions of the "Hello, World" service are examples of this type. Services like this must create some form of a wrapper process which will, at a minimum, do discovery to publish the proxy on lookup services. This wrapper can do as we did in our examples—stay active to manage leases—or it can use a leasing service and shut down after the proxy has been published with a lookup service.

Table 10–1 summarizes the leasing strategies commonly taken by services. The first column, *Service Architecture*, denotes how the service is structured. All services have proxies; some may have active back-end services, or devices that can handle their leasing for them. Others must take alternative approaches.

I should also note that this table only shows leasing strategies for services, which have a variety of implementation characteristics and expected lifetimes. Clients—applications that are merely consumers of Jini services—may have entirely different behaviors. In most cases, a client exists solely to make use of a service to accomplish some task. The task has a natural lifetime and the client will typically be running until the task is complete. Once the task is finished, the client's job is done, and it will usually cease running at that point. Since most clients will use resources leased from Jini services, they will need to continually renew the leases held on those resources. In such cases, it makes sense for a client's process to manage the leases used by that client, rather than delegating to a third party.

The Perils of Leasing

Clearly, applications that have some device or process that is naturally associated with the service, and can handle leases for it, map most directly to the Jini model. And, while Jini is explicitly designed to accommodate the model where leases can be delegated to external services, this model has some

Table 10–1 Leasing Strategies

Service Architecture	*Leasing Strategy*
Always-active back-end process written in Java	Back-end process handles lease renewal for the service proxy.
Always-active back-end process not written in Java	An external "wrapper" process manages Jini participation and lease renewal. This wrapper can do leasing itself internally, or can delegate it to an external leasing service.
Rarely-active back-end process	Either wake up the back-end process periodically to handle lease renewals, or defer to an external leasing delegate.
Device with embedded JVM	The device handles lease renewal for the service proxy.
Device without embedded JVM	Create an external wrapper for the device that runs on a nearby computer; this wrapper may defer to an external leasing service for lease renewal.
Proxy-only	Create an external wrapper for the proxy; this wrapper may stay running to do lease management, or may defer to an external leasing service for lease renewal.

weaknesses compared to allowing services to handle lease management themselves.

The external lease service is designed to automatically renew leases for a longer period of time than is typically granted in a single lease. This strategy, while it makes certain types of services possible (those that don't have any long-lived component, or have a back end that cannot for some reason do lease management), also weakens the durability of a Jini community because it separates the process performing the service from the process performing its leasing. This weakness happens in two ways.

First, using an external service to do leasing extends the "effective" duration of a lease, without requiring the extra proof-of-interest that such a duration would normally expect. That is, once a service asks a leasing service to renew its leases for the next month or year, the leasing service will handle this even if the original service dies. As long as the leasing service continues showing proof-of-interest by renewing the lease, most lease grantors will be more than happy to grant the renewal. Put succinctly, lease delegation grants the power of lease renewal without the natural lease expiration that would happen when a service goes away; the service process can crash without bringing down lease renewal with it.

Second, using an external service introduces another point of failure into the system: the leasing service itself. Since a resource consumer does not have to periodically check the leasing service, the leasing service can die without any of its services becoming aware of its death. Not only is the service unable to contact the leasing service to check or update the status of its leases, but the leases granted by the original grantor may silently expire without the service being any the wiser.

Obviously, using a third-party lease manager that runs in a separate JVM is a two-edged sword. There are situations in which such a strategy is very useful. For example, if a hardware device (like an air conditioner) is installed that will almost certainly never move or crash, a leasing service could perpetually renew its leases with little fear that the hardware will go away. Despite these benefits, however, leasing by an external process can seriously weaken the robustness and durability of a Jini community in which it is used, and you should think seriously about whether it makes sense for you to follow this strategy.

Delegation to an External JVM Versus Delegation to an Internal Class

Even though the basic code for `LeaseRenewalManager` and `LeaseService` look very similar, I need to reiterate the fundamental differences between them. While the `LeaseRenewalManager` class shown earlier in this chapter is a "third party" in the sense that it is a separate object meant to do lease negotiations, it is not a lease renewal *service*, and does not suffer from the same weaknesses of using an external process to do leasing. This is because the `LeaseRenewalManager` utility class is used *within* the back-end process that manages leases. When the back-end process fails, the lease renewal class also fails, and the system cleans up after itself in a normal way. By tying lease management to the service in this way, you gain the expected lease benefits of reliability and self-healing. It is only when lease management is done in a separate process, isolated from the service on whose behalf it is working, that we run into trouble.

Summary

This chapter has looked at the rationale behind leasing as a way to bring self-healing to distributed systems, and has tackled the issues around building lease consumers. Leasing is a fundamental part of Jini, and you'll certainly be using it when you lease service and event registrations as a lease consumer, and probably at other times as well. In most of these cases, you'll be using the high-level APIs described in this chapter. But at times you may need to get under the hood to tinker with the lower-level APIs, or—as you become more proficient with Jini—even build services that expose resources via leasing.

1.1 Update

As noted in the Preface to the Third Printing, there is a proposed LeaseRenewalService being considered for the 1.1 release of Jini. This service has a different programming model than the service presented here; see the preface for further details.

I have kept this example in the book because I believe it illustrates some important techniques, and shows a viable design alternative for this important service. But for most real-world applications, Sun's leasing service should be considered, as its implementations will almost certainly be more robust that any service designed for presentation in a few pages.

What's Next?

In the next chapter we'll look at the other half of the leasing equation—building services that export leased resources. The techniques we'll look at there will let you come "full circle," exporting leases that can be managed by clients using the classes described in this chapter!

EXPORTING LEASED RESOURCES

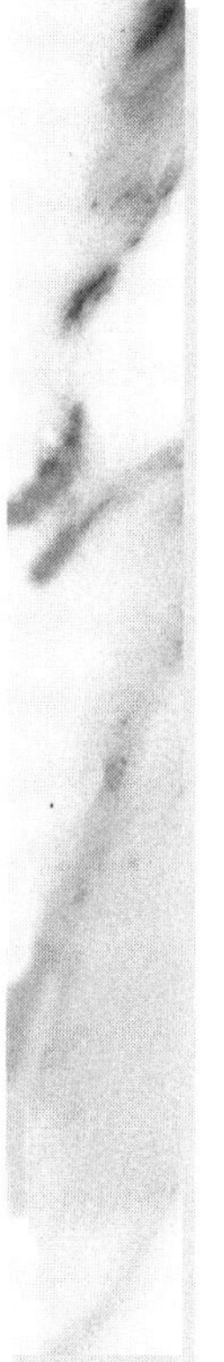

Topics in This Chapter

- Custom lease implementations
- How to use the Landlord paradigm
- How to use "cookies" to identify leased resources
- Creating a service that exports leased resources
- A custom object storage service

Chapter 11

In the last chapter, you saw how to use, renew, and manage leases that you hold on resources granted by a service. Knowledge about how to use leases in this way—being a lease consumer—is essential for being able to program in Jini. Since service and event registrations are leased, you have to be able to be an effective lease consumer to write even the simplest Jini services and clients.

But there is another side to the leasing equation, which we'll talk about in this chapter. Here, you'll see how to be an effective lease *grantor*. Many times you'll be writing a service that will export some resource to consumers. In such cases you may very well find it beneficial to lease these resources. By leasing the resources you export to others, your own programs can take advantage of all the benefits that leasing brings to Jini communities: Resources can be automatically freed when clients forget, or are unable, to release their resources themselves. You've already seen what the consumer of a lease has to do. But what are the steps that the grantor must follow?

In this chapter we'll look at the idioms and strategies for lease granting, and see the responsibilities that lease grantors have. We'll also investigate a set of "helper" classes that Sun provides that can make certain types of lease grantors easier to write. You can use these classes if you wish—they may make your life easier—but by the end of this chapter you should be able to write your own service-side lease granting code "from scratch" if you need to.

In any case, you should have a greater understanding of the "under the hood" details of how leasing is implemented in Jini.

Finally, we'll look at an example of a simple Jini storage service that leases object storage to its clients. This example illustrates how to write an effective lease grantor, and uses the Sun-provided "helper" classes.

Leasing Interfaces and Implementations

As you shall see, while Jini provides and standardizes a basic infrastructure for leasing—including the actual `Lease` interface and a few lease-related exception types—the core Jini interfaces actually say *nothing* about how leasing must be implemented by applications. In fact, when lease holders work with `Lease` objects, they are actually manipulating an *implementation-specific* lease type that has been provided to them by the lease grantor.

Let's look a bit more closely at how this works. Every lease grantor, whether a lookup service or an event generator or any other service that uses leasing as a way to control access to its resources, can decide for itself how it should best implement leasing. When it returns a lease to a resource consumer, all the grantor must do is return some object—any object—that implements the `Lease` interface. When the holders of this `Lease` object call methods on it to renew the lease, cancel the lease, and so on, the object they hold that implements the `Lease` interface actually sends a message back to the lease grantor, telling it that the holder wishes to change the state of the lease. The details of how this communication is done are private to the *particular* lease implementation returned by the grantor, and so the actual `Lease`-implementing object returned is also specific to the grantor. In a nutshell, Jini only specifies the client-side interfaces for dealing with leases; lease grantors can implement these interfaces in any way they see fit.

This strategy makes Jini tremendously flexible, and able to work over any number of communication substrates. Particular lease implementations can communicate with lease grantors via RMI, CORBA, or "raw" sockets. They could potentially even communicate over non-TCP networks, or via infrared links, as long as the chosen communications medium is supported by both the lease grantor and the lease holder.

But while this approach is flexible, it also means that providers of leases have a bit more work to do than they might otherwise. They have to decide how to implement leasing internally, and construct implementations of their

own proprietary lease protocols as well as the Lease implementations that will hide these protocols behind the standard leasing APIs. They also must take care of the internal tasks of cleaning up after expired leases.

Fortunately, Jini provides a set of classes in the com.sun.jini.lease and com.sun.jini.lease.landlord packages that serve as great starting points for constructing lease providers. Be sure to note, however, that since these classes are not part of the net.jini package hierarchy, they are subject to change. But since these classes aren't standardized, there is also no requirement that you use them. If they save you time, great. If not, you may be better off building a completely custom leasing implementation for your service. Of the services provided by Sun's sample implementation of Jini 1.0, only the JavaSpaces service and the transaction manager service use these classes; the lookup service does not.

The Landlord Paradigm

Let's look at what these leasing packages provide in the way of support for building lease grantors. The most important interface is com.sun.jini.lease.Landlord. This interface defines an API that can be used with a particular lease implementation to construct most of the implementation of a lease grantor. You will create a new object that implements the Landlord interface, and is responsible for managing the resources that you are granting under lease to consumers.

Once you've provided an implementation of Landlord, you can simply "plug in" a particular lease implementation that Sun gives you that understands how to communicate with Landlord implementations. This lease type is called LandlordLease, and it is a class that implements the Lease interface, and can be shipped as-is to clients when they ask for a lease.

Let's look first at the Landlord interface, since this is the first bit of code you'll have to write if you're creating a lease provider.

```
package com.sun.jini.lease.landlord;

import java.rmi.Remote;
import net.jini.core.lease.LeaseMapException;
import net.jini.core.lease.UnknownLeaseException;

public interface Landlord extends Remote {
      public void cancel(Object cookie)
```

```
            throws UnknownLeaseException, RemoteException;
        public void cancelAll(Object[] cookies)
            throws LeaseMapException, RemoteException;
        public void renew(Object cookie, long extension)
            throws LeaseDeniedException, UnknownLeaseException,
                           RemoteException;
        public Landlord.RenewResults renewAll(Object[]
                                          cookies,
                                          long[] extensions)
            throws RemoteException;
}
```

This is a relatively simple interface to implement, since it has only four methods. The `cancel()` and `cancelAll()` methods cancel leases, and the `renew()` and `renewAll()` methods renew leases for a specified duration. These methods are invoked when a client holding a `LandlordLease` invokes `cancel()`, `renew()`, and so on. The `cancelAll()` and `renewAll()` versions are invoked when a set of leases batched together into a `LeaseMap` is canceled or renewed as a group.

But what are the "cookie" arguments in all of these methods? A cookie is a unique token that you use internally to identify leased resources; you decide on the cookies you will use when you build your landlord implementation. When you ship out a lease to a client, you embed in it a cookie for the resource it represents. When a caller invokes `cancel()` or `renew()` on this lease, the lease performs an RMI method invocation back to your `Landlord` implementation, passing the cookie that uniquely identifies the leased resource. It's up to you to decide on an intelligent mapping between cookies and resources.

Even though `Landlord` is only an interface, it does dictate certain implementation details for you. In particular, your `Landlord` implementation must be a `RemoteObject`, since the `LandlordLeases` that you will send to clients use RMI to communicate back to the `Landlord`.

One other detail to mention here is the return value of the `renewAll()` method. The object that is returned from this call is an instance of `RenewResults`, which is a nested class defined inside the `Landlord` interface. This class simply contains an array of renewal times for the leases that were successfully renewed, and an array of exceptions for the leases that were denied.

I've talked about how `Landlords` and `LandlordLeases` communicate with each other, and how they use cookies to convey information that uniquely identifies leased resources. But so far I haven't said anything about *how* `LandlordLeases` get created and how they get returned.

For the latter part—how leases get returned—you're on your own. Jini, and the `Landlord` interface, define no particular interfaces for getting leases from resource providers. The way leases are asked for and returned is up to the particular service that grants leases. You've even seen a couple of different ways to ask for and receive leases so far in the standard Jini services: you ask for lookup registrations by calling `register()` on a lookup service, and the lease is returned in a `ServiceRegistration`; you ask for event solicitations by calling `notify()` on a lookup service, and the lease is returned in an `EventRegistration`. The particular APIs you decide on to allow clients to ask for resources and get leases are completely up to you, and should be chosen based on what makes sense for your particular service and the resources you are exporting.

As for how leases get created, the `Landlord` classes do have something to say. The `com.sun.jini.lease.LandlordLeaseFactory` interface defines an API for "factory" objects that can be used to create `LandlordLeases`. The `Factory` class, which is defined as a static nested class within the `LandlordLease` class, provides a `LandlordLeaseFactory` implementation that creates these leases.

The way you use this factory is simple. Once you've decided on the API that clients will use to ask for leases, you implement this API by calling into the factory for `LandlordLeases` to have it create leases that you will return to clients.

The `LandlordLeaseFactory` API has only one method:

```
package com.sun.jini.lease.landlord;

import net.jini.core.lease.Lease;
import net.jini.core.lease.LeaseDeniedException;

public interface LandlordLeaseFactory {
      public Lease newLease(Object cookie,
                            Landlord landlord,
                            long duration)
                               throws LeaseDeniedException;
}
```

The factory class inside `LandlordLease` implements `newLease()` to return new `LandlordLeases`. You pass it the cookie that uniquely identifies the resource associated with the new lease, a reference to the `Landlord` object that the lease will call back to, and the duration to assign to the lease. The duration here is the *actual* duration that you are granting the lease for—the client may have asked for a longer value, but here you pass the duration that you've decided to grant the lease for.

Core Tip: Don't grant leases for *more* time than asked.

When a caller asks for a lease and supplies a requested duration, you are free to grant a lease that is of a duration less than or equal to the requested duration. But you should never grant a lease for longer than the requested duration.

Granting extended leases is simply asking clients to do more work than they would normally do—such as canceling their leases explicitly when they no longer need them.

Identifying Leased Resources

So far we've seen how `LandlordLeases` communicate with `Landlords`, and how these leases get created by `LandlordLeaseFactories`. Let's now revisit how to associate leases with leased resources, and how to identify resources with the cookies received from client leases.

When you create your `Landlord` implementation, you must decide on a type of object to use as the "cookie" values that you bind into leases, and that uniquely identify leased resources.

When you write your service that exports leased resources, only you understand the internals of how these resources will be stored and arranged. If the resources are kept internally in a hash table, then the hash code of the individual objects may suffice to uniquely identify them. Such an arrangement would also permit the resource that is associated with a given lease to be quickly found given the hash code. So, in this set up, using the hash code as the cookie value that you stuff into leases is a good approach to maintaining this association between leases you dole out and the resources you keep track of internally.

Other services may have different arrangements for how their leased resources are stored. In almost every case, an effective cookie type will be one that allows quick access to the underlying resource whenever it comes in to the `Landlord`. Second, cookies should be relatively secure so that if a client manages to get a hold of a cookie by some means, it cannot forge a lease to a resource that it doesn't hold. Finally, a good cookie type will always *uniquely* identify the *association* between the lease and the resource. That is, for any given pair of resource and its lease, there should only be one cookie that identifies this pair.

Let's look at this last requirement in a bit more detail. Suppose the resource you are leasing access to is an item in a fixed-length array (we'll come back to this hypothetical situation in our example for this chapter). Clients might ask for a lease on a slot in the array. Clearly, the index of the item

in the array is one choice for a cookie that uniquely identifies the resource—such a value always identifies only one array item and, when it is returned to the `Landlord`, it can be used to find the associated resource very quickly.

Unfortunately, this cookie only identifies the resource, not the lease; effective cookies must identify *both* parts of the association. Let's look at what can happen if you don't include some identifier for the lease in the cookie. Suppose you grant a lease to a particular item in the array, say item 12, and ship out a lease containing this cookie to a client. Now suppose that this client holds on to the lease for a long period of time, past the lease's expiration time, without renewing it. Now, if the holder of the now-expired lease object contacts the grantor to renew the lease, the cookie—the number 12—will be sent to the landlord without any way of knowing that the lease containing this cookie has already expired. This situation is particularly problematic if the grantor has already issued *new* leases to clients on this same slot 12 in the array—it now has no way to identify or distinguish the expired leases from the newly granted ones.

Because of situations like this, it is necessary to design cookie types in such a way that they not only allow unique and quick access to the underlying resource, but that they also distinguish leases from one another.

Implementing the Landlord Interface

Let's now look at how to build implementations of the `Landlord` interface. These implementations will vary depending on what type of resource you are granting access to, but the basic structure of most `Landlord` implementations will have at least some similarities.

First, and as mentioned, landlords need to be able to track the resources that they expose via leasing, and map from cookies that they receive into leases. They should design these cookies so that they can tell if a client is using a lease that has already expired, or is otherwise no longer valid, so that they can report `UnknownLeaseException` back to the caller.

Second, landlords need to decide on their policies for granting leases. This means that they should decide what the maximum lease duration they will grant is, and when they should deny leases. Some landlords may always grant a requested lease for any resource, as long as it is within certain bounds. Other landlords may grant different lease times depending on the resource that is being asked for.

Finally, landlords also need to do their own cleanup and management of resource deallocation whenever leases expire. That is, Jini doesn't provide any classes that developers can use that will automatically deallocate resources whenever leases expire. So, when you build your landlord implementation, you'll need to figure out how best to implement deallocation.

A common implementation approach would be to have a thread that wakes up periodically and scans all the resources to see which are held by expired leases. Those resources could then be deallocated and any necessary bookkeeping could be done to flag that the resources are available for re-leasing. Another strategy would be to only do the work to determine if a resource should be deallocated "on demand." That is, whenever the landlord gets another request to cancel or renew a lease, it could then scan over the resources it holds to assess which can be deallocated.

Strategies like the first are more appropriate when there is a possibly large set of resources that the service grants access to, and freeing unused resources as soon as possible will be a win. Strategies like the second are simpler to implement and may be beneficial if the number (or total size) of leased resources is small, and the time required to do any deallocation is small enough to not unduly slow down the implementation of `cancel()` or `renew()`.

Landlords must take care of how they allocate memory. In particular, they probably will want to create "surrogate" data structures that hold the information needed for lease implementations (expiration times, cookies, and so forth), and not use actual lease objects internally in the landlord.

This is particularly true in the case of the `LandlordLease` implementation that comes with Jini. You might be tempted to just use these `LandlordLease` objects internally to do your lease bookkeeping—after all, they have expiration times and cookies, and all the other tidbits of information that you need to implement leasing. But recall that these objects are meant to be serialized and returned to clients, and that they contain within them remote references to the landlord itself. So, if your landlord uses these objects internally for bookkeeping, changing the values of their expiration times merely has the effect of calling back to the landlord itself! So you will need to create your own bookkeeping data structures that maintain information about expiration times and cookies and keep these associated with leased resources. Other implementations of the `Lease` interface may afford other strategies. For example, if your lease is a remote object, you can keep the one "true" copy of the lease yourself, and return RMI stubs for it to clients. In this case, it may make sense to use the actual remote lease object as the bookkeeping object for your lease implementation.

Jini provides a handful of interfaces that you can use to assist in the implementation of your landlord, although there is no requirement to use these and, in the case of very simple landlords, the work required to use them may outweigh the benefit you might get.

The com.sun.jini.lease.LeasedResource interface provides a way for you to associate with your resources any extra information that's required to do leasing. This interface provides methods for fetching the cookie associated with a resource, and getting and setting the current expiration time for the lease on the resource. If the resources you lease implement this interface, you can easily scan over them, determine which have expired, and map resources into cookies.

The com.sun.jini.lease.LeasePolicy interface works in cooperation with LeasedResources to implement a particular leasing policy. This interface has methods that allow you to determine if a LeasedResource has already expired, and that will compute an actual granted lease time based on a requested lease time. Particular implementations of this interface, such as LeaseDurationPolicy in the same package, fulfill these requests based on initialized parameters that control maximum and default leasing times.

Finally, the com.sun.jini.lease.LeaseManager interface provides a way to track lease status. Some implementations of LeasePolicy, including the LeaseDurationPolicy one that comes with Jini, allow the use of a LeaseManager to monitor leasing. Think of the LeaseManager as a listener interface that objects can implement to get callbacks whenever leases are initially granted or renewed.

Again, some of these interfaces may help; others may not be worth the work. In the example we'll see shortly, I'll use the LeasedResource interface as a handy tool to associate bookkeeping information with resources, but ignore the other lease helper interfaces.

An Example

Let's look now at an example of how you might implement a lease grantor using the Landlord tools that come with Jini (see Listing 11–1). The program shown is a provider of storage "slots"—this means that the program keeps a fixed number of items that it is willing to grant to callers for storage of their objects. Once the slots run out, new clients cannot acquire storage. Slots are leased so that if clients die or do not renew their interest, the slot provider can clean house and deallocate slots.

This example is a (very!) scaled down example of how a more general Jini storage engine might work—such an engine could provide storage of arbitrary Java objects, under lease to consumers.

Let's work through some of the design decisions in this example. First, the slot resources are implemented as a fixed-length array. Thus, there is a natural way to refer to the individual resources—the index of a slot within the array uniquely identifies it. So this index can serve as *part* of the cookie that we'll stuff into leases so that we can map them back on to resources later. But we also need a way to uniquely identify the leases that we've granted. For this task, let's take a simple approach—the slot provider keeps a counter. Whenever a new lease is issued, it is assigned the current value of the counter and the counter is incremented. So, the cookies that we will use are a tuple consisting of both the index of the resource and the unique identifier for the lease.

Since we never need to map from the lease counter number *back* into a lease, we don't need to keep around a hash table or other data structure that maintains all of our leases. We only need to know when a request comes in if the resource specified by the cookie is still held by the lease specified in the cookie.

Each slot in the table is a class that implements the `LeasedResource` interface, and contains an arbitrary object as a value (this is the object that clients can use to store data in). Each slot knows its expiration time, and the cookie that is associated with the lease that holds that resource. Since slots know their expiration time, the landlord can easily iterate over them and identify ones that have expired. Since slots remember the cookies of the leases that are associated with them, the landlord can easily walk the slots and see if any given cookie matches the cookie for a particular slot.

So we've now decided on how our resources will be stored, and how the bookkeeping information needed for leasing will be bound into the resources. We still need to decide on a policy for granting leases, and a strategy for cleaning up unused resources.

The policy used in this example is quite simple—it grants any requested lease up to a maximum time of 10 minutes. Requests for leases longer than 10 minutes are truncated down to this maximum value.

Since our landlord implementation only allows access to a fixed (and small) number of resources, we won't use a thread to wake up and deallocate stored objects. Instead, let's use the "on demand" approach. Whenever the landlord needs to make a decision to cancel or renew a lease, it scans over the `LeasedResources` it has and, at that time, deallocates any unused data.

First, let's look at the interface that consumers of slots will use to communicate with slot providers.

The interface here, which is a remote interface—it uses RMI for communication between the slot consumer and slot provider—has only two methods. The first, `leaseFreeSlot()`, passes in an object that the slot consumer

Listing 11–1 `SlotProvider.java`

```
package corejini.chapter10;

import java.rmi.Remote;
import java.rmi.RemoteException;
import net.jini.core.lease.UnknownLeaseException;

public interface SlotProvider extends Remote {
    public SlotResult leaseFreeSlot(Object value,
                                    long duration)
                                  throws RemoteException;
    public Object getValue(Object key)
            throws RemoteException, UnknownLeaseException;
}
```

wishes to be stored in a free slot, along with a requested duration. The method returns a `SlotResult` object (Listing 11–2) if a slot is available, or null if no slots are free.

If a consumer successfully acquires a slot, it can then access the data stored in its slot by passing in a special "key" that identifies the data held there. (In this particular application, only the owner of a slot can access the data held there—the key is a way to ensure that applications can't read each others' slots. You could easily think of modifications to this program to allow sharing of objects among clients.)

The `SlotResult` return value contains the index of the slot, the lease on the slot, and a key to be used to fetch the value back out of the slot again. This key is effectively "opaque," meaning that the client cannot tell what's in it, and shouldn't care; it's merely a token to gain access to the stored data.

Listing 11–2 `SlotResult.java`

```
package corejini.chapter10;

import net.jini.core.lease.Lease;
import java.io.Serializable;

public class SlotResult implements Serializable {
    protected int index;
    protected Lease lease;
    protected Object key;
```

Listing 11–2 `SlotResult.java` **(continued)**

```
    SlotResult(int index, Lease lease, Object key) {
        this.index = index;
        this.lease = lease;
        this.key = key;
    }

    public int getIndex() {
        return index;
    }
    public Lease getLease() {
        return lease;
    }
    public Object getKey() {
        return key;
    }
    public String toString() {
        return "slot " + index + " leased until " +
            lease.getExpiration();
    }
}
```

Now let's look at the provider of slots, Listing 11–3. This is code that will implement the remote `SlotProvider` interface, and will grant access to slots on a leased basis. Note that the code shown here, for simplicity, is not a Jini service. Instead, it is a "stand-alone" RMI program that grants access to slots. The goal here is to show how leasing works internally, not how to build yet another Jini program that interacts with lookup and discovery.

Listing 11–3 `SlotProviderImpl.java`

```
package corejini.chapter10;

import com.sun.jini.lease.*;
import com.sun.jini.lease.landlord.*;
import net.jini.core.lease.*;
import java.rmi.RemoteException;
import java.rmi.Naming;
import java.rmi.server.UnicastRemoteObject;
import java.net.InetAddress;
import java.util.Map;
import java.util.HashMap;
import java.io.Serializable;
```

Listing 11–3 `SlotProviderImpl.java` (continued)

```
class CookieType implements Serializable {
    int index;
    int count;

    CookieType(int index, int count) {
        this.index = index;
        this.count = count;
    }

    public boolean equals(Object o) {
        if (!(o instanceof CookieType))
            return false;

        CookieType other = (CookieType) o;

       return other.index == index && other.count == count;
    }

    public String toString() {
        return "idx=" + index + ", count=" + count;
    }
}

public class SlotProviderImpl extends UnicastRemoteObject
    implements SlotProvider {
    protected LeasedSlot[] slotMap = new LeasedSlot[8];
    protected MyLandlord landlord = null;
    protected LandlordLease.Factory factory =
            new LandlordLease.Factory();
    protected static int nextCount = 0;

    static class LeasedSlot implements LeasedResource {
        protected CookieType cookie;
        protected long expiration;
        protected Object value;

        public LeasedSlot(int index) {
            this(index, -1);
        }
        public LeasedSlot(int index, int count) {
            this.cookie = new CookieType(index, count);
            this.expiration = 0;
        }
```

Listing 11–3 `SlotProviderImpl.java` **(continued)**

```
        public Object getCookie() {
            return cookie;
        }
        public long getExpiration() {
            return expiration;
        }
        public void setExpiration(long expiration) {
            this.expiration = expiration;
        }
        Object getValue() {
            return value;
        }
        void setValue(Object value) {
            this.value = value;
        }
        void setCookieCount(int count) {
            cookie.count = count;
        }
        int getCookieCount() {
            return cookie.count;
        }
    }

    class MyLandlord extends UnicastRemoteObject
            implements Landlord {
       protected static final int MAX_LEASE = 1000 * 60 * 10;

        public MyLandlord() throws RemoteException {
            super();
        }

        public long getRealDuration(long duration) {
           if (duration > MAX_LEASE || duration == Lease.ANY){
                return MAX_LEASE;
            } else {
                return duration;
            }
        }

        public void cancel(Object cookie)
                    throws UnknownLeaseException {
            long currentTime = System.currentTimeMillis();

            System.out.println("+++ landlord cancel: " +
                                          cookie);
```

Listing 11–3 `SlotProviderImpl.java` **(continued)**

```
        LeasedSlot slot = validateSlot(cookie);

        slot.setCookieCount(-1);
        slot.setValue(null);
    }

    public void cancelAll(Object[] cookies)
                throws LeaseMapException {
        System.out.println("landlord cancel all: ");
        Map exceptionMap = null;
        LeaseMapException lme = null;

        for (int i=0 ; i<cookies.length ; i++) {
            try {
                cancel(cookies[i]);
            } catch (UnknownLeaseException ex) {
                if (lme == null) {
                    exceptionMap = new HashMap();
                    lme =
                     new LeaseMapException("cancelAll"
                                   + " failed",
                                     exceptionMap);
                }
             Lease lease = factory.newLease(cookies[i],
                                   landlord, 0);
             exceptionMap.put(lease, ex);
            }
        }

        if (lme != null)
            throw lme;
    }

    public long renew(Object cookie, long extension)
                throws UnknownLeaseException {
        System.out.println("+++ landlord renew " +
                     cookie + "for " + extension);

         LeasedSlot slot = validateSlot(cookie);

        extension = getRealDuration(extension);
        slot.setExpiration(extension +
                         System.currentTimeMillis());
        return extension;
    }
```

Listing 11–3 `SlotProviderImpl.java` **(continued)**

```
        public Landlord.RenewResults renewAll(Object[]
                                              cookies,
                                          long[] extensions) {
            long[] granted = new long[cookies.length];
            Exception[] denied = null;

            for (int i=0 ; i<cookies.length ; i++) {
                try {
                    long result = renew(cookies[i],
                                        extensions[i]);
                    granted[i] = result;
                } catch (Exception ex) {
                    if (denied == null) {
                      denied = new Exception[cookies.length
                                             + 1];
                    }
                    denied[i+1] = ex;
                    granted [i] = -1;
                }
            }

            Landlord.RenewResults results =
                new Landlord.RenewResults(granted, denied);
            return results;
        }
    }

    public SlotProviderImpl() throws RemoteException {
        super();

        for (int i=0 ; i<slotMap.length ; i++) {
            slotMap[i] = new LeasedSlot(i);
        }

        landlord = new MyLandlord();
    }

    public synchronized SlotResult leaseFreeSlot(Object
                                                 value,
                                                 long duration)
        throws RemoteException {
        long currentTime = System.currentTimeMillis();
        duration = landlord.getRealDuration(duration);

        // return the first unused free slot
        for (int i=0 ; i<slotMap.length ; i++) {
           LeasedSlot slot = slotMap[i];
```

Listing 11–3 `SlotProviderImpl.java` (continued)

```
            if (slot.getCookieCount() == -1 ||
               slot.getExpiration() < currentTime) {
               slot.setExpiration(duration + currentTime);
               slot.setValue(value);
               slot.setCookieCount(nextCount++);

               System.out.println("+++ setting slot " + i +
                                        " to " + value);
               System.out.println("    cookie is " +
                                        slot.getCookie());

                Lease lease =
                     factory.newLease(slot.getCookie(),
                                  landlord,
                                  duration + currentTime);
                return new SlotResult(i, lease,
                                        slot.getCookie());
            }
        }

        // no available slots
        return null;
    }

    public synchronized Object getValue(Object key)
            throws RemoteException, UnknownLeaseException{
         LeasedSlot slot = validateSlot(key);

         return slot.getValue();
    }

    LeasedSlot validateSlot(Object cookie)
            throws UnknownLeaseException {
         long currentTime = System.currentTimeMillis();

         if (!(cookie instanceof CookieType)) {
              throw new UnknownLeaseException("Bad type");
         }

         int index = ((CookieType) cookie).index;
         int count = ((CookieType) cookie).count;

         if (index < 0 || index >= slotMap.length) {
              throw new UnknownLeaseException("Bad data");
         }
```

Listing 11–3 `SlotProviderImpl.java` **(continued)**

```
        LeasedSlot slot = slotMap[index];

        if (slot.getCookieCount() == -1) {
          throw new UnknownLeaseException("Slot not under" +
                                                      " lease");
        }

        if (slot.getExpiration() < currentTime) {
             slot.setCookieCount(-1);
             slot.setValue(null);
             throw new UnknownLeaseException("Already " +
                                                   "expired");
        }

        if (!slot.getCookie().equals(cookie)) {
          throw new UnknownLeaseException("Wrong cookie for"
                      + " slot; slot has been released.");
        }

        return slot;
    }

    public static void main(String[] args) {
        if (args.length != 1) {
            System.err.println("Usage: SlotProvider " +
                                        "<binding_string>",
            System.exit(1);
        }

        try {
            String host =
                 InetAddress.getLocalHost().getHostName();
            String url = "rmi://" + host + "/" + args[0];
            SlotProviderImpl spi = new SlotProviderImpl();
            Naming.rebind(url, spi);
            System.out.println("SlotProvider bound to " +
                                          url);
        } catch (Exception ex) {
          System.err.println("Couldn't create SlotProvider:"
                                      + ex.getMessage());
            System.exit(1);
        }
    }
}
```

The first class here, `CookieType`, defines the cookies that the slot provider will use to associate leases and resources. The `CookieType` class holds two separate values: an index, which is used to identify a particular resource, and a unique counter, which is used to identify a lease. Whenever a cookie of this type comes in, the slot provider can quickly identify the resource it refers to by looking up the index. And, if the resource stores the counter value of the lease that owns it, the provider can easily see if an incoming cookie was sent by the lease that holds the resource, or another, out-of-date lease.

The `CookieType` class is `Serializable` since it will be transmitted along with leases to clients.

The `SlotProviderImpl` class is what actually implements the slot-providing interfaces. The class extends `UnicastRemoteObject` and implements `SlotProvider`. When a client contacts the slot provider, it will use the methods in the `SlotProvider` interface; this is also the same interface that a proxy would use to communicate with a back-end slot provider, if the code here were implemented as a Jini service. The resources it doles out to clients are elements from an array of `LeasedSlots`. The class also maintains an implementation of `Landlord`, which we'll see shortly, and a counter value that will be incremented whenever new leases are created.

Let's look first at the `LeasedSlot` class that makes up the elements of the resource array. `LeasedSlot` implements `LeasedResource`, so it has methods on it to get the cookie associated with a slot, get the expiration time, and so on. Each slot maintains three pieces of information: the cookie for the slot, the expiration time of the lease that currently owns the slot, and any object that a client may have stored here. If a slot is unowned, its cookie will be set to a special value indicating that the slot is available for leasing. Unowned or expired slots may have zero (uninitialized) expiration times, or may still have the expiration time of the lease that last owned them.

The next nested class that we see here is the landlord that will be used to interact with leases and manage slots. The class `MyLandlord` implements the `Landlord` interface, and extends `UnicastRemoteObject`, so it can work "out of the box" with the Sun-provided `LandlordLease` class. Even though the landlord is a remote object, its methods will never be seen directly by clients—they only access the methods on this class indirectly, through the lease objects that they hold.

The method `getRealDuration()` implements the "policy" for the landlord—the maximum lease duration and the default lease duration are the same, 10 minutes, and any requested lease is granted as long as it is under this value. Requests for leases longer than 10 minutes are shortened to this value.

The next few methods implement the `Landlord` interface. The `cancel()` method takes a cookie that may identify a lease/resource pairing. The method calls `validateSlot()` to make sure that the cookie does indeed represent a valid slot, and that the slot is indeed held by the lease represented by the cookie. The validation check, defined in the outer `SlotProviderImpl`, makes sure that the cookie is of the needed type (`CookieType`), that its index is within range, that the item referred to by the index is in fact leased, that it's not already expired, and that the slot is owned by the lease represented by the cookie. If any of these conditions are not true, `validateSlot()` raises an `UnknownLeaseException`. Otherwise, it returns the slot identified by the cookie.

Once `cancel()` has a valid slot in its hands, it frees the resources associated with the slot by setting the `value` member of the `LeasedSlot` to null, and setting the cookie `count` data to –1, which indicates that the slot is no longer under lease.

The implementation of `cancelAll()` iteratively calls `cancel()` for all the cookies passed to it. If any cancellation fails, the method creates a new `LeaseMapException` containing the failed lease and an exception that indicates why the cancellation failed. Note that the code here actually creates *new* leases to send back to the client in this case. The slot provider implementation never hangs on to the leases it sends to clients, so it simply creates new ones as needed for error reporting. The implementation of `equals()` on the `LandlordLease` class considers two leases to be the same if their cookies are the same and they have the same landlord. So clients will be able to take these new leases and compare them with the leases they hold using `equals()`.

The `renew()` and `renewAll()` methods work much the same as `cancel()` and `cancelAll()`; `renew()` first validates the incoming cookie as referring to a legitimate slot, and then computes the actual new duration to use for the lease by calling `getRealDuration()`. The new duration is stored in the `LeasedSlot`. The `renewAll()` method iterates through the incoming cookies and calls `renew()` for each. The results of the complete operation are returned in a `RenewResults` object, which contains an array of new lease times, and an array of exceptions. If the renewal succeeds, then the corresponding item in the `granted` array is set to the new lease duration. If the renewal fails, then the *next* item in the `denied` array is set—that is, failure of item *i* to renew causes the *i+1* element in the exceptions array to be set. And element *i* of the granted array is sent to –1

The `MyLandlord` class takes care of all the mechanics of lease management for the slot provider. When new leases are created, they are initialized to contain a reference to this landlord, and everything in the cancellation and renewal process happens automatically.

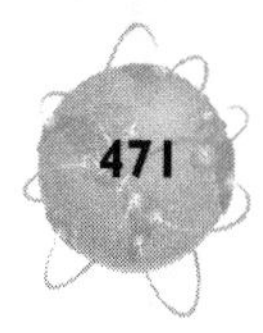

We still need to look at the remainder of the `SlotProviderImpl` class to see how it works; in particular, we need to see how it issues leases for new slots. When the `SlotProviderImpl` is first created, it initializes its array of `LeasedSlots` and creates an instance of `MyLandlord` to handle lease cancellations and renewals.

Clients, when they need a slot, will go through the `leaseFreeSlot()` method. This method takes a value that the client wishes to store, and a requested lease duration. It will return a `SlotResult` if a slot was granted, or null if no more slots are available. The implementation of this method is where new leases get created. The code converts the requested duration into an actual duration based on the policy implemented by `MyLandlord`. It then iterates through the array of slots, looking for any slot that is unleased or already expired. The first time it finds such a slot, it sets its expiration to the computed expiration time, stores the client-supplied value, and initializes a new cookie by incrementing the lease counter to get a unique number. The factory is called to produce a new lease with that cookie and expiration time, and a `SlotResult` is returned to the client. The `key` value that is returned in the `SlotResult` to identify the client's data is simply the cookie value.

Note that it is the `leaseFreeSlot()` method that is responsible for freeing data associated with an expired lease. If a client explicitly cancels a lease, then the `MyLandlord` class will free its data. But data held by expired leases are only cleaned up when a new slot is needed. This is an example of the "on demand" style of resource deallocation mentioned earlier; an alternative would be to have a thread that periodically wakes up and scans the slot array for expired data that can be freed.

The `getValue()` method is used by a client to retrieve the data stored in its slot, given a key to that data returned in the `SlotResult`. The `validateSlot()` method is called to make sure that the key is legitimate, and that the data stored in the corresponding slot is owned by the holder of the key. If it is, then the value is returned.

Finally, the `main()` for the slot provider implementation creates a new `SlotProviderImpl` and binds it into the RMI registry at a name supplied on the command line. Since the code here isn't a Jini service, we cannot rely on discovery and lookup for a slot consumer to rendezvous with the provider. So the code allows the person running the provider to supply a name that the client can use to find it; more on this when we talk about compiling and running the example.

Let's look now at a simple client (Listing 11–4) that will use the slot provider to store data.

Listing 11–4 `SlotClient.java`

```
package corejini.chapter10;

import java.rmi.*;
import net.jini.core.lease.Lease;
import com.sun.jini.lease.LeaseRenewalManager;

public class SlotClient implements Runnable {
    protected SlotProvider provider = null;
    protected LeaseRenewalManager mgr = null;

    public SlotClient() {
        mgr = new LeaseRenewalManager();
    }

    public void setSlotProvider(SlotProvider sp) {
        provider = sp;
    }

    public void run() {
        SlotResult res1, res2, res3;

        while (true) {
            try {
                res1 = provider.leaseFreeSlot("Hello", 10000);
                if (res1 != null) {
                    mgr.renewUntil(res1.getLease(), Lease.ANY,
                                   null);
                } else {
                    System.out.println("No more slots!");
                }

                res2 = provider.leaseFreeSlot("there", 10000);
                if (res2 != null) {
                    mgr.renewUntil(res2.getLease(),
                             System.currentTimeMillis() +
                             (1000 * 20), null);
                } else {
                    System.out.println("No more slots!");
                }

                res3 = provider.leaseFreeSlot("World!",
                                              10000);
```

Listing 11–4 `SlotClient.java` (continued)

```
            if (res3 != null) {
              mgr.renewUntil(res3.getLease(), Lease.ANY,
                                   null);
            } else {
                System.out.println("No more slots!");
            }

            try {
                System.err.println("Sleeping for a " +
                                         "while...");
                Thread.sleep(1000 * 30);
            } catch (InterruptedException ex) {
            }

            try {
                if (res3 != null) {
                  System.out.println("Value of slot: " +
                      provider.getValue(res3.getKey()));
                  System.out.println("Cancelling lease");
                      mgr.cancel(res3.getLease());
                  System.out.println("After cancel.");
                  System.out.println("Value of slot: " +
                      provider.getValue(res3.getKey()));
                }
            } catch (Exception ex) {
                System.err.println("Error: " +
                                   ex.getMessage());
            }

            try {
                System.err.println("Sleeping for a "
                                         + "while...");
                Thread.sleep(1000 * 30);
            } catch (InterruptedException ex) {
            }

        } catch (RemoteException ex) {
            System.err.println("Bogus: " +
                                   ex.getMessage());
            ex.printStackTrace();
        }
    }
}
```

Listing 11–4 `SlotClient.java` (continued)

```
    public static void main(String[] args) {
        if (args.length != 1) {
            System.err.println("Usage: SlotClient <url>");
            System.exit(1);
        }
        try {
            SlotProvider sp = (SlotProvider)
                 Naming.lookup(args[0]);
            SlotClient slotClient = new SlotClient();
            slotClient.setSlotProvider(sp);
            new Thread(slotClient).start();
        } catch (Exception ex) {
           System.err.println("Couldn't start SlotClient:" +
                                       ex.getMessage());
            System.exit(1);
        }
    }
}
```

The `SlotClient` class is an application which iteratively acquires and releases slots from a `SlotProvider`. When the `SlotClient` is started, it creates a `LeaseRenewalManager` to take care of the leases returned by the `SlotProviderImpl`. We've now come full circle! We're actually supplying the leases that will be managed by the `LeaseRenewalManager` class.

The bulk of the code here is in the `run()` method for the class, which continually acquires resources. During each iteration of the loop, the method tries to get three slots. Each is initially leased for 10 seconds and, if a slot can be successfully grabbed, it will be renewed. At each iteration, the first is renewed indefinitely, using the `Lease.ANY` flag. The second is set to expire 20 seconds from the current time. And the third is also renewed indefinitely. After the three slots are acquired, the code sleeps for a few seconds, and then fetches the value of the third resource to show that it can be successfully retrieved. The lease on this resource is then canceled, and so further attempts to fetch its value result in an `UnknownLeaseException`. After another sleep, the entire process repeats itself.

The program will continue acquiring one new, indefinitely leased resource each time through the loop. After a while, it will exhaust the resources available in our `SlotProviderImpl`, and no new slots can be acquired.

Compiling and Running the Examples

On Windows: first, compile the main program files for both the "service" implementation and the client. The Java compiler should build all the class files needed by each, so you can compile the `SlotProviderImpl` into the `service` directory and the `SlotProviderClient` into the `client` directory.

```
javac -classpath C:\jini1_0\lib\jini-core.jar;
                          C:\jini1_0\lib\jini-ext.jar;
                          C:\jini1_0\lib\sun-util.jar;
                          C:\service
            -d C:\service
      C:\corejini\chapter10\SlotProviderImpl.java

javac -classpath C:\jini1_0\lib\jini-core.jar;
                          C:\jini1_0\lib\jini-ext.jar;
                          C:\jini1_0\lib\sun-util.jar;
                          C:\client
            -d C:\client
      C:\corejini\chapter10\SlotProviderClient.java
```

Next, you need to build the RMI stubs for the two remote classes in this example: the `SlotProviderImpl` and the nested `MyLandlord` class. Make sure that the stubs wind up in the `service-dl` directory since they'll need to be downloadable by clients.

```
rmic -classpath C:\jdk1.2\jre\lib\rt.jar;
                         C:\jini1_0\lib\jini-core.jar;
                         C:\jini1_0\lib\jini-ext.jar;
                         C:\jini1_0\lib\sun-util.jar;
                         C:\service
       -d C:\service-dl
corejini.chapter10.SlotProviderImpl
corejini.chapter10.SlotProviderImpl.MyLandlord
```

Finally you're set to run! Make sure you pass in a security policy file, a correct code base, and a file to use for persistent storage for the service. Start the service first. Note that it doesn't need a security policy file, since it won't be downloading any code (it's not a "real" Jini service, and therefore doesn't need to download a lookup service proxy). You'll have to give a name to the slot provider so that the client can rendezvous with it later. This can be any arbitrary string, I've used "foo."

```
java -cp C:\jini1_0\lib\jini-core.jar;
                C:\jini1_0\lib\jini-ext.jar;
                C:\jini1_0\lib\sun-util.jar;
                C:\service
          -Djava.rmi.server.codebase=http://myhost:8085/
      corejini.chapter10.SlotProviderImpl foo
```

And then start the client. The client needs no codebase since it exports no downloadable code. To allow the client to connect with the provider, you must pass in an RMI URL on the command line. This should have the host on which the provider is running, followed by the string that you just used (the provider will print the URL you should use when it starts).

```
java -cp C:\jini1_0\lib\jini-core.jar;
                C:\jini1_0\lib\jini-ext.jar;
                C:\jini1_0\lib\sun-util.jar;
                C:\service
          -Djava.security.policy=C:\policy
      corejini.chapter10.SlotProviderClient
                rmi://turbodog.parc.xerox.com/foo
```

On Solaris: first, compile the main program files for both the "service" implementation and the client. The Java compiler should build all the class files needed by each, so you can compile the `SlotProviderImpl` into the `service` directory and the `SlotProviderClient` into the `client` directory.

```
javac -classpath /files/jini1_0/lib/jini-core.jar:
                        /files/jini1_0/lib/jini-ext.jar:
                        /files/jini1_0/lib/sun-util.jar:
                        /files/service
          -d /files/service
      /files/corejini/chapter10/SlotProviderImpl.java

javac -classpath /files/jini1_0/lib/jini-core.jar:
                        /files/jini1_0/lib/jini-ext.jar:
                        /files/jini1_0/lib/sun-util.jar:
                        /files/client
          -d /files/client
      /files/corejini/chapter10/SlotProviderClient.java
```

Next, you need to build the RMI stubs for the two remote classes in this example: the `SlotProviderImpl` and the nested `MyLandlord` class. Make sure that the stubs wind up in the `service-dl` directory since they'll need to be downloadable by clients.

```
rmic -classpath /jdk1.2/jre/lib/rt.jar:
                        /files/jini1_0/lib/jini-core.jar:
                        /files/jini1_0/lib/jini-ext.jar:
                        /files/jini1_0/lib/sun-util.jar:
                        /files/service
       -d /files/service-dl
corejini.chapter10.SlotProviderImpl
corejini.chapter10.SlotProviderImpl.MyLandlord
```

Finally you're set to run! Make sure you pass in a security policy file, a correct code base, and a file to use for persistent storage for the service. Start the service first. Note that it doesn't need a security policy file, since it won't be downloading any code (it's not a "real" Jini service, and therefore doesn't need to download a lookup service proxy). You'll have to give a name to the slot provider so that the client can rendezvous with it later. This can be any arbitrary string, I've used "foo."

```
java -cp /files/jini1_0/lib/jini-core.jar:
                  /files/jini1_0/lib/jini-ext.jar:
                  /files/jini1_0/lib/sun-util.jar:
                  /files/service
             -Djava.rmi.server.codebase=http://myhost:8085/
      corejini.chapter10.SlotProviderImpl foo
```

And then start the client. The client needs no codebase since it exports no downloadable code. To allow the client to connect with the provider, you must pass in an RMI URL on the command line. This should have the host on which the provider is running, followed by the string that you just used (the provider will print the URL you should use when it starts).

```
java -cp /files/jini1_0/lib/jini-core.jar:
                  /files/jini1_0/lib/jini-ext.jar:
                  /files/jini1_0/lib/sun-util.jar:
                  /files/service
             -Djava.security.policy=/files/policy
      corejini.chapter10.SlotProviderClient
                  rmi://turbodog.parc.xerox.com/foo
```

Summary

This chapter has looked at the grantor side of leasing in Jini. In the last two chapters, we've seen a complete leasing loop—all the way from clients asking for leased resources, to services that grant leases, and back to the clients that must manage their leases. We've also looked at some common APIs that Sun provides for granting leases, using the landlord paradigm. These utility classes should be useful for a range of applications—Sun even uses them internally in the reference implementations of the Jini transaction manager and the JavaSpaces services—and can be applied to the leasing needs of many of the services you will write. But even if these classes aren't sufficient for you, or don't provide the abstractions you need, you should have a deep enough understanding of lease granting from this chapter to write your own custom leasing infrastructure.

What's Next?

So far in this book we've talked about a lot of the things that services need to do—participate in discovery, manage their leases, and so on. In the next chapter,we'll pull together all of the things that you as a service writer need to do to ensure that your services are "well-behaved" in the Jini environment.

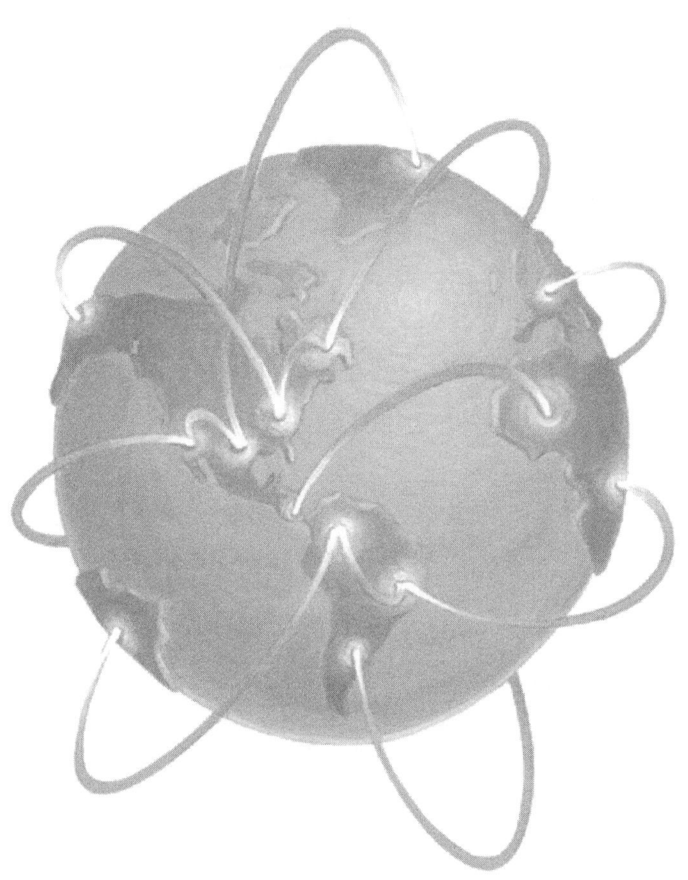

THE WELL-BEHAVED SERVICE

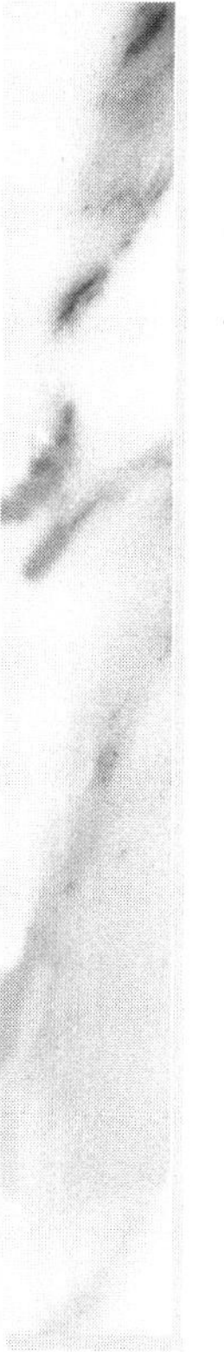

Topics in This Chapter

- Service responsibilities
- Creating administrable services
- Service user interfaces

Chapter 12

While Jini takes great care to make it unlikely that a single service can—through bad programming or software failure—disrupt an entire community, there are still a number of responsibilities that services have "to play well with others." We've looked at most of these responsibilities already: Jini services must follow the join protocol. This ensures that services will try at all costs to persistently maintain any configuration information that users have placed on them. It also provides guidelines for how Jini services connect to their communities—they must wait for a random amount of time before launching into discovery to prevent packet storms, for instance.

For most services, the join protocol represents the required essentials of being a Jini service; you should not deploy services that do not follow the join protocol, as they can disrupt other services in a community and will be difficult to manage.

But beyond these base requirements, there are a number of other jobs that a service can do to ensure that it is useful and useable in a range of contexts. Services should describe themselves through the use of attributes. Services can and should provide administrative interfaces that allow users to configure them. And services that are suitable for direct user interaction should provide user interface components that allow end users to interact with them directly.

In this chapter, we'll look at these "extra" requirements that can make the difference between a merely useable service and a well-tuned, product-quality service.

The Responsibilities of a Service

We've already spent a fair amount of time investigating the minimum requirements of services in Chapter 8. The join protocol, described there, lists the specifics of what services must do in order to work reliably and manageably in a Jini community. To recap:

- Services should wait a random amount of time when they start to prevent packet storms on their networks.
- Services should perform multicast discovery, joining any groups they have been configured to join, or the unnamed "public" group if they have not yet been configured.
- Services should use unicast discovery to connect to any explicitly configured URLs for lookup services.
- Services must renew their leases with all their lookup services until told to deregister with a lookup service.
- If a service loses contact with a lookup service found through unicast discovery, it must attempt periodically to reestablish contact with it.
- When a service is asked to change the set of attributes associated with it, it must make this change at all lookup servers it is registered with.
- Services must save configuration information persistently, so that it will be used even after restarts or crashes. This persistent information includes the service's unique ID, any lookup groups it should join, its attributes, and its explicitly configured lookup services.

Fortunately for all of us, we never see most of this complexity! The `JoinManager` class handles all of these interactions, with the exception of persistence.

In the examples in previous chapters, you've seen how to use the `JoinManager`, and how to create services that persistently store their configuration data. With this knowledge in hand, you can create reliable, fully functioning Jini services.

But well-behaved services can go even further; I've mentioned a number of the extra steps services can take already. They can describe themselves by attaching attributes to their proxies, as described in Chapter 7. The standard set of attributes can be used as a way to communicate information in a well-known format to clients, but services can also provide custom attributes.

Services can also provide administrative interfaces that allow users, or other programs, to configure them. At a minimum, services should support the `JoinAdmin` interface, which controls their interaction with the join protocol. But there are other standard administrative interfaces available, and many services will also provide custom administrative interfaces.

Finally, services can provide complete user interfaces that allow end users to control them. Even though a service's proxy may implement Java interfaces that might not be known to a given client—which effectively means that the client cannot interact programmatically with the service—a service's user interface (UI) may still allow *people* to interact with it directly.

This chapter covers this extra ground that services can cover to ensure that they're as useful as possible. I'll talk about how to implement administrable services, and show an example of an administrative object for the `LeaseService` created earlier. We'll also look at how to attach user interfaces to services.

If you're deploying services for "real world" use, either internally in your company or as a commercial product, you should definitely try to provide these additional features for your service.

Core Note: Know and Use the Jini Technology Compatibility Kit

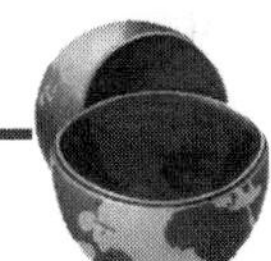

Sun makes available a set of tools called the Jini Technology Compatibility Kit (TCK) that can be used to test a service's compliance with the `Join Protocol`*, and other aspects of being a "well-behaved" Jini service. In fact, passing the requirements of the TCK is necessary for services that wish to use the Jini compatible logo from Sun.*

The TCK is freely available from Sun, and you don't have to be a commercial licensee to use it. You can download it, free of charge, to test your own services, to verify whether third-party services that don't bear the Jini compatible logo are well-behaved, and to ensure that even logo-bearing services do what they claim.

The Jini TCK is available at:

`http://developer.java.sun.com/developer/products/jini/product.offerings.html`

Again, nothing requires you to pass the compatibility kit's tests, and nothing requires you to take the extra steps mentioned in this chapter to ensure

that your service is well-behaved. It's just that if you want to "legally" call yourself a Jini service and use the Jini trademarks, you must pass the compatibility tests.

At the time of this writing, the TCK is at version 1.0, and will certainly grow over time.

Service Administration

Chapter 8 briefly introduced the notion of service administration, and showed some of the common administrative interfaces for services. In this section, we'll look a bit more deeply at administration, and look at an example of how to create an administrable service.

Administration through Delegation

Service administration follows a *delegation* model. This means that, rather than having a service's proxy object implement all of the required administrative interfaces, the proxy can return a "surrogate" object that understands how to do administration.

There are a number of reasons for this. First, it allows developers to create the administrative interfaces for a service independently from the service's core functionality. You can build what your service *does* first, and then worry about how to control it.

Second, administrative interfaces may be quite large. By keeping this functionality out of the proxy, you can speed up download times, and reduce the storage requirement in Jini lookup services. Administrative delegate objects are only fetched when needed.

Finally, by providing the ability for administration to be mediated by an object separate from the proxy, developers can choose the best implementation strategy for each. For example, the administrative object for a service may be simply an RMI stub that communicates directly with the back-end portion of a service. Other service proxies may create the administrative object locally when asked. Still others may ask the back-end part of the service for an administrative object when needed. If Jini required the proxy to implement the administrative interfaces directly, this flexibility would be lost.

These benefits of delegation don't, however, *require* you to create a separate administrative object. A developer can choose to implement the administrative

interfaces directly in the service proxy itself. When asked for its administrative object, such a service proxy would simply return a reference to itself.

Administrative Interfaces

We already looked at the basic Jini administrative interfaces in Chapter 8. A service proxy that can provide an administration delegate object should implement the `net.jini.admin.Administrable` interface. The object returned by the `getAdmin()` call may implement several common administrative interfaces. Table 12–1 lists the standard interfaces.

Table 12–1 Standard Administrative Interfaces

Package	*Interface*	*Description*
`com.sun.jini.admin`	`DestroyAdmin`	Controls the termination of a service.
`net.jini.lookup`	`DiscoveryAdmin`	Controls how a lookup service interacts with groups and other lookup services.
`net.jini.admin`	`JoinAdmin`	Controls a service's participation in the join protocol. Should be implemented by all services.
`com.sun.jini.admin`	`StorageLocation Admin`	Controls the location of a service's persistent storage.

In addition to these standard interfaces, certain services may implement their own custom administrative interfaces. For example, a storage engine may support controls that allow users to configure the maximum amount of storage it will grant.

Implementation of Administrative Delegates

Creators of services have great freedom in how they choose to implement their administrative delegate objects. Some administration objects will be simply RMI stub objects that communicate directly with the back-end service. Others will be more complex objects that "wrap" some protocol that they use to communicate with the service.

There is, however, one restriction that the writers of administrative objects should follow: in general, it's a good idea to not use GUI classes directly in your administrative delegates.

Why is this? Clearly programmatic administration of services isn't the only thing we'll want to do; we'll also want to be able to directly control services through front-end graphical interfaces. If a service provides a custom administration API, it would certainly be useful if it could supply a user interface that allowed us to work with it!

The reason for this guideline is that not all platforms will have all Java packages available to them. The services you write should be not only *useable* but also *controllable* from as many platforms as possible. Suppose that a service proxy is sent to a machine that has only a limited set of the Java class libraries (such as a PDA or cell phone); most likely, devices like this will be lacking many of the full-blown user interface libraries. Now, if the administrative object for this service relies on such libraries—perhaps because it is a subclass of `JFrame` or `Component`, then these machines will be completely unable to even instantiate the administrative object! Even though clients may be perfectly capable of interacting with the object programmatically, they are prevented from doing so because of the constraints placed on the object by its developer. The moral of the story is that you should make your administrative objects as minimal as possible, so that they can be run as widely as possible.

Of course, services can still provide custom GUIs for their administration objects, as well as for themselves; they should, however, take care to not *require* their users to have a full set of class libraries to work. A bit later in this chapter we'll see how to attach user interfaces to services and administration objects.

An Example: Administering the LeaseService

Let's explore an example of how to create an administrable service, using the `LeaseService` from the previous chapter as a starting point. The `LeaseService` is well-behaved in every way—it follows the join protocol, and takes great care to make any configuration information persistent—with one exception: it is not administrable.

As mentioned before, every service should support the `JoinAdmin` interface at a minimum. This interface allows users (and programs) to control how the service interacts with the join protocol. Without this interface, you cannot control which groups the service joins, or which lookup services it registers with. So services should consider this interface to be a requirement.

Additionally, services may want to implement several of the other standard interfaces, or even custom interfaces. In the example we'll create for the `LeaseService`, we'll implement the "big three:" `JoinAdmin`, `DestroyAdmin`, and `StorageLocationAdmin`. You could easily imagine a custom administrative interface for this service—perhaps that allows users to tune leasing policy variables, such as maximum and default lease times. But we'll focus only on the standard interfaces here.

The original `LeaseService` of Chapter 10 was already carefully set up to allow it to be extended with administration—its proxy object implements `Administrable`, and does a remote method invocation back to the service process to fetch an administration object when it is called. The only thing that was lacking from that example was that the back-end service always returned null when asked for its administration object.

To improve the `LeaseService`, we'll subclass it and override `getAdmin()` to return a "real" administrative object. We'll also add some extra remote methods that this administrative object will use to communicate with the back-end service to actually change service parameters.

The organization of this example illustrates a very common approach to implementing administration: the service's proxy contacts the back end when it is asked for an administrative object. The back end then returns a serialized administrative object that is initialized with a remote reference that it can use to speak a "private" administrative protocol with the back end.

Let's look at the code (Listing 12–1). We'll start off by examining the administrative object that is returned by the proxy's `getAdmin()` call. This is the actual object that clients will operate on to perform administration.

Listing 12–1 `LeaseAdminProxy.java`

```
// This is the actual admin object that gets returned to
// clients
package corejini.chapter12;

import net.jini.core.entry.Entry;
import net.jini.core.discovery.LookupLocator;
import net.jini.admin.JoinAdmin;
import com.sun.jini.admin.DestroyAdmin;
import com.sun.jini.admin.StorageLocationAdmin;
import java.io.IOException;
import java.io.Serializable;
import java.rmi.RemoteException;
```

Listing 12–1 `LeaseAdminProxy.java` **(continued)**

```
public class LeaseAdminProxy implements JoinAdmin,
        DestroyAdmin, StorageLocationAdmin, Serializable {
    protected AdminLeaseService.RemoteLeaseAdmin remote;

    LeaseAdminProxy(AdminLeaseService.RemoteLeaseAdmin
                                    remote) {
        this.remote = remote;
    }

    // implement DestroyAdmin
    public void destroy() throws RemoteException {
        remote.destroy();
    }

    // implement StorageLocationAdmin
    public void setStorageLocation(String loc)
                    throws IOException, RemoteException {
        remote.setStorageLocation(loc);
    }


    public String getStorageLocation()
                    throws RemoteException {
        return remote.getStorageLocation();
    }

    // implement JoinAdmin
    public Entry[] getLookupAttributes()
                    throws RemoteException {
        return remote.getLookupAttributes();
    }

    public void addLookupAttributes(Entry[] attrs)
                    throws RemoteException {
        remote.addLookupAttributes(attrs);
    }

    public void modifyLookupAttributes(Entry[] tmpls,
                                       Entry[] attrs)
                    throws RemoteException {
        remote.modifyLookupAttributes(tmpls, attrs);
    }
```

Listing 12–1 `LeaseAdminProxy.java` **(continued)**

```
    public String[] getLookupGroups()
                    throws RemoteException {
        return remote.getLookupGroups();
    }

    public void addLookupGroups(String[] groups)
                    throws RemoteException {
        remote.addLookupGroups(groups);
    }

    public void removeLookupGroups(String[] groups)
                    throws RemoteException {
        remote.removeLookupGroups(groups);
    }

    public void setLookupGroups(String[] groups)
                    throws RemoteException {
        remote.setLookupGroups(groups);
    }

    public LookupLocator[] getLookupLocators()
                        throws RemoteException {
        return remote.getLookupLocators();
    }
    public void addLookupLocators(LookupLocator[] locs)
                        throws RemoteException {
        remote.addLookupLocators(locs);
    }

    public void removeLookupLocators(LookupLocator[] locs)
                        throws RemoteException {
        remote.removeLookupLocators(locs);
    }
    public void setLookupLocators(LookupLocator[] locs)
                        throws RemoteException {
        remote.setLookupLocators(locs);
    }
}
```

The administrable object, called `LeaseAdminProxy`, implements the three administrative interfaces, and is also `Serializable`, since it will be sent from the back end to the client via the proxy's `getAdmin()` method. When the administration object is created, it is initialized with a reference to a remote object that implements the interface the proxy uses to communicate with the back-end service. This interface is nested in the new `LeaseService` subclass that supports administration, and is called `RemoteLeaseAdmin`.

All of the methods on the administrative proxy are simply forwarded to the `RemoteLeaseAdmin` in the service back end. As you'll see, the local administrative APIs are essentially the same as the remote ones in this case. So one possible implementation strategy would be to simply use the stub for the remote interface *as* the administration object. Here, I've taken the approach of creating a separate proxy that calls through to a remote interface, because this is the more general approach, and reflects the way most administrative objects are likely to be built. By separating the implementation of the proxy from the remote protocol, you could imagine more complicated administration objects that cache results locally, or use a more complex protocol to communicate with the back end. Each could evolve independently of the other.

Let's now look at the subclass of `LeaseService`.

The code in Listing 12–2 is a subclass of `LeaseService`, and inherits all of its old methods. Only the `getAdmin()` method is overridden, because it must return the administrative object for the service instead of the null value that the original service returned. I've also added a few extra methods here that allow the proxy to communicate with the back end to perform administrative tasks.

The `AdminLeaseService` class defines a nested interface called `RemoteLeaseAdmin` which defines the way the administrative proxy will communicate with the back end. As mentioned, the local and remote interfaces are—in the case of this example—the same. So the remote interface merely extends the necessary administrative APIs, as well as `Remote`. The nested class `RemoteLeaseAdminImpl` provides an implementation of the interface that the administrative objects sent out to clients will communicate with.

The first methods in the `AdminLeaseService` are, unfortunately, necessary to work around bugs that appear in some versions of Sun's `javac` compiler. The bug prevents inner classes from accessing members contained in their nesting class's superclass. The `getJoinManager()` method and friends simply return members defined in the `LeaseService` class so that they can be accessed by the inner `RemoteLeaseAdminImpl`.

`RemoteLeaseAdminImpl` is a `UnicastRemoteObject`, since the administration object will communicate with it remotely using RMI. This class implements all the various methods that the administration object uses to control the service.

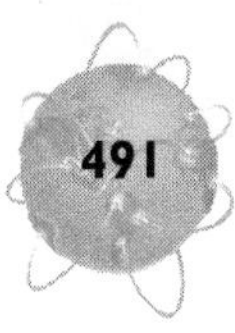

Listing 12–2 `AdminLeaseService.java`

```
package corejini.chapter11;

import java.io.*;
import java.rmi.*;
import java.rmi.server.*;
import net.jini.core.discovery.LookupLocator;
import net.jini.core.entry.Entry;
import com.sun.jini.lookup.JoinManager;
import com.sun.jini.lease.LeaseRenewalManager;
import net.jini.admin.JoinAdmin;
import com.sun.jini.admin.DestroyAdmin;
import com.sun.jini.admin.StorageLocationAdmin;
import corejini.chapter10.LeaseService;

public class AdminLeaseService extends LeaseService {
    protected RemoteLeaseAdmin remoteAdmin = null;
    protected LeaseAdminProxy admin = null;
    protected static boolean done = false;
    protected static Thread thread = null;

    // work around inner class bugs
    JoinManager getJoinManager() {
        return joinManager;
    }

    LeaseRenewalManager getLeaseManager() {
        return leaseManager;
    }
    void setStorageLoc(String loc) {
        storageLoc = loc;
    }
    String getStorageLoc() {
        return storageLoc;
    }

     // All of our administration interfaces
    public interface RemoteLeaseAdmin extends Remote,
        JoinAdmin, StorageLocationAdmin, DestroyAdmin {
    }
```

Listing 12–2 AdminLeaseService.java

```
    public class RemoteLeaseAdminImpl
                  extends UnicastRemoteObject
                  implements RemoteLeaseAdmin {
        RemoteLeaseAdminImpl() throws RemoteException {
            super();
        }

        public void destroy() {
            File locFile = new File(getStorageLoc());
            synchronized (AdminLeaseService.this) {
                // stop doing lookup/discovery
                getJoinManager().terminate();
                // empty out the lease manager.
                getLeaseManager().clear();
                // zap persistent storage
                locFile.delete();
                // shut down thread
                done = true;
                thread.interrupt();
            }
        }

        public void setStorageLocation(String loc)
                         throws RemoteException {
            synchronized (AdminLeaseService.this) {
                try {
                    // pick up the current file and move it.
                    File newLocFile = new File(loc);
                    File oldLocFile =
                             new File(getStorageLoc());

                    BufferedReader reader =
                        new BufferedReader(
                             new FileReader(oldLocFile));
                    BufferedWriter writer =
                        new BufferedWriter(
                             new FileWriter(newLocFile));

                    char[] buffer = new char[1024];
                    int n;
                    while ((n = reader.read(buffer)) > 0) {
                        writer.write(buffer, 0, n);
                    }
```

Listing 12–2 `AdminLeaseService.java`

```
                reader.close();
                 writer.close();

                 setStorageLoc(loc);
                 oldLocFile.delete();
            } catch (IOException ex) {
                throw new RemoteException(
                                          ex.toString());
            }
        }
    }

    public String getStorageLocation() {
        return getStorageLoc();
    }

    public Entry[] getLookupAttributes() {
        return getJoinManager().getAttributes();
    }

    public void addLookupAttributes(Entry[] attrs)
                              throws RemoteException {
        getJoinManager().addAttributes(attrs, true);
        try {
            AdminLeaseService.this.checkpoint();
        } catch (IOException ex) {
            throw new RemoteException(ex.toString());
        }
    }

    public void modifyLookupAttributes(Entry[] tmpls,
                                       Entry[] attrs)
                              throws RemoteException {
        getJoinManager().modifyAttributes(tmpls,
                                       attrs, true);
        try {
            AdminLeaseService.this.checkpoint();
        } catch (IOException ex) {
            throw new RemoteException(ex.toString());
        }
    }
```

Listing 12–2 AdminLeaseService.java

```
    public String[] getLookupGroups() {
        return getJoinManager().getGroups();
    }

    public void addLookupGroups(String[] groups)
                  throws RemoteException {
        try {
            getJoinManager().addGroups(groups);
            AdminLeaseService.this.checkpoint();
        } catch (IOException ex) {
            throw new RemoteException(ex.toString());
        }
    }

    public void removeLookupGroups(String[] groups)
                         throws RemoteException {
        try {
            getJoinManager().removeGroups(groups);
        } catch (IOException ex) {
        }
        try {
            AdminLeaseService.this.checkpoint();
        } catch (IOException ex) {
            throw new RemoteException(ex.toString());
        }
    }

    public void setLookupGroups(String[] groups)
                     throws RemoteException {
        try {
            getJoinManager().setGroups(groups);
        } catch (IOException ex) {
        }
        try {
            AdminLeaseService.this.checkpoint();
        } catch (IOException ex) {
            throw new RemoteException(ex.toString());
        }
    }
```

Listing 12–2 AdminLeaseService.java

```
          public LookupLocator[] getLookupLocators() {
            return getJoinManager().getLocators();
        }

        public void addLookupLocators(LookupLocator[] locs)
                        throws RemoteException {
            getJoinManager().addLocators(locs);
            try {
                AdminLeaseService.this.checkpoint();
            } catch (IOException ex) {
                throw new RemoteException(ex.toString());
            }
        }

         public void removeLookupLocators(LookupLocator[]
                                                  locs)
                            throws RemoteException {
            getJoinManager().removeLocators(locs);
            try {
                AdminLeaseService.this.checkpoint();
            } catch (IOException ex) {
                throw new RemoteException(ex.toString());
            }
        }

        public void setLookupLocators(LookupLocator[] locs)
                            throws RemoteException {
            getJoinManager().setLocators(locs);
            try {
                AdminLeaseService.this.checkpoint();
            } catch (IOException ex) {
                throw new RemoteException(ex.toString());
            }
        }
    }

    public AdminLeaseService(String storageLoc)
                    throws RemoteException, IOException,
                                ClassNotFoundException {
        super(storageLoc);
    }
```

Listing 12–2 `AdminLeaseService.java`

```
    // override getAdmin()
    public Object getAdmin() {
        try {
            if (remoteAdmin == null) {
                remoteAdmin = new RemoteLeaseAdminImpl();
            }
            if (admin == null) {
                admin = new LeaseAdminProxy(remoteAdmin);
            }

            return admin;
        } catch (RemoteException ex) {
             System.err.println("Error creating admin: " +
                                   ex.getMessage());
            ex.printStackTrace();
            return null;
        }
    }
    public static void main(String[] args) {
        if (args.length != 1) {
            System.err.println("Usage: LeaseService " +
                                      "<storage_loc>");
            System.exit(1);
        }

        try {
            AdminLeaseService src =
                new AdminLeaseService(args[0]);
            while (!done) {
                try {
                    thread = Thread.currentThread();
                    Thread.sleep(Long.MAX_VALUE);
                } catch (InterruptedException ex) {
                }
            }
        } catch (Exception ex) {
            System.err.println("Trouble starting: " +
                                      ex.getMessage());
            ex.printStackTrace();
        }
        System.exit(1);
    }
}
```

The `destroy()` method is used to shut down the service. It terminates the join process, clears out the lease manager, and deletes the persistent storage associated with the service. It also causes the thread that keeps the "wrapper" process to stop by setting the `done` flag to true. See the implementation of `main()` to see how the flag is used.

The implementation of `setStorageLocation()` tries to "pick up and move" the persistent storage file to the new specified location. The old file is copied to the new and, if no exceptions are raised, the old file is deleted.

The `getStorageLocation()` method is typical of the "get" methods implemented here. It simply returns the current storage location string stored in the superclass. The other "get" methods fetch data out of the `JoinManager` maintained in the superclass.

With the exception of the `destroy()` method, and the various storage location-related methods, everything else controls aspects of the `JoinManager`. The `addLookupGroups()` method is typical of these—it updates the list of lookup groups in the `JoinManager`, and then calls `checkpoint()` to flush the change out to persistent storage. If you're unfamiliar with inner class syntax, you may be confused by the line `AdminLeaseService.this.checkpoint()`. This code merely specifies that the `checkpoint()` method lives in the outer `AdminLeaseService` class, and not in the `RemoteLeaseAdmin` inner class.

The only other two distinguished methods in the class are `getAdmin()`, which overrides the null-returning version in the superclass. This version creates the `RemoteLeaseAdminImpl` the first time it is used, and then creates and returns a `LeaseAdminProxy` initialized with the remote object.

The `main()` routine creates a new `AdminLeaseService` object and then loops forever—or until the `destroy()` method shuts the service down. The mail thread is recorded so that it can be stopped by `destroy()`.

Providing User Interfaces for Services

In all of the service examples so far, services have been accessed programmatically—through the Java interfaces that they support. This arrangement works fine when both a client and a service can agree ahead of time on what interfaces they will use to work with one another. In fact, because this agreement on interfaces is so important, Sun and its partners are working to define a standard set of interfaces for common network services and devices.

To put it simply, if a client and a service cannot agree on what interfaces they will use, there is essentially no way for them to work together program-

matically. If a client finds a service that implements an unknown interface, with methods it does not recognize, the client will have no way of understanding the semantics of the interface—what the service, and all of its methods, actually *do* and how to use them.

But the situation is not as dire as it might seem. Even though a *program* might be unable to use a service that implements no known interfaces, an actual human *user* may have no problem with such a service. Even if a user wouldn't know a remote method call from a bowling ball, he or she is very likely to be able to work with a service that presents an intuitive user interface that hides the programmatic interface.

So providing intelligent user interfaces for services is important for most services, and virtually essential for those that do not implement standard interfaces. By providing a UI for your service, you make it *directly* accessible to users from programs like browsers that can display the UIs for particular services. So if you have a digital camera and a service that creates thumbnails of images, and the camera has never heard of the thumbnail interface, you may still be able to use these services together if they provide flexible user interfaces, perhaps by directly dragging snapped photos out of the camera's UI and onto the thumbnail service's UI.

In this section we'll look at how to go about building, and delivering, user interfaces for Jini services.

Several Approaches to Providing UIs

There are several ways one might deliver a user interface for a service. One way would be to make the service's proxy, in addition to implementing the programmatic interfaces that allow clients to drive the service, also implement the needed UI functionality itself. So, your service proxy might be a subclass of `JFrame` that, when made visible, could display a complete user interface that would allow people to interact with the service.

The downsides of such an approach are exactly the same as the downsides of having administrative objects implement UI functionality directly—if a given client platform doesn't have the necessary UI classes, it will be unable to use the service *at all*, even in a programmatic way. If your service proxy extends a class that is not available in a particular client, that client will not be able to instantiate it and the proxy will be unuseable there.

Another approach, and a better one, would be to mirror the style of the `Administrable` interface—provide a new interface that proxies could implement, perhaps called "Interfaceable," that returns the GUI for a client. While this approach is far better than having the proxy implement the user interface

functionality directly, it does have problems. Most importantly, it provides only *one* way to get an interface for a service. Since Jini services may be accessed from any number of devices and machines, each with its own UI capabilities, we'd like a more flexible approach that would allow services to provide multiple UIs—including UIs optimized for desktop computers, voice or telephony interfaces, and perhaps graphical UIs optimized for small devices like cell phones and PDAs. So any methods on "Interfaceable" should provide some way for clients to specify what sort of interface they are interested in.

A third approach, and the one taken here, provides user interfaces for services as attributes attached to service proxies. This design provides a lot of flexibility—you can have multiple attributes attached to services, each containing a particular UI implementation. Clients can quickly find the particular UI implementation they need, or can even search for services that implement UI functionality. And, if a client doesn't have the class libraries needed for a *particular* UI, the failure to load the desired attribute will be reflected in a very convenient way—by an `UnuseableEntryException` being raised—without affecting the loading of other attributes or the service proxy itself. This approach is not without its problems though. Specifically, you must take great care when using serialization to transmit a complex object—like a user interface component—as an `Entry`. I'll talk about this more in the example.

Unfortunately, Sun has not, as of the writing of this book, defined a set of standard interfaces that service user interfaces should implement so that they can be located and used by clients. Sun's position is that they wish to encourage the larger Jini community to develop de facto interfaces for service user interfaces, including not only graphical user interfaces, but potentially even auditory, telephone, or other interfaces. Certainly such interfaces will appear in the future, and we can make some educated guesses about what they will look like.

In all probability, these classes will extend some common Java UI class, such as `JApplet`, `JPanel`, or `JFrame`. They will implement the `Entry` interface (so that they can be attached as attributes). And, most likely, they will support an interface that allows them to be initialized for display by passing in the service's proxy object to them. This is so that the UI can be properly created based on the details about the service that can be retrieved from its proxy.

In the rest of this chapter, we'll look at an example of a simple service user interface that's constructed as a `JFrame` attribute; this user interface provides a basic "splash screen" that identifies the `LeaseService` from the previous chapter in a graphically interesting way. The UI also provides a way to access the service's administrative functions. More complicated services could, obviously, support more complicated user interfaces. A storage service might provide graphs and charts showing storage utilization over time. But here, rather than focus on the ins-and-outs of building large-scale Java user interfaces, we'll focus on how to create service UIs that are useable in the context of Jini.

Figure 12–1 shows the UI for the `LeaseService`. This "splash screen"-style interface identifies the service, and provides a button that allows users to administer it. Even though the browser code we looked at earlier provides a way to access a service's administrative functions, other browsers might not support this ability. So the user interface we'll construct has it "built in."

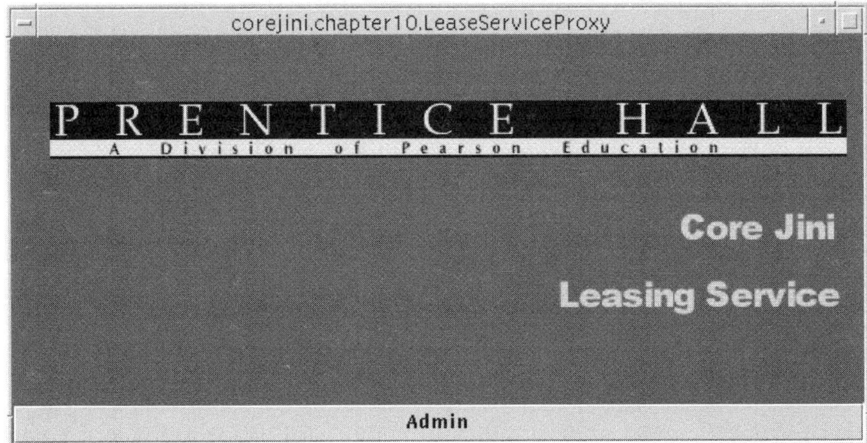

Figure 12–1 A splash screen for the LeaseService

The `SplashScreen` class (Listing 12–3) is an extension of `JFrame`, and implements the `Entry` interface, since it will be sent to clients as an attribute.

Listing 12–3 `SplashScreen.java`

```
// A simple frame to display a splash screen

package corejini.chapter11;

import javax.swing.*;
import java.awt.*;
import java.awt.event.*;
import java.io.*;
import java.rmi.RemoteException;
import net.jini.admin.Administrable;
import net.jini.core.entry.Entry;
import corejini.chapter9.AdminPanel;
```

Listing 12–3 `SplashScreen.java` (continued)

```
public class SplashScreen extends JFrame implements Entry {
    protected final static String ICON =
                "SplashScreen.gif";
    protected final static String DEFAULT =
                "Core Jini / Leasing Service";

    public SplashScreen() {
        super("Uninitialized splash screen");
    }

    public SplashScreen(Object proxy) {
        super(proxy.getClass().getName());
        setProxy(proxy);
    }


    // Set the proxy object that the splash screen is for
    public void setProxy(Object proxy) {
         Object admin = null;

         if (proxy == null) {
             return;
        }

        setTitle(proxy.getClass().getName());

        try {
            if (proxy instanceof Administrable) {
                admin = ((Administrable) proxy).getAdmin();
            }
        } catch (RemoteException ex) {
        }

        addWindowListener(new WindowAdapter() {
            public void windowClosing(WindowEvent ev) {
                setVisible(false);
                dispose();
            }
        });

        JLabel label;
        byte[] buffer = null;
```

Listing 12–3 `SplashScreen.java` (continued)

```
    // Fetch the splash screen image as a resource
    // This gets it using the same class loader that
    // loaded this object.
    try {
        InputStream resource =
                getClass().getResourceAsStream(ICON);
        if (resource == null) {
            label = new JLabel(DEFAULT);
        } else {
            BufferedInputStream in =
                new BufferedInputStream(resource);
            ByteArrayOutputStream out =
                new ByteArrayOutputStream(1024);

            buffer = new byte[1024];
            int n;
                while ((n = in.read(buffer)) > 0) {
                out.write(buffer, 0, n);
            }
            in.close();
            out.flush();

            buffer = out.toByteArray();

            if (buffer.length == 0) {
                label = new JLabel(DEFAULT);
            } else {
                label =
                    new JLabel(new ImageIcon(buffer));
            }
        }
    } catch (IOException ex) {
        label = new JLabel(DEFAULT);
    }

    getContentPane().add(label, "Center");
```

Listing 12–3 `SplashScreen.java` (continued)

```
        if (admin != null) {
            final Object fadmin = admin;
            JButton button = new JButton("Admin");
            button.addActionListener(new ActionListener() {
              public void actionPerformed(ActionEvent ev){
                    JFrame frame =
                    new JFrame("Lease Service Admin");
                    frame.getContentPane().add(
                                        new AdminPanel(admin),
                                                    "Center");
                    frame.pack();
                    frame.addWindowListener(
                        new WindowAdapter() {
                      public void windowClosing(
                                        WindowEvent ev) {
                            setVisible(true);
                            dispose();
                      }
                  });


                frame.setVisible(true);
                }
            });
            getContentPane().add(button, "South");
        }

        pack();
        setVisible(true);
    }
}
```

When instances of the `SplashScreen` attribute are sent to clients, they will be transmitted as serialized objects, and reconstituted upon arrival at the client. When a `SplashScreen` attribute is reconstituted, it will create an as-yet invisible frame with a title bar that says "Uninitialized splash screen." When a client application wishes to initialize the splash screen and make it visible, it calls the `setProxy()` method on it, passing in the proxy object for the `LeaseService`. This method is one API that both the consumer of these attributes and the attribute writer must agree on. As Jini evolves, it will certainly standardize on interfaces that will be used to initialize user interface attributes; in this example, though, both parties agree on the `setProxy()` call.

Core Alert: Take care when sending serialized UI components

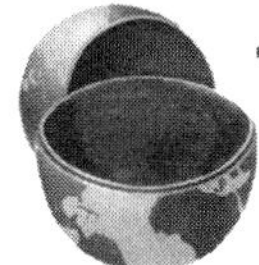

In this example, I'm sending a very simple graphical component to a client as a serialized object. But in general, you should be very careful when returning UI components from services to clients. For one thing, if a service creates a UI component (say, a `JTextArea`*) and attaches it as an attribute, the UI component is initially constructed inside the service. Just naively sending it to the client may not work, as listeners inside the component may point to objects inside the server. So you may need to supply an "initialize" method that clients will invoke on returned objects that correctly set up their state for execution inside the client.*

Note that the second approach mentioned in the section "Several Approaches to Providing UIs," earlier in this chapter, provides a reasonable alternative. That solution would be to require that the proxies for services implement a `getUI()` *method that returns an interface component. Since this method is implemented on the proxy, any UI components can be instantiated inside the client as needed. A* `getUI()` *method could take as an argument a java Class object indicating the sort of UI component the client is interested in (graphical, auditory, and so on).*

Using a method on the service's proxy to get an interface is analogous to the way administration works. For the example here, though, attaching a simple interface as an attribute works just fine. The moral here is that there is no single approach that may be right for all situations.

When the proxy is set in the attribute, it loads a resource that contains the image to be displayed in the splash screen, and creates a button that can be used to bring up the administrative GUI panel we created earlier.

There are a couple of points to make about this code. First, when you create GUI attributes—or any attributes for that matter—you need to ensure that they are properly serializable. The code shown here implements `Entry`, which is a claim to the system that we know what we're doing. But this class has to take special care to make sure that it will behave properly when transmitted to clients.

In particular, note that the code here doesn't hold on to any references to the proxy object. You might think that, rather than forcing the client to call `setProxy()` to tell the GUI about its proxy object, the service that created the proxy could "pre-initialize" it with the proxy. But if the code retains a reference to the proxy object, it will be sent along with the rest of the attribute to the client when it is serialized. Since the client presumably *already* has the service's proxy—retrieved via a call to `lookup()`, or through an event—this is almost certainly not what we want!

Also note the call to `getResource()`. This method loads a "resource" (in this case an image file) by using the class loader that loaded the attribute itself. Since the attribute was originally published by some service, that service must take care to set the codebase when it runs so that the URL that points to the attribute's code, as well as this image file, can be found by clients. The codebase set by the publishing service will be used to fetch the attribute's code and resources whenever the serialized `SplashScreen` object is reconstituted at the client.

This is an important point and deserves restating—when you set a codebase URL in your service, any downloadable classes your clients need will be loaded from this URL, as will any supporting classes or files. So, for example, in this program you would put both the splash screen GUI code and the image itself on a directory exported by an HTTP server, and set the codebase to point to this server. When a client needs the GUI class, it will be retrieved via a class loader initialized to load from the codebase URL. And when this class then needs to load the image resource, it will be fetched using the same class loader that loaded the GUI code. Setting a codebase is a way to ensure that, no matter who needs to use your classes or any of their supporting files, they can be properly fetched from the correct location at run time.

Finally, note the use of member data here. The `SplashScreen` implementation is not readily searchable by the data contained in it. Clients *can* find it by looking for the classes and interfaces it implements. But because there is no public, nonstatic, nontransient data here, the contents of the `SplashScreen` attribute are not searchable. This is fine for the example here, but in more complicated attributes you may want to make sure that they expose searchable data to clients.

Now that we've seen how the `SplashScreen` attribute works, lets look at another extension of the `LeaseService` that publishes these attributes.

This class (Listing 12–4) is an extension of `AdminLeaseService` that simply attaches a couple of attributes to the published proxy object. Here, you see how to attach a `ServiceInfo` object, and the new `SplashScreen` user interface shown earlier. The attributes are added by simply calling out to the `JoinManager`, stored in the original `LeaseService` class, and then checkpointing to make sure the change is saved.

Listing 12–4 `AttrLeaseService.java`

```
// Extend the administrable lease service to attach a GUI
// attribute to it.

package corejini.chapter11;

import java.io.IOException;
import java.rmi.RemoteException;
import net.jini.core.entry.Entry;
import com.sun.jini.lookup.JoinManager;
import net.jini.lookup.entry.ServiceInfo;

public class AttrLeaseService extends AdminLeaseService {
    public AttrLeaseService(String storageLoc)
                    throws RemoteException, IOException,
                                ClassNotFoundException {
        super(storageLoc);

        Entry[] entries = new Entry[2];

        entries[0] = new ServiceInfo("Prentice-Hall",
                                     "LeaseService",
                                     "LeaseService",
                                     null,
                                     "Prentice-Hall",
                                     "v1.0");
        entries[1] = new SplashScreen();
        joinManager.addAttributes(entries);
             checkpoint();
    }
        public static void main(String[] args) {
        if (args.length != 1) {
            System.err.println("Usage: LeaseService " +
                                         "<storage_loc>");
            System.exit(1);
        }
```

Listing 12–4 `AttrLeaseService.java` **(continued)**

```
        try {
            AttrLeaseService src =
                new AttrLeaseService(args[0]);
            while (!done) {
                try {
                    thread = Thread.currentThread();
                    Thread.sleep(Long.MAX_VALUE);
                } catch (InterruptedException ex) {
                }
            }
        } catch (Exception ex) {
            System.err.println("Trouble starting: " +
                                          ex.getMessage());
            ex.printStackTrace();
        }
        System.exit(1);
    }
}
```

Summary

In this chapter we've looked at not only what the basic requirements of Jini services are, but also how to make services more well-behaved. Custom Jini services should always support join administration, and may support other standard or custom administrative interfaces as appropriate. And, if your service exposes some concept that would "make sense" to end users—and particularly if your service doesn't implement a well-known programmatic interface—you should seriously consider adding a custom user interface to your service via an attribute.

What's Next

In the next chapter, we'll pull everything we've learned so far about services together. Chapter 13 presents a complete service, designed to allow access to a host-connected printer. This service uses persistence, follows the join protocol, and is administrable. We'll also look at a sample toolkit that can be used to build new services.

A COMPLETE EXAMPLE: THE PRINT SERVICE

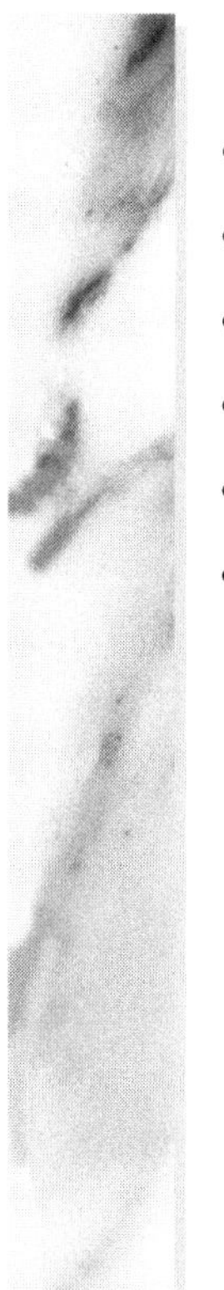

Topics in This Chapter

- A complex, full-featured service
- A toolkit for service writers
- Service persistence
- Custom administration interfaces
- Custom attributes
- Generating events to clients

Chapter 13

In this chapter, we'll look in detail at a long example—a full-featured Jini service that can provide printing support to clients. The patterns you'll see here are common across many types of Jini services, so you may be able to reuse whole chunks of code from this example in your applications. In fact, certain pieces of the code are "pulled out" into a toolkit of sorts for service writers.

In particular, we'll look at how services can checkpoint themselves to persistent storage to ensure reliability and crash recovery, how to support service administration and custom user interfaces for services, and—a new topic for us here—how custom services can generate events to clients to inform them of changes in the state of the service. And, perhaps more important than simply focusing on the individual requirements for a Jini service, we'll also look at how the various parts of the service mesh together.

The printing service that we'll examine here is meant to be a "gateway" between the Jini world and a host-attached printer. The printing service offers clients an API for printing data and controlling certain print parameters (number of copies and paper orientation). The service itself uses the standard Java printing APIs to cause data sent to it to be rendered onto the default printer on whatever host the service is running on. The architecture here follows a very common Jini model, namely that of a software service that controls and mediates access to attached hardware, making it accessible through the Jini interfaces.

Requirements for a Printing Service

Let's begin by looking at what exactly a printing service needs to do. Obviously, at the most basic level, a printing service must support some interface that allows clients to send data to it to be printed. We'd like to make our printing service as general purpose as possible; that is, we'd like to be able to send it any type of data for printing. And, even if the print service does not "know" how to print a particular type of data (JPEG files, or some other complex format, for example), the APIs for printing should not limit the types of data that are sent. One way to make arbitrary data printable is to require that the client send to the service a way for the service to render the data onto a printer.

In addition to simply sending data to the print service, a client needs to have some way of communicating various print parameters to the service, such as paper orientation (portrait versus landscape) and the number of copies to print. For its part, the print service must have some way to inform the client when a print job has completed successfully, or when it has failed. Since printing may take a long time, messages about print completion should be delivered asynchronously as *events* so that clients can continue processing while printing happens in the background.

Print administration is also important. A client may wish to determine how many items are in a service's print queue, and select the service with the shortest queue. So we'll need a way to fetch information like this. And, since we'd like to be able to display the print queue to the user, we'll need a user interface that can present this information in a useful way.

Finally, in addition to all of the *specific* requirements of printing, our service must be a well-behaved, full-featured Jini service. This means that it must be able to recover after crashes by saving its state to persistent storage. Even if a service crashes or is shut down in the middle of printing, we'd like any pending print jobs—including the current one—to be resumed when the print service restarts. Ensuring this behavior takes a bit of careful coding. Being a well-behaved service also means that our printing service must be fully administrable—not only for controlling and viewing the print queue, but also for controlling the service's participation in the join protocol and other common aspects of participating in Jini communities.

A Service Writer's Toolkit

Many Jini services follow similiar patterns: they consist of a proxy as well as a "wrapper" application that implements the back-end portion of the service. This wrapper not only provides some portion of the service's processing, but also takes care of publishing the service's proxy, and the lease management that's needed to maintain the proxy. Services such as this typically need to checkpoint themselves to persistent storage so that they can recover after crashes. And most of the administrative tasks of these services are also the same: they allow users to configure their join protocol parameters and the location of their persistent storage. They may also allow users to shut them down.

Rather than having to rebuild all of this infrastructure every time we write a new service, we can define a set of Java classes that serve as a *toolkit* for creating common types of services. We'll use these classes later in this chapter to build our print service and, indeed, use them in later chapters as we explore different types of services. You can use these classes as well, if you find yourself designing services that follow the patterns supported by these classes.

The service toolkit defined here provides a number of functions to service writers. In particular:

- The toolkit takes care of persistent data, by checkpointing the state of the service to stable storage. If you use these classes, you can extend the checkpoint and restore behavior to read and write whatever data is particular to your new service to persistent storage.
- The toolkit handles creation of a `JoinManager`, as well as initializing the `JoinManager` with whatever persistent state may be saved from the last run.
- The tookit takes care of providing administrative interfaces for the `JoinAdmin`, `StorageLocationAdmin`, and `DestroyAdmin` interfaces. By using the toolkit classes, your service will "automatically" use these interfaces, and you can extend the code to support your own custom administrative interfaces.

The code here is useful for a particular set of services: namely, those that fit into the classic mold where the proxy communicates with a back end to do some processing. In the server tookit shown here, communication happens via RMI: the class from which new services will be derived is an extension of `UnicastRemoteObject`. Likewise, the administrative object is itself an RMI stub which communicates using RMI to a back-end object that implements administration.

There are two classes and one interface that you should understand to use this package. The most important is `BasicUnicastService`. This class should be the superclass of any service that uses this framework. You can subclass `BasicUnicastService` to add your own functionality, and a `main()` routine specific to the needs of your service.

`BasicUnicastService` defines a nested interface that its subclasses can use if they need to add specialized behavior for dealing with persistent storage. This interface, called `BasicUnicastService.RestoreListener`, can be implemented by subclasses; its one method, `restored()` will be called when the service is restored after a restart or crash, to give the subclass an opportunity to initialize itself from the persistent data.

Finally, administration is performed by a class called `BasicUnicastAdmin`. This is an object that actually implements all of the administrative functions for a service, and exposes an RMI interface to clients. Clients access instances of `BasicUnicastAdmin` by calling methods on its RMI stub object, which is returned from proxies when `getAdmin()` is invoked. If your service needs specialized administrative behavior, you can easily subclass `BasicUnicastAdmin` to add the behavior you need.

A Superclass for Services

Let's start off by looking at `BasicUnicastService` as shown is Listing 13–1.

Listing 13–1 `BasicUnicastService.java`

```
package corejini.chapter13;

import net.jini.core.lease.*;
import net.jini.core.lookup.*;
import net.jini.core.entry.*;
import net.jini.core.discovery.*;
import com.sun.jini.lookup.*;
import com.sun.jini.lease.*;
import java.rmi.*;
import java.rmi.server.*;
import java.io.*;
import java.lang.reflect.*;
```

Listing 13–1 `BasicUnicastService.java` **(continued)**

```
public abstract class BasicUnicastService
                         extends UnicastRemoteObject
                         implements ServiceIDListener {
    protected JoinManager joinManager;
    protected String storageLoc;
    protected File file = null;
    protected ServiceID serviceID = null;
    protected LeaseRenewalManager leaseManager;
    protected RestoreListener restoreListener = null;
    protected Object proxy = null;

    static class PersistentData implements Serializable {
        ServiceID serviceID;
        Entry[] attrs;
        String[] groups;
        LookupLocator[] locs;
        Object subclassData;

        PersistentData(ServiceID serviceID, Entry[] attrs,
                                 String[] groups,
                       LookupLocator[] locs,
                                 Object subclassData) {
            this.serviceID = serviceID;
            this.attrs = attrs;
            this.groups = groups;
            this.locs = locs;
            this.subclassData = subclassData;
        }
    }

    // subclasses that want to be informed after a
    // restore should implement this interface
    public interface RestoreListener {
        public void restored(Object subclassData);
    }

    public BasicUnicastService(String storageLoc)
                    throws RemoteException {
        super();

        this.storageLoc = storageLoc;
        file = new File(storageLoc);
    }
```

Listing 13–1 BasicUnicastService.java (continued)

```
    // administration will call this to shut down.
    // clients can override.
    protected void shutdown() {
        System.exit(1);
    }

    // Return the service's proxy object.
    protected abstract Object getProxy();

    // subclasses override to return initial attributes
    protected Entry[] getAttributes() {
        return new Entry[0];
    }

    public void serviceIDNotify(ServiceID id) {
        serviceID = id;
        try {
            checkpoint();
        } catch (IOException ex) {
            System.err.println("Trouble checkpointing: " +
                               ex.getMessage());
        }
    }

    protected void checkpoint() throws IOException {
        checkpoint(null);

    }
    protected void checkpoint(Object subclassData)
                      throws IOException {
        PersistentData data;

        data = new PersistentData(serviceID,
                      joinManager.getAttributes(),
                      joinManager.getGroups(),
                      joinManager.getLocators(),
                      subclassData);
         ObjectOutputStream out = new
           ObjectOutputStream(new FileOutputStream(file));

        out.writeObject(data);
        out.flush();
        out.close();
    }
```

Listing 13–1 `BasicUnicastService.java` **(continued)**

```
    protected void restore() throws IOException,
                                  ClassNotFoundException {
        ObjectInputStream in = new
            ObjectInputStream(new FileInputStream(file));
        PersistentData data =
            (PersistentData) in.readObject();

        if (data == null) {
            System.err.println("No data in storage file.");
        } else {
            serviceID = data.serviceID;
            leaseManager = new LeaseRenewalManager();
            joinManager = new JoinManager(data.serviceID,
                                          proxy,
                                          data.attrs,
                                          data.groups,
                                          data.locs,
                                          leaseManager);
            if (restoreListener != null) {
               restoreListener.restored(data.subclassData);
            }
        }
    }

    // subclasses override this to do their own
    // initialization behavior.
    protected void initialize()
            throws IOException, ClassNotFoundException {
        if (this instanceof RestoreListener) {
            restoreListener = (RestoreListener) this;
        }

        proxy = getProxy();

        if (file.exists()) {
            restore();
        }

        if (joinManager == null) {
            leaseManager = new LeaseRenewalManager();
            joinManager = new JoinManager(proxy,
                                      getAttributes(),
                                      this, leaseManager);
        }
    }
}
```

The BasicUnicastService class is a remote object which extends UnicastRemoteObject. This means that it will use RMI for communication with its proxy objects. Instances of BasicUnicastService are meant to be constructed with a string that indicates the location of the service's persistent storage.

Creation of a BasicUnicastService is a two-stage process. First, a new instance of the class is created. Second, the initialize() method is called, which "begins" the service proper. Separating the stages of creation gives subclasses more freedom in deciding where and how to add their own custom behaviors. In general, most subclasses will call the BasicUnicastService constructor in *their* constructors; the main() routine for the service will then call initialize() on the newly constructed object.

Several of the methods on this class are meant to be overridden by subclasses. In particular, getProxy(), getAttributes(), initialize(), and shutdown() can profitably be overidden by subclasses. Of these, getProxy() is abstract, because BasicUnicastService cannot provide a reasonable default implementation of it—only a particular subclass knows what proxy object it will use. The others provide what are hopefully sensible default behaviors that many subclasses will be able to use unchanged.

The getProxy() and getAttributes() methods simply return the service's proxy object and any initial attributes that should be set on it, respectively.

The initialize() method, by default, checks to see if this—meaning the particular subclass of BasicUnicastService in use at run time—implements the RestoreListener interface. If it does, then this is installed as a listener that will be called when data is restored from persistent storage. The initialize() method then gets the proxy for the service, and attempts to do a restoration of the state of the service by calling restore(). If restore() completes, then it will create a JoinManager initialized from the restored data; otherwise, initialize() will create a "fresh" JoinManager.

The shutdown() method is invoked from the service termination administrative APIs just before the service is destroyed. Services can do any special cleanup jobs that they may require here; by default, shutdown() simply exits the JVM.

Let's look at how checkpointing and restoration work. The nested class PersistentData is used to contain all of the information written to stable storage. It contains all of the information needed for the join protocol (the service's ID, attributes, groups, and explicit lookup locators), as well as an untyped object called subclassData. This object can be used by subclasses to store any information particular to their code. When checkpoint() is called, it builds a new PersistentData record by fetching the information out of the JoinManager, as well as any subclass-specific information passed to it. Subclasses can use this mechanism to pass their own data, specific to their service, to checkpoint() so that it will be saved and recovered.

Restoration of persistent information after a restart is accomplished by restore(). This method is only called once—when the service is first started. It reads the saved data off stable storage, constructs a JoinManager initialized with the recovered information, and calls out to its RestoreListener passing it the subclass-specific data it recovered.

When you look at the printing service, you'll see how subclasses can use this code. Basically the steps they must follow are simple: they should override at least getProxy(), along with any other methods they may need to change, and provide a main() routine that creates a subclass of BasicUnicastService and calls initialize() on it.

A Tool for Administration

Let's now look at how to support administrable BasicUnicastServices. When you create a subclass of BasicUnicastService, you will need to create a proxy object for your subclass. If your service is to be administrable, then this proxy should implement the Administrable interface and return an object which can be used to manage the service as it runs.

Since many of these administrative tasks are common across services—shutting down the service, changing its join parameters, and so forth—many services can share a common implementation of administration.

In this section we will look at a class called BasicUnicastAdmin that cooperates with a BasicUnicastService to administer it. Instances of BasicUnicastAdmin are created with a reference to the service that they will manage. These objects implement all the methods in JoinAdmin, StorageLocationAdmin, and DestroyAdmin. BasicUnicastAdmin is itself an RMI server object, and the RMI-generated stub for it is a perfectly acceptable object to return from the service proxy when getAdmin() is called.

Let's look at the code for this object as shown in Listing 13–2.

Listing 13–2 `BasicUnicastAdmin.java`

```
// A class for handling common administrative chores.
package corejini.chapter13;

import com.sun.jini.lookup.JoinManager;
import net.jini.admin.JoinAdmin;
import com.sun.jini.admin.DestroyAdmin;
import com.sun.jini.admin.StorageLocationAdmin;
import net.jini.core.entry.Entry;
import net.jini.core.discovery.LookupLocator;
import java.rmi.*;
import java.rmi.server.*;
import java.io.*;

public class BasicUnicastAdmin extends UnicastRemoteObject
    implements BasicUnicastAdmin.RemoteUnicastAdmin {
    protected BasicUnicastService service;

     interface RemoteUnicastAdmin extends JoinAdmin,
            DestroyAdmin, StorageLocationAdmin, Remote {
    }

    protected BasicUnicastAdmin(BasicUnicastService
                                                     service)
        throws RemoteException {
        super();
        this.service = service;
    }

    public synchronized void destroy() {
        File locFile = new File(service.storageLoc);
        service.joinManager.terminate();
        locFile.delete();
        service.shutdown();
    }

    public synchronized void setStorageLocation(String
                                                     loc)
        throws RemoteException {
        try {
            File newLocFile = new File(loc);
            File oldLocFile = new File(service.storageLoc);

            BufferedReader reader =
                new BufferedReader(
                                 new FileReader(oldLocFile));
            BufferedWriter writer =
                new BufferedWriter(
                                 new FileWriter(newLocFile));
```

Listing 13–2 `BasicUnicastAdmin.java` **(continued)**

```
            char[] buffer = new char[1024];
            int n;
            while ((n = reader.read(buffer)) > 0) {
                writer.write(buffer, 0, n);
            }
            reader.close();
            writer.close();

            service.storageLoc = loc;
            oldLocFile.delete();
        } catch (IOException ex) {
            throw new RemoteException(ex.toString());
        }
    }

    public String getStorageLocation() {
        return service.storageLoc;
    }
    public Entry[] getLookupAttributes() {
        return service.joinManager.getAttributes();
    }

    public void addLookupAttributes(Entry[] attrs)
        throws RemoteException {
        service.joinManager.addAttributes(attrs, true);
        try {
            service.checkpoint();
        } catch (IOException ex) {
            throw new RemoteException(ex.toString());
        }
    }

    public void modifyLookupAttributes(Entry[] tmpls,
                                       Entry[] attrs)
        throws RemoteException {
        service.joinManager.modifyAttributes(tmpls,
                                             attrs, true);
        try {
            service.checkpoint();
        } catch (IOException ex) {
            throw new RemoteException(ex.toString());
        }
    }
```

Listing 13–2 `BasicUnicastAdmin.java` **(continued)**

```
    public String[] getLookupGroups() {
        return service.joinManager.getGroups();
    }
    public void addLookupGroups(String[] groups)
        throws RemoteException {
        try {
            service.joinManager.addGroups(groups);
        } catch (IOException ex) {
        }
        try {
            service.checkpoint();
        } catch (IOException ex) {
            throw new RemoteException(ex.toString());
        }
    }
    public void removeLookupGroups(String[] groups)
        throws RemoteException {
        try {
            service.joinManager.removeGroups(groups);
        } catch (IOException ex) {
        }
        try {
            service.checkpoint();
        } catch (IOException ex) {
            throw new RemoteException(ex.toString());
        }
    }
    public void setLookupGroups(String[] groups)
        throws RemoteException {
        try {
            service.joinManager.setGroups(groups);
        } catch (IOException ex) {
        }
        try {
            service.checkpoint();
        } catch (IOException ex) {
            throw new RemoteException(ex.toString());
        }
    }
    public LookupLocator[] getLookupLocators() {
        return service.joinManager.getLocators();
    }
```

Listing 13–2 `BasicUnicastAdmin.java` **(continued)**

```
    public void addLookupLocators(LookupLocator[] locs)
        throws RemoteException {
        service.joinManager.addLocators(locs);
        try {
            service.checkpoint();
        } catch (IOException ex) {
            throw new RemoteException(ex.toString());
        }
    }

    public void removeLookupLocators(LookupLocator[] locs)
        throws RemoteException {
        service.joinManager.removeLocators(locs);
        try {
            service.checkpoint();
        } catch (IOException ex) {
            throw new RemoteException(ex.toString());
        }
    }

    public void setLookupLocators(LookupLocator[] locs)
        throws RemoteException {
        service.joinManager.setLocators(locs);
        try {
            service.checkpoint();
        } catch (IOException ex) {
            throw new RemoteException(ex.toString());
        }
    }
}
```

`BasicUnicastAdmin` extends `UnicastRemoteObject`, since it uses RMI to communicate with its stub object located in the client. The class implements a nested remote interface, `BasicUnicastAdmin.RemoteUnicastAdmin`, which defines the set of methods on the class that are callable remotely; these are the methods of the various Jini administrative interfaces. Although `BasicUnicastAdmin` could have been designed to implement the various individual administrative interfaces directly, using a separate interface—`RemoteUnicastAdmin`—can lead to a cleaner design by encapsulating *all* the common administrative interfaces. That is, this separate interface is a design choice, not a requirement.

New instances of BasicUnicastAdmin are initialized with a reference to the BasicUnicastService that they will manage. All the various methods on the administrative implementation change or retrieve information from the service object, and cause the service object to checkpoint itself after a change. The actual implementations of these methods are similar to the ones you saw in Chapter 12.

To use BasicUnicastAdmin in your own services, you would simply instantiate a new instance of the class in your service's wrapper the first time one of your proxies is asked for an administrative object. By returning the RMI-generated stub for BasicUnicastAdmin to the client, you can expose the administrative methods to it.

If your service needs to define custom administrative interfaces, in addition to the standard interfaces supported here, you can easily subclass BasicUnicastAdmin to provide the extra needed functionality.

In the rest of this chapter, we'll build a print service that leverages the service tookit code we've just looked at. You'll see how to subclass Basic-UnicastService to create new RMI-based services, and how to extend the functionality of BasicUnicastAdmin to support custom administrative interfaces.

Defining the Print Service API

Now that we've looked at some tools that we can use to create Jini services, we can begin building atop these tools to create our printing service.

The first thing you need to do when defining any Jini service is to create the API that clients will use to communicate with it. This is the API that the service's proxy object will implement; clients may look for objects that implement this interface when they search lookup services.

In the example service shown in Listing 13–3, we'll use a very simple interface, called Printer, with a single method for controlling printing. This method will take as parameters the data to be printed, a token indicating the paper orientation, the number of copies to print, and a reference to a remote listener object that will be called back when printing completes, either successfully or unsuccessfully.

The format integer here should be one of the special formatting tokens defined in the java.awt.print.PageFormat class: either PORTRAIT, LANDSCAPE, or REVERSE_LANDSCAPE. The copies argument is simply the desired number of copies; data is the data to be printed; and listener is an object

Listing 13–3 `Printer.java`

```
// This is the interface that the proxy implements

package corejini.chapter13;

import java.rmi.RemoteException;

public interface Printer {
    public void print(int format, int copies, Object data,
                      PrintListener listener)
        throws RemoteException;
}
```

that will be called back when the status of printing changes. The `listener` can be null if the client doesn't care about being informed of the status of its print jobs.

The Java printing model in Java 2 uses a "callback" printing model, where a method on an object will be invoked whenever the printing subsystem needs to render a page onto a printer. The objects that are called to control printing must implement either the `java.awt.print.Printable` or the `java.awt.print.Pageable` interface. The object that you pass as the `data` parameter here should implement either one of these interfaces to be printable. The object will be sent to the service, which will use it to control the rendering of the object onto a printer.

At the end of this chapter, I've provided a list of some simple extensions you can make to this code. One possible modification is an *extensible* printing model, where clients can preregister renderers for particular types. Then, if an object is sent which is not `Printable` or `Pageable`, but has an installed renderer for it, the print service can still print it. For now, though, you should make sure that all objects you send implement one of the two Java printing interfaces.

Communicating with Clients: Events and Listeners

You saw in the previous section how clients can install a listener that will be called whenever the status of a print request changes. As you'll see, the printing service queues up print requests from clients, and dispatches them one at a time. Since the time between when a client submits a print request and the time it is actually printed (or fails to print) may be quite long, you need to use an asynchronous notification scheme for telling clients about what's happening to their print jobs.

The standard Java event and listener paradigm will do the job here. Clients can, when they issue a print request, pass in a listener that will be sent an event whenever the status of the print request changes. Since the events will be passed between separate JVMs, and will be delivered using a remote method implemented by the client, you'll have to use Jini's remote event facilities. We'll look more closely at remote events in the next chapter, but you only need to understand some pretty simple details to figure out how events are being used here.

First, let's look at the listener interface (Listing 13–4).

Listing 13–4 `PrintListener.java`

```
// A RemoteEventListener for print events

package corejini.chapter13;

import net.jini.core.event.RemoteEventListener;

public interface PrintListener extends RemoteEventListener{
}
```

If you recall the discussion we had way back in Chapter 3, you'll remember that `RemoteEventListener` is the interface that recipients of remote events should implement. This interface has one method, called `notify()`, that is called whenever an event generator delivers an event to a recipient. The `PrintListener` class is a simple, no-method extension to the `RemoteEventListener` interface; in fact, the new interface is defined here only so that you can extend `PrintListener` independently in the future if you have to.

The `notify()` method of `RemoteEventListener` is defined to take a `RemoteEvent` as a parameter. The printing service that you'll see in a bit will actually deliver `PrintServiceEvents`, which are subclasses of `RemoteEvent`. This new event type contains extra information that clients can use to determine if a print request has succeeded or, if it has failed, why it has failed.

The `PrintServiceEvent` class (Listing 13–5) is a subclass of `RemoteEvent`. It contains within it an `Exception` that indicates why the client's

Listing 13–5 `PrintServiceEvent.java`

```
// A remote event that signals printer completion/failure

package corejini.chapter13;

import java.io.Serializable;
import net.jini.core.event.RemoteEvent;

public class PrintServiceEvent extends RemoteEvent
    implements Serializable {
    protected Exception ex;

    PrintServiceEvent(PrintProxy proxy, long seq,
                                    Exception ex) {
        super(proxy, 0 /* type */, seq, null);
        this.ex = ex;
    }

    public Exception getException() {
        return ex;
    }
    public boolean printJobFinished() {
        return ex == null;
    }
}
```

print request failed, or will be set to null if the print request completed successfully. The `getException()` method returns the nested exception, and the `printJobFinished()` method can be used to determine whether or not the print request completed.

Note that the constructor for this class is package protected, because only the printing service will ever generate new events. When a new `PrintServiceEvent` is created, it is initialized with a proxy object that indicates the source of the event (this proxy can be used to communicate back with the printing service), an event type ID and a sequence number that together uniquely identify the event, and the exception. We'll look at type IDs and sequence numbers in more detail in the next chapter, but basically these are a way for clients to uniquely identify and distinguish particular events. In the printing example, sequence numbers are monotonically increasing, and are saved to persistent storage so that they will never be reused. The service could be better behaved by not using zero as the value of all its event type IDs, but this is good enough for now. See Chapter 14 for more details.

The Remote Printing Interface

Now that we've looked at the APIs for printing and for notification, we can look at the remote printing interface (Listing 13–6). This is the set of methods and conventions that the proxy object will use to communicate back with the printing service running on some remote machine on the network.

Listing 13–6 `RemotePrinter.java`

```
// This is the interface that the proxy uses to communicate
// with the service's back end.

package corejini.chapter13;

import java.rmi.Remote;
import java.rmi.RemoteException;
import net.jini.admin.Administrable;

public interface RemotePrinter extends Remote,
                                        Administrable {
    public void print(int format, int copies, Object data,
                      PrintListener listener)
        throws RemoteException;
}
```

As might be expected, the remote printing API looks similar to the local printing API. The `RemotePrinter` interface extends `Remote`, so we know that the service proxy will use RMI for communication with the printing service. The `print()` method has the same parameters as the local version, and the interface extends `Administrable`, so it also supports a `getAdmin()` method that will fetch an administrative proxy object from the remote printing service.

The Print Service Proxy

All the pieces are now in place to develop the proxy object (Listing 13–7) that will be sent to clients of the printing service. You can think of this proxy as a bit of code that mediates between the local printing APIs provided by the `Printer` interface, and the remote printing APIs provided by the `RemotePrinter` interface.

The methods of the proxy object do a bit of type checking on their arguments, so that some types of failures can be detected locally, without having to do a complete round-trip to the service.

Listing 13–7 `PrintProxy.java`

```
// This is the actual proxy object that will be sent to
// clients.

package corejini.chapter13;

import java.io.Serializable;
import java.rmi.RemoteException;
import net.jini.admin.Administrable;
import java.awt.print.PageFormat;

public class PrintProxy implements Serializable,
                Administrable, Printer {
    protected RemotePrinter remote;

    PrintProxy(RemotePrinter remote) {
        this.remote = remote;
    }

    public void print(int format, int copies, Object data,
                     PrintListener listener)
        throws RemoteException {
        switch (format) {
        case PageFormat.LANDSCAPE:
        case PageFormat.PORTRAIT:
        case PageFormat.REVERSE_LANDSCAPE:
            break;
        default:
            throw new IllegalArgumentException(
                                "Bogus page format");
        }

        if (data == null) {
            throw new NullPointerException("data");
        }

        remote.print(format, copies, data, listener);
    }
```

Listing 13–7 `PrintProxy.java` **(continued)**

```
    public Object getAdmin() throws RemoteException {
        return remote.getAdmin();
    }
    public boolean equals(Object o) {
        if (o instanceof PrintProxy) {
            return ((PrintProxy) o).remote.equals(remote);
        } else {
            return false;
        }
    }

    // Two objects that are equals() must have the same
    // hashCode() value. So here I override hashCode() to
    // return the hash code of the remote object.
    public int hashCode() {
            return remote.hashCode();
    }
}
```

The `PrintProxy` class implements a handful of useful interfaces: it is `Serializable` since it will be sent over the wire; it is `Administrable` since it can provide an administrative proxy for controlling the service; and it is a `Printer` since it exposes the local printing API to clients.

Whenever the proxy is created, it is initialized with a reference to an object implementing the `RemotePrinter` interface; this reference will be used to communicate with the back-end remote printing service.

The two main methods here, `print()` and `getAdmin()`, forward these invocations to the remote printing service. But `print()` also embeds a bit of intelligence to check the values of the `format` and `data` arguments; bogus values here will cause exceptions to be raised locally, without the need to go to the printing service to determine that a failure has occurred.

Finally, the `equals()` method reports that two `PrintProxies` are equal if they refer to the same printing service. This implementation of `equals()` is a convenience to clients so that the proxy objects returned as the sources of `PrintServiceEvents` can be easily compared against the proxies that clients already hold. Likewise, here I've reimplemented `hashCode()` to have correct semantics. The value returned from this method must be the same for any two objects that are `equals()`; since `equals()` is based on whether two proxies refer to the same remote object, I've changed `hashCode()` to simply return the hash value of the remote object.

Printer Administration APIs and UIs

We've seen that the `PrintProxy` can provide an administrative object for the printing service, by going through the `RemotePrinter` interface to fetch one from the back-end service. This administrative object, as we will see, is a subclass of `BasicUnicastAdmin` that implements the "big three" administrative interfaces (`JoinAdmin`, `DestroyAdmin`, and `StorageLocationAdmin`), but also implements a *custom* administrative interface that clients can use to view particular aspects of the print service.

The custom administrative API defined here is quite simple—it provides a way to view the jobs currently queued by the printing service—but it serves as an example of a custom administrative interface. And, since this custom interface is likely to be known to only a handful of specially written clients that have advance knowledge of how to use it, we'll need to provide a user interface that can allow *anyone* to directly interact with it without having to understand the programmatic interface.

First, let's look at the API for the custom print administration interface as shown in Listing 13–8.

Listing 13–8 `PrintAdmin.java`

```
// A simple interface for printer administration

package corejini.chapter13;

import java.util.Vector;
import java.rmi.RemoteException;

public interface PrintAdmin {
    public Vector getJobs() throws RemoteException;
}
```

This interface has one method, `getJobs()`, that returns the currently queued jobs. You can easily extend the APIs here to provide a richer set of administrative functions, perhaps to reorder or delete print jobs. The `getJobs()` method returns a vector of `JobRecords`, each of which contains information about the queued job. We'll see the definition of `JobRecord` a bit later when we look at the implementation of the printing service.

But next, let's look at a custom user interface for viewing objects that implement `PrintAdmin`. This interface can be attached as an attribute and sent along with the printing service's proxy object. Clients can then instantiate the attribute and initialize it by passing the service's administrative object to it.

Figure 13–1 shows a screenshot of the user interface. The UI consists of a simple list box containing the queued jobs, in order of first to last. The "refresh" button contacts the service to retrieve a fresh list of jobs.

Print Admin Panel

Current Print Jobs

portrait, 1 copies, Hello World

portrait, 1 copies, Hello Again

portrait, 1 copies, Hello World

Refresh

Figure 13–1 The PrintAdminPanel GUI

The code that implements this user interface and can be used as an attribute is shown in Listing 13–9.

Listing 13–9 `PrintAdminPanel.java`

```
// A user interface for PrintAdmin objects

package corejini.chapter13;

import net.jini.core.entry.Entry;
import java.awt.*;
import java.awt.event.*;
import javax.swing.*;
import java.util.Vector;
import java.rmi.RemoteException;

public class PrintAdminPanel extends JPanel
                 implements Entry {
    public PrintAdminPanel() {
        super();
    }
```

Listing 13–9 `PrintAdminPanel.java` **(continued)**

```
    public void setAdmin(final PrintAdmin admin) {
        setLayout(new BorderLayout());

        add(new JLabel("Current Print Jobs"), "North");

        final JList list = new JList();
        add(list, "Center");
          JButton refreshButton = new JButton("Refresh");


            refreshButton.addActionListener(
                 new ActionListener() {
            public void actionPerformed(ActionEvent ev) {
                Vector jobs = null;
                try {
                    jobs = admin.getJobs();
                         } catch (RemoteException ex) {
                   System.err.println("Error getting jobs:"
                                     + ex.getMessage());
                }
                list.setListData(jobs);
            }
        });

        add(refreshButton, "South");

        // force a refresh
        refreshButton.doClick();
    }
}
```

The `PrintAdminPanel` is a subclass of `JPanel` and implements `Entry`. As such, it can be embedded in other Swing components, and can be attached to a service's proxy object as an attribute.

When a `PrintAdminPanel` is transmitted to a client it is fully constructed, but as yet uninitialized, invisible, and has no contents. Clients that wish to display the `PrintAdminPanel` initialize it by calling `setAdmin()` and passing in the administrative object for the printing service. This method creates the user interface for the panel. Clients can then install the panel in a `JFrame` or other component to make it visible.

Internals of the Print Service

With the details of the local and remote printing APIs, as well as the administrative interfaces out of the way, we can now begin to look at the implementation of the internals of the printing service. The printing service follows many of the same patterns we've seen earlier in this book (a "wrapper" application that implements the back-end portion of the service, and manages the Jini obligations of the service), and so can be built atop the infrastructure classes from earlier in this chapter.

The service's back-end subclasses `BasicUnicastService`, and so communicates with its proxies via RMI. It creates a class to perform administration which is a subclass of `BasicUnicastAdmin`, with additional methods to support the `PrintAdmin` interface.

Let's look at the heart of this code (Listing 13–10).

Listing 13–10 `PrintService.java`

```
// This is the actual print service back end.

package corejini.chapter13;

import java.awt.print.*;
import java.io.*;
import java.util.*;
import java.rmi.server.UnicastRemoteObject;
import java.rmi.*;
import net.jini.core.lease.*;
import net.jini.core.lookup.*;
import net.jini.core.entry.*;
import net.jini.core.discovery.*;
import com.sun.jini.lookup.*;
import net.jini.admin.JoinAdmin;
import com.sun.jini.admin.DestroyAdmin;
import com.sun.jini.admin.StorageLocationAdmin;
import net.jini.lookup.entry.*;
public class PrintService extends BasicUnicastService
    implements RemotePrinter,
               BasicUnicastService.RestoreListener {
    protected Vector queue = new Vector();
    protected Hashtable agents = new Hashtable();
    protected PrintThread printThread;
    protected boolean done = false;
    protected PrintRecord currentRecord = null;
    protected PrintAdmin remoteAdmin = null;
    protected long lastEventSeqNo = 0;
```

Listing 13–10 `PrintService.java` **(continued)**

```
    // override to get correct shutdown behavior
    protected void shutdown() {
        done = true;
        notify();
        super.shutdown();
    }

    public PrintService(String storageLoc)
                                throws RemoteException {
        super(storageLoc);
    }
    // override base implementation to also save
    // PrintServiceData
    protected void checkpoint() throws IOException {
        checkpoint(new PrintServiceData(currentRecord,
                                        queue,
                                        lastEventSeqNo));
    }

    // override base implementation
    protected void initialize()
            throws IOException, ClassNotFoundException {
        super.initialize();

        printThread = new PrintThread();
        printThread.start();
    }

    // override base implementation
    protected Entry[] getAttributes() {
        Entry[] entries = new Entry[2];
        entries[0] = new ServiceInfo("Prentice-Hall",
                                    "PrintService",
                                    "PrintService",
                                    null,
                                    "Prentice-Hall",
                                    "v1.0");
        entries[1] = new PrintAdminPanel();
        return entries;
    }

    // override base implementation
    protected Object getProxy() {
        return new PrintProxy(this);
    }
```

Listing 13–10 `PrintService.java` (continued)

```
    // implement RestoreListener
    public void restored(Object subclassData) {
        PrintServiceData data = (PrintServiceData)
                                        subclassData;
        currentRecord = data.currentRecord;
        queue = data.queue;
        lastEventSeqNo = data.lastEventSeqNo;
    }

    public void print(int format, int copies, Object data,
                      PrintListener listener) {
        Object agent = getPrintAgent(data);
        PrintRecord record = new PrintRecord(format,
                                     copies, data,
                                     agent, listener);
        queuePrinting(record);
    }

    public Object getAdmin() throws RemoteException {
        if (remoteAdmin == null) {
            remoteAdmin = new PrintAdminImpl(this);
        }

        return remoteAdmin;
    }

    Object getPrintAgent(Object data) {
        if (data instanceof Printable) {
            return data;
        }
        if (data instanceof Pageable) {
            return data;
        }

        // build a list of data's classes and search for
        // them, most specific to least.
        Vector classes = getClasses(data);

        for (int i=0, size=classes.size() ; i<size ; i++) {
            Object o = agents.get(classes.elementAt(i));
            if (o != null) {
                return o;
            }
        }
```

Listing 13–10 `PrintService.java` **(continued)**

```
        System.out.println("No print agent found");
        return null;
    }

    Vector getClasses(Object data) {
        Vector classes = new Vector();
        Class nextClass = data.getClass();

        while (nextClass != null) {
            classes.addElement(nextClass);
            Class[] interfaces = nextClass.getInterfaces();
            for (int i=0, size=interfaces.length ; i<size ;
                                                        i++) {
                classes.addElement(interfaces[i]);
            }

            nextClass = nextClass.getSuperclass();
        }

        return classes;
    }

    void queuePrinting(PrintRecord record) {
        queue.addElement(record);
        try {
            checkpoint();
        } catch (IOException ex) {
            System.err.println("Trouble checkpointing; " +
                               "couldn't save job: " +
                               ex.getMessage());
        }

        synchronized(this) {
            notify();
        }
    }
```

Listing 13–10 PrintService.java (continued)

```
class PrintThread extends Thread {
   public void run() {
       while (!done) {
           PrintRecord record = null;

        //
        // Grab the next item off the queue.  Check
        // currentRecord, since we may be
        // initialized with a print job in-progress
        // after a restore.
        //
        if (currentRecord == null) {
                synchronized (PrintService.this) {
                    if (queue.size() != 0) {
                         record = (PrintRecord)
                                   queue.elementAt(0);

                         currentRecord = record;
                         queue.removeElementAt(0);

                       try {
                           checkpoint();
                       } catch (IOException ex) {
                           System.out.println(
                             "Couldn't checkpoint; " +
                             "job not saved: " +
                             ex.getMessage());
                       }
                   }
               }
           } else {
               record = currentRecord;
           }
```

Listing 13–10 `PrintService.java` (continued)

```
        //
        // Print it, if we have something to print.
        //
        if (record != null) {
            Exception ex = printRecord(record);
            if (record.listener != null) {
                PrintServiceEvent ev =
                    new PrintServiceEvent((
                            PrintProxy) proxy,
                            lastEventSeqNo++,
                                        ex);
                try {
                    record.listener.notify(ev);
                } catch (Exception ex2) {
                    System.err.println(
                      "Trouble sending event: " +
                          ex2.getMessage());
                }
            }

            currentRecord = null
            try {
                checkpoint();
            } catch (IOException ex2) {
                System.out.println(
                        "Couldn't checkpoint; " +
                        "job not saved: " +
                        ex2.getMessage());
            }
        }

        //
        // Wait for more stuff on the queue...
        //
        if (queue.size() > 0)
             continue;
```

Listing 13–10 `PrintService.java` **(continued)**

```
            synchronized(PrintService.this) {
                try {
                     PrintService.this.wait();
                } catch (InterruptedException ex) {
                }
              }
            }
        }

        Exception printRecord(PrintRecord record) {
            Exception ex = null;

            PageFormat format = new PageFormat();
            format.setOrientation(record.format);

            PrinterJob job = PrinterJob.getPrinterJob();
            job.setCopies(record.copies);
            job.defaultPage(format);

            if (record.agent instanceof Pageable) {
                job.setPageable((Pageable) record.agent);
                try {
                   job.print();
                } catch (Exception ex2) {
                   ex = ex2;
                }
            } else if (record.agent instanceof Printable) {
                job.setPrintable((Printable)
                                 record.agent, format);
               try {
                   job.print();
               } catch (Exception ex2) {
                   ex = ex2;
               }
            } else {
                ex = new IllegalArgumentException(
                                         "Bad agent");
            }

            return ex;
        }
    }
```

Listing 13–10 `PrintService.java` **(continued)**

```
    public static void main(String[] args) {
        try {
            if (args.length != 1) {
                System.err.println("Usage: PrintService " +
                                   "<datafile>");
                System.exit(1);
            }

            PrintService service =
                         new PrintService(args[0]);
            service.initialize();
            System.out.println("Print Service Started");
        } catch (Exception ex) {
            System.err.println("Error starting service: " +
                               ex.getMessage());
            System.exit(1);
        }
    }
}
```

In addition to extending `BasicUnicastService`, the `PrintService` class also implements the `RemotePrinter` interface, which clients will use to communicate with it, and `RestoreListener`, so that it can have a chance to update the data particular to itself after it is restored.

When the service is run, its `main()` routine instantiates a new `PrintService` object with a command-line argument that indicates the location of the service's persistent storage. In the constructor for `PrintService`, this argument is passed to the constructor for `BasicUnicastService` which handles the actual restoration of old data, or creation of the service for the first time.

After creating a `PrintService` object, `main()` calls `initialize()`, which is overridden from the base `BasicUnicastService` superclass. The `initialize()` method calls `BasicUnicastService.initialize()` which, as you have seen, sets up the `RestoreListener`, and then tries to restore the service, or creates a "fresh" `JoinManager` if this is the first time the service has been run. The rest of `PrintService`'s version of `initialize()` creates and starts a `PrintThread`, which is a thread that monitors and dispatches the print queue.

The `PrintService` class overrides a few key methods that are used to determine the behavior of `BasicUnicastService`. The `getProxy()` method is implemented to return a new `PrintProxy`; `getAttributes()`

creates and returns two attributes that will be attached to the service's entry wherever it is registered. The first of these is a `ServiceInfo` attribute that describes the printing service; the second is the `PrintAdminPanel` that can provide a user interface to print administration.

The `PrintService` class also initializes some "working" storage that it will use as it runs. The `queue` vector contains the current queue of submitted print requests; `agents` is a list of mappings from `Class` objects to print "agents" or "handlers" that know how to render objects of those classes onto a printer; `proxy` is the print proxy that will be sent to clients.

As we'll see in this example, the notion of print agents is used to separate the data that's being printed from the code that knows how to print it. In this example's current form, all objects sent to the print service should implement `Printable` or `Pageable` so that they can effectively "be their own agents." But the mechanisms here provide a way for you to extend this example to create new printing code that can be used to render objects of *arbitrary* types. I'll talk about how to do this at the end of the chapter.

After initialization, a new `PrintThread` object is created and started. This thread monitors the print request queue and handles printing the requests stored there. It will sleep if the print queue becomes empty, and will be awakened if new items are added. This separate thread allows printing to happen in the background, separate from any other threads in the system that might be servicing administrative calls, performing join duties, and so on.

The facilities in `PrintService` for handling persistent data build on those provided by `BasicUnicastService`. Here the `checkpoint()` call is overridden to call the superclass' version, passing it an instance of `PrintServiceData` to be saved in addition to the information already saved by `BasicUnicastService`. The `PrintServiceData` object contains the print job currently being serviced (if there is one), the contents of the print queue, and the last sequence number used in an outgoing event.

Since `PrintService` implements the `RestoreListener` interface, its `restored()` method will be called after the service is resumed, with the subclass-specific data passed as an argument. In the case of `PrintService`, this data will be an instance of `PrintServiceData` (since this is the type of the "extra" data passed to `checkpoint()`). The `restored()` method initializes the currently printing job, the print queue, and the last event sequence number from this data.

The `checkpoint()` method will be called "automatically" by `BasicUnicastService` any time that data under its control changes. So, for example, the state of the service is checkpointed whenever a service ID is assigned to it, or from the various administrative methods. But `checkpoint()` is also

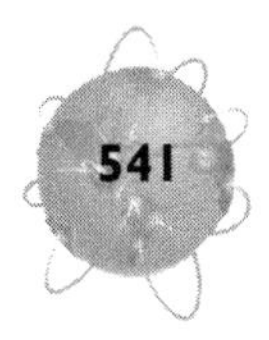

called directly from `PrintService` whenever any data specific to this subclass of `BasicUnicastService` changes. So checkpointing is done from the `PrintThread` as print jobs are dispatched. It is important to make sure that your services save their state any time they make a change that will need to be reflected across restarts; they need to make sure that changed data is reliably saved to disk.

Printing

Let's look at the actual mechanics of printing now. The main entry point for printing is the `print()` method. This method takes the data to be printed, some parameters to control printing, and—optionally—a listener that will be called when printing completes, either successfully or unsuccessfully.

The `print()` method first calls `getPrintAgent()` to get an "agent" that knows how to print the data that has just been received. An agent in this context is simply an object that implements either `Printable` or `Pageable`, so that it can be used with Java's printing subsystem, and "understands" how to render a particular type of data. If the object that is passed to `getPrintAgent()` is itself `Printable` or `Pageable`, then it is simply returned—the object is "self-printing," as it already knows how to print itself. Otherwise, the object to be printed is introspected and all the classes and interfaces that it extends or implements are found. These are, in turn, looked up in a hashtable to see if any printing agents have been installed for any of these particular types. This is an avenue for future expansion—you can "preregister" agents for common types, such as strings of text and images, and make these printable by the service. Clients could even transmit new print agents to the service to extend its abilities at run time.

Once a print agent has been found for the data, the `print()` method creates a new `PrintRecord` (described below) to hold the information about the request, and queues the record by calling `queuePrinting()`.

The `queuePrinting()` method adds the new record to the end of the print queue, and checkpoints the state of the service. This checkpoint is necessary so that if the service crashes after receiving the print request, but before it can be completed, the service can resume printing without losing data. After checkpointing, `queuePrinting()` calls `notify()` (defined in `java.lang.Object`) to wake up the `PrintThread` if it is waiting for new data to appear in the queue.

The `PrintThread` class is where the heart of printing and queue management lives. One `PrintThread` instance will be created and started whenever the service is run. The `run()` method on this thread essentially sits in a big loop, processing items in the job queue. At the start of a pass, it looks to see if there is currently a job in progress. This will be the case if, for instance, the service crashed while printing and then resumed—the `PrintThread` should dispatch any current print job before moving on to the rest of the queue. If no job was in progress, then it dequeues the item at the head of the print queue, makes this the currently processed job, and checkpoints itself to remember that it is processing this item.

After grabbing an item to print, the thread actually prints it by calling `printRecord()`. This method handles the interaction with the Java printing subsystem by creating a new `PrinterJob`, initializing it with the parameters specified in the client's print request, and then beginning printing. This method causes the `PrintThread` to block until finished, at which point it returns any exception that may have occurred, or null if printing completed successfully.

Back in the `PrintThread`, after `printRecord()` finishes, the client's listener is notified, if one has been provided, by delivering a new `PrintServiceEvent` to it. This event has a fresh sequence number, generated by incrementing the count of used sequence numbers. If event delivery fails—most likely because the client that issued the request has crashed or terminated before the job completed—an exception will be raised and caught, and the service will continue processing normally. The current print job is cleared to indicate that no work is in progress—the job has been completely dispatched—and the state of the service is checkpointed again. Checkpointing also saves the last used sequence number, to ensure that sequence numbers are never reused, and that clients can readily distinguish multiple events from this service.

Finally, if more print jobs are waiting to be printed, the thread continues processing jobs. Otherwise, it blocks by calling `wait()`, which causes it to sleep until new jobs are added and `notify()` is called.

Persistent Data Formats

The `checkpoint()` and `restored()` methods rely on two nested classes to store data. The first is `PrintServiceData` (Listing 13–11), which contains all the persistent state of the `PrintService` which is not already held by its superclass, `BasicUnicastService`. Instances of `PrintServiceData` will be read from and written to the persistent storage file as the service runs. This class contains the currently executing job, the contents of the entire print queue, and the last used sequence number.

Listing 13–11 `PrintServiceData`

```
// This holds the print service's persistent data.

static class PrintServiceData implements Serializable {
    PrintRecord currentRecord;
    Vector queue;
    long lastEventSeqNo;

    PrintServiceData(PrintRecord currentRecord,
                    Vector queue, long lastEventSeqNo) {
        this.currentRecord = currentRecord;
        this.queue = queue;
        this.lastEventSeqNo = lastEventSeqNo;
    }
}
```

The current record as well as the items in the queue are instances of `PrintRecord` (Listing 13–12). Each `PrintRecord` contains information needed to dispatch one print request: the format of the request (portrait, landscape, etc.), the number of desired copies, the data to print, the "agent" that knows how to print it, and the listener that will be called when the job finishes.

Listing 13–12 `PrintRecord`

```
// Each print record is a particular job.

static class PrintRecord implements Serializable {
    int format;
    int copies;
    Object data;
    Object agent;
    PrintListener listener;

    PrintRecord(int format, int copies, Object data,
                Object agent, PrintListener listener) {
        this.format = format;
        this.copies = copies;
        this.data = data;
        this.agent = agent;
        this.listener = listener;
    }
}
```

Implementing Print Service Administration

The final big piece of the puzzle is the implementation of administration for the printing service. In this particular case, administration is implemented by a separate nested object that is a subclass of `BasicUnicastAdmin`. The administrative object that the print service returns to callers is actually the *stub* for this implementation. This arrangement is different than the approach from Chapter 12. In that chapter, the administrative object is a separate proxy that forwards its methods on to a remote object that lives in the back-end portion of the service. Here, I've simply used the remote object's stub as the administrative object, as there is no difference in the API that is presented to clients and the API that's implemented "natively" by the remote administration object. (Using an RMI-generated stub is actually just the "degenerate" case of the sort of proxy that I've used all along in this book—that is, it's a serializable object that gets sent over the wire so that clients can use the back end. But in the case of the RMI stub, the proxy is automatically generated by `rmic`, and consists of only remote methods, no local ones.)

By basing the implementation of the administrative object on `BasicUnicastAdmin`, the service gets an implementation of `JoinAdmin`, `StorageLocationAdmin`, and `DestroyAdmin` "for free." The subclass need only implement the methods particular to `PrintAdmin`.

Let's look at how this works (see Listing 13–13). The service's `getAdmin()` method creates an instance of `PrintAdminImpl` the first time it is called, and returns this to its caller. The caller, in this case, will be the `PrintProxy` object, which will simply return this object to callers. Since the stubs for remote objects are returned in place of the actual remote implementations in RMI calls, clients will, after calling `getAdmin()` on their `PrintProxies`, have an RMI stub that refers directly to the underlying `PrintAdminImpl` object.

Listing 13–13 `RemotePrintAdmin, PrintAdminImpl`

```
    // This interface groups together all the
    // administration interfaces

    interface RemotePrintAdmin
            extends BasicUnicastAdmin.RemoteUnicastAdmin,
                              PrintAdmin, Remote {
   }
```

Listing 13–13 `RemotePrintAdmin, PrintAdminImpl` **(continued)**

```
// An implementation of the RemotePrintAdmin interface.
// Since the code here extends BasicUnicastAdmin, all
// the "basic" interfaces are already handled; this code
// only needs to implement getJobs().

class PrintAdminImpl extends BasicUnicastAdmin
    implements RemotePrintAdmin {

    PrintAdminImpl(PrintService s)
                         throws RemoteException {
        super(s);
    }

    public Vector getJobs() {
        Vector jobs = new Vector();
        synchronized (PrintService.this) {
            if (currentRecord != null) {
                jobs.addElement(
                  new JobRecord(currentRecord, true));
            }

            for (int i=0, size=queue.size() ; i<size ;
                                               i++) {
                jobs.addElement(new JobRecord(
                                  (PrintRecord)
                                  queue.elementAt(i),
                                          false));
            }
        }
        return jobs;
    }
}
```

Here you see the `RemotePrintAdmin` interface, which is a "remote" version of the `PrintAdmin` interface. This interface must be declared so that the RMI stubs compiler will know which methods on `PrintAdminImpl` are meant to be callable remotely.

`PrintAdminImpl` implements all the particular administrative interfaces; the implementations of `JoinAdmin`, `DestroyAdmin`, and `StorageLocationAdmin` are gained by subclassing `BasicUnicastAdmin`, and the object also implements the `RemotePrintAdmin` interface, by returning details about the currently queued print jobs when asked. Rather than returning "private," implementation-specific details about the listeners registered with print jobs, and so on, the implementation of `getJobs()` returns a vector of `JobRecords` (Listing 13–14). These `JobRecords` contain some of the same information as `PrintRecords`, but without some of the internal details used by `PrintRecords`. `JobRecords` contain a string describing the printed data, without containing the data itself.

Listing 13–14 `JobRecord`

```
// JobRecords are returned from the getJobs() method.

public static class JobRecord implements Serializable {
   boolean current;
   int format;
   int copies;
   String dataName;
   int jobid;

   JobRecord(PrintRecord rec, boolean current) {
       this.current = current;
       this.format = rec.format;
       this.copies = rec.copies;
       this.dataName = rec.data.toString();
       this.jobid = rec.hashCode();
   }

   public boolean getCurrent() {
       return current;
   }
   public int getFormat() {
       return format;
   }
   public int getCopies() {
       return copies;
   }
   public String getDataName() {
       return dataName;
   }
   public int getJobID() {
       return jobid;
   }
   public String toString() {
       StringBuffer buf = new StringBuffer();
```

Listing 13–14 `JobRecord` (continued)

```
            if (current) {
                buf.append("[CURRENT] ");
            }
            switch (format) {
            case PageFormat.PORTRAIT:
                buf.append("portrait, ");
                break;
            case PageFormat.LANDSCAPE:
                buf.append("landscape, ");
                break;
            case PageFormat.REVERSE_LANDSCAPE:
                buf.append("reverse, ");
                break;
            }
            buf.append(copies + " copies, ");
            buf.append(dataName);

            return buf.toString();
        }
    }
```

A Print Client

Now we can build a simple client (Listing 13–15) to test out the service. This client will use discovery to find lookup services and then search for `PrintServices` there. Once such a service is found, the client will issue a couple of print requests, and register itself as the listener for these jobs so that it can determine whether they succeed or fail. The client will also download the `PrintAdminPanel` attribute for the service and use this to create a UI for the printing service.

When a `PrintAdminPanel` attribute is found, it is initialized by calling the `setAdmin()` method on it. As mentioned in the last chapter, it would be great if there were a standardized interface that administrative user interfaces implemented that allowed this task to be generalized across different user interface classes. But without this ability in Jini at the time of writing, I've had to explicitly "know" that this `setAdmin()` method exists on `Print-AdminPanel` here.

Listing 13–15 `Client.java`

```
// A client of the print service

package corejini.chapter13;

import net.jini.discovery.*;
import net.jini.core.lookup.*;
import net.jini.core.event.*;
import net.jini.core.entry.*;
import net.jini.admin.*;
import java.io.*;
import java.awt.print.*;
import java.awt.*;
import java.rmi.*;
import java.rmi.server.*;
import java.awt.event.*;
import javax.swing.*;

public class Client implements Runnable {
    ServiceTemplate template;

    // An inner class for discovery
    class Discoverer implements DiscoveryListener {
        public void discovered(DiscoveryEvent ev) {
            ServiceRegistrar[] regs = ev.getRegistrars();
            for (int i=0 ; i<regs.length ; i++) {
                doit(regs[i]);
            }
        }
        public void discarded(DiscoveryEvent ev) {
        }
    }

    public Client() throws IOException {
        Class[] types = { Printer.class };
        template = new ServiceTemplate(null, types, null);

        LookupDiscovery disco =
            new LookupDiscovery(
                                LookupDiscovery.ALL_GROUPS);
        disco.addDiscoveryListener(new Discoverer());
    }
```

Listing 13–15 `Client.java` (continued)

```
void doit(ServiceRegistrar reg) {
    Printer printer = null;
    Entry[] attributes = null;

    try {
        ServiceMatches matches = reg.lookup(template,
                                    Integer.MAX_VALUE);
        if (matches.totalMatches > 0) {
            printer = (Printer)
                         matches.items[0].service;
           attributes = matches.items[0].attributeSets;
        } else {
            printer = null;
        }
    } catch (Exception ex) {
        System.err.println("Doing lookup: " +
                                  ex.getMessage());
        ex.printStackTrace();
    }

    if (printer == null)
        return;

    System.out.println("Got a printer!");

          // issue a couple of print requests.
    try {
        printer.print(PageFormat.PORTRAIT, 1,
                   new PrintableString("Hello World"),
                      new Listener());
        printer.print(PageFormat.LANDSCAPE, 1,
                   new PrintableString("Hello Again"),
                      new Listener());
    } catch (Exception ex) {
        System.out.println("Trouble printing: " +
                                  ex.getMessage());
        ex.printStackTrace();
    }

    PrintAdminPanel panel = null;

    for (int i=0, size=attributes.length ; i<size; i++){
        if (attributes[i] instanceof PrintAdminPanel)
            panel = (PrintAdminPanel) attributes[i];
    }
```

Listing 13–15 `Client.java` **(continued)**

```
        if (panel != null) {
            try {
                panel.setAdmin((PrintAdmin)
                                  ((Administrable)
                                  printer).getAdmin());
            } catch (RemoteException ex) {
                System.err.println("Error getting admin: "
                                      + ex.getMessage());
                ex.printStackTrace();
            }

            final JFrame frame =
                new JFrame("Print Admin Panel");
            frame.getContentPane().add(panel);
            frame.pack();
            frame.setVisible(true);
            frame.addWindowListener(new WindowAdapter() {
               public void windowClosing(WindowEvent ev) {
                   frame.setVisible(false);
                   frame.dispose();
               }
            });
        }
    }

    // An inner class for handling events.
    class Listener extends UnicastRemoteObject
                            implements PrintListener {
        Listener() throws RemoteException {
            super();
        }
        public void notify(RemoteEvent e) {
            if (!(e instanceof PrintServiceEvent)) {
                return;
            }
            PrintServiceEvent ev = (PrintServiceEvent) e;
            if (ev.printJobFinished()) {
                System.out.println(
                         "Job finished successfully!");
            } else {
                System.out.println("Job failed:  " +
                         ev.getException().getMessage());
                ev.getException().printStackTrace();
            }
        }
    }
```

Listing 13–15 `Client.java` **(continued)**

```
        public void run() {
        while (true) {
            try {
                Thread.sleep(Integer.MAX_VALUE);
            } catch (InterruptedException ex) {
            }
        }
    }


    // A string that implements Printable
    static class PrintableString
                    implements Printable, Serializable {
        String s;
        PrintableString(String s) {
            this.s = s;
        }
        public int print(Graphics g, PageFormat pf,
                    int page) throws PrinterException {
            if (page >= 1) {
                return Printable.NO_SUCH_PAGE;
            }
            g.drawString(s, 20, 60);
            return Printable.PAGE_EXISTS;
        }
        public String toString() {
            return s;
        }
    }

    public static void main(String[] args) {
        try {
            Client client = new Client();
            new Thread(client).start();
        } catch (Exception ex) {
           System.err.println("Bogus: " + ex.getMessage());
            System.exit(1);
        }
    }
}
```

Print jobs are issued to the service by passing it instances of a class called `PrintableString`. This is a simple class, implemented by the client, that wraps a Java string and provides an implementation of the `Printable` interface needed to tell the service how to render a particular data type. `PrintableString` has a `print()` method that renders its string in the default font on the page.

The client also provides a class called `Listener` which implements `PrintListener` to receive `PrintServiceEvents`. Whenever events are received, the `Listener` class prints out details about the success or failure of the print job.

Compiling and Running the Examples

To run the sample code here, first compile the service and the client to their respective directories. You'll then have to run `rmic` on the three classes that implement remote interfaces: `Client.Listener`, `PrintService`, and `PrintService.PrintAdminImpl`. In addition to any RMI-generated stubs, the proxy for the printing service must be downloadable by the client. So be sure to copy it to the `service-dl` directory.

On Windows:

```
javac -classpath C:\jini1_0\lib\jini-core.jar;
                             C:\jini1_0\lib\jini-ext.jar;
                             C:\jini1_0\lib\sun-util.jar;
                             C:\service
            -d C:\service
           C:\files\corejini\chapter13\PrintService.java
javac -classpath C:\jini1_0\lib\jini-core.jar;
                             C:\jini1_0\lib\jini-ext.jar;
                             C:\jini1_0\lib\sun-util.jar;
                             C:\client
            -d C:\client
           C:\files\corejini\chapter13\Client.java
```

```
rmic -classpath C:\jdk1.2\jre\lib\rt.jar;
                             C:\jini1_0\lib\jini-core.jar;
                             C:\jini1_0\lib\jini-ext.jar;
                             C:\jini1_0\lib\sun-util.jar;
                             C:\client
            -d C:\client-dl
        corejini.chapter13.Client.Listener

rmic -classpath C:\jdk1.2\jre\lib\rt.jar;
                             C:\jini1_0\lib\jini-core.jar;
                             C:\jini1_0\lib\jini-ext.jar;
                             C:\jini1_0\lib\sun-util.jar;
                             C:\service
            -d C:\service-dl
        corejini.chapter13.PrintService
        corejini.chapter13.PrintService.PrintAdminImpl
cd C:\service\corejini\chapter13
copy PrintProxy.class
            C:\service-dl\corejini\chapter13
```

On Solaris:

```
javac -classpath /files/jini1_0/lib/jini-core.jar:
                         /files/jini1_0/lib/jini-ext.jar:
                         /files/jini1_0/lib/sun-util.jar:
                         /files/service
             -d /files/service
            /files/corejini/chapter13/PrintService.java
javac -classpath /files/jini1_0/lib/jini-core.jar:
                         /files/jini1_0/lib/jini-ext.jar:
                         /files/jini1_0/lib/sun-util.jar:
                         /files/client
             -d /files/client
            /files/files/corejini/chapter13/Client.java

rmic -classpath /files/jdk1.2/jre/lib\rt.jar:
                         /files/jini1_0/lib/jini-core.jar:
                         /files/jini1_0/lib/jini-ext.jar:
                         /files/jini1_0/lib/sun-util.jar:
                         /files/client
            -d /files/client-dl
        corejini.chapter13.Client.Listener
```

```
rmic -classpath /jdk1.2/jre/lib/rt.jar:
                         /files/jini1_0/lib/jini-core.jar:
                         /files/jini1_0/lib/jini-ext.jar:
                         /files/jini1_0/lib/sun-util.jar:
                         /files/service
             -d /files/service-dl
         corejini.chapter13.PrintService
         corejini.chapter13.PrintService.PrintAdminImpl
cd /files/service/corejini/chapter13
copy PrintProxy.class
             /files/service-dl/corejini/chapter13
```

Invoke the service by providing it with a location for its persistent storage, along with the service's codebase and a policy file. The client will download and use stubs and proxies, so it also needs a security policy file. And since it exports its event listener stub as well as its `PrintableString` class, it needs a codebase. Be sure to use the appropriate separate codebases for the client and the service.

On Windows:

```
java -cp C:\jini1_0\lib\jini-core.jar;
                    C:\jini1_0\lib\jini-ext.jar;
                    C:\jini1_0\lib\sun-util.jar;
                    C:\service;
                    C:\service-dl
        -Djava.rmi.server.codebase=http://myhost:8085/
        -Djava.security.policy=C:\policy
        corejini.chapter13.PrintService C:\storage

java -cp C:\jini1_0\lib\jini-core.jar;
                    C:\jini1_0\lib\jini-ext.jar;
                    C:\jini1_0\lib\sun-util.jar;
                    C:\client;
                    C:\client-dl
        -Djava.rmi.server.codebase=http://myhost:8086/
        -Djava.security.policy=C:\policy
        corejini.chapter13.Client
```

On Solaris:

```
java -cp /files/jini1_0/lib/jini-core.jar:
                   /files/jini1_0/lib/jini-ext.jar:
                   /files/jini1_0/lib/sun-util.jar:
                   /files/service:
                   /files/service-dl
      -Djava.rmi.server.codebase=http://myhost:8085/
      -Djava.security.policy=/files/policy
      corejini.chapter13.PrintService /var/storage

java -cp /files/jini1_0/lib/jini-core.jar:
                   /files/jini1_0/lib/jini-ext.jar:
                   /files/jini1_0/lib/sun-util.jar:
                   /files/client:
                   /files/client-dl
      -Djava.rmi.server.codebase=http://myhost:8086/
      -Djava.security.policy=/files/policy
      corejini.chapter13.Client
```

Ideas for Future Work

I've already hinted at one of the big possible improvements you could make to this code: You can allow the printing of objects that do not directly implement `Pageable` or `Printable` by using the "agents" framework already present here. You could even consider "widening" the administrative interface to allow clients to transmit new print agents for particular data types to the print service; the print service could store these persistently so that downloaded agents could be available across restarts.

In general, the administrative interface shown here could be improved in several ways. Obvious extensions include the ability to reorder and delete print jobs. The administrative interfaces could also generate events—unlike the events you've already seen that indicate the disposition of *particular* print jobs, these events might tell a systems administrator whether a printer is out of paper or needs service.

Finally, the print service shown here lacks a nonadministrative GUI. That is, while there is a special user interface for interacting with the custom `PrintAdmin` API, there is no special user interface for common printing tasks. Such an interface might take the form of a printer icon that is responsive to drag-and-drop operations—dropping an item on the printer could cause it to be added to the print queue. With this ability, the Jini print service could appear on a "desktop" browser application as a printer, and allow any sort of data to be dropped onto it.

Summary

This chapter has presented a set of toolkit classes for building services, as well as a complete example of a Jini service for printing. From this code, you've seen how to create services with persistent state and custom administrative interfaces. You've also seen how to generate events when the status of a print job changes.

The overall form of the printing service and the toolkit class that it is based on is typical of many Jini services: the system is architected as a front-end proxy that communicates using RMI with a back end. This back end brings some resource—in this case a printer attached to a host computer—into the "Jini world."

When you create your own Jini services, you should find that you're dealing with many of the same tasks and problems that we've looked at here.

What's Next?

In this chapter, you saw a few simple uses of Jini remote events. The next chapter covers this topic in depth. You'll see how to receive remote events, and how to be a proper and well-behaved generator of remove events. You'll also understand how to create "pluggable" pipelines of events that can interconnect Jini services, and extend the basic event delivery machinery already present in Jini.

IN DEPTH: REMOTE EVENTS

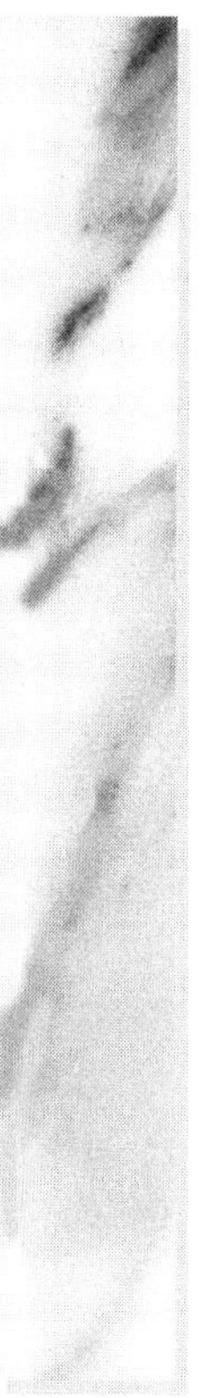

Topics in This Chapter

- How the Jini event model works
- What makes remote events different than local events
- A toolkit class for handling event registration leases
- Building a simple event generator/listener pair
- The rationale behind third-party event delegates
- An event mailbox delegate

Chapter 14

You've already seen in this book some examples of how Jini uses remote events, primarily in the context of lookup service events. You've seen how lookup services will generate events to inform interested parties about changes in the services that are members of a community.

But Jini's mechanisms for notification can be used in many other situations. In some cases, you will write clients that interact with services that generate events to inform consumers when there is a change in their state. So we'll look in more detail at how to be a proper consumer of remote events.

In other situations, you will be writing your own custom services and applications that will *generate* events. You'll need to understand the patterns that you can use to track your listeners and lease their registrations. You'll also need to understand the idioms of remote communication facilitated by Jini.

But in either circumstance—whether you are consuming or producing Jini events—you should understand why the Jini event architecture was designed as it was. Events in Jini have a superficial similarity with the "classic" Java event paradigm used in local applications. But remote events have some important differences, which we'll look at in this chapter. Foremost among these differences is the ability to create "generic" chunks of code that can be composed together to form a distributed event "pipeline" of processing.

In this chapter we'll look at the design rationale behind Jini events, we'll see how to build real applications that use and produce events, and we'll explore Jini's ability to create generic event handlers.

The Need for Notifications

If you're used to programming in Java—or any other modern programming language or environment for that matter—you understand the importance of an *asynchronous notification* mechanism for allowing you to deal with occurrences outside your own program. Asynchronous notification simply means that your program is told, or "notified," whenever something "interesting" happens externally. The "asynchronous" part comes from the fact that notification happens at or about the time that the interesting thing happens, not just when your program happens to ask whether something interesting has happened.

Asynchronous notifications can be contrasted to *polling*, which is another way for programs to learn about changes in some state external to themselves. In polling, a program explicitly checks regularly to see if an interesting change has taken place. Polling has its advantages. For one, the external change can be dealt with when the program is ready to deal with it. But polling has many downsides as well. Most importantly, the polling program must be structured to periodically check the changing entity. Often, the requirements that polling imposes on a program can radically alter the "natural" structure of the program. For instance, if you're polling you'd better make sure that no single operation you perform will last longer than the minimum sampling interval between polls. Otherwise there's a chance you could fail to notice an important change.

The alternative is the approach that asynchronous notifications take—rather than having the program check for the change, the program is told that it has changed. The change is dealt with by code in the program, but—here is the key—in a separate flow of control from the main execution of the program. Essentially you provide a "handler" (often called a *callback*) that specifies what will happen whenever an interesting change is detected. Because you are relieved of the burden of constantly checking for that change—since you are explicitly told when the change happens—you don't have to structure your code around polling. And because the code that responds to changes is separated logically from the code that does the other work of the application, your program can be more cleanly structured than otherwise.

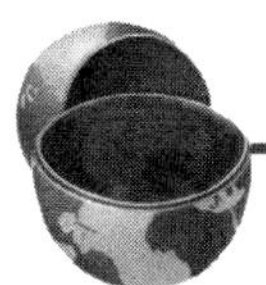

Core Note: How asynchronous notification *really* works

I've glossed over many of the details of how asynchronous notification actually works, in the interest of showing the benefits of using asynchronous callbacks. The truth is that there has to be some bit of code in your application that detects the delivery of the notification from the external entity and knows how to invoke your callback.

The code that does this actually uses polling to do its work. This code, often called a dispatcher, hangs out waiting on notifications and then maps particular types of notifications into invocations of particular callbacks. How this works varies from system to system. In many windowing toolkits, including the X Window System's Xt toolkit, the dispatcher is simply a procedure that you turn control of your program over to. Once the dispatcher is running, it grabs notifications and fires callbacks, and everything happens in the same thread of control—the program's main thread. Such systems impose restrictions on how long any single callback can take—since as long as a callback is running, the dispatcher is blocked and no notifications can be received.

Other systems, including Java, use separate threads of control to dispatch notifications and invoke callbacks (Java actually has its own terminology for this, as we'll see shortly). The main benefit of a threaded dispatcher is that the dispatcher need not be blocked while a callback is executing. The downside is that callbacks run in separate threads from the application's main thread, and so you must take care to properly synchronize access to data shared between your callback and your main application code.

If there's a moral here it's that there's no such thing as a free lunch.

So we've talked about asynchronous notifications in the abstract, but the title of this chapter has the word "events" in it, and we have yet to talk about what asynchronous notifications have to do with events. Events are simply objects that encapsulate some change—a window has appeared on the screen, a button has been pressed, a Web page has finished loading. In virtually every system that uses events, events are categorized into types to provide *specific* information about the change that has taken place. In Java's AWT for example, there are `MouseEvents`, `WindowEvents`, `KeyEvents`, and so on. Each of these event classes has information that describes a *particular* change in the state of the windowing system.

To continue bringing these abstract ideas about notification into concrete Java terms, Java also uses *listeners* as the way to associate the code with particular event types. Listeners are analogous to callbacks as described earlier—you can install a listener for a particular event and, when that event is received, the dispatcher will invoke your listener to do its job. In Java's AWT, there are about as many listener types as there are event types—`MouseListener`, `WindowListener`, `KeyListener`, and so on. Each of these listeners is an interface with methods that the dispatcher will call when certain events are received. So the methods of `MouseListener` are called when particular mouse-related situations arise; these methods are different than the methods on the other listener classes, because each is tailored specifically for its individual task.

This discussion of notifications, events, and listeners may seem pretty academic. Certainly if you've been doing any Java programming at all—and most readers of this book will be already rather handy with Java—then you already know all of this. But my goal here is to bring out some of the key assumptions that are implicit and very often not even thought about in the Java model—namely that there are specific types of events that are dispatched to specific listeners. This assumption is one of the subtle differences between the "normal" Java event model and the Jini model. Understanding the rationale behind why Java does things the way it does will help highlight the differences in Jini when we get to them.

And, of course, a second reason for going into all this detail is that events are quite simply a fundamental part of any programming model, not to be taken lightly.

Jini Event Design Center

Now that we've talked a bit about what events are and why they're useful, we can look at how Jini uses events, and what features of an event system the Jini designers felt were the most important to focus on.

First and foremost, the events that Jini propagates between services and service consumers are *remote events*. This means that the event objects that capture some change in state are sent across VM boundaries: the entity that is sending the event resides in a different VM, and usually even on a different host, than the entity that receives it.[1] The "remoteness" of these events entails all of the difficulties covered in Chapter 2 in the discussion about distributed systems—a sender or a receiver can fail, the time required to send the event can be quite large, and so on. I'll talk specifically about the implications of using events remotely in the next section.

1. Of course, most Jini applications will also generate and consume local events as well—any application with a graphical interface will certainly use events, for example. So Jini adds only the mechanisms for sending events between entities on different VMs.

Second, in Jini, event listeners are designed to be *composable*. This means that you can take a set of event listeners and "stack" them together—the output of one listener becomes the input of the next one in the stack.

You could imagine doing something like this in AWT. For example, you could write a class that implements `MouseListener`, but also supports the `addMouseListener()` method so that "downstream" listeners could receive events from it. But unlike in the AWT event model, where you would have to create a separate type of listener for each of the dozen or so events that AWT generates (`MouseEvents`, `WindowEvents`, `KeyEvents`, `ActionEvents`, and so on), Jini supports the ability for you to write *one* type of listener that can be "plugged in" for *any* type of remote event.

In practice, this means that if you write a class that generates events, you can send those events to any type of Jini event listener without knowing the details of the listener or requiring it to implement any special interfaces, beyond the basic Jini event listener interface. And the flip-side of this is that any Jini event listener can receive any type of event from any event generator.

Why is this useful and why have the Jini creators considered this design point to be so crucial to the architecture of a remote event system? We'll find out in the next section when we look more closely at how remoteness affects an event system.

How Remote Events Differ from Local Events

Chapter 3 touched quickly on some of the differences between remote and local events, but I want to visit these again quickly because these differences manifest themselves throughout the Jini event architecture. Here is another situation where simply making one component of a system remote has great consequences on the architecture of the system.

Because a system running across VMs on disparate hosts is such a different creature than a system running entirely in a single VM, there are a number of implications for an event system designed to work in such a setting. The most important of these are:

- Out of order delivery
- Partial failures
- Latency versus computation trade-offs

Let's quickly revisit each of these to see how they affect remote events.

Out of Order Delivery

In general, it's much more difficult to ensure that messages sent across a network are received in the same order they were sent, especially when messages are sent to multiple consumers. While a remote event delivery system *could* make such guarantees at the expense of performance (using reliable protocols or custom sequencing techniques), the performance hit may be unwieldy for some applications. Further, guaranteeing *global* in-order delivery is extremely hard—if one recipient crashes, do you hold up delivery of events to the other parties to maintain order? These types of guarantees require delivery policies that understand the semantics of the applications involved—whether they require in-order delivery, and how much they're willing to pay for it.[2]

Partial Failures

If you're sending a local event to a component in the same VM, you generally are assured that if you send the event it will be delivered. Any crash or failure that brings down the recipient is almost certain to bring down the sender as well, resulting in a total failure of the application.

Contrast this to the remote setting, where partial failures can occur. In such a setting, the sender may generate an event that goes undelivered because the recipient has failed. The addition of the possibility of partial failure brings a separate parameter of control not present in the local case—if an event cannot be delivered, what should the sender do? Should it try to resend? Should it discard the event? Should it queue the event and hold on to it until the receiver asks for it? If so, how long should it be held?

Local-only event delivery mechanisms simply have no way to express such constraints, because they aren't present in the local-only setting.

Latency Versus Computation

In the local case, events can be generated, sent, and delivered very quickly. Look at AWT for examples of this—you can get an event every time the

2. I should note that even in Java's local AWT event dispatch system, there are no guarantees of in-order delivery. But in general, such a guarantee could be made far more easily than in a remote setting.

mouse pointer moves across the screen. In most cases, the work that an application will do when an event is received (update the display, write some data to disk) completely dominates the time required for the event machinery to generate and dispatch the event.

Such is not the case in the remote setting. There, delivery of an event involves serializing the information in the event, sending it across a network, and deserializing it on the other end. The time required to do this can be several orders of magnitude larger than local delivery, and will almost certainly dominate the time spent by an application to respond to or handle the event.

This disparity in delivery times has architectural implications for applications in the remote setting: in general, events will be sent far less frequently than in the local case, and will contain as much information as necessary to allow the application to process the event without the need for another network round-trip. Because the cost of remote events is so high relative to local events, applications may take steps to batch remote events together or make other provisions to try to offset the cost. Again, here we see the semantics of the particular applications involved imposing constraints on the event subsystem.

In all these cases, applications need the ability to express their desires about event *policies*: meaning how and even whether events are delivered. Put simply, there is a much wider variance in what applications may expect from an event delivery system in the remote case than in the local case. There are no single answers for all applications. Some applications may require in-order delivery at all costs; others may not care about order at all. Some applications may insist that events never be dropped, possibly requiring that they be logged for later delivery; others may be perfectly capable of tolerating lost messages. Since there is such latitude in the space of what applications may reasonably require, any useful remote event system must make provisions for applications to specify their own constraints and behaviors.

Addressing Application Semantics

Jini's event model addresses the need to accommodate different application semantics by providing a way for applications to extend, at run time, the event model itself. It does this by supporting the composable event handlers described earlier. That is, if an application needs some special behavior, such as in-order events, or storage of events, or guaranteed delivery, it can simply write a handler that provides this behavior and "plug it in."

Paradoxically, the sorts of behaviors that can be added are open-ended, even though the Jini event programming model says *nothing* about such behaviors in its APIs. That is, there is no call to `enableInOrderDelivery()` or `storeEventsUntilDeliverable()`. Instead, Jini provides only the bare minimum set of APIs for event delivery, but defines these APIs in such a way that developers can write new behaviors without having to understand the semantics of the events themselves. So you can write code that provides in-order delivery behavior and use it with *any* type of Jini remote event, without having to understand what those events *mean*.

Further, such behaviors can be added either by the generators of events or by the consumers of events. So if you're writing a new service that sends events periodically, and it's important to you that clients receive your events if at all possible, you can create a "reliable delivery" event handler and forward your events to it. This handler could then try to ensure that events are delivered on to their final destinations. Alternatively, the decision to use such an event handler could be made by the consumer of the events. So if you are writing an application that will only periodically wake up to receive events, you can create a "store and forward" event handler and arrange for events destined for you to be sent there. When your application is active it can contact the event handler to have its events forwarded.

The ability to extend the event model to accommodate such new, application-specified behaviors was an important goal for the Jini designers. And the solution they came up with—composable, application-provided event handlers that can work with any type of event—is elegant and minimal. An alternative like providing "control knobs" in the API for setting and tuning any number of delivery parameters would have only increased the work for event generators—since they would now have to implement *all* these potential delivery policies—but would still likely fall short of the requirements of many applications. The Jini approach is extremely flexible while being minimal and easy to understand.

The Jini Event Programming Model

With this introduction and rationale behind us, let's look at the programming model Jini uses for remote events. As you've seen already, Jini provides an *extremely* minimal set of APIs for dealing with events. But the size of the API set belies the range of tasks it can be applied to.

There are really only two important classes and interfaces. RemoteEvent defines a common superclass for all Jini remote events. And RemoteEventListener defines a single method that event consumers must implement to receive events. Jini does not define any standard interface to event generators. Instead, the particulars of how clients will ask to receive events will vary from generator to generator. We've already seen how the notify() call on Jini ServiceRegistrars works, which is an example of a service-specific way to ask to receive events.

The RemoteEvent Class

Let's look first at the relevant details of RemoteEvent:

```
public class RemoteEvent
                     extends java.util.EventObject {
     protected Object source;
     protected long eventID;
     protected long seqNum;
     protected MarshalledObject handback;

     public RemoteEvent(Object source, long eventID,
                          long seqNum,
                          MarshalledObject handback);
     public long getID();
     public long getSequenceNumber();
     public MarshalledObject
                          getRegistrationObject();
}
```

The RemoteEvent class extends java.util.EventObject, as all Java events do. EventObject implements Serializable, so RemoteEvents can be transmitted over the wire to other Java VMs and reconstituted as needed. The "source" of a RemoteEvent is the object that generated the event. Obviously, this will vary from event generator to event generator.

Event Types

RemoteEvents have a few details that are designed to support the uses to which they will be applied in Jini. First, every RemoteEvent has an identifier that uniquely describes the "type" of the event relative to the entity that generated it.

Each unique identifier should represent some distinct type of occurrence in the event generator, *not* each and every instance of an event object. So a printer service might use one event type to indicate that the printer is out of paper, and another event type to indicate that the printer has jammed. In such a use, multiple instances of "out of paper" events would have the same event identifier that indicates the type of the event.

In Sun's sample implementation of the Jini lookup service, a new event identifier is assigned to each distinct registration. That is, the implementation defines the "distinct occurrence" that warrants an event to be a match of the particular service template provided by a client. You could imagine other services that define the space of their identifiers in different ways. As we'll see when we talk about customizing the event pipeline, though, using a separate type identifier for each client registration can be a big help when using event delegates.

The set of identifiers that a service may generate is unique only to it. Put another way, there is not any global namespace of event identifiers. A printer service may use the integers 1 and 2 to indicate special printer conditions, while a Jini lookup service might use these same numbers to indicate different occurrences specific to it.

In addition to using these type identifiers, Jini services are also free to use subclasses of `RemoteEvent` to describe state changes. You've already seen one example of this in the Jini lookup service. The lookup service sends `ServiceEvents` to describe changes in the registrations with a particular lookup service. These `ServiceEvents` contain information specific to the change at hand, but are still `RemoteEvents` and so they can be used, operated on, and forwarded by any code that understands basic `RemoteEvents`.

Sequence Numbers, Idempotency, and Ordering

Each event also contains a *sequence number* that can be used by consumers to determine whether they may have received events out of order. Jini is fairly flexible about how event generators set and use sequence numbers, but there are two basic requirements. First, the Jini specifications dictate that any object that generates events use a different sequence number for those events if and only if the events refer to two distinct occurrences within the event generator. Second, Jini dictates that for any two events *A* and *B* from the same generator and with the same event identifier, then *A* occurred before *B* if and only if the sequence number of *A* is lower than the sequence number of *B*.

Let's look at an example of how such sequence numbering would work in our familiar printer service. A printer service might define an event type to indicate that the printer is out of paper, and generate events to interested

parties whenever this happens. The first requirement imposed by Jini *mandates* that the service *cannot* use the same sequence number in events that result from two occurrences of the printer running out of paper. And also, the service has to use the *same* sequence numbers for events generated from the same "out of paper" occurrence.

This requirement is imposed so that clients that process events can be *idempotent*. That is, that they can, if they choose, be written in such a way that they only deal with the underlying occurrence once, regardless of how many events they may receive notifying them of the underlying occurrence. So if a flaky event generator or a third-party event handler somehow sends multiple events for the same out of paper occurrence, clients can do the right thing by handling these events only once.

The second requirement—that sequence numbers be increasing in value—mandates that if the printer runs out of paper twice, then the sequence number for the events that result from the second occurrence will be higher than the sequence numbers that resulted from the first. This requirement is so that event consumers can tell if they have received events out-of-order. Some consumers, for instance, may simply discard events that arrive after a "logically-later" event that they have already dealt with.

This requirement produces what is known as a *strict ordering* of events. Given any two events that resulted from different occurrences, you can tell which happened later. Note that this strict ordering requirement doesn't say that generators cannot skip sequence numbers—a generator could increment sequence numbers by ten or a hundred for every occurrence that produces events. Because this is true, clients are limited in the information they can infer from sequence numbers. Clearly, they can infer ordering information, since sequence numbers increase. But if the sequence numbers of two events differ by, say, a hundred, then the client cannot determine if no events, one event, or even a hundred events transpired between the two.[3]

For the most part, implementing these requirements is trivial—event generators can keep a counter for sequence numbers, and make sure that for any event-worthy occurrence they use the same sequence number for any and all events that result from that occurrence. After each round of events is sent off, they simply increment the sequence counter. Event consumers can choose to pay attention to sequence numbers if they wish, or simply deal with the conse-

3. Although if the sequence numbers differ by exactly 1, that is if the sequence number of event *A* is n and the sequence number of event *B* is $n+1$, then a client can be assured that *no* events came between *A* and *B*, because there is no "gap" for other events to hide in.

quences of potentially receiving multiple events that correspond to the same occurrence, or out-of-order events. In most cases, this won't be a big deal.

But event generators can optionally make an even stronger guarantee over and above these "baseline" guarantees designed to support idempotency and ordering. Services can, if they choose, guarantee that not only do their sequence numbers increase, but that sequence numbers are not skipped. This allows consumers to take two sequence numbers from the same generator and with the same type identifier and determine *exactly* how many intervening events (from the same generator and of the same type) have been generated. A client that received such events would then be able to precisely determine whether it has missed any events and, if so, how many. This guarantee provides what is known as a *full ordering* of events.

The implementation of a service that provides full ordering of events is not much more difficult than a service that provides only the baseline guarantees. Recall that the baseline guarantees can be satisfied by having a global counter within the generator, and incrementing that counter whenever there is an event-worthy occurrence, no matter what the event type. To provide full ordering, a service only needs to make sure that there are *separate* counters for each event type (so that each increases separately from the others), and that counters are incremented by exactly one each time an event-worthy occurrence takes place.

Be sure to remember that *all* these guarantees about sequence numbers are only made for events from a single event generator and with the same event ID. So the sequence numbers of two events from different generators, or two events from the same generator but with different IDs, cannot be compared.

Table 14–1 summarizes the guarantees that services may be able to make about event sequencing:

Table 14–1 Event Sequencing Guarantees

Idempotency	Events have different sequence numbers if and only if they correspond to different occurrences in the event generator	Required by the Jini spec
Strict Ordering	Sequence numbers are increasing, but the event generator may "skip" sequence numbers	Required by the Jini spec
Full Ordering	Sequence numbers are increasing, and are not skipped	Optionally implemented by services

Currently, there is no easy way for services to "advertise" what level of strictness in event sequencing they provide. Clearly, the logical way to do this would be as an attribute on the service's registration with a lookup service, but as of this writing, there is no standard attribute that describes the guarantees a service is willing to make.

Application-Specified Return Data

The final component of `RemoteEvent` is the `MarshalledObject` that is returned by the `getRegistrationObject()` method. This object is a way for an event consumer to have data particular to it "handed back" when a `RemoteEvent` is received. Recall that a `MarshalledObject` is simply the serialized version of whatever object you provide, along with codebase information to allow the implementation of the object to be retrieved later if needed.

Although Jini defines no "standard" interface for event generators, most generators will provide a registration method that allows clients to ask to receive events. Whatever the particulars of these registration methods, they should allow a way for the client to pass in a `MarshalledObject` to be associated with the registration. The event generator should then return this `MarshalledObject` whenever an event is sent to the consumer.

By using this ability to associate arbitrary data with event registrations, clients can simplify some of their bookkeeping chores. Clients can use this "hand back" object to associate client-specific context with event registrations.

The RemoteEventListener Interface

After `RemoteEvent`, the most important interface you must understand is `RemoteEventListener`. This is the interface that any consumer of `RemoteEvents` must implement; fortunately, implementing it is very easy, as the interface has only one method:

```
public interface RemoteEventListener
            extends java.rmi.Remote,
                    java.util.EventListener {
            public void notify(RemoteEvent ev)
                    throws UnknownEventException,
                           java.rmi.RemoteException;
}
```

Whenever an event generator sends an event to you, the `notify()` method on an object that you have designated as a listener for remote events will be called. The actual event that is delivered may be a subclass of `RemoteEvent`, as you've already seen in our look at notifications from lookup services—lookup services actually send a subclass of `RemoteEvent` called `ServiceEvent` that contains more detailed information about state changes than a generic `RemoteEvent`.

The basic paradigm here is quite simple—you just register for events, using whatever mechanisms are provided by the service you want events from, and then those events get delivered via the `notify()` method.

There are a few points about event delivery that you should be aware of, though. First, the `RemoteEventListener` method extends `java.rmi.Remote`. This means that the interface itself defines an RMI communication protocol between the event consumer and the event generator. This means that your implementation of `RemoteEventListener` *must* be an RMI server object, typically a `java.rmi.server.UnicastRemoteObject`.

This is an important point—while I've used RMI in the examples in this book for any number of tasks, this is actually the *only* place in the core Jini APIs where the use of RMI is *required* by the specification.[4] Even though methods on other Jini classes may be declared to raise `RemoteException`, there is no requirement that those interfaces be implemented by RMI remote objects. In such cases, the RMI `RemoteException` class is used as a "generic" exception class to indicate all the sorts of failures that can occur in distributed systems. Implementations of these core interfaces built on a communications substrate other than RMI would simply map their exceptions into `RemoteException`.

Core Note: The use of RMI in Jini

As noted, remote events are the only place in Jini where the use of RMI is really required. What does this really mean?

Well, classes like `RemoteException` *get used all over the place in Jini. But the interfaces such as* `ServiceRegistrar` *and* `Lease` *that contain methods that raise these exceptions do not extend* `java.rmi.Remote`*. This means that they can be implemented by any communications*

4. There is actually, one other place in Jini where RMI is required: if you're writing a service that participates in transactions (as we'll see in Chapter 16), then you must use RMI. But remember that in Jini transactions are implemented as a separate service *on top* of the basic Jini infrastructure. So remote events are the only place in the common APIs that require RMI.

technology. The RMI `RemoteException` *class was simply chosen as a convenient way to represent the failures that may happen in distributed systems, regardless of the underlying communications substrate.*

Of course, this doesn't mean that the implementations of these interfaces do not use RMI, merely that they don't have to. In fact, all the Sun sample implementations of the core Jini services do use RMI extensively. But the fact that the specifications and interfaces do not require RMI means that developers can reimplement these services to be based on another communications mechanism.

The reason that Jini dictates a particular communication mechanism for events is that event delivery is one of the only places in Jini where the implementation of the communication between client and service is not done via a proxy provided by the service. In all other cases—communication with lookup services, communication with other Jini services, communication with lease grantors—the actual communication happens through code provided to the client by the service, and so the service is free to choose the communication technology it will use.

Another point to make is that event consumers must take care when implementing the `notify()` method. RMI uses *synchronous* calls, which means that when a service invokes the `notify()` method on your event listener remotely, the service blocks until your code returns. If your code takes a long time before it completes, you will prevent the service from delivering events to others. So it's important that you try to limit the amount of work done in `notify()`. Most times, you will simply place the received event on a queue and then return; the work of dealing with the particular queued events is delegated to a separate thread.[5]

Dealing with Errors

Event delivery errors can happen in the consumer or in the generator. You'll notice that `RemoteEventListener`, the interface implemented by the consumer, declares `notify()` as raising an `UnknownEventException`. Consumers are allowed to raise this exception from `notify()` if they ever receive an event

5. Services that are concerned with performance and robustness may insulate themselves from ill-behaved clients by handing off the invocation of `notify()` to a separate short-lived thread. This allows the service to continue doing other work—including notifying other clients—without having to completely block until `notify()` returns.

with an unexpected type identifier, or from an unexpected source. This situation indicates that, somehow, either the service or the client has gotten confused, and that unanticipated and unwanted events are being exchanged between them. By raising `UnknownEventException` the client is claiming that it doesn't want to receive that particular type of event from that event generator again.

On the part of the generator, if it calls the `notify()` method on a client and receives an `UnknownEventException`, it is free to cancel the client's event registration for that particular type of event. This would ensure that the client never receives that type of event from the generator again.

Other Event Interfaces

The `RemoteEvent` and `RemoteEventListener` interfaces are the most central APIs defined by the Jini remote event model. There is, however, one more common class that, although not required, will be used frequently by Jini applications. This class is `EventRegistration`, which encapsulates the information associated with a particular client's solicitation of events.

The reason that this class is not "required" by all Jini event generators is that the interfaces to event generators are not standardized—event generators may or may not return an `EventRegistration` as their needs dictate. The class is commonly used, however, and is defined as a return value from `ServiceRegistrar`'s event solicitation method.

You've already seen this class before, so I won't dwell too long on it. But you should make sure that you understand how the members of `EventRegistration` will be set and used. Let's look at the particulars of this class.

```
public class EventRegistration
                implements java.io.Serializable {
        protected long eventID;
        protected Object source;
        protected Lease lease;
        protected long seqNum;

        public EventRegistration(long eventID,
                                 Object source,
                                 Lease lease,
                                 long seqNum);
        public long getID();
        public Object getSource();
        public Lease getLease();
        public long getSequenceNumber();
}
```

EventRegistrations are serializable since, obviously, they will need to be sent to clients who are registering for events.

The Lease object referenced here is a representation of the client's lease on its event registration. While event generators don't strictly *have* to lease their event registrations, they are strongly advised to—leasing ensures that any event generator you write will be able to clean up after ill-behaved or crashed clients. You've already seen lots of details on leasing, and explanations for why leasing is important, so I won't go into more details here. Review Chapter 10 if you want a refresher on leasing.

The other members of EventRegistration require a bit more explanation. If you're writing an event generator that returns these EventRegistration objects to clients, you need to make sure you properly set up all these fields.

The source object indicates the generator that will deliver remote events. This should be set to the same source that will be used in all RemoteEvents generated for this event registration; clients must be able to take the source from a RemoteEvent they receive and compare it to the source in the registration.

Likewise, the event ID should be the identifier that will be used in all RemoteEvents for this registration. A client should be able to take a RemoteEvent and identify the registration that caused that event given the combination of source and event ID in the event.

Finally, the sequence number in the registration should identify the *last* sequence number used by the generator for events of the specified type at the time the registration was granted. Clients can store this number and then compare it to subsequently received events; this will allow them to determine whether they may have missed any events after the registration.

As you'll see, correctly setting the source and event ID is necessary so that third-party event handlers can correctly route events to a desired destination. The sequence number must be returned so that clients can determine if they may have missed any events between when the registration occurred and when they actually receive their first event.

At this point we've looked at the entire set of APIs used by Jini to deal with remote events! Let's jump into some example programs next.

An Example: Heartbeat Events

In this example we'll look at a Jini service that generates "heartbeat events." These are events that are sent periodically to clients. Clients can ask to

receive heartbeat events at certain intervals, such as every minute, every hour, every day, or every week.

The semantics of these events are very simple. In fact, for most clients, simply having an internal thread periodically awaken to generate a notification would be sufficient, and far more lightweight than relying on some external service to generate timer events.[6] But by keeping the amount of application-specific code to a minimum here, we can focus in on the mechanics of event registration, leasing, and delivery—which are, after all, the main goals of this chapter.

This is the first example in the book that implements a real event generator with proper leasing behavior (the example in Chapter 13 sent `PrintServiceEvents` when a job completed, but the registration process was implicitly "hidden" behind print job submission, and registrations were never actually leased). So here we'll look at a more complete event generator as well as a more prototypical event consumer.

To keep the example interesting, I'll be creating some "helper" classes that can be used to support leased event registrations. These classes can easily work in conjunction with the `BasicUnicastService` classes you saw in Chapter 13. You should be able to reuse these classes in many of your own applications.

Let's look at the classes to help with event registrations before diving into the service itself.

A Toolkit for Event Registrations

You've already seen in Chapter 13 how it's possible to build a simple "toolkit" for managing tasks common to many services. In this section, we'll look at how to abstract away some of the common functionality needed to handle the leasing and managing of event registrations. Much of this work is simple bookkeeping—keeping lists of registrations, expiring leases as necessary, handling the chores of being a lease landlord. As such, much of this work can be handled comfortably by a library of code that can be applied to different applications.

6. This heartbeat service isn't as daft as it might first appear, however. Services that are inactive for long periods of time, such as a weekly backup service, might use the RMI activation framework to "deactivate" themselves. Having an external service send a message once per week could be the trigger that caused such a service to reactivate itself.

The main class here is called `BasicRegistrationLandlord`. This class follows the standard landlord paradigm you've already seen in Chapter 11, and in fact, works much the same way as the landlord in the `SlotProvider` example—it implements a simple, default leasing policy; it uses RMI for communication with the `LandlordLeases` that are sent to clients; and registrations are kept in a simple data structure that can be easily scanned.

Each event registration is represented internally by an instance of a class called `Registration`. Each `Registration` maintains the cookie that uniquely identifies the lease on the registration, the `RemoteEventListener` that will be notified when an event is delivered, the `MarshalledObject` that will be returned to the listener, and the current expiration time of the registration.

Whenever the `BasicRegistrationLandlord` needs to cancel or renew leases, it scans a `Vector` of `Registration` objects, looking for the `Registration` that contains a particular cookie. Once it finds it, it updates the `Registration`'s expiration time if it is renewing it, or removes it from the list if it is canceling it.

Let's look at the code for `Registration` as shown in Listing 14–1.

Listing 14–1 `Registration.java`

```
// This class represents one event registration
// with a BasicRegistrationLandlord

package corejini.chapter14;

import java.io.Serializable;
import java.rmi.MarshalledObject;
import net.jini.core.event.RemoteEventListener;

class Registration implements Serializable {
    protected Object cookie;
    protected RemoteEventListener listener;
    protected MarshalledObject data;
    protected long expiration;

    // To maintain a registration we need to remember
    // the cookie for the registration, who the listener
    // is, the client-provided data, and its expiration
    // time.
```

Listing 14–1 `Registration.java` **(continued)**

```
    Registration(Object cookie,
                 RemoteEventListener listener,
                 MarshalledObject data, long expiration) {
        this.cookie = cookie;
        this.listener = listener;
        this.data = data;
        this.expiration = expiration;
    }

    Object getCookie() {
        return cookie;
    }

    RemoteEventListener getListener() {
        return listener;
    }

    MarshalledObject getData() {
        return data;
    }
     long getExpiration() {
        return expiration;
    }

    void setExpiration(long expiration) {
        this.expiration = expiration;
    }

    // Subclasses can override this if they need to do
    // special things at cancellation/expiration time.
    // The default implementation does nothing.
    protected void cancelled() {
    }
}
```

This simple class maintains the items necessary for keeping and using a registration, namely the cookie that represents the lease on the registration, the listener that will be called when an event needs to be delivered, the `MarshalledObject` data that should be returned to the consumer, and the expiration time for the registration.

This class is only used internally by the `BasicRegistrationLandlord` and its callers—it is never exposed to lease holders or other event consumers.

Let's now look at the `BasicRegistrationLandlord` class (Listing 14–2), which manages sets of event registrations.

Listing 14–2 BasicRegistrationLandlord.java

```
// This class implements some basic functionality to
// lease event registrations. It can work in conjunction
// with the BasicUnicastService from Chapter 13.

package corejini.chapter14;

import net.jini.core.lease.Lease;
import net.jini.core.lease.LeaseMapException;
import net.jini.core.lease.UnknownLeaseException;
import com.sun.jini.lease.landlord.Landlord;
import com.sun.jini.lease.landlord.LandlordLease;
import java.rmi.server.UnicastRemoteObject;
import java.rmi.RemoteException;
import java.util.*;

public class BasicRegistrationLandlord
                extends UnicastRemoteObject
                implements Landlord {
    // A simple leasing policy...10 minute leases.
    protected static final int DEFAULT_MAX_LEASE
                                        = 1000 * 60 * 10;
    protected int maxLease = DEFAULT_MAX_LEASE;
    // Assume that registrations are kept in
    // a vector maintained by our clients.
    protected Vector regs;
    // A factory for making landlord leases.
    protected LandlordLease.Factory factory;

    public BasicRegistrationLandlord(Vector regs,
                        LandlordLease.Factory factory)
        throws RemoteException {
        this.regs = regs;
        this.factory = factory;
    }

    // Change the maximum lease time from the default.
    public void setMaxLease(int maxLease) {
        this.maxLease = maxLease;
    }

    // Apply the policy to a requested duration
    // to get an actual expiration time.
    public long getExpiration(long request) {
        if (request > maxLease || request == Lease.ANY)
            return System.currentTimeMillis() + maxLease;
        else
            return System.currentTimeMillis() + request;
    }
```

Listing 14–2 `BasicRegistrationLandlord.java` **(continued)**

```
    // Cancel the lease represented by 'cookie'
    public void cancel(Object cookie)
        throws UnknownLeaseException {
        for (int i=0, size=regs.size() ; i<size ; i++) {
            Registration reg =
                         (Registration) regs.elementAt(i);
            if (reg.cookie.equals(cookie)) {
                reg.cancelled();
                regs.removeElementAt(i);
                return;
            }
        }
        throw new UnknownLeaseException(cookie.toString());
    }

    // Cancel a set of leases
    public void cancelAll(Object[] cookies)
        throws LeaseMapException {
        Map exceptionMap = null;
        LeaseMapException lme = null;

        for (int i=0 ; i<cookies.length ; i++) {
            try {
                cancel(cookies[i]);
            } catch (UnknownLeaseException ex) {
                if (lme == null) {
                    exceptionMap = new HashMap();
                    lme = new LeaseMapException(
                                  "cancelAll failed",
                                  exceptionMap);
                }
                Lease lease = factory.newLease(cookies[i],
                                                  this, 0);
                exceptionMap.put(lease, ex);
            }
        }

        if (lme != null)
            throw lme;
    }
```

Listing 14–2 `BasicRegistrationLandlord.java` **(continued)**

```
    // Renew the lease specified by 'cookie''
    public long renew(Object cookie, long extension)
        throws UnknownLeaseException {

        for (int i=0, size=regs.size() ; i<size ; i++) {
            Registration reg =
             (Registration) regs.elementAt(i);
            if (reg.getCookie().equals(cookie)) {
                long expiration =
                     getExpiration(extension);
                reg.setExpiration(expiration);
                return expiration -
                     System.currentTimeMillis();
            }
        }
        throw new UnknownLeaseException(cookie.toString());
    }

    // Renew a set of leases.
    public Landlord.RenewResults renewAll(Object[] cookies,
                                          long[] extensions) {
        long[] granted = new long[cookies.length];
        Exception[] denied = null;

        for (int i=0 ; i<cookies.length ; i++) {
            try {
                granted[i] = renew(cookies[i],
                                extensions[i]);
            } catch (Exception ex) {
                if (denied == null) {
                    denied =
                         new Exception[cookies.length+1];
                }
                denied[i+1] = ex;
            }
        }

        Landlord.RenewResults results =
            new Landlord.RenewResults(granted, denied);
        return results;
    }
}
```

Let's look at how this code works. The BasicRegistrationLandlord class is a Landlord that works with Sun's LandlordLease implementation of leasing. So BasicRegistrationLandlord extends UnicastRemoteObject since, as you will recall, LandlordLeases communicate back to their landlords via RMI. The class also implements the Landlord interface, which defines the contract that LandlordLeases expect.

This new landlord manages a single vector of Registration objects. Each Registration is a landlord-internal representation of an event registration made by a client. When a BasicRegistrationLandlord is created, it is initialized with a vector of Registrations and a factory for making new leases (you can refer back to Chapter 11 on exporting resources via leasing if you need to review the details of factories and how the landlord paradigm works).

Many of the methods here are similar to those in the examples of Chapter 11: the setMaxLease() method controls the leasing policy by setting the maximum lease duration which will be issued; getExpiration() takes a requested duration and returns an actual lease expiration time, given whatever policy is in effect.

But the "meat" of the work here is done by the methods to cancel and renew event registration leases. The cancel() method scans the vector of Registration objects looking for one with a cookie that matches the input parameter. If it is found, it is removed from the set of managed registrations and its cancelled() method is called. While in the implementation of Registration shown here, cancelled() does nothing, subclasses of Registration could override this method to allow some special type of behavior to happen upon cancellation. If the input cookie is not found, then an UnknownLeaseException method is raised—presumably a client has held on to a lease longer than its expiration time.

The renew() method works in much the same way—it scans the vector, looking for a matching cookie. If it is found, the expiration date of the corresponding Registration object is updated. If it is not found, an UnknownLeaseException is raised.

The two methods that deal with multiple leases at once—cancelAll() and renewAll() simply iterate through the cookies passed to them and call the underlying cancel() and renew() methods.

Note that there is nothing in the BasicRegistrationLandlord class that is specific to event registrations—all the particular details about events are hidden away in the Registration class. So by substituting a different Registration class you can use this code for managing many sorts of LandlordLeases.

A Simple Event Generator

Now that we've built up some tools for handling registrations of events, let's look at an event generator. This event generator, called `HeartbeatGenerator`, allows clients to register for "heartbeat" events at various intervals. Clients can ask that they receive events on every minute, hourly, daily, or weekly. These registrations are leased to clients using the landlord techniques seen earlier.

The generator itself makes only a "best effort" attempt at sending events. If the generator crashes and then restarts, it does not send "make up" events for the time that it was down. Again, the goal here is to focus on the strategies for building event generators and clients, not on all the application details that might be necessary in a more robust generator of heartbeat events.

Let's look at the code as shown in Listing 14–3.

Listing 14–3 `HeartbeatGenerator.java`

```
// A simple service that sends periodic events.

package corejini.chapter14;

import corejini.chapter13.BasicUnicastService;
import corejini.chapter13.BasicUnicastAdmin;
import net.jini.core.lease.Lease;
import net.jini.core.lease.UnknownLeaseException;
import net.jini.core.event.RemoteEvent;
import net.jini.core.event.RemoteEventListener;
import net.jini.core.event.EventRegistration;
import net.jini.core.event.UnknownEventException;
import com.sun.jini.lease.landlord.LandlordLease;
import java.rmi.Remote;
import java.rmi.RemoteException;
import java.rmi.MarshalledObject;
import java.rmi.server.UnicastRemoteObject;
import java.io.Serializable;
import java.io.IOException;
import java.util.Vector;
```

Listing 14–3 `HeartbeatGenerator.java` **(continued)**

```
// The cookie class for our leases. This class
// identifies leases by their unique event type
// identifiers and the period they're registering
// for.
class HeartbeatCookie implements Serializable {
    int period;
    long eventType;

    HeartbeatCookie(int period, long eventType) {
        this.period = period;
        this.eventType = eventType;
    }
    public boolean equals(Object other) {
        if (!(other instanceof HeartbeatCookie))
            return false;

        HeartbeatCookie cookie = (HeartbeatCookie) other;

        return cookie.period == period &&
                          cookie.eventType == eventType;
    }
}

// The heartbeat service is a BasicUnicastService
// (see Chapter 13).
public class HeartbeatGenerator
        extends BasicUnicastService
        implements BasicUnicastService.RestoreListener,
           Runnable, HeartbeatGenerator.HeartbeatRequest {
    // 10 minutes
    protected static final int MAX_LEASE = 1000 * 60 * 10;
    protected boolean done = false;
    protected long tickCount = 0;
    // Lists of registrants.
    protected Vector minute = new Vector();
    protected Vector hour = new Vector();
    protected Vector day = new Vector();
    protected Vector week = new Vector();
```

Listing 14–3 `HeartbeatGenerator.java` **(continued)**

```
    // Separate landlords for each list.
    protected BasicRegistrationLandlord minuteLandlord;
    protected BasicRegistrationLandlord hourLandlord;
    protected BasicRegistrationLandlord dayLandlord;
    protected BasicRegistrationLandlord weekLandlord;
    protected long lastEventSeqNo = 0;
    protected LandlordLease.Factory factory =
        new LandlordLease.Factory();

    // public static final int EVENT_TYPE = 1;
    protected long nextEventType = 1;

    public static final int  MINUTE=1,
                             HOUR=2,
                             DAY=3,
                             WEEK=4;

    // Saves our class-specific data when we persist
    static class Registrations implements Serializable {
         Vector minute;
         Vector hour;
         Vector day;
         Vector week;
         long nextEventType;
         long lastEventSeqNo;

         Registrations(Vector minute, Vector hour,
                       Vector day, Vector week,
                       long nextEventType,
                       long lastEventSeqNo) {
             this.minute = minute;
             this.hour = hour;
             this.day = day;
             this.week = week;
             this.nextEventType = nextEventType;
             this.lastEventSeqNo = lastEventSeqNo;
         }
    }
```

Listing 14–3 `HeartbeatGenerator.java` (continued)

```
    // We send particular subclasses of RemoteEvent
    public static class HeartbeatEvent extends RemoteEvent
        implements Serializable {
        int period;

        HeartbeatEvent(Object proxy, long eventType,
                       long seq, MarshalledObject data,
                       int period) {
            super(proxy, eventType, seq, data);
            this.period = period;
        }
        public int getPeriod() {
            return period;
        }
    }

    // Callers speak this interface to ask us to send
    //heartbeats
    public interface HeartbeatRequest extends Remote {
        public EventRegistration register(int period,
                            MarshalledObject data,
                            RemoteEventListener listener,
                            long duration)
            throws RemoteException;
    }

    public HeartbeatGenerator(String storageLoc)
                  throws RemoteException {
        super(storageLoc);

        minuteLandlord =
            new BasicRegistrationLandlord(minute, factory);
        hourLandlord =
            new BasicRegistrationLandlord(hour, factory);
        dayLandlord =
            new BasicRegistrationLandlord(day, factory);
        weekLandlord =
            new BasicRegistrationLandlord(week, factory);
    }
```

Listing 14–3 `HeartbeatGenerator.java` **(continued)**

```
// Initialize the superclass and start the
// leasing thread.
protected void initialize()
        throws IOException, ClassNotFoundException {
    super.initialize();
    new Thread(this).start();
}

// Save the specific registration data
protected void checkpoint() throws IOException {
    checkpoint(new Registrations( minute, hour,
                                  day, week,
                                  nextEventType,
                                  lastEventSeqNo));
}

// Use the RMI-generated stub as the proxy
protected Object getProxy() {
    return this;
}

// Restore class-specific data.
public void restored(Object subclassData) {
    Registrations regs = (Registrations) subclassData;
    minute = regs.minute;
    hour = regs.hour;
    day = regs.day;
    week = regs.week;
    nextEventType = regs.nextEventType;
    lastEventSeqNo = regs.lastEventSeqNo;
}

 public synchronized EventRegistration register(
                          int period,
                          MarshalledObject data,
                          RemoteEventListener listener,
                          long duration) {
    // Build a cookie based on the table and token
    void eventType = nextEventType++;
    HeartbeatCookie cookie =
            new HeartbeatCookie(period, eventType);
```

Listing 14–3 `HeartbeatGenerator.java` **(continued)**

```
// The landlord we'll use for the lease.
BasicRegistrationLandlord landlord;

// The registration vector we'll add it to.
Vector regs;

switch (period) {
case MINUTE:
    landlord = minuteLandlord;
    regs = minute;
    break;
case HOUR:
    landlord = hourLandlord;
    regs = hour;
    break;
case DAY:
    landlord = dayLandlord;
    regs = day;
    break;
case WEEK:
    landlord = weekLandlord;
    regs = week;
    break;
default:
    throw new IllegalArgumentException(
                                  "Bad period");
}

// Create the lease and registration, and add the
// registration to the appropriate list.
long expiration = landlord.getExpiration(duration);
Registration reg = new Registration(cookie,
                              listener,
                              data, expiration);
Lease lease = factory.newLease(cookie, landlord,
                              expiration);
regs.addElement(reg);

// Return an event registration to the client.
EventRegistration evtreg =
    new EventRegistration(eventType, proxy,
                                  lease, 0);
```

Listing 14–3 `HeartbeatGenerator.java` **(continued)**

```
        try {
            checkpoint();
        } catch(IOException ex) {
            System.err.println("Error checkpointing: " +
                               ex.getMessage());
        }

        return evtreg;
    }

    protected void sendHeartbeat() {
        tickCount++;

        // minute listeners
        sendHeartbeats(minute, MINUTE);

        // hour listeners
        if (tickCount % 60 == 0) {
            sendHeartbeats(hour, HOUR);
        }

        // day listeners
        if (tickCount % (60 * 24) == 0) {
            sendHeartbeats(day, DAY);
        }

        // week listeners
        if (tickCount % (60 * 24 * 7) == 0) {
            sendHeartbeats(week, WEEK);
        }
    }

    protected void sendHeartbeats(Vector regs, int period){
        // First, scavenge the list for dead registrations
        // in reverse order (to make us immune from
        // compaction)
        long now = System.currentTimeMillis();
        for (int i=regs.size()-1 ; i >= 0 ; i--) {
            Registration reg = (Registration)
                                          regs.elementAt(i);
            if (reg.expiration < now) {
                reg.cancelled();
                regs.removeElementAt(i);
            }
        }
```

Listing 14–3 `HeartbeatGenerator.java` **(continued)**

```
        // Now, message the remaining listeners
        for (int i=0, size=regs.size() ; i<size ; i++) {
            Registration reg = (Registration)
                                     regs.elementAt(i);
            HeartbeatCookie cookie =
                        (HeartbeatCookie) reg.getCookie();
            long eventType = cookie.eventType;

            try {
                HeartbeatEvent ev =
                     new HeartbeatEvent(proxy,
                                        entType,
                                        lastEventSeqNo++,
                                        reg.data,
                                        period);
                reg.listener.notify(ev);
            } catch (RemoteException ex) {
                 // Just complain...
                 System.err.println(
                      "Error notifying remote listener: "
                                  + ex.getMessage());
            } catch (UnknownEventException ex) {
                 // Cancel the registration... Here I'll
                 // do this by setting its expiration so
                 // that it'll be dropped the next time
                 // through.
                 System.err.println("Unknown event: " +
                               ex.getMessage());
                 reg.expiration = 0;
            }
        }
    }

    public void run() {
        long timeToSleep = 60 * 1000;
        while (true) {
            long nextWakeup = System.currentTimeMillis() +
                                             timeToSleep;
            try {
                Thread.sleep(timeToSleep);
            } catch (InterruptedException ex) {
            }
```

Listing 14–3 `HeartbeatGenerator.java` **(continued)**

```
            long currentTime = System.currentTimeMillis();
            // see if we're at the next wakeup time
            if (currentTime >= nextWakeup) {
                nextWakeup = currentTime + (60 * 1000);
                // notify
                sendHeartbeat();
            }
            timeToSleep = nextWakeup -
                                System.currentTimeMillis();
        }
    }

    public static void main(String[] args) {
        try {
            if (args.length != 1) {
                System.err.println(
                         "Usage: HeartbeatGenerator " +
                         "<storageloc>");
                System.exit(1);
            }

            HeartbeatGenerator gen =
                         new HeartbeatGenerator(args[0]);
            gen.initialize();
            System.out.println("Heartbeat started.");
        } catch (Exception ex) {
            System.err.println("Error starting: " +
                                ex.getMessage());
            System.exit(1);
        }
    }
}
```

This code is based on the `BasicUnicastService` you saw in the last chapter, so many of the concepts here will be familiar to you. The service is structured around separate vectors of `Registration` objects, one vector per "period" that clients can register for (per-minute events, per-hour events, and so on). For each of these, there is a separate `BasicRegistrationLandlord` that handles the management tasks for that period.

Event Types and Sequence Numbers

Two of the main decisions that any event generator has to make are how to use event type identifiers, and how to use sequence numbers.

Let's look first at how this service uses event type identifiers. Earlier in this chapter I talked about how events are delivered with particular event type identifiers in them. And remember that the `EventRegistration` objects that are returned to clients contain in them the event type identifier that the client has just registered to receive. The event type identifier is meant to uniquely distinguish some type of occurrence in the generator that causes events to be fired. For this service, I grant a separate event type identifier for each and every client registration; when a client registers to receive, say, hourly heartbeat events, a new event type number is generated and returned to the client.

This strategy is similar to that employed by Sun's implementation of the lookup service, where each registration for notifications by a client is given a separate event type identifier. As we'll see when we talk about third-party event delegates, using separate event type identifiers for each registration is quite useful for allowing third-party delegates to know how to route events to "downstream" receivers.

For sequence numbers, the `HeartbeatGenerator` keeps a global sequence number counter (called `lastEventSeqNo`). This counter is incremented by one every time a new event is sent. This service only tries to send an event once when the "due date" comes up for a client. Since there are no retries, the code here doesn't have to do anything special to ensure that multiple events from the same "due date" have the same sequence numbers. Thus, satisfying the requirements for idempotency and strict ordering is easy here.

Note that since each client registration has a different event ID, any single client may see skips in the sequence numbers of events delivered to it. For example, if a client has asked to receive weekly events, it will see gaps in sequence numbers caused by the fact that other clients, who are receiving events at smaller intervals, have been sent the events with the intervening sequence numbers.

So the service here only implements the two required sequence number guarantees. It ensures that distinct sequence numbers are generated if and only if there are two distinct occurrences—in this case, the passing of the "due date" for sending an event. The code does this by only sending one event for each occurrence, and ensuring that sequence numbers are never reused. Likewise, the service also guarantees that sequence numbers are uniformly increasing. The service does this by keeping a global counter and incrementing it each time a new sequence number is needed.

The service *does not* provide the optional "full ordering" guarantee. To provide this guarantee is a relatively simple task though: in the `Registration` object for each client registration, the service would store the last used sequence number for that *particular* client—or, more accurately, that particular event type identifier, since full ordering imposes restrictions on sequence numbers relative to a particular type identifier.

Defining a Cookie Type

The class `HeartbeatCookie` defines the "cookie type" for the application's leases. You'll recall from Chapter 11 that the definition of a cookie type for a lease is dependent on the particular application that will grant the lease—cookies are meant to be used by the grantor of a lease to uniquely identify the leased resource and the holder of the lease. For this application, the cookie type is defined to hold an integer that represents the period—this is used to identify which registration vector the lease is stored in—and the event type identifier that was returned to the client when it registered for events.

Given this cookie definition—period and event ID—the service can uniquely find each and every active registration. First, it can identify which `Registration` vector to search and then, since each `Registration` is graced with a separate event ID, it can search for that ID in the vector. Essentially, the event ID becomes a unique token for identifying client registrations.

Persistent Data

You'll remember from the last chapter that much of the work of being a `BasicUnicastService` has to do with dealing with persistent data—checkpointing data periodically, and recovering after a crash.

The service here has several key pieces of data that must be reliably saved and recovered. These data are grouped together by the `Registrations` class. Instances of this class maintain references to the four vectors of client `Registration` objects, the last-used event type, and the last-used sequence number.

Whenever `checkpoint()` is called, this information is saved to disk, along with whatever other data was saved by the `BasicUnicastService` superclass (mainly data used by the `JoinManager`). And when the service is restored from persistent storage, an instance of `Registrations` is loaded off disk and used to reset the various registration vectors and counters.

Registering for and Sending Events

The event-centric portions of this code have to do with how the service handles clients' requests for event registrations, and how events are sent to clients. Let's look at the registration process first.

The `HeartbeatGenerator` service exports a single method to allow clients to register to receive heartbeat events. Remember that Jini provides no "standard" interfaces for event generators—each generator can decide for itself how it will allow clients to solicit events. Here, the `register()` method takes the period that specifies how often the client wishes to receive events, a `MarshalledObject` containing arbitrary data to be returned to the client when the event occurs, a `RemoteEventListener` to send the events to, and a requested lease duration.

When a new request comes in, the service generates a new event type identifier to serve as the ID for events for this registration. This type identifier will also uniquely identify the registration, and be used in cookie values. A new `HeartbeatCookie` is created based on the period and the type identifier; this cookie will be used in the leasing process as described in Chapter 11.

After this, a new `Registration` is created that holds the data specific to this particular client's registration—the cookie, the listener to send events to, the client-provided hand-back data, and the current expiration time. A new lease is created, the registration is added to the appropriate vector of `Registration` objects, and a new `EventRegistration` is created and returned to the client.

If a client calls `register()` multiple times with the same parameters, the service will dutifully install multiple registrations for it. So the client will receive separate events for each period it has registered for, and each will have a different event type ID.

Note that `Registration` is the service-internal information needed to handle registrations; `EventRegistration` is the information returned to the client, which contains the event type identifier, the "source" of the events (in this case, the proxy object for the service), the lease, and the last-known sequence number for this event type. Here, the last known sequence number for the client's event type is zero, since the service has never before sent any events to it.

After updating these state variables, the service is checkpointed to disk.

The actual delivery of events is handled by a separate thread. The service's `run()` method wakes up every minute to deliver any events that need to be sent. After each batch of events is delivered, `run()` figures in the time required to actually process all of the events, so that its timer doesn't "drift" off. (We want to ensure that we send events roughly every minute, rather than every minute plus whatever time is required to do the delivery. The code here subtracts out delivery time when deciding how long to sleep for the next interval.)

Whenever the thread wakes up, `sendHeartbeat()` is called to process the appropriate registration vectors: minute registrations are sent each time the thread wakes, hourly registrations are sent every 60th wake up, and so on. The `sendHeartbeats()` method takes care of the actual delivery.

This method first scans the registration vector, expiring any out-of-date event registrations. This "lazy" clean-up method—where registrations are only discarded just before we try to use them—keeps the code from having to have a separate lease expiration thread and simplifies the design.

After expiring any out-of-date registrations, the code processes all the remaining `Registration` objects in the vector. For each, it generates a new `HeartbeatEvent` with a unique sequence number, and initializes it with the source for the event (the service's proxy object), the client's particular event type identifier, the `MarshalledObject` data the client has asked to be returned to it, and the period for which this event is being sent. Note that the proxy and event type are *exactly* what was returned to the client in the `EventRegistration` object—this is required so that clients can compare these values in events that they receive with the values originally returned to them in their `EventRegistrations`.

Once the actual event object has been constructed, it is delivered to the client by calling the `notify()` method on the `RemoteEventListener` provided by the client. This call uses RMI to transport the event to the client's VM, possibly on a different machine somewhere on the network.

There are two ways that `notify()` can fail. The first is with a `RemoteException`. This exception will be raised if the client crashes or is unreachable because of network problems. The service here complains when this happens—by printing a message—but otherwise takes no action. It will continue trying to resend events to the client in the future, until its registration expires. So if the client recovers or the network is repaired, the client will receive events normally.

The other way `notify()` can fail is with an `UnknownEventException`. Recall that this exception is raised by clients when they receive an event with an unexpected type or source. Most probably this is caused by either a bug in the service (it delivers an event with a type different than the one returned in the client's `EventRegistration`), or a bug in the client (the client has simply failed to track its event registrations reliably). In either case, when the client raises this exception it is claiming that it no longer wishes to receive events of this type. So the `HeartbeatGenerator` service drops the client's registration. In this code, it does this by setting its expiration time to zero, so that it will be lazily cleaned up the next time events are delivered.

A Client to Test the HeartbeatGenerator

Now that we've got a service that generates heartbeat events, we can look at a simple client to exercise the service. This application, called `HeartbeatClient`, simply contacts all the Jini lookup services until it finds a `HeartbeatGenerator`. Once the service has been located, it solicits events for each of the four supported periods (minute, hour, day, and week), and renews its leases eternally.

Listing 14–4 provides the code for the client.

Listing 14–4 `HeartbeatClient.java`

```
// A simple client to test the HeartbeatGenerator
// service.

package corejini.chapter14;

import net.jini.discovery.DiscoveryListener;
import net.jini.discovery.DiscoveryEvent;
import net.jini.discovery.LookupDiscovery;
import net.jini.core.lookup.ServiceRegistrar;
import net.jini.core.lookup.ServiceEvent;
import net.jini.core.lookup.ServiceTemplate;
import net.jini.core.event.RemoteEvent;
import net.jini.core.event.EventRegistration;
import net.jini.core.event.RemoteEventListener;
import com.sun.jini.lease.LeaseRenewalManager;
import com.sun.jini.lease.LeaseRenewalEvent;
import com.sun.jini.lease.LeaseListener;
import net.jini.core.lease.Lease;
import java.io.IOException;
import java.rmi.RemoteException;
import java.rmi.server.UnicastRemoteObject;

public class HeartbeatClient implements Runnable {
    ServiceTemplate template;
    HeartbeatGenerator.HeartbeatRequest gen = null;
    LeaseRenewalManager leaseManager =
                              new LeaseRenewalManager();
    EvtListener listener;

    // An inner class for discovery listening
```

Listing 14–4 `HeartbeatClient.java` (continued)

```
    public class DiscListener
                  implements DiscoveryListener {
        public void discovered(DiscoveryEvent ev) {
            ServiceRegistrar[] regs = ev.getRegistrars();
            for (int i=0 ; i<regs.length ; i++) {
                doit(regs[i]);
            }
        }

        public void discarded(DiscoveryEvent ev) {
        }
    }

    // an inner class for event listening
    class EvtListener extends UnicastRemoteObject
        implements RemoteEventListener {
        EvtListener() throws RemoteException {
        }
        public void notify(RemoteEvent e) {
            if (!(e instanceof
                    HeartbeatGenerator.HeartbeatEvent)) {
                return;
            }

            HeartbeatGenerator.HeartbeatEvent ev =
                (HeartbeatGenerator.HeartbeatEvent) e;

            switch (ev.getPeriod()) {
            case HeartbeatGenerator.MINUTE:
                System.out.println("Came from MINUTE");
                break;
            case HeartbeatGenerator.HOUR:
                System.out.println("Came from HOUR");
                break;
            case HeartbeatGenerator.DAY:
                System.out.println("Came from DAY");
                break;
            case HeartbeatGenerator.WEEK:
                System.out.println("Came from WEEK");
                break;
            default:
                System.out.println("Unknown!");
                break;
            }
        }
    }
```

Listing 14–4 `HeartbeatClient.java` **(continued)**

```
    public HeartbeatClient() throws IOException,
            RemoteException {
        Class[] types =
            { HeartbeatGenerator.HeartbeatRequest.class };
        template = new ServiceTemplate(null, types, null);

        listener = new EvtListener();

        LookupDiscovery disco =
            new LookupDiscovery(
                            LookupDiscovery.ALL_GROUPS);
        disco.addDiscoveryListener(new DiscListener());
    }

    void doit(ServiceRegistrar reg) {
        if (gen != null) // bail once we've found it.
            return;

        try {
            gen = (HeartbeatGenerator.HeartbeatRequest)
                reg.lookup(template);
        } catch (Exception ex) {
            System.err.println("Doing lookup: " +
                                   ex.getMessage());
        }

        if (gen == null)
            return;

        // sign us up for events!
        EventRegistration evt;
        try {
            evt = gen.register(HeartbeatGenerator.MINUTE,
                    null, listener, Lease.ANY);
            leaseManager.renewUntil(evt.getLease(),
                     Lease.ANY, null);

            evt = gen.register(HeartbeatGenerator.HOUR,
                    null, listener, Lease.ANY);
            leaseManager.renewUntil(evt.getLease(),
                     Lease.ANY, null);
```

Listing 14–4 `HeartbeatClient.java` **(continued)**

```
            evt = gen.register(HeartbeatGenerator.DAY,
                    null, listener, Lease.ANY);
            leaseManager.renewUntil(evt.getLease(),
                     Lease.ANY, null);

            evt = gen.register(HeartbeatGenerator.WEEK,
                    null, listener, Lease.ANY);
            leaseManager.renewUntil(evt.getLease(),
                     Lease.ANY, null);

        } catch (RemoteException ex) {
           System.err.println("Bogus: " + ex.getMessage());
        }
    }

    public void run() {
        while (true) {
            try {
                Thread.sleep(Integer.MAX_VALUE);
            } catch (InterruptedException ex) {
            }
        }
    }

    public static void main(String[] args) {
        try {
            HeartbeatClient client = new HeartbeatClient();
            new Thread(client).start();
        } catch (Exception ex) {
           System.err.println("Bogus: " + ex.getMessage());
            System.exit(1);
        }
    }
}
```

This is an extremely simple client to exercise the `HeartbeatGenerator` service. The client defines a separate inner class to participate in the Jini discovery process. The client only continues searching until it has found a single `HeartbeatGenerator`. At that point, it registers for events to be delivered every minute, hour, day, and week. The leases for these event registrations are handed off to a `LeaseRenewalManager` so that they will be renewed indefinitely.

The client also defines a separate inner class to receive events. When heartbeat events are delivered, they come through this class's `notify()` method. The client simply ensures that they are indeed `HeartbeatEvents` and then displays whether the event was sent because of the minute timer, the hour timer, and so on.

Compiling and Running the Heartbeat Examples

Let's now build and run the `HeartbeatGenerator` and `HeartbeatClient` programs. First, let's compile the code needed for the service, and build the necessary RMI stubs. Both `BasicRegistrationLandlord` and `Heartbeat-Generator` extend `java.rmi.server.UnicastRemoteObject`, so you have to build stubs for them.

On Windows:

```
javac -classpath C:\jini1_0\lib\jini-core.jar;
                              C:\jini1_0\lib\jini-ext.jar;
                              C:\jini1_0\lib\sun-util.jar;
                              C:\service
     -d C:\service
     C:\files\corejini\chapter14\HeartbeatGenerator.java

rmic -classpath C:\jdk1.2\jre\lib\rt.jar;
                             C:\jini1_0\lib\jini-core.jar;
                             C:\jini1_0\lib\jini-ext.jar;
                             C:\jini1_0\lib\sun-util.jar;
                             C:\service
            -d C:\service-dl
            corejini.chapter14.BasicRegistrationLandlord
            corejini.chapter14.HeartbeatGenerator
```

On Solaris:

```
javac -classpath     /files/jini1_0/lib/jini-core.jar:
                     /files/jini1_0/lib/jini-ext.jar:
                     /files/jini1_0/lib/sun-util.jar:
                     /files/service
                -d /files/service
        /files/corejini/chapter14/HeartbeatGenerator.java

    rmic -classpath  /files/jdk1.2/jre/lib/rt.jar:
                     /files/jini1_0/lib/jini-core.jar:
                     /files/jini1_0/lib/jini-ext.jar:
                     /files/jini1_0/lib/sun-util.jar:
```

```
                /files/service
            -d /files/service-dl
        corejini.chapter14.BasicRegistrationLandlord
        corejini.chapter14.HeartbeatGenerator
```

After this, you need to build the files necessary for the client program. Note that the client also needs the `HeartbeatRequest` interface, which is the interface that the service's proxy implements. This interface is contained within the service's code, but is actually used by both the service and the client. So you'll have to copy it out to the client's directory. Since `HeartbeatClient`'s `EvtListener` class extends `UnicastRemoteObject`, you'll have to run `rmic` to generate its stubs.

On Windows:

```
javac -classpath C:\jini1_0\lib\jini-core.jar;
                           C:\jini1_0\lib\jini-ext.jar;
                           C:\jini1_0\lib\sun-util.jar;
                           C:\client
         -d C:\client
         C:\files\corejini\chapter14\HeartbeatClient.java

rmic -classpath C:\jdk1.2\jre\lib\rt.jar;
                          C:\jini1_0\lib\jini-core.jar;
                          C:\jini1_0\lib\jini-ext.jar;
                          C:\jini1_0\lib\sun-util.jar;
                          C:\client
            -d C:\client-dl
            corejini.chapter14.HeartbeatClient.EvtListener

cd C:\service
copy HeartbeatGenerator$HeartbeatRequest.class
                          C:\client
```

On Solaris:

```
javac -classpath     /files/jini1_0/lib/jini-core.jar:
                     /files/jini1_0/lib/jini-ext.jar:
                     /files/jini1_0/lib/sun-util.jar:
                     /files/client
                 -d /files/client
            /files/corejini/chapter14/HeartbeatClient.java

    rmic -classpath  /files/jdk1.2/jre/lib/rt.jar:
                     /files/jini1_0/lib/jini-core.jar:
                     /files/jini1_0/lib/jini-ext.jar:
```

```
                    /files/jini1_0/lib/sun-util.jar:
                    /files/client
               -d /files/client-dl
          corejini.chapter14.HeartbeatClient.EvtListener

cd /files/service
cp HeartbeatGenerator$HeartbeatRequest.class
                /files/client
```

Finally you're set to run the applications! Start the service first, then the client. Be sure to give the service a pathname to use for its stable storage. As usual, replace "myhost" with the hostname on which the client's and the service's HTTP servers are running, and set the appropriate port number.

On Windows:

```
java -cp C:\files\jini1_0\lib\jini-core.jar;
            C:\files\jini1_0\lib\jini-ext.jar;
            C:\files\jini1_0\lib\sun-util.jar;
            C:\service
        -Djava.rmi.server.codebase=http://myhost:8085/
        -Djava.security.policy=C:\policy
    corejini.chapter14.HeartbeatGenerator C:\tmp\hb

java -cp C:\files\jini1_0\lib\jini-core.jar;
            C:\files\jini1_0\lib\jini-ext.jar;
            C:\files\jini1_0\lib\sun-util.jar;
            C:\client
        -Djava.rmi.server.codebase=http://myhost:8086/
        -Djava.security.policy=C:\policy
    corejini.chapter14.HeartbeatClient
```

On Solaris:

```
java -cp /files/jini1_0/lib/jini-core.jar:
            /files/jini1_0/lib/jini-ext.jar:
            /files/jini1_0/lib/sun-util.jar:
            /files/service
        -Djava.rmi.server.codebase=http://myhost:8085/
        -Djava.security.policy=/files/policy
    corejini.chapter14.HeartbeatGenerator /tmp/hb

java -cp /files/jini1_0/lib/jini-core.jar:
            /files/jini1_0/lib/jini-ext.jar:
            /files/jini1_0/lib/sun-util.jar:
            /files/client
```

```
      -Djava.rmi.server.codebase=http://myhost:8086/
      -Djava.security.policy=/files/policy
  corejini.chapter14.HeartbeatClient
```

As the service starts up, you should see it report:
Heartbeat generator started.

And then—for as long as you leave the client and the server running—you should see the client output messages to the effect of:
Came from MINUTE
Came from MINUTE
Came from MINUTE

If either you're very bored or very tenacious, you can leave this up long enough to get the hourly, daily, and weekly messages.

This example has shown how to create a simple event client—much like you've seen before—and also a rather robust event generator. This generator takes care of event registration leases, manages sequence numbers correctly, and assigns event type identifiers to allow client registrations to be clearly distinguished from one another.

In the remainder of this chapter, we'll look at how to build an event handling delegate service, and use this service "in between" the `HeartbeatGenerator` and a client.

Third-Party Event Delegates

This chapter has already talked a lot about how Jini was designed to support "third-party" event delegates—these are chunks of code that can add new application-provided functionality to an event system. Further, these delegates are "generic" in the sense that they can operate on any type of event, from any source.

In Jini, these delegates are typically implemented as Jini services that run in separate VMs from the original "upstream" generator, or the final "downstream" receiver. Delegates can be added by either the receiving client or by the sending service, and multiple delegates can be composed together.

Let's review briefly why event delegates are important, and how event delegates can be used in a Jini community. As you've seen in this chapter, the Jini event programming model says nothing about quality of service guarantees, such as what policies a service should follow when an event cannot be delivered to a client, what ordering should be imposed on events, and so forth. These sorts of policies don't just affect performance; they can also drive the entire architecture of a client application.

For example, imagine a client application that is inactive for large periods of time. If this client needed to receive events, then each delivery would cause the client to be reactivated. If the frequency of events is high, then the client may spend nearly all of its time simply reactivating itself so that it can receive an event!

This is a very real example of how the standard event delivery mechanisms in Jini may need to be augmented by applications to support their particular semantics and constraints. In the case of the activatable client, we'd like to have a way for events to be queued up and retrieved periodically. Essentially what we need is a "mailbox" for events, that receives events until the client goes to "pick up its mail." Such an event mailbox service could be used not only by Jini clients, but by other services as well.

In the last example of this chapter, we'll look at building just such an event mailbox service.

Designing for Composition

Jini supports composable event delegates by relying on a very *standard* and very *narrow* set of APIs for event delivery. By *standard* I mean that every single remote event, no matter what its type, is delivered to a `RemoteEventListener` through the `notify()` method. Because there is no other way for Jini remote events to be delivered, you know that if you are a `RemoteEventListener` you can receive any type of event.

This situation is in stark contrast to, say, AWT's event model. In AWT there are maybe a dozen separate types of events, each with its own listener classes. Because of the many ways to receive events, it's very difficult to create a "generic" listener—you'd have to implement all dozen or so listener interfaces with all their methods. And if a new event type showed up in the future, you'd be out of luck since you can only implement the event listener interfaces that you know about at compile time.

By relying on only one listener interface, Jini allows your code to listen for any type of remote event, including remote events that may not even be defined at the time your code is written.

The *narrowness* of the Jini APIs means simply that there are very few methods you need to worry about to receive events. In fact, there's only *one*—the `notify()` method. This makes the job of writing a new event listener almost trivial; there are no exotic or rarely used methods that you have to understand in order to "plug in" to the Jini event system.

These properties are present in Jini by design, not by accident. And they mean that any entity, whether it's an event generator or an event receiver, can add event delegates to the delivery path between the two. Multiple delegates can even be composed together on the delivery path—sometimes called the *event pipeline*—to enable rich new behaviors.

Composition in Practice

Let's move away from the abstract and talk about what composable event delegates mean in practice. I've said that both generators and receivers can add delegates to the event pipeline.

Services that need to enforce some particular event delivery behaviors may choose to provide these behaviors through delegation for a couple of reasons. First, using a delegate may enable the service writer to use a cleaner design for the service than might otherwise be possible. If a huge chunk of code is going to be necessary to ensure that the service's events are delivered in-order at all costs, then the service writer may decide to separate that chunk of code into a separate "in-order event delegate service."

Second, event-generating services may use delegates simply to leverage third-party code. If there are a host of useful delegates available to you, why not take advantage of them rather than reinventing their functionality?

Services and clients that *receive* events may have many more reasons to use delegates, however. A service that is rarely active may not wish to be awakened every time an event is delivered. Such a service could use an event mailbox as described earlier.

Some clients may find that an event generator does not provide fine-grained facilities for describing the events to be sent. For example, some clients may find the search facilities provided through `ServiceTemplates` and the Jini lookup service to be too limiting. A client that needs to find all storage services with a "free space" attribute greater than some specified value would fall into this category. Such a client could create a service that acts as an "event filter delegate." This delegate would receive a more general set of events from a lookup service, and then filter these based on some query provided by the client. Only the events that pass the filter would be forwarded on to the client. So in the case of a client that is only interested in storage services with some minimum amount of free space available, the delegate would register with a lookup service to receive events about all storage services that have any value in the "free space" attribute. The delegate would then forward

only those events that refer to storage services with free space greater than, say, a megabyte.

How Events are Delivered through the Pipeline

Let's ignore, for the moment, the process of setting up a series of delegates, and focus on what happens when an event is actually delivered from an original generator, through a series of delegates, and down to the intended receiver.

Every delegate, as well as the final receiver, implements the `RemoteEventListener` method, so `RemoteEvents` can be delivered through the `notify()` method on each of these entities. In most cases, each delegate will be implemented as a service that may be providing some event processing to any number of clients. So this raises a question: If a delegate is processing and forwarding events from several upstream generators, and these are possibly intended for several downstream receivers, how does the generator know how to route the events?

The answer is that each downstream entity must tell the delegate "before" it in the pipeline that the downstream entity should receive all events from a certain source and with a certain event type that are delivered to the delegate. The delegate keeps a mapping that indicates which downstream listener to send events to, given the source and type of the events.

Figure 14–1 shows an example of a delegate processing events to and from a number of entities. Here you see three event generators sending events to a single delegate. The delegate keeps a mapping table internally so that it can remember how to route events from each of these generators on to the downstream receivers.

This mapping is established through a registration process that is analogous to the process when an event listener asks a generator to send it events; in fact, you could say that this *is* exactly the same process, since delegates are not only listeners, but generators as well!

Setting up the Pipeline

So events can be routed through a pipeline of delegates by using the source and event type contained in every event, and routing to an associated downstream listener. But how is this association first created?

Each type of delegate will define its own interfaces for allowing it to be hooked into a pipeline. The situation here is the same as for all other event generators—there are no "standard" interfaces for generators (or delegates),

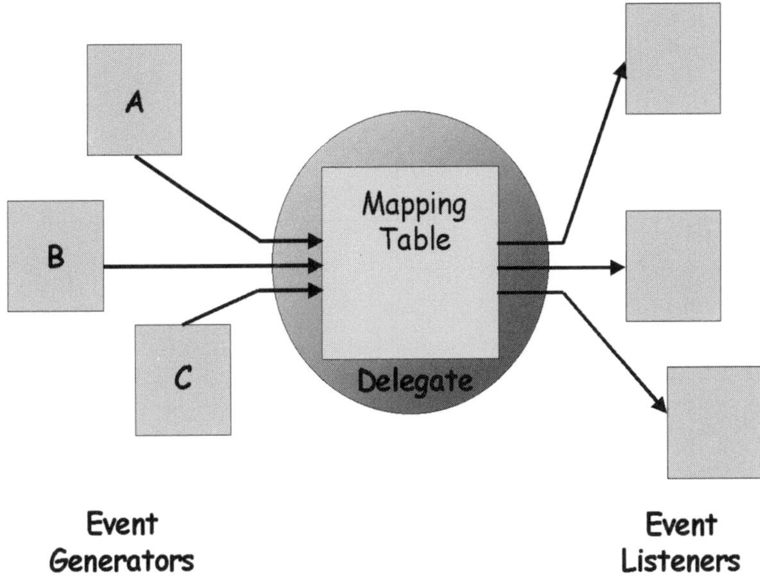

Figure 14–1 An event delegate routes events from multiple generators

because each entity that generates events supports its own way to ask for events that make sense for its particular application domain. You ask lookup services for events by giving them a `ServiceTemplate`. Other services may have completely different notions of when events should be sent, and therefore support completely different mechanisms for asking that events be sent.

In general, either the original generator or the original listener will set up the event pipeline; the code idioms they follow are quite different, however. Let's look at each.

Pipelines from the Generator Perspective

Event generators have a somewhat easier task than listeners when they create an event pipeline. Typically, an event generator that wishes to use a delegate to enhance its event processing will obtain a reference to the delegate before it allows clients to solicit events from it. The service will typically register the delegate as its *only* event listener—so all events sent by the service will go straight to the delegate.

When a client contacts the service to receive events, the client passes in a listener to which events should be sent. The service then registers with the delegate—using whatever delegate-specific registration interfaces it supports—and tells the delegate to route events from the service, and of a certain type known to the service, to the `RemoteEventListener` supplied by the client.

In this case, the service already knows everything it needs to construct the pipeline. The service can assign every client registration a unique event identifier, and make sure it never sends any events with that identifier until the registration process is complete, and the client-supplied listener has been registered with the delegate.

Let's talk through an example. Suppose you want to create a reimplementation of the Jini lookup service that routes all its outgoing events through a delegate. The first thing you would do is acquire a reference to the delegate service you intend to use. This delegate would implement `RemoteEventListener` (since it needs to receive your outgoing events), and would presumably have some registration method that would take as parameters an event source, and event type, and a `RemoteEventListener`. Any events received by the delegate that had the specified source and type would be forwarded on to that listener. The reimplemented lookup service would send *all* its events to the delegate, regardless of final source.

The only other significant change would come in the `notify()` method on the service which, you will remember, is how clients ask to receive events from lookup services (the method name `notify()` is unfortunately overloaded in Java and Jini). When the service processes the client's request for registration, it generates a unique event ID for the client and tells the delegate to route events of that type that it receives to the client-supplied listener.

From this point, whenever the service generated any events, they would go directly to the delegate, which would route them to the client-supplied listener based on the source and type information in the event.

Pipelines from the Listener Perspective

Because they are not "inside" the registration process (as generators are when they use delegates) listeners have a somewhat difficult time setting up an event processing pipeline. The steps that a consumer will take to create an event pipeline vary in the specifics because each delegate has its own interfaces. But in general, there are a number of steps that will be largely common, no matter what the particulars of the delegates or other generators.

When you build an event pipeline from within a listener, you must:

1. Start with the original generator, which is the most upstream entity, and work downstream.
2. Ask each in turn to deliver events to the next most downstream entity.
3. Continue until the ultimate receiver has been added as a listener for events. At this point everything is "wired together."

The difficulty from the perspective of the listener is in providing each stage in the pipeline with accurate routine information. Typically a client won't know the information needed for routing (source and event type) for a given stage in the pipeline until the listener registration is already complete. In programmatic terms, you don't get back the `EventRegistration` until you've already solicited events and passed in a `RemoteEventListener`, so you cannot build up the pipeline from the listener out to the generator. Since the listener hasn't yet been told about the source or types of the events you've just signed it up to receive, it cannot know how to route any events from the upstream source (and, in fact, it cannot know the routing information yet since you don't have this information until after you've already gotten back the event registration).

Unfortunately, constructing an event pipeline "backwards"—from the original generator down to the final listener—has race conditions, because the generator may send an event before the pipeline is fully constructed. The alternative, working from the original listener back to the generator, is not workable when the listener is constructing the pipeline, as it doesn't know the source and event type information needed to route events until it has already registered a listener. If events enter the pipeline before it is fully constructed, a delegate may receive an event before it has a destination to send it to.

One solution to this problem is to have delegates hold on to "unknown" events they receive for a period of time, in the anticipation that they may shortly be called with information that will tell them how to route such events. Alternatively, they could simply drop events that are received with an unknown source and type until the pipeline is fully constructed.

Here's some pseudocode that shows how a listener may create an event pipeline between it and a Jini lookup service. Assume that we have a set of delegates, say of an imaginary class `Delegate`, each with a register method that takes a source, an event type, and a downstream listener. Each `Delegate` is itself a `RemoteEventListener` so that it can receive events. Let's say that the code doing this is a `RemoteEventListener`, and is the final destination for the events, and that the original generator is a Jini lookup service.

```
class Delegate implements RemoteEventListener {
        // ...
        void register(Object source,
                      long eventID,
                      RemoteEventListener downstream);
        // ...
}

void createPipeline(ServiceRegistrar reg,
                    ServiceTemplate tmpl) {
        // These would actually be proxies for delegate
        // services.
        Delegate d1 = new Delegate();
        Delegate d2 = new Delegate();
        Delegate d3 = new Delegate();

        EventRegistration evtreg =
                     reg.notify(tmpl, d1
                          /* ...some args omitted...*/);

        d1.register(evtreg.getSource(),
                    evtreg.getID(),
                    d2);
        d2.register(evtreg.getSource(),
                    evtreg.getID(),
                    d3);
        d3.register(evtreg.getSource(),
                    evtreg.getID(),
                    this);    // final destination
}
```

This pseudocode follows the "work backward" approach, connecting each upstream generator to the next downstream listener. Only at the end of the setup process is the entire pipeline constructed and fully functional. You'll note here how the initial registration with the Jini lookup service is necessary to get the event source and type information needed to tell the delegates how to route events properly.

Here, there's a presumption that the delegates do not change the source and ID of the event, so the original source and ID are passed on to each delegate. The event that finally arrives at the ultimate destination will be indistinguishable from one that hadn't passed through the delegate chain.

Leasing Across Delegates

One other important question we must address in chaining delegates is: How does leasing work? Presumably a delegate won't continue to forward and process events in perpetuity just because we ask it to. This is definitely un-Jini-like! Clearly the answer is to lease event registrations with delegates, just as "normal" event registrations are leased from event generators.

There are a couple of approaches that one could follow here. One strategy would be to have the entity that creates the pipeline do the leasing for *all* the delegates. So, in the pseudocode just shown, the client that is consuming the events would get leases back from the `register()` calls on the delegates, and renew them using a `LeaseRenewalManager` or some other strategy. If the client crashes, the delegates gradually expire the leased registrations and the pipeline dissolves.

Another approach would be to have each entity in the pipeline handle the lease for the registration for the next upstream member of the pipe that it receives events from. So, in the foregoing pseudocode, `d1` might manage the lease for the event registration with the lookup service, `d2` might manage the lease that causes `d1` to continue forwarding events, and so on. The client—the actual final consumer of the events—would only manually handle the final event registration lease from `d3`. Such an arrangement would require that the `register()` calls of the `Delegate` class be extended to take a lease to be managed.

This approach may be marginally less work for the client, and has a certain elegance to it—much like in the single-generator, single-listener model, the listener is responsible for telling the generator to continue sending it events. This approach also works well if the eventual recipient will not be active often enough to perform leasing. Presumably the event processing delegates will be implemented as long-lived services, so handing off lease management to them would allow the ultimate recipient to become inactive as needed.

One downside of this approach is that when a problem occurs, leases expire serially, rather than in parallel as would happen in the first approach. So the total time required for the pipeline to dissolve would be longer.

In the example in this chapter, I'll use the first approach—the client, which is the final receiver of events, handles all the leases for all the delegates.

An Example: An Event Mailbox

Let's move on to the final example of this chapter—an event mailbox service that can store events until they are requested by their final recipient. Receivers can use this mailbox much as just shown—they simply interpose it between the original generator of events and themselves. They must "reserve space" in the mailbox service by telling it about the events they expect to receive. Then, once the mailbox has accumulated events for them, they can fetch these events as a "batch" (causing all stored events to be returned in a vector), or they can ask that the mailbox deliver them individually using the recipient's normal `notify()` method. This allows the "normal" event processing code to be reused for receiving stored events.

This code builds on the `BasicRegistrationLandlord` code shown earlier in this chapter for managing event registration leases. The mailbox service defines its own particular subclass of `Registration`. Recall that this is the class that stores the service-internal information needed to process event registrations. This subclass (Listing 14–5) is called `EventMailboxRegistration`.

Listing 14–5 `EventMailboxRegistration.java`

```
// A subclass of registration that holds a
// vector of to-be-delivered events.

package corejini.chapter14;

import java.io.Serializable;
import java.rmi.MarshalledObject;
import java.util.Vector;
import net.jini.core.event.RemoteEvent;
import net.jini.core.event.RemoteEventListener;

class EventMailboxRegistration extends Registration
                implements Serializable {
    // This is the actual set of saved events for each
    // client.
    protected Vector mailbox = new Vector();
```

Listing 14–5 `EventMailboxRegistration.java` **(continued)**

```
    EventMailboxRegistration(Object cookie,
                             RemoteEventListener listener,
                             MarshalledObject data,
                             long expiration) {
        super(cookie, listener, data, expiration);
    }

    // Override cancelled to null the mailbox
    protected void cancelled() {
        mailbox = null;
    }

    // Return the saved event vector.
    Vector getMailbox() {
        return mailbox;
    }

    // Add to the saved event vector
    void appendEvent(RemoteEvent ev) {
        mailbox.addElement(ev);
    }

    // Return the saved event vector, clearing it.
    Vector getAndFlushMailbox() {
        Vector rv = getMailbox();
        mailbox = new Vector();
        return rv;
    }
}
```

The `Registration` superclass holds the lease cookie, the `RemoteEventListener` specified by the client, the `MarshalledObject` that should be returned to the client, and the current expiration time for the registration. The `EventMailboxRegistration` subclass adds only storage for the set of events that are being kept for the client. This class will be used internally by `EventMailbox` to store client-by-client information to process events.

The EventMailbox Service

Let's look now at the `EventMailbox` class (Listing 14–6), which implements the store-and-forward event delegate service.

Listing 14–6 `EventMailbox.java`

```
// A "mailbox" for events--a service that stores
// events until asked.

package corejini.chapter14;

import corejini.chapter13.BasicUnicastService;
import corejini.chapter13.BasicUnicastAdmin;
import net.jini.core.lease.Lease;
import net.jini.core.lease.UnknownLeaseException;
import net.jini.core.event.RemoteEvent;
import net.jini.core.event.RemoteEventListener;
import net.jini.core.event.EventRegistration;
import net.jini.core.event.UnknownEventException;
import com.sun.jini.lease.landlord.Landlord;
import com.sun.jini.lease.landlord.LandlordLease;
import java.rmi.Remote;
import java.rmi.RemoteException;
import java.rmi.server.UnicastRemoteObject;
import java.io.IOException;
import java.io.Serializable;
import java.util.Vector;
import java.util.Hashtable;

// Define a new type of cookie to use for our
// leases.
class MailboxCookie implements Serializable {
    protected Object source;
    protected long eventType;

    MailboxCookie(Object source, long eventType) {
        this.source = source;
        this.eventType = eventType;
    }
```

Listing 14–6 `EventMailbox.java` **(continued)**

```
    public boolean equals(Object o) {
        if (!(o instanceof MailboxCookie))
            return false;

        MailboxCookie cookie = (MailboxCookie) o;

        return cookie.eventType == eventType &&
            cookie.source.equals(source);
    }
}

// EventMailbox is a BasicUnicastService (see Ch. 13)
public class EventMailbox extends BasicUnicastService
            implements Runnable,
            BasicUnicastService.RestoreListener,
            EventMailbox.EventMailboxRequest {
    protected LandlordLease.Factory factory =
        new LandlordLease.Factory();
    // Vectors of Registrations keyed by source
    protected Hashtable mailboxes = new Hashtable();
    // Landlords keyed by source.
    protected Hashtable landlords = new Hashtable();

    // Defines the remote interface that clients will
    // use to communicate with the service.
    public interface EventMailboxRequest
        extends RemoteEventListener, Remote {
        // Get a mailbox.
        public EventRegistration acquireMailbox(Object src,
                                                long eventType,
                                                 long duration)
            throws RemoteException;
        // Get events in a batch.
        public Vector getEvents(Object source,
                                long eventType)
             throws RemoteException,
             UnknownLeaseException;
        // Have events redelivered
        public void deliverEvents(Object source,
                               long eventType,
                               RemoteEventListener listener)
            throws RemoteException, UnknownLeaseException;
    }
```

Listing 14–6 `EventMailbox.java` **(continued)**

```
    // serialized data object
    static class MailboxData implements Serializable {
        Hashtable mailboxes;

        MailboxData(Hashtable mailboxes) {
            this.mailboxes = mailboxes;
        }
    }

    protected EventMailbox(String storageLoc)
                      throws RemoteException {
        super(storageLoc);
    }

    public void initialize()
         throws IOException, ClassNotFoundException {
         super.initialize();
         new Thread(this).start();
    }

    protected void checkpoint() throws IOException {
        super.checkpoint(new MailboxData(mailboxes));
    }

    protected Object getProxy() {
        return this;
    }

    public void restored(Object subclassData) {
        MailboxData data = (MailboxData) subclassData;
        mailboxes = data.mailboxes;
    }

    // Events from generators come in through this method.
    public void synchronized notify(RemoteEvent ev) {
        Object source = ev.getSource();
        Vector regs = (Vector) mailboxes.get(source);
        // If we don't have an entry for this source, we
        // don't complain with an UnknownEventException--
        // that would prevent us from getting any future
        // events from that source. Instead we just
        // silently ignore it.
```

Listing 14–6 `EventMailbox.java` **(continued)**

```
        if (regs == null) {
            System.err.println("Unknown source.");
            return;
        }

        // Iterate through the list looking for the
        // matching cookie.
        for (int i=0, size=regs.size() ; i<size ; i++) {
            EventMailboxRegistration reg =
                (EventMailboxRegistration)
                                regs.elementAt(i);

            MailboxCookie cookie = (MailboxCookie)
                                        reg.getCookie();

            // File the event into the matching mailbox.
            if (cookie.source.equals(source)) {
                System.out.println("Saved event");
                reg.appendEvent(ev);
                return;
            }
        }

        // If we don't find a matching mailbox,
        // just ignore it.
        System.out.println("No registration.");
    }

    // Consumers or generators can install a request for
    // mailboxing through this call.
    public EventRegistration acquireMailbox(Object source,
                                            long eventType,
                                            long duration)
        throws RemoteException {
        // Create a cookie for the mailbox and its lease
        MailboxCookie cookie =
                    new MailboxCookie(source, eventType);

        // Create a new vector for this source, if we
        // need to. Also get the landlord for this
        // source.
```

Listing 14–6 EventMailbox.java (continued)

```
        Vector regs;
        BasicRegistrationLandlord landlord;
        if ((regs = (Vector) mailboxes.get(source))
                                            == null) {
            regs = new Vector();
            landlord = new BasicRegistrationLandlord(regs,
                                            factory);
            mailboxes.put(source, regs);
            landlords.put(source, landlord);
        } else {
            landlord = (BasicRegistrationLandlord)
                landlords.get(source);
        }

        // Compute the expiration time.
        long expiration = landlord.getExpiration(duration);
        EventMailboxRegistration emr = new
            EventMailboxRegistration(cookie, null, null,
                                    expiration);
        Lease lease = factory.newLease(cookie, landlord,
                                            expiration);

        // Add the registration to the list of mailboxes.
        regs.addElement(emr);

        // Return an event registration to the client
        EventRegistration mbr =
            new EventRegistration(eventType, source,
                                  lease, 0);

        try {
            checkpoint();
        } catch (IOException ex) {
            System.err.println("Error checkpoint: " +
                               ex.getMessage());
        }

        System.out.println("Acquired new mailbox for " +
                           source + ", " + eventType);

        return mbr;
    }
```

Listing 14–6 `EventMailbox.java` **(continued)**

```
public Vector synchronized getEvents(Object source,
                                     long eventType)
    throws UnknownLeaseException {
    System.out.println("Getting events.");
    Vector regs = (Vector) mailboxes.get(source);

    if (regs == null) {
        throw new UnknownLeaseException();
    }

    MailboxCookie cookie = new MailboxCookie(source,
                                             eventType);

    for (int i=0, size=regs.size() ; i<size ; i++) {
        EventMailboxRegistration reg =
            (EventMailboxRegistration)
                                  regs.elementAt(i);
        if (reg.getCookie().equals(cookie))
            return reg.getAndFlushMailbox();
    }

    throw new UnknownLeaseException();
}

 public void synchronized deliverEvents(Object source,
                             long eventType,
                             RemoteEventListener listener)
    throws UnknownLeaseException, RemoteException {
    System.out.println("Redelivering events.");
    Vector regs = (Vector) mailboxes.get(source);

    if (regs == null) {
        throw new UnknownLeaseException();
    }

    MailboxCookie cookie = new MailboxCookie(source,
                                             eventType);

    for (int i=0, size=regs.size() ; i<size ; i++) {
        EventMailboxRegistration reg =
            (EventMailboxRegistration)
                                  regs.elementAt(i);
```

Listing 14–6 `EventMailbox.java` **(continued)**

```
        if (reg.getCookie().equals(cookie)) {
            Vector events = reg.getMailbox();
            // Try to send them. If we get any
             // exceptions, don't flush the mailbox.
            boolean succeeded = true;
            for (int j=0, evsize=events.size() ;
                                      j<evsize ; j++) {
                try {
                    listener.notify((RemoteEvent)
                                 events.elementAt(j));
                } catch (RemoteException ex) {
                 System.err.println("Error sending: "+
                                     ex.getMessage());
                    succeeded = false;
                } catch (UnknownEventException ex) {
                    System.err.println(
                     "Client claims they don't want " +
                       "this event type... removing");

                            Landlord ll = (Landlord)
                      landlords.get(source);

                    if (ll != null) {
                        ll.cancel(reg.getCookie());
                    }

                    return;
                }
            }

            if (succeeded) {
                reg.getAndFlushMailbox();
            }

            return;
        }
    }

    throw new UnknownLeaseException();
}
```

Listing 14–6 `EventMailbox.java` **(continued)**

```
    public void run() {
        while (true) {
            try {
                Thread.sleep(Integer.MAX_VALUE);
            } catch (InterruptedException ex) {
            }
        }
    }

    public static void main(String[] args) {
        if (args.length != 1) {
            System.err.println("Usage: EventMailbox " +
                                                "<storage>");
            System.exit(1);
        }

        try {
            EventMailbox mailbox =
                                new EventMailbox(args[0]);
            mailbox.initialize();
            System.out.println("running!");
        } catch (Exception ex) {
            System.err.println("Error starting mailbox: " +
                                ex.getMessage());
            System.exit(1);
        }
    }
}
```

The `EventMailbox` service extends the `BasicUnicastService` from Chapter 13, and uses many of the conventions of that class. It first defines a new cookie type for maintaining the associations between leases held by clients and internally leased resources. The `MailboxCookie` class maintains the source and event type of an object registration; these will uniquely identify an event registration.

The `EventMailbox` class itself maintains its internal data in the form of two hashtables. The first maintains all the `EventMailboxRegistrations` in effect. It is organized as a hashtable of `Vectors` keyed by event source. Each `Vector` contains the `EventMailboxRegistrations` for that source. Whenever an event arrives, the service can quickly find the particular set of registrations for that source, and then scan the registrations looking for the one that matches the event type at hand.

The second hashtable keeps a mapping from event sources to BasicRegistrationLandlords. Recall that the BasicRegistrationLandlord class understands how to manage a single Vector of Registration objects. Since the service here stores registrations in a hashtable that contains Vectors as values, there is a separate landlord for each source. This hashtable maintains this mapping.

The remote interface EventMailboxRequest defines the protocol that clients will use to communicate with the service. The service's proxy is actually just the automatically generated stub for the EventMailbox service. There are three methods defined by this interface. The first, acquireMailbox(), is used by clients to reserve a mailbox for events of a particular type from a particular source. "Reserving a mailbox" means that the service will begin storing events that it sees that match the parameters, and not simply dispose of them. This method also takes a requested lease duration.

The second method, getEvents(), returns a "batch" of all the events received since the client last checked in. The events are returned as a Vector and the client's mailbox is cleared.

Note that the notify(), getEvents(), and deliverEvents() methods are synchronized. So getEvents() and deliverEvents() will have sole access to the mailbox when they run—new events cannot be stored in the mailbox while they are in the process of delivering or returning events.

The final method, deliverEvents(), causes any stored events to be sent one at a time to the specified RemoteEventListener. After the events have been delivered, the client's mailbox is cleared.

The EventMailbox service follows the usual conventions for storing persistent data. The class MailboxData contains the hashtable of registrations, and is saved to disk every time checkpoint() is called; this same information is restored whenever the service is restarted.

The bulk of the work in this service is in its implementation of notify(), and the three methods defined by the EventMailboxRequest remote interface. Let's look at these in detail.

The notify() method is called whenever an upstream event generator needs to deliver an event to the mailbox delegate. When an event arrives, its source is looked up in the hashtable of registrations to see if any client has registered interest in the source. If there is no Vector of EventMailboxRegistrations for the source, then the service has received a spurious event or—more likely—a client has added it as a listener for an upstream generator, but has not had a chance to acquire a mailbox. Remember that the information needed to acquire a mailbox (the event's source and type) are typically only available from generators (including the Jini lookup service) once the delegate has already been installed as a listener for the generator.

The policy taken by the mailbox service is that it simply drops all events from unknown sources or of unknown types until clients have established a valid mailbox for them.

If there is a `Vector` containing registrations from the event's source, then the registrations are scanned in turn to try to find the particular `EventMailboxRegistration` for the event's source and type. If it is found, then the event is appended to the client's mailbox for later retrieval. Otherwise it is simply dropped.

Whenever a client wants to have the mailbox service begin storing events for it, it calls `acquireMailbox()`. The parameters to this call are the source and type of the events that are to be saved—presumably this is enough information to uniquely identify the destination of the event—and a requested lease duration.

The call creates a new `Vector` to hold registrations from this source, if there is none. If this is the first time that this source has been encountered, a new `BasicRegistrationLandlord` is also created to manage leasing for registrations for events from the source.

The normal leasing mechanics are done here—computing an actual expiration time, creating a cookie and a lease, and so on—the registration is added to the appropriate vector, and an `EventRegistration` is returned to the client. From this point, whenever an event is received that has a source and type that have been specified in a call to `acquireMailbox()`, the event will be saved in a client-specific mailbox until the client retrieves its events, or its lease on the mailbox expires.

The `getEvents()` method simply finds the mailbox for the client given the specified event source and type, and returns the whole `Vector` of events to the client; the mailbox is cleared after this operation. If there is no such mailbox, the service assumes that the client's lease on the mailbox expired, and throws `UnknownLeaseException` to tell the client that its lease is no longer valid.

The `deliverEvents()` method works similarly. The only difference here is that the method takes a `RemoteEventListener` parameter that the service should deliver the events to. The service will call `notify()` in turn for each of the events to deliver them using the "normal" event handling code in the listener. If `notify()` raises an `UnknownEventException`, the service cancels the client's registration. Otherwise, a `RemoteException` while delivering is noted to the standard error output.

Note that here, if a `RemoteException` is raised, the client's event mailbox is not emptied. The service tries to ensure that events are actually delivered to the client before discarding any stored events. If a client crashes in the middle of having its events delivered, it can reconnect later and still retrieve all of its stored events.

A Mailbox Client

Let's now look at the final piece of the puzzle: A client to exercise the `EventMailbox`. This is actually the first client in this book that uses *two* services at once. In this case, it will build an event pipeline containing both the `HeartbeatGenerator` as the ultimate event generator, and the `EventMailbox` as an intermediary between the client and the generator. The `MailboxClient` class is a subclass of `HeartbeatClient`—it can reuse all the behavior in the earlier client for finding `HeartbeatGenerators`, and only extend the code to use the event mailbox as shown in Listing 14–7.

Listing 14–7 `MailboxClient.java`

```
// A subclass of HeartbeatClient that uses a mailbox
// for deferred event delivery.

package corejini.chapter14;

import net.jini.core.lookup.ServiceTemplate;
import net.jini.core.lookup.ServiceRegistrar;
import net.jini.core.event.RemoteEvent;
import net.jini.core.event.EventRegistration;
import com.sun.jini.lease.LeaseRenewalManager;
import net.jini.core.lease.Lease;
import java.io.IOException;
import java.rmi.RemoteException;
import java.util.Vector;

public class MailboxClient extends HeartbeatClient {
    ServiceTemplate mailboxTemplate;
    EventMailbox.EventMailboxRequest mailbox = null;

    public MailboxClient() throws IOException,
                    RemoteException {
        Class[] mbtypes =
            { EventMailbox.EventMailboxRequest.class };
        mailboxTemplate =
            new ServiceTemplate(null, mbtypes, null);
    }
```

Listing 14–7 `MailboxClient.java` **(continued)**

```
void doit(ServiceRegistrar reg) {
    // Bail once we've found a generator and a mailbox.
    if (gen != null && mailbox != null)
        return;

    // find a generator
    if (gen == null) {
        try {
            gen = (HeartbeatGenerator.HeartbeatRequest)
                reg.lookup(template);
        } catch (Exception ex) {
            System.err.println("Doing lookup: " +
                             ex.getMessage());
            ex.printStackTrace();
        }
    }

    // find a mailbox
    if (mailbox == null) {
        try {
           mailbox = (EventMailbox.EventMailboxRequest)
                reg.lookup(mailboxTemplate);
        } catch (Exception ex) {
            System.err.println("Doing lookup: " +
                                 ex.getMessage());
            ex.printStackTrace();
        }
    }

    if (gen == null || mailbox == null)
        return;

    System.out.println("Got both services!");

    // Remember our registrations...
    EventRegistration evtreg = null;
    EventRegistration mbreg = null;

    // sign us up for events!
    try {
        // Tell the generator to send to the mailbox.
        // We do our own leasing for all event
        // registrations.
```

Listing 14–7 MailboxClient.java (continued)

```
        evtreg =
            gen.register(HeartbeatGenerator.MINUTE,
                         null, mailbox, Lease.ANY);
        leaseManager.renewUntil(evtreg.getLease(),
                                Lease.ANY, null);

        // We need to tell the mailbox to hold on to
        // events with this <source, type>. We do this
        // by acquiring a mailbox. We again do our own
        // leasing of this mailbox.
        mbreg =
            mailbox.acquireMailbox(evtreg.getSource(),
                                   evtreg.getID(),
                                   Lease.ANY);
        leaseManager.renewUntil(mbreg.getLease(),
                                Lease.ANY, null);
    } catch (RemoteException ex) {
       System.err.println("Bogus: " + ex.getMessage());
        ex.printStackTrace();
    }

    System.out.println("Sleeping a while...");

    // now wait a while, then ask the mailbox
    // for our events.
    try {
        Thread.sleep(1000 * 60 * 5);
    } catch (InterruptedException ex) {
    }

    System.out.println("Getting events in a batch");

    try {
        Vector events =
                mailbox.getEvents(mbreg.getSource(),
                                  mbreg.getID());
         System.out.println("events:" );
         for (int i=0, size=events.size() ; i<size; i++){
             System.out.println(i + " = " +
                                events.elementAt(i));
         }

    } catch (Exception ex) {
        ex.getMessage();
        ex.printStackTrace();
    }
```

Listing 14–7 `MailboxClient.java` (continued)

```
        System.out.println("Sleeping again...");

        // now wait again, and get them delivered.
        try {
            Thread.sleep(1000 * 60 * 5);
        } catch (InterruptedException ex) {
        }

        System.out.println("Asking for delivery");

        try {
            mailbox.deliverEvents(mbreg.getSource(),
                                  mbreg.getID(),
                                  listener);
        } catch (Exception ex) {
            ex.getMessage();
            ex.printStackTrace();
        }
    }

    public static void main(String[] args) {
        try {
            MailboxClient client = new MailboxClient();
            new Thread(client).start();
        } catch (Exception ex) {
           System.err.println("Bogus: " + ex.getMessage());
            System.exit(1);
        }
    }
}
```

The core of this code is in the `doit()` method. This code is invoked every time a new lookup service is discovered; it searches lookup services until it finds both a `HeartbeatGenerator` and an `EventMailbox`. Once it has these, it goes to work.

The first thing it must do is build the event pipeline. It contacts the `HeartbeatGenerator` and solicits to receive events every minute, and has them delivered to the mailbox service (the proxy for this service implements `RemoteEventListener`, so that it can receive these events). It then has a `LeaseRenewalManager` renew the lease for this event registration indefinitely.

Next, the client calls `acquireMailbox()` on the `EventMailbox` to tell it to store events from the `HeartbeatGenerator`. The `EventRegistration` returned from the `register()` call on the `HeartbeatGenerator` contains the source and type of the events it will send to its listener; by passing these to `acquireMailbox()`, the client is telling the mailbox that matching events should be held for it.

Finally, the code tests out whether this event pipeline really works! It sleeps for five minutes—to allow some time for events to accumulate in the mailbox—and then calls `getEvents()` on the mailbox to fetch all the queued events. These are printed out, and then the client sleeps for another five minutes, and then calls `deliverEvents()` to have the events delivered to it via the "normal" `RemoteEventListener` interface defined in the superclass.

Compiling and Running the Examples

Let's now build and run a little distributed system that consists of the new `EventMailbox`, the `HeartbeatGenerator` from the last example, and the `MailboxClient`. First, let's compile the code needed for the service, and build the necessary RMI stubs. Make sure that you compiled `BasicRegistrationLandlord`, `HeartbeatClient`, and `HeartbeatGenerator` from the last examples, as we'll be needing them again. Since `EventMailbox` extends `java.rmi.server.UnicastRemoteObject`, you'll have to build stubs for it.

On Windows:

```
javac -classpath C:\jini1_0\lib\jini-core.jar;
                               C:\jini1_0\lib\jini-ext.jar;
                               C:\jini1_0\lib\sun-util.jar;
                               C:\service
              -d C:\service
              C:\files\corejini\chapter14\EventMailbox.java

rmic -classpath C:\jdk1.2\jre\lib\rt.jar;
                              C:\jini1_0\lib\jini-core.jar;
                              C:\jini1_0\lib\jini-ext.jar;
                              C:\jini1_0\lib\sun-util.jar;
                              C:\service
             -d C:\service-dl
             corejini.chapter14.EventMailbox
```

On Solaris:

```
javac -classpath     /files/jini1_0/lib/jini-core.jar:
                     /files/jini1_0/lib/jini-ext.jar:
                     /files/jini1_0/lib/sun-util.jar:
                     /files/service
                 -d /files/service
             /files/corejini/chapter14/EventMailbox.java
    rmic -classpath  /files/jdk1.2/jre/lib/rt.jar:
                     /files/jini1_0/lib/jini-core.jar:
                     /files/jini1_0/lib/jini-ext.jar:
```

```
                /files/jini1_0/lib/sun-util.jar:
                /files/service
            -d /files/service-dl
        corejini.chapter14.EventMailbox
```

After this, you need to build the files necessary for the client program. Note that the client also needs the `EventMailboxRequest` interface, which is the interface that the service's proxy implements. This interface is contained within the service's code, but is actually used by both the service and the client. So you'll have to copy it out to the client's directory.

On Windows:

```
javac -classpath C:\jini1_0\lib\jini-core.jar;
                              C:\jini1_0\lib\jini-ext.jar;
                              C:\jini1_0\lib\sun-util.jar;
                              C:\client
             -d C:\client
             C:\files\corejini\chapter14\MailboxClient.java

cd C:\service
copy EventMailbox$EventMailboxRequest.class
                         C:\client
```

On Solaris:

```
javac -classpath     /files/jini1_0/lib/jini-core.jar:
                     /files/jini1_0/lib/jini-ext.jar:
                     /files/jini1_0/lib/sun-util.jar:
                     /files/client
                -d /files/client
            /files/corejini/chapter14/MailboxClient.java

cd /files/service
cp EventMailbox$EventMailboxRequest.class
                /files/client
```

Finally you're set to run the applications! Start the `HeartbeatGenerator` service first, then the `EventMailbox` service, then the client. Be sure to give both the services pathnames to use for their stable storage, and set the hostnames in the codebases appropriately.

On Windows:

```
java -cp C:\files\jini1_0\lib\jini-core.jar;
            C:\files\jini1_0\lib\jini-ext.jar;
            C:\files\jini1_0\lib\sun-util.jar;
            C:\service
        -Djava.rmi.server.codebase=http://myhost:8085/
        -Djava.security.policy=C:\policy
    corejini.chapter14.HeartbeatGenerator C:\tmp\hb
java -cp C:\files\jini1_0\lib\jini-core.jar;
            C:\files\jini1_0\lib\jini-ext.jar;
```

```
            C:\files\jini1_0\lib\sun-util.jar;
            C:\service
        -Djava.rmi.server.codebase=http://myhost:8085/
        -Djava.security.policy=C:\policy
    corejini.chapter14.EventMailbox C:\tmp\mb

java -cp C:\files\jini1_0\lib\jini-core.jar;
            C:\files\jini1_0\lib\jini-ext.jar;
            C:\files\jini1_0\lib\sun-util.jar;
            C:\client
        -Djava.rmi.server.codebase=http://myhost:8086/
        -Djava.security.policy=C:\policy
    corejini.chapter14.MailboxClient
```

On Solaris:

```
java -cp /files/jini1_0/lib/jini-core.jar:
            /files/jini1_0/lib/jini-ext.jar:
            /files/jini1_0/lib/sun-util.jar:
            /files/service
        -Djava.rmi.server.codebase=http://myhost:8085/
        -Djava.security.policy=/files/policy
    corejini.chapter14.HeartbeatGenerator /tmp/hb

java -cp /files/jini1_0/lib/jini-core.jar:
            /files/jini1_0/lib/jini-ext.jar:
            /files/jini1_0/lib/sun-util.jar:
            /files/service
        -Djava.rmi.server.codebase=http://myhost:8085/
        -Djava.security.policy=/files/policy
    corejini.chapter14.EventMailbox /tmp/mb

java -cp /files/jini1_0/lib/jini-core.jar:
            /files/jini1_0/lib/jini-ext.jar:
            /files/jini1_0/lib/sun-util.jar:
            /files/client
        -Djava.rmi.server.codebase=http://myhost:8086/
        -Djava.security.policy=/files/policy
    corejini.chapter14.MailboxClient
```

When you start the `HeartbeatGenerator` service, you should see:
Heartbeat generator started.

After starting the `EventMailbox` you'll see it report:
Running!

Finally, start the `MailboxClient`. It will contact the mailbox server to get a mailbox assigned to it after it solicits events from the `HeartbeatGenera-`

tor. The EventMailbox will print some output when a mailbox is acquired, resulting in something like the following:

Acquired new mailbox for corejini.chapter14.HeartbeatGenerator_Stub [RemoteStub [ref: [endpoint: [13.2.116.134:44273](remote),objID:[b3b823:d6dd277b8b:-8000, 0]]]], 2

This apparent mumbo-jumbo is the string representation of the source that the EventMailbox expects to receive events from. In this case, the client has specified the HeartbeatGenerator as the source and here we see the toString() representation of the RMI stub for the HeartbeatGenerator.

As the HeartbeatGenerator delivers events to the EventMailbox, it will record when events are received. It will also display a message when the client application asks for the events to be delivered to it in a batch, or for the events to be "redelivered" to it via its RemoteEventListener interface:

Saved event in mailbox
Saved event in mailbox
Saved event in mailbox
Saved event in mailbox
Saved event in mailbox
Getting events.
Saved event in mailbox
Saved event in mailbox
Saved event in mailbox
Saved event in mailbox
Saved event in mailbox
Redelivering events.

The client will start up and indicate when it has acquired the service proxies for both the HeartbeatGenerator and the EventMailbox:

Got a generator and a mailbox!

The client will then sleep for a few minutes and get the events in a "batch" from the mailbox. As the events are returned, they are printed. The output below shows the default toString() representation of the HeartbeatEvents:

Sleeping a while...
Getting events in a batch
events:
0 = corejini.chapter14.HeartbeatGenerator$HeartbeatEvent [source=corejini.chapter14.HeartbeatGenerator_Stub[RemoteStub [ref: [endpoint:[13.2.116.134:44273](remote),objID: [b3b823:d6dd277b8b:-8000, 0]]]]]
1 = corejini.chapter14.HeartbeatGenerator$HeartbeatEvent

[source=corejini.chapter14.HeartbeatGenerator_Stub[RemoteStub [ref: [endpoint:[13.2.116.134:44273](remote),objID: [b3b823:d6dd277b8b:-8000, 0]]]]]
2 = corejini.chapter14.HeartbeatGenerator$HeartbeatEvent [source=corejini.chapter14.HeartbeatGenerator_Stub[RemoteStub [ref: [endpoint:[13.2.116.134:44273](remote),objID: [b3b823:d6dd277b8b:-8000, 0]]]]]
3 = corejini.chapter14.HeartbeatGenerator$HeartbeatEvent [source=corejini.chapter14.HeartbeatGenerator_Stub[RemoteStub [ref: [endpoint:[13.2.116.134:44273](remote),objID: [b3b823:d6dd277b8b:-8000, 0]]]]]
4 = corejini.chapter14.HeartbeatGenerator$HeartbeatEvent [source=corejini.chapter14.HeartbeatGenerator_Stub[RemoteStub [ref: [endpoint:[13.2.116.134:44273](remote),objID: [b3b823:d6dd277b8b:-8000, 0]]]]]

The client will then sleep again, and then ask for redelivery of any events stored at the mailbox. This time, when the events are received, they come in via the `notify()` method implemented in the `HeartbeatClient` example earlier in the chapter:

Sleeping again...
Asking for delivery
Came from MINUTE
Came from MINUTE
Came from MINUTE
Came from MINUTE
Came from MINUTE

This example has shown how a client can interpose a third-party event delegate between itself and an existing event generator. The important thing to realize here is that the generator, the `HeartbeatGenerator`, is completely unchanged from the first example of this chapter. The client has added new functionality to the event delivery pipeline, without having to know anything about the `HeartbeatGenerator` other than how to ask it for events, and without needing to make any modifications to the `HeartbeatGenerator`! This functionality has been added solely by the client, with no involvement or knowledge required by the event generator.

Using code like the `EventMailbox` shown here, you can have your clients augment the functionality provided by the event generators they find in a Jini community. And once you've got a "toolbox" of event-handling delegates, you can use them freely with any event generator.

Summary

This chapter has looked at Jini's philosophy for remote events, and the actual programmatic interfaces for building event generators and event consumers. The first example in this chapter showed how to construct a generator/consumer pair for simple "heartbeat" events. The generator in this case performs leasing of its event registrations.

The second example of the chapter looked at how to build an event delegate that could be interposed between an event generator and an event recipient. The fact that the generator knew nothing about the delegate means that you can extend whatever functionality is provided by other delegates in similar ways. And even though this example showed how to use delegation with `HeartbeatEvents`, you can easily use this exact same event mailbox with *any* Jini event source, including Jini lookup services.

1.1 Update

The early access information on the Jini 1.1 release proposes a service called the EventMailbox which will become a standard part of the Jini Software Kit. This service has essentially the same functionality as the service described here, but with slightly different semantics. Namely, once a client has acquired a RemoteEventListener from the EventMailbox and registered it to receive upstream events, the mailbox will designate all events received by that listener for the client, regardless of type.

The relationship between the EventMailboxService presented in this chapter and the upcoming EventMailbox code from Sun mirror the issues around the LeaseRenewalService discussed earlier. While I believe that the exploration of the issues around building the EventMailboxService are important (and warrant retaining the description of that service presented here), Jini developers should certainly rely on the Sun-provided mailbox, as it is likely to become a standard part of many Jini networks.

What's Next?

The final two chapters of this book address a slightly different topic than what we've seen before: they'll talk about common Jini services that are built atop the basic Jini infrastructure. Chapter 15 talks about JavaSpaces, a storage service for objects. JavaSpaces is a service defined and provided by Sun, and will be common enough on most Jini networks that you should know how to leverage and use it.

JAVASPACES

Topics in This Chapter

- What is JavaSpaces?
- Getting and installing JavaSpaces
- The JavaSpaces programming model
- JavaSpaces as a general model for distributed computing

Chapter 15

The chapters so far in this book have focused solely on the infrastructure that forms the underpinnings of Jini communities—the plumbing, if you will, that all collections of services have to agree upon in order to form dynamic federations at run time.

This chapter shifts focus to look at one particular service that is built atop the basic Jini substrate. This service—called JavaSpaces—provides a storage facility for Java objects. Using JavaSpaces, Jini services and clients can create and manipulate "spaces" of Java objects. They can acquire leased storage for Java objects, search for stored objects, and remove stored objects from a space.

In addition to simply providing storage for entities in a Jini community, JavaSpaces can be applied to other uses. The JavaSpaces programming model is quite simple, and yet is powerful and flexible enough that it can be used as the basis for entirely new ways to build distributed applications. Collections of applications can use a JavaSpace as a "shared blackboard" for depositing and retrieving objects. The objects that are stored in a space can represent work to be done (and thus be used to build producer/consumer-style distributed applications), or simple parcels of data (perhaps used to build distributed voting or bidding applications).

In this chapter we'll explore this service, look at its basic programming model, and see how it can be applied to a number of distributed systems programming problems.

What Is JavaSpaces?

Many applications in a distributed setting, just as in a local setting, have a need to store data persistently. The JavaSpaces service provides this capability in the form of a full-fledged Jini service which can be found via lookup and used through its proxy, just like any other Jini service.

But what does it mean to be a "storage service?" If someone tells you simply that they have a storage service, there are a number of questions you might ask them about it. For example, what kinds of things can it store? You could imagine a storage service that holds on to sequences of raw bytes for clients. Such a service would be capable of storing anything, as long as it was first serialized to a byte array. Other services might hold actual objects, like the simple "slot provider" example of Chapter 11, which doles out a fixed number of "slots" for object storage to clients.

You could also ask how you retrieve data from the service. The slot provider in Chapter 11 returned a unique "key" value to the client that could be used to retrieve data stored there. Others services might refer to data by a name provided by the client, or some other mechanism.

JavaSpaces takes a very Java-centric approach. Like the slot provider example in this book, it is not a *data* storage service, but an *object* storage service. That is, it holds complete, live Java objects. In fact, it can *only* hold Java objects. But unlike the slot provider, which never actually made any use of the "objectness" of the items it stored, JavaSpaces fully understands the Java type system, and can leverage type semantics to make it a natural fit for applications that need to store, find, and retrieve Java objects.

A Filesystem for Objects

The goal of JavaSpaces is to provide what might be thought of as a "filesystem for objects." That is, JavaSpaces can provide a ubiquitous, natural way to store and use objects, designed to work naturally with object-oriented applications written in Java. And, much like a filesystem, JavaSpaces can provide a way to *share* objects between applications. So just like an application (or a user) can drop a file into a well-known location on a filesystem for retrieval by another application (or user), JavaSpaces can act as a shared communications medium between Jini-aware clients and services.

But typical filesystems only store simple "bags of bits." In the case of systems like UNIX and Windows, these files don't even really have types associated with them. For the most part, it's up to the applications that use them, and established conventions, that associate some meaning and interpretation to these bags of bits known as files that exist in a filesystem.

JavaSpaces, on the other hand, is a very object-centered storage system. Rather than storing simple untyped data, JavaSpaces leverages Java to store whole objects, with all the benefits that come from being a Java object: strong typing, mobile code, secure execution, and so forth. So in a JavaSpace, the stored entities have actual types and may contain code in them.

Another difference lies in how stored entities are found. In a filesystem, access to previously stored data is done through naming. Every file in a filesystem has a name that's unique within that filesystem. If the name is well-known and agreed upon by all parties that will use it (such as `C:\autoexec.bat` or `/dev/tty`), then it can, by convention, have special properties and be used by any number of parties. Searching in a filesystem is typically done by searching for some portion of the name of the file or—in some cases such as text files—by searching through the actual contents of the file.

In JavaSpaces, names aren't so important. In fact, the "name" of an object is just one of the many attributes of an object that you could use to find it. You can search for objects based on their class, or their superclass, or the interfaces they implement. And you can search for objects based on their attributes, including any attribute that—by convention—is treated as a name.

Attribute-Based Search

So if objects don't necessarily have names that identify them, how do clients use a JavaSpace to store and find objects? The answer is that JavaSpaces uses exactly the same technology as the Jini lookup service for attribute-based searches. Every object stored in a JavaSpace must implement the `net.jini.core.entry.Entry` interface, which means that it can be interpreted as a strongly typed *collection* of the member objects within it. In fact, the only difference between the JavaSpace and Jini lookup service use of attribute searching, is that lookup services define how a *set* of templates can match a *set* of entries; JavaSpaces only has tools for matching single entries.

Recall from Chapter 7 that `Entry` is a no-method "tagging" interface that objects can implement to tell the system that the creator of that object is aware of the special ways such objects will be used in lookup services (members of the object are serialized independently and so forth). `Entry` objects in JavaSpaces have exactly the same semantics: They are treated as collections of the public, nonstatic, nonfinal, nontransient objects that are referred to by them.

Each `Entry` can be searched for via a "template" that is matched against its member objects; templates can be used to search based on either the types or the values of objects, and support "wildcards," exactly as shown in Chapter 7. (So now might be a good time to review the matching rules for attributes in Chapter 7, if they've slipped your mind.)

Since these same concepts are used so extensively in the Jini lookup service, you're already used to them. JavaSpaces uses exactly the same attribute-based search rules as the lookup service, although it uses a different set of APIs for storing objects, searching, and retrieving objects. These APIs are more closely aligned with the needs of a storage service.

Predecessors to JavaSpaces

Much of the work that went into building JavaSpaces is based on earlier research by David Gelernter, a computer scientist at Yale University. Gelernter designed a system called *Linda*, which is in many ways a predecessor of JavaSpaces. The central notions in Linda are *tuples*, which are collections of data grouped together, and the *tuple space*, which is a "shared blackboard" into which applications can deposit and retrieve tuples.

These notions are clear analogs of *entries* and *spaces* in the JavaSpace world. But while JavaSpaces owes much to Linda, there are some important differences between the two. First, Linda tuples do not have the strong typing that the Java language provides. That is, while the individual *elements* of a tuple are typed, the tuple as a whole is not. JavaSpaces provides strong typing for not only `Entry` objects, but also the objects referred to by those `Entries`. This strong typing is important to enable JavaSpaces to mesh nicely with applications that expect the strong typing they find in the Java platform. Furthermore, not only are JavaSpace `Entry` objects strongly typed, but they leverage and use the Java type system, meaning that clients can search based on superclass relationships. Linda allows only value matching.

Second, `Entry` objects in JavaSpaces *are* objects—that is, they not only have data associated with them, but actual methods too. Since complete objects can be stored in JavaSpaces, clients can retrieve not only lifeless data but also the code necessary to operate on this data.

Finally, JavaSpaces meshes well with the Jini conventions and paradigms. Whereas Linda systems typically envision a single, large Linda tuple space, a Jini community will typically have several JavaSpaces services active. Each can support its own, separate storage area for objects. JavaSpaces `Entry` objects are leased by the clients that store them, so the Jini self-healing mandate applies here as well.

The rise in popularity of Java has brought a renewed interest in Linda-descended systems. One of these is the *T Spaces* system from IBM Research. T Spaces is in many ways similar to JavaSpaces, although it is not as minimal. T Spaces provides the ability to modify the behavior of the tuple space through downloaded code, supports database-style indexing and queries, and allows users to set access control security policies on tuples.

Getting and Installing JavaSpaces

Way back in Chapter 1, when you downloaded and installed the basic Jini distribution, I ignored a couple of key services that weren't used in the first part of the book. It's time to go back and take care of the missing pieces now, so let's look at installing the JavaSpaces code on your system. If you've already installed the basic Jini Starter Kit as described in Chapter 1 of this book, you can just install the JavaSpaces Technology Kit "on top of" the existing Jini installation. If you haven't installed the Jini Starter Kit, you should grab it now because JavaSpaces will require the rest of the Jini infrastructure.

Here's the checklist for getting JavaSpaces installed and running on your system.

1. Download JavaSpaces from Sun
2. Unpack the distribution
3. Examine the distribution
4. Set up your environment
5. Start the necessary run-time services (transaction manager and JavaSpaces service)

Let's look at these steps in more detail.

Downloading JavaSpaces from Sun

As of the writing of this book, the JavaSpaces code is available from the Java Developer's Connection Website, just the same as the Jini Starter Kit you downloaded earlier. This site requires a free registration before you can access the code there.

The version of JavaSpaces that I've used in the development of this book is called the "JavaSpaces 1.0" version, which was current at the time this book was written. You may have to adapt the instructions given here a bit to accommodate new versions.

To download the software from the Developer's Connection, register with the site (if you haven't already), and then go to:

```
http://developer.javasoft.com/developer/products/jini/
index.html
```

This page has information on the latest versions of Jini as well as related services such as JavaSpaces, and information on how to submit bugs or requests for improvements. The "Product Offerings" link is where the actual downloadable code comes from, so click on that link now. The JavaSpaces release is called the "JavaSpaces Technology Kit," or JSTK. This software bundle contains Sun's implementation of the JavaSpaces technology, as well as documentation and some example programs.

Download the JSTK now. As of this writing, the ZIP file that contains the software is called `jstk10.zip`. Be sure to check to see if newer versions are available by the time you read this.

Unpacking the Distribution

Once you've downloaded the JavaSpaces Technology Kit ZIP file, you're set to unpack and install it. You should "overlay" the extracted contents of this ZIP file over the already installed Jini release. I'll be using the same naming conventions and directory structure that's used in the rest of this book.

For Windows: You can use your favorite ZIP extraction utility, such as WinZip. Presuming the core Jini software is installed in the `C:\jini1_0` directory, you can simply download the ZIP file to `C:\` and extract it. The contents will be placed under the `jini1_0` directory:

```
cd C:\
unzip jstk10_EA.zip
```

For Solaris: Copy the ZIP file for the JavaSpaces Technology Kit to the directory above where the `jini1_0` directory lives. When you extract the contents, they will be placed inside the `jini1_0` directory. For example, if the current Jini installation lives in `/files/jini1_0`:

```
cd /files
unzip jsdk10.zip
```

Examining the Distribution

The installation process copies some new files into the `jini1_0` directory, and also creates some new subdirectories. You should make sure that you understand what you've just unpacked and where everything lives. Table 15–1 shows the most important changes to the `jini1_0` directory that the JavaSpaces installation produces.

Table 15–1 JavaSpaces Components in the Jini 1.0 Release

`jini1_0/index.html`	The top-level documentation file is updated to reflect JavaSpaces additions.
`jini1_0/doc`	The documentation files are updated to include the Javadoc-generated documentation for JavaSpaces, as well as release notes and instructions on running the examples.
`jini1_0/lib`	New JAR and ZIP files required by JavaSpaces are copied here. The most important are `outrigger.jar` and `transient-outrigger.jar`, which contain the Sun JavaSpaces implementations, and `outrigger-dl.jar`, which is the downloadable code required to use these implementations.
`jini1_0/example`	Support files for a few JavaSpaces-specific examples are copied into this directory.

Once you've installed the JSTK, you should read the `jini1_0/index.html` file for information on release notes and documentation for JavaSpaces.

Set Up Your Environment

Just as with the other essential Jini services you've seen, you should need very little configuration of your environment to run JavaSpaces itself. Presumably, you already have the Java 2 executable directory in your PATH, and you shouldn't need any CLASSPATH set to run the JavaSpace service itself.

In all of the examples in this chapter, I'll be following the guidelines from Chapter 5. When we build and run example programs, the CLASSPATH will

be set on the command line to allow class files for clients and services to be separated. This better "simulates" a multimachine environment and can alleviate debugging headaches down the road.

So the good news is that you shouldn't have to do *anything* in particular to configure your environment differently now that we've introduced JavaSpaces into it.

The bad news is that most of the tricky work comes from configuring the *run-time* environment in which JavaSpaces will run. Let's look at that next.

Start the Run-time Services

JavaSpaces provides a new service for the Jini environment, but it also relies on the existing Jini infrastructure to function correctly. As a "normal" Jini service, JavaSpaces requires the "normal" infrastructure, such as lookup services and HTTP servers to support its downloadable code. But JavaSpaces also requires one service that ships with Jini which you haven't seen yet: the Jini *transaction manager*. Sun's implementation of this service is called *mahalo*.

Just as in Chapter 1, these necessary services can be started via the GUI provided by Sun, or "by hand." I'll walk through the GUI installation first, because it's the easiest and will give you a feel for the steps that are required to start up JavaSpaces. But you should definitely pay attention to the command-line instructions for starting JavaSpaces: having an understanding of the service at this level will be important if you need to move a JavaSpaces installation to a different machine or need to start JavaSpaces at boot time.

Starting Required Services via the GUI

As you saw in Chapter 1, Jini ships with an easy-to-use graphical interface for starting the services that Jini uses. This interface can only start services on the local machine, so if you have a need to run services on a set of machines, you'll either have to run the GUI on each or, perhaps better, just use the command-line instructions. Be sure to recall the Core Alert in Chapter 1 about the bug in the GUI program that prevents lookup services from starting correctly on PCs. While there is a good chance this problem will be fixed by the time you read this, you should be on the lookout for it, just in case.

It's easy to launch and use the GUI application.

On Windows:

```
java -cp C:\jini1_0\lib\jini-examples.jar
    com.sun.jini.example.service.StartService
```

On Solaris:

```
java -cp /files/jini1_0/lib/jini-examples.jar
    com.sun.jini.example.service.StartService
```

Once the program starts up, you'll see the same GUI containing tabbed panes for starting the various services that you saw in Chapter 1. In the following instructions, I'll assume that you've already started a Jini lookup service, as well as an RMI activation daemon on each of the machines on which you will be running the JavaSpaces service or the transaction manager service. For most settings, this can be the same machine that is hosting a lookup service, and so will already be running an activation daemon. (You do not need a separate activation daemon for each activatable service you run on a given machine; one activation daemon can support all services on one machine.)

You do, however, need to make sure that the HTTP services on your network are correctly configured. Just as with any Jini service, JavaSpaces and the transaction manager need to be able to export downloadable code to clients. The downloadable code for these services is installed into the `lib` directory under `jini1_0`. There are two separate JAR files that contain the downloadable code for these services, called `outrigger-dl.jar` and `mahalo-dl.jar`.

If there is already an HTTP server running with its root directory set to the Jini `lib` directory, then you can simply "reuse" this HTTP server to serve up the downloadable code for these two new services. Because the Jini installation places all downloadable code for the "core" services, as well as JavaSpaces, together in one directory, it's easy to use one HTTP server to export the downloadable code for the lookup service, JavaSpaces, and the transaction manager.

If you have not installed the JavaSpaces kit on top of the Jini installation, or do not have an HTTP server running to serve the downloadable JAR files, you will need to start one. See the instructions in Chapter 1 for how to do this.

The common case, though, is the easy one—all the files are installed together and there is one machine that is used for running the Sun-provided Jini services, and already has an HTTP server and an activation daemon running on it. In this case, all you have to do is start the transaction manager and then start the JavaSpaces service.

Click on the *TxnManager* tabbed pane on the GUI to bring up the panel shown in Figure 15–1.

Configuring the transaction manager is easy. All you have to do is provide an absolute path for it to use for its log file. This is the file that the service will use for persistent storage. On Windows, something like `C:\temp\txn_log` is fine; on Solaris, `/tmp/txn_log` works great for development work.

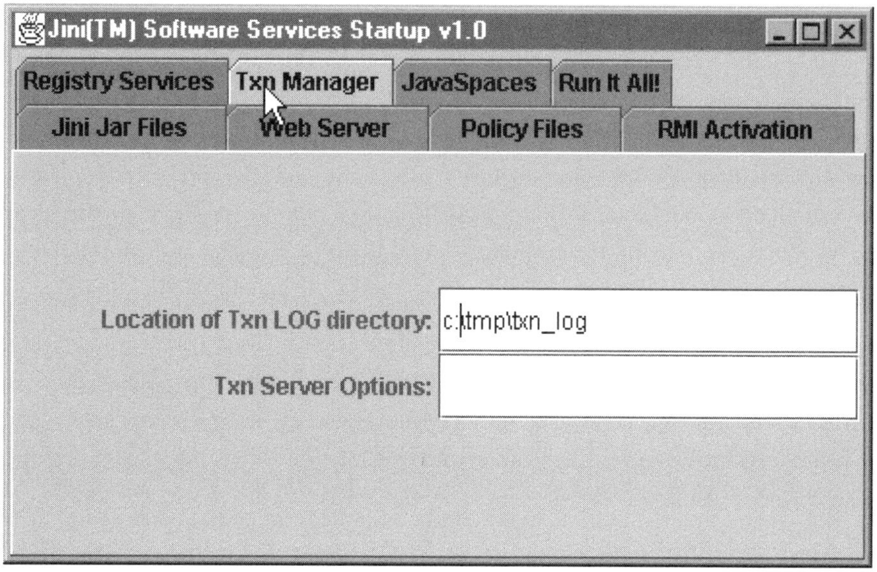

Figure 15–1 Starting the Transaction Manager

The *JavaSpaces* panel (shown in Figure 15–2) provides a way to set the name of the space service you are creating. The default value ("JavaSpaces") is ideal. You can choose whether you wish to start a "transient" or a "persistent" space. I'll talk about what these terms mean a bit later in this chapter. But for now, just leave the menu set for a transient space. The *Location of Persistent Dir* field only needs to be set if you are using a persistent space, so you can ignore it for now.

Once you've got these two services configured, the only thing left is to actually start them up. Go to the *Run it All* panel (Figure 15–3). Assuming that the rest of the needed services are running in appropriate places, all you have to do is start the transaction manager service and then start the JavaSpaces service by clicking on the buttons. You can also use this panel to shut down a service, if you need to.

Starting the Required Services via the Command Line

In this section we'll look at the nitty-gritty details of how to get the services required by JavaSpaces started manually. Understanding how this works will give you some insight into how these services work, and will let you do things like write scripts that can automatically start a service when a machine boots.

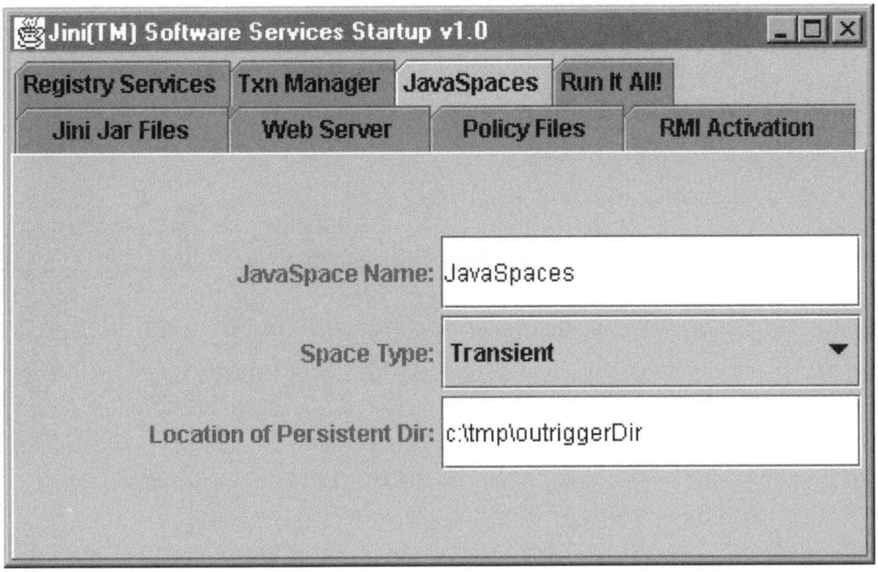

Figure 15–2 Starting a JavaSpaces service

As mentioned in the last section, the services required to use JavaSpaces are—first and foremost—normal Jini services that require lookup services, HTTP servers, and activation daemons. So you need to make sure

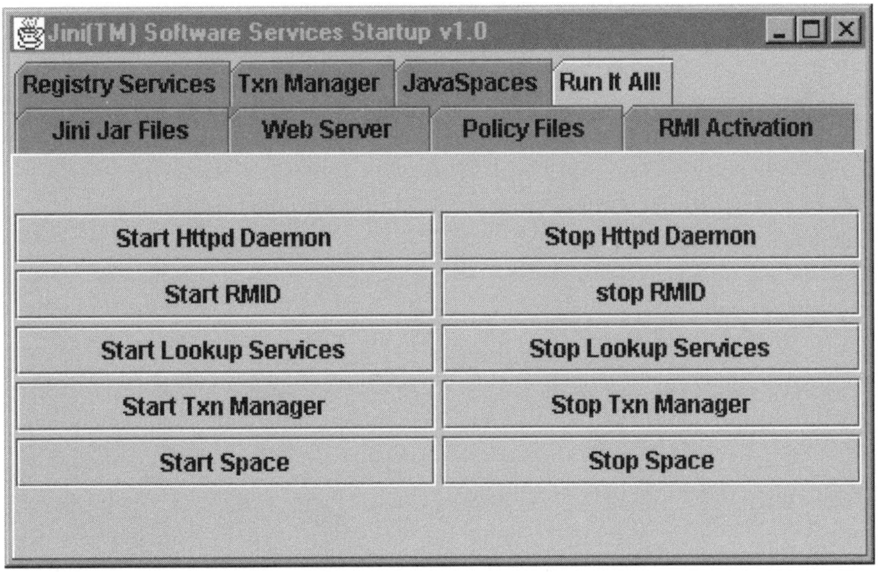

Figure 15–3 Running the Services

that you are running a properly configured lookup service somewhere on your network.

To do JavaSpaces development or use JavaSpaces-aware clients, you must run both the JavaSpaces service as well as the Jini transaction manager service. The latter comes with the standard Jini Starter Kit distribution. Both of these services make use of the RMI activation framework, so each should be run on a machine with an instance of `rmid` running on it. If you're running these services on the same machine or even (as is likely) on the same machine as a Jini lookup service, you can "share" one instance of `rmid` among all of these services.

Also like any other Jini service, JavaSpaces and the transaction manager need to be able to export downloadable code to their clients. The downloadable code for both services lives in the Jini `lib` directory; `outrigger-dl.jar` contains the downloadable code for JavaSpaces, and `mahalo-dl.jar` contains the downloadable code for the transaction manager.

If you're already running a Jini lookup service on your network, then out of necessity you're already running an HTTP server that exports the lookup service's downloadable code. Since the downloadable code for JavaSpaces and the transaction manager live in the same directory (by default) as the downloadable code for the lookup service, you can use this same HTTP server to export *all* the code for these three services. Just make sure that there is an HTTP server running somewhere on your network with its root directory set to point to the location of these JAR files. You'll need to remember the machine name and port number of this HTTP service for use in codebase properties, so that JavaSpaces and the transaction manager can tell their clients where to access downloadable code from.

Let's now start the transaction manager. The startup arguments for the transaction manager look much like the other Jini services we saw in Chapter 1. The basic form of the transaction manager command line is:

```
java -Djava.security.policy=<policy-file>
        -jar <txn-mgr-jar-file>
        -Dcom.sun.jini.mahalo.managerName=<name>
        <txn-mgr-codebase>
        <security-policy-file>
        <log-directory>
        [<lookup-service-group>]
```

This format is similar to the other Jini services. The security policy file controls the security permissions for the JVM that runs the transaction manager and registers it with the RMI activation daemon. The `-jar` option says that the classes to run reside entirely within a JAR file. You can specify a "name" for the transaction manager service (usually "TransactionManager" is just fine), as well as a codebase to provide to clients. This codebase should be set to the hostname and port number of the HTTP server that's exporting the `mahalo-dl.jar` file.

The second security policy file here is used to set the security permissions on any JVMs that are started by the activation daemon to run reactivated code; review Chapter 1 for details on how this works. The log directory is an absolute path to a directory in which the transaction manager will write its persistent state. You should make sure that this directory doesn't exist when you run the transaction manager; it will be created automatically when it is used.

Finally, you can optionally specify the name of a Jini community to join. Passing "public" is a special flag that indicates that the transaction manager should become part of the unnamed public group.

Let's look at the specific command lines for starting the transaction manager on different platforms.

On Windows:

```
java -Djava.security.policy=
          C:\jini1_0\example\txn\policy.all
      -jar C:\jini1_0\lib\mahalo.jar
      -Dcom.sun.jini.mahalo.managerName=
          TransactionManager
      http://myhost:8080/mahalo-dl.jar
      C:\jini1_0\example\txn\policy.all
      C:\temp\txn_log
      public
```

On Solaris:

```
java -Djava.security.policy=
          /files/jini1_0/example/txn/policy.all
      -jar /files/jini1_0/lib/mahalo.jar
      -Dcom.sun.jini.mahalo.managerName=
          TransactionManager
      http://myhost:8080/mahalo-dl.jar
      /files/jini1_0/example/txn/policy.all
      /tmp/txn_log
      public
```

Listings 15–1 and 15–2 provide some simple scripts to automate the startup process for Windows and Solaris (the Solaris script should also work well on other UNIX variants). These scripts are available in the downloadable code package from the Prentice-Hall FTP server as described in the introduction. Be sure you edit the scripts to set the location of your Jini installation, your hostname, and so on.

Listing 15–1 `txnmgr.bat` Script for Windows

```
REM Set this to wherever Jini is installed
set JINI_HOME=C:\jini1_0
REM Set this to the host where the webserver runs
set HOSTNAME=hostname

REM Everything below should work with few
REM changes
set POLICYFILE=%JINI_HOME%\example\txn\policy.all
set JARFILE=%JINI_HOME%\lib\mahalo.jar
set CODEBASE=http://%HOSTNAME%:8080/mahalo-dl.jar
set TXN_POLICYFILE=%POLICYFILE%
set LOG_DIR=C:\temp\txn_log
set GROUP=public

java -Djava.security.policy=%POLICYFILE%
     -jar %JARFILE%
     -Dcom.sun.jini.mahalo.managerName=
         TransactionManager
%CODEBASE% %TXN_POLICYFILE%
%LOG_DIR% %GROUP%
```

Next, let's start up the JavaSpaces service. For the examples in this book, we'll start a "transient" JavaSpace. I'll talk about what this means a bit later in the chapter. The prototypical command line for starting a transient JavaSpace looks like this:

```
java -Djava.security.policy=<policy-file>
      -Djava.rmi.server.codebase=<codebase>
      -jar <jar-file>
      -Dcom.sun.jini.outrigger.spaceName=<name>
      [<group>]
```

Once again, the policy file controls the permissions granted to the JVM. The codebase is set so that clients of the JavaSpaces service will know where to download code needed to use the service. Like the transaction manager, you can specify a name for the service (usually "JavaSpaces" is fine), and can provide the name of a Jini community to join. Passing "public" here indicates that the service should join the unnamed public group.

Here are the command lines for starting a transient JavaSpace for Windows and Solaris.

Listing 15–2 `txnmgr.sh` Script for Solaris

```
#!/bin/sh

# Set this to wherever Jini is installed
JINI_HOME=/files/jini1_0

# Set this to wherever the webserver is running
HOSTNAME=hostname

# everything below should work with few changes
POLICYFILE=$JINI_HOME/example/txn/policy.all
JARFILE=$JINI_HOME/lib/mahalo.jar
CODEBASE=http://$HOSTNAME:8080/mahalo-dl.jar
TXN_POLICYFILE=$POLICYFILE
LOG_DIR=/tmp/txn_log
GROUP=public

java -Djava.security.policy=$POLICYFILE \
-jar $JARFILE\
-Dcom.sun.jini.mahalo.managerName=\
    TransactionManager \
$CODEBASE $TXN_POLICYFILE \
$LOG_DIR $GROUP
```

On Windows:

```
java -Djava.security.policy=
        C:\jini1_0\example\books\policy.all
     -Djava.rmi.server.codebase=
        http://myhost:8080/outrigger-dl.jar
     -jar C:\jini1_0\lib\transient-outrigger.jar
     -Dcom.sun.jini.outrigger.spaceName=JavaSpaces
     public
```

On Solaris:

```
java -Djava.security.policy=
        /files/jini1_0/example/books/policy.all
     -Djava.rmi.server.codebase=
        http://myhost:8080/outrigger-dl.jar
     -jar
        /files/jini1_0/lib/transient-outrigger.jar
     -Dcom.sun.jini.outrigger.spaceName=JavaSpaces
     public
```

Here are two scripts, Listings 15–3 and 15–4, for starting the JavaSpaces service on Windows and Solaris.

Listing 15–3 `javaspaces.bat` Script for Windows

```
REM Set this to wherever Jini is installed
set JINI_HOME=C:\jini1_0
REM Set this to the host where the webserver runs
set HOSTNAME=hostname

REM Everything below should work with few
REM changes
set POLICYFILE=%JINI_HOME%\example\books\policy.all
set JARFILE=%JINI_HOME%\lib\transient-outrigger.jar
set CODEBASE=http://%HOSTNAME%:8080/outrigger-dl.jar
set GROUP=public

java -Djava.security.policy=%POLICYFILE%
    -Djava.rmi.server.codebase=%CODEBASE%
    -jar %JARFILE%
    -Dcom.sun.jini.outrigger.spaceName=JavaSpaces
    %GROUP%
```

Listing 15–4 `javaspaces.sh` Script for Solaris

```
#!/bin/sh

# Set this to wherever Jini is installed
JINI_HOME=/files/jini1_0

# Set this to wherever the webserver is running
HOSTNAME=hostname

# everything below should work with few changes
POLICYFILE=$JINI_HOME/example/books/policy.all
JARFILE=$JINI_HOME/lib/transient-outrigger.jar
CODEBASE=http://$HOSTNAME:8080/outrigger-dl.jar
GROUP=public

java -Djava.security.policy=$POLICYFILE \
    -Djava.rmi.server.codebase=$CODEBASE \
    -jar $JARFILE\
    -Dcom.sun.jini.outrigger.spaceName=JavaSpaces \
    $GROUP
```

Now that you've got the transaction manager and JavaSpaces services up, we can start to look more closely at how to build on top of these services!

Transient and Persistent JavaSpaces

I've talked a few times already about the fact that the Sun release of JavaSpaces ships with two different implementations of the service: a *transient* implementation and a *persistent* implementation. In the installation instructions I've focused solely on the transient JavaSpaces implementation.

The difference between the two is that a transient JavaSpaces service only holds on to the data it stores as long as it is running. Any stored objects will be lost if the service crashes or is otherwise brought down. Persistent JavaSpaces, on the other hand, log their stored objects to the disk, so they can recover their state after they are restarted. These are two different *implementations* of JavaSpaces, but they share exactly the same *interfaces*.

In this book, I've recommended going with the transient space for development and testing. The transient space is a bit faster than the persistent space, and—the primary reason for its use here—is easier to set up. In a production environment, though, ensuring that there is no data loss is typically of primary importance, and so the persistent space would be more appropriate.

In case you run into the terminology in your own explorations, the class that implements the transient JavaSpaces service is called `com.sun.jini.outrigger.TransientSpace`. The class that implements the persistent service is called `com.sun.jini.outrigger.FrontEndSpace` (there used to be a persistent space implementation called `PersistentSpace`, but it's no longer available from Sun). The transient implementation lives in the JAR file `transient-outrigger.jar`, which you used earlier when starting the service, while the persistent implementation is in `outrigger.jar`.

Read the documentation that comes with the JavaSpaces Technology Kit for more details on the persistent space.

The JavaSpaces Programming Model

JavaSpaces espouses the philosophy that less is more. The programming model for using JavaSpaces is very minimal—there are only four types of operations that you can do on a JavaSpace.

- You can write a new object into a JavaSpace.
- You can read an object that's in a JavaSpace.
- You can take an object out of a JavaSpace (this is like a read that removes the just-read item).
- You can ask that the JavaSpace notify you when objects that match a certain template are written into the space.

That's it! You cannot get much simpler than that. These four conceptual operations are actually used via a slightly larger set of methods in the `net.jini.space.JavaSpace` interface; these methods provide overloaded versions of some of the operations, and some ways to speed processing in a space.

All these operations support the common Jini notions of leasing. Stored objects are actually leased. A client must renew the leases for a stored object or the JavaSpace will remove the object. Similarly, the JavaSpaces service leases event registrations, just like a lookup service.

All these operations take `Entry` parameters that specify either the object to be stored (in the case of the write operation), or the template to be matched (in the case of the read, take, and notify operations).

Transactions, in Brief

In addition to lease duration and `Entry` parameters, the write, read, take, and notify operations also allow you to optionally pass a `Transaction` object to them. Transactions are a topic we'll reserve for the last chapter of the book—mainly because they're not used very often, especially in beginning Jini programming—but I'll say just a bit about them here.

Transactions, as you may remember from Chapter 3, are a way to group a related set of operations together. So if you're building a banking application and you need to do a transfer between two accounts, you would typically implement this as two separate operations grouped together by a transaction. The first operation decrements an account by a desired amount, and the second increments a different account by the same amount. By "grouping these into a transaction," you're telling the system that it should ensure that both of the operations complete successfully, or that neither of them complete at all.

Transactions provide a way to guard against partial failures. In the banking example, the *last* thing you want is for only one of the two operations to succeed. If this happens, you've either just robbed one client of money, or given another client free money, depending on which operation succeeds. The system is in an inconsistent state because of a partial failure. With transactions, either the whole thing works or it doesn't. If it works, you're happy, and if it doesn't, at least the system is in a known state and you can try to do the transfer later.

One of the reasons that I've saved transactions until the last chapter is that, of all the current Sun-provided Jini services, JavaSpaces is the only one that uses or supports transactions. And even in the case of JavaSpaces, transactions are optional! Even though all the operations listed above will take a transaction parameter to indicate that they should be run in the context of a transaction, you can simply pass null here. Operations that do not run in the context of a transaction are logically "independent" of one another.

So for the rest of this chapter, I'll mention transactions where appropriate, but won't get into any of the "meat" of transactions until Chapter 16.

JavaSpaces APIs

Let's look at the interface for using JavaSpace services. This interface, `net.jini.space.JavaSpace`, is implemented by the service proxies for JavaSpace services. Like all Jini proxies, you don't know (and generally don't care) how the service proxy *implements* this interface. A particular proxy may communicate using RMI or CORBA or raw sockets with a back-end JavaSpace service. And that service may be implemented using simple in-memory hashtables or with a full-blown database. The one thing that all have in common, though, is that their proxies will implement this one simple interface that allows clients and other Jini services to use them in the same way.

```
package net.jini.space;

public interface JavaSpace {
    public final long NO_WAIT = 0;// don't wait

    Lease write(Entry e, Transaction txn,
             long lease)
          throws RemoteException,
                TransactionException;
    Entry read(Entry tmpl, Transaction txn,
             long timeout)
          throws RemoteException,
                TransactionException,
                UnusableEntryException,
                InterruptedException;
    Entry readIfExists(Entry tmpl, Transaction txn,
                   long timeout)
          throws RemoteException,
```

```
                        TransactionException,
                        UnusableEntryException,
                        InterruptedException;
        Entry take(Entry tmpl, Transaction txn,
                   long timeout)
              throws RemoteException,
                     TransactionException,
                     UnusableEntryException,
                     InterruptedException;
        Entry takeIfExists(Entry tmpl, Transaction txn,
                           long timeout)
              throws RemoteException,
                     TransactionException,
                     UnusableEntryException,
                     InterruptedException;
        EventRegistration notify(Entry tmpl,
                                 Transaction txn,
                                 RemoteEventListener l,
                                 long lease,
                                 MarshalledObject obj)
              throws RemoteException,
                     TransactionException;
        Entry snapshot(Entry e) throws RemoteException;
    }
```

Let's look at the individual methods here in more detail.

Write()

The `write()` method is used to deposit a new `Entry` into a JavaSpace. The arguments are the `Entry` object to be written, the `Transaction` that the write operation should be a part of, and an initial requested lease duration expressed in milliseconds. The `Entry` that is passed to the method is unchanged; it is serialized and a copy of it is stored in the JavaSpace. The method returns a `Lease` object, which can be renewed "manually" by the client, or can be handed off to a `LeaseRenewalManager` or other code for renewal.

If you pass in a `Transaction` to this method, or to any of the other methods in this class, then the operation will not happen until you tell the `Transaction` to "go."[1] This causes the `Transaction` to attempt to perform all of the operations, which will either succeed if all the operations succeed,

1. More accurately, the operation *will* happen, but all of the effects of it will be invisible "outside" the transaction. Again, see Chapter 16 for details.

or fail if one or more of them fails. If any constituent operation fails then all operations are "undone" and it appears as if the transaction never happened.

If you don't want to worry about this sort of thing just yet, you're in luck, because you can always pass null as the transaction parameter and calling `write()` will simply cause an object to be written, independent of any other operations.

If you call `write()` and the call returns without raising an exception, you can be assured that the object has been written into the JavaSpace. If a `RemoteException` is raised, then you cannot tell if the write was successful or not.

Read() and ReadIfExists()

The `read()` and `readIfExists()` methods use the provided template to search the JavaSpace. The template is compared against the `Entry` objects stored in the space according to the attribute matching rules in Chapter 7. If a match exists, an `Entry` will be returned, otherwise null will be returned.

Note that the JavaSpaces API provides no way to return multiple values from a search. You should specify your template so that any object that matches the template will satisfy the use to which you intend to put it. If there are multiple matching objects in the space, there is no guarantee that the same will be returned each time. (Even if there is only one object that matches, a particular JavaSpaces implementation may return *equivalent* yet *distinct* objects each time; that is, JavaSpaces may return two objects that have identical values as reported by `equals()`, but may be separate objects as reported by the `==` operator. So you should be sure that you are aware of this possibility if you plan on comparing objects retrieved from multiple calls to a space.)

Passing in a null template means that *any* `Entry` in the space may be returned.

The difference between these two methods is in how they use their timeout parameters. The `read()` call will return a matching `Entry` if it exists, or wait for the timeout period until a matching `Entry` appears; the `readIfExists()` call will try to return a matching `Entry` immediately if it exists, or null otherwise. It does not wait for a matching `Entry` to appear.

But if `readIfExists()` doesn't wait to see if a matching `Entry` appears, why does it have a timeout parameter? The answer has to do with the way transactions work. When `readIfExists()` is called, the matching `Entry` may be currently involved in a transaction—more accurately, it may be currently affected by some operation that is running as part of a transaction.

For example, the `write()` which placed the matching `Entry` in the JavaSpace in the first place may be one operation in a transaction that has not

fully committed yet. Until the transaction commits, the `write()` hasn't "really" happened yet, and the `readIfExists()` call cannot safely return it (if the transaction were to abort, the `Entry` would be removed from the JavaSpace, since an unsuccessful transaction returns the system to the state that it would be in if the transaction had never happened).

This is where the timeout parameter comes in. The `readIfExists()` call may block for the duration specified by the timeout parameter if the only possible match is involved in a transaction. If the transaction "quiesces" before the timeout period, then the `Entry` will be returned. If the timeout elapses and there is no matching `Entry` available that is not involved in a transaction, then null will be returned.

The `read()` call also considers transactions. It will block waiting until a matching `Entry` appears, or until a matching `Entry` that is involved in a transaction stabilizes. If the timeout elapses before either of these occur, then null will be returned.

The `JavaSpaces` interface defines a constant, `NO_WAIT`, which can be used as a timeout value to mean that these calls should return immediately.

Take() and TakeIfExists()

The `take()` and `takeIfExists()` calls work just like `read()` and `readIfExists()`—they match a template, possibly block until some timeout elapses, and then return a matching `Entry` or null. The difference is that the `read()` methods leave the matched `Entry` in the JavaSpace; the `take()` methods remove it from the space.

Both the `read()` and the `take()` methods can raise two kinds of exceptions. If a `RemoteException` is raised, then there was some network communication problem, and—in the case of `take()`—the removal of the matching `Entry` may or may not have taken place. If this is unacceptable, you can execute the `take()` operation in a transaction and only commit the transaction once you've already got the return value from the `take()`. This lets you separate the acquisition of the return value of the `take()` from the process of making the removal of the item "visible" to other operations.

With both the `read()` and the `take()` methods, an `UnusableEntryException` occurs when the `Entry` that would have been returned cannot be deserialized—typically this is because of version errors or because the class of the `Entry` is not known to the client. When such a case happens during a `take()`, the `Entry` is still removed even though no value will be returned to the client.

Notify()

The `notify()` method works much the same way as the method of the same name on Jini lookup services. The method takes an `Entry` as a template that will be matched against future writes to the JavaSpace. If a new `Entry` is written that matches the template, an event will be sent to the listener specified in the `notify()` call.

In addition to the template, the method takes an optional transaction parameter, the `RemoteEventListener` to send events to, a requested lease duration in milliseconds, and a `MarshalledObject` that contains a serialized object that will be returned in any events generated as a result of this registration. The call returns an `EventRegistration` object containing all the usual details—the source and type of the events that will come as a result of the registration, the `Lease` for the registration, and the last sequence number sent for the event type.

Sun's specification for JavaSpaces dictates that the service use *full ordering* for sequence numbers of events from the service. So if you see an event with sequence number 5 and then see an event with sequence number 10, you know that there have been 5 intervening matches of written `Entry` objects that resulted in events not seen by you, possibly because of network problems or out-of-order delivery.

The JavaSpaces service does not guarantee that events will be delivered to registered clients; instead it makes a "best effort" attempt. If it catches a `RemoteException` while trying to send an event to the client (through the invocation of the `notify()` method of the listener), it will periodically try to resend events until the client's lease expires.

Core Note: Documenting service behavior is important!

The sort of details just listed—how the JavaSpaces service generates sequence numbers, what its event delivery policies are—are important to most writers of clients! Since clients care about such details, there's a lesson here for service writers: While advertising such information at run time via attributes is important, good solid documentation that's available when developers sit down to understand your service is crucial. If you write a new service, documenting such little details can go a long way toward making your service truly useful and useable by other developers.

Snapshot()

The methods just presented represent the core operations in JavaSpaces—they're all you need to know to effectively use JavaSpaces services. But with a little help, you can make your interactions with JavaSpaces much more efficient. This is where the `snapshot()` method comes in.

The process of serializing an object in Java can be very time consuming, especially if the object is large or has a complicated series of references within it (hashtables of vectors, for instance). And yet every time you pass an `Entry` (or any other parameter for that matter) to one of the methods in the `JavaSpace` interface, the parameters must be serialized for transmission to the service. Some clients will have very regular access patterns: They will write the same object many times, or they may use an `Entry` as a template to search over and over again for matching objects.

In such cases, it may be a big win to avoid the cost of having to serialize the same object over and over again. The `read()`, `write()`, etc., methods cannot really do this for you—for them to check to see if an object you pass in is the same as an object you passed in earlier, they would have to go ahead and serialize the passed object anyway to see if it's identical to the first. So there's no win to be gained by having `read()` and friends do this check for you. It's something that you, as the caller of these methods, have to plan on.

This is where `snapshot()` comes in. When you call `snapshot()`, you pass in an `Entry` and get an `Entry` out. The returned `Entry` can be used in any future calls to the same JavaSpace that you called `snapshot()` on, and will avoid the repeated serialization process. Essentially, the `Entry` that you get back from `snapshot()` is a "token" that identifies the original object and can be sent without repeated serializations of the original object. By using the `snapshot()`'ed `Entry` in lieu of the original, you can save a lot of cycles that would have otherwise been spent on serializing the same object over and over again.

There are a few restrictions on how you can use the `Entry` that's returned from `snapshot()`. First, the object is essentially "opaque" to you. It's not the original object you passed in, it's a specialized representation of it that's particular to the JavaSpaces implementation you're talking to. You should be sure not to make any changes to it, or treat it like the original for anything except sending to a JavaSpace.

Since the returned object is a specialized representation of the original `Entry`, it is only valid as a parameter to methods on the JavaSpace that gener-

ated it. So you cannot produce a snapshot of an `Entry` on one JavaSpace service and expect it to work on another.

Likewise, you cannot transfer the snapshot version of an `Entry` to another JVM (say, via an RMI call) and expect it to work. Particular implementations of the JavaSpaces service proxy may be "smart," using a caching scheme to map snapshots of `Entry` objects to whatever they send over the wire to the back-end service. To permit implementations like this, JavaSpaces makes no guarantees that a snapshot of an `Entry` can be used from a VM other than the one in which it was generated.

You cannot compare a snapshot to `Entry` objects that are *returned* from a JavaSpaces server. That is, all of the methods that return `Entry` objects return "nonsnapshot" objects, or "real entries" in other words. Snapshots are only used as input parameters, not return values.

Finally, even though you can call `snapshot()` on a null `Entry`, the JavaSpaces specification makes no guarantees about what value is returned. The particular JavaSpaces implementation you're talking to may return null as the value of the snapshot `Entry`, so you should be aware of this.

Creating snapshots of the `Entry` objects you pass to JavaSpaces can be a big win if you're writing the same data over and over again, or searching using the same templates over and over again.

An Example: Persistent Event Logging with JavaSpaces

In this example we'll put our newly found knowledge of JavaSpaces to work in a pair of programs: The first contacts the lookup services for a Jini community, receives all the events that describe the changes in membership in the community, produces `Entry` objects that represent these changes, and logs them to a JavaSpaces service. The second program can connect up to a JavaSpaces service and copy out the logged history of a Jini community.

This is a rather simple application of JavaSpaces, but it shows the basics of reading and writing data, and shows an example of how to design your classes for easy searchability.

Design for Searchability

What do I mean by "design for searchability?" Recall that `Entry` objects have certain very particular semantics that apply to searching. Every `Entry` that you store in a service is searchable by its type, or by the types or values of the public, nonstatic, nontransient, nonfinal object members within it. This means that if you want to search by a member of an `Entry` that you create, you need to make sure that it meets the criteria for searchability (public, nonstatic, and so on). You also need to make sure that it's an object, rather than a primitive data type, because only objects can be used in a search.

Finally, in addition to the basic rules about the types of objects that can be searched, there's also an element of design here. Namely, because only exact matches count when you're searching by the value of an object, you may need to "pull out" certain aspects of your `Entry` types as members so that they can be searched. For example, if your `Entry` has a hashtable as a member, chances are that it will be hard for a client to produce a hashtable which will be an exact match for the stored one. This means that searching by value for hashtables is quite difficult. If, on the other hand, you can extract certain key elements from the hashtable, and represent them as separate members in the `Entry`, they become more easily searchable.

The lesson here is that even though an `Entry` may contain a bunch of useful data, you may want to represent it differently to make it more easily searchable.

Let's look at the `Entry` classes that will be used for the community logging example. The logging program will record not only information about discovery—what new lookup services have appeared or seem to have gone away—but also information about what services are available. These types of occurrences are different, but share some common information that we would like to record—namely, the group name that the change happened in, and the time of the change.

The approach I've taken here is to define a superclass, called `WatcherEntry`, that's used by all `Entry` classes used by the community watching-and-logging program. Two specific subclasses of it, `DiscoveryEventEntry` and `ServiceEventEntry`, record information specific to discovery and service membership changes.

Let's look at `WatcherEntry` first, as shown in Listing 15–5.

Listing 15–5 `WatcherEntry.java`

```
// This is a superclass for the Entry types that
// we'll use. This stores the time that the
// event arrived, and the group name that was
// being watched.

package corejini.chapter15;

import net.jini.core.entry.Entry;

public class WatcherEntry implements Entry {
    public Long timestamp = null;
    public String group = null;

    public WatcherEntry() {
    }

    public WatcherEntry(String group, long time) {
        this.group = group;
        timestamp = new Long(time);
    }
}
```

This class is the superclass of the other two `Entry` classes we'll define. It implements the `Entry` interface, and has two members which, you will note, satisfy the requirements for searchability. These two members store the group in which the `Entry` records a change, and the timestamp of the change. The timestamp here could be represented as the fundamental type `long`, but I've used the object representation `Long` so that it will be searchable. Since `WatcherEntry` is an `Entry`, and the `Entry` class is `Serializable`, then `WatcherEntry` must have a no-argument constructor to be properly deserialized.

Let's look at the two subclasses that record specific events now, starting with `DiscoveryEventEntry` (see Listing 15–6).

This class extends `WatcherEntry`, so it is still an `Entry` that can be used with JavaSpaces. A new `DiscoveryEventEntry` will be written to the space whenever a new lookup service is discovered, or when the watcher program discards a lookup service because it seems to be down or otherwise misbehaving. Even though a `DiscoveryEvent` may contain information about a

Listing 15–6 `DiscoveryEventEntry.java`

```
// An Entry class that represents a DiscoveryEvent

package corejini.chapter15;

import net.jini.core.lookup.ServiceRegistrar;
import net.jini.core.discovery.LookupLocator;
import java.rmi.RemoteException;

public class DiscoveryEventEntry extends WatcherEntry {
    public ServiceRegistrar reg;
    public LookupLocator locator = null;
    public Boolean discovered = null;

    public DiscoveryEventEntry() {
    }

    public DiscoveryEventEntry(String group,
                               ServiceRegistrar reg,
                               boolean discovered) {
        super(group, System.currentTimeMillis());

        this.reg = reg;
        try {
            this.locator = reg.getLocator();
        } catch (RemoteException ex) {
        }
        this.discovered = new Boolean(discovered);
    }
}
```

whole set of lookup services, a separate `DiscoveryEventEntry` will be written for each lookup service in the set.

The class maintains three pieces of data—the service registrar that was discovered or discarded, the registrar's lookup locator (recall that this is a URL-like class that represents a lookup service), and a flag indicating whether this `DiscoveryEventEntry` is due to a discovery or a discard.

Here you can see the same patterns as before—all of the data is in the form of public objects. And here I've "broken out" some data that's not strictly necessary, but makes searching easier. A lookup service's `LookupLocator` can be easily retrieved from its `ServiceRegistrar`. So any client that retrieves a `DiscoveryEventEntry` could already determine its URL given the `Service-`

Registrar stored here. But ServiceRegistrars are not easily searchable—to search based on a ServiceRegistrar, a client would have to go through discovery itself to fetch a proxy for a lookup service, and then use this in a template to search the space (and, it should be noted, there is no requirement that the proxies returned by a lookup service be exactly the same each time. A proxy may cache state, so even if a client does fetch a proxy and try to search by it, there is no guarantee that it'll match a proxy from an earlier discovery).

But LookupLocators are easy to construct. If a client wishes to see the entire discovery and discard history of one particular Jini lookup service, it only needs the host and port of the lookup service to construct a Lookup-Locator that it can use for searching. This is an example of "designing for searchability"—even though keeping redundant information in the Entry (a locator that could be derived from the other data) may seem wasteful, it's actually a big help in searching. And there are clearly other useful bits of information you could keep in these entries, such as the service ID of the lookup service that's been discovered or discarded.

Let's look now at the ServiceEventEntry class (Listing 15–7).

Listing 15–7 ServiceEventEntry.java

```
// An Entry that represents a ServiceEvent.

package corejini.chapter15;

import net.jini.core.lookup.ServiceID;
import net.jini.core.lookup.ServiceRegistrar;
import net.jini.core.lookup.ServiceItem;
import net.jini.core.lookup.ServiceEvent;
import net.jini.core.entry.Entry;
import net.jini.lookup.entry.Name;

public class ServiceEventEntry extends WatcherEntry {
    public ServiceRegistrar registrar = null;
    public ServiceID serviceID = null;
    // even though these details can be fetched
    // from the service item, breaking them out
    // allows independent searching.
    public ServiceItem serviceItem = null;
    public Object service = null;
    public Integer transition = null;
    public String name = null;

    public ServiceEventEntry() {
    }
```

Listing 15–7 `ServiceEventEntry.java` **(continued)**

```
    public ServiceEventEntry(String group,
                             ServiceEvent ev){
        super(group, System.currentTimeMillis());

        registrar = (ServiceRegistrar) ev.getSource();
        serviceID = ev.getServiceID();
        serviceItem = ev.getServiceItem();
        transition = new Integer(ev.getTransition());
        if (serviceItem != null) {
            service = serviceItem.service;

            // Attach the Name as a separate member, if
            // there is one.
            Entry[] attrs = serviceItem.attributeSets;

            for (int i=0 ; i<attrs.length ; i++) {
                if (attrs[i] instanceof Name) {
                    name = ((Name) attrs[i]).name;
                }
            }
        }
    }
}
```

This example shows more of the same. `ServiceEventEntry` objects are written into the JavaSpaces service whenever a `ServiceEvent` is received by the watcher. It records information about the type of transition that occurred (whether a new service appeared, an existing service disappeared, or an existing service changed), as well as a set of other data that can aid in searching, or can be used by clients that retrieve these objects. For example, the `ServiceRegistrar` and `ServiceItem` objects are likely to be useful to a client that retrieves this `Entry`, but are not very useful for searching. On the other hand, the `ServiceID` and `Name` members are very useful for searching, even though they could be retrieved from the other data in the class, once downloaded. Note, here, how the `Name` attribute is retrieved from the set of attributes attached to the service's proxy, and stored separately to make it more searchable.

A Community Watcher

Now that we've seen the `Entry` types that will be stored and retrieved from the space, let's look at the two programs that will demonstrate how to use JavaSpaces. The first is called `DjinnWatcher`. Once started, this program tries to discover all the lookup services for the group specified on the command line. Whenever a `DiscoveryEvent` arrives, it writes a new `DiscoveryEventEntry` into a JavaSpace.

As the program finds lookup services, it registers with each to receive all types of events from it. This way, the program will be notified when any type of transition occurs in the lookup service, and can store these as `ServiceEventEntry` objects.

Let's look at the program as shown in Listing 15–8.

Listing 15–8 `DjinnWatcher.java`

```
// Watch for DiscoveryEvents and ServiceEvents for
// a given community. Create Entry objects for these
// and write them into a space.

package corejini.chapter15;

import net.jini.space.JavaSpace;
import net.jini.core.lookup.ServiceRegistrar;
import net.jini.core.lookup.ServiceEvent;
import net.jini.core.lookup.ServiceTemplate;
import net.jini.core.lease.Lease;
import net.jini.core.entry.Entry;
import net.jini.core.event.RemoteEvent;
import net.jini.core.event.RemoteEventListener;
import net.jini.core.event.EventRegistration;
import net.jini.discovery.DiscoveryEvent;
import net.jini.discovery.LookupDiscovery;
import net.jini.discovery.DiscoveryListener;
import com.sun.jini.lease.LeaseRenewalManager;
import java.util.Vector;
import java.rmi.RemoteException;
import java.rmi.RMISecurityManager;
import java.rmi.server.UnicastRemoteObject;
import java.io.IOException;
```

Listing 15–8 `DjinnWatcher.java` **(continued)**

```
public class DjinnWatcher implements Runnable {
    protected Class[] types = { JavaSpace.class };
    protected String group;
    protected ServiceTemplate tmpl =
        new ServiceTemplate(null, types, null);
    protected Vector regs = new Vector();
    protected JavaSpace javaSpace = null;
    protected LeaseRenewalManager leaseManager = null;
    protected static final int ALL_FLAGS =
        ServiceRegistrar.TRANSITION_MATCH_NOMATCH |
        ServiceRegistrar.TRANSITION_NOMATCH_MATCH |
        ServiceRegistrar.TRANSITION_MATCH_MATCH;
    protected EvtListener evtListener;
    protected LookupDiscovery disco;

     // An inner class for listening for remote events.
    class EvtListener extends UnicastRemoteObject
        implements RemoteEventListener {
        public EvtListener() throws RemoteException {
        }

        public void notify(RemoteEvent ev) {
            if (!(ev instanceof ServiceEvent))
                return;

            ServiceEvent sev = (ServiceEvent) ev;

            // write the data into the space.
            writeEventData(javaSpace, sev);
        }
    }

    // An inner class for listening for discovery events
    class DiscListener implements DiscoveryListener {
        public void discovered(DiscoveryEvent ev) {
             boolean spaceNotYetFound = (javaSpace == null);
             ServiceRegistrar[] newregs = ev.getRegistrars();
             for (int i=0, size=newregs.length ; i<size ;
                                                 i++) {
                if (!regs.contains(newregs[i])) {
                 // If we don't have a space yet, search
                 // for it. Otherwise, start getting
                 // events from the new registrar!
                 regs.addElement(newregs[i]);
```

Listing 15–8 `DjinnWatcher.java` **(continued)**

```
                if (javaSpace == null) {
                    // This will register for events in
                    // all known registrars.
                    findJavaSpace(newregs[i]);
                } else {
                    registerForEvents(newregs[i]);
                }
            }
        }

        // we only log discovery events received
        // *after* we find a space. So if we're still
        // processing the event that found the space for
        // us, we just bail. spaceNotYetFound records
        // whether the space was found at the time this
        // method started.
        if (spaceNotYetFound)
            return;

        // after adding each to the list, and looking
        // for javaspaces we can log new discovery
        // events if we've found a space already.
        if (javaSpace != null) {
            writeEventData(javaSpace, ev, true);
        }
    }

    public void discarded(DiscoveryEvent ev) {
        ServiceRegistrar[] deadregs =
                                  ev.getRegistrars();
        for (int i=0, size=deadregs.length ; i<size ;
                                             i++) {
            regs.removeElement(deadregs[i]);
        }

        // Log the event, if we've found a space.
        if (javaSpace != null) {
            writeEventData(javaSpace, ev, false);
        }
    }
}
```

Listing 15–8 `DjinnWatcher.java` **(continued)**

```
    public DjinnWatcher(String group)
        throws IOException, RemoteException {
        leaseManager = new LeaseRenewalManager();
        evtListener = new EvtListener();
        this.group = group;

        if (group == null) {
            System.out.println("Watching public group");
            disco = new
                LookupDiscovery(new String[] { "" });
        } else {
            System.out.println("Watching group " + group);
            disco = new
                LookupDiscovery(new String[] { group });
        }

        disco.addDiscoveryListener(new DiscListener());
    }

    protected void findJavaSpace(ServiceRegistrar reg) {
        if (javaSpace != null)
            return;

        try {
            javaSpace = (JavaSpace) reg.lookup(tmpl);
            if (javaSpace == null) {
                return;
            }
            System.out.println("Found a space!");
        } catch (RemoteException ex) {
            System.err.println("Error doing lookup: " +
                               ex.getMessage());
            disco.discard(reg);
            return;
        }

        for (int i=0, size=regs.size() ; i<size ; i++) {
            System.out.println("Registering for events" +
                               "at previously-found " +
                               "registrar: " +
                               regs.elementAt(i));
            registerForEvents((ServiceRegistrar)
                              regs.elementAt(i));
        }
    }
```

Listing 15–8 `DjinnWatcher.java` **(continued)**

```
    // Log discovery events.
    protected void writeEventData(JavaSpace space,
                                  DiscoveryEvent ev,
                                  boolean discovered) {
        System.out.println("Writing DiscoveryEvent " + ev);

        try {
            ServiceRegistrar[] evtregs =
                ev.getRegistrars();
            for (int i=0 ; i<evtregs.length ; i++) {
                DiscoveryEventEntry entry =
                    new DiscoveryEventEntry(group,
                                            evtregs[i],
                                            discovered);
                Lease lease = space.write(entry, null,
                                          60 * 60 * 1000);
                leaseManager.renewUntil(lease,
                                        Lease.ANY,
                                        null);
            }
        } catch (Exception ex) {
            System.err.println("Error writing event: " +
                               ex.getMessage());
        }
    }

    // Log service events.
    protected void writeEventData(JavaSpace space,
                                  ServiceEvent ev) {
        System.out.println("Writing ServiceEvent " + ev);

        try {
            Lease lease;
            ServiceEventEntry entry =
                new ServiceEventEntry(group, ev);

            lease = space.write(entry, null,
                                60 * 60 * 1000);
           leaseManager.renewUntil(lease, Lease.ANY, null);
        } catch (Exception ex) {
            System.err.println("Error writing event: " +
                               ex.getMessage());
        }
    }
```

Listing 15–8 `DjinnWatcher.java` (continued)

```
    protected void registerForEvents(ServiceRegistrar
                                                    reg) {
        try {
            ServiceTemplate search =
                new ServiceTemplate(null, null, null);
            EventRegistration evtreg;
            evtreg = reg.notify(search, ALL_FLAGS,
                                evtListener, null,
                                60 * 60 * 1000);
            leaseManager.renewUntil(evtreg.getLease(),
                                    Lease.ANY, null);
        } catch (RemoteException ex) {
           System.err.println("Error soliciting events: " +
                              ex.getMessage());
            disco.discard(reg);
        }
    }

     public void run() {
        while (true) {
            try {
                Thread.sleep(Integer.MAX_VALUE);
            } catch (InterruptedException ex) {
            }
        }
    }

    public static void main(String[] args) {
        String group = null;

        if (System.getSecurityManager() == null) {
            System.setSecurityManager(
                                new RMISecurityManager());
        }

        if (args.length == 1) {
            group = args[0];
        } else if (args.length > 1) {
            System.err.println("Usage: DjinnWatcher " +
                                        "[<group>]");
        }
```

Listing 15–8 `DjinnWatcher.java` (continued)

```
        try {
            DjinnWatcher dw = new DjinnWatcher(group);
            new Thread(dw).start();
            System.out.println("Cruising!");
        } catch (Exception ex) {
        }
    }
}
```

The `DjinnWatcher` program takes a group name on the command line. You can pass "public" here if you want the program to watch the public group. When the program starts, it creates a `LeaseRenewalManager` to handle its leases on the objects it will store in the JavaSpaces service, and—following our usual pattern—creates an inner class for listening for discovery events and an inner class (which is a remote object) for receiving remote events from lookup services.

Before the `DjinnWatcher` can begin logging events, it must find a JavaSpace through the usual lookup mechanisms. So whenever a new lookup service is discovered, the program looks to see if a JavaSpace is registered there if it has not already found one. When a JavaSpaces service is found for the first time, the program contacts all the previously-found lookup services to register to receive events from them; the program will also register to receive events from all lookup services that it finds in the future.

Note that there is a limitation with this program and its peer (which you'll see in a bit) that you should be aware of. The program only discovers lookup services in the community it's been asked to watch, and only looks for JavaSpaces services in those communities. So you need to make sure that—for the version of the program shown here—you run a JavaSpaces service that's a member of the community you're planning on watching. This is simply a limitation of this program, not a limitation of JavaSpaces. You can easily change the code to find a lookup service in a different community, but this approach is the simplest for illustrating the techniques that are covered in this chapter.

Likewise, the program stores all the `Entry` objects it writes into the *first* JavaSpaces service it encounters. So you should probably only run one JavaSpace for this example.

The `findJavaSpace()` call works just as you would expect—it uses the `lookup()` method on the lookup services it finds to search for a JavaSpaces service. The `registerForEvents()` call also uses methods you've seen before. It calls `notify()` on the lookup service to ask to receive events in the future, and passes the inner `EvtListener` instance as the listener for events. Leasing of the event registration is done by the `LeaseRenewalManager` created earlier.

The program shown here is doing quite a bit of work in the thread that does discovery—it is doing a remote call to search the lookup service for JavaSpaces services, and registering with lookup services to receive events. In a "real" application, you would want to do these slow operations in a separate, short-lived thread so that the discovery process isn't blocked while you're doing other things. But the situation isn't too dire for the little example here.

Also note that the code here calls `discard()` on the discovery listener object whenever a `RemoteException` is caught in `findJavaSpace()` or `registerForEvents()`. Remember that a call to `discard()` tells the discovery machiney that a lookup service is not responding; this allows it to be discovered again, if it returns to the community. Calling `discard()` on a `LookupDiscovery` object causes that object to invoke the `discarded()` method on the discovery listener, so that it can clean up its state as needed.

The main work done by the program is to write `Entry` objects into the JavaSpaces service when it receives a `DiscoveryEvent` or a `ServiceEvent`. These tasks are handled by the two versions of the `writeEventData()` call. One takes a `DiscoveryEvent` and the other takes a `ServiceEvent`. Each `DiscoveryEvent` can contain discovery information for multiple lookup services. So the code here breaks these up into multiple, discrete `DiscoveryEventEntry` objects so that each is represented separately in the log of the history. The `Entry` objects are created and then written into the space (with no transaction), and the lease for the stored object is passed to the `LeaseRenewalManager` for renewal.

The version of `writeEventData()` that takes a `ServiceEvent` is similar. A new `ServiceEventEntry` is constructed from the event and written to the space.

Note here the use of a thread that does nothing but keep the VM from exiting. Since this application uses no other libraries—such as AWT—that would start their own threads, this step is necessary so that the VM doesn't terminate after `main()` completes.

A Consumer of Logged Event Data

Next, let's look at a program that can retrieve stored information about a community and display it. The model that `DjinnConsumer` (Listing 15–9) follows is that, after a `DjinnWatcher` has been running for a while, you can start the consumer, give it a group name, and it will fetch all the accumulated `Entry` objects for the group.

The same limitations that applied to the `DjinnWatcher` implementation apply here—the program will only contact a JavaSpace service that's a member of the group for which the user wants history information, and the program contacts the first JavaSpaces service it finds. So you should make sure that you run a single JavaSpaces service in the group you're logging, unless you decide to modify this program to make it more robust.

Let's look at the code.

Listing 15–9 `DjinnConsumer.java`

```
// Contact a JavaSpaces service and retrieve the
// logged history for a single group.

package corejini.chapter15;

import net.jini.space.JavaSpace;
import net.jini.core.lookup.ServiceTemplate;
import net.jini.core.lookup.ServiceRegistrar;
import net.jini.core.entry.*;
import net.jini.discovery.DiscoveryEvent;
import net.jini.discovery.DiscoveryListener;
import net.jini.discovery.LookupDiscovery;
import java.rmi.RemoteException;
import java.rmi.RMISecurityManager;
import java.io.IOException;

public class DjinnConsumer implements Runnable {
    protected Class[] types = { JavaSpace.class };
    protected String group;
    protected ServiceTemplate tmpl =
        new ServiceTemplate(null, types, null);
    protected JavaSpace javaSpace = null;


    // An inner class for discovery.
    class DiscListener implements DiscoveryListener {
        public synchronized void discovered(DiscoveryEvent
                                                        ev) {
            if (javaSpace != null)
                return;
```

Listing 15–9 `DjinnConsumer.java` **(continued)**

```
            ServiceRegistrar[] regs = ev.getRegistrars();
            for (int i=0, size=regs.length ; i<size ; i++) {
                JavaSpace js = findJavaSpace(regs[i]);
                if (js != null) {
                    javaSpace = js;
                    doit();
                }
            }
        }

        public void discarded(DiscoveryEvent ev) {
        }
    }

    public DjinnConsumer(String group) throws IOException {
        LookupDiscovery disco;
        this.group = group;

        if (group == null) {
            System.out.println("Fetching public history");
            disco = new
                LookupDiscovery(new String[] { "" });
        } else {
            System.out.println("Fetching history for " +
                                                group);
            disco = new
                LookupDiscovery(new String[] { group });
        }

        disco.addDiscoveryListener(new DiscListener());
    }

    // find and return a JavaSpace, if it exists at the
    // registrar.
    protected JavaSpace findJavaSpace(ServiceRegistrar
                                                  reg) {
        if (javaSpace != null)
            return null;
```

Listing 15–9 `DjinnConsumer.java` **(continued)**

```
        try {
            JavaSpace javaSpace = (JavaSpace)
                                  reg.lookup(tmpl);
            if (javaSpace != null) {
                System.out.println("Found a space!");
                return javaSpace;
            }
        } catch (RemoteException ex) {
            System.err.println("Error doing lookup: " +
                               ex.getMessage());
            return null;
        }

        return null;
    }

     protected void doit() {
        System.out.println("Searching for history for " +
                                                group);

        // Make a template to search for the group
        // passed on the command line, any timestamp
        WatcherEntry tmpl = new WatcherEntry();
        tmpl.group = group;
        tmpl.timestamp = null;

        try {
            // Snapshot it, since we'll be using it
            // over and over.
            Entry snapshot = javaSpace.snapshot(tmpl);
            boolean done = false;
            int i = 0;

            while (!done) {
                Entry result =
                         javaSpace.takeIfExists(snapshot,
                                    null,
                                    JavaSpace.NO_WAIT);

                if (result != null) {
                    printResult(i++, result);
                }
```

Listing 15–9 DjinnConsumer.java (continued)

```
                done = (result == null);
            }

            // quit once we've got everything
            System.out.println("Done!");
            System.exit(1);
        } catch (Exception ex) {
            System.err.println("bogus:  " +
                                     ex.getMessage());
            ex.printStackTrace();
        }
    }

    protected void printResult(int i, Entry result) {
        if (result instanceof DiscoveryEventEntry) {
            DiscoveryEventEntry disc =
                (DiscoveryEventEntry) result;
            System.out.println("[" + i + "] " +
                          (disc.discovered.booleanValue() ?
                              "discovered" : "discarded") +
                          " " + disc.locator.toString());
        } else if (result instanceof ServiceEventEntry) {
            ServiceEventEntry serv =
                (ServiceEventEntry) result;
            System.out.println("[" + i + "] " + serv.name +
                          " " +  serv.transition + " " +
                              (serv.service == null ? "" :
                     serv.service.getClass().getName()) +
                                  " " + serv.serviceID);
        } else {
            // Someone else added an entry type?
            System.out.println(result);
        }
    }

    public void run() {
        while (true) {
            try {
                Thread.sleep(Integer.MAX_VALUE);
            } catch (InterruptedException ex) {
            }
        }
    }
```

Listing 15–9 `DjinnConsumer.java` (continued)

```
    public static void main(String[] args) {
        String group = null;

        if (System.getSecurityManager() == null) {
            System.setSecurityManager(
                            new RMISecurityManager());
        }

        if (args.length == 1) {
            group = args[0];
        } else if (args.length > 1) {
            System.err.println("Usage: DjinnConsumer " +
                                            "[<group>]");
        }

        try {
            DjinnConsumer dc = new DjinnConsumer(group);
            new Thread(dc).start();
            System.out.println("Cruising!");
        } catch (Exception ex) {
        }
    }
}
```

This program is a bit shorter than `DjinnWatcher`, as it doesn't have to solicit events from any lookup services, or maintain a list of discovered lookup services, or log any event data.

The code defines an inner class, `DiscListener`, to perform discovery. Whenever a new lookup service is found for the specified group, `findJavaSpace()` is called to search for a JavaSpaces service and, if one is found, the `doit()` method is called to retrieve the `Entry` objects that describe the community's history.

As in the last example, this code is doing a lot of work in the discovery thread—too much for a "real-world" application, but not too bad for an example designed to show off how to use JavaSpaces. Be sure that in your programs if you have to do a lot of computation or invoke any remote calls as a result of discovery, you create a short-lived thread to do the work without blocking the discovery thread.

The most interesting part of the program is in the `doit()` method, so let's look at that. The `DjinnConsumer` is interested in all `Entry` objects that describe the history of the community—whether they're of type `Discovery-`

EventEntry or ServiceEventEntry. The easiest way to search for both is to search for their superclass, WatcherEntry. Here, the fact that JavaSpaces understands the Java type system is a big win: The program can search using a WatcherEntry as a template and find all the specific Entry objects that are of classes derived from it.

In this example, the code needs to find all the objects that describe a particular group, so it creates a WatcherEntry, sets its group member to the group being searched for, and sets the timestamp to null. This says that the code wants to match any Entry that is of class WatcherEntry (or a subclass), and that has an *exact* match in the group field for the group. The timestamp value is treated as a "don't care" since it's null; it's effectively a wildcard value that will match any value of timestamp.

The JavaSpace APIs only allow a client to fetch one item at a time. Since this application will be using the same template over and over again, I've created a "snapshot" of it here. Recall that a snapshot is a way to save yourself the time of serializing an Entry over and over again.

After this, DjinnConsumer sits in a loop, taking matching items out of the JavaSpace until there are no more. A version of the take() call is used so that the code will remove each item as it is matched; takeIfExists() is specifically used because the code should try to remove only items that exist at the time the method is called—we don't want to sit around waiting for new items to appear in the future. To prevent the call from blocking because of objects that may be involved in an "unsettled" transaction, the JavaSpaces.NO_WAIT flag is used. This indicates that even though a potentially matching Entry may be involved in a transaction, the call shouldn't wait for the transaction to complete. In such an event, the method will simply return null to indicate that there are no more matching Entry objects in the space.

When each Entry is retrieved, it is tested for null and then passed to printResult() for display. Remember that the take() and read() methods can return null if they don't match any items, or if the matched items are involved in transactions that don't complete before a timeout period elapses. So you need to make sure that you don't just blindly use a returned result without checking it. The loop continues until takeIfExists() returns null, which the program interprets as exhaustion of the event data, at which point DjinnConsumer exits.

The program as shown here uses the retrieved objects in a very simple way—they are simply printed to standard output in the order they are fetched. You could imagine some more sophisticated visualizations or presentations of the data, or even some less sophisticated ones, such as simply

ordering the data based on timestamp, or removing duplicate services by looking at the service IDs in ServiceEventEntries.

Compiling and Running the Programs

Ok, it's time to get these things running! Unlike most of the previous examples we've looked at, these two programs aren't clients or servers to each other—they're both clients of JavaSpaces, but don't need to share any downloadable code with each other. In fact, it would be completely acceptable to bundle both of these programs and their associated files into the same JAR file, and allow users to run either from the same JAR.

So I'm going to compile them both to the client directory, and forego the enforced separation that we've usually followed when building a client and a server program. Note that even though we're now building a program to use the JavaSpaces APIs, we don't need to include any JavaSpaces JAR files in the classpath! Only the net.jini.space.JavaSpace interface is needed at compile time, and that exists in the jini-ext.jar file; the implementation will be delivered at run time by the Jini infrastructure.

On Windows:

```
javac -classpath C:\jini1_0\lib\jini-core.jar;
                 C:\jini1_0\lib\jini-ext.jar;
                 C:\jini1_0\lib\sun-util.jar;
                 C:\client
       -d C:\client
       C:\files\corejini.chapter15.DjinnWatcher.java
       C:\files\corejini.chapter15.DjinnConsumer.java
```

On Solaris:

```
javac -classpath
          /files/jini1_0/lib/jini-core.jar:
          /files/jini1_0/lib/jini-ext.jar:
          /files/jini1_0/lib/sun-util.jar:
          /files/client
       -d /files/client
       /files/corejini/chapter15/DjinnWatcher.java
       /files/corejini/chapter15/DjinnConsumer.java
```

The only remote object in this example is the nested EvtListener class in DjinnWatcher. You'll need to generate stubs for it via rmic.

On Windows:

```
rmic -classpath C:\jini1_0\lib\jini-core.jar;
                C:\jini1_0\lib\jini-ext.jar;
```

```
                  C:\jini1_0\lib\sun-util.jar;
                  C:\client
        -d C:\client-dl
        corejini.chapter15.DjinnWatcher.EvtListener
```

On Solaris:

```
rmic -classpath /files/jini1_0/lib/jini-core.jar:
                /files/jini1_0/lib/jini-ext.jar:
                /files/jini1_0/lib/sun-util.jar:
                /files/client
        -d /files/client-dl
        corejini.chapter15.DjinnWatcher.EvtListener
```

Now you're set to run! Start up the `DjinnWatcher` program first, and let it run for a while. While it's running, you may want to start or stop some of the services you've seen earlier in the book, just to give the watcher something to record. Be sure to give the watcher a group to watch; here I've used "public."

On Windows:

```
java -cp C:\jini1_0\lib\jini-core.jar;
          C:\jini1_0\lib\jini-ext.jar;
          C:\jini1_0\lib\sun-util.jar;
          C:\client;
          C:\client-dl
       -Djava.rmi.server.codebase=http://myhost:8086
       -Djava.security.policy=C:\policy
       corejini.chapter15.DjinnWatcher public
```

On Solaris:

```
java -cp /files/jini1_0/lib/jini-core.jar:
          /files/jini1_0/lib/jini-ext.jar:
          /files/jini1_0/lib/sun-util.jar:
          /files/client:
          /files/client-dl
       -Djava.rmi.server.codebase=http://myhost:8086
       -Djava.security.policy=/files/policy
       corejini.chapter15.DjinnWatcher public
```

As the watcher runs, you should see output as it finds a JavaSpaces service, and logs events to it. Obviously, the more things going on in your community, the more event traces you'll see.

Watching public group

Found a space!

Registering for events at previously-found registrar: com.sun.jini.reggie.RegistrarProxy@ac2984f

Cruising!
Writing ServiceEvent
com.sun.jini.reggie.RegistrarEvent[source=com.sun.jini.reggie.Registrar-Proxy@ac2984f]
Writing ServiceEvent
com.sun.jini.reggie.RegistrarEvent[source=com.sun.jini.reggie.Registrar-Proxy@ac2984f]
Writing ServiceEvent
com.sun.jini.reggie.RegistrarEvent[source=com.sun.jini.reggie.Registrar-Proxy@ac2984f]
Writing ServiceEvent
com.sun.jini.reggie.RegistrarEvent[source=com.sun.jini.reggie.Registrar-Proxy@ac2984f]
Writing ServiceEvent
com.sun.jini.reggie.RegistrarEvent[source=com.sun.jini.reggie.Registrar-Proxy@ac2984f]
Writing ServiceEvent
com.sun.jini.reggie.RegistrarEvent[source=com.sun.jini.reggie.Registrar-Proxy@ac2984f]

Next, run the consumer program. Note that the consumer, since it exports no downloadable code, doesn't need to have a codebase property set, and doesn't need the `client-dl` stubs directory in its classpath. (It *will*, however, be using downloaded code—namely the proxy for the JavaSpaces service—so it needs a security policy file.) Be sure to use the same group name for the consumer as you did for the watcher.

On Windows:

```
java -cp C:\jini1_0\lib\jini-core.jar;
         C:\jini1_0\lib\jini-ext.jar;
         C:\jini1_0\lib\sun-util.jar;
         C:\client
     -Djava.security.policy=C:\policy
     corejini.chapter15.DjinnConsumer public
```

On Solaris:

```
java -cp /files/jini1_0/lib/jini-core.jar:
         /files/jini1_0/lib/jini-ext.jar:
         /files/jini1_0/lib/sun-util.jar:
         /files/client
     -Djava.security.policy=/files/policy
     corejini.chapter15.DjinnConsumer public
```

When the client runs, it'll fetch all the history for the group you've specified, and dump it to standard out.

Fetching public history
Found a space!
Searching for history for public
[0] null 2 corejini.chapter5.HelloWorldServiceProxy
b227e764-0e84-4bcf-adca-82f9a98445f1
[1] null 2 corejini.chapter10.LeaseServiceProxy
ce95e89f-a06f-419c-b167-87cdbac61caa
[2] null 1 b227e764-0e84-4bcf-adca-82f9a98445f1
[3] null 2 corejini.chapter5.HelloWorldServiceProxy
b227e764-0e84-4bcf-adca-82f9a98445f1
[4] null 2 corejini.chapter10.LeaseServiceProxy
f2a50050-952e-4c49-9379-e2db24ec4dab
Cruising!
Done!

The output here shows five events that were logged for the public group. In this case, there were two separate instances of two services, `HelloWorld-Service` and `LeaseService`, started after the watcher began its logging. We know that these services started, because of the transition number ("2" is the numerical form of the `TRANSITION_NOMATCH_MATCH` flag). The "null" here is where the name of the services would be, if they had names. And the long string of numbers and letters at the end is the service ID for each.

This example has shown a simple pair of applications—a writer and a reader—that can cooperate together to produce and display histories of the activity in a given Jini community. The minimalist JavaSpaces API makes applications like this easy. And JavaSpaces follows the basic paradigms of interaction in Jini—attribute-based search, leased resources, notification using the Jini remote events model—making it a good and useful citizen in many Jini communities.

Applying JavaSpaces to Distributed Computing Problems

This chapter has focused on one particular and obvious use of the JavaSpaces programming model: as a persistent shared repository for objects. Such a use is easy to understand, and has immediate utility for many applications that need to store objects or make them available to others.

But JavaSpaces can also be used in a different way: It can be used as the complete basis for a new distributed systems programming paradigm. This was the original intent of the Linda work on which JavaSpaces was based. While Linda certainly could be used as a simple storage engine, the real goal was to provide a new model for building distributed applications. In this new model, distributed systems would be built around "flows" of objects from application to application, coordinated through the central Linda tuple space.

The idea here is that rather than building custom, remote communication interfaces or protocols for each new distributed application, applications can be defined in terms of the set of objects they write into the tuple space and the set of objects they retrieve from the tuple space. To move the analogy into Java terms, rather than defining and refining new RMI remote interfaces for each new task, the JavaSpaces interfaces would be the common APIs for interaction between applications. Applications would define their own set of `Entry` objects, and associate their own semantics with these objects.

Let's look at a distributed compute server as an example. Say you want to build a program to speed up builds of a large software project—sort of a distributed `make` application. In the traditional approach, you'd define a set of interfaces that the various components of the system would use to talk to each other. A `Controller` object might do the dependency analysis of the source code and farm out each chunk to one of a set of `Builder` processes. The `Controller` might have methods to `createJob()` to start a new build, and `checkJobStatus()` to see how a build is going. Each `Builder` might support methods to `startBuild()` and `stopBuild()` and `checkStatus()` to return the status of a compilation local to that one builder. These interfaces would also likely support event passing, so that the central `Controller` could know when an individual build has finished.

In the JavaSpaces model, each of the tasks that needs to be done for a distributed `make` program would be mapped into the concepts of `Entry` objects in a JavaSpace. For example, a centralized coordinating `Controller` process could write `BuildTask Entry` objects into a JavaSpace, while the separate `Builders` would retrieve these objects whenever they were ready to compile a new chunk of the code. When each `Builder` finished a chunk, it would write a `BuildStatus` object into the space, where it would be retrieved by the `Controller`.

In this model, the JavaSpaces service takes care of the mechanics of event propagation and searching for new tasks. New `Builders` can be added dynamically without having to tell the `Controller`—if you run a new one, it simply begins doing `take()` operations on a space when it finds a new `BuildTask`. So it's easy to dynamically expand the capacity of the system.

And rather than defining separate interfaces for each component of the system, the `JavaSpaces` interface is the only API that components of the system need to understand. Rather than providing a host of new methods that need to be implemented and understood by all parties, the handful of JavaSpaces methods are sufficient to build the entire distributed application. All of the semantics of the task at hand get encoded into the objects stored to and retrieved from the space. And many applications can share this same infrastructure to build their systems.

This distributed `make` case is only one example of the sort of applications that could be built on top of JavaSpaces. Addressing this use of the JavaSpaces paradigm is really beyond the scope of this book. The focus here is on enabling you to build and use Jini services, and understand the mechanics of distributed computing using the tools that Jini provides. JavaSpaces provides another programming model that is logically separate from Jini, but can be used by Jini applications that can benefit from it.

Further Reading

If you're interested in the research that the JavaSpaces work was based on, you can check out the Linda project home page at Yale:

`http://www.cs.yale.edu/HTML/YALE/CS/Linda/linda.html`

The T Spaces work at IBM's Almaden Research Center also shows a tuple space-based approach to building distributed systems. T Spaces is more functional, and also more complex, than JavaSpaces, which has an extremely minimalistic programming model. The home page for this project is at:

`http://www.almaden.ibm.com/cs/TSpaces/index.html`

Finally, the Java Distributed Computing page has information on JavaSpaces, including details of a nifty demo at the 1998 JavaOne conference in San Francisco. There, JavaSpaces was used to build a massively parallel compute server out of the thousands of "JavaRing" devices given to attendees—these devices are literally rings that you wear on your finger, and have an embedded Java VM inside them. Using JavaSpaces, parts of a large fractal

image were parceled out to individual rings for computation, and then reassembled into a whole.

This page is also a good starting point if you're interested in leveraging the JavaSpaces programming model as a way to build distributed applications as flows of objects.

```
http://www.java.sun.com/products/javaspaces/
```

What's Next?

The last chapter in the book addresses the main issue that we punted on in this chapter—transactions! In the next chapter, we'll look at what sorts of safety guarantees transactions can provide, what the Jini model for distributed transactions is, and see how to use transactions to coordinate operations across multiple services.

DISTRIBUTED TRANSACTIONS

Topics in This Chapter

- What are transactions?
- The Jini distributed transaction model
- Building transaction clients
- Using transactions with JavaSpaces

Chapter 16

The final chapter of this book is dedicated to one of the somewhat more seldom used aspects of Jini—distributed transactions. Transactions, as mentioned in Chapter 3, are an important tool for building reliable systems in which computation must span a number of components.

But of the core concepts in Jini—discovery, lookup, leasing, remote events, and transactions—transactions are likely to be the one that you use the least. Of the standard services that ship with Jini, only JavaSpaces uses transactions and even there, transactions are optional.

Still, an understanding of transactions is important for understanding Jini. If you're building Jini-aware programs that need to interact with multiple services, and ensure that results that involve more than one service are carried out accurately, then transactions are the tool that you need.

In this chapter, we'll briefly revisit what transactions can do for us: How transactions can mitigate some of the problems in distributed systems that arise from partial failures, and how transactions can be used to keep a computation in a known state at all times. We'll look at the classical transaction model that you may be familiar with from database programming, and see how the Jini model differs from that. We'll also see how the Jini transaction APIs are used, particularly from the standpoint of a client application using transactions to coordinate a number of services. Finally, we'll look at an example that uses transactions to coordinate multiple JavaSpaces services.

Consistency and the Evils of Partial Failure

Chapter 2 talked about the differences between building stand-alone applications and true distributed systems. As you recall from that chapter, the key distinction between a stand-alone system and a distributed one is the fact that distributed systems can suffer *partial failures*.

A partial failure is when one component of the system fails, leaving other components functioning. Stand-alone systems, in contrast, typically suffer from *total failures* where the entire application (or the machine on which the application is running) simply dies. Paradoxically, while a total failure might on the surface seem to be a much more dire event, partial failures are the source of many of the problems in distributed computing. There are a couple of reasons for this.

First, detecting whether a partial failure exists can sometimes be difficult. You may not even be able to tell reliably that a component has failed in a distributed system. In a stand-alone system, typically either the system is up and running, or it's crashed; there are no "fuzzy" circumstances.

Second, you may not know if the component that is not responding actually did the work you asked it to do. Say you ask a remote database to withdraw $100 from an account and you never get a response back from it. Should you ask it to do the work again, when it comes back up? Should you assume that it completed?

Total failures in a stand-alone system cause work to stop: The system isn't functioning, and nothing will happen until the system is brought back up. But partial failures in a distributed system can cause *inconsistencies* in the state of the system. These inconsistencies may go unnoticed and can even spread through the system unless you're careful.

A Classical Transaction Model

Stand-alone applications can still encounter consistency problems. Think of a stand-alone database, running on a single machine. This database may dutifully process transfers between bank accounts, until one day it crashes unexpectedly. The database cannot predict when it is going to crash, clearly—if it could, then it would take steps not to crash! And so there is the chance that a crash will occur right in the middle of a transfer, say when money has been

removed from one account but not yet added to another. If a crash occurs at just the wrong time, the database could come back up in an inconsistent state—money has been subtracted from the first account but not yet added to the second; this cash is essentially lost to the bit bucket.

To address these problems, the database community adopted the notion of *transactions*. A transaction is a group of computations—such as subtracting an amount from one account and adding it to another—which must be completely executed as a group for the result to be considered valid. Transactions provide a way to "cluster" operations together and make the execution of all of them appear to be like the execution of a single operation: either the operation happens or it doesn't.

You should be sure that you understand that transactions don't guarantee that a set of grouped operations will always succeed. Transactions merely guarantee that the operations will either all succeed or all fail, and that—most importantly—the system can tell which has happened.

Transactions in stand-alone systems most commonly ensure that the system will return to a known state after a crash. In the classical banking example, if the debit and credit operations are grouped together into a transaction, then—even if the system crashes in the middle of the transaction—the system guarantees that it will come back into a known state. Either the transaction will have fully completed, and the system can detect this and carry on with its business, or the transaction will have failed in the middle, in which case none of the component operations take effect and the entire transaction can be retried later.

But even in stand-alone systems, transactions can be used to guard against the failure of individual component operations. In a database, one operation in a transaction may fail because it would cause deadlock or because a disk is full, for instance. Here again, transactions ensure that *none* of the related operations in the transaction take place if any one of them fail.[1]

Core Note: Filesystems have these same problems.

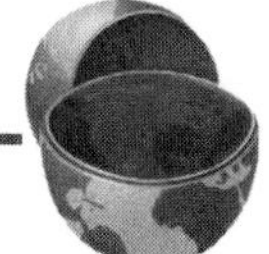

I've focused on databases as an example of a system in which crash recovery can be aided by transactions. But you may not know that everyday computer filesystems have many of these same problems!

1. This example is actually getting close to the errors that can happen in distributed systems, where only one constituent operation in a transaction fails. Still, in the stand-alone case, it is easy to detect that the operation has failed. This is not always the case in a distributed system.

If you've ever flipped the power switch on a Windows machine without properly shutting it down, you may have been greeted by the dreaded "System not properly shut down. Must run scandisk" message. What has happened here is that the system has been unexpectedly shut down, and must check itself for any inconsistencies. In general, the operating system will not allow itself to fully boot until any inconsistencies have been removed. The scandisk program scans the entire disk looking for information that might be in an inconsistent state.

The same benefits that transactions bring to databases can be applied to filesystems as well. "Journaling" or "log-based" filesystems essentially use a transaction model like the one described here to ensure that filesystems come back up into a known state after a crash. By doing filesystem updates in the context of a transaction, you can guard against data loss, prevent inconsistencies, and save yourself the time and hassle of having to run scandisk after a crash.

Just one more example of the power of transactions!

Two-Phase Commit

Let's look at how transactions actually work. We'll start off looking at the basic transaction *protocols*—the steps of the transaction process—in the stand-alone case, before moving on to how transactions work in a distributed setting like Jini.

Most transactions in database systems are based on what is known as the *two-phase commit* protocol, sometimes just called 2PC. While transactions have a lot of special terminology surrounding them, the basics are actually surprisingly simple. Two-phase commit says that to get a group of operations to either all succeed or all fail together in a known way, you have to follow a simple two-step process.

In the first step, called the *prepare* step, a coordinating entity (called the *transaction manager*) tells all the parties involved in the transaction to "get ready" to perform their operations. This means that each of the parties, called a *participant*, has to do a few things: First, the participant computes whatever result is being asked for. But rather than writing the result into some permanent storage (onto the disk, or into the database), the result is just saved in a log file. Second, each participant reports back to the central manager whether it was able to successfully move into this state.

If a participant reports that it has successfully prepared itself to move to the next stage, then this is a guarantee to the transaction manager that the participant is willing and able to move to the next step at some point in the future.

In the second step, called the *commit* step, the manager tallies up all these *votes* from the participants about whether they were able to do the first stage. If any of the participants was not able to move into the prepared stage, then the manager calls off the transaction since it cannot be fully completed. But if all the participants report that they are ready, then the manager writes into a log that it is about to complete the transaction, along with a list of all the prepared participants. It then tells each participant to "go." When each participant receives the "go" message, it copies the result from temporary storage into permanent storage, and tells the manager when it has finished.

You may be wondering what happens if a participant fails after the manager has told it to commit, but before the participant actually updates the permanent record. Isn't it possible, in this case, for the update to be lost? If a participant reports that it has successfully moved to the prepare stage, then this is in effect a *guarantee* to the manager that if the manager contacts it in the future, the participant will be able to commit the change. The manager must continue telling participants to commit until it has heard from all of them. As long as even one participant hasn't responded, the manager keeps trying; it is not allowed to clean up after the transaction until all participants have been updated.

All this may seem complicated, but the good news is that most of the time, you don't need to worry about the actual details of how two-phase commit works. If you're writing applications that are doling out operations to services to be executed under transactions, then the Jini transaction APIs hide most of this complexity from you. (Services that expose operations that can happen within transactions have to have a somewhat greater understanding of the protocol, though.)

With this in mind, let's move on to look at what the Jini transaction model looks like.

Transactions in Jini

Just like so much else in Jini, the Jini transaction model makes a strong separation between interface and implementation. And while usually in Jini this means that objects are described in terms of their Java interfaces, and their implementations are hidden, the Jini transaction model takes this separation one step further.

In Jini, only the two-phase commit protocol itself is standardized. What services do in response to the individual phases of the protocol is up to them. In essence, only the mechanics of the two-phase commit stages are a built-in part of Jini, while the semantics of what transactions "mean" to any given service are not dictated by Jini.

What does this mean in practice? This design decision has several implications.

First, it means that Jini can have one transaction manager that can drive transactions in any number of applications. In more traditional systems, the transaction manager is typically tightly integrated with the rest of the system. In databases, for instance, the transaction manager *is* the database, because transactions are an inseparable part of the database and the transaction manager must have internal knowledge of the database to be able to work.

In contrast, the single Jini transaction manager can drive the two-phase commit protocol for transactions in *any* type of service, even services that the transaction manager has no knowledge of.

Second, it means that Jini as a whole has no way of enforcing *what* any particular service will do when confronted with a transaction. In a database system, transactions are so tightly integrated with the database that operations cannot "escape" from their transaction boundaries, and update data without going through the transaction process.

In Jini, service writers can receive messages from the transaction manager telling them to move to the prepare stage, the commit stage, and so on. But there is no guarantee about what exactly those services will do in response to those messages. Of course, one hopes that if a service writer has gone to the trouble of working with transactions, then the service will preserve sensible transaction semantics.

The approach that Jini takes is very lightweight, and very object oriented. The two-phase commit protocol itself is the "interface" that transaction participants must understand. The "implementation" of the protocol is up to them. So service writers can choose an implementation that makes sense for them. A database service might keep fully redundant, fully reliable logging information to implement two-phase commit. While an on-line game might use a much faster and looser implementation.

The Players in Jini Transactions

There are three main parties involved in Jini transactions: the transaction manager, the transaction participant, and the transaction client. In Jini the transaction manager is actually a full-fledged Jini service that simply runs through the two-phase commit protocol when asked. The transaction manager keeps, for each transaction, a list of participants. For each participant, it will send it a message telling it what stage to move to. Essentially the manager is only in charge of the signaling for the two-phase commit protocol. All transaction manager services, including the one in the sample implementation from Sun, implement the `net.jini.core.transaction.server.TransactionManager` interface.

The participant in a transaction is a program that is performing an operation that is grouped with other operations into a transaction. Typically, this will be a Jini service that is allowing some of its operations to be "transactable"—letting them take a transaction parameter so that the operation can be grouped with others. In Jini, transaction participants implement the `net.jini.core.transaction.server.TransactionParticipant` interface.

Finally, the transaction client is the entity that starts the whole process. This may be a Jini application that needs to perform operations on multiple services and ensure that they all happen together. Or in other cases it may be a Jini service that needs to make use of operations in other services. But whatever the context, there is no required interface that transaction clients must implement. Jini does, however, provide some helper classes that clients can use to make their use of transactions easier. The most important of these is the `net.jini.core.transaction.Transaction` interface, which provides an object representation of a set of operations grouped into a transaction. The `net.jini.core.transaction.TransactionFactory` class provides a useful helper for creating new `Transaction` instances.

The high-level overview of how a transaction is used is pretty simple. First, a client gets a reference to the Jini transaction manager, usually through the standard discovery and lookup process. The client then calls the `TransactionFactory` to create a new `Transaction` object that will be managed by that transaction manager.

After the client has a `Transaction` object, it can begin grouping together the operations that will make up the transaction. In Jini, this is typically done by sending the `Transaction` object off to the individual participants as part of a method call to perform some operation. If you think about the JavaSpaces examples from the last chapter, there was no abstract representation of a *write* operation that could be "added" to a `Transaction`, and the `Transaction` class has no methods for adding operations to it. Instead, in the JavaSpaces case, certain methods on the service that can operate in the context of transactions simply take a `Transaction` argument. The JavaSpaces service takes care of creating some bookkeeping information that remembers that the particular operation is associated with a particular transaction, and then *joins* the transaction by telling the transaction manager that it is controlling one of the member operations.

So while the client is *conceptually* adding operations to the transaction, the programming model and APIs simply look like the client is invoking methods on the services just like normal, only with a `Transaction` object as a parameter.

Once all the member operations have been grouped together, the client then tries to commit the operations by calling the `commit()` method on the `Transaction`. It is this method that begins the two-phase commit process, or rather, it signals the manager to begin the process and handle the messaging of all the member participants.

Up until this point, none of the participating services have actually executed any of the requested operations. So if you've called `write()` on a JavaSpace with a `Transaction` parameter, the write will not actually take effect until you commit the transaction.[2]

At the end of all this, if the `commit()` call successfully completes, then the client can be sure that all the member operations have successfully completed. The call may raise a `net.jini.core.transaction.CannotCommitException` if any participant cannot move to the prepared stage.

This overview really represents about 90 percent of what you need to know to use Jini transactions. For the most part, transaction clients—which are the part of the puzzle you will most commonly be working with—don't need to understand the mechanics of two-phase commit or logging or crash recovery. Transaction participants do need to have a deeper understanding of transactions, though. And there are a few subtleties that will even affect clients.

I'll talk about the subtleties a bit later in the chapter, but for now, let's focus on the Jini transaction programming model, and how it appears to clients.

---

2. Actually, the notion of when and how transactions "take effect" is a bit more complicated than this. Even the effects of operations in uncommitted transactions will be visible to other operations operating under that same transaction. More on this a bit later in the chapter, but for now you can think of the operations as "not happening" until the transaction commits.

Programming with Jini Transactions

In this section we'll look at the Jini transaction interfaces and classes, and see how to build clients that can take advantage of transactions. A bit later, once we've covered the basics, we'll look at a simple example of writing a transaction client that can coordinate operations across multiple JavaSpaces services.

The Transaction Manager

The most important part of the Jini transaction paradigm is the transaction manager. As mentioned before, the transaction manager is itself a service which simply handles stepping through the two-phase commit protocol on behalf of clients. Since the transaction manager is a service, it can be shared among other services and clients in a Jini community.

You've already seen how to run Sun's sample implementation of a transaction manager, called "mahalo," in the last chapter. This implementation, as well as any other alternate implementations that may appear in the future, will implement the `TransactionManager` interface.

I won't present the `TransactionManager` interface here, because it is rarely if ever used directly by clients, but you should know that it exists and that if you are writing new services that participate in transactions you will have to have a greater familiarity with it.

Creating Transactions

Once a client has a reference to a `TransactionManager`, obtained via the usual lookup process, it can create transactions as needed. Clients do not create transactions through the `TransactionManager` directly.[3] Instead, they use the `TransactionFactory` class, which is a part of the `net.jini.core.transaction` package.

3. Clients don't create transactions through the `TransactionManager` directly, even though the manager has a `create()` call. Many of the methods used by the various Jini transaction interfaces look very similar, and it can be difficult to tell when you should use what. This is why I'm neglecting the `Transaction-Manager` API here—to keep the number of superficially similar APIs to a minimum in the interests of cutting down on confusion and focusing on the common tasks that clients will perform.

Let's look at this interface now.

```
package net.jini.core.transaction;

import net.jini.core.lease.LeaseDeniedException;
import java.rmi.RemoteException;

public class TransactionFactory {
    static NestableTransaction.Created
            create(NestableTransactionManager mgr,
                   long leaseTime)
            throws LeaseDeniedException,
                   RemoteException;
    static Transaction.Created
            create(TransactionManager mgr,
                   long leaseTime)
            throws LeaseDeniedException,
                   RemoteException;
}
```

The `TransactionFactory` "fronts" a `TransactionManager`, and provides a more high-level API on top of it. The two static methods here are used to create new transactions, given a Jini `TransactionManager`. You'll notice here that transactions are leased. The `TransactionManager` actually leases transactions to you. If you are executing a transaction that may take a significant time to perform, you will have to handle renewing the leases on the transaction until it is complete.

Leasing governs how long a transaction is left "open" before an attempt is made to commit it. You need to be sure you renew the lease on the transaction at least until you try to commit it. Once a lease has expired on a transaction, you cannot add more participants to it, and you cannot try to commit it. Once you have begun the commit process the transaction manager will continue it even if the lease expires, so you don't have to worry about renewing the leases through the duration of the two-phase commit process. The lease only governs the time you have in which to add participant operations and begin the commit process.

The first version of the `create()` call is used to create transactions that can be "nested" within other transactions. In the Jini model, transactions can be hierarchical. So if you have a computation that depends on the successful completion of some subgroup of operations, you can execute that subgroup in a nested transaction. I'll talk a bit more about nested transactions later in the chapter, but for now let's focus on the second version of the `create()` method.

This method returns an instance of `Created`, a static inner class within the `Transaction` class:

```
public static class Transaction.Created
        implements Serializable {
    public final Lease lease;
    public final Transaction transaction;
    // ... other details elided ...
}
```

This is a simple container class that holds the newly created `Transaction` object, as well as the `Lease` object that can be used to renew or cancel the lease on the transaction.

The Transaction Interface

After a client has successfully found a proxy for a `TransactionManager`, and created a new `Transaction`, most of its operations will be performed through this `Transaction` object. Let's look at the `Transaction` interface.

```
package net.jini.core.transaction;

import java.rmi.RemoteException;

public interface Transaction {
    void abort()
        throws UnknownTransactionException,
            CannotAbortException,
            RemoteException;
    void abort(long waitFor)
        throws UnknownTransactionException,
            CannotAbortException,
            TimeoutExpiredException,
            RemoteException;
    void commit()
        throws UnknownTransactionException,
            CannotCommitException,
            RemoteException;
    void commit(long waitFor)
        throws UnknownTransactionException,
            CannotCommitException,
            TimeoutExpiredException,
            RemoteException;

}
```

The `abort()` method is used to cause a transaction to abort—meaning that the transaction manager essentially cancels the transaction. You can only call `abort()` on a transaction that has not already committed—a committed transaction is considered final and cannot be undone. But if you haven't gone this far, then `abort()` will stop the entire transaction and cause the participants to clean up any state they may have accrued in the process of getting ready to perform the transaction. A call to `abort()` on a transaction that has already committed will raise `CannotAbortException`. This exception will also be raised if the lease on the transaction has expired.

The call will return as soon as the manager records the fact that the transaction is now in the "aborted" state, but before all the participants have been notified of the change. This prevents the client from having to block until all the messages have gone out to the participants.

The `commit()` method is how clients cause the two-phase commit process to begin. Calling `commit()` signals the transaction manager to begin the protocol. If any participant cannot move to the prepare state, or if the lease on the transaction has expired, or if the transaction has already been aborted, then the `CannotCommitException` is raised. At this point, the client can be guaranteed that *none* of the constituent operations have happened.

Otherwise, the method will return as soon as the manager moves into the commit stage. This means that all the participants have moved to the prepare stage, and the manager has recorded the fact that it is *going* to commit, but hasn't necessarily notified all the individual participants. This means that when `commit()` returns, the change is guaranteed to happen, but the effects of it may not have propagated out to all the participants yet. Like the behavior of `abort()`, this behavior keeps clients from having to block as long.

Both `abort()` and `commit()` have versions that take a timeout, expressed as a number of milliseconds. These versions of the calls actually block until all the participants have been notified of the abort or commit operation, or until the timeout elapses. These versions of `abort()` and `commit()` are useful if you want to wait until all the participants in a transaction have a chance to reflect the new data—this method can make stronger guarantees about whether you will see all the results of the abort or commit operation everywhere immediately after you abort or commit. If the timeout elapses before all the participants have been notified, then `TimeoutExpiredException` will be raised. The manager will still continue trying to notify all the participants, but control is returned to you after the timeout.

Core Alert: You can sometimes still see out-of-date data, even with transactions

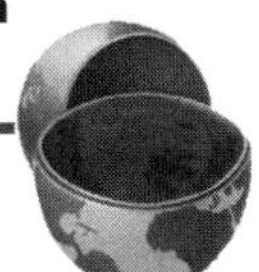

One of the biggest differences with transactions in a distributed setting, as opposed to transactions in a stand-alone setting, is that in certain circumstances, you can still see out-of-date data. This can happen when a client tells the transaction manager to begin the commit process, but not all participant services have yet been notified to move from the prepare to the commit phase. Once the transaction manager has collected all the votes from participants and knows that all participants are ready in the prepare stage, then it knows that at some point, it will be able to complete the transaction. But the process of notifying all the participants may take an arbitrarily long time.

Stand-alone systems don't have this problem since the individual components can typically be notified of the commit phase virtually instantly. But you should be aware that there may be a time window in which you can see temporarily inconsistent results, even when using transactions.

All these calls can raise `UnknownTransactionException` in addition to whatever other exceptions they may raise. This exception is analogous to the `UnknownLeaseException` you saw in Chapter 10—if you hold on to a `Transaction` object long enough that it becomes unknown to the transaction manager, and then try to use it, you'll get an `UnknownTransactionException`. Common reasons for this exception are when you hold on to a previously aborted or committed transaction for which the transaction manager has already cleaned up its bookkeeping records.

Transaction Participants

Each service that exposes "transactable" methods will play the role of a Jini transaction participant. The `TransactionParticipant` interface is used to coordinate communication between the manager and the participant—the manager will invoke the methods defined by the `TransactionParticipant` interface as it moves all the participants through the two-phase commit process.

`TransactionParticipant` is a `java.rmi.Remote` interface, which means that all participants must speak the RMI protocol. The fact that Jini dictates that `TransactionParticipants` use RMI guarantees that the standard transaction manager will have a way to communicate with all participants, without requiring the manager to download proxy objects for the participants.

Even though you should know that the `TransactionParticipant` interface exists and understand the role it plays, I won't go into the details of it here because it's virtually never used by clients. The `TransactionParticipant` interface is *only* used between managers and participants to regulate the two-phase commit process; it has nothing to say about how clients add new operations to transactions.

Instead, and as you've already seen with JavaSpaces, the particulars about how services allow operations to be added to transactions are up to the individual services. In the case of JavaSpaces, operations are added by simply passing a `Transaction` instance to one of the normal JavaSpaces methods. There are no standardized methods supported by all participants to add operations to a transaction.[4]

Using Transactions with JavaSpaces

Let's look at a simple example of using transactions with the one service we have that currently supports them: JavaSpaces. By using transactions with JavaSpaces you can coordinate operations across any number of spaces, transferring objects, updating data sets, and so on, reliably even in the face of partial failures.

Listing 16–1 shows the basics of working with transactions as a client: it securely moves `Entry` objects between two JavaSpaces. Such a program might be useful for transferring datasets from a JavaSpace running on a slow desktop machine to a large compute server, for example.

Here I'm using transactions for the data movement, because it's important that no data be lost. If I were to simply take an `Entry` out of one space without performing the operation under a transaction, my client (or the destination JavaSpace) could crash before the data could be written to its destination. Transactions ensure that each move happens completely or not at all.

---

4. In fact, unless you read the documentation for JavaSpaces, you'd never even know that it can participate in transactions. The proxy for JavaSpaces doesn't itself implement `TransactionParticipant`, so you cannot test it to see if you can use transactions with it. Instead, the class that implements the participant functionality for JavaSpaces is hidden within the implementation of the service. This really isn't a problem, since to do pretty much *anything* to a service requires that you know ahead of time what methods it supports and how to use them.

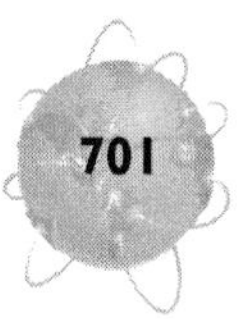

Let's look at the program.

Listing 16–1 `EntryMover.java`

```
// Safely move a set of Entry objects from one JavaSpace
// to another.

package corejini.chapter16;

import net.jini.space.JavaSpace;
import net.jini.core.lookup.ServiceTemplate;
import net.jini.core.lookup.ServiceMatches;
import net.jini.core.lookup.ServiceRegistrar;
import net.jini.core.lookup.ServiceID;
import net.jini.core.entry.Entry;
import net.jini.core.lease.Lease;
import net.jini.core.transaction.Transaction;
import net.jini.core.transaction.TransactionFactory;
import net.jini.core.transaction.CannotCommitException;
import net.jini.core.transaction.UnknownTransactionException;
import net.jini.core.transaction.server.TransactionManager;
import com.sun.jini.lease.LeaseRenewalManager;
import net.jini.discovery.LookupDiscovery;
import net.jini.discovery.DiscoveryListener;
import net.jini.discovery.DiscoveryEvent;
import net.jini.lookup.entry.Name;
import java.util.Vector;
import java.rmi.RemoteException;
import java.rmi.RMISecurityManager;
import java.io.IOException;

public class EntryMover implements Runnable {
    protected Class[] spaceTypes = { JavaSpace.class };
    protected ServiceTemplate spaceTmpl =
        new ServiceTemplate(null, spaceTypes, null);
    protected Class[] txnTypes =
            { TransactionManager.class };
    protected ServiceTemplate txnTmpl =
        new ServiceTemplate(null, txnTypes, null);
    protected Vector regs = new Vector();
    protected LeaseRenewalManager leaseMgr =
        new LeaseRenewalManager();
    protected JavaSpace js1 = null, js2 = null;
    protected TransactionManager txn = null;
    // This is the ID of any already found JavaSpace.
    // We need to keep it to weed out duplicates.
    protected ServiceID id = null;
```

Listing 16–1 `EntryMover.java` **(continued)**

```
    // An inner class for discovery.
    class Discoverer implements DiscoveryListener {
        public void discovered(DiscoveryEvent ev) {
            System.out.println("Discovered!");
            ServiceRegistrar[] newregs = ev.getRegistrars();
            for (int i=0, size=newregs.length; i<size; i++){
                if (!regs.contains(newregs[i])) {
                    regs.addElement(newregs[i]);
                    findServices((ServiceRegistrar)
                                               newregs[i]);
                }
            }
        }
        public void discarded(DiscoveryEvent ev) {
        }
    }

    public EntryMover() throws IOException {
        LookupDiscovery disco = new
            LookupDiscovery(LookupDiscovery.ALL_GROUPS);
        disco.addDiscoveryListener(new Discoverer());
    }

    // Find all the services we'll need, and then call
    // doit()!
    protected void findServices(ServiceRegistrar reg) {
        if (js1 != null && js2 != null && txn != null ) {
            return;
        }

        ServiceMatches matches = null;

        if (js1 == null || js2 == null) {
            System.out.println("Searching for JavaSpace");
            try {
                matches = reg.lookup(spaceTmpl,
                                     Integer.MAX_VALUE);
            } catch (RemoteException ex) {
                System.err.println("Error doing lookup: " +
                                   ex.getMessage());
                return;
            }
```

Listing 16–1 `EntryMover.java` **(continued)**

```
        for (int i=0 ; i<matches.totalMatches ; i++) {
              // If we haven't found a space yet, or if
              // this is a  new space, then use it.
             if (js1 == null) {
                 js1 = (JavaSpace)
                         matches.items[i].service;
                 System.out.println("Found first " +
                                    "JavaSpace!");
                 id = matches.items[i].serviceID;
             } else if (js2 == null &&
                       !id.equals(
                     matches.items[i].serviceID)) {
                 js2 = (JavaSpace)
                         matches.items[i].service;
                 System.out.println("Found second " +
                                    "JavaSpace!");
             }
         }
     }

     if (txn == null) {
       System.out.println("Searching for txn mgr");
       try {
           txn = (TransactionManager)
                               reg.lookup(txnTmpl);
           if (txn != null) {
               System.out.println("Found it!");
           }
       } catch (RemoteException ex) {
           System.err.println("Error: " +
                             ex.getMessage());
           ex.printStackTrace();
       }
     }

     // If we've got two spaces and a transaction
     // manager, then do it!
     if (js1 != null && js2 != null && txn != null)
         doit();
}
```

Listing 16–1 EntryMover.java (continued)

```
    // Load up the first space with some data, and then
    // move it out under transactions.
    protected void doit() {
        System.out.println("Writing to first space");
        for (int i=0 ; i<10 ; i++) {
            Name name = new Name(Integer.toString(i));
            try {
                Lease l = js1.write(name, null, 60 * 1000);
                System.out.println("Wrote: " + name);
                leaseMgr.renewUntil(l, Lease.ANY, null);
            } catch (Exception ex) {
                System.err.println("Trouble writing: " +
                                   ex.getMessage());
                ex.printStackTrace();
            }
        }

        System.out.println("Moving to second space");

        Name nameTmpl = new Name(null);

        Entry e = null;
        boolean done = false;
        int idx=0;
        Vector uncommits = new Vector();

        while (!done) {
            try {
                Transaction.Created c =
                    TransactionFactory.create(txn,
                                              10 * 60 * 1000);

                // Manage the lease on the transaction,
                // just in case.
                leaseMgr.renewUntil(c.lease, Lease.ANY,
                                    null);

                // Take under a transaction
                e = js1.takeIfExists(nameTmpl,
                                     c.transaction,
                                     JavaSpace.NO_WAIT);

                if (e == null) {
                    done = true;
                    continue;
                }
```

Listing 16–1 `EntryMover.java` **(continued)**

```
        // Write under the same transaction
        System.out.println("Moving: " + e);
        Lease l = js2.write(e, c.transaction,
                                   60 * 1000);
        leaseMgr.renewUntil(l, Lease.ANY, null);


         // Commit!
         if (idx++ % 2 == 0) {
            System.out.println("Committing!");
            c.transaction.commit();
         } else {
            uncommits.addElement(c.transaction);
         }
    } catch (RemoteException ex) {
       System.err.println("Trouble communicating:"
                              + ex.getMessage());
    } catch (CannotCommitException ex) {
        System.err.println("Couldn't commit: " +
                           ex.getMessage());
    } catch (UnknownTransactionException ex) {
       System.err.println("Unknown transaction: " +
                           ex.getMessage());
    } catch (Exception ex) {
        System.err.println("Other problem: " +
                           ex.getMessage());
    }
}

// Dump out the contents of the spaces, then
// commit the remaining transactions, then
// dump again.

System.out.println("Contents of space 1: ");
dumpContents(js1);

System.out.println("Contents of space 2: ");
dumpContents(js2);
```

Listing 16–1 `EntryMover.java` **(continued)**

```
        System.out.println("Committing remaining " +
                                "transactions.");
        for (int i=0, size=uncommits.size() ; i<size ;
                                                i++) {
            Transaction t = (Transaction)
                uncommits.elementAt(i);
            try {
                t.commit();
            } catch (RemoteException ex) {
                System.err.println("Trouble communicating:"
                                + ex.getMessage());
            } catch (CannotCommitException ex) {
                System.err.println("Couldn't commit: " +
                            ex.getMessage());
            } catch (UnknownTransactionException ex) {
               System.err.println("Unknown transaction: " +
                            ex.getMessage());
            }
        }

        System.out.println("Contents of space 1: ");
        dumpContents(js1);

        System.out.println("Contents of space 2: ");
        dumpContents(js2);
    }

    protected void dumpContents(JavaSpace js) {
        try {
            Name nameTmpl = new Name(null);

            Entry e = null;
            while ((e = js.takeIfExists(nameTmpl, null,
                                JavaSpace.NO_WAIT))
                                        != null) {
                System.out.println("Removing: " + e);
            }
        } catch (Exception ex) {
            System.err.println(ex.getMessage());
            ex.printStackTrace();
        }
    }
```

Listing 16–1 `EntryMover.java` (continued)

```
    public void run() {
        while (true) {
            try {
                Thread.sleep(Integer.MAX_VALUE);
            } catch (InterruptedException ex) {
            }
        }
    }

    public static void main(String[] args) {
        try {
            if (System.getSecurityManager() == null) {
                System.setSecurityManager(
                             new RMISecurityManager());
            }
            EntryMover mover = new EntryMover();
            new Thread(mover).start();
        } catch (Exception ex) {
           System.err.println("Error: " + ex.getMessage());
            ex.printStackTrace();
        }
    }
}
```

This program uses discovery to find lookup services, and then searches those lookup services until it finds the other services it needs to do its job. The program requires two separate JavaSpaces and a transaction manager service to work. The `findServices()` method is called each time a new lookup service is found until the necessary complement of services has been located. Once everything is in order, the program calls `doit()` to exercise the Jini transaction manager.

The interesting part of this program is in the `doit()` method, so let's look at it. The method first writes a set of `Name` entries into the first JavaSpace. This is so that it will have some data to later extract. The program writes ten entries, each of which has a distinct name so that we can see later which have been successfully moved. Note that the writes are *not* done under a transaction, since they do not depend on the success or failure of any other operations.

After this, the program sits in a loop, moving `Name` objects as it finds them. For each iteration, the program creates a new `Transaction` by calling out to the `TransactionFactory`. That is, for each move a separate transaction is created under which the move will be performed (remember, a single move is the *combination* of a take and a write). Thus, although the client retrieves a single transaction *manager*, it creates many transactions to be processed by that manager on behalf of the client. The program asks for a 10-minute lease, and passes the lease off to a `LeaseRenewalManager` just in case the transaction takes longer to execute than expected.

The heart of the move code is two JavaSpaces operations that happen under the same transaction. First, `takeIfExists()` is called on the first space to remove an entry, and then `write()` is called on the second space to copy it to there, completing the move. This pair of operations happens under the same transaction to ensure that either they both happen (and the entry is moved) or neither happened (and the entry stays where it is); this way, no entries are lost. Because the move happens under a transaction, the move is not *actually* completed until the transaction under which it operates commits.

Just to make things a little more exciting, only half of the transactions are committed immediately. The uncommitted transactions are kept on a list so that they can be committed later.

After the loop completes—because there are no more entries to be moved—the code prints out the contents of the two spaces, commits the remaining transactions, and then prints the contents of the two spaces again.

Let's build and run the program to see what it does.

Compiling and Running the EntryMover

On Windows:

```
javac -classpath C:\jini1_0\lib\jini-core.jar;
                 C:\jini1_0\lib\jini-ext.jar;
                 C:\jini1_0\lib\sun-util.jar;
                 C:\client
          -d C:\client
          C:\files\corejini\chapter16\EntryMover.java
```

On Solaris:

```
javac -classpath
              /files/jini1_0/lib/jini-core.jar:
              /files/jini1_0/lib/jini-ext.jar:
              /files/jini1_0/lib/sun-util.jar:
              /files/client
          -d /files/client
          /files/corejini/chapter16/EntryMover.java
```

Now you're set to run it. Before you start, make sure that you've got a transaction manager and *two* separate JavaSpaces running! If you have a lookup service browser running, you can check to see if these necessary services are available on your network. Be sure that you distinguish between a single JavaSpaces service that might be registered on several lookup services, and two separate instances of the JavaSpaces service—you'll actually need two separate JavaSpaces instances running here. Refer back to the instructions in Chapter 15 for details on running these.

On Windows:

```
java -cp C:\jini1_0\lib\jini-core.jar;
         C:\jini1_0\lib\jini-ext.jar;
         C:\jini1_0\lib\sun-util.jar;
         C:\client
      -Djava.security.policy=C:\policy
      corejini.chapter16.EntryMover
```

On Solaris:

```
java -cp /files/jini1_0/lib/jini-core.jar:
         /files/jini1_0/lib/jini-ext.jar:
         /files/jini1_0/lib/sun-util.jar:
         /files/client
      -Djava.security.policy=/files/policy
      corejini.chapter16.EntryMover
```

Let's look at the output of the `EntryMover` program. First, you should see the program searching for and finding the pair of JavaSpaces and the transaction manager.

Searching for JavaSpace
Found first JavaSpace!
Searching for txn mgr
Found it!
Searching for JavaSpace
Found second JavaSpace!

After this, the `EntryMover` will set up some data for it to move. It will write 10 `Name` entries into the first space:

Writing to first space
Wrote: net.jini.lookup.entry.Name(name=0)
Wrote: net.jini.lookup.entry.Name(name=1)
Wrote: net.jini.lookup.entry.Name(name=2)

Wrote: net.jini.lookup.entry.Name(name=3)
Wrote: net.jini.lookup.entry.Name(name=4)
Wrote: net.jini.lookup.entry.Name(name=5)
Wrote: net.jini.lookup.entry.Name(name=6)
Wrote: net.jini.lookup.entry.Name(name=7)
Wrote: net.jini.lookup.entry.Name(name=8)
Wrote: net.jini.lookup.entry.Name(name=9)

Now here comes the interesting part! The program will begin moving data from the first space to the second. Each move consists of two operations—a `takeIfExists()` and a `write()`—which are grouped together under a transaction. The even numbered moves will be committed immediately, while the others will be deferred. We'll see the results of all this in just a bit.

Moving to second space
Moving: net.jini.lookup.entry.Name(name=0)
Committing...
Moving: net.jini.lookup.entry.Name(name=1)
Moving: net.jini.lookup.entry.Name(name=2)
Committing...
Moving: net.jini.lookup.entry.Name(name=3)
Moving: net.jini.lookup.entry.Name(name=4)
Committing...
Moving: net.jini.lookup.entry.Name(name=5)
Moving: net.jini.lookup.entry.Name(name=6)
Committing...
Moving: net.jini.lookup.entry.Name(name=7)
Moving: net.jini.lookup.entry.Name(name=8)
Committing...
Moving: net.jini.lookup.entry.Name(name=9)

Finally, let's look at the results of these moves. The `dumpContents()` method is a destructive way to print out the contents of a JavaSpace. That is, it works by actually taking items out of the space and displaying them. Remember that only the even numbered transactions were committed—the odd transactions are still pending, and so we shouldn't see the effects of them here:

Contents of space 1:
Contents of space 2:
Removing: net.jini.lookup.entry.Name(name=0)

Removing: net.jini.lookup.entry.Name(name=2)
Removing: net.jini.lookup.entry.Name(name=4)
Removing: net.jini.lookup.entry.Name(name=6)
Removing: net.jini.lookup.entry.Name(name=8)

Sure enough, the first space is empty and the second space shows all the entries put there from the committed transactions only. Now the program will commit the remaining transactions, and we'll see what the results are.

Committing remaining transactions.
Contents of space 1:
Contents of space 2:
Removing: net.jini.lookup.entry.Name(name=1)
Removing: net.jini.lookup.entry.Name(name=3)
Removing: net.jini.lookup.entry.Name(name=5)
Removing: net.jini.lookup.entry.Name(name=7)
Removing: net.jini.lookup.entry.Name(name=9)

Remember that the `dumpContents()` method removes the items it displays. So all the even numbered entries from the first part of example have now been removed. But here you see that the data from the newly committed transactions have appeared in the second space!

Here, transactions have given us exactly what we want: They provide a way to ensure consistency in the data by grouping operations together. So far, you've seen how to build applications that are simple transaction clients. In the next section, we'll look at some of the more subtle aspects of transactions.

Other Transaction Issues and Idioms

This section highlights some of the subtle points of dealing with transactions, as well as some not-so-subtle, but seldom-used aspects of the programming model.

Transactions and Visibility

Earlier in this chapter when I said that operations grouped into a transaction don't actually take place until the transaction is committed, I told a white lie.

The more accurate truth is that the operations *do* happen; they're just not visible "outside" the transaction.

Let's look at what this means in terms of the example program you've just seen. In that program, a series of move operations were done under transactions, but only half of the transactions were immediately committed. When the `dumpContents()` method was called, it only showed the data that had been moved by committed transactions. This might lead you to believe that the JavaSpaces involved in the transactions simply queued up the `takeIfExists()` and `write()` calls until the word came down from the transaction manager to invoke them. But in fact, this is not what happens.

What actually happens is that the `takeIfExists()` and `write()` operations *do* take place immediately. But their effects are constrained so that they can only be detected by operations that are members of the same transaction!

So the reason `dumpContents()` didn't see the uncommitted moves *wasn't* because the spaces hadn't done anything yet. It was because `dumpContents()` itself made calls to `takeIfExists()` to fetch entries for display, and *that* call wasn't a member of the transaction that did the move. In the `EntryMover` example, you can go back and change the code so that `dumpContents()` uses one of the uncommitted transactions for its call to `takeIfExists()` and it will suddenly be able to see the results of all the operations in this uncommitted transaction.

The very logical reason for this is that the operations grouped together in a transaction are meant to be logically related. So it makes sense for them to all "see" the effects of one another. So in the `EntryMover` example the `write()` clearly needs to be able to use the entry returned by `takeIfExists()` if it is to work properly.

This is a general fact of life in the transactions world that you should be aware of. What actually happens when you use transactions is more complex than simply queueing up operations until all participants are ready to go. Transactions have implications for the visibility of the effects of operations.

You can even use these terms to describe what happens when you don't pass *any* transaction to one of the JavaSpaces methods. What effectively happens is that you get a "transient" transaction that only contains one member operation and commits immediately. So the effects of any of these operations with a null transaction argument is immediately visible to all parties.

Nesting Transactions

If you have very complex sets of operations that you need to group together into transactions, you may think about decomposing the problem down into constituent parts which are themselves composed of many operations. To support situations like this, Jini allows *nested transactions*. Nested transactions are transactions in which member operations are themselves transactions.

The semantics work just the same as in "normal" transactions—for the transaction to succeed, all of its constituent members must succeed. So if one of the members is itself a transaction, all of *its* member operations must succeed.

Nested transactions follow the usual transaction visibility rules—the effects of members of a transaction are only visible to other members of the transaction. The effects of operations in a parent transaction are visible to operations in its subtransactions. The effects of subtransactions are only visible in the parent when the subtransaction commits. (This is analogous to what happens with individual operations in a transaction—the effects of that operation are visible, even within the transaction, only when it is performed. The commit of a subtransaction is analogous to performing a primitive operation.)

You've already seen, in the interface for `TransactionFactory`, a method for creating "nestable" transactions—meaning transactions that can be nested within other transactions. This method returns a `NestableTransaction.Created` container that holds a `NestableTransaction` and its lease. And the method takes as an argument a `NestableTransactionManager`, which is a subinterface of the regular `TransactionManager`.

Core Note: Mahalo doesn't support nested transactions

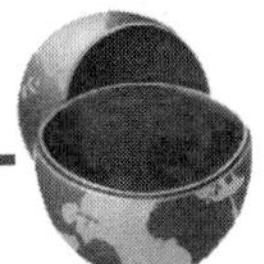

Even though the Jini specifications have quite a bit to say about nested transactions, and the semantics of nested transactions are clearly defined, Sun's implementation of `mahalo`*—its transaction manager—does not support nested transactions. So be careful about creating applications that may require nested transaction functionality. While this functionality is certainly coming, it's not available at the time of this writing.*

Events and Sequence Numbers

If you looked carefully at the interface for the JavaSpaces service, you may have noticed that not only do the expected calls like `read()`, `write()`, and `take()` allow a transaction parameter, but so does `notify()`. You may have been curious about why an event registration was allowed to happen inside a transaction, and even what it means for an event registration to happen inside a transaction!

Basically, you can register to receive events within a transaction. This means that you will be able to see any events that arise from changes caused by other member operations in the transaction: This much is probably what you expected. In a nutshell, you will receive events caused by other operations in your transaction, even though these same operations will be invisible eventwise (just as they are invisible resultwise) to anyone outside the transaction, until the transaction commits. Once the transaction commits, then any listeners outside the transaction will receive events about any changes, just as they normally would.

But being able to ask for events from within a transaction context has implications for how event sequence numbers and types work and how event registration leases are used.

First, an event generator that allows event registrations to happen under transactions *must* use a different event type ID for events that are delivered inside transactions versus those delivered outside, even if those events are of the same logical "type." So, for instance, if a printer service generates out-of-paper events that generally have the same type ID regardless of their destination, that service would have to use a *different* ID for out-of-paper events sent to recipients that registered for events under a transaction.

This requirement is so that third-party event delegates won't blindly forward events to recipients that should only be visible to parties that are members of a certain transaction. Recall that such delegates rely on the event type ID to know how to route the event to downstream listeners. By using a separate type ID, recipients outside the transaction won't receive the events, and recipients inside the transaction can simply tell the delegate to deliver within-transaction events to them. (Of course, if your service doesn't support event registrations within a transaction, you don't have to worry about any of this.)

A second implication has to do with how sequence numbers are generated for events delivered within a transaction scope. Events sent because of an

occurrence visible only inside a transaction will have a different sequence number than events sent because of the *same* occurrence if it happens outside the transaction, or when the transaction commits. This is because operations that occur within a transaction, even event deliveries, must be isolated from operations that occur outside a transaction.

Finally, the duration of an event registration that occurs within a transaction is bounded by the duration of the transaction. So even if you ask for a long event registration lease, if the transaction completes (either by committing or aborting), the lease on the event registration will be terminated, even if it hasn't yet expired.

Using Transactions to Hide Data

An interesting twist on the transaction visibility rules can be applied in situations where you need it. The fact that operations that are within a transaction are only visible to other operations within the transaction is not just useful for ensuring that uncommitted data keeps from "polluting" other operations. It can also be used as a nifty way to hide data. By grouping operations into a transaction, you can prevent any other programs from messing with your data, whether intentionally or unintentionally.

Let's look at the `EntryMover` as an example. This is actually a pretty ill-behaved program. It writes a few `Name` entries into a space, and then copies out *all* of the `Name` entries in that space! If some other applications had a brisk trade in `Name` entries going, we've just scuttled them!

While using transactions as an impromptu information hiding strategy isn't an approach based in "real" systems security principles, it can be useful in a number of scenarios. One of the scenarios in which it's most useful is when you want to protect yourself from the inadvertent—rather than the determined and malicious—stray program.

You may be wondering how this works. At some point, if you're working with transactions you'll either have to commit your changes (making them visible to others), or abort the changes (in which case they simply "won't exist"). How can you get any benefit out of this?

The answer is to use operations within a transaction that can return results to a calling program. Let's look at how to do this in JavaSpaces. Say you wish to use JavaSpaces to privately exchange some data with another program. You create a transaction, and then write new objects into the space. You then send the transaction object to the receiver. Essentially this transaction acts like a "key" which allows the receiver access to the data. The key can be exchanged with another client using some means you devise yourself, and which both you and the other client agree upon. Some ways might include sending it over a socket, or through an RMI call, or even putting it in a JavaSpace, wrapped in an `Entry`!

The receiver then performs take operations on the space, using the key. Once all the data has been fetched, the receiver can simply abort the transaction, and the space will clean up all the tentative entries, as if they had never existed. Of course, the receiver will already have the objects in its hands, returned from the take operations.

Again, using transactions for data hiding shouldn't be thought of as a robust approach to system security. But it can help guard against damage done by clumsy programs.

Summary

This chapter has provided an overview of the fundamentals of Jini's distributed transaction model, with a particular focus on the view of transactions from the client. We've looked at how transactions can be used to guard against partial failures, and at Jini's unique transaction model, which separates the two-phase commit protocol from the semantics of transactions.

The example in this chapter has illustrated how to use transactions as a JavaSpaces client, which for the near future will be the most common use of transactions (at least until other transactable services appear). And you've seen some of the deeper implications of using transactions, such as how transactions affect remote event delivery. Using the techniques described here, you should be ready to interact with any number of transaction-supporting services, as they appear on the market.

Part 3

APPENDICES

Appendix A

AN RMI PRIMER

This appendix presents a quick-and-dirty primer to the Java Remote Method Invocation (RMI) technology. RMI has been in Java since the days of JDK1.1, but has been significantly enhanced and expanded for the Java 2 release. Jini takes advantage of classes and features that exist only in the Java 2 version of RMI.

This appendix covers the basics of RMI as it exists in Java 2. We'll talk about how to design, compile, and build RMI programs, how to use serialization, how class loading works in RMI, security implications, and how to use the RMI activation framework. This appendix isn't meant to provide full, in-depth coverage of this technology—that could easily be a book in itself! Rather, it's meant to provide enough information about the basics to get you up and running quickly.

Overview of RMI

RMI provides a way for Java applications running in different Java Virtual Machines (JVMs), possibly even on different host computers, to talk to one another. In this sense, RMI is very much like Remote Procedure Call (RPC) systems that you may be used to: RMI allows a Java program on one machine to call out to a Java method defined by an object that exists on another machine.

But, as we'll see, RMI has some properties that make it unique, and really distinguish it from remote procedure call systems, or even other distributed object systems.

Remote Interfaces

An object that will expose methods that can be invoked by objects on other machines is called a *remote* object. In client/server terminology, this object is the *server*, and the object that invokes methods on it is the *client*. But while it may help you to think of clients and servers for purposes of understanding how a pair of objects interact, RMI doesn't impose any other restrictions on the communication patterns of clients and servers. A server may itself be a client of another object, and a single Java program can—and often will—contain both client and server objects. So it isn't really fair to call RMI a client/server system; it's much more rich than that. But for purposes of clarity, I'll use the term "client" to refer to an object that is invoking methods on a remote object, and use the term "server" to refer to the remote object that is allowing its methods to be called remotely.

Before a client can call a method on an object—remote or not—the client must know the interface that the object implements. For example, if someone hands you a plain `java.lang.Object`, you only know how to do a few things to it: call `equals()`, `toString()`, and the other methods that are defined by this class. And even though the object may be a more specific type, such as a `Vector` or a `JPanel`, unless you know more specific information about the type of the object, you cannot use it.

The same is true in RMI, just as it's true in "plain" Java. For a client to invoke a method on a server, it must know what methods the server makes available to it. This set of APIs is called the server's *remote interface*, and it defines the set of methods that can be invoked from outside the server's JVM. Of course, any given server object may also have any number of "local" methods that can only be called by objects that live in the server's JVM.

In RMI, the remote interface of a server is simply a Java interface that extends the `java.rmi.Remote` interface. By extending `Remote`, you're in effect telling RMI that it should create the necessary machinery to allow any methods in your interface to be called remotely. A particular server object that you write, then, is simply an implementation of this remote interface.

Stubs and Skeletons

The Java Virtual Machine only knows how to perform local method invocations: When you write a program that invokes a method on an object, this machinery gets executed to run the method. So then how do remote invocations work? The answer is that a bit of extra machinery is needed; in the case of RMI, this machinery is implemented in Java code layered atop the JVM, and is not part of the JVM itself.

The first extra bit of functionality RMI requires is a way for the server that implements the remote interface to be able to accept network connections from clients, take data read from those connections, and "turn them into" Java method invocations locally. Second, when a client makes an invocation on a remote object, it must actually make a local invocation on some local object that serves as a representation for the remote object. (It must always directly invoke a local object, because this is all the JVM knows how to do.) This local object then takes care of connecting to the server and sending it data to cause the invocation to happen. Once the invocation has finished, any return data must be sent back to the client and reconstituted.

On the server side, this extra functionality is handled by two different classes. First, to handle the network communication, the server object typically will extend a class that knows how to take care of the networking chores involved in RMI. Most of the time, servers will extend a class called `jini.rmi.server.UnicastRemoteObject`. This class has all the necessary "smarts" to take care of the low-level networking details that must be done to send messages to the server.

But `UnicastRemoteObject` is just a "generic" class that can be extended to provide networking support for all kinds of remote server objects. How do the *specific* methods on a *particular* server object get called? The answer is that a second object, called a *skeleton*, handles taking the data received from the network, figuring out which operation to invoke on the server, and returning the results. The skeleton is paired with a particular server object, because it has to understand what methods are available on a server, and what arguments and return values they have. You can think of a skeleton as providing an "insulation layer" between the server object, which is written pretty much as a normal "local" Java object, and the network.

On the client side the situation is similar, but a little simpler. The object *making* a remote call doesn't have to do anything special to "export" itself, or make itself callable from other JVMs. All the client-side machinery has to do is map from local object invocations on the object that represents the server to actual network communication. In RMI, the local object that lives

inside the client and handles the chores of packing and unpacking the data and managing the network connection to a server is called a *stub*. Whenever a client "invokes" a method on a remote object, it is actually invoking a method on a local stub object—because this is all the JVM can do inherently. This stub then sends a message to the remote JVM, where it is received, and "translated" by the server-side skeleton into a local method call. Figure A–1 shows how this happens.

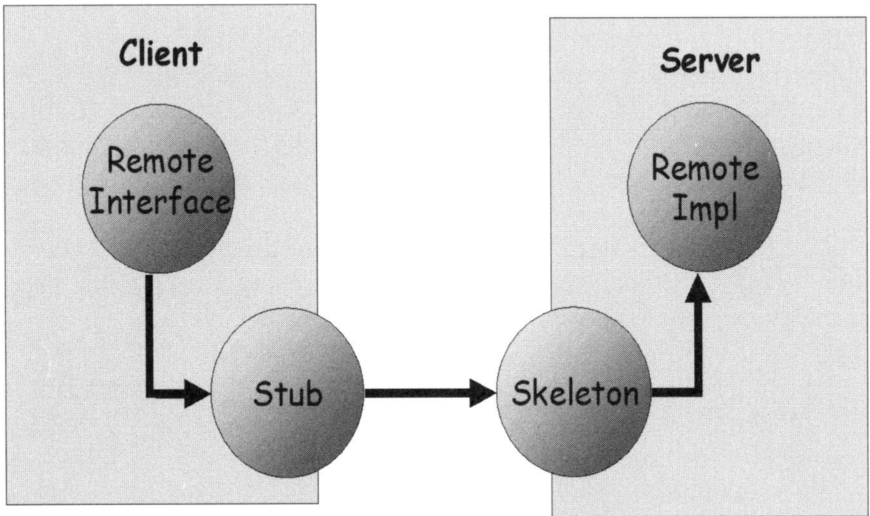

Figure A–1 Clients and servers communicate through stubs and skeletons

All this may seem like a lot of work, and in fact, RMI is doing quite a bit "under the covers" to make all this remote communication happen. But the good thing is that for the most part *all* this machinery is hidden from both clients and servers.[1] Servers virtually never see their skeletons—even though a skeleton is what actually invokes the remote methods on a server, the server can "believe" that clients are invoking them directly.

Clients actually "see" the stubs for a remote server, but in general, think of the stubs as just being the remote object itself. In RMI, the stub for a server object implements the *exact same* remote interface as the server itself: It has the same methods, raises the same exceptions, and has the same parameters and return types. Stubs even implement the `Remote` interface, so they look

1. And, as we'll see shortly, you don't even have to write the stubs and skeletons yourself. RMI will create them for you.

like any other remote object. So for all intents and purposes, when you're writing a client, you write your code in terms of the remote interface you're calling out to. You never have to know that it's actually the stub that you're talking to, and not the remote object directly.

Serialization

I said in the preceding section that the stubs and skeletons take care of the networking details, such as packing and unpacking arguments and return values to and from remote calls. So if I have a remote method that takes some input parameters and returns a result, the stubs and skeletons take care of turning these parameters and return values into streams of bytes that can be sent over a network and reconstituted at the other end.

The mechanism for turning an object into streams of bytes and then reconstituting them is called *serialization*, and is a necessary part of RMI, as well as an important part of many other applications.

In the Java language, any object that implements the `java.io.Serializable` interface can be turned into a stream of bytes and then later reconstituted. The `Serializable` interface actually adds no methods that you have to implement; it's merely a "tagging" interface that you use as an indication to Java that you're allowing a given class to be serialized.[2]

Without serialization, RMI would have no way to send complex Java objects across the wire—either as arguments to a method invocation or as return values. Any type that you use as a parameter or return value to or from a remote method invocation *must* be serializable. Primitive types such as `int`, `boolean`, and so on are considered to be serializable, so you can also send or return these in any RMI call.

There are a few other requirements that your classes must meet if they are to be serializable. Even though your class may implement the `Serializable` interface, there are things it can do that prevent it from being serialized. Even worse, these problems cannot be detected at compile time, and so you discover them when you get a `java.io.NotSerializableException` at run time.

2. While you don't have to implement any methods to be serializable, you *can* implement certain methods to override the default serialization behavior. A full discussion of how to do this is outside the scope of this appendix, but look at the documentation for the `Serializable` class for details on how to do this, if you're interested.

The first thing your class must do is ensure that it has a public, no-argument constructor. The presence of this constructor is required for the class to be properly deserialized. Second, you must make sure that your class contains no references to objects that are themselves not serializable. This is why Java cannot fully determine whether your classes are serializable at compile time: You may have an object that would otherwise be serializable, but contains a `Vector` of both serializable and nonserializable objects. If a member of an object cannot be serialized, then the object itself cannot be serialized.

Serialization is deceptively simple. While in most cases, developers can simply tag an object as `Serializable` and then forget about it, there are cases when you may need to take more care with serialization. See the Further Reading section at the end of the appendix for some pointers to more information on serialization.

Parameters and Return Values

With the overview of serialization and stubs complete, let's look at exactly how parameter passing works in RMI. First, lets look at the simple case—what happens when you pass a reference to a nonremote object as an argument to an RMI method call.

Any parameter or return value that you use in an RMI call must be serializable. RMI will transparently serialize the objects or primitive types you pass or return in remote methods. The fact that RMI serializes the data it sends has some important implications. Unlike local method calls, which pass references to objects, RMI copies the arguments and return values of remote method calls. So the semantics of input and output objects are "pass by value" rather than "pass by reference."

The treatment of remote objects as parameters or return values is a bit different. Let's look next at what happens when you pass a remote object into a remote method as an argument, or return it from a remote method as a result.

RMI works some more "under the covers" magic when it comes to using references to remote objects. Say in the implementation of your server, one of your remote methods returns a reference to `this`. In your server, `this` refers to the actual server implementation object that lives in the server's VM. But remember that clients always deal with stubs as a way to represent the server; they have no way to *directly* refer to any object in another VM, so they have to use the stub as a proxy for a remote object. So what we would like to have happen when the server returns a reference to itself is that the client should receive a reference to the server's stub.

To make this happen, remote methods look for input and output parameters that are references to objects that implement `Remote`. Whenever one of these is seen, it is silently replaced with the corresponding stub as appropriate. So if a server returns a reference to itself as the result of a method, RMI "converts" this to a stub so that the client can use it.

This transparent argument swapping ensures the "invisibility" of stubs in both services and clients. Again, both services and clients have the illusion that they're working with local objects, because even things like the `this` reference work and can be exchanged between JVMs.

The effect of this strategy is that remote objects maintain the "pass by reference" semantics or "normal" Java. When you pass a remote object in or out of a method call, what you actually get is a "live" reference to that remote object that can be used by either the client or the server. Passing a remote object doesn't copy the entire object; rather, it just copies the stub, which can be thought of as a reference to a remote object. (And stubs are, in fact, serializable, which means that they are actually passed in remote methods just as nonremote serializable objects are.)

Dynamic Code Loading

Simply saying that all parameter and return types must be serializable glosses over a problem that we haven't addressed yet. Serialization only packages up the member data within an object; it doesn't package up the code that implements the object. So if you send a serialized object to someone else, how can they use it if they don't get the code?

This single question—What to do with objects that you may receive that you don't have the code for—leads to one of the biggest differences between RMI and "traditional" remote procedure call or distributed object systems. RMI allows a JVM to dynamically download the *implementation* of a class as needed, not just the data contained in a particular object.

Let's look at what this means in practice. Say you've defined a remote interface that can sort collections of data. This interface might have a method called `sort()` that is defined to take a `java.util.Set` (this interface is a part of the Java 2 "collections framework;" it's essentially an interface that describes the things you can do to a set of data). This method might be defined to return an object that implements the `java.util.SortedSet` interface.

The Java collections framework defines an implementation of `Set` called `HashSet`. As you might expect, this implementation uses a hashtable internally, and has certain performance characteristics based on this implementation. Likewise, the collections framework comes with an implementation of `SortedSet` called `TreeSet` that uses a tree data structure internally.

All is fine here, because the server supports a simple method that takes and returns common, known types. But what happens if a client writer decides that he or she needs to use a new, custom implementation of `Set` internally, maybe called `FastSet`? Perhaps this set uses some exotic data structure for performance or space reasons. The `sort()` method is defined to simply take objects that implement `Set`. In the local case, we know we could pass the new `FastSet` and everything would work, because `sort()` only cares that its inputs speak the `Set` interface. This is an example of *polymorphism* in an object-oriented language: As long as you know what interface you want to speak, you don't *care* how that interface is implemented.

But this situation presents a problem in the remote case. In the remote case, the server has never even *heard* of `FastSet`, and it certainly doesn't have the implementation of it available. What we would like to have happen is for the implementation of `FastSet` to be sent to the server, which would allow the server to work on the new `FastSet` and return its results, just like it would in the local case.

It turns out this is exactly what RMI does, and this technique is the source of much of its power. Unlike traditional distributed "object" systems, where a remote object may lose the ability to have unknown subclasses passed into it, RMI allows true "remote polymorphism," where objects work as parameters and returns to and from remote methods just like they would in local methods.

Let's see how this would work in practice. Normally, a Java application finds the implementations of all the classes it needs by looking in its *classpath*—a set of directories and JAR files that contain necessary class files. RMI extends this basic notion with the concept of a *codebase*. You can think of the codebase as a new location for classfiles that is provided dynamically to a Java program so that it can access some new class implementations it didn't previously have access to.

In RMI, any program that will *export* classes that may need to be downloadable by others must set a codebase that indicates where the implementations of these classes come from. The codebase isn't used to tell the exporting program where to get the classes from. Rather, the codebase is sent to the downloading program, tagged on to the serialization of the object's data. Once the receiver gets the serialized object it can reconstitute it and, if it

doesn't have the class available locally, download it from the location indicated in the codebase.

Essentially the codebase is a way for one program to extend another's classpath at run time, for particular classes. And whereas the classpath typically contains only path names, the codebase will contain URLs that indicate from where the classes can be downloaded.

A misunderstanding of how codebases work is one of the most common problems faced by beginning RMI programmers. The RMI protocol itself doesn't handle transmitting class implementations around the network. Instead, RMI uses an external facility—the ability of Java programs to copy bytecodes from URLs and securely execute them—to provide downloadable code. RMI only supports the mechanisms for "annotating" serialized data streams with the codebase that says where to get the bytecodes that implement the serialized class.

In the most common scenario, downloadable code will be placed in a directory served by an HTTP server. Any program that exports downloadable code will then set a codebase that contains an `http` URL that indicates the location of the classes on that server. Codebases are set via properties to the server object's JVM, passed on the command line.

Most new RMI developers commonly think of using downloadable code to support "custom" implementations of types used as parameter or return values in remote method calls. But RMI actually uses dynamic code loading to transmit the stubs for a remote object to a client. This way, the client *only* has to know about the remote interface that the server object implements. The actual stubs that facilitate communication with the server are provided by the server itself. This allows the server to do things such as use custom stubs, or stubs that use custom network protocols, if it chooses. So even the most simple RMI programs will need to support downloadable code, to move stubs around if for no other reason.

Security Implications

Clearly there are security implications to being able to download code from another application on the fly. The situation is much like an applet: You're running code that you got from someone else, and you hope that it's not malicious. But just like applets, which provide a restricted environment for downloaded code, RMI can provide a secure environment for running the code that you get from other programs.

In Java, application security is provided by having a `SecurityManager` installed in the run time environment. To prevent malicious downloaded code from doing harm, RMI will not remotely load *any* code if there is no `SecurityManager` active in the downloading program—instead, the program must be able to find all necessary classes, including stubs, on the local classpath.

While this situation may be workable for debugging, it's not appropriate for a production environment. To enable downloadable code, you must run with a security manager set. RMI provides a simple security manager, called the `java.rmi.RMISecurityManager`, which can be used. In Java 2, security managers typically are configurable by a *security policy*, which is a file passed on the command line to a Java program. A security policy can define certain "permissions" for the code in an application, based on where the code comes from. So, for instance, you can express notions like, "All code signed by Dave can write to this particular directory, and connect to this particular host on the Internet," or, "any code downloaded from this site has no filesystem access."

While a full discussion of Java 2 security is outside the scope of this book, you can check the Further Reading section at the end of this appendix for some pointers to good material to get you started. But the basics of what you need to know about security and RMI is that if you use a security manager, which you *must* do if you want to use downloadable code, then you *must* set a security policy that tells that security manager what sorts of operations are allowable.

When a security manager is in effect, it controls the behavior of not only downloaded code, but local code as well. By default, almost nothing is allowed, so you'll need a policy file that at least allows your program to access the URLs for remote code.

Chapter 5 of this book presents a "promiscuous" policy file that allows any sort of accesses. This policy is used in all of the examples in the book, because it makes testing and experimentation easier. But for deployment, you should craft a more careful policy file that restricts access more appropriately.

Marshalled Objects

One other handy item in your bag of tricks as an RMI programmer is the `MarshalledObject` class. This class, introduced in Java 2, provides a way to represent the serialized form of an object. In general, when you serialize an object, you can write it to a byte array, to a file, or to any other stream of content. The `MarshalledObject` class provides another "container" for the bytes that make up a serialized object.

MarshalledObjects are created by passing an object to them in the constructor; this object is serialized and stored within the MarshalledObject, and can be later retrieved by using the get() method on MarshalledObject.

So why would you ever want to use an object to represent a serialized object? Isn't the whole point of serialization to turn the object into something that's not objectlike for transmission or storage?

The answer is that, very often, a program will need to hold on to the serialized representation of an object without immediately reconstituting it. The MarshalledObject class provides a convenient and standard way to do this.

Suppose, for instance, that you're writing a storage service for objects. Clients may pass in objects that implement Serializable for storage by the service. Now, in many cases, the storage service will have no need to reconstitute the objects that are sent to it for safekeeping: The storage service never *looks at* or *uses* the objects, it just holds on to them. If clients pass Serializable objects to the storage service through RMI, then those objects will be automatically reconstituted when they arrive at the storage service, which can be an expensive operation, and is simply not useful for this particular application.

In such a case, the storage service could define its interfaces so that it takes MarshalledObjects as values to store. MarshalledObjects are themselves Serializable, so they can be transmitted over the wire to the service. But when they are reconstituted, they become simply MarshalledObjects, not whatever arbitrarily complex application-defined class is stored within the MarshalledObject.

So using MarshalledObject is a good way to transmit and represent objects that shouldn't be automatically reconstituted. But this class provides another handy feature—storing and fetching objects out of a MarshalledObject uses RMI-style serialization semantics. So when you store an object in a MarshalledObject, it is stored with codebase information that indicates where the implementation of the object can be found. Retrieving an object out of a MarshalledObject instance uses this location information to dynamically load the class, if necessary. Also like RMI, when you store a remote object in a MarshalledObject, the remote object is silently replaced with its stub.

This feature of MarshalledObjects makes them useful as a self-contained representation of everything a client or service might need to know to reconstitute and use an object.

So far we've talked about the basic structure of RMI applications, how parameters are passed and used, how code is downloaded, and how security works. Now let's turn these abstract notions into concrete details about how to build RMI applications.

Building with RMI

Let's look at a quick example of how to write a simple RMI program. While the previous sections focused on the conceptual details of how RMI works, this section looks at the pragmatic details of how to actually go through the steps of writing, building, and running an RMI program.

The first thing you need to do is create the remote interface that will define how a client and server will talk to one another. In Listing A–1, I've defined a simple remote interface, called `NextNumber`, that has a single method. The idea is that a client passes an `int` to this method, which returns the next larger `int` as a result (this is a pretty trivial example, but the goal here is to work out the details of RMI, not focus on a full-fledged application).

Listing A–1 `NextNumber.java`

```
// A remote interface for getting increasing numbers

package corejini.appendixa;

import java.rmi.Remote;
import java.rmi.RemoteException;

public interface NextNumber extends Remote {
    public int getNextNumber(int n) throws RemoteException;
}
```

This interface defines a single method, `getNextNumber()`, which both takes and returns a simple `int`. There are only a couple of things you really must note about this remote interface. The first is that it extends `Remote`. This is the signal to RMI that the interface will be used as a way for a client to speak to a server object that lives in a different JVM. The second is that the `getNextNumber()` method is declared to raise `RemoteException`. In general, *every* method that is callable remotely must be declared to raise this exception in its interface. RMI will cause a client to see this exception if there is trouble communicating with a remote server object.

Now that we've seen the common interface that the server will implement and the client will call, let's look at the implementation of this interface that the server provides in Listing A–2.

Listing A–2 `NextNumberImpl.java`

```
// A server object that implements the NextNumber
// remote interface

package corejini.appendixa;

import java.rmi.RemoteException;
import java.rmi.RMISecurityManager;
import java.rmi.Naming;
import java.rmi.server.UnicastRemoteObject;
import java.net.InetAddress;
import java.net.UnknownHostException;
import java.net.MalformedURLException;

public class NextNumberImpl extends UnicastRemoteObject
    implements NextNumber {
    public NextNumberImpl() throws RemoteException {
        if (System.getSecurityManager() == null) {
            System.setSecurityManager(
                new RMISecurityManager());
        }

        try {
            String host =
                InetAddress.getLocalHost().getHostName();
            String url = "rmi://" + host + "/nextNumber";
            Naming.rebind(url, this);
            System.out.println("Server bound to: " + url);
        } catch (UnknownHostException ex) {
            System.err.println("Couldn't get local host");
            System.exit(1);
        } catch (RemoteException ex) {
            System.err.println("Couldn't contact " +
                               "rmiregistry.");
            System.err.println("Are you sure you're running "
                                + rmiregistry?");
            System.exit(1);
        } catch (MalformedURLException ex) {
            // Shouldn't happen
            System.exit(1);
        }
    }

    public int getNextNumber(int n) {
        return n+1;
    }
```

Listing A–2 NextNumberImpl.java

```
    public static void main(String[] args) {
      try {
          NextNumberImpl server = new NextNumberImpl();
      } catch (RemoteException ex) {
          System.err.println("Trouble creating server: " +
                                         ex.getMessage());
          ex.printStackTrace();
        }
    }
}
```

This class has a `main()` routine, which creates an instance of `NextNumberImpl`, which implements the remote interface. As you see here, `NextNumberImpl` extends `UnicastRemoteObject`—which means that it has the "smarts" necessary to be a remote object—and it implements `NextNumber`—which means that it provides a concrete implementation of the interface that the clients will know how to speak.

Let's look at the constructor for this object. The first thing the code does is to set a security manager. In this case, strictly speaking, there will be no downloaded code: The interfaces are defined to take and return primitive types (`ints`), and the server doesn't need to download any stubs (remember that it's the *client* that downloads the *server's* stub object). But virtually all RMI programs of any complexity *will* need to use downloadable code, so I've gone ahead and set the security manager here, just to reinforce the point.

Next, the code must address an issue that we haven't discussed yet: How does the client find the server after it's running? This is called the *rendezvous problem*. There may be many `NextNumberImpls` running on the network. How does the client specify which one it wants?

RMI provides a process called the *registry*, which is used to map from string names to remote objects. You can think of the registry as a name server that clients can contact when they need to find a remote object. Clients pass a name in and get a remote object out. The registry actually stores the stubs for the remote objects, so that clients can just download them and go.

The `Naming` class shown here supports interactions with the registry. Here, the code creates a URL-style string that provides a name for it. The string consists of a protocol part ("rmi"), followed by the local host name, and then a unique name for the server ("nextNumber"). This complete URL will be printed out when the server runs; you can pass this string to a client program so that it can find the server at run time.

I won't spend a lot of time talking about the registry here, because it's not used much in the rest of this book—instead, the programs in this book, even the ones that use RMI, use Jini's lookup and discovery protocols to find remote programs.

This registry binding process can raise several exceptions if it cannot get the host name for the local host, or if the registry is not running, or if you pass it a bogus URL. The code here just exits if any of these happen.

Next you see the actual implementation of the `getNextNumber()` method. Perhaps surprisingly, this method is implemented *exactly* like a purely local version of the same method! The RMI machinery that's in place means that you only have to write the core application logic for remote methods, and RMI takes care of everything else.

Let's move on and look at the client side of the RMI equation. In Listing A–3, you'll see a simple client program that can contact the registry to find the server, and invoke its method remotely.

Listing A–3 `NextNumberClient.java`

```
// A client to test the NextNumber server

package corejini.appendixa;

import java.rmi.Remote;
import java.rmi.RemoteException;
import java.rmi.RMISecurityManager;
import java.rmi.NotBoundException;
import java.rmi.Naming;
import java.net.MalformedURLException;

public class NextNumberClient {
    public static void main(String[] args) {
         if (args.length != 1) {
              System.err.println("Usage: NextNumberClient "
                                       + "<url>");
              System.exit(1);
         }

         if (System.getSecurityManager() == null) {
              System.setSecurityManager(
                   new RMISecurityManager());
         }
```

Listing A–3 `NextNumberClient.java` **(continued)**

```
        Remote r = null;

        try {
            r = Naming.lookup(args[0]);
        } catch (RemoteException ex) {
            System.err.println("Couldn't contact registry.");
            System.err.println("Are you sure you're running "
                                     + "rmiregistry?");
            System.exit(1);
        } catch (NotBoundException ex) {
            System.err.println("There is no object bound to "
                                     + args[0]);
            System.err.println("Are you sure you ran the " +
                                     "server?");
            System.exit(1);
        } catch (MalformedURLException ex) {
            System.err.println("The string " + args[0] +
                                 " is not a valid RMI URL");
            System.err.println("Make sure you use a " +
                          "properly-formatted rmi: // URL");
            System.exit(1);
        }

        try {
          if (r instanceof NextNumber) {
              NextNumber nn = (NextNumber) r;
              System.out.println("Next number after 1 is " +
                                     nn.getNextNumber(1));
              System.out.println("Next number after 2 is " +
                                     nn.getNextNumber(2));
              System.out.println("Next number after 3 is " +
                                     nn.getNextNumber(3));
          } else {
              System.err.println("Uh oh, the name " +
                                   args[0] +
                                   " isn't a NextNumber");
            }
        } catch (RemoteException ex) {
            System.err.println("Couldn't start client: " +
                                     ex.getMessage());
            ex.printStackTrace();
        }
    }
}
```

The client program consists only of a `main()` that contacts the registry to find a `NextNumber` server, and then calls the `getNextNumber()` method on it repeatedly to test it out.

The client program expects to get an RMI-formatted URL on the command line, which should name an instance of the server object. This should be the same URL that the server prints out when it starts. Next, the client installs an RMI security manager. The client application *will* be downloading code from the server—in this case, the stubs for the server. So the code here needs to install a security manager so that the code can be loaded remotely.

You should, however, note one of the common "gotchas" with RMI development: If you neglect to install a security manager, but happen to have the stubs in your classpath, then the program will continue to work normally because it will simply load the stubs in the "standard" way from the local classpath. But this same program will break if the classes cannot be found locally. So, even for testing, it's a good idea to go through all the steps that would be required to deploy this program in an actual remote setting where it doesn't have local access to the stubs.

After setting the security manager, the code calls the `lookup()` method on the `Naming` class, passing it the URL from the command line. This call asks the registry to return the stub for the object named by the URL. The method may fail in a number of ways—if the registry isn't running, or if the URL is bogus, or if there is no remote object bound to that name. In all of these cases, the program simply exits.

Finally, after fetching the object, we're ready to do some work! The code checks to make sure that the remote object it got back is indeed a `NextNumber`. This remote object should be the stub for the `NextNumberImpl` server, which implements the `NextNumber` interface. If this isn't the case, then someone else has bound another type of remote object to the URL passed on the command line, and the program exits. If the remote object returned from the registry *is* a `NextNumber`, then the program calls the `getNextNumber()` method on it a few times, printing the results.

Note here, how the code must trap any `RemoteExceptions` that are raised by the calls to `getNextNumber()`. The server may crash, or the network may become partitioned, or any number of other network-related failures can happen. RMI presents all of these as `RemoteExceptions`.

This is a pretty simple example—no code is being downloaded except for the stubs for the `NextNumberImpl`—but it shows the basics of what you have to do to work with RMI. Next, let's walk through how to get this code up and running.

Compiling the Example

The first step to getting everything running is to compile the server, the client, and the interface. The warning noted in the last section—that clients and servers must take care that they do not "accidentally" load classes from their classpaths that should be loaded remotely—applies here. For this example, I'll be compiling everything into the same directory. But in general, this is a bad idea that can mask many problems in coding and configuration that only show up at run time.

Read Chapter 5 for details on the "proper" way to configure your environment. The guidelines there cover details like compiling clients and servers into separate directories, setting up separate HTTP servers to export the downloadable code needed for each, and so on. The rest of this Core Jini book follows those guidelines to ensure that there is no unwanted "crosstalk" of classes between clients and servers.

The first step, on either Windows or Solaris, is to compile all the files:

```
javac NextNumber.java
        NextNumberImpl.java
        NextNumberClient.java
```

If you look in the directory, you should see `.class` files for each of these. You may be wondering about where the stub and skeleton classes come from. We haven't written any of these classes, but clearly they get used extensively by RMI.

The answer is that there is a separate step in the compilation process to create stubs and skeletons for remote objects. RMI uses a *stubs compiler* program to generate these classes; the compiler is called `rmic`, and it lives with the rest of the standard Java tools. Unlike `javac`, which takes pathnames, `rmic` takes fully qualified Java class names. The class names you pass it are the classes that *implement* remote interfaces. So, in this case where we have one remote implementation, you would run `rmic` on `NextNumberImpl`:

```
rmic corejini.appendixa.NextNumberImpl
```

If you now look at the contents of the directory, you'll see a couple of new class files there: `NextNumberImpl_Stub.class` and `NextNumberImpl_Skel.class`. These are the stub and skeleton classes, generated by `rmic` from the `NextNumberImpl` class file. If you're curious about what these classes actually do, you can pass the `-keepgenerated` option to `rmic`, which tells it to leave Java source files for the stubs and skeletons in the directory.

Running the Programs

The first thing you must do before you run these programs is start the RMI registry process! Many developers try to experiment with RMI and run into trouble because they forget this simple first step. The registry lives in the `bin` directory in the standard Java distribution. You can run it by typing `rmi-registry` on the command line. You should *at least* run the registry on the machine on which your server object will live; in general, it's helpful to run a registry on every machine on your network that may potentially support RMI programs.

Let's now run the client and server programs. The server in this case needs to export downloadable code (its stub class), and the client needs to be able to access this code. In a production environment, the way you would typically do this is to place the stub class on an HTTP server somewhere on your network. Alternatively, you could even implement a tiny, low-function HTTP server within the RMI server program yourself.

HTTP servers are configured to use one directory on the filesystem of the computer on which they run as their "root" directory. This is the directory that they serve content out of. To make a class file accessible from an HTTP server, you'd place it under the server's root directory, creating separate directories for each package name in the fully qualified class name.

So, for example, suppose you have an HTTP server running on Windows with a root directory of `C:\http`, the stub class for this example would live at `C:\http\corejini\appendixa\NextNumberImpl_Stub.class`. On Solaris, with a root directory of `/var/http`, the class would live at `/var/http/corejini/appendixa/NextNumberImpl_Stub.class`. Alternatively, you could bundle any required classes into a JAR file and place the JAR file in the HTTP server's root directory.

In the following examples, I'll assume that you've placed the stubs file appropriately on an HTTP server running on the machine `myhost`. We'll be using this hostname to construct a codebase to tell clients where they can find the downloadable code. If the class file is installed as just described, then the codebase URL would be `http://myhost/`. If the class file is installed in a JAR file in the server's root directory, then you would name the JAR file in the codebase; for example, `http://myhost/stubs.jar`.

After you're all set for downloadable code, you also need to take care of security. Remember that as long as code is running with a security manager, it must have a security policy that allows it access to filesystems and network resources. In Chapter 5 of this book, I'll be using a policy file that grants all permissions to code—essentially allowing them unfettered access to the system. Recall the warnings earlier in this appendix about using this policy file in a production system, but it will serve our purposes fine for now.

Both the codebase and the policy file are passed as properties to the JVM on the command line. Let's look at how to run the server. Assume for this example that the policy file lives in `C:\files\policy` on Windows and `/files/policy` on Solaris.

On Windows:

```
java -Djava.security.policy=C:\files\policy
        -Djava.rmi.server.codebase=http://myhost/
        corejini.appendixa.NextNumberImpl
```

On Solaris:

```
java -Djava.security.policy=/files/policy
        -Djava.rmi.server.codebase=http://myhost/
        corejini.appendixa.NextNumberImpl
```

The server should print the URL that it binds itself to in the registry; for instance, on my workstation it reports:

Server bound to: rmi://turbodog.parc.xerox.com/nextNumber

Be sure to remember this string as you'll have to pass it on the command line to the client. Speaking of which, let's now run the client. The client has a security manager, so it too needs to have a policy file passed to it. But unlike the server, the client exports no downloadable code. So you don't have to set a codebase, because the client doesn't have to tell anyone where to get class files from. Be sure you pass the URL that the server prints out on the command line.

On Windows:

```
java -Djava.security.policy=C:\files\policy
        corejini.appendixa.NextNumberClient
          rmi://turbodog.parc.xerox.com/nextNumber
```

On Solaris:

```
java -Djava.security.policy=/files/policy
        corejini.appendixa.NextNumberClient
          rmi://turbodog.parc.xerox.com/nextNumber
```

After all this work, the output isn't particularly spectacular: The client will simply print out as it invokes messages on the server.

Next number after 1 is 2
Next number after 2 is 3
Next number after 3 is 4

This example does show all the basics that you need to know to work with RMI, though.

In case you didn't try this example because you don't have an HTTP server running on your network, or don't want to take the time to copy class files to it, you should try to run it anyway. The client will "fall back" to using the local class path, which will mean that the example will probably work anyway—since you probably built the client and the server in the same directory.

Again, even though things may work this way, it isn't the recommended way to develop RMI-based software because it hides problems that can show up later when the client and the server *don't* share the same filesystem.

The next section covers one last aspect of RMI that is useful when developing Jini applications: the RMI activation framework.

The Activation Framework

The final topic we must address in this primer on RMI is *activation*. Activation is, simply, a way for Java to start remote server objects "on demand" as they are needed. In the example program in this appendix, you saw how the `NextNumberImpl` server was written—it consisted of a `main()` routine that created and registered a remote object, and then continued running. The server object was only available to clients as long as the program was running.

Activation, introduced in Java 2, provides a way to structure your programs around remote objects that are only "live" when they are necessary, and can basically "go to sleep" when they are not needed. The process of making an object "go to sleep" is called *deactivation*; the reawakening of an object is called *activation*. The facilities provided by the RMI activation framework can be extremely useful when you have remote objects that may need to do work only rarely, or when you have large numbers of remote objects, and the cost of keeping them all "live" at the same time may be prohibitive.

But beyond these two fairly obvious uses of activation, it brings an additional benefit as well: Because activation provides a way for server objects to be started as needed, it can be a powerful tool for creating software that can automatically recover after a crash. If an activatable remote object is shut down or crashes, or the machine on which it is running crashes, activation can be used as a way to bring it back to life when it is needed.

Players in Activation

The high-level description of activation above begs the question: If activatable objects can be reconstituted and made live on demand, who is doing the activation?

The answer is that activation is implemented by a set of cooperating entities. First, there is the activatable object itself. This is the remote server object that may be activated and deactivated as necessary. Second, there is a "wrapper" program that takes care of telling the RMI activation subsystem about this new activatable server object. This wrapper program will typically call out to a few methods to provide details about how the activatable object should be activated, when it is needed, and then exits. The wrapper is analogous to the `main()` program in the `NextNumberImpl`—it handles the chores of setting up the remote server object. But in the case of `NextNumberImpl` program, the wrapper must continue running for as long as the server is to be callable. Both of these classes—the activatable object and the program that sets it up—are written by you.

The third entity is a standard part of the Java 2 distribution, and is the most important part of the activation picture: the RMI activation daemon, or `rmid`. The activation daemon should be run on any computer on which activatable objects may be started and stopped; there only needs to be one instance of `rmid` on any computer, no matter how many activatable objects will be run there. It is the activation daemon that records the information needed to restart activatable objects.

You may be wondering exactly *where* a newly activated object will be run. Instantiating and running newly activated remote server objects *inside* the activation daemon would be problematic—`rmid` would get bogged down doing many things other than simply handling activation and, perhaps even worse, this strategy would mean that remote objects from different applications would be sharing the same JVM. Each of these remote objects may have different security restrictions, and may require different levels of permissions set for them.

So the activation daemon uses the fourth and final entity of the activation framework to take care of actually "hosting" activated objects: *activation groups*. Activation groups are essentially complete, separate instances of the Java Virtual Machine that exist solely to host groups of activated objects. These fresh JVMs are started as needed by `rmid`. In many cases, a whole set of activatable objects created by one wrapper program can share the same JVM. So the activation framework provides a way for wrappers to describe the characteristics of the activation group that will run their activatable

objects. Wrappers can use different activation groups to run different activatable objects, and can select security policy files for the JVMs that will run their objects.

This constellation of entities—activatable objects, the wrapper programs that create them, the activation daemon, and JVMs associated with activation groups—cooperate together to support objects which can be activated on demand.

I've decided to cover activation, which many will think of as an "advanced" topic, in this book because it can be so useful for writing Jini services. Activation is helpful for creating long-lived remote server objects that can automatically recover after a crash—which, in a nutshell, is a pretty reasonable description of the functionality that a Jini service must provide.

Using the Activation Framework

Chapter 5 of this book presents an example of using activation, so I won't cover the programmatic details and APIs of using activation in depth here. But I will give a quick overview of what you have to do to use the activation framework. These details will largely be the same no matter what sort of activatable object you're writing. I'll present the steps below, and then give a bit more detail on each.

1. Make sure the activation daemon is running on your system!
2. Create the implementation for your activatable object. This will be the remote server object that can be started on demand.
   - Extend the `java.rmi.Activatable` class if you're creating a new activatable object.
   - Declare a two-argument constructor that takes a `java.rmi.activation.ActivationID` and a `java.rmi.MarshalledObject`.
   - Implement the remote methods on your activatable object, as you normally would.
3. Create the implementation for your wrapper program. This program handles the "set up" for the activatable server object.
   - Make sure you install a security manager, typically a `java.rmi.RMISecurityManager`.
   - Create a `java.rmi.activation.ActivationGroup` that contains the information necessary to start a JVM with the appropriate parameters to run your activatable object.

- Create a `java.rmi.activation.ActivationDesc` that contains the information needed for the activation subsystem to properly activate your object. Register the `ActivationDesc` with the activation daemon so that it has the information to recreate your object. Registering will return the stub for your activatable object.
- You can either bind your activatable object in the RMI registry (if you want callers to find it by name), or simply pass its stub to any interested parties.

Let's look at these steps in a bit more detail. The first one, running the activation daemon, is easy. You simply type `rmid`; the executable lives in the standard Java `bin` directory.

Creating your activatable object is likewise pretty easy—in fact, creating an activatable remote object is essentially no harder than creating a standard, nonactivatable remote object, although the two do follow slightly different patterns. First, an activatable object should extend `java.rmi.activation.Activable`, rather than `java.rmi.server.UnicastRemoteObject`. The `Activatable` class is itself a subclass of `UnicastRemoteObject`, so you still inherit all of this functionality.[3] Also, whereas nonactivatable remote objects must have a no-argument constructor, activatable remote objects must instead have a two-argument constructor. The first argument is the `ActivationID`, which provides a unique identifier for the activatable object, as well as some other information. The second argument is a `MarshalledObject`. As we'll see, the wrapper program can provide an arbitrary `MarshalledObject` instance that will be passed to the activatable object when it is instantiated; this mechanism provides a simple one-shot way for the wrapper to pass data to the activatable object.

The constructor for your activatable object must also call the superclass constructor on `Activatable`. There are a number of variants of the `Activatable` constructor, and you should check the API documentation for specific details. In most cases, the simplest constructor should be used, which takes an `ActivationID` (which should be the same one passed to your activatable object's constructor), and a port number (which should typically be zero).

These two tasks—extending `Activatable` and providing the special constructor—are the only "special" things you have to do to create an activatable

3. The activation framework also provides a way to create activatable objects which are *not* subclasses of `Activatable`. The discussion of how to do this is outside the scope of this primer; see the Further Reading section at the end of this appendix for more details.

remote object. After doing these, you simply implement the remote methods of your implementation, just as you normally would.

The construction of the wrapper program is a little more complicated, but typically follows a pretty fixed pattern. The wrapper will need to communicate with the activation daemon, and possibly the RMI registry. Both of these are themselves RMI programs, and so the wrapper must be prepared to use the stubs downloaded from these services. So the first step in any wrapper is to install a security manager, so that it can execute downloadable code. And, recall, once you've installed a security manager, you'll have to pass a policy file to the wrapper's JVM as well.

Next, the wrapper must prepare information to tell the activation system about how to create activation group JVMs to run its activatable objects. Since activatable objects are run in separate JVMs, the wrapper needs to set up any information that would normally be passed in on the command line to a JVM. At a minimum, this typically includes a security policy file for the JVMs started to hold activated objects.[4] This information is contained within a class called an `ActivationGroupDesc`, which describes how the activation system should create activation groups. This information is "registered" with the activation system, and can be started as needed.

While the activation group descriptor contains information about how to start JVMs to run activatable objects, you still need to create a description of how to instantiate and run those activatable objects within their activation group. So the next thing the wrapper does is create an activation descriptor (`ActivationDesc`) which contains information such as the codebase URL that indicates where the activatable object's implementation can be retrieved, and an arbitrary `MarshalledObject` that will passed to the activatable object's constructor when it is created.

Finally, this activation descriptor is "registered" with the activation subsystem. The registration process tells the activation framework that a new activatable object is available and ready to be called; the server object will be created as necessary. When the object is registered, an RMI stub for it will be returned. Note that at this point, the activatable object need not be "live" for there to be a stub for it. This stub can be passed around, or bound to a name in the RMI registry, all without causing the object to be activated until one of its remote methods is called.

---

4. In the installation and set-up instructions for Jini in Chapter 1 of this book, you may have noticed that many of the Jini services require *two* security policy files on the command line. This is an indication that these services are implemented using activation—one policy file is used to set permissions for the wrapper, and another is used to set permissions on any JVMs started by the activation system.

Once the wrapper has set up the necessary information to describe the object and the activation group that should run it, it can simply exit. The activation subsystem will take care of instantiating the object the first time one of its remote methods are called.

"Lazy" References

One of the benefits of activation is that you can think of references to activatable objects as being "lazy." That is, references to these objects contain the persistent handle information that allows the activation subsystem to know which object should be started, if it is not already running. After an activatable reference is used the first time, a "regular" remote reference is used to contact the server object directly, without having to go through the activation system again.

Because the activation system can convert one of these persistent handles to a "live" remote reference as needed, references to activatable objects are *always* useable, even across restarts of the object. References to a normal remote object, on the other hand, become invalid after the object has crashed and then been restarted. References to activatable objects provide a useful way to have a persistent reference to a server object that is valid even across restarts.

Deactivation

Even though the activation framework will automatically start an activatable object the first time it is needed, it will not automatically deactivate objects when they are no longer required. The reason for this is simple—the decision about when to deactivate an object is best left to the object itself. Some objects may prefer to never deactivate themselves, while others may use complicated heuristics that are based on the number of times a method has been invoked over a period of time.

But regardless of how or whether they decide to do it, activatable objects can deactivate themselves as needed. You can call the `Activatable.inactive()` method, passing an `ActivationID`, to deactivate an object.

Activatable objects can also be *unregistered*. While deactivation is a temporary state—a deactivated object will be reactivated when it is needed—unregistering an object means that it is removed from the activation system. You can call `Activatable.unregister()`, passing in an `ActivationID`, to unregister an object. This allows you to "clean up" activatable objects that you no longer wish to use.

Getting the Most from the Activation Daemon

There are a couple of commonly overlooked ways to exploit the activation daemon that can be helpful when building systems with activatable components. The first is that you can set up your programs to be automatically restarted when the activation daemon restarts. Recall that the activation daemon records persistent information about the activatable objects it knows about. When you create the activation descriptor for your object, you can optionally say that you would like the object to be restarted when the activation daemon starts, as opposed to on-demand restarting.

This feature is useful if you know that your activatable objects are likely to be heavily used, and you want them started as soon as possible. If you've configured `rmid` to start when your computer boots, this feature can be used to launch activatable objects at boot time.

The activation daemon stores its persistent state in a log in the filesystem. By default, this log is a directory called `log` under the directory from which `rmid` was started. You can pass the `-log` option to `rmid` to change the location of the log directory. When `rmid` starts, it consults its log directory (if it exists) to recover information about activatable objects it knows about, and to launch any objects that have requested restart service.

The activation daemon also provides a handy way to shut itself down. If you need to stop the `rmid` process for some reason (perhaps because its log is on a filesystem that is full), you can run `rmid -stop`. This command line will cause any currently running `rmid` process to shut down.

Further Reading

This appendix has taken a very shallow look at a topic that is actually quite deep. If you're not familiar with RMI or Java 2, there may be a number of topics that you would like to read up on.

The new security architecture is one of the biggest changes that Java 2 has brought, and many developers are confused by it. The book *Just Java 1.2*, by Peter van der Linden, has an entire chapter devoted to Java 2 security, and is worth checking out.

If you just want the high-level overview, the following URL has details on the Java 2 security permissions mechanism:

```
http://www.javasoft.com/products/jdk/1.2/docs/guide/
security/permissions.html
```

This page at the JavaSoft Website has the details about the syntax of policy files. This information will be useful if you want to customize the policy file used by the examples in this book into something more robust:

```
http://www.javasoft.com/products/jdk/1.2/docs/guide/
security/PolicyFiles.html
```

If you want more details about RMI, you should check out Sun's page on the RMI implementation in Java 2. This page includes low-level specifications, examples, release notes, and API documentation. It also has coverage of the RMI activation framework:

```
http://www.javasoft.com/products/jdk/1.2/docs/guide/rmi/
index.html
```

If you want to read up on serialization, this Sun page has specifications, examples, and so on about all the ins-and-outs of object serialization:

```
http://www.javasoft.com/products/jdk/1.2/docs/guide/
serialization/index.html
```

Finally, the Frequently Asked Questions (FAQ) list for both RMI and serialization is available from Sun at:

```
http://www.javasoft.com/products/jdk/1.2/docs/guide/rmi/
faq.html
```

Appendix B

COMMON JAVA AND JINI SYSTEM PROPERTIES

This final appendix provides a reference to the many properties commonly used when developing Jini applications. Properties, as you remember, are special settings that can be used to tune the behavior of the Java runtime and class libraries. Properties are typically passed as arguments on the command line when the Java virtual machine is started, using the `-D` option.

So, for instance, to set the `java.rmi.server.codebase` property to `http://myhost/`, you would type:

```
java -Djava.rmi.server.codebase=http://myhost/
```

Properties can also be set programmatically, as is typically done when setting up an activation group descriptor for configuring the parameters of a JVM launched from the activation framework.

Tables B–1 thru B–6 list the properties used by the RMI and activation packages in Sun's reference implementation of Java 2, as well as properties dictated by the Jini specifications, and properties particular to Sun's sample implementation of Jini.

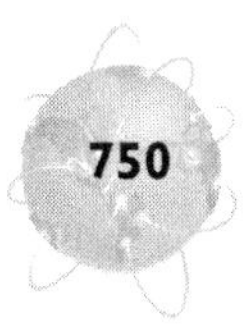

Table B–1 RMI Server Properties	
java.rmi.server.codebase	This property specifies where the implementations of classes that are exported by the VM on which it is set can be found. The property will be passed to VMs that need to download code remotely, effectively augmenting their classpaths at run time. Sets of URLs can be specified separated by spaces (you may have to enclose the value of the property in quotes on your platform, to keep the spaces from being parsed incorrectly).
java.rmi.server.disableHttp	RMI can "tunnel" through HTTP to allow invocation of remote methods through firewalls. If set to "true," HTTP tunneling is turned off. The default is "false" (tunneling is enabled).
java.rmi.server.hostname	By default, RMI uses the IP address of the host on which a remote object is exported to construct references to it. If this property is set, its value is treated as the hostname or IP address of the server and is used instead of the IP address that would be used otherwise. This property can be helpful if an RMI server uses DHCP and references to it should not contain a fixed IP address. By default, this property is not set.
java.rmi.dgc.leaseValue	This property sets the lease duration that RMI grants to clients that reference remote objects, specified in minutes. The default is 10 minutes.
java.rmi.server.logCalls	If set to true, an RMI server will log calls to `System.err`. The property is set to false by default.
java.rmi.server.useCodebaseOnly	This property, if set to true, disables local loading of classes referenced by remote methods—meaning that classes are only loaded from the codebase URLs, not from the local class path. This property can be useful for ensuring that there is no "crosstalk" between clients and services because they share a classpath.

Table B–1 RMI Server Properties (continued)	
java.rmi.server.useLocalHostname	If this property is set to true, then RMI will embed hostnames—rather than IP addresses—in references to remote objects. This property can be overridden by setting `java.rmi.server.hostname`, in which case the value specified there is always used.

Table B–2 RMI Activation Properties	
java.rmi.activation.port	This property indicates the port number on which the `ActivationSystem` is exported. This property should be set if the `rmid` activation daemon runs on a port other than the default.
java.rmi.activation.activator.class	This property specifies the class that implements the `java.rmi.activation.Activator` interface, which is used to control how clients communicate with the activation daemon. This property is used to name the implementation class so that the appropriate stub class can be found.

Table B–3 Jini Discovery Properties	
net.jini.discovery.debug	If this property is set to any value, debugging information about the Jini discovery and join protocols will be printed to `System.err`.
net.jini.discovery.mtu	This property indicates the maximum allowable size of multicast packets on your system. It must be a value between 512 and the actual maximum size your network supports. This property can be used to increase the allowed size of multicast request and announcement messages. Its default value is 512.

Table B–3 Jini Discovery Properties (continued)	
net.jini.discovery.ttl	This property sets the time-to-live (TTL) parameter used by multicast request and announcement. This value controls the "radius" of multicast messages. The value must be set to an integer between 1 and 255; the default is 15.
net.jini.discovery.timeout	This property sets the amount of time a client or service will wait for a response from a lookup service, when using the unicast discovery protocol. The value should be set to the timeout, in milliseconds. The default is 60,000 (1 minute).

Table B–4 "Reggie" (Sample Lookup Service) Properties	
net.jini.discovery.announce	This property controls how often the reggie lookup service will announce its presence via multicast announcement. The value is expressed in milliseconds, and the default is 120,000 milliseconds (every 2 minutes).
com.sun.jini.reggie.unicastTimeout	When reggie responds to a discovering entity performing unicast discovery, this property controls the timeout period for which reggie will try to send a unicast response. The value is expressed in milliseconds, and the default is 60,000 (1 minute).
com.sun.jini.reggie.proxy.debug	Setting this property to any value causes the service proxy for reggie to print out debugging information to `System.err` as it runs. You should be sure to set this property on a client that has downloaded the service proxy; not the lookup service itself.

Table B–5 "Mahalo" (Sample Transaction Manager) Properties	
com.sun.jini.use.registry	If this property is set to a non-null value, then mahalo will bind itself to the RMI registry, in addition to registering itself with the Jini lookup service. This facility is only present to allow debugging and development of mahalo, and shouldn't be used in practice.
com.sun.jini.rmiRegistryPort	This property controls the port on which mahalo looks for the RMI registry. This property only works in conjunction with the `com.sun.jini.use.registry` property above.
com.sun.jini.mahalo.managerName	This property sets the "name" of the mahalo instance. When mahalo is bound into the RMI registry, the name sets the name that the service is bound to. When mahalo is registered with the Jini lookup service, an attribute of type `net.jini.lookup.entry.Name` is created with this value and attached to the service's registration.

Table B–6 "Outrigger" (Sample JavaSpaces Service) Properties	
com.sun.jini.use.registry	If this property is set to a non-null value, then outrigger will bind itself to the RMI registry, in addition to registering itself with the Jini lookup service. This facility is only present to allow debugging and development of outrigger, and shouldn't be used in practice.
com.sun.jini.rmiRegistryPort	This property controls the port on which outrigger looks for the RMI registry. This property only works in conjunction with the `com.sun.jini.use.registry` property above.

Table B–6 "Outrigger" (Sample JavaSpaces Service) Properties	
com.sun.jini.outrigger.spaceName	This property sets the "name" of the outrigger instance. When outrigger is bound into the RMI registry, the name sets the name that the service is bound to. When outrigger is registered with the Jini lookup service, an attribute of type `net.jini.lookup.entry.Name` is created with this value and attached to the service's registration.
com.sun.jini.outrigger.backend.vm.options	This property is used to set command line arguments to the VM which will run the `BackEndSpace` part of a persistent JavaSpaces service. You must set the property on the VM running the `FrontEndSpace`, which is the portion of the persistent space directly launched on the command line.
com.sun.jini.outrigger.java	This property controls the name of the Java virtual machine used to run the `BackEndSpace` portion of a persistent JavaSpace. By default, the executable "java" is used.
com.sun.jini.outrigger.backend.gcInterval	This property controls how aggressive the `BackEndSpace` portion of a persistent JavaSpace will be in invoking the garbage collector. Persistent JavaSpaces consist of a `FrontEndSpace` that writes log entries to a spool which is consumed by a `BackEndSpace`. The value of the property controls how many log entries must be written before the persistent store is garbage collected. The default is 5. This property must be set on the JVM running the `BackEndSpace`.

Index

A

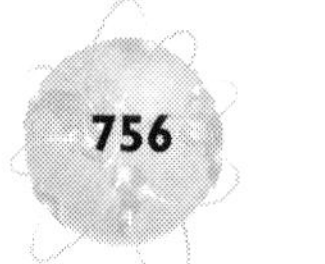

B

C

D

E

I

J

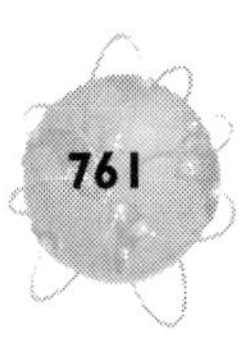

K

L

M

N

O

P

S

T

U

V

W

X

Z